SAS® Procedures Guide
Version 6
Third Edition

SAS Institute Inc.
SAS Campus Drive
Cary, NC 27513

The correct bibliographic citation for this manual is as follows: SAS Institute Inc., *SAS® Procedures Guide, Version 6, Third Edition,* Cary, NC: SAS Institute Inc., 1990. 705 pp.

SAS® Procedures Guide, Version 6, Third Edition

The SAS® System is an integrated system of software providing complete control over data access, management, analysis, and presentation. Base SAS software is the foundation of the SAS System. Products within the SAS System include SAS/ACCESS® SAS/AF® SAS/ASSIST® SAS/CALC® SAS/CONNECT® SAS/CPE® SAS/DMI® SAS/EIS® SAS/ENGLISH® SAS/ETS® SAS/FSP® SAS/GRAPH® SAS/IML® SAS/IMS-DL/I® SAS/INSIGHT® SAS/LAB® SAS/OR® SAS/PH-Clinical® SAS/QC® SAS/REPLAY-CICS® SAS/SHARE® SAS/STAT® SAS/TOOLKIT® SAS/TUTOR® SAS/DB2™ SAS/LOOKUP™ SAS/NVISION™ and SAS/SQL-DS™ software. Other SAS Institute products are SYSTEM 2000® Data Management Software, with basic SYSTEM 2000, CREATE™ Multi-User™ QueX™ Screen Writer™ and CICS interface software; NeoVisuals® software; JMP® JMP IN® JMP Serve® and JMP *Design*® software; SAS/RTERM® software; and the SAS/C® Compiler and the SAS/CX® Compiler. MultiVendor Architecture™ and MVA™ are trademarks of SAS Institute Inc. SAS Video Productions™ and the SVP logo are service marks of SAS Institute Inc. SAS Institute also offers SAS Consulting® Ambassador Select™ and On-Site Ambassador™ services. *Authorline® SAS Communications® SAS Training® SAS Views®* the SASware Ballot® and *Observations*™ are published by SAS Institute Inc. All trademarks above are registered trademarks or trademarks of SAS Institute Inc. in the USA and other countries. ® indicates USA registration.

The Institute is a private company devoted to the support and further development of its software and related services.

Other brand and product names are registered trademarks or trademarks of their respective companies.

Doc SS1, Ver 24.4, 111489

Contents

Illustrations

Figures

Tables

Credits

Documentation

Composition	James R. Byron, Gail C. Freeman, Lori R. Head, Cynthia M. Hopkins, Blanche W. Phillips, Craig R. Sampson, Pamela A. Troutman, June Zglinski
Graphics	Laura B. Hill, Ginny Matsey
Proofreading	Jennifer M. Ginn, Beth A. Heiney, Hanna P. Hicks, Beryl C. Pittman, Josephine P. Pope, Toni P. Sherrill, John M. West, Susan E. Willard
Technical Review	Johnny B. Andrews, Scott L. Bass, Patricia L. Berryman, Ed Blair, Lisa B. Brown, Gloria N. Cappy, Ann E. Carpenter, Leslie B. Clinton, Darylene C. Colbert, Thomas B. Cole, Oita C. Coleman, Ellen B. Daniels, Katherine M. DeRusso, David A. Driggs, Tony Fisher, Richard B. Fitzgerald, Annette T. Harris, Amerie Helton, Linda C. Helwig, R. Brian Hess, F. W. Hester, Scott K. Isaacs, Deborah J. Johnson, Christina A. Keene, Jennifer A. Kendall, Amy S. Kosarin, Elizabeth C. Langston, Sally B. Langthorn, Rusti Ludwick, A. Darrell Massengill, Jeffrey R. McDermott, Susan A. McGrath, James A. McKenzie, Jean W. Moorefield, Rebeccah K. Neff, Diane D. Olson, Lynn H. Patrick, Denise M. Poll, Joy Polzin, Richard A. Ragland, Lisa M. Ripperton, Richard G. Roach, Eddie Routten, James T. Rowles, Alissa R. Schleich, David C. Schlotzhauer, Sandra D. Schlotzhauer, Douglas J. Sedlak, David B. Shamlin, W. David Shinn, Veronica L. Shores, Joseph G. Slater, Michael K. Stockstill, Mark E. Stranieri, Jana D. Van Wyk, Amanda W. Womble, Ken D. Worsham
Writing and Editing	Catherine C. Carter, Rick V. Cornell, Susan E. Johnston, Regina C. Luginbuhl, Gary R. Meek, Sonja R. Moore, Kathryn A. Restivo, Holly S. Whittle, Helen F. Wolfson

Software

The procedures were implemented primarily by the Information Products Department of the Applications Division. The Statistical Research Division, Core Development Division, Host Systems Division, and Internal Database Department also made significant contributions.

Program development includes designing, programming, debugging, and supporting the software as well as providing preliminary documentation and reviewing later documentation. Most Version 6 procedures were converted from Version 5 procedures (in PL/I), but several were written from scratch and many greatly enhanced. In addition, Release 6.06 includes several new procedures.

In the list below, an asterisk follows the name of the developer currently supporting each procedure. Other developers listed worked on the procedure previously.

APPEND	Stephen M. Beatrous, Bary A. Gold*
CALENDAR	Heman H. Robinson,* Jack J. Rouse
CATALOG	Bary A. Gold,* Rebecca A. Perry
CHART	Katherine Ng, Heman H. Robinson,* Mark V. Schaffer
CIMPORT	Philip F. Busby, Sue Her, LanChien Hsueh*
COMPARE	Mark R. Little*
CONTENTS	Stephen M. Beatrous, Bary A. Gold*
COPY	Stephen M. Beatrous, Bary A. Gold*
CORR	Yang C. Yuan*
CPORT	Philip F. Busby, Sue Her, LanChien Hsueh*
DATASETS	Stephen M. Beatrous, Bary A. Gold*
FORMAT	Richard D. Langston*
FORMS	Rajen H. Doshi,* Karen H. Cross
FREQ	William M. Stanish*
MEANS	Nancy L. Agnew,* Katherine Ng
OPTIONS	Mark V. Schaffer*
PMENU	Claire S. Cates*
PLOT	Christopher R. Olinger,* Heman H. Robinson, Brian T. Schellenberger
PRINT	Darylene C. Colbert, Bary A. Gold,* Warren S. Sarle, Brian T. Schellenberger
PRINTTO	Randal K. Whitehead*
RANK	David F. Ross,* Brian T. Schellenberger
SORT	Rajen H. Doshi,* Dale D. Ingold, Katherine Ng
SPELL	Bud Whitmeyer*
SQL	Lewis Church, Henrietta H. Cummings, Paul M. Kent*
STANDARD	David F. Ross,* Brian T. Schellenberger
SUMMARY	Nancy L. Agnew,* Katherine Ng
TABULATE	Nancy L. Agnew,* Alan R. Eaton, Katherine Ng, Jack J. Rouse
TIMEPLOT	Jane E. Pierce*
TRANSPOSE	David F. Ross,* Warren S. Sarle, Brian T. Schellenberger
UNIVARIATE	Yang C. Yuan*
V5TOV6	Philip F. Busby, Rajen H. Doshi, Anthony L. Friebel, Bary A. Gold*, Richard D. Langston, Mark R. Little

Support Groups

Development Testing	Linda W. Binkley, Leslie B. Clinton, Elizabeth C. Langston, Linda L. Wharton, Amanda W. Womble
Technical Support	Johnny B. Andrews, Gregory C. Cooper, David A. Driggs, Christina A. Keene, Lynn H. Patrick, Meg Pounds, Eddie Routten, David C. Schlotzhauer, Yvonne Selby
Quality Assurance	Jack J. Berry, Patricia L. Berryman, Katherine M. DeRusso, John W. Gillikin, Gerardo I. Hurtado, Deborah J. Johnson, Susan A. McGrath, Joy Polzin, Richard A. Ragland, Kari L. Richardson, Mark E. Stranieri, Scott S. Sweetland
Source Management	James H. Boone, Karen H. Cross, Merle A. Finch, Robert P. Janka

Acknowledgments

Many people make significant and continuing contributions to the development of SAS Institute's software products. First among them are SAS users who have served as chairpersons for the SAS Users Group International (SUGI). They are Sally Carson, Helene Cavior, Dr. Michael Farrell, Rudolf J. Freund, Bob Hamer, Dr. Ronald W. Helms, Donald Henderson, Gerry Hobbs, Julian Horwich, Kenneth L. Koonce, Rich La Valley, Dr. Ramon C. Littell, J. Philip Miller, Pat Hermes Smith, Dr. Rodney Strand, and Dr. William Wilson.

Others who have contributed to the development and implementation of Release 6.06 of base SAS software include Ray Barnes, Upjohn Pharmaceutical Co.; Marjorie Bedinger, Health Care Financing Administration; Mark Bercov, Gulf Canada; Dick Blocker, Washington University; Wilbert P. Byrd, Clemson University; George Chao, Arnar-Stone Laboratories; Ray Danner, National Institute of Health; Sandra Donaghy, North Carolina State University; Paul Fingerman, Boeing Computer Services; Charles Gates, Texas A&M University; Harold Gugel, General Motors Corporation; Donald Guthrie, University of California, Los Angeles; Frank Harrell, Duke University; Jim Harrington, Monsanto Research; David Hurst, University of Alabama at Birmingham; Emilio A. Icaza, Louisiana State University; Janet Lind, San Diego Processing Corporation; Jon Mauney, Consultant; H.W. "Barry" Merrill, Merrill Consultants; Robert D. Morrison, Oklahoma State University; Richard M. Patterson, Auburn University; Jim Penny, University of North Carolina at Greensboro; Pete Rikard, Virginia Commonwealth University; John Ruth, University of Toronto; William L. Sanders, University of Tennessee; Robert Schechter, Scott Paper Company; Dale Trone, Proctor & Gamble; Jim Walker, Legent; Glenn Ware, University of Georgia.

The final responsibility for the SAS System lies with SAS Institute alone. We hope that you will always let us know your feelings about the system and its documentation. It is through such communication that the progress of SAS software continues to be accomplished.

Using This Book

PURPOSE

The *SAS Procedures Guide, Version 6, Third Edition* provides complete reference information for all procedures in Release 6.06 base SAS software.

"Using This Book" contains important information that will assist you as you use this book. This information includes how much experience with base SAS software is required before using this book, how to use this book, and what conventions are used in text and example code. In addition, **Additional Documentation**, found near the end of "Using This Book," provides references to other books that contain information on related topics.

AUDIENCE

The *SAS Procedures Guide* is written for users who have not used the SAS System but who have some computer programming experience and know the fundamentals of programming logic. It is also written for experienced SAS users.

PREREQUISITES

The following table summarizes the SAS System concepts you need to understand in order to use the *SAS Procedures Guide*.

You need to know how to	Refer to
invoke the SAS System at your site.	instructions provided by the SAS Software Consultant at your site.
use base SAS software. You need varying amounts of familiarity with the SAS System, depending on which procedures you want to use.	*SAS Introductory Guide, Third Edition* for a brief introduction; *SAS Language and Procedures: Usage, Version 6, First Edition* for a more thorough introduction; and *SAS Language: Reference, Version 6, First Edition* for complete reference information on the SAS language.
allocate SAS data libraries and assign librefs.	*SAS Language: Reference, Version 6, First Edition*.

HOW TO USE THIS BOOK

This section describes how this book is organized and provides an overview of the information in it.

Organization

This book begins with the changes and enhancements for Version 6 base SAS procedures. "Changes and Enhancements" briefly describes new procedures and changes to existing procedures. The first four chapters of this book provide overviews of the four types of base SAS procedures:

- elementary statistics
- reporting
- scoring
- utility.

Each of the remaining chapters discusses a procedure. Appendix 1 indicates which SAS statements you can use with the procedures. Appendix 2 describes the impact of the engine you are using on the processing capabilities of the base SAS procedures.

Summary of Procedures

The base SAS procedures and a brief description of each follow:

APPEND procedure
   adds the observations from one SAS data set to the end of another SAS data set.

BMDP procedure
   calls any BMDP® program to analyze data in a SAS data set. This procedure is described in system-dependent documentation.

CALENDAR procedure
   displays data from a SAS data set in a monthly calendar format. PROC CALENDAR can also display holidays in the month and process data for multiple calendars with varying work schedules.

CATALOG procedure
   manages entries in SAS catalogs. PROC CATALOG is an interactive, non–full-screen procedure that allows you to display the contents of a catalog, copy a catalog or selected entries within a catalog, and rename, exchange, or delete entries within a catalog.

CHART procedure
   produces vertical and horizontal bar charts (also called *histograms*), block charts, pie charts, and star charts. These charts are useful as a visual representation of the values of a single variable or several variables.

CIMPORT procedure
   restores a transport file created by the CPORT procedure to its original form (a SAS data library, a SAS catalog, or a SAS data set) in the format appropriate to the host operating system. Coupled with the CPORT procedure, PROC CIMPORT enables you to move SAS catalogs and data sets from one operating system to another.

COMPARE procedure
   compares the contents of two SAS data sets. You can also use PROC COMPARE to compare the values of different variables within a single

---

BMDP is a registered trademark of BMDP Statistical Software, Inc.

data set. PROC COMPARE can produce a variety of reports on the comparisons it performs.

CONTENTS procedure
prints descriptions of the contents of one or more files from a SAS data library.

CONVERT procedure
converts BMDP, OSIRIS, and SPSS® system files to SAS data sets. The procedure is described in system-dependent documentation.

COPY procedure
copies an entire SAS data library or selected members of the library. Optional features enable you to limit processing to specific types of library members.

CORR procedure
computes correlation coefficients between variables, including Pearson product-moment and weighted product-moment correlations. Three nonparametric measures of association (Spearman's rank-order correlation, Kendall's tau-b, and Hoeffding's measure of dependence, D) can also be produced. In addition, the CORR procedure computes partial correlations (Pearson's partial correlation, Spearman's partial rank-order correlation, and Kendall's partial tau-b) and Cronbach's coefficient alpha. Some univariate descriptive statisitics are also generated.

CPORT procedure
writes SAS data sets and catalogs into a special format in a transport file. Coupled with the CIMPORT procedure, PROC CPORT enables you to move SAS catalogs and data sets from one operating system to another.

DATASETS procedure
enables you to list, copy, rename, and delete SAS files and to manage indexes for and append SAS data sets in a SAS data library. It provides all the capabilities of the APPEND, CONTENTS, and COPY procedures.

FORMAT procedure
defines your own informats and formats for character or numeric variables. Options for the FORMAT procedure print the contents of a format library, create a control data set for writing other informats and formats, or read a control data set to create informats and formats.

FORMS procedure
produces labels for envelopes, mailing labels, external tape labels, file cards, and any other printer forms that have a regular pattern.

FREQ procedure
produces one-way to n-way frequency and cross-tabulation tables. For two-way tables, it computes tests and measures of association. For n-way tables, it does stratified analysis, computing statistics within, as well as across, strata.

MEANS procedure
produces simple, univariate descriptive statistics for numeric variables. You can use the OUTPUT statement to request that PROC MEANS output statistics to a SAS data set.

OPTIONS procedure
lists the current values of all SAS system options.

OSIRIS is a registered trademark of Columbia Computing Services.
SPSS is a registered trademark of SPSS, Inc.

PDS procedure
lists, deletes, and renames the members of a partitioned data set. This procedure is described in system-dependent documentation.

PDSCOPY procedure
copies partitioned data sets from disk to tape, disk to disk, tape to tape, or tape to disk. This procedure is described in system-dependent documentation.

PLOT procedure
graphs one variable against another, producing a printer plot. The coordinates of each point on the plot correspond to the two variables' values in one or more observations of the input data set.

PMENU procedure
defines PMENU facilities for windows created by using the WINDOW statement in base SAS software, the %WINDOW macro statement, the BUILD procedure of SAS/AF software, or the Screen Control Language (SCL) PMENU function with SAS/AF and SAS/FSP software.

PRINT procedure
prints the observations in a SAS data set, using all or some of the variables. PROC PRINT can also print totals and subtotals for numeric variables.

PRINTTO procedure
defines destinations for SAS procedure output and the SAS log.

RANK procedure
computes ranks for one or more numeric variables across the observations of a SAS data set. The ranks are output to a new SAS data set. Alternatively, PROC RANK produces normal scores or other rank scores.

RELEASE procedure
releases unused space at the end of a disk data set in an MVS environment. This procedure is described in system-dependent documentation.

SORT procedure
sorts observations in a SAS data set by one or more variables, storing the resulting sorted observations in a new SAS data set or replacing the original data set.

SOURCE procedure
provides an easy way to back up and process library data sets. This procedure is described in system-dependent documentation.

SPELL procedure
checks the spelling in an external file or in SAS catalog entries of type HELP or CBT. It also maintains dictionaries.

SQL procedure

implements the Structured Query Language (SQL™) for Version 6 of the SAS System. SQL is a standardized, widely used language that retrieves and updates data in tables and views based on those tables.

STANDARD procedure

standardizes some or all of the variables in a SAS data set to a given mean and standard deviation and produces a new SAS data set containing the standardized values.

SUMMARY procedure

computes descriptive statistics on numeric variables in a SAS data set and outputs the results to a new SAS data set.

TABULATE procedure

displays descriptive statistics in tabular form. The value in each table cell is calculated from the variables and statistics that define the pages, rows, and columns of the table. The statistic associated with each cell is calculated on values from all observations in that category.

TAPECOPY procedure

copies an entire tape volume or files from one or more tape volumes to one output tape volume. This procedure is described in system-dependent documentation.

TAPELABEL procedure

lists the label information of an IBM® standard-labeled tape volume under the MVS operating system. This procedure is described in system-dependent documentation.

TIMEPLOT procedure

plots one or more variables over time intervals.

TRANSPOSE procedure

transposes a data set, changing observations into variables and vice versa.

UNIVARIATE procedure

produces simple descriptive statistics (including quantiles) for numeric variables.

V5TOV6 procedure

converts members of a SAS data library or a file of formats from Version 5 to Version 6 format on the same operating system.

What You Should Read

This section recommends which sections of this book you should read, depending on your level of experience with base SAS software.

If you are	You should read
new to the SAS System	the first four chapters, which serve as an overview of the four types of procedures (elementary statistics, reporting, scoring, and utility). You should then refer to the "Summary of Procedures" section, earlier in "Using This Book," to determine which procedure you need to reference. The procedures are described in alphabetic order, one procedure per chapter, beginning with Chapter 5. For information on SAS statements that you can use within a procedure, consult Appendix 1.
an experienced SAS user	"Changes and Enhancements" in the front of this book to find the summary of changes and enhancements to the procedures for Release 6.06. You should then refer to "Summary of Procedures," earlier in "Using This Book," to determine which procedure you need to reference. The procedures are described in alphabetic order, one procedure per chapter, beginning with Chapter 5. For information on SAS statements that you can use within a procedure, consult Appendix 1.
using SAS/ACCESS interface products, using data sets on tape, or using compressed data sets	Appendix 2, which describes how the engine you use affects the processing capabilities of the base SAS procedures.

Reference Aids

The *SAS Procedures Guide* is organized to make information easy to find. The following features are provided for your easy reference:

Table of Contents   lists the chapter titles and the page numbers of each.

List of Illustrations   lists all figures in this book.

List of Tables   lists all tables in this book.

Changes and Enhancements

provides information about changes that have been made to base SAS software since Release 5.18. It also points out new features of Release 6.06 software. You should carefully read this section if you are going to run Version 5 programs under Release 6.06 or if you want to learn about new features of Release 6.06.

Index   provides the page numbers where specific topics,
          procedures, statements, and options are discussed.
          Where an index entry has more than one page
          reference, boldface is used to indicate the primary
          reference for that entry, if one exists.

The first four chapters are overviews of the four types of procedures. Starting
with Chapter 5, the procedures are presented in alphabetic order, one chapter
per procedure. Within the discussion of each procedure, statements are also discussed in alphabetic order as are the required arguments and options supported
by each statement. The structure of the procedure chapters generally follows a
standard format. The sections you will find in all chapters are discussed in the
following list:

ABSTRACT   summarizes the procedure's function.

INTRODUCTION describes the procedure's function in more detail and
                  defines terms that are necessary to the description of the
                  procedure.

SPECIFICATIONS shows the syntax of the procedure. The syntax is
                  followed by a description of

                  • the PROC statement.
                  • required arguments and options for the PROC
                    statement (in alphabetic order).
                  • subordinate statements used with the PROC
                    statement and their required arguments and options.
                    (Statements appear in alphabetic order as do the
                    required arguments and options supported by each
                    statement.)

DETAILS   discusses various details, such as the way the procedure
                  handles missing values, the appearance of the printed
                  output, and the structure of an output data set.

EXAMPLES   shows various ways of using the procedure.

You should be familiar with the graphics inside the front and back covers. The
graphic inside the front cover provides a functional overview of the SAS System.
The graphic inside the back cover provides an overview of base SAS software
and the use of each procedure. You can use these graphics to determine which
SAS software or base SAS procedures you should use.

CONVENTIONS

This section explains the various conventions used in presenting text, SAS language syntax, file and library references, examples, and printed output in this
book. The following terms are used in discussing syntax:

keyword   is a literal that is a primary part of the SAS language. (A
          literal must be spelled exactly as shown, although it can
          be entered in uppercase or lowercase.) Keywords in this
          book are statement names.

argument   is an element that follows a keyword. It is either literal or
user-supplied. It has a built-in value or has a value
assigned to it.

Arguments that you must use are *required arguments*.
Other arguments are *optional arguments*, or more simply,
options.

value   is an element that follows an equal sign. It assigns a
value to an argument. It may be a literal or a user-
supplied value.

Typographical Conventions

You will see several type styles used in this book. The following list explains the
meaning of each style:

roman   is the standard type style used for most text in this book.

UPPERCASE ROMAN

is used for SAS statements, variables' names, and other
SAS language elements when they appear in the text.
However, you can enter these elements in your own SAS
code in lowercase, uppercase, or a mixture of the two.

italic   is used to define new terms and to emphasize important
information.

bold   is used for headings and references to sections within
text. It is also used to emphasize important sentences
and primary index entries.

`monospace`   is used to show examples of SAS statements. In most
cases, this book uses lowercase type for SAS code, with
the exception of some title characters. You can enter
your own SAS code in lowercase, uppercase, or a
mixture of the two. The SAS System always changes your
variable names to uppercase, but character variable
values remain in lowercase if you have entered them
that way. Enter any titles and footnotes exactly as you
want them to appear on your output.

Monospace is also used to show the values of
character variables and labels in text.

Syntax Conventions

Type styles have special meanings when used in the presentation of base SAS
software syntax in this book. The following list explains the style conventions for
the syntax sections:

UPPERCASE BOLD

identifies SAS keywords such as the names of statements
and procedures (for example, **PROC APPEND**).

UPPERCASE ROMAN

identifies arguments and values that are literals (for
example, LIST and FORMAT=SASLIB).

italic   identifies arguments or values that you supply. Items in italic can represent user-supplied values that are either

- nonliteral values assigned to an argument (for example, *number-of-midpoints* in LEVELS=*number-of-midpoints*)
- nonliteral arguments (for example, FREQ *variable*).

In addition, an item in italics can be the generic name for a list of arguments from which the user can choose (for example, *entry-list*).

The following symbols are used to indicate other syntax conventions:

< > (angle brackets)   identify optional arguments. Any argument not enclosed in angle brackets is required.

| (vertical bar)   indicates that you can choose one value from a group. Values separated by bars are mutually exclusive.

... (ellipsis)   indicates that the argument or group of arguments following the ellipsis can be repeated any number of times. If the ellipsis and the following argument are enclosed in angle brackets, they are optional.

The following examples illustrate these syntax conventions. These examples contain selected syntax elements, not complete syntax.

PROC CATALOG CATALOG=<*libref.*>*catalog* <KILL>;

- **PROC CATALOG** is in uppercase bold because it is a SAS keyword, the name of a statement. The remaining elements in this statement are arguments and values for arguments.
- CATALOG= is not enclosed in angle brackets because it is a required argument. It is in uppercase to indicate that it is a literal and must be spelled as shown.
- *libref.* is enclosed in angle brackets because it is an optional part of the value for the CATALOG= argument. It is in italic because it is a value you must supply. In this case, the value must be a valid libref.
- *catalog* is not enclosed in angle brackets because it is a required part of the value for the CATALOG= argument. It is in italic because it is a value you must supply. In this case, the value is the name of a SAS catalog.
- KILL is enclosed in angle brackets because it is an optional argument. It is in uppercase to indicate that it is a literal and must be spelled as shown.
- The ending semicolon (;) is not enclosed in angle brackets because it is required.

CHANGE *old-name-1*=*new-name-1* <...*old-name-n*=*new-name-n*>;

- **CHANGE** is in uppercase bold because it is a SAS keyword, the name of a statement. The remaining elements in this statement are arguments and values for arguments.
- *old-name-1*=*new-name-1* is not enclosed in angle brackets because it is a required argument with a required value. The words are in italic because they are values you must supply. In this case, *old-name-1* represents the name of an existing SAS catalog, and *new-name-1* represents a new name for that catalog. Note that because the equal sign is not in italic, you must enter it as shown.

- *old-name-n*=*new-name-n* is enclosed in angle brackets because additional user-supplied arguments and values are optional. The ellipsis indicates that you can use as many pairs of old and new names as you want. Again, you must enter the equal sign as shown.

PROC OPTIONS <SHORT | LONG>;

- SHORT | LONG is enclosed in angle brackets because it is optional. The vertical bar indicates that you can use either SHORT or LONG but not both. The use of uppercase indicates that you must spell the option you select as shown.

Conventions for Examples and Output

Most of the programs in this book were run using the following SAS system options:

- NODATE
- LINESIZE=132
- PAGESIZE=60.

SAS programs that use only these options do not contain an OPTIONS statement. However, any SAS program that uses other options or specifies different values for these options includes an appropriate OPTIONS statement.

Your output may differ from the output shown in the book if you run the example programs with different options or different values for those options.

Output from procedures is enclosed in boxes. Your output may differ slightly from the output shown in this book. This is a function of whether a floating-point processor is used in your computer, rather than a problem with the software. In all situations, the differences should be minor.

Some **Printed Output** sections in the procedure chapters include a numbered list. These numbers correspond to the circled numbers in the example output.

References to Libraries and Files

This book uses the SAS LIBNAME and FILENAME statements to associate logical references (librefs and filerefs) with SAS data libraries and external files. On some operating systems you can use operating system control language to make these associations. On the VSE operating system, you must use operating system control language.

Additional Documentation

SAS Institute provides many publications about software products of the SAS System and how to use them on specific hosts. For a complete list of SAS publications, you should refer to the current *Publications Catalog*. The catalog is produced twice a year. You can order a free copy of the catalog by writing to the following address:

SAS Institute Inc.
Book Sales Department
SAS Campus Drive
Cary, NC 27513

In addition to the *SAS Procedures Guide*, you will find these other documents helpful when using base SAS software:

- *SAS Language and Procedures: Introduction, Version 6, First Edition* (order #A56074) provides information for users who are unfamiliar with the SAS System or any other programming language.
- *SAS Language: Reference, Version 6, First Edition* (order #A56076) provides detailed reference information about SAS language statements, functions, formats, informats, the SAS Display Manager System, the SAS Text Editor, or any other element of base SAS software except procedures.
- *SAS Language and Procedures: Usage, Version 6, First Edition* (order #A56075) provides task-oriented examples of the major features of base SAS software.
- *SAS Language and Procedures: Usage 2, Version 6, First Edition* (order #A56078) provides more advanced task-oriented examples of the major features of base SAS software.
- *SAS Guide to the SQL Procedure: Usage and Reference, Version 6, First Edition* (order #A56070) provides information on how to retrieve and update data sets using the SQL procedure and on how to create SQL views.
- *SAS Guide to TABULATE Processing, 1987 Edition* (order #A5664) provides detailed information on how to summarize values for all observations in a data set and print the summaries in table format using the TABULATE procedure.
- *SAS Guide to the REPORT Procedure: Usage and Reference, Version 6, First Edition* (order #A56088) provides information on producing customized reports.
- *SAS Guide to Macro Processing, Version 6, Second Edition* (order #A56041) provides a tool for extending and customizing your SAS programs.
- SAS documentation for your host system provides information about the operating-system specific features of the SAS System for your operating system.

Changes and Enhancements to Base SAS® Procedures

INTRODUCTION

This section briefly describes the new base SAS software procedures and summarizes the major changes to existing procedures since Release 5.18.

NEW PROCEDURES

The CATALOG Procedure

The CATALOG procedure manages the entries in a SAS catalog. It provides capabilities similar to those that the DATASETS procedure offers for SAS data set management. With PROC CATALOG, you can display the contents of a catalog, copy or move a catalog or selected entries, rename or delete entries in a catalog, and exchange names of pairs of catalog entries. PROC CATALOG replaces the CATOUT procedure.

The PMENU Procedure

The PMENU procedure builds action bars and pull-down menus that can be associated with a window created with the WINDOW or %WINDOW statement in base SAS software or with SAS/AF or SAS/FSP software.

The SPELL Procedure

The SPELL procedure checks the spelling in an external file or in SAS catalog entries of type HELP or CBT. It also maintains dictionaries.

The SQL Procedure

The SQL procedure implements the Structured Query Language (SQL), a standardized, widely used language that creates, retrieves, and updates data in tables or in views based on those tables.

The V5TOV6 Procedure

The V5TOV6 procedure converts members of a SAS data library or a file of formats from Version 5 format to Version 6 format on the same operating system.

CHANGES AND ENHANCEMENTS TO EXISTING PROCEDURES

The APPEND Procedure

The utility function of the APPEND procedure is now also available with the APPEND statement in the DATASETS procedure.

The BROWSE Procedure

The SAS System provides a procedure more powerful than the BROWSE procedure for reading SAS data sets. This procedure, the FSBROWSE procedure, is part of SAS/FSP software. PROC BROWSE is no longer documented, but it is still available in Release 6.06. If you need documentation for the BROWSE procedure, refer to *SAS User's Guide: Basics, Version 5 Edition*.

The CALENDAR Procedure

The CALENDAR procedure has many new features. These features increase the CALENDAR procedure's compatibility with the SAS/OR project management procedures, CPM and GANTT.

PROC CALENDAR now creates multiple calendars. You can define any number of calendars using different schedules and associate these different schedules with each calendar. Use the CALID statement with the OUTPUT= option to create multiple calendars.

PROC CALENDAR now creates multiple schedules. You can change or modify general work patterns with the WORKDATA= and CALEDATA= data sets in addition to the DATA= and HOLIDATA= data sets documented in previous versions of PROC CALENDAR. The new WORKDATA= data set enables you to control daily work schedules. The CALEDATA= data set enables you to create weekly work schedules. The INTERVAL= and DAYLENGTH= options also are useful in modifying work patterns.

PROC CALENDAR enables you to determine the duration and display of a project. You can use the START or ID statement to specify the starting date for an activity. Use the HOLISTART statement to indicate the start of a holiday and the OUTSTART statement to specify the day of the week on which the calendar begins. Use the HOLIFIN statement to determine when a holiday activity ends and the OUTFIN statement to choose the last day of the week displayed in your calendar. You can control the length of time that an activity lasts with the appropriate use of the DUR, HOLIDUR, and OUTDUR statements.

The CHART Procedure

There have been various improvements in printed output. The headings for pie, block, and star charts have been enhanced, and no headings are printed for horizontal bar and vertical bar charts. Other printing improvements include scaling, centering, and spacing changes. A new option, NOHEADER, suppresses the default heading normally printed at the top of block, pie, and star charts.

The FORMCHAR= option, which supports system-dependent form characters, is now available.

The NOSPACE option is now always in effect. If the specified line size does not allow room for spaces between the bars, the CHART procedure can print a vertical bar chart without spaces between bars. If space is still insufficient, a horizontal bar chart is printed instead.

The CIMPORT Procedure

The CIMPORT procedure can import SAS data libraries, SAS catalogs, and, if the transport file was created with the CPORT procedure from Release 6.03 or later, SAS data sets.

The CIMPORT procedure supports the following new options:

EXCLUDE=	excludes individual catalog entries from the import process.
INFILE=	specifies the transport file to read.
MODEV5	copies source of Version 5 SAS/AF PROGRAM entries without modification.
NOCOMPRESS	suppresses compression of binary zeros and blanks in SAS catalogs and data sets created by PROC CIMPORT.
NOOPT	imports source of Version 5 SAS/AF PROGRAM entries without optimizing.
OPT	imports source of Version 5 SAS/AF PROGRAM entries to optimized Version 6 programs.
SELECT=	selects individual catalog entries to import.
TAPE	directs PROC CIMPORT to read from tape.

Some devices on some operating systems support options that specify the background color for Version 5 catalogs that you import. See the SAS documentation for your host system for details.

The COMPARE Procedure

The definition of the RELATIVE method has changed to include a constant in the denominator so that the method does not break down when the values compared approach zero.

The contents and formats of the reports that the COMPARE procedure generates have changed substantially.

In addition, the PROC COMPARE statement supports the following new options:

BRIEFSUMMARY
BRIEF
> produces a short comparison summary and suppresses the four default summary reports.

LISTALL
LIST
> lists all variables and observations found in only one data set.

LISTBASE
> lists all observations and variables found in the base data set but not in the comparison data set.

LISTBASEOBS
> lists all observations found in the base data set but not in the comparison data set.

LISTBASEVAR
> lists all variables found in the base data set but not in the comparison data set.

LISTCOMP
> lists all observations and variables found in the comparison data set but not in the base data set.

LISTCOMPOBS

lists all observations found in the comparison data set but not in the base data set.

LISTCOMPVAR

lists all variables found in the comparison data set but not in the base data set.

LISTEQUALVAR

prints a list of variables whose values are judged equal at all observations, in addition to the default list of variables whose values are judged unequal.

LISTOBS

lists all observations found in only one data set.

LISTVAR

lists all variables found in only one data set.

MAXPRINT=

specifies the maximum number of differences to print for each variable within a BY group and, optionally, the total number of differences to print.

NODATE

suppresses the display in the data set summary report of the creation dates and the last modified dates of the base and comparison data sets.

NOVALUES

suppresses the report of the value comparison results.

OUTALL

writes an observation to the output data set for each observation in the base data set and for each observation in the comparison data set. The OUTALL option also writes observations to the output data set containing the differences and percent differences between the values in matching observations.

OUTBASE

writes an observation to the output data set for each observation in the base data set.

OUTCOMP

writes an observation to the output data set for each observation in the comparison data set.

OUTDIF

writes an observation to the output data set for each pair of matching observations. The values in the observation include values for the differences between the values in the pair of observations. The OUTDIF option is the default unless you specify the OUTBASE, OUTCOMP, or OUTPERCENT option. If you use any of these options, you must explicitly invoke the OUTDIF option.

OUTSTATS=

writes summary statistics for all pairs of matching variables to the specified SAS data set.

PRINTALL

invokes the following options: ALLVARS, ALLOBS, ALLSTATS, LISTALL, and WARNING.

TRANSPOSE

prints the reports of value differences by observation instead of by variable.

The CONTENTS Procedure

The following options have no effect with the CONTENTS procedure in Version 6:

HISTORY
NOSOURCE

The output produced by PROC CONTENTS has changed to include information on indexes and other new features of SAS data sets in Version 6.

The utility function of PROC CONTENTS is now available with the CONTENTS statement in the DATASETS procedure.

The COPY Procedure

The following options have been replaced by the use of the transport engine name in the LIBNAME statement and are no longer available:

EXPORT
IMPORT

The following options are not available with the COPY procedure in Version 6:

NOHISTORY
PROTECT=

The utility function of PROC COPY is now also available with the COPY statement in the DATASETS procedure.

The CORR Procedure

The ALPHA, CSSCP, and SINGULAR= options have been added to the PROC CORR statement. The PARTIAL statement is new. It enables you to compute Pearson's partial correlation, Spearman's partial rank-order correlation, or Kendall's partial tau-b.

The CPORT Procedure

The CPORT procedure can export SAS catalogs and SAS data sets. The CPORT procedure supports the following new options:

EXCLUDE= excludes individual catalog entries from the transport file.

FILE= specifies a previously defined fileref or the filename of the transport file to write to. If you do not use the FILE= option, the CPORT procedure writes to a file with the reserved fileref SASCAT.

MEMTYPE= limits the type of SAS file PROC CPORT writes to the transport file.

SELECT= selects individual catalog entries for the transport file.

TAPE directs the output from PROC CPORT to tape. By default, output goes to disk.

TRANSLATE= translates the specified characters from one ASCII or EBCDIC value to another.

OUTLIB= is an additional option name that you can use for the OUT= option.

The DATASETS Procedure

The DATASETS procedure is no longer a full-screen procedure; however, it still runs interactively (that is, you can continue to submit procedure statements after you submit a RUN statement).

The FORCE option in the PROC DATASETS statement functions differently. The FORCE option now works like the FORCE option in the APPEND statement to force unlike SAS data sets to append.

The following options are no longer available with the DATASETS procedure:

- the NOFS and PROTECT= options in the PROC DATASETS statement
- the PROTECT= and READ= options in the MODIFY statement.

The following new subordinate statements have been added:

APPEND statement
  appends observations from one SAS data set to the end of another SAS data set; thus, the utility function of PROC APPEND is now available within the PROC DATASETS step.

CONTENTS statement
  describes the contents of one or more SAS files in the SAS data library referenced by the LIBRARY= option in the PROC DATASETS statement. This statement provides the same utility function as that provided by PROC CONTENTS.

COPY statement
  copies one or more SAS files from one SAS library into another library. You can also use the SELECT and EXCLUDE statements in conjunction with the COPY statement; thus, the same utility functions as those provided by PROC COPY are available within the PROC DATASETS step.

INDEX CREATE statement
  creates simple and composite indexes on Release 6.06 or later SAS data sets.

INDEX DELETE statement
  deletes simple and composite indexes on Release 6.06 or later SAS data sets.

REPAIR statement
  repairs data sets and catalogs damaged by hardware failures or abnormal termination of the operating system.

The EDITOR Procedure

The SAS System provides a procedure more powerful than the EDITOR procedure for editing SAS data sets. This procedure, the FSEDIT procedure, is part of SAS/FSP software. PROC EDITOR is no longer documented, but it is still available in Release 6.06. If you need documentation for the EDITOR procedure, refer to *SAS User's Guide: Basics, Version 5 Edition*.

The FORMAT Procedure

User-written formats created using the FORMAT procedure are now stored in a SAS catalog. The INVALUE statement, which enables you to create informats, has a new option: UPCASE. In addition, you can use the DEFAULT=, MIN=, and MAX= options in the INVALUE statement.

The CNTLIN= and CNTLOUT= options in the PROC FORMAT statement read and write special SAS data sets that contain descriptive information about some or all of the informats and formats in a catalog. Use the SELECT or EXCLUDE statement to limit the effects of the CNTLIN= and CNTLOUT= options to selected formats and informats.

The FMTLIB and PAGE options in the PROC FORMAT statement produce printed descriptions of the contents of a format catalog. These options produce output similar to the output produced by the SUGI Supplemental Library procedure, FMTLIB.

The DECK option is not available with PROC FORMAT in Version 6.

The FORMS Procedure

FILE= is an additional option name that you can use instead of DDNAME= or DD= to refer to the external file into which the FORMS procedure writes its printed output.

ACROSS= is an additional option name that you can use instead of NACROSS to specify the number of form units to print across the page.

The default value for the WIDTH= option is now the width of the widest line, instead of 40.

The FREQ Procedure

A new option, EXACT, provides Fisher's exact test for tables that are larger than 2×2. For 2×2 tables, Fisher's exact test is performed if the CHISQ option is specified. In Release 6.06, both the left-tailed and right-tailed p values are produced. Previously, a single one-tailed p value was reported for the tail that produced the smaller p value.

The NOPERCENT option now has an effect for one-way frequencies and frequencies in list format. It suppresses printing of percentages and cumulative percentages.

The ALPHA= option allows values between 0.0001 and 0.9999. If you specify a value of 0, the limit of 0.0001 is actually used. See Chapter 20, "The FREQ Procedure," for details.

The MEANS and SUMMARY Procedures

The MEANS and SUMMARY procedures are now the same program. Certain differences exist in the default actions for PROC MEANS versus PROC SUMMARY, but the same statements and options are available for both procedures, including the CLASS statement in PROC MEANS.

A major difference between the two procedures is that, by default, PROC SUMMARY produces no printed output. The PRINT= option is available if you want to override the default and print output.

Another difference between PROC MEANS and PROC SUMMARY is that if you omit the VAR statement, PROC SUMMARY gives a simple count of observations, while PROC MEANS analyzes all numeric variables in the input data set except for the variables used in the BY, FREQ, WEIGHT, and CLASS statements.

Additionally, the way the MEANS procedure treats ID variables has changed from previous versions. Currently, the values from the observation containing the MAXIMUM value for the first ID variable are output. In Version 5, the values in the first observation for each BY group were output for the ID variables.

You can specify two new options in the OUTPUT statement, MINID and MAXID. These options enable you to associate lists of ID variables with the minimum or maximum of different analysis variables.

PROC SUMMARY now computes skewness and kurtosis.

The limit on the number of class value interactions has changed. On many machines, the number is in the 200 million range (up from 32,767). The maximum number of class variables allowed is now 30.

Appearance of Output

The printed output differs from previous versions. The changes are noticeable in the following:

- default statistics
- line-size specifications
- naming conventions
- BY-group processing.

In Release 6.06, the following statistics are printed by default: mean, standard deviation, minimum, and maximum. This differs from Version 5, where additional statistics were printed if the LINESIZE= option allowed it. Output is centered by default. Names of some statistics are printed differently, for example, MINIMUM VALUE and MAXIMUM VALUE are now printed Minimum and Maximum, respectively. The MEANS and SUMMARY procedures now print the name of each statistic with an initial uppercase letter rather than with all uppercase letters. Also, the position of the statistical title line when you use a BY statement has changed. If you have only one analysis variable, it is printed at the top of the page. If you have more than one, they are printed as in previous versions. To illustrate output differences between versions, the following code is used with the same data under both Release 6.06 and Release 5.18:

```
options linesize=120 nodate;
proc means;
    title 'Statistics For All Numeric Variables';
run;
```

The output produced under Release 5.18 is shown in **Output 1**. The output produced under Release 6.06 is shown in **Output 2**.

Output 1 PROC MEANS Output Using Release 5.18

```
                    Statistics For All Numeric Variables                                      1

VARIABLE    N      MEAN      STANDARD      MINIMUM      MAXIMUM     STD ERROR
                             DEVIATION      VALUE        VALUE      OF MEAN

HEIGHT     37   65.63243243   5.8398561   51.3000000   78.000000   0.96006642
WEIGHT     36   98.35555556  16.8519680   50.5000000  128.000000   2.80866133
TIME       37    1.51351351   0.5067117    1.0000000    2.000000   0.08330289
```

Output 2 PROC MEANS Output Using Release 6.06

```
                       Statistics For All Numeric Variables                                   1

       Variable   N       Mean      Std Dev      Minimum      Maximum
       ----------------------------------------------------------------
       HEIGHT    37   65.6324324   5.8398561   51.3000000    78.0000000
       WEIGHT    36   98.3555556  16.8519680   50.5000000   128.0000000
       TIME      37    1.5135135   0.5067117    1.0000000     2.0000000
       ----------------------------------------------------------------
```

Complete documentation for both PROC MEANS and PROC SUMMARY is found under PROC MEANS.

The OPTIONS Procedure

The format of the output from the OPTIONS procedure has changed slightly. Options are divided into configuration options (those that can be specified only when you invoke the system) and session options. Host-specific options are listed separately.

The PLOT Procedure

The PLOT procedure can now be used interactively.

To plot all unique combinations of a list of variables, you can now specify a variable list. For example, the following PLOT statement plots the combinations A*B, A*C, and B*C:

```
plot (a b c);
```

Scaling for PLOT procedure output has changed, so plots may look different from plots produced by earlier releases.

The PROC PLOT statement supports the following new options:

FORMCHAR= specifies the characters to use to construct the borders of the plot.

HPERCENT= specifies the percentage of the horizontal page to use for each plot.

NOMISS excludes observations with missing values from calculation of the axes.

VPERCENT= specifies the percentage of the vertical page to use for each plot.

VTOH= specifies the aspect ratio (vertical to horizontal) of the characters on the output device.

The PLOT statement supports the following new options:

BOX draws a border around the entire plot.

HEXPAND expands the horizontal axis to minimize the margins at the sides of the plot.

HREVERSE reverses the order of the values on the horizontal axis.

SLIST= specifies plotting symbols for multiple contour levels.

VEXPAND expands the vertical axis to minimize the margins above and below the plot.

The PRINTTO Procedure

The PRINTTO procedure supports two new options, LOG= and PRINT=, that change the destination of the SAS log or SAS output in the middle of a SAS program or session.

The RANK Procedure

The NPLUS1 option has been added to the PROC RANK statement, enabling you to request fractional ranks where the denominator is $n+1$ rather than n, where n is the number of observations having nonmissing values of the ranking variable.

The SORT Procedure

The NODUPKEY option is new for the PROC SORT statement. This option checks for and eliminates records with duplicate keys. The FORCE option is a new option that is required if you want to sort and replace a data set that has been subsetted or has indexes defined for it. The FORCE option destroys any existing indexes.

Three new options specify alternate sorting sequences: ASCII, EBCDIC, and SORTSEQ=. Specify either the ASCII or EBCDIC option to use a sorting sequence other than the one native to your environment. Use the SORTSEQ= option to specify any of the supported collating sequences.

The options listed below are available in limited environments. Refer to the SAS documentation for your host system for information on the following options:

DIAG
LEAVE=n
LIST
L
MESSAGE
M
SORTSIZE=parameter
SIZE=parameter
SORTWKNO=number
TECHNIQUE=xxxx
T=xxxx

The STANDARD Procedure

If you specify the PRINT option, the STANDARD procedure prints the input frequency, mean, and standard deviation for each variable standardized. The NOPRINT option is the default.

The TABULATE Procedure

The PROC TABULATE statement has a new option, VARDEF=, that specifies the divisor to use in the calculation of variances.

The TIMEPLOT Procedure

The NPP option for the PLOT statement suppresses the printing of values of plotted variables.

There is no longer a restriction on the number of CLASS statements.

The UNIVARIATE Procedure

The ROUND= option for the PROC UNIVARIATE statement is new. Use the ROUND= option to specify the units used to round the variable values.

The OUTPUT statement has the following new percentile options:

PCTLNAME=   specifies percentile names in the same order as the
             PCTLPTS= option.

PCTLPTS=   specifies percentile values ranging from 0 to 100.

PCTLRPRE=   specifies prefix names in order of the variables in the
             VAR statement.

The PCTLDEF= option now equals 5 rather than 4 by default. Two new statistics are available, PROBN and PROBS. PROBN gives the probability for testing the hypothesis that the data come from a normal distribution. PROBS gives the probability of a greater absolute value for the centered, signed rank statistic.

SAS® Elementary Statistics Procedures

INTRODUCTION

The following SAS procedures compute univariate or bivariate statistics, such as means, sums, standard deviations, and correlations:

CORR   computes bivariate correlations and other measures of association.

MEANS and SUMMARY

compute elementary univariate statistics within groups of observations. The groups are defined by variables in a CLASS statement. The statistics can be printed or output to a SAS data set.

TABULATE   prints complex tables of elementary statistics.

UNIVARIATE   computes univariate statistics, including quantiles, and draws distributional plots.

Other procedures that compute elementary statistics include the following:

CHART   draws bar, block, pie, and star charts of counts, percentages, means, or sums.

FREQ   computes frequency distributions for categorical variables and does multi-way crosstabulations. The FREQ procedure computes a wide variety of descriptive and inferential statistics.

Comparison of Procedures

Table 1.1 indicates the statistics available from each procedure. **Table 1.2** summarizes some other important features. An X indicates that the statistic or feature is available.

Table 1.1   Statistics Available from Each SAS Elementary Statistics Procedure

Statistic	MEANS	UNIVARIATE	SUMMARY	TABULATE	CORR
Number of missing values	x	x	x	x	
Number of nonmissing values	x	x	x	x	x
Number of values	x		x		
Sum of weights	x	x	x	x	x
Mean	x	x	x	x	x
Sum	x	x	x	x	x
Minimum	x	x	x	x	x
Maximum	x	x	x	x	x
Range	x	x	x	x	x
Uncorrected sum of squares	x	x	x	x	x
Corrected sum of squares	x	x	x	x	x
Variance	x	x	x	x	x
Standard deviation	x	x	x	x	x

(continued)

Table 1.1 Statistics Available from Each SAS Elementary Statistics Procedure (*continued*)

Statistic	MEANS	UNIVARIATE	SUMMARY	TABULATE	CORR
Standard error	x	x	x	x	
Coefficient of variation	x	x	x	x	
Skewness	x	x	x		
Kurtosis	x	x	x		
Student's t	x	x	x	x	
Prob> $|t|$	x	x	x	x	
Median		x			x
Quartiles		x			
Mode		x			
Pearson correlation					x

Table 1.2 Features of Each SAS Elementary Statistics Procedure

Feature	MEANS	UNIVARIATE	SUMMARY	TABULATE	CORR
Printed output	x	x	x	x	x
Output to a SAS data set	x	x	x		x
CLASS statement	x		x	x	
BY statement	x	x	x	x	x

Efficiency

Quantiles, including the median, require time proportional to $n\log(n)$ for large sample sizes, so PROC UNIVARIATE may require more time than other elementary statistics procedures. PROC UNIVARIATE also requires more storage space because the data are held in core.

If you need to compute statistics for each of several groups of observations, you can use any of the previous procedures with a BY statement to specify the groups. However, BY-group processing requires sorting or indexing the data set, which can be expensive for large data sets. The SUMMARY, MEANS, and TABULATE procedures can produce statistics across a classification without sorting.

Keywords and Formulas

A standardized set of keywords is used to refer to the univariate statistics in SAS procedures. These keywords are used in SAS statements to request statistics for printing or storing in an output data set.

The following notations are used where summation is over all nonmissing values:

x_i the ith nonmissing observation on the variable

w_i the weight associated with x_i if a WEIGHT statement is specified, otherwise 1

n the number of nonmissing observations

$\bar{x}$ $= \Sigma w_i x_i / \Sigma w_i$

d $= n$ if VARDEF$=$N is specified,

   $= n-1$ if VARDEF$=$DF is specified,

   $= \Sigma w_i$ if VARDEF$=$WEIGHT $|$ WGT is specified,

   $= \Sigma w_i - 1$ if VARDEF$=$WDF is specified

s^2 $= \Sigma w_i (x_i - \bar{x})^2 / d$

z_i $= (x_i - \bar{x})/s$ standardized variables.

The formulas and standard keywords for each statistic are given below. In some formulas a keyword is used to designate the corresponding statistic.

N   number of nonmissing observations

NMISS   number of missing observations

MIN   minimum value

MAX   maximum value

RANGE   MAX$-$MIN, the range

SUM $\Sigma w_i x_i$, the weighted sum

SUMWGT Σw_i, the sum of weights

MEAN $\bar{x}$, the arithmetic mean

USS $\Sigma w_i x_i^2$, the uncorrected sum of squares

CSS $\Sigma w_i (x_i - \bar{x})^2$, the sum of squares corrected for the mean

VAR s^2, the variance

COVARIANCE $\mathrm{cov}_{xy} \Sigma w_i (x_i - \bar{x}_w)(y_i - \bar{y}_w)/d$, the covariance

STD s, the standard deviation

STDERR $s/\sqrt{n}$, the standard error of the mean

CV $100\, s/\bar{x}$, the percent coefficient of variation

SKEWNESS $\Sigma z_i^3 \times n/(n-1)(n-2)$, measures sidedness

KURTOSIS $\Sigma z_i^4 \times n(n+1)/(n-1)(n-2)(n-3) - 3(n-1)^2/(n-2)(n-3)$, measures heaviness of tails

T $t = \bar{x}^* \sqrt{n}/s$, Student's t for H_0: population mean$=0$

PRT   the two-tailed p-value for Student's t with $n-1$ degrees of freedom, the probability under the null hypothesis of obtaining an absolute value of t greater than the t-value observed in this sample

MEDIAN   the middle value when the x_i are arranged in order of value and n is odd; the mean of the two middle values when n is even.

QUARTILE   the values such that the upper quarter of the x_i values are larger and the lower quarter of the x_i values are smaller

MODE   the most frequent value of x_i.

Data Requirements for Univariate Statistics

Statistics are reported as missing if they cannot be computed. The N and NMISS statistics are computed regardless of the number of missing or nonmissing observations. The SUM, MEAN, MAX, MIN, RANGE, USS, and CSS statistics will be computed if there is at least one nonmissing observation. The requirements for other statistics are as follows:

- The VAR, STD, STDERR, CV, T, and PRT statistics require at least two nonmissing observations.
- The SKEWNESS statistic requires at least three nonmissing observations.
- The KURTOSIS statistic requires at least four nonmissing observations.
- The SKEWNESS, KURTOSIS, T, and PRT statistics require that STD be greater than 0.
- The SKEWNESS and KURTOSIS statistics are not computed if a WEIGHT statement is used.
- The CV statistic requires that MEAN not equal 0.

STATISTICAL BACKGROUND

The rest of this chapter provides a brief introduction to some of the statistical concepts necessary for interpreting the output of SAS procedures for elementary statistics. For a more thorough discussion, consult an introductory statistics textbook such as Moore (1979), Ott (1977), or Snedecor and Cochran (1976).

POPULATION AND PARAMETERS

Usually, there is a clearly defined set of elements in which you are interested. This set of elements is called the *universe*, and a set of values associated with these elements is called a *population* of values. The statistical term *population* has nothing to do with people per se. A statistical population is a collection of values, not a collection of people. For example, a universe may be all the students at a particular school, and there could be two populations of interest: one of height values and one of weight values. Or, a universe could be the set of all widgets manufactured by a particular company, while the population of values could be the length of time each widget is used before it fails.

A population of values can be described in terms of its *cumulative distribution function*, which gives the proportion of the population less than each possible value. A discrete population can also be described by a *probability function* giving the proportion of the population equal to each possible value. A continuous population can often be described by a *density function*, which is the derivative of the cumulative distribution function. A density function can be approximated by a histogram that gives the proportion of the population lying within each of a series of intervals of values such as produced by the CHART procedure. A probability density function is like a histogram with an infinite number of infinitely small intervals.

In technical literature, when the term *distribution* is used without qualification, it generally refers to the cumulative distribution function. In informal writing, *distribution* sometimes means the density function instead. Often the word *distribu-*

tion is used simply to refer to an abstract population of values rather than some concrete population. Thus, the statistical literature refers to many types of abstract distributions, such as normal distributions, exponential distributions, Cauchy distributions, and so on. When a phrase such as *normal distribution* is used, it frequently does not matter whether the cumulative distribution function or the density function is intended.

It may be expedient to describe a population in terms of a few measures that summarize interesting features of the distribution. One such measure, computed from the population values, is called a *parameter*. Many different parameters can be defined to measure different aspects of a distribution.

The most commonly used parameter is the (arithmetic) *mean*. If the population contains a finite number of values, the population mean is computed as the sum of all the values in the population divided by the number of elements in the population. For an infinite population, the concept of the mean is similar but requires more complicated mathematics.

We write $E(x)$ to denote the mean of a population of values symbolized by x, such as height, where E stands for *expected value*. We can also consider expected values of derived functions of the original values. For example, if x represents height, then $E(x^2)$ is the expected value of height squared, that is, the mean value of the population obtained by squaring every value in the population of heights.

Samples and Statistics

It is often impossible to measure all of the values in a population. A collection of measured values is called a *sample*. A mathematical function of a sample of values is called a *statistic*. A statistic is to a sample as a parameter is to a population. It is customary to denote statistics by Roman letters and parameters by Greek letters. For example, the population mean is often written as μ, whereas the sample mean is written as $\bar{x}$. The branch of mathematics called *statistics* is largely concerned with the study of the behavior of sample statistics.

Samples can be selected in a variety of ways. Most SAS procedures assume that the data constitute a *simple random sample*, which means that the sample was selected in such a way that all possible samples were equally likely to be selected.

Statistics from a sample can be used to make inferences, or reasonable guesses, about the parameters of a population. For example, if you take a random sample of 30 students from the high school, the mean height for those 30 students is a reasonable guess, or *estimate*, of the mean height of all the students in the high school. Other statistics, such as the standard error, can provide information about how good an estimate is likely to be.

For any population parameter, there are many statistics that can be used to estimate it. Often, however, there is one particular statistic that is customarily used to estimate a given parameter. For example, the sample mean is the usual estimator of the population mean. In the case of the mean, the formulas for the parameter and the statistic are the same. In other cases, the formula for a parameter may be different from that of the most commonly used estimator. It should not be assumed that the most commonly used estimator is the best estimator in all applications.

Measures of Location

Measures of location include the mean, the median, and the mode. These measures can generally be thought of as describing the center of a distribution. In the definitions below, notice that if the entire sample is changed by adding a fixed amount to each observation, then these measures of location are shifted by the same fixed amount.

The Mean

As discussed above, the population mean $\mu = E(x)$ is usually estimated by the sample mean:

$$\bar{x} = \Sigma\, x_i\, /\, n \quad .$$

The Median

The population median is the central value, lying above and below half of the population values. The sample median is the middle value when the data are arranged in ascending or descending order. For an even number of observations, the midpoint between the two middle values is usually reported as the median.

The Mode

The mode is the value at which the density of the population is at a maximum. Some densities have more than one local maximum (peak) and are said to be *multimodal*. The sample mode is the value that occurs most often in the sample. If there is a tie for most-often-occurring sample value, the UNIVARIATE procedure reports the lowest such value. If the population is continuous, then all sample values occur once and the sample mode has little use.

Quantiles

Quantiles, including percentiles, quartiles, and the median, are useful for a detailed study of a distribution. For a set of measurements arranged in order of magnitude, the pth percentile is the value that has $p\%$ of the measurements below it and $(100-p)\%$ above it. The median is the 50th percentile. Since it may not be possible to divide your data so that you get exactly the desired percentile, a more precise definition is used (see Chapter 42, "The UNIVARIATE Procedure").

The upper quartile of a distribution is the value below which 75% of the measurements fall (the 75th percentile). Twenty-five percent of the measurements fall below the lower quartile value. The UNIVARIATE and RANK procedures can be used to calculate any desired quantiles.

Example 1: Quantiles and Measures of Location

The data in the following example are artificially generated by a call to a pseudo-random-number function. The UNIVARIATE procedure computes a variety of quantiles and measures of location, and outputs the values to a SAS data set. A DATA step then uses the SYMPUT routine to assign the values of the statistics to macro variables. The macro variables are used in the macro %FORMGEN to produce value labels for the FORMAT procedure. The resulting format is used with the CHART procedure to display the values of the statistics on a histogram.

The program below produces **Output 1.1**.

```
title 'Example of Quantiles and Measures of Location';

data random;
  drop n;
  do n=1 to 1000;
     x=floor(exp(rannor(314159)*.8+1.8));
     output;
  end;
run;

proc univariate;
   var x;
   output out=location mean=mean mode=mode median=median
       q1=q1 q3=q3 p5=p5 p10=p10 p90=p90 p95=p95 max=max;
run;

proc print;
run;

data _null_;
   set location;
   call symput('MEAN',round(mean,1));
   call symput('MODE',mode);
   call symput('MEDIAN',round(median,1));
   call symput('Q1',round(q1,1));
   call symput('Q3',round(q3,1));
   call symput('P5',round(p5,1));
   call symput('P10',round(p10,1));
   call symput('P90',round(p90,1));
   call symput('P95',round(p95,1));
   call symput('MAX',min(50,max));
run;

%macro formgen;
   %do i=1 %to &max;
      %let value=&i;
      %if &i=&p5     %then %let value=&value   p5;
      %if &i=&p10    %then %let value=&value   p10;
      %if &i=&q1     %then %let value=&value   q1;
      %if &i=&mode   %then %let value=&value   mode;
      %if &i=&median %then %let value=&value   median;
      %if &i=&mean   %then %let value=&value   mean;
      %if &i=&q3     %then %let value=&value   q3;
      %if &i=&p90    %then %let value=&value   p90;
      %if &i=&p95    %then %let value=&value   p95;
      %if &i=&max    %then %let value=>=&value;
      &i="&value"
   %end;
%mend;
```

```
proc format print;
   value stat %formgen;
run;

proc chart data=random;
   vbar x / midpoints=1 to &max by 1;
   format x stat.;
   footnote  'P5  =  5TH PERCENTILE';
   footnote2 'P10 = 10TH PERCENTILE';
   footnote3 'P90 = 90TH PERCENTILE';
   footnote4 'P95 = 95TH PERCENTILE';
   footnote5 'Q1  =  1ST QUARTILE  ';
   footnote6 'Q3  =  3RD QUARTILE  ';
run;
```

Output 1.1 Example of Quantiles and Measures of Location

```
              Example of Quantiles and Measures of Location                          1
                          Univariate Procedure

Variable=X

         Moments                    Quantiles(Def=5)                  Extremes

N          1000  Sum Wgts    1000   100% Max   62    99%   37.5    Lowest  Obs   Highest  Obs
Mean      7.605  Sum         7605    75% Q3     9    95%   21.5       0(   941)    44(   216)
Std Dev 7.381698 Variance 54.48946   50% Med    5    90%   16         0(   756)    44(   486)
Skewness 2.730385 Kurtosis 11.18706  25% Q1     3    10%    2         0(   402)    57(   319)
USS      112271  CSS      54434.97    0% Min    0     5%    1         0(   358)    61(   951)
CV      97.06375 Std Mean 0.23343                     1%    0         0(   323)    62(   147)
T:Mean=0 32.57939 Prob>|T|  0.0001   Range     62
Num ¬= 0    989  Num > 0     989     Q3-Q1      6
M(Sign)   494.5  Prob>|M|  0.0001    Mode       3
Sgn Rank 244777.5 Prob>|S|  0.0001
```

```
              Example of Quantiles and Measures of Location                          2
        OBS    MEAN    MAX   Q3   MEDIAN   Q1    P95    P90   P10   P5   MODE

         1    7.605    62    9      5       3   21.5    16     2    1     3
```

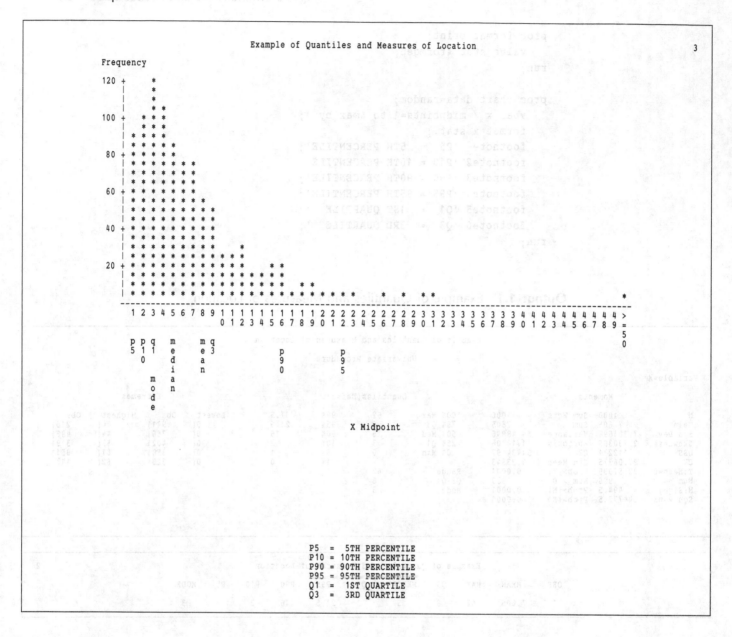

Example of Quantiles and Measures of Location

P5 = 5TH PERCENTILE
P10 = 10TH PERCENTILE
P90 = 90TH PERCENTILE
P95 = 95TH PERCENTILE
Q1 = 1ST QUARTILE
Q3 = 3RD QUARTILE

Measures of Variability

Another group of statistics important for studying the distribution of a population measures the *variability*, or spread, of values. In the definitions given in the sections that follow, notice that if the entire sample is changed by the addition of a fixed amount to each observation, then the values of these statistics are unchanged. The values of these statistics are changed, however, if each observation in the sample is multiplied by a constant.

The Range

The sample range is the difference between the largest and smallest values in the sample. For many populations, at least in statistical theory, the range is infinite, so the sample range may not tell you much about the population. The sample range tends to increase as the sample size increases. If all sample values are multiplied by a constant, the sample range is multiplied by the same constant.

The Interquartile Range

The interquartile range is the difference between the upper and lower quartiles. If all sample values are multiplied by a constant, the sample interquartile range is multiplied by the same constant.

The Variance

The population variance, usually denoted by σ^2 when it is clear what population is being considered, is the expected value of the squared difference of the values from the population mean:

$$\sigma^2 = E(x - \mu)^2 \quad .$$

The sample variance, denoted s^2, is usually computed as

$$s^2 = \Sigma (x_i - \bar{x})^2 / (n - 1) \quad .$$

The difference between a value and the mean is called a *deviation from the mean*. Thus, the variance is the mean of the squared deviation. When all the values lie close to the mean, the variance is small but never less than zero. When values are more scattered, the variance is larger. If all sample values are multiplied by a constant, the sample variance is multiplied by the square of the constant.

Sometimes values other than $n-1$ are used in the denominator. The VARDEF option controls what divisor is used.

The Standard Deviation

The standard deviation is the square root of the variance, or root-mean-square deviation from the mean, in either population or sample. The usual symbols are σ for the population and s for a sample. The standard deviation is expressed in the same units as the observations, rather than in squared units. If all sample values are multiplied by a constant, the sample standard deviation is multiplied by the same constant.

Coefficient of Variation

The coefficient of variation is a unitless measure of relative variability. It is defined as the ratio of the standard deviation to the mean expressed as a percentage. The coefficient of variation is meaningful only if the variable is measured on a ratio scale. If all sample values are multiplied by a constant, the sample coefficient of variation remains unchanged.

Measures of Shape

Skewness

The variance is a measure of the overall size of the deviations from the mean. Since the formula for the variance squares the deviations, both positive and negative deviations contribute to the variance in the same way. In many distributions, positive deviations may tend to be larger in magnitude than negative deviations, or vice versa. *Skewness* is a measure of the tendency of the deviations to be larger in one direction than in the other. For example, the data in the last example are skewed to the right.

Population skewness is defined as

$$E(x - \mu)^3 / \sigma^3 \quad .$$

Since the deviations are cubed rather than squared, the signs of the deviations are maintained. Cubing the deviations also emphasizes the effects of large deviations. The formula includes a divisor of σ^3 to remove the effect of scale, so multiplying all values by a constant does not change the skewness. Skewness can thus be interpreted as a tendency for one tail of the population to be heavier than the other.

The sample skewness is calculated as

$$n / (n - 1)(n - 2) \Sigma_{i=1}^{n} (x_i - \bar{x})^3 / s^3 \quad .$$

Skewness can be positive or negative and is unbounded.

Kurtosis

The heaviness of the tails of a population affects the behavior of many statistics. Hence it is useful to have a measure of tail heaviness. One such measure is *kurtosis*. The population kurtosis is usually defined as

$$E(x - \mu)^4 / \sigma^4 - 3$$

although some statisticians omit the subtraction of 3. Since the deviations are raised to the fourth power, positive and negative deviations make the same contribution, while large deviations are strongly emphasized. Because of the divisor σ^4, multiplying each value by a constant has no effect on kurtosis.

Population kurtosis must lie between -2 and positive infinity, inclusive. If m_3 represents population skewness and m_4 represents population kurtosis, then

$$m_4 \geq m_3^2 - 2 \quad .$$

The sample kurtosis is calculated as

$$n(n + 1)/(n - 1)(n - 2)(n - 3) \Sigma_{i=1}^{n} (x_i - \bar{x})^4/s^4 - 3(n - 1)(n - 1)/(n - 2)(n - 3) \quad .$$

There is a myth in the statistical literature that kurtosis measures the *peakedness* of a density. This myth stubbornly persists despite repeated debunking (Kaplansky 1945; Ali 1974; Johnson, Tietjen, and Beckman 1980). Heavy tails have much more influence on kurtosis than does the shape of the distribution near the mean.

Sample skewness and kurtosis are rather unreliable estimators of the corresponding parameters in small samples. Trust them only if you have a very large sample. However, large values of skewness or kurtosis may merit attention even in small samples because such values indicate that statistical methods based on normality assumptions (see the next section) may be inappropriate.

The Normal Distribution

One especially important family of theoretical distributions is the *normal* or *Gaussian* distribution. A normal distribution is a smooth symmetric function often referred to as "bell-shaped." Its skewness and kurtosis are both zero. A normal distribution can be completely specified by only two parameters: the mean and the standard deviation. Approximately 68% of the values in a normal population are within one standard deviation of the population mean; approximately 95% of the values are within two standard deviations of the mean; and about 99.7% are within three standard deviations. Use of the term *normal* to describe this particular kind of distribution does not imply that other kinds of distributions are necessarily abnormal or pathological.

Many statistical methods are designed under the assumption that the population being sampled is normally distributed. Nevertheless, most real-life populations do not have normal distributions. Before using any statistical method based on normality assumptions, you should consult the statistical literature to find out how sensitive the method is to nonnormality and, if necessary, check your sample for evidence of nonnormality.

Example 2: Normal Distribution

The following data are sampled from a normal distribution with mean 50 and standard deviation 10. The statements below generate **Output 1.2**.

```
title 'Sample of 10000 Observations from a Normal Distribution';
title2 'with Mean=50 and Standard Deviation=10';
data normal;
   drop n;
   do n=1 to 10000;
      x=10*rannor(53124)+50;
      output;
   end;
run;

proc univariate normal;
   var x;
run;

proc format;
   picture msd
      20='20.0 MEAN-3*STD' (noedit)
      30='30.0 MEAN-2*STD' (noedit)
      40='40.0 MEAN-STD  ' (noedit)
      50='50.0 MEAN      ' (noedit)
      60='60.0 MEAN+STD  ' (noedit)
      70='70.0 MEAN+2*STD' (noedit)
      80='80.0 MEAN+3*STD' (noedit)
   other='00.0';
run;

proc chart;
   vbar x / midpoints=20 to 80 by 2;
   format x msd.;
run;
```

Output 1.2 Sample from a Normal Distribution

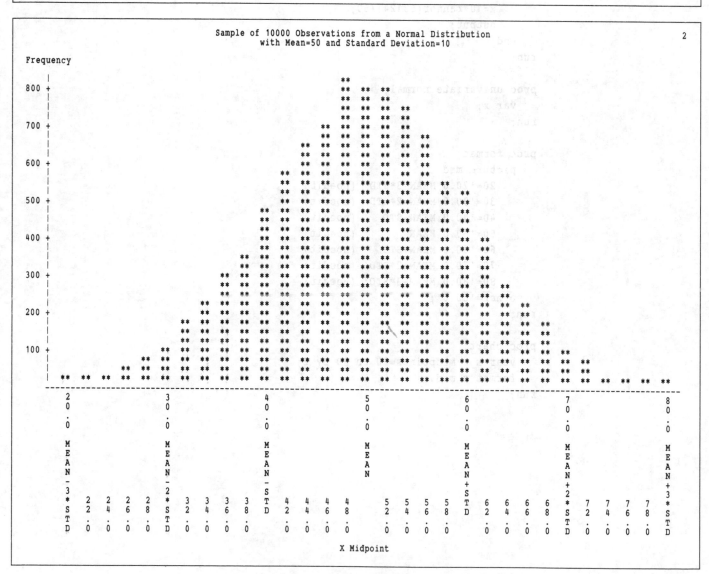

```
                Sample of 10000 Observations from a Normal Distribution                    1
                          with Mean=50 and Standard Deviation=10

                                    Univariate Procedure

Variable=X

            Moments                        Quantiles(Def=5)                    Extremes

N            10000  Sum Wgts     10000   100% Max   90.21051   99%    72.678      Lowest  Obs     Highest  Obs
Mean       50.03237  Sum        500323.7  75% Q3    56.72798   95%  66.22214    13.69709( 3124)  83.51076( 7791)
Std Dev    9.920139  Variance   98.40915  50% Med   50.06492   90%  62.66782    14.70881( 9117)  84.00529( 2403)
Skewness   -0.01993  Kurtosis   -0.01638  25% Q1    43.44618   10%  37.11393    15.80234( 5642)  87.48835(  208)
USS        26016378  CSS        983993.1   0% Min   13.69709    5%  33.54542    17.02475( 1735)  88.30869( 4766)
CV         19.82744  Std Mean   0.099201                        1%  26.91889    18.20598( 5048)  90.21051( 2444)
T:Mean=0   504.3516  Prob>|T|    0.0001  Range      76.51343
Num ¬= 0     10000  Num > 0      10000  Q3-Q1      13.28179
M(Sign)       5000  Prob>|M|     0.0001  Mode       13.69709
Sgn Rank   25002500  Prob>|S|    0.0001
D:Normal   0.006595  Prob>D        >.15
```

```
                Sample of 10000 Observations from a Normal Distribution                    2
                          with Mean=50 and Standard Deviation=10

Frequency

   800 +                             **
       |                             ** ** **
       |                             ** ** **
       |                             ** ** ** **
   700 +                          ** ** ** ** **
       |                          ** ** ** ** **
       |                       ** ** ** ** ** ** **
       |                       ** ** ** ** ** ** **
   600 +                       ** ** ** ** ** ** **
       |                    ** ** ** ** ** ** ** **
       |                    ** ** ** ** ** ** ** **
       |                    ** ** ** ** ** ** ** **
   500 +                    ** ** ** ** ** ** ** ** **
       |                    ** ** ** ** ** ** ** ** **
       |                 ** ** ** ** ** ** ** ** ** **
       |                 ** ** ** ** ** ** ** ** ** **
   400 +                 ** ** ** ** ** ** ** ** ** **
       |                 ** ** ** ** ** ** ** ** ** ** **
       |              ** ** ** ** ** ** ** ** ** ** ** **
       |              ** ** ** ** ** ** ** ** ** ** ** **
   300 +           ** ** ** ** ** ** ** ** ** ** ** ** **
       |           ** ** ** ** ** ** ** ** ** ** ** ** ** **
       |           ** ** ** ** ** ** ** ** ** ** ** ** ** **
       |        ** ** ** ** ** ** ** ** ** ** ** ** ** ** **
   200 +     ** ** ** ** ** ** ** ** ** ** ** ** ** ** ** ** **
       |     ** ** ** ** ** ** ** ** ** ** ** ** ** ** ** ** ** **
       |     ** ** ** ** ** ** ** ** ** ** ** ** ** ** ** ** ** ** **
       |  ** ** ** ** ** ** ** ** ** ** ** ** ** ** ** ** ** ** ** **
   100 +  ** ** ** ** ** ** ** ** ** ** ** ** ** ** ** ** ** ** ** ** **
       |  ** ** ** ** ** ** ** ** ** ** ** ** ** ** ** ** ** ** ** ** ** **
       |  ** ** ** ** ** ** ** ** ** ** ** ** ** ** ** ** ** ** ** ** ** ** ** **
       |**  ** ** ** ** ** ** ** ** ** ** ** ** ** ** ** ** ** ** ** ** ** ** ** ** **
       ------------------------------------------------------------------------------------
          2         3         4         5         6         7         8
          0         0         0         0         0         0         0
          .         .         .         .         .         .         .
          0         0         0         0         0         0         0

          M         M         M         M         M         M         M
          E         E         E         E         E         E         E
          A         A         A         A         A         A         A
          N         N         N         N         N         N         N
          -         -         -                   +         +         +
          3         2         S                   S         2         3
          *         *         T                   T         *         *
          S  2  2  2  2  S  3  3  3  3  T  4  4  4  4  5  5  5  5  D  6  6  6  6  S  7  7  7  7  S
          T  2  4  6  8  T  2  4  6  8  D  2  4  6  8  2  4  6  8     2  4  6  8  T  2  4  6  8  T
          D  0  0  0  0  D  0  0  0  0     0  0  0  0  0  0  0  0     0  0  0  0  D  0  0  0  0  D

                                          X Midpoint
```

Sampling Distribution of the Mean

If you repeatedly draw samples of size *n* from a population and compute the mean of each sample, then the sample means themselves have a distribution. Consider a new population consisting of the means of all the samples that could possibly be drawn from the original population. The distribution of this new population is called a *sampling distribution*.

It can be proven mathematically that if the original population has mean μ and standard deviation σ, then the sampling distribution of the mean also has mean μ, but its standard deviation is $\sigma/\sqrt{n}$. The standard deviation of the sampling distribution of the mean is called the *standard error of the mean*. The standard error of the mean provides an indication of the accuracy of a sample mean as an estimator of the population mean.

If the original population has a normal distribution, then the sampling distribution of the mean is also normal. If the original distribution is not normal but does not have excessively long tails, then the sampling distribution of the mean can be approximated by a normal distribution for large sample sizes.

Example 3:   Sampling Distributions

The following DATA step creates a sample of 1000 observations from an exponential distribution generated by the RANEXP function. The theoretical population mean is 1.00, while the sample mean is 1.01, to two decimal places. The population standard deviation is 1.00, the sample standard deviation 1.04.

This is an example of a nonnormal distribution. The population skewness is 2.00, which is close to the sample skewness of 1.97. The population kurtosis is 6.00, but the sample kurtosis is only 4.80. The statements below generate **Output 1.3**.

```
title 'Sample of 1000 Observations from an Exponential Distribution';

data expo;
   drop n;
   do n=1 to 1000;
      x=ranexp(18746363);
      output;
   end;
run;

proc chart;
   vbar x / axis=300 midpoints=0.05 to 4.95 by .1;
run;

proc univariate;
run;
```

Output 1.3   Sample from an Exponential Distribution

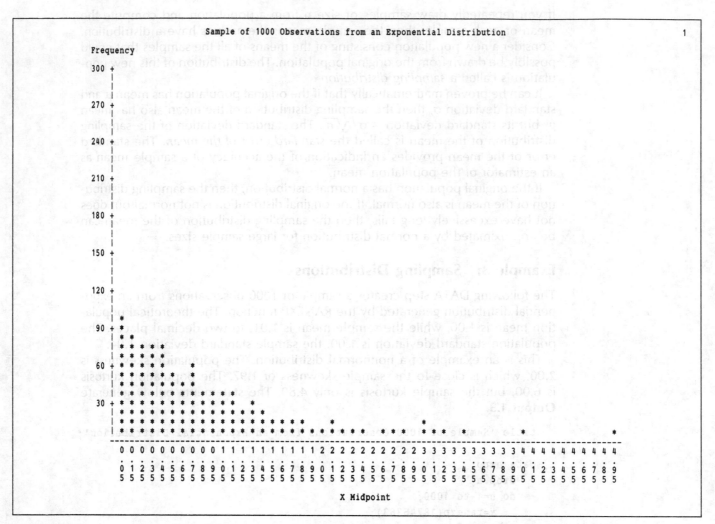

Variable=X

	Moments			Quantiles(Def=5)			Extremes			
N	1000	Sum Wgts	1000	100% Max	6.639068	99% 5.044917	Lowest	Obs	Highest	Obs
Mean	1.011762	Sum	1011.762	75% Q3	1.357334	95% 3.134823	0.000554(	333)	5.782202(	148)
Std Dev	1.043712	Variance	1.089334	50% Med	0.689502	90% 2.378036	0.001248(	630)	6.006787(	906)
Skewness	1.969631	Kurtosis	4.801506	25% Q1	0.294814	10% 0.10219	0.002223(	858)	6.135398(	855)
USS	2111.908	CSS	1088.245	0% Min	0.000554	5% 0.051928	0.002533(	452)	6.608973(	213)
CV	103.1578	Std Mean	0.033005			1% 0.011956	0.003967(	947)	6.639068(	50)
T:Mean=0	30.65475	Prob>|T|	0.0001	Range	6.638513					
Num ¬= 0	1000	Num > 0	1000	Q3-Q1	1.06252					
M(Sign)	500	Prob>|M|	0.0001	Mode	0.000554					
Sgn Rank	250250	Prob>|S|	0.0001							

The next DATA step draws 1000 different samples from the same population as the previous DATA step. Each sample contains ten observations. The MEANS procedure computes the mean of each sample. In the data set created by PROC MEANS, each observation represents the mean of a sample of ten observations from an exponential distribution. Thus, the data set is a sample from the sampling distribution of the mean for an exponential population.

PROC UNIVARIATE displays statistics for this sample of means. Notice that the mean of the sample of means is .99, almost the same as the mean of the original population. Theoretically, the standard deviation of the sampling distribution is $\sigma/\sqrt{n} = 1.00/\sqrt{10} = .32$, whereas the standard deviation of this sample from the sampling distribution is .30. The skewness (.54) and kurtosis ($-.006$) are closer to zero in the sample from the sampling distribution than in the original sample from the exponential distribution, since the sampling distribution is closer to a normal distribution than is the original exponential distribution. A histogram of the 1000 sample means is shown using the CHART procedure. The shape of the histogram is much closer to a bell-like normal density, but it is still distinctly lopsided. The statements below produce **Output 1.4**.

```
title '1000 Sample Means with 10 Observations per Sample';
title2 'Drawn from an Exponential Distribution';
data samp10;
   drop n;
   do sample=1 to 1000;
      do n=1 to 10;
         x=ranexp(433879);
         output;
      end;
   end;

proc means noprint;
   output out=mean10 mean=mean;
   var x;
   by sample;
run;

proc chart;
   vbar mean/axis=300  midpoints=0.05 to 4.95 by .1;
run;

proc univariate;
   var mean;
run;
```

Output 1.4 Sample Drawn from an Exponential Distribution

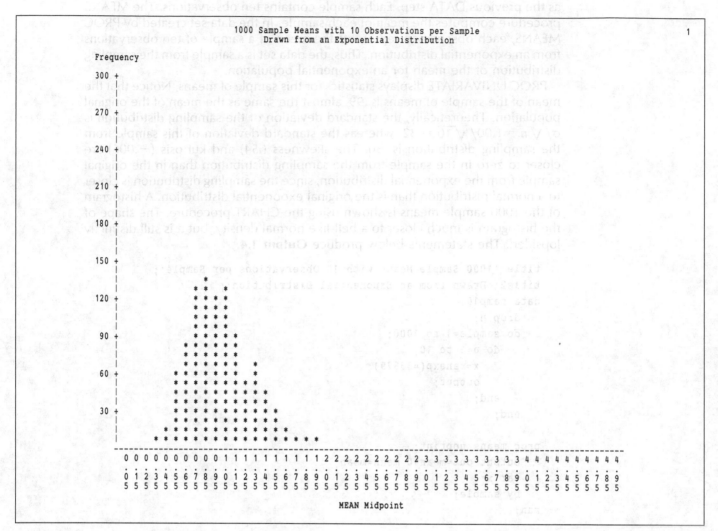

In the following DATA step, the size of each sample is increased to 50. The standard deviation of the sampling distribution is smaller than in the previous example because the size of each sample is larger. Also, the sampling distribution is even closer to a normal distribution, as can be seen from the histogram and the skewness. This example produces **Output 1.5**.

```
options linesize=120 pagesize=60;
title '1000 Sample Means with 50 Observations per Sample';
title2 'Drawn from an Exponential Distribution';
data samp50;
    drop n;
    do sample=1 to 1000;
        do n=1 to 50;
            x=ranexp(72437213);
            output;
        end;
    end;

proc means noprint;
    output out=mean50 mean=mean;
    var x;
    by sample;
run;

proc chart;
    vbar mean / axis=300  midpoints=0.05 to 4.95 by .1;

proc univariate;
    var mean;
run;
```

Output 1.5 An Exponential Distribution with Increased Sample Size

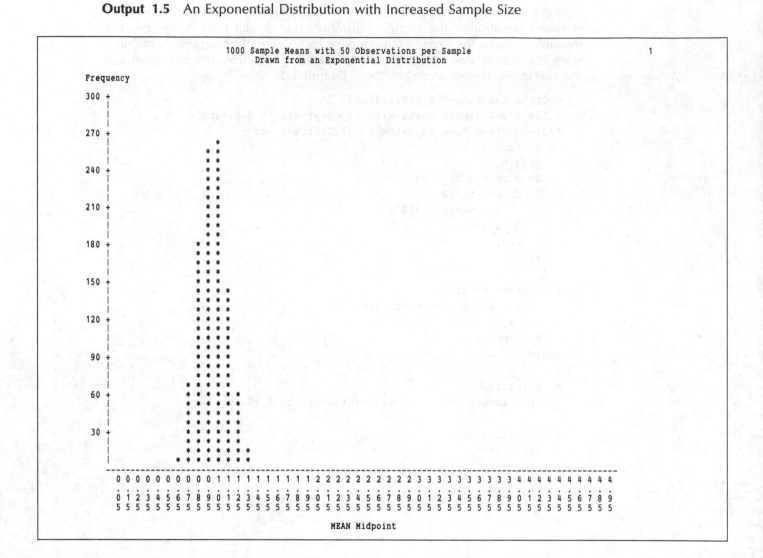

1000 Sample Means with 50 Observations per Sample
Drawn from an Exponential Distribution

MEAN Midpoint

```
                    1000 Sample Means with 50 Observations per Sample          2
                         Drawn from an Exponential Distribution

                                  Univariate Procedure

Variable=MEAN

              Moments                                          Quantiles(Def=5)

N                1000  Sum Wgts      1000          100% Max  1.454957   99%  1.337016
Mean         0.996797  Sum        996.797           75% Q3   1.086515   95%  1.231508
Std Dev      0.138154  Variance  0.019087           50% Med  0.996023   90%  1.179223
Skewness     0.190626  Kurtosis  -0.14386           25% Q1   0.896953   10%  0.814906
USS          1012.672  CSS       19.06745            0% Min   0.584558    5%  0.780783
CV            13.8598  Std Mean  0.004369                                 1%  0.706588
T:Mean=0     228.1619  Prob>|T|    0.0001          Range     0.870399
Num ¬= 0         1000  Num > 0        1000         Q3-Q1     0.189562
M(Sign)           500  Prob>|M|    0.0001          Mode      0.584558
Sgn Rank       250250  Prob>|S|    0.0001


                                      Extremes

                   Lowest     Obs      Highest     Obs
                   0.584558(    121)   1.375359(    179)
                   0.670252(     13)   1.378008(    382)
                   0.67143(     714)   1.391916(    528)
                   0.67221(     235)   1.403003(    308)
                   0.680194(    440)   1.454957(     91)
```

Testing Hypotheses

The purpose of the statistical methods discussed so far is to estimate a population parameter by means of a sample statistic. Another class of statistical methods is used for testing hypotheses about population parameters or for measuring the amount of evidence against a hypothesis.

Consider the universe of students discussed earlier. Let the variable X be the number of pounds by which a student's weight deviates from the ideal weight for a person of the same sex, height, and build. You want to find out whether the population of students is, on the average, underweight or overweight. To this end, you have taken a random sample of X values from nine students, with results as given in the following DATA step:

```
data x;
   title 'Deviations from Normal Weight';
   input x @@;
   cards;
-7 -2 1 3 6 10 15 21 30
;
```

You can define several hypotheses of interest. One hypothesis is that, on the average, the students are of exactly ideal weight. If μ represents the population mean of the X values, you can write this hypothesis, called the *null* hypothesis, as $H_0: \mu=0$. The other two hypotheses, called *alternative* hypotheses, are that the students are underweight on the average, $H_1: \mu<0$, and that the students are overweight on the average, $H_2: \mu>0$.

The null hypothesis is so called not because the hypothesized parameter value is zero, but because the hypothesis specifies a particular value for the parameter. The null hypothesis is not credible because the mean of a continuous variable is almost never exactly equal to any known value. The null hypothesis can be considered a straw man to be knocked down by statistical evidence, and you can decide between the alternative hypotheses according to which way it falls.

A naive way to approach this problem would be to look at the sample mean $\bar{x}$ and decide among the three hypotheses according to the following rule:

- If $\bar{x} < 0$, decide on H_1: $\mu < 0$.
- If $\bar{x} = 0$, decide on H_0: $\mu = 0$.
- If $\bar{x} > 0$, decide on H_2: $\mu > 0$.

The trouble with this approach is that there may be a high probability of making an incorrect decision. If H_0 is true, you are nearly certain to make a wrong decision because the chances of $\bar{x}$ being exactly zero are almost nil. If μ is slightly less than zero, so that H_1 is true, there may be nearly a 50% chance that $\bar{x}$ will be greater than zero in repeated sampling, so the chances of incorrectly choosing H_2 would also be nearly 50%. Thus, you have a high probability of making an error if $\bar{x}$ is near zero. In such cases, there is not enough evidence to make a confident decision, so the best response may be to reserve judgment until you can obtain more evidence.

The question is, how far from zero must $\bar{x}$ be for you to be able to make a confident decision? The answer can be obtained by considering the sampling distribution of $\bar{x}$. If X has a roughly normal distribution, then $\bar{x}$ has an approximately normal sampling distribution. The mean of the sampling distribution of $\bar{x}$ is μ. Assume temporarily that σ, the standard deviation of X, is known to be 12. Then the standard error of $\bar{x}$ for samples of nine observations is $\sigma/\sqrt{n} = 12/\sqrt{9} = 4$.

You know that about 95% of the values from a normal distribution are within two standard deviations of the mean, so about 95% of the possible samples of nine X values have a sample mean $\bar{x}$ between $0 - 2 \times 4$ and $0 + 2 \times 4$, or between -8 and 8. Consider the chances of making an error with the following decision rule:

- If $\bar{x} < -8$, decide on H_1: $\mu < 0$.
- If $-8 \leq \bar{x} \leq 8$, reserve judgment.
- If $\bar{x} > 8$, decide on H_2: $\mu > 0$.

If H_0 is true, then in about 95% of the possible samples $\bar{x}$ will be between the *critical values* -8 and 8, so you will reserve judgment. In these cases the statistical evidence is not strong enough to fell the straw man. In the other 5% of the samples you will make an error; in 2.5% of the samples you will incorrectly choose H_1, and in 2.5% you will incorrectly choose H_2.

If H_1 is true, you will make an error only if $\bar{x}$ is greater than 8. To calculate the chances of this occurrence you need to know the actual value of μ, but the chance of an error cannot exceed 2.5%. Similarly, the chance of an incorrect decision if H_2 is true cannot exceed 2.5%.

Thus, using this decision rule, you will make an incorrect decision in at most about 5% of the possible samples. The price you pay for controlling the chances of making an error is the necessity of reserving judgment when there is not sufficient statistical evidence to reject the null hypothesis.

Significance and Power

The probability of rejecting the null hypothesis if it is true is called the *significance level* of the statistical test. In this example, an $\bar{x}$ value less than -8 or greater than 8 is said to be *statistically significant* at the 5% level. You can adjust the significance level according to your needs by choosing different critical values. For example, critical values of -4 and 4 would produce a significance level of about 32%, while -12 and 12 would give a significance level of about 0.3%.

The decision rule stated above is a *two-tailed* test because the alternative hypotheses allow for population means either smaller or larger than the value specified in the null hypothesis. If you were interested only in the possibility of the students being overweight on the average, you could use a *one-tailed* test:

- If $\bar{x} \leq 8$, reserve judgment.
- If $\bar{x} > 8$, decide on H_2: $\mu > 0$.

For this one-tailed test, the significance level is 2.5%, half that of the two-tailed test.

The probability of rejecting the null hypothesis if it is false is called the *power* of the statistical test. The power depends on the true value of the parameter. In the example, assume the population mean is 4. The power for detecting H_2 is the probability of getting a sample mean greater than 8. The critical value 8 is one standard error higher than the population mean 4. The chance of getting a value at least one standard deviation greater than the mean from a normal distribution is about 16%, so the power for detecting the alternative hypothesis H_2 is about 16%. If the population mean were 8, the power for H_2 would be 50%, whereas a population mean of 12 would yield a power of about 84%.

The smaller the significance level, the less the chance of making an incorrect decision, but the higher the chance of having to reserve judgment. In choosing a significance level, you should consider the resulting power for various alternatives of interest.

Student's *t* Distribution

Unfortunately, you could not really use the decision rule described above because you do not know the value of σ. You could, however, use s as an estimate of σ. Consider the following statistic:

$$t = (\bar{x} - \mu_0) / (s / \sqrt{n})$$

which is the difference between the sample mean and the hypothesized mean μ_0 divided by the estimated standard error of the mean. A t statistic for the null hypothesis that $\mu = 0$ can be obtained along with related statistics using the MEANS procedure:

```
proc means data=x n mean std stderr t prt;
run;
```

If the null hypothesis is true and the population is normally distributed, then the t statistic has what is called a *Student's t distribution* with $n - 1$ *degrees of freedom*. This distribution looks very similar to a normal distribution, but the tails of the Student's t distribution are heavier. As the sample size gets larger, the sample standard deviation becomes a better estimator of the population standard deviation, and the t distribution gets closer to a normal distribution.

You can base a decision rule on the t statistic:

- If $t < -2.3$, decide on H_1: $\mu < 0$.
- If $-2.3 \leq t \leq 2.3$, reserve judgment.
- If $t > 2.3$, decide on H_2: $\mu > 0$.

The value 2.3 was obtained from a table of Student's *t* distributions in a statistics text to give a significance level of 5% for 8 (that is, 9−1) degrees of freedom. If you do not have a statistics text handy, you can print a table of the *t* distributions using a DATA step. The statements below produce **Output 1.6**.

```
data x;
   title 'Deviations from Normal Weight';
   input x @@;
   cards;
-7 -2 1 3 6 10 15 21 30
;
data _null_;
   title;
   file print;
   array p p1-p7;
   retain p1 .10 p2 .05 p3 .025 p4 .01 p5 .005 p6 .0025 p7 .001;
   put '            TABLE OF STUDENT''S T DISTRIBUTION'
    / '            ---------------------------------'
    // ' DF              TWO-TAILED SIGNIFICANCE LEVEL'
    / '    -------------------------------------------------------'
    / '    ' @;
   do i=1 to 7;
      pc=100*p(i);
      put pc best7. '%' @;
      end;
   put /;
   do df=1 to 30, 35 to 50 by 5, 60 to 100 by 10, 200 to 1000 by 100;
      put df 4. @;
      do i=1 to 7;
         b=betainv(p(i),df/2,.5);
         f=df*(1-b)/b;
         t=sqrt(f);
         put t 8.3 @;
         end;
      put;
      end;
   run;
```

Output 1.6 Output of a Table Showing the *t* Distribution

	Deviations from Normal Weight				1
Analysis Variable : X					

N	Mean	Std Dev	Std Error	T	Prob>|T|
9	8.5555556	11.7591572	3.9197191	2.1826961	0.0606

```
            TABLE OF STUDENT'S T DISTRIBUTION
            -----------------------------------

  DF                TWO-TAILED SIGNIFICANCE LEVEL
  --          ----------------------------------------------------
            10%      5%     2.5%      1%     0.5%    0.25%    0.1%

    1       6.314  12.706  25.452  63.657 127.321 254.647 636.619
    2       2.920   4.303   6.205   9.925  14.089  19.962  31.599
    3       2.353   3.182   4.177   5.841   7.453   9.465  12.924
    4       2.132   2.776   3.495   4.604   5.598   6.758   8.610
    5       2.015   2.571   3.163   4.032   4.773   5.604   6.869
    6       1.943   2.447   2.969   3.707   4.317   4.981   5.959
    7       1.895   2.365   2.841   3.499   4.029   4.595   5.408
    8       1.860   2.306   2.752   3.355   3.833   4.334   5.041
    9       1.833   2.262   2.685   3.250   3.690   4.146   4.781
   10       1.812   2.228   2.634   3.169   3.581   4.005   4.587
   11       1.796   2.201   2.593   3.106   3.497   3.895   4.437
   12       1.782   2.179   2.560   3.055   3.428   3.807   4.318
   13       1.771   2.160   2.533   3.012   3.372   3.735   4.221
   14       1.761   2.145   2.510   2.977   3.326   3.675   4.140
   15       1.753   2.131   2.490   2.947   3.286   3.624   4.073
   16       1.746   2.120   2.473   2.921   3.252   3.581   4.015
   17       1.740   2.110   2.458   2.898   3.222   3.543   3.965
   18       1.734   2.101   2.445   2.878   3.197   3.510   3.922
   19       1.729   2.093   2.433   2.861   3.174   3.481   3.883
   20       1.725   2.086   2.423   2.845   3.153   3.455   3.850
   21       1.721   2.080   2.414   2.831   3.135   3.432   3.819
   22       1.717   2.074   2.405   2.819   3.119   3.412   3.792
   23       1.714   2.069   2.398   2.807   3.104   3.393   3.768
   24       1.711   2.064   2.391   2.797   3.091   3.376   3.745
   25       1.708   2.060   2.385   2.787   3.078   3.361   3.725
   26       1.706   2.056   2.379   2.779   3.067   3.346   3.707
   27       1.703   2.052   2.373   2.771   3.057   3.333   3.690
   28       1.701   2.048   2.368   2.763   3.047   3.321   3.674
   29       1.699   2.045   2.364   2.756   3.038   3.310   3.659
   30       1.697   2.042   2.360   2.750   3.030   3.300   3.646
   35       1.690   2.030   2.342   2.724   2.996   3.258   3.591
   40       1.684   2.021   2.329   2.704   2.971   3.227   3.551
   45       1.679   2.014   2.319   2.690   2.952   3.203   3.520
   50       1.676   2.009   2.311   2.678   2.937   3.184   3.496
   60       1.671   2.000   2.299   2.660   2.915   3.156   3.460
   70       1.667   1.994   2.291   2.648   2.899   3.137   3.435
   80       1.664   1.990   2.284   2.639   2.887   3.122   3.416
   90       1.662   1.987   2.280   2.632   2.878   3.111   3.402
  100       1.660   1.984   2.276   2.626   2.871   3.102   3.390
  200       1.653   1.972   2.258   2.601   2.839   3.062   3.340
  300       1.650   1.968   2.253   2.592   2.828   3.049   3.323
  400       1.649   1.966   2.250   2.588   2.823   3.043   3.315
  500       1.648   1.965   2.248   2.586   2.820   3.039   3.310
  600       1.647   1.964   2.247   2.584   2.817   3.036   3.307
  700       1.647   1.963   2.246   2.583   2.816   3.034   3.304
  800       1.647   1.963   2.246   2.582   2.815   3.033   3.303
  900       1.647   1.963   2.245   2.581   2.814   3.032   3.301
 1000       1.646   1.962   2.245   2.581   2.813   3.031   3.300
```

In the current example, the value of the t statistic is 2.18, so using a 5% significance level you must reserve judgment. If you had elected to use a 10% significance level, the critical value of the t distribution would have been 1.86 and you could have rejected the null hypothesis. The sample size is so small, however, that the validity of your conclusion depends strongly on how close the distribution of the population is to a normal distribution.

Probability Values

Another way to report the results of a statistical test is to compute a *probability value* or *p-value*. A p-value gives the probability in repeated sampling of obtaining a statistic as far in the direction(s) specified by the alternative hypothesis as is the value actually observed. A two-tailed p-value for a t statistic is the probability of obtaining an absolute t-value greater than the observed absolute t-value. A one-tailed p-value for a t statistic for the alternative hypothesis $\mu > \mu_0$ is the probability of obtaining a t-value greater than the observed t-value. Once the p-value is computed, you can perform a hypothesis test by comparing the p-value with the desired significance level. If the p-value is less than the significance level of the test, the null hypothesis can be rejected. In the example, the two-tailed p-value, labeled PR> |T| on the PROC MEANS output, is .0606, so the null hypothesis could be rejected at the 10% significance level but not at the 5% level.

A p-value is a measure of the strength of the evidence against the null hypothesis. The smaller the p-value, the stronger the evidence for rejecting the null hypothesis.

Bivariate Measures

Bivariate statistics measure the degree of dependence between two variables. Bivariate measures for continuous variables are available in the CORR procedure. These include correlations, rank correlations, and measures of concordance. Bivariate measures are discussed in detail in Chapter 15, "The CORR Procedure."

REFERENCES

Ali, M.M. (1974), "Stochastic Ordering and Kurtosis Measure," JASA, 69, 543–545.

Fisher, R.A. (1973), *Statistical Methods for Research Workers*, 14th Edition, New York: Hafner Publishing Company.

Johnson, M.E., Tietjen, G.L., and Beckman, R.J. (1980), "A New Family of Probability Distributions With Applications to Monte Carlo Studies," JASA, 75, 276–279.

Kaplansky, I. (1945), "A Common Error Concerning Kurtosis," JASA, 40, 259–263.

Moore, D.S. (1979), *Statistics: Concepts and Controversies*, San Francisco: W.H. Freeman and Company.

Ott, L. (1977), *An Introduction to Statistical Methods and Data Analysis*, North Scituate, Mass.: Duxbury Press.

Snedecor, G.W. and Cochran, W.C. (1976), *Statistical Methods*, 6th Edition, Ames, Iowa: Iowa State University Press.

Chapter 2

SAS® Reporting Procedures

INTRODUCTION

A reporting procedure produces a display of information. Depending on the procedure you use, the display can be a listing of data, an organized display of data, or a graphical display such as a plot or a bar chart. Most descriptive and statistical procedures also produce reports to display results, but the procedures described in this chapter are specialized for reporting.

PRINT   prints values from a SAS data set.

FORMS   prints mailing list labels or other data laid out in repetitive forms.

CHART   charts frequencies and other statistics with bar charts and other pictorial representations.

PLOT   plots variables in a scatter diagram.

TABULATE   displays descriptive statistics in tabular format.

CALENDAR   prints data in the form of a summary or schedule calendar.

TIMEPLOT   plots one or more variables over time intervals.

In addition to these procedures, the PUT statement in the DATA step can be used to program custom reports. (See the discussion of the PUT statement in *SAS Language: Reference, Version 6, First Edition*.)

THE PRINT PROCEDURE

The PRINT procedure provides an easy way to list the data in a SAS data set. The simplest invocation

```
proc print;
run;
```

prints the most recently created SAS data set. Each variable in the data set forms a column of the report; each observation of the data set forms a row of the report.

If you want variables to form rows and observations to form columns, use the TRANSPOSE procedure to change variables into observations and vice versa before you print the data set.

PROC PRINT can

- use FORMAT statements to associate formats with variables
- use TITLE and FOOTNOTE statements to define up to ten title and ten footnote lines
- use LINESIZE= and PAGESIZE= system options to control size
- use an ID variable to identify observations
- print any subset of the variables
- use the WHERE statement or the FIRSTOBS= and LASTOBS= data set options to print a subset of observations
- separate groups of observations according to BY groups
- print the number of observations in each BY group or in the entire data set
- calculate and print totals for numeric variables for all observations or according to BY groups
- print variable labels as column headings
- divide the report into sections when there are too many variables to fit across the page.

You tell PROC PRINT what to do, not how to do it. While other SAS reporting methods may require programming, no programming is required with PROC PRINT. However, the PRINT procedure may be too limited for some applications because you must do most computations ahead of time in DATA steps.

The following example creates a SAS data set and then prints it twice using PROC PRINT, once in a very simple manner and again using formats, totals, variable labels, and an ID variable. The statements below produce **Output 2.1**.

```
libname report 'SAS-data-library';

data report.a;
   input year sales cost;
   profit=sales-cost;
   cards;
1981 12132 11021
1982 19823 12928
1983 16982 14002
1984 18432 14590
;
run;

proc print data=report.a;
   title 'Simple PROC PRINT Report';
run;

proc print data=report.a split='*';
   label sales='Sales for * Year'
         cost='Total Cost'
         profit='Profit Before *Taxes';
   format sales cost profit dollar10.2;
   id year;
   sum sales cost profit;
   title 'PROC PRINT with Totals, Formats, Labels, and ID Variable';
run;
```

Output 2.1 Two PROC PRINT Reports

```
                         Simple PROC PRINT Report                                1

           OBS    YEAR    SALES     COST    PROFIT

            1     1981    12132    11021    1111
            2     1982    19823    12928    6895
            3     1983    16982    14002    2980
            4     1984    18432    14590    3842
```

```
        PROC PRINT with Totals, Formats, Labels, and ID Variable                 2
                    Sales for                    Profit Before
           YEAR       Year        Total Cost        Taxes

           1981    $12,132.00     $11,021.00      $1,111.00
           1982    $19,823.00     $12,928.00      $6,895.00
           1983    $16,982.00     $14,002.00      $2,980.00
           1984    $18,432.00     $14,590.00      $3,842.00
                   ==========     ==========      ===============
                   $67,369.00     $52,541.00     $14,828.00
```

THE FORMS PROCEDURE

The FORMS procedure prints mailing labels and other types of repetitive forms.
The example below adds labeling variables to the data in order to identify the
fields on the form units. The forms are laid out three units across a page. The statements below produce **Output 2.2**.

```
    libname report 'SAS-data-library';

    data report.b;
       set report.a;
        tyear='YEAR  = ';
       tsales='SALES = ';
        tcost='COST  = ';
    run;

    proc forms data=report.b lines=3 w=20 d=1 a=3 between=5;
       format sales cost comma10.2 year 10.;
       line 1 tyear year;
       line 2 tsales sales;
       line 3 tcost cost;
    run;
```

Output 2.2   PROC FORMS Report

```
                                              The SAS System                                              1

YEAR   =        1981     YEAR   =        1982     YEAR   =        1983
SALES  =   12,132.00     SALES  =   19,823.00     SALES  =   16,982.00
COST   =   11,021.00     COST   =   12,928.00     COST   =   14,002.00

YEAR   =        1984
SALES  =   18,432.00
COST   =   14,590.00
```

THE CHART PROCEDURE

The CHART procedure draws a variety of charts: horizontal and vertical bar charts, block charts, pie charts, and star charts. The procedure can chart frequencies, percentages, means, and sums. The statements below produce **Output 2.3**, a block chart of the PROFIT variable from the PRINT procedure example.

```
libname report 'SAS-data-library';

proc chart data=report.a;
    title 'PROC CHART Report on Profit';
    format profit dollar10.2;
    block year / sumvar=profit discrete symbol='X';
run;
```

Output 2.3   PROC CHART Report

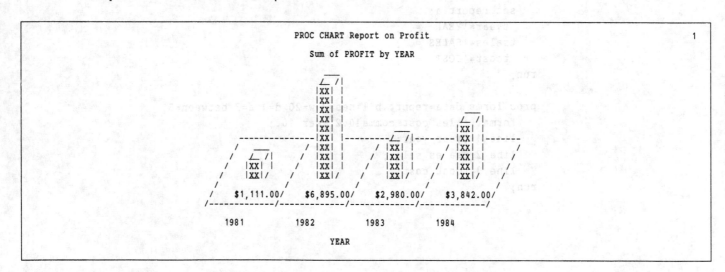

THE PLOT PROCEDURE

The PLOT procedure produces two-dimensional plots, with the values of one variable on the vertical axis and the values of the other variable on the horizontal axis. The following example plots three variables against YEAR. The three variables appear on the same plot, identified by different plotting characters. The statements below produce **Output 2.4**.

```
libname report 'SAS-data-library';

proc plot data=report.a;
    title 'PROC PLOT Report';
    label profit='Dollars'
          year='Year';
    plot profit*year='P'
         sales*year='S'
         cost*year='C' / overlay vpos=20 hpos=32;
run;
```

Output 2.4   PROC PLOT Report

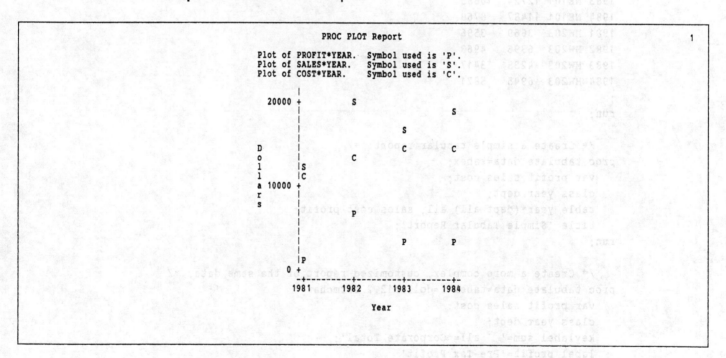

THE TABULATE PROCEDURE

The TABULATE procedure creates tabular reports. You have a great deal of control over the appearance of these reports. For example, you can apply labels and formats to column titles and row titles, and you can format the values in table cells. The procedure supports the CLASS statement, which groups data by category to produce statistics. The universal class variable, ALL, summarizes statistics for a category.

The following example uses the data from the PRINT procedure example with figures for SALES and COST broken down by department. The first PROC TABULATE step simply shows the departmental figures grouped and summed by year. The second PROC TABULATE step customizes the same table by using formats, labels, formatting characters, and other features of PROC TABULATE. The statements below produce **Output 2.5**.

```
data tabex;
   input year dept $ sales cost;
   profit=sales-cost;
   cards;
1981 NE101  8463   7425
1982 NE101 13427   8019
1983 NE101 12724  10685
1984 NE101 11487   8769
1981 MW203  3669   3596
1982 MW203  6396   4963
1983 MW203  4258   3417
1984 MW203  6945   5821
;
run;


   /* Create a simple tabular report. */
proc tabulate data=tabex;
   var profit sales cost;
   class year dept;
   table year*(dept all) all, sales cost profit;
   title 'Simple Tabular Report';
run;


   /* Create a more complex, customized report of the same data. */
proc tabulate data=tabex f=dollar12.2 formchar='              ';
   var profit sales cost;
   class year dept;
   keylabel sum=' ' all='Corporate Total';
   label profit='Pre-Tax Profit'
         sales='Total Revenues'
          dept='Department'
          cost='Total Costs';
   table year=' '*(dept all) all='Total -- All Years',
         sales cost profit
         / box='Year End Position -- 1981-1984' rts=24;
   title 'Customized Tabular Report';
run;
```

Output 2.5   Two PROC TABULATE Reports

```
                              Simple Tabular Report                                  1
        --------------------------------------------------------------
        |                       |   SALES   |   COST    |  PROFIT   |
        |                       |-----------+-----------+-----------|
        |                       |    SUM    |    SUM    |    SUM    |
        |-----------------------+-----------+-----------+-----------|
        |YEAR     |DEPT         |           |           |           |
        |---------+-------------|           |           |           |
        |1981     |MW203        |   3669.00 |   3596.00 |     73.00 |
        |         |-------------+-----------+-----------+-----------|
        |         |NE101        |   8463.00 |   7425.00 |   1038.00 |
        |         |-------------+-----------+-----------+-----------|
        |         |ALL          |  12132.00 |  11021.00 |   1111.00 |
        |---------+-------------+-----------+-----------+-----------|
        |1982     |DEPT         |           |           |           |
        |         |-------------|           |           |           |
        |         |MW203        |   6396.00 |   4963.00 |   1433.00 |
        |         |-------------+-----------+-----------+-----------|
        |         |NE101        |  13427.00 |   8019.00 |   5408.00 |
        |         |-------------+-----------+-----------+-----------|
        |         |ALL          |  19823.00 |  12982.00 |   6841.00 |
        |---------+-------------+-----------+-----------+-----------|
        |1983     |DEPT         |           |           |           |
        |         |-------------|           |           |           |
        |         |MW203        |   4258.00 |   3417.00 |    841.00 |
        |         |-------------+-----------+-----------+-----------|
        |         |NE101        |  12724.00 |  10685.00 |   2039.00 |
        |         |-------------+-----------+-----------+-----------|
        |         |ALL          |  16982.00 |  14102.00 |   2880.00 |
        |---------+-------------+-----------+-----------+-----------|
        |1984     |DEPT         |           |           |           |
        |         |-------------|           |           |           |
        |         |MW203        |   6945.00 |   5821.00 |   1124.00 |
        |         |-------------+-----------+-----------+-----------|
        |         |NE101        |  11487.00 |   8769.00 |   2718.00 |
        |         |-------------+-----------+-----------+-----------|
        |         |ALL          |  18432.00 |  14590.00 |   3842.00 |
        |---------+-------------+-----------+-----------+-----------|
        |ALL                    |  67369.00 |  52695.00 |  14674.00 |
        --------------------------------------------------------------
```

```
                             Customized Tabular Report                              2

      Year End Position --      Total                   Pre-Tax
      1981-1984                 Revenues   Total Costs   Profit

         1981     Department

                  MW203         $3,669.00    $3,596.00      $73.00

                  NE101         $8,463.00    $7,425.00   $1,038.00

                  Corporate
                  Total        $12,132.00   $11,021.00   $1,111.00

         1982     Department

                  MW203         $6,396.00    $4,963.00   $1,433.00

                  NE101        $13,427.00    $8,019.00   $5,408.00

                  Corporate
                  Total        $19,823.00   $12,982.00   $6,841.00

         1983     Department

                  MW203         $4,258.00    $3,417.00     $841.00

                  NE101        $12,724.00   $10,685.00   $2,039.00

                  Corporate
                  Total        $16,982.00   $14,102.00   $2,880.00
```

(continued on next page)

(continued from previous page)

1984	Department			
	MW203	$6,945.00	$5,821.00	$1,124.00
	NE101	$11,487.00	$8,769.00	$2,718.00
	Corporate Total	$18,432.00	$14,590.00	$3,842.00
Total -- All Years		$67,369.00	$52,695.00	$14,674.00

THE CALENDAR PROCEDURE

Use the CALENDAR procedure if you have either daily data on some activity or data representing events, each of which is identified by a date. In both cases, PROC CALENDAR displays the data in the form of a monthly calendar. You can specify formats for variables, missing value options, and customized borders for the calendar. You can also specify the calendar to cover all the days in a month or only weekdays (Monday-Friday). This procedure is useful for two main applications:

- daily reporting, such as daily tallies of sales or usage. You can also collect sums and means.
- scheduling (making calendars of events).

The statements below produce a summary calendar that displays telephone calls received by a library during daytime and evening hours. Variables are printed using picture formats created by the FORMAT procedure, and sums and means of the variables appear in the legend. These statements produce **Output 2.6**:

```
libname report 'SAS-data-library';

data report.tel;
   input date : date. day night @@;
   cards;
 1OCT85 33 48   2OCT85 29 10   3OCT85 18 35   4OCT85 18 23
 5OCT85 36 45   6OCT85 25 44   7OCT85 28 40   8OCT85 29 49
 9OCT85 31 17  10OCT85 20  .  11OCT85 19 29  12OCT85 30 11
13OCT85 28 49  14OCT85 27 46  15OCT85 20 36  16OCT85 27 48
17OCT85 20 39  18OCT85 27 46  19OCT85 20 36  20OCT85 27 48
21OCT85 33 48  22OCT85 29 10  23OCT85 18 35  24OCT85 18 23
25OCT85 36 45  26OCT85 25 44  27OCT85 28 40  28OCT85 29 49
29OCT85 31 17  30OCT85 20  .  31OCT85 19 29
;
run;

proc format;
   picture ddd other='000 DAY';
   picture nnn other='000 NIGHT';
run;
```

```
proc calendar data=report.tel header=small legend;
   start date;
   var day night;
   sum day night;
   mean day night;
   label day='Daytime Calls' night='Night Calls';
   format day ddd. night nnn. ;
   title 'Telephone Calls Received at City Library';
run;
```

Output 2.6   PROC CALENDAR Report

```
                  Telephone Calls Received at City Library                    1

                               October  1985

    --------------------------------------------------------------------------
    | Sunday  |  Monday |  Tuesday | Wednesday | Thursday |  Friday | Saturday |
    |---------+---------+----------+-----------+----------+---------+----------|
    |         |         |    1     |     2     |    3     |    4    |    5     |
    |         |         |          |           |          |         |          |
    |         |         |  33 DAY  |  29 DAY   |  18 DAY  |  18 DAY |  36 DAY  |
    |         |         |  48 NIGHT|  10 NIGHT |  35 NIGHT|  23 NIGHT| 45 NIGHT|
    |---------+---------+----------+-----------+----------+---------+----------|
    |    6    |    7    |    8     |     9     |    10    |    11   |    12    |
    |         |         |          |           |          |         |          |
    |  25 DAY |  28 DAY |  29 DAY  |  31 DAY   |  20 DAY  |  19 DAY |  30 DAY  |
    |  44 NIGHT| 40 NIGHT| 49 NIGHT|  17 NIGHT |      .   |  29 NIGHT| 11 NIGHT|
    |---------+---------+----------+-----------+----------+---------+----------|
    |   13    |    14   |    15    |    16     |    17    |    18   |    19    |
    |         |         |          |           |          |         |          |
    |  28 DAY |  27 DAY |  20 DAY  |  27 DAY   |  20 DAY  |  27 DAY |  20 DAY  |
    |  49 NIGHT| 46 NIGHT| 36 NIGHT|  48 NIGHT |  39 NIGHT|  46 NIGHT| 36 NIGHT|
    |---------+---------+----------+-----------+----------+---------+----------|
    |   20    |    21   |    22    |    23     |    24    |    25   |    26    |
    |         |         |          |           |          |         |          |
    |  27 DAY |  33 DAY |  29 DAY  |  18 DAY   |  18 DAY  |  36 DAY |  25 DAY  |
    |  48 NIGHT| 48 NIGHT| 10 NIGHT|  35 NIGHT |  23 NIGHT|  45 NIGHT| 44 NIGHT|
    |---------+---------+----------+-----------+----------+---------+----------|
    |   27    |    28   |    29    |    30     |    31    |         |          |
    |         |         |          |           |          |         |          |
    |  28 DAY |  29 DAY |  31 DAY  |  20 DAY   |  19 DAY  |         |          |
    |  40 NIGHT| 49 NIGHT| 17 NIGHT|      .    |  29 NIGHT|         |          |
    --------------------------------------------------------------------------


                   --------------------------------------
                   | Legend        |  Sum   |   Mean    |
                   |               |        |           |
                   | Daytime Calls |   798  |   25.742  |
                   | Night Calls   |  1039  |   35.828  |
                   --------------------------------------
```

THE TIMEPLOT PROCEDURE

The TIMEPLOT procedure produces a plot and a listing of observations in the data set similar to those produced by the PLOT and PRINT procedures. However, a plot produced by PROC TIMEPLOT has these features:

- The vertical axis always represents the sequence of observations in the data set; thus, if the observations are arranged chronologically, the vertical axis represents time.
- The horizontal axis contains values of the variables you are examining.
- A plot can occupy more than one page.
- Each observation appears on a separate line; no observations are hidden, as can occur with PROC PLOT.
- Each observation in the plot is accompanied by a listing of the values plotted.

The following example overlays plots of U.S. and world cotton production on the same axes. A vertical reference line appears at the mean value of each variable, and a horizontal line connects the values within each observation. The statements below produce **Output 2.7**.

```
libname report 'SAS-data-library';

data report.cotton;
   input year us world @@;
   label us='US Cotton Production'
      world='World Cotton Production';
   cards;
1940 12.6 31.2 1975  8.3 54.0
1950 10.0 30.6 1976 10.6 57.4
1960 14.2 46.2 1977 14.4 63.5
1965 15.0 55.0 1978 10.9 60.2
1970 10.2 53.6 1979 14.6 65.7
1972 13.7 62.9 1980 11.1 65.5
1973 13.0 63.3 1981 15.6 70.8
1974 11.5 64.3 1982 12.0 67.4
;
run;

proc sort;
   by year;
run;

proc timeplot data=report.cotton;
   plot us world / overlay ref=mean(us world) hiloc pos=64;
   id year;
   title 'Trends in Cotton Production';
   title2 'Selected Years 1940-1982';
   title4 '(Millions of Bales)';
run;
```

Output 2.7   PROC TIMEPLOT Report

```
                           Trends in Cotton Production                              1
                             Selected Years 1940-1982

                                 (Millions of Bales)

   YEAR          US          World      min                                    max
             Cotton         Cotton      8.3                                    70.8
           Production    Production     *-------------------------------------------*
   1940        12.60         31.20      |    U----------------W                     |
   1950        10.00         30.60      | U-|-----------------W                     |
   1960        14.20         46.20      |   | U-----------------------------W       |
   1965        15.00         55.00      |   |    U----------------------------------W|
   1970        10.20         53.60      | U-|-----------------------------------W    |
   1972        13.70         62.90      |   | U---------------------------------|-----W |
   1973        13.00         63.30      |   |U---------------------------------|------W |
   1974        11.50         64.30      |  U|----------------------------------|------W |
   1975         8.30         54.00      |U---|-----------------------------W   |       |
   1976        10.60         57.40      |  U-|--------------------------------W |       |
   1977        14.40         63.50      |   | U--------------------------------|------W |
   1978        10.90         60.20      |  U|-------------------------------|--W       |
   1979        14.60         65.70      |   | U--------------------------------|--------W |
   1980        11.10         65.50      |  U|--------------------------------|--------W |
   1981        15.60         70.80      |   | U--------------------------------|----------W|
   1982        12.00         67.40      |   U--------------------------------|--------W |
                                        *-------------------------------------------*
```

REPORTS WRITTEN WITH PUT STATEMENTS

You can use the PUT statement in a DATA step to create customized reports for which you perform every calculation and specify the line and column for each part of the report. Using PUT statements for report writing is documented in detail in *SAS Language: Reference*. **Output 2.8** is an example of a report produced with PUT statements.

In the example below, you want to print the observations as columns and the variables as rows in a report. This is most conveniently done with the N=PS feature (see the **FILE Statement** in *SAS Language: Reference*) and by computing column positions with program statements. The variable C indexes column positions corresponding to observations from the data and a column for the total. The statements below produce **Output 2.8**.

```
libname report 'SAS-data-library';

data _null_;
   file print n=ps;
   title 'PUT Statement Report';
```

```
     do c=25 to 61 by 12;      /* C is the printing column.  */


         /* Bring in an observation here.                 */
         /* Each observation contains values for the four */
         /* variables YEAR, SALES, COST, and PROFIT.      */
         /*                                               */
     set report.a end=eof;
         /* Compute gross profit and accumulate totals.   */
     totsales+sales;
     totcgs+cost;
     totprof+profit;


         /* Print out a column for this year. */
     put #5
         'Year'              ac year    10.
     // 'Gross Revenue'      ac sales   10.2
      / 'Cost of Goods Sold' ac cost    10.2
      /                      ac '=========='
      / 'Gross Profit'       ac profit  10.2;


         /* At end of data */
     if eof then
        do;
           c=c+12; /* Advance pointer to next column of report. */


           /* Compute margin and print totals. */
           pctmarg=100*totprof/totcgs;
           put #5 ac '    Total'
              // ac totsales  10.2
               / ac totcgs    10.2
               / ac '=========='
               / ac totprof   10.2
              // 'Profit Margin Percent of Cost' ac pctmarg 10.2;
        end;
     end;
  run;
```

Output 2.8   PUT Statement Report

```
                                      PUT Statement Report                                                1


Year                    1981      1982      1983      1984     Total

Gross Revenue        12132.00  19823.00  16982.00  18432.00  67369.00
Cost of Goods Sold   11021.00  12928.00  14002.00  14590.00  52541.00
                     ========  ========  ========  ========  ========
Gross Profit          1111.00   6895.00   2980.00   3842.00  14828.00

Profit Margin Percent of Cost                                   28.22
```

Chapter 3

SAS® Scoring Procedures

Scoring procedures are utilities that produce an output data set with new variables that are transformations of data in the input data set. PROC RANK produces rank scores across observations. PROC SCORE multiplies values from two SAS data sets, one containing coefficients and the other raw data. PROC STANDARD transforms each variable individually. These procedures each produce an output data set but little or no printed output.

RANK   ranks the observations of each numeric variable and outputs ranks or rank scores.

SCORE   constructs new variables that are linear combinations of old variables according to a scoring data set. This procedure is used with other statistical procedures that output scoring coefficients. See the *SAS/STAT User's Guide, Version 6, Fourth Edition* for information about PROC SCORE.

STANDARD   standardizes variables to a given mean and standard deviation.

Chapter 4

SAS® Utility Procedures

A utility procedure performs a specific type of intermediate processing or data manipulation. Following is a list and brief description of SAS utility procedures that are fully described in this book. In addition, check the SAS documentation for your host system for any additional procedures available.

APPEND	appends data from one SAS data set to the end of another SAS data set.
CATALOG	manages entries in SAS catalogs.
CIMPORT	converts a transport sequential file created by the CPORT procedure (usually on a different operating system) into its original form as a SAS catalog or data set.
COMPARE	compares the contents of two SAS data sets.
CONTENTS	describes the contents of a SAS data library or specified members of the library.
COPY	copies a SAS data library or selected members of the library.
CPORT	converts a SAS catalog or data set into a transport sequential file that can be re-created by the CIMPORT procedure (usually on a different operating system) into its original form as a SAS catalog or data set.
DATASETS	manages a SAS data library.
FORMAT	defines output formats for labeling values and informats for reading data.
PMENU	creates action bars and pull-down menus for user-written windows.
SORT	sorts a SAS data set according to one or more variables.
SPELL	creates dictionaries and verifies spelling in a text file using a standard dictionary or dictionaries you have created.
TRANSPOSE	turns a SAS data set on its side, changing variables into observations and observations into variables.
V5TOV6	converts Version 5 SAS data sets, catalogs, IML workspaces, formats, and informats into Release 6.06 or later data sets and catalog entries.

Chapter 5

The APPEND Procedure

ABSTRACT

The APPEND procedure adds the observations from one SAS data set to the end of another SAS data set.

INTRODUCTION

The APPEND procedure operates only on SAS data sets. Refer to Chapter 6, "SAS Files," in *SAS Language: Reference, Version 6, First Edition* to familiarize yourself with SAS data sets and related terminology.

Often you need to add new observations to a SAS data set. If you use the SET statement in a DATA step to concatenate two data sets, the SAS System must process all the observations in both data sets to create a new one. The APPEND procedure bypasses the processing of data in the original data set and adds new observations directly to the end of the original data set.

The APPEND statement in the DATASETS procedure (described in Chapter 17) works in the same way the APPEND procedure does.

SPECIFICATIONS

The PROC APPEND statement is the only statement associated with the APPEND procedure.

PROC APPEND Statement

PROC APPEND BASE=*SAS-data-set* <DATA=*SAS-data-set*> <FORCE>;

where *SAS-data-set* can be a one- or two-level name. If *SAS-data-set* is a one-level name, the libref is the default libref, usually WORK.

Use the APPEND procedure to append observations from the DATA= data set to the BASE= data set. This statement can be used only with SAS data sets.

Requirements

The following argument is required on the PROC APPEND statement:

BASE=*SAS-data-set*
OUT=*SAS-data-set*

> name the data set to which you want to add observations. If PROC APPEND cannot find an existing data set with this name, it creates a new data set. In other words, you can use PROC APPEND to create a data set by specifying a new data set name in the BASE= argument. The OUT= argument is equivalent to the BASE= argument. Either the BASE= or the OUT= argument must be specified.

Options

The APPEND procedure can be used with these options:

DATA=*SAS-data-set*
NEW=*SAS-data-set*

> name the SAS data set containing observations to be added to the end of the SAS data set specified by the BASE= argument. If the DATA= option is omitted, the most recently created SAS data set is used. The NEW= option is equivalent to the DATA= option.
>
> Note: You can use the WHERE= data set option or a WHERE statement in the PROC APPEND step to limit which observations from the DATA= data set are added to the BASE= data set as shown in this example:

```
proc append base=test1 data=test2(where=(x=2));
run;
```

> Refer to Chapter 9, "SAS Language Statements," and Chapter 15, "SAS Data Set Options," in *SAS Language: Reference* for more information on the WHERE statement and the WHERE= data set option.

FORCE

> forces PROC APPEND to concatenate data sets when the DATA= data set contains variables that either
>
> - are not in the BASE= data set
> - do not have the same type as the variables in the BASE= data set
> - are longer than the variables in the BASE= data set

Refer to **Concatenating Data Sets with Different Descriptions** later in this chapter for more information on how the FORCE option works.

DETAILS

Usage Notes

When the APPEND procedure creates a new data set, the BASE= data set becomes the current SAS data set. Appending to an existing data set does not change which data set is the current SAS data set.

Using PROC APPEND can be more efficient than using a SET statement in the DATA step to concatenate two data sets, especially if the BASE= data set is large. Consider the following example:

```
data large;
   set large small;
```

To perform this concatenation, the SAS System must read all observations in both the LARGE and SMALL data sets. With the APPEND procedure you can add the observations in the SMALL data set to the end of the LARGE data set without reading the observations in LARGE. For example, the following statement offers a much more efficient way to concatenate the two data sets:

```
proc append base=large data=small;
```

This procedure is especially useful if observations are frequently added to a SAS data set (for example, in production programs that are constantly appending data to a journal-type data set).

If all variables in the BASE= data set have the same length and type as the variables in the DATA= data set and if all variables exist in both data sets, the procedure executes faster than a DATA step with a SET statement that concatenates the data sets. You can use the CONTENTS procedure or the CONTENTS statement of PROC DATASETS to see the variable lengths and types.

Caution: If there is a system failure or if some other type of interruption occurs while the procedure is executing, the BASE= data set may not be properly updated; it is possible that not all, perhaps none, of the observations will be added to the BASE= data set.

Concatenating Compressed Data Sets

You can concatenate compressed SAS data sets (those created with the COMPRESS=YES data set option). Either or both of the BASE= and DATA= data sets can be compressed. If you specify COMPRESS=YES and REUSE=NO (or omit the REUSE= data set option) when you create the BASE= data set, the observations from the DATA= data set are added to the end of the BASE= data set.

You may encounter problems, however, if you specify COMPRESS=YES and REUSE=YES when the BASE= data set is created. When you append to data sets created with REUSE=YES, observations from the DATA= data set are not necessarily added to the end of the BASE= data set; the observations may be inserted into the middle of the BASE= data set to make use of available space. For example, if you have deleted several observations from the BASE= data set, several observations from the DATA= data set could be inserted into the space freed by the deleted observations.

Concatenating Data Sets with Different Descriptions

If you are concatenating two SAS data sets that do not have the same variables with the same attributes, PROC APPEND works as described in the next two sections.

Data Sets with Different Variables

If the DATA= data set contains variables that are not in the BASE= data set, you must use the FORCE option on the PROC APPEND statement to force PROC APPEND to concatenate the two data sets. Note that the extra variables from the DATA= data set are not included in the BASE= data set; you receive a message to warn you that variables are being dropped.

If the BASE= data set contains a variable that is not in the DATA= data set, PROC APPEND concatenates the data sets, but the observations from the DATA= data set have a missing value for the variable that was not in the DATA= data set. The FORCE option is not needed in this case.

Data Sets with Variables That Have Different Attributes

If a variable has different attributes in the BASE= data set than it does in the DATA= data set, the attributes in the BASE= data set prevail.

If the variables have different formats, informats, and labels, PROC APPEND concatenates the data sets and uses the format, informat, or label from the BASE= data set for all observations.

If the length of a variable is longer in the BASE= data set than in the DATA= data set, the concatenation succeeds, and the length of the variable is the same as it originally was in the BASE= data set.

If the length of a variable is longer in the DATA= data set than in the BASE= data set, or if the same variable is a character variable in one data set and a numeric variable in the other, PROC APPEND fails to concatenate the files unless you specify the FORCE option.

Using the FORCE option has the following consequences:

- The length specified in the BASE= data set remains the same. The SAS System truncates values from the DATA= data set to fit them into the length specified in the BASE= data set.
- The type specified in the BASE= data set remains the same. The procedure replaces values of the wrong type (all values for the variable in the DATA= data set) with missing values.

Output Data Set

Observations from the DATA= data set are added to the BASE= data set. If the BASE= data set does not exist, PROC APPEND creates a new SAS data set consisting of the observations in the DATA= data set. The output data set (BASE=) becomes the current SAS data set.

Printed Output

Messages pertaining to procedure processing appear in the SAS log, but no printed output is produced.

EXAMPLES

Example 1:   Appending an Update File

In the following example, a temporary data file called ADD contains information on average temperatures in cities around the country. It is appended to an existing permanent data set, EXP.MASTER. The PRINT procedure lists the permanent file before and after the execution of PROC APPEND. The following statements produce **Output 5.1:**

```
data add;
   input city $ 1-11 month $10. temp;
   cards;
Raleigh     July        77.5
Raleigh     January     40.5
Miami       August      82.9
Miami       January     67.2
Los Angeles August      69.5
Los Angeles January     54.5
;
run;


libname exp 'SAS-data-library';


proc print data=exp.master;
   title 'Master Before ADD Data Appended';
run;


proc append base=exp.master data=add;
run;


proc print data=exp.master;
   title 'Master After ADD Data Appended';
run;
```

Output 5.1   The BASE= Data Set Before and After the PROC APPEND Step

```
                      Master Before ADD Data Appended                        1

         OBS      CITY          MONTH       TEMP

          1      Honolulu      August      80.7
          2      Honolulu      January     72.3
          3      Boston        July        73.3
          4      Boston        January     29.2
          5      Duluth        July        65.6
          6      Duluth        January      8.5
```

```
                      Master After ADD Data Appended                         2

         OBS      CITY          MONTH       TEMP

          1      Honolulu      August      80.7
          2      Honolulu      January     72.3
          3      Boston        July        73.3
          4      Boston        January     29.2
          5      Duluth        July        65.6
          6      Duluth        January      8.5
          7      Raleigh       July        77.5
          8      Raleigh       January     40.5
          9      Miami         August      82.9
         10      Miami         January     67.2
         11      Los Angeles   August      69.5
         12      Los Angeles   January     54.5
```

Example 2: Using PROC APPEND with the FORCE Option

This example illustrates one use of the FORCE option. Weather data are gathered each day and stored in a SAS data set named ACCUM.WEATHER. The following statements produce **Output 5.2**, which shows the information contained in ACCUM.WEATHER.

```
libname accum 'SAS-data-library';

proc print data=accum.weather;
   format date date7.;
   title 'Weather Information Before Appending';
run;
```

Output 5.2 Printed Output for ACCUM.WEATHER

```
                     Weather Information Before Appending                                1

                     OBS      DATE     TEMP    SUNHRS

                      1     01JAN90     35      9.30
                      2     02JAN90     34      9.33
                      3     03JAN90     37      9.35
                      4     04JAN90     38      9.39
```

The following statements create the new day's weather information, print it, and then append the new weather information to ACCUM.WEATHER. The results appear in **Output 5.3**.

```
data daily;
   input date mmddyy8. temp sunhrs precip;
   cards;
01-05-90 35 9.40 1.1
;
run;

proc print data=daily;
   format date date7.;
   title 'New Weather Information Including PRECIP';
run;

libname accum 'SAS-data-library';

proc append base=accum.weather data=daily force;
run;

proc print data=accum.weather;
   format date date7.;
   title 'Weather Information After Appending';
run;
```

Notice that the data set DAILY contains the variable PRECIP for which no corresponding variable exists in the BASE= data set, ACCUM.WEATHER. With the FORCE option in effect, the observation is appended to ACCUM.WEATHER, but the variable PRECIP is dropped from the ACCUM.WEATHER data set.

Output 5.3 FORCE Option Causes Variable to Be Dropped

```
                    New Weather Information Including PRECIP                          1

        OBS        DATE      TEMP     SUNHRS     PRECIP

         1       05JAN90      35        9.4        1.1
```

```
                    Weather Information After Appending                              2

            OBS        DATE      TEMP    SUNHRS

             1       01JAN90      35      9.30
             2       02JAN90      34      9.33
             3       03JAN90      37      9.35
             4       04JAN90      38      9.39
             5       05JAN90      35      9.40
```

Chapter 6
The BMDP Procedure

ABSTRACT

The BMDP procedure calls any BMDP program to analyze data in a SAS data set. This procedure is described in system-dependent documentation.

52

The CALENDAR Procedure

ABSTRACT

The CALENDAR procedure displays data from a SAS data set in a monthly calendar format. PROC CALENDAR can also display holidays in the month and process data for multiple calendars with varying work schedules.

INTRODUCTION

The CALENDAR procedure can produce two types of calendars: *summary* and *schedule*. A *summary calendar* displays activities that last one day and can include sum and mean calculations. A schedule calendar displays activities that last for several days. It enables you to schedule activities around holidays, weekends, or other nonwork periods.

Both the schedule and summary calendars can span multiple pages and may include any number of months.

You can use the CALID statement to produce a *multiple calendar,* a calendar containing information from several sources.

Introductory Examples

The examples that follow illustrate the uses of summary and schedule calendars. The **EXAMPLES** section later in this chapter contains more examples illustrating many features of PROC CALENDAR.

Summary Calendar

The statements below produce a summary calendar displaying the number of meals served daily in a hospital cafeteria. The START statement specifies that the variable DATE in the data set ACT contains the starting date of each activity. This data set lists the dates in order. If your data are not in order, use the SORT procedure or create an appropriate index. For summary calendars, the START statement is the only required statement. The following statements produce **Output 7.1**:

```
title 'Meals Served in Community Hospital Cafeteria';
options pagesize=60 linesize=132 nodate;

data act;
   input date date7. brkfst lunch dinner;
   cards;
01Dec91      123 234 123
02Dec91      123 234 238
03Dec91      188 188 198
04Dec91      123 183 176
05Dec91      200 267 243
06Dec91      176 165 177
07Dec91      156  . 167
08Dec91      198 143 167
09Dec91      178 198 187
10Dec91      165 176 187
```

```
11Dec91        187 176 231
12Dec91        176 187 222
13Dec91        187 187 123
14Dec91        164 187 231
15Dec91        187 165 167
16Dec91        187 198 156
17Dec91        198 187 156
18Dec91        187 165 178
19Dec91        187 176 156
20Dec91        156 211 199
21Dec91        176 156 143
22Dec91        165 167 211
23Dec91        187 176   .
24Dec91        185 167 167
25Dec91        187 178 187
26Dec91        167 156 198
27Dec91        167 239 267
28Dec91        267 287 256
29Dec91        276 243 234
30Dec91        267 287 256
31Dec91        243 231 243
;
run;

proc calendar;
    start date;
    sum brkfst lunch dinner;
    mean brkfst lunch dinner;
run;
```

Output 7.1   Summary Calendar Showing Meals Served

```
                         Meals Served in Community Hospital Cafeteria                        1
 -------------------------------------------------------------------------------------------
|                                                                                           |
|                                   December  1991                                          |
|-------------------------------------------------------------------------------------------|
| Sunday    |  Monday   |  Tuesday  | Wednesday |  Thursday |  Friday   |  Saturday |
|-----------+-----------+-----------+-----------+-----------+-----------+-----------|
|    1      |    2      |    3      |    4      |    5      |    6      |    7      |
|           |           |           |           |           |           |           |
|       123 |       123 |       188 |       123 |       200 |       176 |       156 |
|       234 |       234 |       188 |       183 |       267 |       165 |         . |
|       123 |       238 |       198 |       176 |       243 |       177 |       167 |
|-----------+-----------+-----------+-----------+-----------+-----------+-----------|
|    8      |    9      |   10      |   11      |   12      |   13      |   14      |
|           |           |           |           |           |           |           |
|       198 |       178 |       165 |       187 |       176 |       187 |       164 |
|       143 |       198 |       176 |       176 |       187 |       187 |       187 |
|       167 |       187 |       187 |       231 |       222 |       123 |       231 |
|-----------+-----------+-----------+-----------+-----------+-----------+-----------|
|   15      |   16      |   17      |   18      |   19      |   20      |   21      |
|           |           |           |           |           |           |           |
|       187 |       187 |       198 |       187 |       187 |       156 |       176 |
|       165 |       198 |       187 |       165 |       176 |       211 |       156 |
|       167 |       156 |       156 |       178 |       156 |       199 |       143 |
|-----------+-----------+-----------+-----------+-----------+-----------+-----------|
|   22      |   23      |   24      |   25      |   26      |   27      |   28      |
|           |           |           |           |           |           |           |
|       165 |       187 |       185 |       187 |       167 |       167 |       267 |
|       167 |       176 |       167 |       178 |       156 |       239 |       287 |
|       211 |         . |       167 |       187 |       198 |       267 |       256 |
|-----------+-----------+-----------+-----------+-----------------------------------|
|   29      |   30      |   31      |           |
|           |           |           |           |
|       276 |       267 |       243 |           |
|       243 |       287 |       231 |           |
|       234 |       256 |       243 |           |
 ----------------------------------------------
```

```
                    ----------------------------------
                   |        |    Sum    |    Mean      |
                   | BRKFST |     5733  |   184.935    |
                   | LUNCH  |     5914  |   197.133    |
                   | DINNER |     5844  |   194.800    |
                    ----------------------------------
```

In a summary calendar, each piece of information for a given day is the value of a variable for that day. The variables can be either numeric or character, and you can format them as you require. You can use the SUM and MEAN options to collect sums and means for any numeric variables. PROC CALENDAR displays these statistics on your printed output in a box below the calendar.

Schedule Calendar

The statements below produce a schedule calendar that displays activities planned by a busy executive. The START and DUR statements specify the variables that contain the starting date and the duration of each activity, respectively. With a schedule calendar, you must use either a DUR or FIN statement, as well as a START statement. The following statements product **Output 7.2**:

```
options pagesize=60 linesize=132 nodate;
title 'Summer Planning Calendar:  '
'Julia Q. Wydget, President';
title2 'Better Products Inc.';

data act;
   input date : date7. happen $ 9-36 who $ 38-48 long;
   cards;
01JUL91 Dist. Mtg.                     All          1
02JUL91 Mgrs. Meeting                  District 6   2
03JUL91 Interview                      JW           1
05JUL91 VIP Banquet                    JW           1
08JUL91 Sales Drive                    District 6   5
08JUL91 Trade Show                     Knox         3
11JUL91 Mgrs. Meeting                  District 7   2
11JUL91 Planning Council               Group II     1
12JUL91 Seminar                        White        1
14JUL91 Co. Picnic                     All          1
15JUL91 Sales Drive                    District 7   5
16JUL91 Dentist                        JW           1
17JUL91 Bank Meeting                   1st Natl     1
18JUL91 NewsLetter Deadline            All          1
18JUL91 Planning Council               Group III    1
19JUL91 Seminar                        White        1
22JUL91 Inventors Show                 Melvin       3
24JUL91 Birthday                       Mary         1
25JUL91 Planning Council               Group IV     1
25JUL91 Close Sale                     WYGIX Co.    2
;
run;

proc calendar data=act;
   start date;
   dur long;
run;
```

Output 7.2   Schedule Calendar Showing Activities

```
                    Summer Planning Calendar:  Julia Q. Wydget, President                    1
                                 Better Products Inc.
 ---------------------------------------------------------------------------------------------
|                                                                                             |
|                                           July 1991                                         |
 ---------------------------------------------------------------------------------------------
|   Sunday    |    Monday   |   Tuesday   |  Wednesday  |  Thursday   |    Friday   |  Saturday |
 ---------------------------------------------------------------------------------------------
|             |      1      |      2      |      3      |      4      |      5      |     6     |
|             |             |             |             |             |             |           |
|             |             |             |+=Interview/JW==+|         |             |           |
|             |+Dist. Mtg./All=+|+=====Mgrs. Meeting/District 6=====+|  |+VIP Banquet/JW=+|     |
 ---------------------------------------------------------------------------------------------
|     7       |      8      |      9      |     10      |     11      |     12      |    13     |
|             |             |             |             |             |             |           |
|             |             |             |             |+Planning Counci+|+=Seminar/White=+|   |
|             |+=====================Trade Show/Knox===================+|+=====Mgrs. Meeting/District 7=====+|  |
|             |+==================================Sales Drive/District 6===================================+|  |
 ---------------------------------------------------------------------------------------------
|    14       |     15      |     16      |     17      |     18      |     19      |    20     |
|             |             |             |             |             |             |           |
|             |             |             |             |+Planning Counci+|           |           |
|             |             |+==Dentist/JW===+|+Bank Meeting/1s+|+NewsLetter Dead+|+=Seminar/White=+| |
|+Co. Picnic/All=+|+================================Sales Drive/District 7===================================+|  |
 ---------------------------------------------------------------------------------------------
|    21       |     22      |     23      |     24      |     25      |     26      |    27     |
|             |             |             |             |             |             |           |
|             |             |             |             |             |             |           |
|             |             |             |+=Birthday/Mary=+|+======Close Sale/WYGIX Co.========+|  |
|             |+================Inventors Show/Melvin================+|+Planning Counci+|       |
 ---------------------------------------------------------------------------------------------
|    28       |     29      |     30      |     31      |             |             |           |
|             |             |             |             |             |             |           |
|             |             |             |             |             |             |           |
|             |             |             |             |             |             |           |
|             |             |             |             |             |             |           |
 ---------------------------------------------------------------------------------------------
```

In a schedule calendar, the duration of an activity is shown by a continuous line through each day of the activity. Values of variables for each activity are printed on the same line, separated by slashes (/). Each activity begins and ends with a plus sign (+). If an activity continues from one week to another, PROC CALENDAR displays arrows (< >) at the points of continuation.

   Note: The length of the activity lines is determined by the space specified in the LINESIZE= option. In the output above, you could increase the 12 spaces allowed activities with a one-day duration by increasing the line size or by using the WEEKDAYS option to suppress the display of weekend activities. Omitting the weekend activities provides more space for printing of Monday through Friday activities.

SPECIFICATIONS

The CALENDAR procedure is controlled by the following statements:

> **PROC CALENDAR** *<standard-option-list><summary-option-list>*
> *<schedule-option-list>*;
> **START** *variable*;
> **BY** *variable-list*;
> **CALID** *variable* </ OUTPUT=*option*>;
> **DUR** *variable*;
> **FIN** *variable*;
> **HOLISTART** *variable*;
> > **HOLIDUR** *variable*;
> > **HOLIFIN** *variable*;
> > **HOLIVAR** *variable*;
> **MEAN** *variable-list* </ FORMAT=*format-name*>;
> **OUTSTART** *day-of-week*;
> > **OUTDUR** *number-of-days*;
> > **OUTFIN** *day-of-week*;
> **SUM** *variable-list* </ FORMAT=*format-name*>;
> **VAR** *variable-list*;

Table 7.1 lists the statements and options available in the CALENDAR procedure according to function. In this section, the PROC CALENDAR statement is described first, and the other statements follow in alphabetic order.

Table 7.1   Summary of PROC CALENDAR Functions

Function	Statements	Options
Request summary calendar	START, SUM, MEAN	
Request schedule calendar	START, DUR, FIN	
Request multiple calendars	START, CALID	CALEDATA=, DAYLENGTH=, HOLIDATA=, INTERVAL=, OUTPUT=, WORKDATA=
Specify holidays	HOLISTART, HOLIDUR, HOLIFIN, HOLIVAR	HOLIDATA=

(continued)

Table 7.1 (*continued*)

Function	Statements	Options
Control display	OUTSTART, OUTDUR, OUTFIN	DATETIME, FILL, FORMCHAR=, HEADER=, INTERVAL=, LEGEND, MISSING, OUTPUT=, WEEKDAYS=
Specify grouping	BY, CALID	
Specify varied work schedules	CALID, START, DUR, FIN	CALEDATA=, DAYLENGTH=, INTERVAL=, WEEKDAYS, WORKDATA=

Only a few of these statements are required. The CALID statement is required for multiple calendars; a DUR or FIN statement is required for schedule calendars; the HOLIDATA= option and the HOLISTART statement are required if you want your calendar to contain holidays. The PROC CALENDAR and START statements are required for both types of calendars.

PROC CALENDAR Statement

> **PROC CALENDAR** <*standard-option-list*> <*summary-option-list*>
> <*schedule-option-list*>;

The options supported by the PROC CALENDAR statement are divided into three groups:

standard-option-list
  specifies options for summary and schedule calendars.

summary-option-list
  specifies options for summary calendars only.

schedule-option-list
  specifies options for schedule calendars only.

Table 7.2   Summary of Options Available in the PROC CALENDAR
Statement

Class	Options
Standard options	
Options to read data sets	DATA=
	CALEDATA=
	HOLIDATA=
	WORKDATA=
Options to control printing	MISSING
	FILL
	FORMCHAR=
	DATETIME
	HEADER=
	INTERVAL=
	WEEKDAYS
Summary options	LEGEND
	MEANTYPE=
Schedule option	DAYLENGTH=

CALEDATA=*SAS-data-set*
  specifies the SAS data set that contains weekly work schedules for
  multiple calendars. The CALEDATA= data set is not required, but it is
  useful if you are using multiple calendars or a nonstandard work
  schedule. See **Calendar Data Set** later in this chapter for more
  information on the CALEDATA= data set.

DATA=*SAS-data-set*
  specifies the activities data set, a SAS data set that contains activities to
  display in the output. PROC CALENDAR requires an activities data set. If
  you omit the DATA= option, the most recently created SAS data set is
  used. The activities data set contains starting dates for all activities, and
  variables to display for each activity. Activities must be sorted or
  indexed by starting date. See **Activities Data Set** later in this chapter for
  more information on the activities data set.

  Note: You can use the WHERE= data set option with the DATA=
  option to limit which observations are available for comparison. Refer to
  Chapter 9, "SAS Language Statements," and Chapter 15, "SAS Data Set
  Options," in *SAS Language: Reference, Version 6, First Edition* for more
  information on the WHERE statement and the WHERE= data set option.

DATETIME
  specifies that START and FIN variables contain values in DATETIME.
  format. If you omit the DATETIME option, PROC CALENDAR assumes
  that the START and FIN values are in DATE. format.

DAYLENGTH=*hours*
  gives the number of hours in a standard working day. The hour value
  you specify must be a SAS TIME value. The DAYLENGTH= option
  applies only to schedule calendars. PROC CALENDAR ignores this
  option if you specify it for a summary calendar.

  The DAYLENGTH= option is useful when you use the DUR
  statement and your work schedule contains days of varying lengths, for

example, a 5 1/2-day work week. In a work week with varying day lengths, you need to set a standard daylength to use in calculating duration times. For example, an activity with a duration of 3.0 workdays lasts 24 hours if DAYLENGTH=8:00, or 30 hours if DAYLENGTH=10:00.

If you prefer, instead of specifying the DAYLENGTH= option, you can specify the length of the working day using a D_LENGTH variable in the CALEDATA= data set. Using this method, you can specify different standard day lengths for different calendars.

If you specify both the DAYLENGTH= option and a D_LENGTH variable, PROC CALENDAR uses the DAYLENGTH= value only when the D_LENGTH value is missing. If you specify neither the DAYLENGTH= option nor a D_LENGTH variable, the length of the working day defaults to 24 hours if INTERVAL=DAY, and to 8 hours if INTERVAL=WORKDAY.

Note: When INTERVAL=DAY and you have no CALEDATA= data set, specifying a DAYLENGTH= value has no effect. For more information on setting the length of the standard workday, see **Calendar Data Set** later in this chapter.

FILL
displays all months between the first and last activity, start and finish dates inclusive, including months that contain no activities. If you do not specify the FILL option, PROC CALENDAR omits months with no activities.

FORMCHAR <(index-list)> ='formchar-string'
defines the characters used to print outlines and dividers for the calendar cells as well as all identifying markers (such as asterisks and arrows) used to indicate holidays or continuation of activities in PROC CALENDAR output. PROC CALENDAR uses 17 of the SAS form characters. You can use any character or hexidecimal string to customize the appearance of your calendar. You can set format characters using the SAS system option FORMCHAR= or the PROC CALENDAR option FORMCHAR=; and you can set all the format characters or only selected ones. See **Formatting Your Output** later in this chapter for more information on the FORMCHAR= option.

HOLIDATA=SAS-data-set
specifies the SAS data set containing the holidays you want to display in the output. The holidays data set is not required; you can produce calendars without using the HOLIDATA= option. However, if you want your calendar to contain holidays, you must use a HOLIDATA= data set and the HOLISTART statement.

The holidays data set contains the variable HOLISTART, whose values are the starting dates for all holidays, and contains the variable HOLIVAR, whose values are the names of the holidays. The HOLISTART variable is required when you use the HOLIDATA= option. The holidays data set need not be sorted. PROC CALENDAR marks holidays in the calendar output with asterisks (*) when space permits, as in the partial calendar shown below.

```
|----------------------------------------------------------------------------------------------------------------------------|
|    Sunday     |    Monday     |    Tuesday    |   Wednesday   |   Thursday    |    Friday     |   Saturday    |
|---------------+---------------+---------------+---------------+---------------+---------------+---------------|
|               |               |               |               |               |             1 |             2 |
|               |               |               |               |               |***New Year's****|             |
|---------------+---------------+---------------+---------------+---------------+---------------+---------------|
|             3 |             4 |             5 |             6 |             7 |             8 |             9 |
|               |               |               |               |               |               |               |
|----------------------------------------------------------------------------------------------------------------------------|
```

See **Holidays Data Set** later in this chapter for more information on the holidays data set.

HEADER=SMALL | MEDIUM | LARGE
specifies the type of heading to use in printing the name of the month. HEADER=SMALL prints the month and year on one line. HEADER=MEDIUM, the default, prints the month and year in a box 4 lines high. HEADER=LARGE prints the month 7 lines high using asterisks (*). The year is included if space is available. An example appears below:

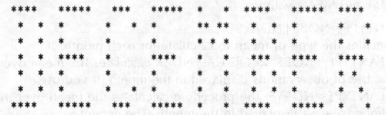

INTERVAL=DAY | WORKDAY
specifies the units of the DUR and HOLIDUR variables. If INTERVAL=DAY, PROC CALENDAR treats the values of the DUR and HOLIDUR variables in units of 24-hour days. For instance, a DUR value of 3.0 is treated as 72 hours. When INTERVAL=DAY, the default, the default calendar work schedule consists of seven working days, all starting at 00:00 with a length of 24:00.

If INTERVAL=WORKDAY, the default calendar work schedule consists of five working days, Monday through Friday, all starting at 09:00 with a length of 08:00. When WORKDAY is specified, PROC CALENDAR treats the values of the DUR and HOLIDUR variables in units of working days, as defined in the DAYLENGTH= option, the CALEDATA= data set, or the default calendar. For example, if the working day is 8 hours long, a DUR value of 3.0 is treated as 24 hours. The INTERVAL= option also specifies the default calendar.

In the absence of a CALEDATA= data set, PROC CALENDAR uses the work schedule defined in a default calendar. For more information on the default calendar, see **The Default Calendar** later in this chapter.

For more information on the INTERVAL= option and the specification of working days, see **Multiple Calendars** and **Calendar Data Set** later in this chapter.

LEGEND

prints text identifying the variables whose values appear in the calendar. This identifying text, or legend box, appears at the bottom of the page for each month if space permits; otherwise, it is printed on the following page. PROC CALENDAR identifies each variable by name or by label if one exists. The order of variables in the legend matches their order in the calendar. The LEGEND option applies only to summary calendars. PROC CALENDAR ignores this option if you specify it for a schedule calendar. An example is shown below.

```
         -----------
        |  Legend  |
        |          |
        |  TASK    |
        |  DUR     |
        |  COST    |
         -----------
```

If you use the SUM and MEAN statements, the legend box also contains SUM and MEAN values.

MEANTYPE=NOBS | NDAYS

specifies the type of mean to calculate for each month. If MEANTYPE=NOBS, PROC CALENDAR calculates the mean over the number of observations displayed in the month. If you use MEANTYPE=NDAYS, the procedure calculates the mean over the number of days displayed in the month. The default is MEANTYPE=NOBS. The MEANTYPE= option applies only to summary calendars. PROC CALENDAR ignores this option if you specify it for a schedule calendar.

Normally, PROC CALENDAR displays all days for each month. However, it may omit some days if you use the OUTSTART, OUTDUR and OUTFIN statements.

MISSING

the MISSING option is interpreted in several ways, depending on the type of calendar you use. For a summary calendar, if there is a day without an activity scheduled and you use the MISSING option, the values of variables for that day are printed using the SAS or user-defined format specified for missing values. If you do not use the MISSING option, days with no activities scheduled do not contain values. See **Example 3** for one use of the MISSING option. See **Missing Values in Input Data Sets** later in this chapter for more information on missing values.

If you use the MISSING option with a schedule calendar, it specifies that missing values of variables appear in the label of an activity, using the format specified for missing values. If you do not use the MISSING option, PROC CALENDAR ignores missing values in labelling activities.

WEEKDAYS

suppresses the display of Saturdays and Sundays in the output. It also specifies that the value of the INTERVAL= option is WORKDAY. The WEEKDAYS option is thus an alternative to using the combination of INTERVAL=WORKDAY and the statements OUTSTART Monday and OUTFIN Friday. For example, the following two groups of statements produce the same results:

```
proc calendar interval=workday;     proc calendar weekdays;
   start date;                          start date;
   outstart Monday;                     run;
   outfin Friday;
run;
```

WORKDATA=*SAS-data-set*

specifies the SAS data set that defines the work pattern during a standard working day. Each numeric variable in the WORKDATA= data set (also referred to as the workdays data set) denotes a unique shift pattern during one working day. The workdays data set is not required, but it is useful when you use the CALEDATA= data set. See **Workdays Data Set** later in this chapter for more information.

BY Statement

BY *variable-list*;

A BY statement causes PROC CALENDAR to process activities separately for each unique group of BY values in the DATA= data set. For example, if you specify a BY variable named BYVAR and the observations in your activities data set contain three different values for BYVAR, you get three sets of calendar output, one for each BYVAR value. When you use a BY statement, PROC CALENDAR expects your activities data set to be sorted first by the BY variables and then by the START variable, or to have an appropriate index. If your input data set is not sorted or indexed, you can do one of the following:

- Use the SORT procedure with a similar BY statement to sort the data.
- If appropriate, use the BY statement options NOTSORTED or DESCENDING.
- Use the DATASETS procedure to create an index on the BY variables you want to use. For more information on using the BY statement with indexed data sets, see Chapter 17, "The DATASETS Procedure."

CALID Statement

CALID *variable* </ OUTPUT=*option*>;

The CALID statement processes activities in groups defined by the values of a calendar identifier variable. The CALID variable can be either character or numeric. If the CALID variable is not in the holiday or calendar data sets, PROC CALENDAR looks for a default variable, _CAL_, in these data sets. You can specify a _CAL_ variable in your input statement. See **Multiple Calendars** later in this chapter for an example using the _CAL_ variable. With the CALID statement, you can schedule activities for multiple calendars according to the conventions of SAS/OR software.

The OUTPUT= option is the only option available with the CALID statement. The general form is

OUTPUT=SEPARATE | COMBINE | MIX

The OUTPUT= option controls the amount of space required to display output for multiple calendars. If OUTPUT=SEPARATE, PROC CALENDAR produces a separate page for each value of the CALID variable. PROC CALENDAR expects the actitivites to be sorted, first by the CALID variable, then by the START variable. If OUTPUT=SEPARATE and your activities are not already in sorted order, you must use an appropriate index or use the SORT procedure to sort your data, for example,

```
proc sort data=act;
   by _cal_ date;
run;
```

OUTPUT=COMBINED is the default format. It produces one page for each month containing activities and subdivides each day by the CALID value. Variables are sorted by the START variable.

OUTPUT=MIX format requires the least space for output because it produces one page for each month containing activities, but it does not identify activities by the CALID value. Variables are sorted by the START variable.

If you use OUTPUT=COMBINE or OUTPUT=MIX, you need only sort the data set by the START variable.

EXAMPLES later in this chapter includes output showing all three formats for multiple summary and schedule calendars.

DUR Statement

DUR *variable*;
DURATION *variable*;

The DUR or DURATION statement specifies the variable containing the duration of each activity and is used to produce schedule calendars. To produce a schedule calendar, you can give either DUR or FIN statements with the START statement. If you give both the DUR and FIN statements, only the FIN statement is used.

Duration is measured inclusively from the start of the activity (as given in the START variable). The duration may be a real or integral value. In the output, any activity lasting part of a day is displayed as lasting a full day.

The unit of the duration variable may be set to DAY or WORKDAY using the INTERVAL= option. The default unit is DAY, which is a 24-hour period. If INTERVAL=WORKDAY, the length of the duration unit is the length of the standard working day, which may be set using the DAYLENGTH= option or a D_LENGTH variable in the CALEDATA= data set. If neither of these are used the daylength defaults to 8 hours.

For more information on activity durations, see **Activities Data Set** and **Calendar Data Set** later in this chapter.

FIN Statement

FIN *variable*;
FINISH *variable*;

The FIN or FINISH statement specifies the variable in the DATA= data set that contains the finishing date of each activity. A FIN statement is used to produce a schedule calendar. The values in the FIN variable must be in either SAS date or datetime values. If you use datetime values, specify the DATETIME option in the PROC CALENDAR statement.

To produce a schedule calendar, you can use either a DUR or a FIN statement with the START statement. If you give both the DUR and FIN statements, PROC CALENDAR uses only the FIN statement. To produce a summary calendar, neither the DUR nor the FIN statements are necessary.

HOLIDUR Statement

HOLIDUR *variable*;
HOLIDURATION *variable*;

The HOLIDUR or HOLIDURATION statement specifies the variable that contains the duration of each holiday. Duration is measured inclusively from the start of the holiday (as given in the HOLISTART variable). The duration may be a real or integral value. In the output, any holiday lasting at least half a day appears as lasting a full day.

You set the unit of the holiday duration variable in the same way as the unit of the duration variable, using the INTERVAL= and DAYLENGTH= options and the CALEDATA= data set.

For more information on holiday durations, see **Holiday Data Set** later in this chapter.

HOLIFIN Statement

HOLIFIN *variable*;
HOLIFINISH *variable*;

The HOLIFIN or HOLIFINISH statement specifies the variable in the HOLIDATA= data set containing the finishing date of each holiday. The values contained in the HOLIFIN variable may be either SAS date or datetime values.

HOLISTART Statement

HOLISTART *variable*;
HOLISTA *variable*;
HOLIDAY *variable*;

The HOLISTART statement specifies a variable in the HOLIDATA= data set that contains the starting date of each holiday. The HOLISTART statement is required when you use the HOLIDATA= option.

The HOLIDATA= data set need not be sorted. If two or more holidays occur on the same day, PROC CALENDAR uses only the first observation. The values contained in the HOLISTART variable may be either SAS date or datetime values.

When you use a HOLISTART statement, you can use either the HOLIDUR statement, the HOLIFIN statement, both, or neither. If you use both, then in your holidays data set you can give values for either variable. When a holiday contains values for both the HOLIDUR and HOLIFIN variables, PROC CALENDAR uses only the HOLIFIN value. If you use neither the HOLIDUR nor HOLIFIN statements, all holidays last only one day.

HOLIVAR Statement

HOLIVAR *variable*;
HOLIVARIABLE *variable*;
HOLINAME *variable*;

The HOLIVAR statement specifies a variable in the HOLIDATA= data set whose value is used to label the holidays. Typically, this variable contains the names of the holidays; but the variable can be either character or numeric, and you can format the HOLIVAR variable as you like.

MEAN Statement

> **MEAN** *variable-list* </ FORMAT=*format-name*>;

The MEAN statement specifies numeric variables for which mean values are to be calculated for each month. The means appear at the bottom of the calendar page, if there is room; otherwise they appear on the following page. The means appear in the legend box if the LEGEND option is used, as shown below.

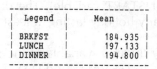

```
 -----------------------------
 | Legend  |   Mean    |
 |         |           |
 | BRKFST  |   184.935 |
 | LUNCH   |   197.133 |
 | DINNER  |   194.800 |
 -----------------------------
```

You can use as many MEAN statements as you want. PROC CALENDAR automatically displays variables named in a MEAN statement for each activity in the output, even if the variable is not listed in the VAR statement.

You can format MEAN values by using the FORMAT= option:

FORMAT=*format-name*
F=*format-name*
> names a SAS or user-defined format to be used in displaying the means requested. The BEST. format is the default.

OUTDUR Statement

> **OUTDUR** *number-of-days*;
> **OUTDURATION** *number-of-days*;

The OUTDUR or OUTDURATION statement specifies in days the length of the week to be displayed. For example, the combination of statements

```
outstart monday;
outdur 5;
```

produces a calendar displaying weeks with only the days Monday through Friday.

If you use the OUTDUR statement, you must use also an OUTSTART statement.

OUTFIN Statement

> **OUTFIN** *day-of-week*;
> **OUTFINISH** *day-of-week*;

The OUTFIN or OUTFINISH statement specifies the last day of the week to display in the calendar output. For example, the combination of statements

```
outstart monday;
outfin friday;
```

produces a calendar displaying only the days Monday through Friday, and is equivalent to the example in **OUTDUR Statement** above.

If you use the OUTFIN statement, you must also use the OUTSTART statement.

OUTSTART Statement

> **OUTTSTART** *day-of-week;*
> **OUTSTA** *day-of-week;*

The OUTSTART or OUTSTA statement specifies the starting day of the week. For example, the statement

    outstart monday;

produces a calendar with weeks that start on Monday and end on Sunday.

When you use the OUTSTART statement, you can use either the OUTDUR statement, the OUTFIN statement, both, or neither. If you give both statements, only the OUTFIN statement is used. If you use neither the OUTDUR nor OUTFIN statements, the week displayed is seven days long.

START Statement

> **START** *variable;*
> **STA** *variable;*
> **DATE** *variable;*
> **ID** *variable;*

The START statement specifies the variable in the DATA= data set containing the starting date of each activity. This statement is required for both summary and schedule calendars. Values of the START variable must be in either SAS DATE or DATETIME values. If you use DATETIME values, specify the DATETIME option in the PROC CALENDAR statement.

For summary calendars, activities always finish on the same date they start, so the START statement is the only required statement. Schedule calendars require a DUR or FIN statement in addition to the START statement. If you give both the DUR and FIN statements, PROC CALENDAR uses the FIN statement.

SUM Statement

> **SUM** *variable-list* </ FORMAT=*format-name*>;

The SUM statement specifies numeric variables to total for each month. The sum appears at the bottom of the calendar page, if there is room; otherwise, it appears on the following page. The sum appears in the LEGEND box if you specify the LEGEND option, as shown below.

You can use as many SUM statements as you like. PROC CALENDAR automatically displays variables named in a SUM statement in the calendar output, even if the variables are not named in the VAR statement.

You can format SUM values by using the FORMAT option:

FORMAT=*format-name*
F=*format-name*
    names a SAS or user-defined format to use in displaying the sums requested. The BEST. format is the default.

VAR Statement

    VAR *variable-list*;
    VARIABLE *variable-list*;

The VAR or VARIABLE statement specifies the variables for each activity in the DATA= data set that you want to display. Variables can be either character or numeric, and you can format them as you want.

PROC CALENDAR displays variables in the order that they appear in the VAR statement. All variables except BY, CALID, START, DUR, and FIN variables are displayed, insofar as LINESIZE= and PAGESIZE= specifications permit. If you do not use a VAR statement, the procedure displays all variables in the DATA= data set in the order that they are found in the activities data set. Any variable named in a SUM or MEAN statement is displayed for each activity in the calendar output, even if it you do not name the variable in a VAR statement.

DETAILS

Summary and Schedule Calendars

PROC CALENDAR determines whether your output appears in summary or schedule format based on the absence or presence of the DUR and FIN statements. If you use neither the DUR nor the FIN statement and your activities last for only one day, your calendar is output in summary format. If you use either the DUR or the FIN statement, your activities may last for more than one day, so your calendar output appears in schedule format.

The principal differences between summary and schedule calendars are as follows:

- Sums and means can be calculated only in a summary calendar.
- Activities can be scheduled around holidays and nonwork periods only in a schedule calendar.

Use a summary calendar if your activities last for only one day, or if you are interested in sum and mean calculations. Use a schedule calendar if your activities could last for several days, or if you are interested in scheduling activities around holidays and nonwork periods.

Multiple Calendars

A *multiple calendar* contains information from several sources. You can design both summary and schedule multiple calendars. The CALID statement is required. It creates multiple calendars and specifies the variable that identifies the calendar. Options on the CALID statement control the appearance of the output. The multiple-calendar feature was added specifically to enable PROC CALENDAR to process the output of PROC CPM in SAS/OR software.

For example, recall the summer planning calendar for the busy executive Julia Q. Wydget used in **Introductory Examples** earlier in this chapter. She may want to create a calendar combining her work schedule with her home schedule. Her home schedule includes the activities of her husband, Fred, and daughter Meagan. The statements below produce **Output 7.3**.

```
options pagesize=60 linesize=132 nodate;
title   'Summer Planning Calendar:  '
'Julia Q. Wydget, President';
title2  'Better Products Inc.';
title3  'Work and Home Schedule';

data act;
  input date:date7. happen $ 10-34 who $ 35-47 _CAL_ $ long;
  cards;
01JUL91  Dist. Mtg.            All          CAL1    1
02JUL91  Mgrs. Meeting         District 6   CAL1    2
03JUL91  Interview             JW           CAL1    1
05JUL91  VIP Banquet           JW           CAL1    1
06JUL91  Beach trip            family       CAL2    2
08JUL91  Sales Drive           District 6   CAL1    5
08JUL91  Trade Show            Knox         CAL1    3
09JUL91  Orthodontist          Meagan       CAL2    1
11JUL91  Mgrs. Meeting         District 7   CAL1    2
11JUL91  Planning Council      Group II     CAL1    1
12JUL91  Seminar               White        CAL1    1
14JUL91  Co. Picnic            All          CAL1    1
14JUL91  Business trip         Fred         CAL2    2
15JUL91  Sales Drive           District 7   CAL1    5
16JUL91  Dentist               JW           CAL1    1
17JUL91  Bank Meeting          1st Natl     CAL1    1
17JUL91  Real estate agent     Family       CAL2    1
18JUL91  NewsLetter Deadline   All          CAL1    1
18JUL91  Planning Council      Group III    CAL1    1
19JUL91  Seminar               White        CAL1    1
22JUL91  Inventors Show        Melvin       CAL1    3
24JUL91  Birthday              Mary         CAL1    1
25JUL91  Planning Council      Group IV     CAL1    1
25JUL91  Close Sale            WYGIX Co.    CAL1    2
27JUL91  Ballgame              Family       CAL2    1
;
run;

data vac;
  input hdate:date7.  holiday $ 11-25 _CAL_ $ ;
  cards;
04JUL91    Independence        CAL1
29JUL91    vacation            CAL2
;
run;

proc calendar data=act holidata=vac;
  calid _CAL_ / output=combine;
  start date ;
  holistart hdate;
  holivar holiday;
  dur long;
run;
```

Output 7.3 Producing a Multiple Calendar

```
                    Summer Planning Calendar:  Julia Q. Wydget, President                          1
                                     Better Products Inc.
                                     Work and Home Schedule
     ---------------------------------------------------------------------------------------------
    |                                                                                             |
    |                                          July  1991                                         |
    |                                                                                             |
     ---------------------------------------------------------------------------------------------
    |       Sunday    |    Monday    |   Tuesday    |   Wednesday   |   Thursday   |    Friday     |   Saturday   |
    +-----------------+--------------+--------------+---------------+--------------+---------------+--------------+
    |                 |      1       |      2       |      3        |      4       |      5        |      6       |
    | CAL1            |              |              |+=Interview/JW=+|**Independence**|             |              |
    |                 |+Dist. Mtg./All+|+====Mgrs. Meeting/District 6=====+|      |+VIP Banquet/JW+|              |
    | CAL2            |              |              |               |              |               |+Beach trip/fam>|
    +-----------------+--------------+--------------+---------------+--------------+---------------+--------------+
    |       7         |      8       |      9       |     10        |     11       |     12        |     13       |
    | CAL1            |              |              |               |+Planning Counc+|+Seminar/White+|            |
    |                 |+=================Trade Show/Knox=================+|+===Mgrs. Meeting/District 7====+|    |
    |                 |+=================================Sales Drive/District 6==================================+|
    | CAL2           |<Beach trip/fam+|           |+Orthodontist/M+|              |               |              |
    +-----------------+--------------+--------------+---------------+--------------+---------------+--------------+
    |      14         |     15       |     16       |     17        |     18       |     19        |     20       |
    | CAL1            |              |              |               |+Planning Counc+|             |              |
    |                 |              |+==Dentist/JW==+|+Bank Meeting/1+|+NewsLetter Dea+|+Seminar/White=+|       |
    |                 |+Co. Picnic/All+|+================================Sales Drive/District 7================================+|
    | CAL2           |+======Business trip/Fred=======+|          |+Real estate ag+|             |              |
    +-----------------+--------------+--------------+---------------+--------------+---------------+--------------+
    |      21         |     22       |     23       |     24        |     25       |     26        |     27       |
    | CAL1            |              |              |+Birthday/Mary=+|+======Close Sale/WYGIX Co.=======+|        |
    |                 |+=============Inventors Show/Melvin=============+|+Planning Counc+|           |              |
    | CAL2            |              |              |               |              |               |+Ballgame/Famil+|
    +-----------------+--------------+--------------+---------------+--------------+---------------+--------------+
    |      28         |     29       |     30       |     31        |              |               |              |
    | CAL2            |****vacation****|            |               |              |               |              |
    |                 |              |              |               |              |               |              |
    |                 |              |              |               |              |               |              |
     ---------------------------------------------------------------------------------------------
```

Notice the use of the _CAL_ variable to create the separate calendars. The value
CAL1 refers to the work schedule; the value CAL2 to the home schedule. The
HOLIDATA= option identifies the holidays data set. PROC CALENDAR reads
the data values specified in the VAC data set into the calendar. The
OUTPUT=COMBINE option prints both calendars on one page and separates
CAL1 and CAL2.

Using the CALID Variable

The previous example shows how you can use the _CAL_ variable to define a
multiple calendar variable. You can also use other variables instead. The CALID
variable can be character or numeric.

   You can use the CALID variable to define distinct work and vacation periods.
For instance, in the previous example, the value CAL1 defines one calendar; the
value CAL2 defines another. You could use a CALID variable to specify different
work shifts as well.

   The WORKDATA=, CALEDATA=, and DAYLENGTH= options are useful in
defining special work schedules. When you combine calendars using the holidays

or calendar data sets, PROC CALENDAR treats the variable values in the following way:

- Every value of the CALID variable that appears in either the holidays or calendar data sets defines a calendar.
- If a CALID value appears in the HOLIDATA= data set but not in the CALEDATA= data set, the work schedule of the default calendar is used.
- If a CALID value appears in the CALEDATA= data set but not in the HOLIDATA= data set, the holidays of the default calendar are used.
- If a CALID value appears in the DATA= data set but not in the HOLIDATA= or CALEDATA= data sets, the work schedule and holidays of the default calendar are used.

If the CALID variable is not found in the holiday or calendar data sets, PROC CALENDAR looks for the default variable _CAL_ instead. If neither the CALID variable nor a _CAL_ variable appear in a data set, the observations in that data set are applied to a default calendar.

The Default Calendar

The *default calendar* is a special calendar defined by PROC CALENDAR. It is used when you do not specify the CALID statement or when, as outlined above, the CALID variable is not defined in a data set that you are using. Its definition and uses are described here.

If you have not specified a CALID variable and are not using a CALEDATA= or WORKDATA= data set, the default calendar is defined by the INTERVAL= and DAYLENGTH= options in the PROC CALENDAR statement. The value for the INTERVAL= option can be either DAY or WORKDAY.

If INTERVAL=DAY, then work is scheduled for all seven days of the week; otherwise, Saturday and Sunday are nonworking days. For example, if you use INTERVAL=DAY, then in the absence of a CALEDATA= data set, this value specifies a seven-day weekly work schedule for the default calendar. You can modify this calendar if the schedule is computed using SAS datetime values, because the length of the working day is determined by the values of the DAYLENGTH= option.

If you use INTERVAL=WORKDAY, you specify a five-day work schedule, Monday through Friday. Starting times for work days are 00:00 when INTERVAL=DAY, and 09:00 when INTERVAL=WORKDAY. The default is DAYLENGTH=24:00 when INTERVAL=DAY, and DAYLENGTH=8:00 when INTERVAL=WORKDAY.

All the holidays specified in the HOLIDATA data set refer to this default calendar and all the activities in the project follow it. If you do not use a CALID variable, the default calendar is the only calendar used for all the activities in the project.

If you use a CALID variable that identifies distinct calendars, you can use an observation in the CALEDATA= data set to define the work week structure for the default calendar. Use the value 0 (if the CALID variable is numeric) or the value DEFAULT (if the CALID variable is character) to identify the default calendar. In the absence of such an observation, the default calendar is defined by the INTERVAL= and DAYLENGTH= options, as before. The default calendar is used to substitute default work patterns for missing values in the calendar data set or to set default work-week structures for newly defined calendars in the holidays data set.

Input Data Sets

You may need several data sets to produce a calendar, depending on the complexity of your application. PROC CALENDAR can process between one and four input data sets. These are the

- activities data set
- holidays data set
- calendar data set
- workdays data set.

Each data set is described in the sections that follow.

Activities Data Set

An activities data set is required for all applications. If you do not specify an activities data set using the DATA= option, PROC CALENDAR uses the most recently created SAS data set. Only one activities data set is allowed.

Each observation in the activities data set contains one activity. One variable of the data set must contain the starting date of the activities, and you must name this variable in the START statement. If you are producing a schedule calendar, you must include either durations or finishing dates for activities, and name the variable in a DUR or FIN statement. The activities data set must always be sorted or indexed by the START variable and by the CALID variable if you use one. If you use the BY statement, the activities data set must be sorted or indexed by the BY variables. Other variables in the data set are used to label the activities in the calendar output.

Listed below are the statements that create the two activities data sets for the summary and schedule calendars in **Introductory Examples** earlier in this chapter. In both data sets, the variable DATE contains the starting dates of the activities. Variables displayed for each activity are BRKFST, LUNCH, and DINNER in the summary data set, and HAPPEN and WHO in the schedule data set. In the schedule data set, the variable LONG contains activity durations. This variable, LONG, will be used in the DUR or FIN statement.

```
title 'Summary Calendar';            title 'Schedule Calendar';
data act;                            data act;
  input date date7.                    input date:date7.
    brkfst lunch dinner;               happen $ 9-30 who $ 31-40 long;
  cards;                               cards;
01Dec91  123 234 123                 01JUL91 Dist. Mtg.            All         1
02Dec91  123 234 238                 02JUL91 Mgrs. Meeting         District 6  2
03Dec91  188 188 198                 03JUL91 Interview             JW          1
04Dec91  123 183 176                 05JUL91 VIP Banquet           JW          1
05Dec91  200 267 243                 08JUL91 Sales Drive           District 6  5
06Dec91  176 165 177                 08JUL91 Trade Show            Knox        3
07Dec91  156  .  167                 11JUL91 Mgrs. Meeting         District 7  2
08Dec91  198 143 167                 11JUL91 Planning Council      Group II    1
09Dec91  178 198 187                 12JUL91 Seminar               White       1
10Dec91  165 176 187                 14JUL91 Co. Picnic            All         1
11Dec91  187 176 231                 15JUL91 Sales Drive           District 7  5
12Dec91  176 187 222                 16JUL91 Dentist               JW          1
13Dec91  187 187 123                 17JUL91 Bank Meeting          1st Natl    1
14Dec91  164 187 231                 18JUL91 Newsletter Deadline   All         1
15Dec91  187 165 167                 18JUL91 Planning Council      Group III   1
16Dec91  187 198 156                 19JUL91 Seminar               White       1
17Dec91  198 187 156                 22JUL91 Inventors Show        Melvin      3
```

```
18Dec91  187 165 178        24JUL91 Birthday          Mary        1
19Dec91  187 176 156        25JUL91 Planning Council   Group IV    1
20Dec91  156 211 199        25JUL91 Close Sale         WYGIX Co.   2
21Dec91  176 156 143        ;
22Dec91  165 167 211        run;
23Dec91  187 176  .
24Dec91  185 167 167
25Dec91  187 178 187
26Dec91  167 156 198
27Dec91  167 239 267
28Dec91  267 287 256
29Dec91  276 243 234
30Dec91  267 287 256
31Dec91  243 231 243
;
run;
```

For summary calendars, only one activity can be displayed on a given date; so if more than one activity has the same START value, only the last observation read is used. In such situations, you may find PROC SUMMARY useful to collapse your data set to contain one activity per starting date.

Activities can occur on any day of the week in a summary calendar. For schedule calendars, activities are scheduled based on information in the HOLIDATA=, WORKDATA=, and CALEDATA= data sets.

Holidays Data Set

You can use a holidays data set to mark holidays on your calendar output. If you are producing a schedule calendar, PROC CALENDAR does not schedule activities on holidays. PROC CALENDAR does not require a holidays data set, but if you choose to use this feature, you must use the HOLISTART statement and the HOLIDATA= option.

Each observation in the holidays data set contains one holiday. One variable of the data set must contain the starting date of the holidays, and you must name it in the HOLISTART statement. Another variable should contain the names of the holidays; you can specify this variable with a HOLIVAR statement. For example, in the holidays data set below, DATE is the HOLISTART variable, and NAME is the HOLIVAR variable.

```
data hol;
  input date: date7. name & $ 15.;
  cards;
1JAN91  New Year's
30JUN91 Inventory
4JUL91  Independence
29JUL91 Vacation
2SEP91  Labor Day
25DEC91 Christmas
;
run;
```

You do not need to sort or index the holidays data set.

Holidays defined in the HOLIDATA= data set cannot occur during nonwork periods defined in the work schedule. For instance, you cannot schedule Sunday as a vacation day if the work week is defined as Monday through Friday. When such a conflict occurs, the holiday is rescheduled to the next available working period following the nonwork day.

PROC CALENDAR calculates time using SAS datetime values even when your data are in DATE. format; it calculates time in minutes and seconds. It automatically calculates the holidays using this specification as well. Because of this, you may receive the following messages from PROC CALENDAR on your log:

```
NOTE: All holidays are assumed to start at the time/date specified
      for the holiday variable and last one DTWRKDAY.
WARNING: The units of calculation are SAS datetime values while
         all the holiday variables are not. All holidays are
         converted to SAS datetime values.
```

Scheduling Activities and Holidays

You can easily schedule activities using multiple calendars. For example, consider the 1986 work and holiday schedule for Julia Q. Wydget, President of Better Products, Inc. The DATA step below defines her work schedule to include only work periods from 09:00 to 17:00 Monday through Friday. In 1986, July 5th and 6th fell on Saturday and Sunday. For the calendar shown below she specified INTERVAL=WORKDAY but neglected to schedule July 4th as a holiday.

```
options linesize=132;
data act;
input date:date7. happen $ 9-36 who $ 38-40 _CAL_ $ 50 -53 long;
cards;
03JUL86 project                     JW       CAL1   3
07JUL86 finish                      JW       CAL1   1
;
run;

proc calendar data=act  interval=workday;
    start date;
    dur long;
run;
```

Part of the calendar produced is a shown below.

```
                                    The SAS System                                                              1
|--------------------------------------------------------------------------------------------------------------|
|                                                                                                              |
|                                        July  1986                                                            |
|--------------------------------------------------------------------------------------------------------------|
|   Sunday   |    Monday    |   Tuesday   |  Wednesday  |   Thursday   |    Friday   |   Saturday   |
|------------+--------------+-------------+-------------+--------------+-------------+--------------|
|            |              |      1      |      2      |      3       |      4      |      5       |
|            |              |             |             |              |             |              |
|            |              |             |             |              |             |              |
|            |              |             |             |              |             |              |
|            |              |             |             | +=========project/JW/CAL1=========>|    |
|------------+--------------+-------------+-------------+--------------+-------------+--------------|
|     6      |      7       |      8      |      9      |     10       |     11      |     12       |
|            |              |             |             |              |             |              |
|            |              |             |             |              |             |              |
|            | +finish/JW/CAL1=+|          |             |              |             |              |
|            | <project/JW/CAL1+|          |             |              |             |              |
|------------+--------------+-------------+-------------+--------------+-------------+--------------|
```

Ms. Wydget realized her mistake and rescheduled July 4 as a holiday using the HOLIDATA= option with a default HOLISTART date of 09:00 on Friday, July 4th. As with the activities data set, she can specify the length of the holiday with either a HOLIDUR or a HOLIFIN statement. Since Ms. Wydget did not use a HOLIDUR or HOLIFIN statement, the default, INTERVAL=WORKDAY, determines the length of the holiday.

```
data act;
input date:date7. happen $ 9-36 who $ 38-40 _CAL_ $ long;
cards;
03JUL86 project                    JW          CAL1    3
07JUL86 finish                     JW          CAL1    1
;
run;

data vac;
  input date:date7.  holiday $ 11-25 _CAL_ $;
cards;
04jul86    Independence          CAL1
;
run;

proc calendar data=act holidata=vac interval=workday;
   calid _CAL_  / output=mixed;
   start date;
   dur long;
   holistart date;
   holivar  holiday;
run;
```

Part of the calendar produced is shown below.

```
                                   The SAS System                                          1
------------------------------------------------------------------------------------------
|                                                                                        |
|                                    July  1986                                          |
|                                                                                        |
--------------------------------------------------------------------------------------------
|  Sunday     |   Monday    |   Tuesday   |  Wednesday  |  Thursday   |   Friday    |  Saturday  |
--------------------------------------------------------------------------------------------
|             |             |     1       |     2       |     3       |     4       |     5      |
|             |             |             |             |             |             |            |
|             |             |             |             |             |             |            |
|             |             |             |             |+==project/JW===>|**Independence***|  |
--------------------------------------------------------------------------------------------
|     6       |     7       |     8       |     9       |    10       |    11       |    12      |
|             |             |             |             |             |             |            |
|             |+===finish/JW===+|         |             |             |             |            |
|             |<===========project/JW===========+|      |             |             |            |
--------------------------------------------------------------------------------------------
```

Ms. Wydget could specify the holiday using a HOLIFIN variable with a value of Saturday, July 5th, at 17:00. Then the holiday occurs between the hours of 09:00 and 17:00 on Friday, July 4th only, because July 5th and 6th are nonwork periods.

Suppose instead of giving a HOLIFIN variable, Ms. Wydget gave a HOLIDUR variable with a value of 2.0, as shown in the code below. In this case, the holiday is rescheduled for the next available 16-hour work period, which is between the hours of 09:00 and 17:00 on July 4th and 7th.

```
data act;
input date:date7. happen $ 9-36 who $ 38-40 _CAL_ $ long;
cards;
03JUL86 project                      JW         CAL1  3
07JUL86 finish                       JW         CAL1  1
;
run;

data vac;
input date:date7.  holiday $ 11-25  dur _CAL_ $;
cards;
04jul86    Independence            2            CAL1
;
run;

proc calendar data=act holidata=vac interval=workday;
   calid _CAL_ / output=mixed;
   start date;
   dur long;
   holistart date;
   holivar  holiday;
   holidur dur;
run;
```

Part of the calendar produced is shown below.

```
                             The SAS System                                    1
--------------------------------------------------------------------------------
|                                                                              |
|                               July  1986                                     |
|------------------------------------------------------------------------------|
| Sunday  |  Monday  |  Tuesday |  Wednesday |  Thursday |  Friday  |  Saturday |
|---------------------------------------------------------------------------- |
|         |          |    1     |     2      |     3     |    4     |    5      |
|         |          |          |            |           |          |           |
|         |          |          |            |           |          |           |
|         |          |          |            |+==project/JW===>|**Independence***|
|-------------------------------------------------------------------------------|
|    6    |    7     |    8     |     9      |    10     |    11    |    12     |
|         |          |          |            |           |          |           |
|         |          |          |            |           |          |           |
|         |**Independence***|+===finish/JW===+|          |          |           |
|         |**Independence***|<===========project/JW============>|    |           |
|-------------------------------------------------------------------------------|
```

Note that while PROC CALENDAR can schedule activities only in a schedule calendar, holidays are scheduled around nonwork periods in both summary and schedule calendars. In scheduling holidays, PROC CALENDAR uses the work schedule for the default calendar, or it can define a schedule in the CALEDATA= and WORKDATA= data sets.

Calendar Data Set

You can use a calendar data set, specified with the CALEDATA= option, to specify work schedules for different calendars. Each observation in the CALEDATA= data set contains one weekly work schedule.

The data set created in the DATA step shown below contains work schedules for two calendars, CALONE and CALTWO. Here, the variables _SUN_, _MON_, and so forth contain the names of workshifts. Valid workshift names are WORKDAY, which is the default workshift; HOLIDAY, which is a nonwork period; or names of variables in the WORKDATA= data set, in this case SHIFT1 and SHIFT2.

```
data cale;
    input _Sun_ $  1- 8  _Mon_ $  9-16  _Tue_ $ 17-24
          _Wed_ $ 25-32  _Thu_ $ 33-40  _Fri_ $ 41-48
          _Sat_ $ 49-56  _cal_ $ 57-64  d_length time6. ;
    cards;
holiday workday workday workday workday workday holiday calone  8:00
    holiday shift1  shift1  shift1  shift1  shift2  holiday caltwo  9:00
;
```

The variable _CAL_ is the CALID variable containing the name of the calendar used. This variable serves as a pointer, indicating the values, CALONE and CALTWO, used for the different work schedules. If this variable is not present, the first observation in this data set defines the work schedule for the default calendar. If the CALID variable contains a missing value, the character or numeric value for the default calendar (DEFAULT or 0) is used. See **The Default Calendar** earlier in this chapter for further details.

The variable D_LENGTH contains the length of the standard workday to be used in calendar calculations. If this variable is not used, you can set the workday length with the DAYLENGTH= option. Missing values for this variable default to the number of hours specified in the DAYLENGTH= option; if the DAYLENGTH= option is not used, the day length defaults to 24 hours if INTERVAL=DAY, or 8 hours if INTERVAL=WORKDAY.

You can use the CALEDATA= data set with or without a WORKDATA= data set. Work shifts not defined in a WORKDATA= data set start at 00:00 if INTERVAL=DAY or 09:00 if INTERVAL=WORKDAY. Their length is specified by a D_LENGTH variable or by the DAYLENGTH= option, or they default to 24:00 if INTERVAL=DAY or 08:00 if INTERVAL=WORKDAY.

Workdays Data Set

You can use a workdays data set, specified with the WORKDATA= option, to define the daily work shifts named in a CALEDATA= data set. Each variable in the WORKDATA= data set contains one daily schedule of alternating work and nonwork periods.

The data set created in the DATA step shown below contains specifications for two work shifts. The variable SHIFT1 specifies a 10-hour workday, with an hour off for lunch, and the variable SHIFT2 specifies a 4-hour half-workday.

```
data work;
    input shift1 time6. shift2 time6.;
    cards;
 7:00   7:00
12:00  11:00
13:00   .
17:00   .
;
run;
```

The missing values default to 00:00 in the first observation; to 24:00 in all other observations. Two consecutive values of 24:00 define a zero-length time period, which is ignored.

If you associate the work shifts in this WORKDATA= data set with the weekly work schedules defined in the CALEDATA= data set of the previous section, the first schedule in the CALEDATA= data set, CALONE, specifies a standard work-week of five 8-hour days. The second schedule, CALTWO, specifies four 10-hour days, followed by a 4-hour half-day. Thus, the daily work schedules in this work-days data set together with the weekly work schedules in the calendar data set define two different 40-hour workweeks by using calendars CALONE and CALTWO.

For more examples of the use of DATA=, HOLIDATA=, WORKDATA=, and CALEDATA= data sets, see **EXAMPLES** later in this chapter.

Missing Values in Input Data Sets

Table 7.3 summarizes the treatment of missing values for variables in the data sets used by PROC CALENDAR.

Table 7.3 Treatment of Missing Values in PROC CALENDAR

Data Set	Variable	Treatment of Missing Values
DATA=	CALID	default calendar value is used
	STA	observation is not used
	DUR	1.0 is used
	FIN	START value + daylength is used
	VAR	if a summary calendar or the MISSING option is specified, the missing value is used; otherwise, no value is used
	SUM, MEAN	for a summary calendar, 0 is used; otherwise, no value is used

(continued)

Table 7.3 (continued)

Data Set	Variable	Treatment of Missing Values
CALEDATA=	CALID	default calendar value is used
	SUN, _MON_,	corresponding shift for default calendar is used
	D_LENGTH	if available, DAYLENGTH= value is used; otherwise, if INTERVAL=DAY, 24:00 is used; otherwise 8:00 is used
HOLIDATA=	CALID	all known calendar values are used
	HOLISTART	observation is not used
	HOLIDUR	if available, HOLIFIN value is used instead of HOLIDUR value; otherwise 1.0 is used
	HOLIFIN	if available, HOLIDUR value is used instead of HOLIFIN value; otherwise, HOLISTART value + day length is used
	HOLIVAR	no value is used
WORKDATA=	any	for the first observation, 00:00 is used; otherwise, 24:00 is used

Formatting Your Output

The SAS system option FORMCHAR= and the FORMCHAR= option in the PROC CALENDAR statement both define the characters used to print output. If you set the FORMCHAR= option on the PROC CALENDAR statement, it affects only the output produced by that PROC CALENDAR step; if you set the SAS system option FORMCHAR=, it affects all procedure output that uses the FORMCHAR= option.

PROC CALENDAR uses 17 of the first 20 SAS format characters. The following table shows these format characters, together with their default character, their hexadecimal values, and their use in PROC CALENDAR.

Table 7.4 Format Characters Used in PROC CALENDAR

Position	Name	Default	Hex Value	Use in PROC CALENDAR
1	vertical bar	|	7C	calendar outlines
2	horizontal bar	–	2D	calendar outlines
3	upper left	–	2D	calendar outlines
4	upper middle	–	2D	calendar outlines
5	upper right	–	2D	calendar outlines
6	middle left	|	7C	calendar outlines
7	middle middle	+	2B	calendar outlines
8	middle right	|	7C	calendar outlines
9	lower left	–	2D	calendar outlines
10	lower middle	–	2D	calendar outlines
11	lower right	–	2D	calendar outlines
12	vertical thick	+	2B	activity start and finish
13	horizontal thick	=	3D	activity line
14	vertical dash	|	7C	not used
15	horizontal dash	–	2D	not used
16	slash	/	2F	activity value separator
17	backslash	\	5C	not used
18	left arrow	<	3C	activity continuation
19	right arrow	>	3E	activity continuation
20	asterisk	*	2A	holiday marker

You can use the FORMCHAR= option to customize the appearance of your PROC CALENDAR output by substituting your own characters for the default. For example, using

```
formchar(12 13)='*-'
```

changes the start and finish marker for activities from a plus sign (+) to an asterisk (*) and the activity line from a double line (=) to a single line (-). Then, activity lines normally drawn as

```
+==================ACTIVITY==================+
```

appear as

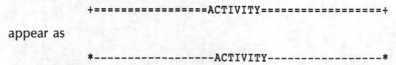

```
*------------------ACTIVITY------------------*
```

If your printer supports an *extended character set*, one that includes graphics characters in addition to the regular alphanumeric characters, you can can greatly improve the appearance of your output using the FORMCHAR= option. For example, the hexadecimal codes in the statements below refer to characters in an extended character set on an IBM 6670 printer, which was used to produce the following version of the schedule calendar shown earlier in **Introductory Examples**.

```
proc calendar formchar='fabfacccbceb8fecabcbbbafbf4f6061e04c6eaf'x
   weekdays data=act;
   id date;
   sum brkfst lunch dinner;
   mean brkfst lunch dinner;
run;
```

Output 7.4   Schedule Calendar Using Extended Character Set

```
         Meals Served in Community Hospital Cafeteria

                          DECEMBER  1991

  MONDAY        TUESDAY       WEDNESDAY      THURSDAY        FRIDAY

    2             3             4             5             6
         123           188           123           200           176
         234           188           183           267           165
         238           198           176           243           177

    9            10            11            12            13
         178           165           187           176           187
         198           176           176           187           187
         187           187           231           222           123

   16            17            18            19            20
         187           198           187           187           156
         198           187           165           176           211
         156           156           178           156           199

   23            24            25            26            27
         187           185           187           167           167
         176           167           178           156           239
                       167           187           198           267

   30            31
         267           243
         287           231
         256           243


            SUM           MEAN
  BRKFST    4021          182.77273
  LUNCH     4332          196.90909
  DINNER    4145          197.38095
```

The FORMCHAR set used above, or the more standard

```
formchar = 'fabfacccbceb8fecabcbbb4e7e4f6061e04c6eaf'x
```

gives good results on an IBM 6670 printer with typestyle 27 or 225, with input character set 216. If you use an IBM 1403, 3211, or 3203-5 printer or equivalent, with a TN (text) print train, the following specification is recommended:

```
formchar = '4fbfacbfbc4f8f4fabbfbbb4e7e4f6061e04c6eaf'x
```

Appropriate format characters for other printers can be found in the operating manuals for the printer.

Printed Output

The quantity of printed output produced by PROC CALENDAR depends on

- the range of dates in the activities data set
- whether the FILL option is specified
- the BY statement
- the CALID statement.

PROC CALENDAR always prints one calendar for every month that contains any activities. If you specify the FILL option, you'll get one calendar for every month between the first and last activities, including months that contain no activities. Using the BY statement prints one set of output for each BY value. Using the CALID statement with OUTPUT=SEPARATE prints one set of output for each value of the CALID variable.

The format of printed output produced by PROC CALENDAR depends on two factors: the size of the page, and the characters used to print the output. PROC CALENDAR always attempts to fit the calendar within a single page, as defined by the SAS system options PAGESIZE= and LINESIZE=. If your PAGESIZE= and LINESIZE= values do not allow sufficient room, PROC CALENDAR may print the legend box on a separate page. In the worst cases, PROC CALENDAR truncates or omits values to make the output fit the page and prints messages to that effect in the SAS log.

You can control the characters used to print your output. See the previous section, **Formatting Your Output**, for more information.

Each page of printed output for summary and schedule calendars includes the following

1. any titles specified
2. BY and CALID lines, if used
3. month, year, and day headings
4. monthly calendars displaying activities and holidays
5. for summary calendars, a legend box if a legend is requested.

EXAMPLES

Example 1: Summary Calendar

The following statements produce an enhanced version of the summary calendar shown in **Introductory Examples**. Here, a HOLIDATA= data set has been added, with HOLISTART and HOLIVAR statements, to display holidays. Also, the FORMAT procedure has been added to display values more clearly. Finally, three labels are added to display more descriptive titles in the legend box.

```
options pagesize=60 linesize=132 nodate;
title 'Meals Served in Community Hospital Cafeteria';
data act;
   input date date. brkfst lunch dinner;
   cards;
01Dec91        123 234 123
02Dec91        123 234 238
03Dec91        188 188 198
04Dec91        123 183 176
05Dec91        200 267 243
06Dec91        176 165 177
07Dec91        156   . 167
08Dec91        198 143 167
```

```
09Dec91              178 198 187
10Dec91              165 176 187
11Dec91              187 176 231
12Dec91              176 187 222
13Dec91              187 187 123
14Dec91              164 187 231
15Dec91              187 165 167
16Dec91              187 198 156
17Dec91              198 187 156
18Dec91              187 165 178
19Dec91              187 176 156
20Dec91              156 211 199
21Dec91              176 156 143
22Dec91              165 167 211
23Dec91              187 176   .
24Dec91              185 167 167
25Dec91              187 178 187
26Dec91              167 156 198
27Dec91              167 239 267
28Dec91              267 287 256
29Dec91              276 243 234
30Dec91              267 287 256
31Dec91              243 231 243
;
run;


data hol;
   input date: date7. name & $12.;
   cards;
25Dec91 Christmas
;
run;


proc format;
   picture bfmt    other = '999 Brkfst';
   picture lfmt    other = '999 Lunch ';
   picture dfmt    other = '999 Dinner';
run;


proc calendar data=act holidata=hol;
   start date;
   holistart date;
   holivar name;
   format brkfst bfmt.;
   format lunch  lfmt.;
   format dinner dfmt.;
   sum  brkfst lunch dinner / format=4.0;
   mean brkfst lunch dinner / format=6.2;
   label brkfst = 'Breakfasts Served'
         lunch  = '  Lunches Served'
         dinner = '   Dinners Served';
run;
```

Output 7.5   Summary Calendar with Holidays, Sums, and Means

```
                              ❶  Meals Served in Community Hospital Cafeteria                    1
      -----------------------------------------------------------------------------------
      |                                                                                 |
      |                                 December  1991                                  |
      |   ❸                                                                             |
      |----------+----------+----------+----------+----------+----------+---------------|
      |  Sunday  |  Monday  | Tuesday  | Wednesday| Thursday |  Friday  |   Saturday    |
      |----------+----------+----------+----------+----------+----------+---------------|
      |    1     |    2     |    3     |    4     |    5     |    6     |     7         |
      |          |          |          |          |          |          |               |
      | 123 Brkfst| 123 Brkfst| 188 Brkfst| 123 Brkfst| 200 Brkfst| 176 Brkfst| 156 Brkfst    |
   ❹  | 234 Lunch | 234 Lunch | 188 Lunch | 183 Lunch | 267 Lunch | 165 Lunch |     .         |
      | 123 Dinner| 238 Dinner| 198 Dinner| 176 Dinner| 243 Dinner| 177 Dinner| 167 Dinner    |
      |----------+----------+----------+----------+----------+----------+---------------|
      |    8     |    9     |    10    |    11    |    12    |    13    |     14        |
      |          |          |          |          |          |          |               |
      | 198 Brkfst| 178 Brkfst| 165 Brkfst| 187 Brkfst| 176 Brkfst| 187 Brkfst| 164 Brkfst    |
      | 143 Lunch | 198 Lunch | 176 Lunch | 176 Lunch | 187 Lunch | 187 Lunch | 187 Lunch     |
      | 167 Dinner| 187 Dinner| 187 Dinner| 231 Dinner| 222 Dinner| 123 Dinner| 231 Dinner    |
      |----------+----------+----------+----------+----------+----------+---------------|
      |    15    |    16    |    17    |    18    |    19    |    20    |     21        |
      |          |          |          |          |          |          |               |
      | 187 Brkfst| 187 Brkfst| 198 Brkfst| 187 Brkfst| 187 Brkfst| 156 Brkfst| 176 Brkfst    |
      | 165 Lunch | 198 Lunch | 187 Lunch | 165 Lunch | 176 Lunch | 211 Lunch | 156 Lunch     |
      | 167 Dinner| 156 Dinner| 156 Dinner| 178 Dinner| 156 Dinner| 199 Dinner| 143 Dinner    |
      |----------+----------+----------+----------+----------+----------+---------------|
      |    22    |    23    |    24    |    25    |    26    |    27    |     28        |
      |          |          |          |*Christmas**|        |          |               |
      | 165 Brkfst| 187 Brkfst| 185 Brkfst| 187 Brkfst| 167 Brkfst| 167 Brkfst| 267 Brkfst    |
      | 167 Lunch | 176 Lunch | 167 Lunch | 178 Lunch | 156 Lunch | 239 Lunch | 287 Lunch     |
      | 211 Dinner|     .     | 167 Dinner| 187 Dinner| 198 Dinner| 267 Dinner| 256 Dinner    |
      |----------+----------+----------+----------+----------+----------+---------------|
      |    29    |    30    |    31    |          |          |          |               |
      |          |          |          |          |          |          |               |
      | 276 Brkfst| 267 Brkfst| 243 Brkfst|          |          |          |               |
      | 243 Lunch | 287 Lunch | 231 Lunch |          |          |          |               |
      | 234 Dinner| 256 Dinner| 243 Dinner|          |          |          |               |
      -----------------------------------------------------------------------------------


                          --------------------------------
                          |                  | Sum  | Mean |
                          |                  |      |      |
                       ❺  | Breakfasts Served| 5733 | 184.94 |
                          | Lunches Served   | 5914 | 197.13 |
                          | Dinners Served   | 5844 | 194.80 |
                          --------------------------------
```

Example 2:   Summary Calendar with MEAN Values by Observation

This example shows mean usage of a bank's computer center each business day. By default, PROC CALENDAR calculates MEAN values based on the number of observations, so the weekends and holidays are not considered in the calculations. The following statements produce **Output 7.6**:

```
options pagesize=60 linesize=132 nodate;
libname bank 'SAS-data-library ';
title1 'System Performance Summary';
title2 'First National Bank Computer Center';

data bank.act;
   input date: date. jobs act cpu;
   cards;
02May88 873 22.1  7.6
03May88 881 23.8 11.7
04May88 940 24.0  7.7
05May88 194  5.3  1.5
06May88 154 17.4  7.1
09May88 807 24   10.5
```

```
10May88 829 23.4 10.5
11May88 915 24   10.6
12May88 388 21    6.9
13May88   .   .    .
16May88 806 24.0 10.0
17May88 848 23.6 10.5
18May88 906 23   10.1
19May88 103 23.4 18.7
20May88 103 20.1 20
23May88 729 24    4.9
24May88 652 21.3 12.2
25May88 809 23.8 12.3
26May88 168 15.8 10.7
27May88  85  7    5.6
31May88 100 11.1  1.8
;

proc format;
picture jfmt  . = '000 jobs' (noedit)
        other = '000 jobs';
picture afmt  . = '00.0 act' (noedit)
        other = '00.0 act';
picture cfmt  . = '00.0 cpu' (noedit)
        other = '00.0 cpu';
run;

title3 'Mean Usage per Business Day';
proc calendar data=bank.act;
   start date;
   format jobs jfmt.
          act afmt.
          cpu cfmt.;
   sum  jobs act cpu / format = 7.0;
   mean jobs act cpu / format = 6.1;
   label jobs = 'Jobs Run'
         act = 'Active Hours'
         cpu = 'Cpu Hours';
run;
```

Output 7.6   Summary Calendar with MEAN Values by Observation

```
                          System Performance Summary                                1
                        First National Bank Computer Center
                           Mean Usage per Business Day

     -------------------------------------------------------------------------
     |                                                                       |
     |                              May   1988                               |
     |                                                                       |
     |-----------------------------------------------------------------------|
     | Sunday  |  Monday  | Tuesday  |Wednesday | Thursday |  Friday  | Saturday |
     |---------+----------+----------+----------+----------+----------+--------|
     |    1    |    2     |    3     |    4     |    5     |    6     |    7   |
     |         |          |          |          |          |          |        |
     |         | 873 jobs | 881 jobs | 940 jobs | 194 jobs | 154 jobs |        |
     |         | 22.1 act | 23.8 act | 24.0 act |  5.3 act | 17.4 act |        |
     |         |  7.6 cpu | 11.7 cpu |  7.7 cpu |  1.5 cpu |  7.1 cpu |        |
     |---------+----------+----------+----------+----------+----------+--------|
     |    8    |    9     |    10    |    11    |    12    |    13    |   14   |
     |         |          |          |          |          |          |        |
     |         | 807 jobs | 829 jobs | 915 jobs | 388 jobs | 000 jobs |        |
     |         | 24.0 act | 23.4 act | 24.0 act | 21.0 act | 00.0 act |        |
     |         | 10.5 cpu | 10.5 cpu | 10.6 cpu |  6.9 cpu | 00.0 cpu |        |
     |---------+----------+----------+----------+----------+----------+--------|
     |   15    |   16     |    17    |    18    |    19    |    20    |   21   |
     |         |          |          |          |          |          |        |
     |         | 806 jobs | 848 jobs | 906 jobs | 103 jobs | 103 jobs |        |
     |         | 24.0 act | 23.6 act | 23.0 act | 23.4 act | 20.1 act |        |
     |         | 10.0 cpu | 10.5 cpu | 10.1 cpu | 18.7 cpu | 20.0 cpu |        |
     |---------+----------+----------+----------+----------+----------+--------|
     |   22    |   23     |    24    |    25    |    26    |    27    |   28   |
     |         |          |          |          |          |          |        |
     |         | 729 jobs | 652 jobs | 809 jobs | 168 jobs |  85 jobs |        |
     |         | 24.0 act | 21.3 act | 23.8 act | 15.8 act |  7.0 act |        |
     |         |  4.9 cpu | 12.2 cpu | 12.3 cpu | 10.7 cpu |  5.6 cpu |        |
     |---------+----------+----------+----------+----------+----------+--------|
     |   29    |   30     |    31    |          |          |          |        |
     |         |          |          |          |          |          |        |
     |         |          | 100 jobs |          |          |          |        |
     |         |          | 11.1 act |          |          |          |        |
     |         |          |  1.8 cpu |          |          |          |        |
     -------------------------------------------------------------------------

                    ---------------------------------
                    |                | Sum  | Mean   |
                    |                |      |        |
                    | Jobs Run       | 11290| 564.5  |
                    | Active Hours   |   402|  20.1  |
                    | Cpu Hours      |   191|   9.5  |
                    ---------------------------------
```

Example 3:   Summary Calendar with MEAN Values by Day

This example is identical to **Example 2** except that the options
MEANTYPE=NDAYS and MISSING have been added. MEANTYPE=NDAYS
causes MEAN values to be calculated based on the number of days displayed,
rather than the number of observations in the activities data set. In this example,
this causes weekends and holidays to be included in the mean calculations.
The MISSING option causes PROC CALENDAR to print missing values on days
with no observations. In this example, this causes missing values for weekends
and holidays to be printed in the display. The effect of adding both the MISSING
and MEANTYPE= options is to transform the calendar from a summary of activities by business day to a summary of activities over all days. The statements below
produce **Output 7.7**.

```
proc format;
picture jfmt  . = '000 jobs' (noedit)
        other = '000 jobs';
picture afmt  . = '00.0 act' (noedit)
        other = '00.0 act';
picture cfmt  . = '00.0 cpu' (noedit)
        other = '00.0 cpu';
run;
```

```
title1 'System Performance Summary';
title2 'First National Bank Computer Center';
title3 'Mean Usage per Day';
proc calendar missing data=bank.act meantype=ndays;
   start date;
   format jobs jfmt.
          act afmt.
          cpu cfmt.;
   sum  jobs act cpu / format = 7.0;
   mean jobs act cpu / format = 6.1;
   label jobs = 'Jobs Run Daily'
         act = 'Active Hours' cpu = 'Cpu Hours';
run;
```

Output 7.7 Summary Calendar MEAN by Values Day

```
                        System Performance Summary                            1
                     First National Bank Computer Center
                              Mean Usage per Day

-------------------------------------------------------------------------------
|                                                                             |
|                              May   1988                                     |
|                                                                             |
|-----------------------------------------------------------------------------|
| Sunday  | Monday  | Tuesday |Wednesday| Thursday| Friday  | Saturday |
|---------+---------+---------+---------+---------+---------+---------|
|    1    |    2    |    3    |    4    |    5    |    6    |    7    |
|         |         |         |         |         |         |         |
| 000 jobs| 873 jobs| 881 jobs| 940 jobs| 194 jobs| 154 jobs| 000 jobs|
| 00.0 act| 22.1 act| 23.8 act| 24.0 act|  5.3 act| 17.4 act| 00.0 act|
| 00.0 cpu|  7.6 cpu| 11.7 cpu|  7.7 cpu|  1.5 cpu|  7.1 cpu| 00.0 cpu|
|---------+---------+---------+---------+---------+---------+---------|
|    8    |    9    |   10    |   11    |   12    |   13    |   14    |
|         |         |         |         |         |         |         |
| 000 jobs| 807 jobs| 829 jobs| 915 jobs| 388 jobs| 000 jobs| 000 jobs|
| 00.0 act| 24.0 act| 23.4 act| 24.0 act| 21.0 act| 00.0 act| 00.0 act|
| 00.0 cpu| 10.5 cpu| 10.5 cpu| 10.6 cpu|  6.9 cpu| 00.0 cpu| 00.0 cpu|
|---------+---------+---------+---------+---------+---------+---------|
|   15    |   16    |   17    |   18    |   19    |   20    |   21    |
|         |         |         |         |         |         |         |
| 000 jobs| 806 jobs| 848 jobs| 906 jobs| 103 jobs| 103 jobs| 000 jobs|
| 00.0 act| 24.0 act| 23.6 act| 23.0 act| 23.4 act| 20.1 act| 00.0 act|
| 00.0 cpu| 10.0 cpu| 10.5 cpu| 10.1 cpu| 18.7 cpu| 20.0 cpu| 00.0 cpu|
|---------+---------+---------+---------+---------+---------+---------|
|   22    |   23    |   24    |   25    |   26    |   27    |   28    |
|         |         |         |         |         |         |         |
| 000 jobs| 729 jobs| 652 jobs| 809 jobs| 168 jobs|  85 jobs| 000 jobs|
| 00.0 act| 24.0 act| 21.3 act| 23.8 act| 15.8 act|  7.0 act| 00.0 act|
| 00.0 cpu|  4.9 cpu| 12.2 cpu| 12.3 cpu| 10.7 cpu|  5.6 cpu| 00.0 cpu|
|---------+---------+---------+---------+---------+---------+---------|
|   29    |   30    |   31    |         |         |         |         |
|         |         |         |         |         |         |         |
| 000 jobs| 000 jobs| 100 jobs|         |         |         |         |
| 00.0 act| 00.0 act| 11.1 act|         |         |         |         |
| 00.0 cpu| 00.0 cpu|  1.8 cpu|         |         |         |         |
-------------------------------------------------------------------------------

              -----------------------------------
              |                | Sum   | Mean   |
              | Jobs Run Daily | 11290 | 364.2  |
              | Active Hours   |   402 |  13.0  |
              | Cpu Hours      |   191 |   6.2  |
              -----------------------------------
```

Example 4:   Summary Calendar with Separated Output

The next three examples show the effect of the options of the CALID statement when you create multiple summary calendars. These examples all display the costs of drilling a well, with the various tasks involved scheduled on two calendars. All three examples use the four data sets created below.

```
libname well 'SAS-data-library';
data well.act;
   input task $ 1-16 dur 21-30 date datetime. _cal_ $ cost;
   cards;
Drill Well          3.50        01JUL85:12:00:00    CAL1    1000
Lay Power Line      3.00        04JUL85:12:00:00    CAL1    2000
Assemble Tank       4.00        05JUL85:08:00:00    CAL1    1000
Build Pump House    3.00        08JUL85:12:00:00    CAL1    2000
Pour Foundation     4.00        11JUL85:08:00:00    CAL1    1500
Install Pump        4.00        15JUL85:14:00:00    CAL1     500
Install Pipe        2.00        19JUL85:08:00:00    CAL1    1000
Erect Tower         6.00        20JUL85:08:00:00    CAL1    2500
Deliver Material    2.00        01JUL85:12:00:00    CAL2     500
Excavate            4.75        03JUL85:08:00:00    CAL2    3500
;
run;

data well.hol;
   input date date. holiday $ 11-25 _cal_ $;
   cards;
04JUL85    Independence        CAL1
07JUL85    Vacation            CAL2
;
run;

data well.cal;
   input _sun_ $ _sat_ $ _cal_ $;
   cards;
Holiday Holiday  CAL1
Holiday Halfday  CAL2
;
run;

data well.wor;
   input halfday time8.;
   cards;
08:00
12:00
;
run;
```

The activities data set contains the tasks, their durations, starting dates, calendars, and costs. The holidays data set contains one holiday for two different calendars, CAL1 and CAL2. The calendar data set specifies that one calendar operates on a 5-day week, and the other on a 5 1/2-day week. The workdays data set specifies a work shift for the half day; the days Monday through Friday use the default work shift.

The statements below use OUTPUT=SEPARATE to produce one page of output for each calendar. Activities are sorted first by the CALID variable, then by the START variable.

```
options pagesize=60 linesize=132 nodate;
title 'Well Drilling Cost Summary:  Output=Separate';

proc sort data=well.act;
   by _cal_ date;
run;

proc calendar data=well.act
     holidata=well.hol  caledata=well.cal workdata=well.wor
          datetime legend;
   calid _cal_ / output=separate;
   start date;
   format cost dollar9.2;
   sum cost / format=dollar9.2;
   holistart date;
   holivar holiday;
   outstart Monday;
   outfin Saturday;
run;
```

Output 7.8 Summary Calendars with Separated Output

```
                    Well Drilling Cost Summary:  Output=Separate                          1
❷ ··········································_CAL_=CAL1··········································

   ---------------------------------------------------------------------------------------
   |                                                                                     |
   |                                    July  1985                                       |
   |-------------------------------------------------------------------------------------|
   |   Monday    |   Tuesday   |  Wednesday  |   Thursday   |    Friday   |   Saturday   |
   |-------------+-------------+-------------+--------------+-------------+--------------|
   |      1      |      2      |      3      |      4       |      5      |      6       |
   |             |             |             |***Independence***|          |              |
   | Drill Well  |             |             | Lay Power Line | Assemble Tank |           |
   |        3.5  |             |             |           3  |           4  |              |
   |     $1,000.00 |           |             |     $2,000.00 |    $1,000.00 |             |
   |-------------+-------------+-------------+--------------+-------------+--------------|
   |      8      |      9      |     10      |     11       |     12      |     13       |
   | Build Pump House |        |             | Pour Foundation |           |              |
   |          3  |             |             |           4  |             |              |
   |     $2,000.00 |           |             |     $1,500.00 |             |             |
   |-------------+-------------+-------------+--------------+-------------+--------------|
   |     15      |     16      |     17      |     18       |     19      |     20       |
   | Install Pump |           |             |              | Install Pipe | Erect Tower |
   |          4  |             |             |              |           2  |          6  |
   |      $500.00 |           |             |              |    $1,000.00 |    $2,500.00 |
   |-------------+-------------+-------------+--------------+-------------+--------------|
   |     22      |     23      |     24      |     25       |     26      |     27       |
   |             |             |             |              |             |              |
   |             |             |             |              |             |              |
   |             |             |             |              |             |              |
   |-------------+-------------+-------------+--------------+-------------+--------------|
   |     29      |     30      |     31      |              |             |              |
   |             |             |             |              |             |              |
   |             |             |             |              |             |              |
   |             |             |             |              |             |              |
   ---------------------------------------------------------------------------------------


                            -------------------------
                            | Legend   |    Sum     |
                            |          |            |
                            | TASK     |            |
                            | DUR      |            |
                            | COST     | $11500.00  |
                            -------------------------
```

```
                        Well Drilling Cost Summary:  Output=Separate                        2
......................................_CAL_=CAL2.......................................
|--------------------------------------------------------------------------------------|
|                                                                                      |
|                                     July   1985                                      |
|                                                                                      |
|--------------------------------------------------------------------------------------|
|   Monday    |   Tuesday   |  Wednesday  |  Thursday   |   Friday    |  Saturday   |
|-------------+-------------+-------------+-------------+-------------+-------------|
|     1       |     2       |     3       |     4       |     5       |     6       |
|             |             |             |             |             |             |
| Deliver Material          | Excavate    |             |             |             |
|           2 |             |        4.75 |             |             |             |
|     $500.00 |             |   $3,500.00 |             |             |             |
|-------------+-------------+-------------+-------------+-------------+-------------|
|     8       |     9       |    10       |    11       |    12       |    13       |
|*****Vacation*****         |             |             |             |             |
|             |             |             |             |             |             |
|             |             |             |             |             |             |
|-------------+-------------+-------------+-------------+-------------+-------------|
|    15       |    16       |    17       |    18       |    19       |    20       |
|             |             |             |             |             |             |
|             |             |             |             |             |             |
|             |             |             |             |             |             |
|-------------+-------------+-------------+-------------+-------------+-------------|
|    22       |    23       |    24       |    25       |    26       |    27       |
|             |             |             |             |             |             |
|             |             |             |             |             |             |
|             |             |             |             |             |             |
|-------------+-------------+-------------+-------------+-------------+-------------|
|    29       |    30       |    31       |             |             |             |
|             |             |             |             |             |             |
|             |             |             |             |             |             |
|             |             |             |             |             |             |
|--------------------------------------------------------------------------------------|

                              |  Legend  |     Sum    |
                              |          |            |
                              |  TASK    |            |
                              |  DUR     |            |
                              |  COST    | $4,000.00  |
```

Example 5:   Summary Calendars with Combined Output

This example uses OUTPUT=COMBINE to produce one page of output for two
calendars, with the activities grouped by calendar. Activities are sorted only by
the START variable if you use OUTPUT=COMBINE.

```
options pagesize=60 linesize=132 nodate;
title 'Well Drilling Cost Summary:  Output=Combine';

proc sort data=well.act;
   by date;
run;
```

```
proc calendar data=well.act
     holidata=well.hol caledata=well.cal workdata=well.wor
          datetime legend;
  calid _cal_ / output=combine;
  start date;
  format cost dollar9.2;
  sum cost / format=dollar9.2;
  holistart date;
  holivar holiday;
  outstart Monday;
  outfin Saturday;
run;
```

Output 7.9 Summary Calendars with Combined Output

```
                    Well Drilling Cost Summary:  Output=Combine                        1
   -------------------------------------------------------------------------------------
  |                                                                                     |
  |                                      July  1985                                     |
  |                                                                                     |
  |-------------------------------------------------------------------------------------|
  |     Monday    |   Tuesday   |  Wednesday  |   Thursday   |   Friday    |   Saturday  |
  |---------------+-------------+-------------+--------------+-------------+-------------|
  |       1       |      2      |      3      |      4       |      5      |      6      |
  | CAL1 | Drill Well.........|.............| Lay Power Line| Assemble Tank|............|
  |      |        3.5 |        |             |           3  |          4  |            |
  |      |   $1,000.00 |       |             |    $2,000.00 |   $1,000.00 |            |
  | CAL2 | Deliver Material |  | Excavate    |              |             |            |
  |---------------+-------------+-------------+--------------+-------------+-------------|
  |       8       |      9      |     10      |      11      |     12      |     13      |
  | CAL1 | Build Pump House |  |             | Pour Foundation|           |             |
  |      |          3 |        |             |           4  |             |             |
  |      |   $2,000.00 |       |             |    $1,500.00 |             |             |
  |      |             |       |             |              |             |             |
  |---------------+-------------+-------------+--------------+-------------+-------------|
  |      15       |     16      |     17      |      18      |     19      |     20      |
  | CAL1.| Install Pump.......|.............|..............| Install Pipe | Erect Tower |
  |      |            4|       |             |              |           2 |           6 |
  |      |     $500.00 |       |             |              |   $1,000.00 |   $2,500.00 |
  |      |             |       |             |              |             |             |
  |---------------+-------------+-------------+--------------+-------------+-------------|
  |      22       |     23      |     24      |      25      |     26      |     27      |
  |      |             |       |             |              |             |             |
  |      |             |       |             |              |             |             |
  |      |             |       |             |              |             |             |
  |      |             |       |             |              |             |             |
  |---------------+-------------+-------------+--------------+-------------+-------------|
  |      29       |     30      |     31      |              |             |             |
  |      |             |       |             |              |             |             |
  |      |             |       |             |              |             |             |
  |      |             |       |             |              |             |             |
  |      |             |       |             |              |             |             |
   -------------------------------------------------------------------------------------
```

```
                    Well Drilling Cost Summary:  Output=Combine                          2
                  ------------------------------------
                  |         | Legend |     Sum    |
                  |.........|........|............|
                  | DEFAULT | TASK   |            |
                  |         | DUR    |            |
                  |         | COST   |    $0.00   |
                  |.........|........|............|
                  | CAL1    | TASK   |            |
                  |         | DUR    |            |
                  |         | COST   | $11500.00  |
                  |.........|........|............|
                  | CAL2    | TASK   |            |
                  |         | DUR    |            |
                  |         | COST   | $4,000.00  |
                  |=========|========|============|
                  |         | TASK   |            |
                  |         | DUR    |            |
                  |         | COST   | $15500.00  |
                  ------------------------------------
```

Example 6:   Summary Calendars with Mixed Output

This example uses OUTPUT=MIX to produce one page of output for both calendars, without grouping the activities by calendar. Activities are sorted by START variable.

```
options pagesize=66 linesize=132 nodate ;
title 'Well Drilling Cost Summary:  Output=Mix';

proc sort data=well.act;
   by date;
run;

proc calendar data=well.act
      holidata=well.hol caledata=well.cal workdata=well.wor
          datetime legend;
   calid _cal_ / output=mix;
   start date;
   format cost dollar9.2;
   sum cost / format=dollar9.2;
   holistart date;
   holivar holiday;
   outstart Monday;
   outfin Saturday;
run;
```

Output 7.10 Summary Calendar with Mixed Output

```
                          Well Drilling Cost Summary:  Output=Mix                        1
-------------------------------------------------------------------------------------------
|                                                                                         |
|                                        July  1985                                       |
|-----------------------------------------------------------------------------------------|
|   Monday    |   Tuesday   |  Wednesday  |  Thursday   |   Friday    |  Saturday   |
|-----------------------------------------------------------------------------------------|
|     1       |     2       |     3       |     4       |     5       |     6       |
|             |             |             |***Independence***|         |             |
| Deliver Material|         | Excavate    | Lay Power Line | Assemble Tank |           |
|           2 |             |        4.75 |           3 |           4 |             |
|     $500.00 |             |   $3,500.00 |   $2,000.00 |   $1,000.00 |             |
|-----------------------------------------------------------------------------------------|
|     8       |     9       |     10      |     11      |     12      |     13      |
|             |             |             |             |             |             |
| Build Pump House|         |             | Pour Foundation |           |             |
|           3 |             |             |           4 |             |             |
|   $2,000.00 |             |             |   $1,500.00 |             |             |
|-----------------------------------------------------------------------------------------|
|     15      |     16      |     17      |     18      |     19      |     20      |
|             |             |             |             |             |             |
| Install Pump|             |             |             | Install Pipe| Erect Tower |
|           4 |             |             |             |           2 |           6 |
|     $500.00 |             |             |             |   $1,000.00 |   $2,500.00 |
|-----------------------------------------------------------------------------------------|
|     22      |     23      |     24      |     25      |     26      |     27      |
|             |             |             |             |             |             |
|             |             |             |             |             |             |
|-----------------------------------------------------------------------------------------|
|     29      |     30      |     31      |             |             |             |
|             |             |             |             |             |             |
|             |             |             |             |             |             |
-------------------------------------------------------------------------------------------

                          -------------------------------
                          |  Legend   |     Sum         |
                          |-----------|-----------------|
                          |  TASK     |                 |
                          |  DUR      |                 |
                          |  COST     |  $14500.00      |
                          -------------------------------
```

Example 7:   Schedule Calendar

This example produces an enhanced version of the schedule calendar shown in
Introductory Examples. Here, a HOLIDATA= data set has been added with
HOLISTART and HOLIVAR statements to print holidays in the calendar output.
Also, OUTSTART and OUTFIN statements are used to begin the week on Monday
and end it on Friday. The statements below produce **Output 7.11**.

```
title 'Summer Planning Calendar:  Julia Q. Wydget, President';
title2 'Better Products Inc.';
options pagesize=60 linesize=132 nodate;
data act;
   input date:date7. happen $ 9-36 who $ 37-48 long;
   cards;
01JUL91 Dist. Mtg.                   All         1
02JUL91 Mgrs. Meeting                District 6  2
03JUL91 Interview                    JW          1
05JUL91 VIP Banquet                  JW          1
08JUL91 Sales Drive                  District 6  5
08JUL91 Trade Show                   Knox        3
11JUL91 Mgrs. Meeting                District 7  2
11JUL91 Planning Council             Group II    1
12JUL91 Seminar                      White       1
15JUL91 Sales Drive                  District 7  5
16JUL91 Dentist                      JW          1
17JUL91 Bank Meeting                 1st Natl    1
18JUL91 NewsLetter Deadline          All         1
18JUL91 Planning Council             Group III   1
19JUL91 Seminar                      White       1
19JUL91 Co. Picnic                   All         1
22JUL91 Inventors Show               Melvin      3
24JUL91 Birthday                     Mary        1
25JUL91 Planning Council             Group IV    1
25JUL91 Close Sale                   WYGIX Co.   2
;
run;

data hol;
   input date: date7. dur name & $15.;
   cards;
04JUL91  1  Independence
29JUL91  3  Vacation
;
run;

proc calendar data=act holidata=hol;
   start date;
   dur long;
   holistart date;
   holivar name;
   holidur dur;
   outstart Monday;
   outfin Friday;
run;
```

Output 7.11   Schedule Calendar with Holidays

```
                     Summer Planning Calendar:  Julia Q. Wydget, President                          1
                                      Better Products Inc.
 -------------------------------------------------------------------------------------------------
|                                                                                                 |
|                                          July 1991                                              |
|-------------------------------------------------------------------------------------------------|
|      Monday      |      Tuesday      |     Wednesday     |      Thursday      |      Friday       |
|------------------+-------------------+-------------------+-------------------+-------------------|
|        1         |         2         |         3         |         4         |         5         |
|                  |                   |                   |******Independence*******|              |
|                  |                   |                   |                   |                   |
|                  |                   |+=====Interview/JW======+|                |                   |
|+====Dist. Mtg./All=====+|=============Mgrs. Meeting/District 6============+|    |+====VIP Banquet/JW=====+|
|------------------+-------------------+-------------------+-------------------+-------------------|
|        8         |         9         |        10         |        11         |        12         |
|                  |                   |                   |                   |                   |
|                  |                   |                   |+Planning Council/Group +|+=====Seminar/White=====+|
|+===============Trade Show/Knox================+|=============Mgrs. Meeting/District 7=============+|
|+=====================================Sales Drive/District 6=======================================+|
|------------------+-------------------+-------------------+-------------------+-------------------|
|        15        |        16         |        17         |        18         |        19         |
|                  |                   |                   |                   |                   |
|                  |                   |                   |+Planning Council/Group +|+=====Co. Picnic/All=====+|
|                  |+======Dentist/JW=======+|+=Bank Meeting/1st Natl=|+NewsLetter Deadline/All+|+=====Seminar/White=====+|
|+==========================================Sales Drive/District 7=================================+|
|------------------+-------------------+-------------------+-------------------+-------------------|
|        22        |        23         |        24         |        25         |        26         |
|                  |                   |                   |                   |                   |
|                  |                   |                   |                   |                   |
|                  |                   |+=====Birthday/Mary=====+|+==============Close Sale/WYGIX Co.=================+|
|+===========================Inventors Show/Melvin=====================+|+Planning Council/Group +|    |
|------------------+-------------------+-------------------+-------------------+-------------------|
|        29        |        30         |        31         |                   |                   |
|********Vacation*********|********Vacation*********|********Vacation*********|             |                   |
|                  |                   |                   |                   |                   |
|                  |                   |                   |                   |                   |
 -------------------------------------------------------------------------------------------------
```

Example 8:   Schedule Calendar with Separated Output

The next three examples show the three different output formats for multiple
schedule calendars. These examples use the same four data sets as in the well-
drilling examples for summary calendars.

The statements below use OUTPUT=SEPARATE to produce one page of output for each calendar. For separated output, the activities are sorted first by the
CALID variable, then by the START variable.

```
title 'Well Drilling Work Schedule:  Output=Separate';
options pagesize=60 linesize=132 nodate ;

proc sort data=well.act;
   by _cal_ date;
run;
```

```
proc calendar data=well.act
    holidata=well.hol
    caledata=well.cal workdata=well.wor datetime;
  calid _cal_ / output=separate;
  start date;
  dur dur;
  format cost dollar9.2;
  holistart date;
  holivar holiday;
  outstart Monday;
  outfin Saturday;
run;
```

Output 7.12 Schedule Calendar with Separated Output

```
                              Well Drilling Work Schedule:  Output=Separate                                    1
.................................................. _CAL_=CAL1 ..................................................
 ---------------------------------------------------------------------------------------------------------------
|                                                                                                               |
|                                                  July  1985                                                   |
|                                                                                                               |
| -------------------------------------------------------------------------------------------------------------|
|    Monday      |    Tuesday     |   Wednesday    |    Thursday    |     Friday     |    Saturday    |          |
| ---------------+----------------+----------------+----------------+----------------+----------------|
|       1        |       2        |       3        |       4        |       5        |       6        |          |
|                |                |                |****Independence****|             |                |          |
|                |                |                |                |                |                |          |
|                |                |                |                |+Assemble Tank/$1,0>|            |          |
|                |                |                |                |+Lay Power Line/$2,>|            |          |
|+===================Drill Well/$1,000.00===================>|       |<Drill Well/$1,000.+|           |          |
| ---------------+----------------+----------------+----------------+----------------+----------------|
|       8        |       9        |      10        |      11        |      12        |      13        |          |
|                |                |                |                |                |                |          |
|                |                |                |                |                |                |          |
|+========================Build Pump House/$2,000.00==========================+|                      |          |
|<=========Assemble Tank/$1,000.00==========================+|                  |                     |          |
|<=======Lay Power Line/$2,000.00========+|          |+=======Pour Foundation/$1,500.00=======>|    |          |
| ---------------+----------------+----------------+----------------+----------------+----------------|
|      15        |      16        |      17        |      18        |      19        |      20        |          |
|                |                |                |                |                |                |          |
|                |                |                |                |                |                |          |
|+========================================Install Pump/$500.00============================================+|     |
|<===================Pour Foundation/$1,500.00===================+|          |+Install Pipe/$1,00>|      |          |
| ---------------+----------------+----------------+----------------+----------------+----------------|
|      22        |      23        |      24        |      25        |      26        |      27        |          |
|                |                |                |                |                |                |          |
|                |                |                |                |                |                |          |
|+============================================Erect Tower/$2,500.00============================================>|  |
|<=======Install Pipe/$1,000.00=========+|          |                |                |               |          |
| ---------------+----------------+----------------+----------------+----------------+----------------|
|      29        |      30        |      31        |                |                |                |          |
|                |                |                |                |                |                |          |
|                |                |                |                |                |                |          |
|                |                |                |                |                |                |          |
|<Erect Tower/$2,500+|            |                |                |                |               |          |
 ---------------------------------------------------------------------------------------------------------------
```

```
-----------------------------------------------------------------------------------------------
|                                          July  1985                                          |
|---------------------------------------------------------------------------------------------|
|    Monday    |    Tuesday    |   Wednesday   |    Thursday   |    Friday    |   Saturday     |
|--------------+---------------+---------------+---------------+--------------+----------------|
|      1       |      2        |      3        |      4        |      5       |      6         |
|              |               |               |               |              |                |
|              |               |               |               |              |                |
|              |               |  +=============================Excavate/$3,500.00=============================>|
|+==================Deliver Material/$500.00==================+|              |                |
|--------------+---------------+---------------+---------------+--------------+----------------|
|      8       |      9        |     10        |     11        |     12       |     13         |
|******Vacation******|         |               |               |              |                |
|              |               |               |               |              |                |
|              |  <===========Excavate/$3,500.00===========+|               |                |
|--------------+---------------+---------------+---------------+--------------+----------------|
|     15       |     16        |     17        |     18        |     19       |     20         |
|              |               |               |               |              |                |
|              |               |               |               |              |                |
|              |               |               |               |              |                |
|--------------+---------------+---------------+---------------+--------------+----------------|
|     22       |     23        |     24        |     25        |     26       |     27         |
|              |               |               |               |              |                |
|              |               |               |               |              |                |
|              |               |               |               |              |                |
|--------------+---------------+---------------+---------------+--------------+----------------|
|     29       |     30        |     31        |               |              |                |
|              |               |               |               |              |                |
|              |               |               |               |              |                |
|              |               |               |               |              |                |
-----------------------------------------------------------------------------------------------
```

Example 9:   Schedule Calendar with Combined Output

This example uses OUTPUT=COMBINE to produce one page of output for both calendars, with the activities grouped by calendar. For combined output, the activities are sorted by the START variable only.

```
options pagesize=66 linesize=132 nodate ;
title 'Well Drilling Work Schedule:  Output=Combine';

proc sort data=well.act;
   by date;
run;
```

```
proc calendar data=well.act
   holidata=well.hol caledata=well.cal workdata=well.wor datetime;
calid _cal_ / output=combine;
start date;
dur dur;
format cost dollar9.2;
holistart date;
holivar holiday;
outstart Monday;
outfin Saturday;
run;
```

Output 7.13 Schedule Calendar with Combined Output

```
                        Well Drilling Work Schedule:  Output=Combine                          1
      -------------------------------------------------------------------------------------
     |                                                                                       |
     |                                    July   1985                                        |
     |                                                                                       |
     |------------------------------------------------------------------------------------- |
     |   Monday    |    Tuesday    |   Wednesday   |    Thursday   |    Friday   |  Saturday  |
     |-------------+---------------+---------------+---------------+-------------+------------|
     |      1      |       2       |       3       |       4       |      5      |      6     |
|.........................................................................................|
|CAL1 |             |               |               |***Independence****|+Assemble Tank/$1,>|  |
|     |             |               |               |               |+Lay Power Line/$2>|     |
|     |+==================Drill Well/$1,000.00==================>|<Drill Well/$1,000+|       |
|CAL2 |             |               |+====================================Excavate/$3,500.00====================>|
|     |+================Deliver Material/$500.00================+|             |            |
|-------------+---------------+---------------+---------------+-------------+------------|
|      8      |       9       |      10       |      11       |     12      |     13     |
|.........................................................................................|
|CAL1 |+=========================Build Pump House/$2,000.00=========================+|      |
|     |<=========================Assemble Tank/$1,000.00==========================+|       |
|     |<======Lay Power Line/$2,000.00=======+|               |+======Pour Foundation/$1,500.00======>|
|CAL2 |*****Vacation******|<=========Excavate/$3,500.00==========+|             |            |
|     |             |               |               |               |             |            |
|-------------+---------------+---------------+---------------+-------------+------------|
|     15      |      16       |      17       |      18       |     19      |     20     |
|.........................................................................................|
|CAL1 |+=====================================Install Pump/$500.00=====================================+|
|     |<================Pour Foundation/$1,500.00================+|+Install Pipe/$1,0>|     |
|     |             |               |               |               |             |            |
|     |             |               |               |               |             |            |
|     |             |               |               |               |             |            |
|-------------+---------------+---------------+---------------+-------------+------------|
|     22      |      23       |      24       |      25       |     26      |     27     |
|.........................................................................................|
|CAL1 |+====================================Erect Tower/$2,500.00====================================>|
|     |<=======Install Pipe/$1,000.00========+|               |             |            |
|     |             |               |               |               |             |            |
|     |             |               |               |               |             |            |
|     |             |               |               |               |             |            |
|-------------+---------------+---------------+---------------+-------------+------------|
|     29      |      30       |      31       |               |             |            |
|.........................................................................................|
|CAL1 |<Erect Tower/$2,50+|               |               |               |             |            |
|     |             |               |               |               |             |            |
|     |             |               |               |               |             |            |
|     |             |               |               |               |             |            |
|     |             |               |               |               |             |            |
      -------------------------------------------------------------------------------------
```

Example 10:   Schedule Calendar with Mixed Output

This example uses OUTPUT=MIX to produce one page of output for both calendars, without grouping the activities by calendar. For mixed output, the activities are sorted by the START variable only.

```
options pagesize=66 linesize=132 nodate ;
title 'Well Drilling Work Schedule:  Output=Mix';

proc sort data=well.act;
   by date;
run;

proc calendar data=well.act
     holidata=well.hol caledata=well.cal workdata=well.wor datetime;
   calid _cal_ / output=mix;
   start date;
   dur dur;
   format cost dollar9.2;
   holistart date;
   holivar holiday;
   outstart Monday;
   outfin Saturday;
run;
```

Output 7.14 Schedule Calendar with Mixed Output

```
                          Well Drilling Work Schedule:  Output=Mix                          1
-----------------------------------------------------------------------------------------------
|                                                                                             |
|                                             July  1985                                      |
|---------------------------------------------------------------------------------------------|
|    Monday     |    Tuesday    |   Wednesday   |    Thursday   |     Friday    |   Saturday   |
|---------------+---------------+---------------+---------------+---------------+--------------|
|       1       |       2       |       3       |       4       |       5       |       6      |
|               |               |               |               |               |              |
|               |               |               |               |+Assemble Tank/$1,0>|          |
|               |               |               +===============================Excavate/$3,500.00=========================>|
|+====================Deliver Material/$500.00==================+|****Independence****|+Lay Power Line/$2,>|          |
|+====================Drill Well/$1,000.00=====================>|****Independence****|<Drill Well/$1,000.+|          |
|---------------+---------------+---------------+---------------+---------------+--------------|
|       8       |       9       |      10       |      11       |      12       |      13      |
|               |               |               |               |               |              |
|               |               |               |               |               |              |
|+==========================Build Pump House/$2,000.00==========================+|              |
|<==========================Assemble Tank/$1,000.00============================+|              |
|<=======Lay Power Line/$2,000.00========+|               |               |               |          |
|******Vacation******|<===========Excavate/$3,500.00===========+|+=======Pour Foundation/$1,500.00=======>|          |
|---------------+---------------+---------------+---------------+---------------+--------------|
|      15       |      16       |      17       |      18       |      19       |      20      |
|               |               |               |               |               |              |
|               |               |               |               |               |              |
|               |               |               |               |               |              |
|+===========================================Install Pump/$500.00============================================+|          |
|<=================Pour Foundation/$1,500.00=================+|               |+Install Pipe/$1,00>|          |
|---------------+---------------+---------------+---------------+---------------+--------------|
|      22       |      23       |      24       |      25       |      26       |      27      |
|               |               |               |               |               |              |
|               |               |               |               |               |              |
|               |               |               |               |               |              |
|+=================================Erect Tower/$2,500.00======================================>|          |
|<========Install Pipe/$1,000.00=========+|               |               |               |          |
|---------------+---------------+---------------+---------------+---------------+--------------|
|      29       |      30       |      31       |               |               |              |
|               |               |               |               |               |              |
|               |               |               |               |               |              |
|               |               |               |               |               |              |
|<Erect Tower/$2,500+|               |               |               |               |          |
-----------------------------------------------------------------------------------------------
```

For MIXED output schedule calendars, holidays are printed on the same line as the activities scheduled around them. For example, scheduling of the **Excavate** activity was affected by the holiday labelled **Vacation** on July 8th; and so that holiday is labelled on the line of the activity it affected. Scheduling of the activity **Excavate** was not affected by the holiday **Independence** on July 4th. That holiday occurs in calendar **CAL1**, while **Excavate** occurs in calendar **CAL2**. So on July 4th the activity **Excavate** continues through the holiday. The holiday **Independence** did affect the scheduling of both the activities **Drill Well** and **Lay Power Line**. This resulted in the holiday **Independence** being printed twice.

Example 11: Schedule Calendar with Holidays Only

You can produce a schedule calendar that displays only holidays by using an activities data set containing only two activities, both with zero durations. Activities with zero durations are not displayed, but the months containing them are printed; the FILL option causes all months between the dates of the two activities to be printed.

The statements below generate a calendar of holidays only. If you removed the holidays data set and statements, a set of blank calendars containing no activities or holidays is output. **Output 7.15** shows the first several calendars produced by these statements.

```
data acts;
   input sta:date7. act $ 11-30 dur;
   cards;
01JAN88    Start                  0
31DEC88    Finish                 0
 ;
run;

data holidays;
   input sta:date7. act $ 11-30 dur;
   cards;
01JAN88    New Year's             1
01APR88    Good Friday            1
30MAY88    Memorial Day           1
04JUL88    Independence Day       1
05SEP88    Labor Day              1
24NOV88    Thanksgiving           2
26DEC88    Christmas              3
 ;
run;

options pagesize=30 linesize=132;
proc calendar data=acts holidata=holidays fill;
   start sta;
   dur dur;
   holistart sta;
   holidur dur;
   holivar act;
run;
```

Output 7.15   Schedule Calendars with Holidays Only

```
                                    The SAS System                                           1
 -------------------------------------------------------------------------------------------
 |                                  January 1988                                            |
 -------------------------------------------------------------------------------------------
 | Sunday   |   Monday   |  Tuesday   | Wednesday  |  Thursday  |   Friday   |  Saturday    |
 -------------------------------------------------------------------------------------------
 |          |            |            |            |            |     1      |      2        |
 |          |            |            |            |            |***New Year's****|           |
 -------------------------------------------------------------------------------------------
 |    3     |     4      |     5      |     6      |     7      |     8      |      9        |
 -------------------------------------------------------------------------------------------
 |   10     |    11      |    12      |    13      |    14      |    15      |     16        |
 -------------------------------------------------------------------------------------------
 |   17     |    18      |    19      |    20      |    21      |    22      |     23        |
 -------------------------------------------------------------------------------------------
 |   24     |    25      |    26      |    27      |    28      |    29      |     30        |
 -------------------------------------------------------------------------------------------
 |   31     |            |            |            |            |            |               |
 -------------------------------------------------------------------------------------------
```

```
                                    The SAS System                                           2
 -------------------------------------------------------------------------------------------
 |                                  February 1988                                           |
 -------------------------------------------------------------------------------------------
 | Sunday   |   Monday   |  Tuesday   | Wednesday  |  Thursday  |   Friday   |  Saturday    |
 -------------------------------------------------------------------------------------------
 |          |     1      |     2      |     3      |     4      |     5      |      6        |
 -------------------------------------------------------------------------------------------
 |    7     |     8      |     9      |    10      |    11      |    12      |     13        |
 -------------------------------------------------------------------------------------------
 |   14     |    15      |    16      |    17      |    18      |    19      |     20        |
 -------------------------------------------------------------------------------------------
 |   21     |    22      |    23      |    24      |    25      |    26      |     27        |
 -------------------------------------------------------------------------------------------
 |   28     |    29      |            |            |            |            |               |
 -------------------------------------------------------------------------------------------
```

```
                                    The SAS System                                           3
 -------------------------------------------------------------------------------------------
 |                                   March 1988                                             |
 -------------------------------------------------------------------------------------------
 | Sunday   |   Monday   |  Tuesday   | Wednesday  |  Thursday  |   Friday   |  Saturday    |
 -------------------------------------------------------------------------------------------
 |          |            |     1      |     2      |     3      |     4      |      5        |
 -------------------------------------------------------------------------------------------
 |    6     |     7      |     8      |     9      |    10      |    11      |     12        |
 -------------------------------------------------------------------------------------------
 |   13     |    14      |    15      |    16      |    17      |    18      |     19        |
 -------------------------------------------------------------------------------------------
 |   20     |    21      |    22      |    23      |    24      |    25      |     26        |
 -------------------------------------------------------------------------------------------
 |   27     |    28      |    29      |    30      |    31      |            |               |
 -------------------------------------------------------------------------------------------
```

```
                                    The SAS System                                          4
-------------------------------------------------------------------------------------------
|                                                                                         |
|                                     April  1988                                         |
|-----------------------------------------------------------------------------------------|
|   Sunday    |    Monday    |   Tuesday    |  Wednesday   |  Thursday    |    Friday    |   Saturday   |
|-------------+--------------+--------------+--------------+--------------+--------------+--------------|
|             |              |              |              |              |      1       |      2       |
|             |              |              |              |              |***Good Friday***|           |
|-------------+--------------+--------------+--------------+--------------+--------------+--------------|
|     3       |      4       |      5       |      6       |      7       |      8       |      9       |
|-------------+--------------+--------------+--------------+--------------+--------------+--------------|
|    10       |     11       |     12       |     13       |     14       |     15       |     16       |
|-------------+--------------+--------------+--------------+--------------+--------------+--------------|
|    17       |     18       |     19       |     20       |     21       |     22       |     23       |
|-------------+--------------+--------------+--------------+--------------+--------------+--------------|
|    24       |     25       |     26       |     27       |     28       |     29       |     30       |
-------------------------------------------------------------------------------------------
```

```
                                    The SAS System                                          5
-------------------------------------------------------------------------------------------
|                                                                                         |
|                                      May  1988                                          |
|-----------------------------------------------------------------------------------------|
|   Sunday    |    Monday    |   Tuesday    |  Wednesday   |  Thursday    |    Friday    |   Saturday   |
|-------------+--------------+--------------+--------------+--------------+--------------+--------------|
|     1       |      2       |      3       |      4        |     5        |      6       |      7       |
|-------------+--------------+--------------+--------------+--------------+--------------+--------------|
|     8       |      9       |     10       |     11       |     12       |     13       |     14       |
|-------------+--------------+--------------+--------------+--------------+--------------+--------------|
|    15       |     16       |     17       |     18       |     19       |     20       |     21       |
|-------------+--------------+--------------+--------------+--------------+--------------+--------------|
|    22       |     23       |     24       |     25       |     26       |     27       |     28       |
|-------------+--------------+--------------+--------------+--------------+--------------+--------------|
|    29       |     30       |     31       |              |              |              |              |
|             |**Memorial Day***|           |              |              |              |              |
-------------------------------------------------------------------------------------------
```

Chapter 8

The CATALOG
Procedure

ABSTRACT

Use the CATALOG procedure to manage entries in SAS catalogs. PROC CATALOG is an interactive, non-full-screen procedure that allows you to

- display the contents of a catalog
- copy a catalog or selected entries within a catalog
- rename, exchange, or delete entries within a catalog.

The CATALOG procedure replaces the Version 5 CATOUT procedure.

INTRODUCTION

A catalog is a type of SAS file that can be stored in a SAS data library. Catalogs are used by the FORMAT, PMENU, and SPELL procedures, the SAS macro facility, and the SAS Display Manager System. Catalogs are also used by other SAS products, such as SAS/FSP, SAS/AF, SAS/IML, and SAS/GRAPH software, to store several types of information.

A catalog can have entries of many different types. Each entry type stores a different kind of information. For example, a data entry screen, a format, a help screen, and a KEYS entry each has its own entry type.

For more information on SAS data libraries and catalogs, including a complete list of catalog entry types, refer to Chapter 6, "SAS Files," in *SAS Language: Reference, Version 6, First Edition*.

Also, see **CATALOG Window** in Chapter 17, "SAS Display Manager Windows," in *SAS Language: Reference* to learn how to use the full-screen CATALOG window to manage entries in a SAS catalog. You may prefer to use the CATALOG window from a SAS full-screen window environment instead of PROC CATALOG; the window can do most of what the procedure does.

SPECIFICATIONS

The CATALOG procedure is controlled by the following statements:

> **PROC CATALOG** CATALOG=<*libref.*>*catalog* <ENTRYTYPE=*etype*> <KILL>;
>   **CONTENTS** <OUT=*SAS-data-set*> <FILE=*fileref*>;
>   **COPY** OUT=<*libref.*>*catalog* <*option-list*>;
>   **SELECT** *entry-list* </ ENTRYTYPE=*etype*>;
>   **EXCLUDE** *entry-list* </ ENTRYTYPE=*etype*>;
>   **CHANGE** *old-name-1=new-name-1* <*...old-name-n=new-name-n*>
>   </ ENTRYTYPE=*etype*>;
>   **EXCHANGE** *name-1=other-name-1* <*...name-n=other-name-n*>
>   </ ENTRYTYPE=*etype*>;
>   **DELETE** *entry-list* </ ENTRYTYPE=*etype*>;
>   **SAVE** *entry-list* </ ENTRYTYPE=*etype*>;

Entries are uniquely identified in the SAS System by a four-level name of the form *libref.catalog.entry.etype*. You specify *libref.catalog* in the CATALOG= option in the PROC CATALOG statement. Then, when executing statements within PROC CATALOG, you can specify *entries* with one-level or two-level names:

- A two-level name is specified as *entry.etype*, where *entry* is a valid SAS name and *etype* is a valid entry type (see the description for the ENTRYTYPE= option).
- A one-level name is specified as *entry*. You can use it only if you have specified *etype* elsewhere (as you will see, you can do that in the PROC CATALOG statement or in an ENTRYTYPE= option within other statements).

Table 8.1 summarizes how to use the statements of the CATALOG procedure. The options listed in the last column of the table are used on the statements listed in the middle column.

Table 8.1   Summary of PROC CATALOG Functions

Function	Statements	Options
Limit processing to a specified type of entry	PROC CATALOG	ENTRYTYPE=
Print the contents of a catalog	CONTENTS	OUT=, FILE=
Copy or move all entries in a catalog to another SAS data library	COPY	MOVE
Copy selected entries in a catalog to another SAS data library	COPY, SELECT, EXCLUDE	
Change the names of catalog entries	CHANGE	
Switch the names of two catalog entries	EXCHANGE	
Delete entries from a catalog	PROC CATALOG DELETE, SAVE	KILL

Procedure Execution

The CATALOG procedure is interactive. Once you submit a PROC CATALOG statement, you can continue to enter and execute statements without repeating the PROC CATALOG statement. You terminate the procedure by submitting a QUIT statement, by submitting another DATA or PROC statement, or by leaving the SAS System with an ENDSAS statement or a BYE display manager command. Note: When you enter a QUIT, DATA, or PROC statement, any previous statements are executed before the CATALOG procedure terminates.

RUN Groups

When you use the CATALOG procedure, you specify subordinate procedure statements to make changes to catalog entries. The changes for a given group of statements take effect when a RUN statement is encountered. You may have more than one RUN statement among the set of procedure statements. A *RUN group* is a set of procedure statements ending with a RUN statement. Error handling is based in part on the division of statements into RUN groups, as the next section describes.

Error Handling

If an error is encountered, statements in the current RUN group are not executed, and execution proceeds to the next RUN group. Even if the error occurs in the 20th statement of a 20-statement RUN group, none of the statements in the RUN group takes effect. For example, suppose that the following statements are submitted as a group, complete with a misspelled DELETE statement:

```
proc catalog catalog=misc entrytype=help;
   copy out=drink;
      select coffee tea;
   del juices;
   exchange glass=plastic;
run;

   change calstats=nutri;
run;
```

Since the DELETE statement is incorrectly specified as DEL, the SAS System does not execute it, the COPY statement, or the EXCHANGE statement. However, because the CHANGE statement is in a different RUN group, it is executed. Be careful when setting up batch jobs in which one RUN group's statements depend on the effects of a previous RUN group, especially when deleting and renaming entries.

Using the ENTRYTYPE= Option in Subordinate Statements

The ENTRYTYPE= (or ET=) option in the PROC CATALOG statement specifies the entry type for all statements that follow. However, if the ENTRYTYPE= option is not specified in the PROC CATALOG statement, you can specify the ENTRYTYPE= option in other statements by using a slash or parentheses as described below:

/ ENTRYTYPE=etype

   after a slash, identifies the type of all entry names preceding it.
   However, if a preceding entry is followed immediately by
   (ENTRYTYPE=etype), that entry has the type specified by the
   ENTRYTYPE= option in parentheses.

   Specifying / ENTRYTYPE=etype does not override an ENTRYTYPE=
   option in the PROC CATALOG statement.

   The following statement deletes A.HELP, B.FORMAT, and C.HELP:

```
delete a b (entrytype=format) c / entrytype=help;
```

   All statements in PROC CATALOG except the CONTENTS statement
   allow you to specify ENTRYTYPE= as an option.

(ENTRYTYPE=etype)

   in parentheses, identifies the type of the entry just preceding it. You can
   also specify the entry type for a specific entry by using a two-level name
   in the form entry.etype. This form is equivalent to using the
   (ENTRYTYPE=etype) option. These forms are useful mainly to specify
   exceptions to a / ENTRYTYPE= option. Note the following points about
   (ENTRYTYPE=etype):

   1. An ENTRYTYPE= option in parentheses cannot override an
      ENTRYTYPE= option in the PROC CATALOG statement.
   2. For the CHANGE and EXCHANGE statements, the ENTRYTYPE=
      option in parentheses is specified only once for each pair of
      names following the second name in the pair.

There is no default entry type when no ENTRYTYPE= option is specified in the PROC CATALOG statement.

For example, the following program causes an error and is not processed because there is no default entry type assumed for entry A:

```
proc catalog cat=train;
   delete a b (entrytype=list) c.screen;
run;
```

PROC CATALOG Statement

PROC CATALOG CATALOG=<*libref.*>*catalog* <ENTRYTYPE=*etype*> <KILL>;

The PROC CATALOG statement begins the procedure and specifies the catalog to be processed.

Requirement

The CATALOG= argument is required in the PROC CATALOG statement:

CATALOG=<*libref.*>*catalog*
CAT=<*libref.*>*catalog*
C=<*libref.*>*catalog*

   refers to the SAS catalog to be processed. If the CATALOG= argument is not specified here, the procedure fails because there is no default catalog name.

Options

The following options can be specified in the PROC CATALOG statement:

ENTRYTYPE=*etype*
ET=*etype*

   specifies an entry type to make available for processing if a one-level entry name is used in a subordinate statement. If the ENTRYTYPE= option is specified in the PROC CATALOG statement, then an ENTRYTYPE= option in a subordinate statement cannot override it. However, if the ENTRYTYPE= option is not specified in the PROC CATALOG statement, then each statement operates on an entry type named in its own ENTRYTYPE= option. There is no default entry type. See **Using the ENTRYTYPE= Option in Subordinate Statements** earlier in this chapter.

   For example, consider a catalog with entries A.PROGRAM, B.PROGRAM, and C.PROGRAM. The following statements issue an error message and do not delete any entries because the ENTRYTYPE= option in the PROC CATALOG statement conflicts with the one in the DELETE statement:

```
proc catalog cat=sample entrytype=help;
   delete a b c / entrytype=program;
run;
```

   The next example deletes A.PROGRAM, B.PROGRAM, and C.PROGRAM:

```
proc catalog cat=sample;
   delete a b c / entrytype=program;
run;
```

KILL

   deletes all entries in a SAS catalog. The KILL option does not, however, remove the empty catalog from the SAS data library that it is in.

   Caution: Do not attempt to limit the effects of the KILL option. The ENTRYTYPE= option is ignored when the KILL option is specified. In addition, you cannot use the SAVE statement with the KILL option. The KILL option deletes all entries before any other statements are processed, so the SAVE statement has no effect.

CHANGE Statement

CHANGE *old-name-1=new-name-1* <*...old-name-n=new-name-n*>
        </ ENTRYTYPE=*etype*>;

Use the CHANGE statement to rename one or more entries. Specify the old entry name on the left side of the equal sign and the new entry name on the right. You may include as many renaming pairs as you want. For example, the following statements change PERSIA.PROGRAM to IRAN.PROGRAM and RUSSIA.PROGRAM to USSR.PROGRAM:

```
proc catalog catalog=arms entrytype=program;
    change persia=iran russia=ussr;
run;
```

You can change only the name of an entry, not its type. A catalog entry type cannot be changed.

The ENTRYTYPE= option in the CHANGE statement specifies an entry type to make available for processing if the ENTRYTYPE= option is not specified in the PROC CATALOG statement. See **Using the ENTRYTYPE= Option in Subordinate Statements** earlier in this chapter for information on how to use the ENTRYTYPE= option in this statement.

CONTENTS Statement

CONTENTS <OUT=*SAS-data-set*> <FILE=*fileref*>;

Use the CONTENTS statement to list the contents of a catalog in the procedure output listing or to put a list of the contents into a SAS data set or an external file. If you omit both of the options, the output is sent to the procedure output listing, for example, the OUTPUT window of display manager.

Options

The following options can be specified in the CONTENTS statement:

FILE=*fileref*
  sends the contents to an external file, where *fileref* is a SAS fileref. If *fileref* is given but no FILENAME statement was issued to specify it, then the file is named according to host-dependent rules for external files. Refer to the SAS documentation for your host system.

OUT=*SAS-data-set*
  sends the contents to a SAS data set, where *SAS-data-set* is specified by a one- or two-level data set name. The libref WORK is used if a one-level data set name is specified. When the statement executes, you get a message on the SAS log telling you that a data set has been created. The data set contains six variables:

LIBNAME	the libref
MEMNAME	the catalog name
NAME	the names of entries
TYPE	the types of entries
DATE	the dates entries were last modified
DESC	the descriptions of entries.

COPY Statement

COPY OUT=<*libref.*>*catalog* <*option-list*>;

Use the COPY statement to copy some or all of the entries in one catalog to another catalog. Use SELECT or EXCLUDE statements after the COPY statement to limit which entries are copied. A COPY statement's effect ends at a RUN statement or at the beginning of a statement other than the SELECT or EXCLUDE statements.

Requirement

The following argument is required in the COPY statement:

OUT=<*libref.*>*catalog*
names the catalog to which entries are copied. The OUT= argument is required.

Options

The following options can be specified in the COPY statement:

ENTRYTYPE=*etype*
ET=*etype*
specifies an entry type to make available for processing if a one-level entry name is used. Refer to **Using the ENTRYTYPE= Option in Subordinate Statements** earlier in this chapter for information on how to use this option.

IN=<*libref.*>*catalog*
specifies the catalog to copy. The IN= option overrides a CATALOG= argument specified in the PROC CATALOG statement.

MOVE
deletes the original catalog or entries after the new copy is made. Whenever a MOVE command takes all entries out of a catalog, that catalog is deleted from the library.

NOEDIT
prevents the copied version of the following SAS/AF entry types from being edited by the BUILD procedure:
CBT
HELP
MENU
PROGRAM
SYSTEM

If you specify the NOEDIT option for an entry that is not one of these types, it is ignored.

NOSOURCE
NOSRC
omits copying the source lines when you copy a SAS/AF PROGRAM entry. If you specify this option for an entry other than a PROGRAM entry, it is ignored.

DELETE Statement

> **DELETE** *entry-list* </ ENTRYTYPE=*etype*>;

Use the DELETE statement to delete entries from a catalog. The ENTRYTYPE=
option in the DELETE statement specifies an entry type to make available for processing if the ENTRYTYPE= option is not used in the PROC CATALOG statement. See **Using the ENTRYTYPE= Option in Subordinate Statements** earlier in
this chapter for information on how to use the ENTRYTYPE= option in this statement.

EXCHANGE Statement

> **EXCHANGE** *name-1*=*other-name-1* <...*name-n*=*other-name-n*>
> </ ENTRYTYPE=*etype*>;

Use the EXCHANGE statement to exchange the names of two entries. The entries
must have the same entry type. For example, if your catalog contains the entries
A.PROGRAM and B.PROGRAM, the following statements change the name of
the entry A.PROGRAM to B.PROGRAM, and the name of B.PROGRAM to
A.PROGRAM:

```
libname mylib 'SAS-data-library';

proc catalog cat=mylib.sample;
   exchange a.program=b.program;
run;
```

You may specify one-level entry names if you also include an ENTRYTYPE=
option in the PROC CATALOG statement or in the EXCHANGE statement.

The ENTRYTYPE= option in the EXCHANGE statement specifies an entry type
to make available for processing if the ENTRYTYPE= option is not used in the
PROC CATALOG statement. See **Using the ENTRYTYPE= Option in Subordinate
Statements** earlier in this chapter for information on how to use the ENTRYTYPE=
option in this statement.

EXCLUDE Statement

> **EXCLUDE** *entry-list* </ ENTRYTYPE=*etype*>;

Use the EXCLUDE statement with the COPY statement to specify which entries
are not to be copied. The SELECT and EXCLUDE statements cannot be used at
the same time in a single COPY statement RUN group, but one or the other can
be used multiple times.

The ENTRYTYPE= option in the EXCLUDE statement specifies an entry type
to make available for processing if the ENTRYTYPE= option is not used in the
PROC CATALOG statement. See **Using the ENTRYTYPE= Option in Subordinate
Statements** earlier in this chapter for information on how to use the ENTRYTYPE=
option in this statement.

The following example copies everything in MYLIB.SAMPLE to WORK.FEED
except CORN.HELP, BARLEY.PROGRAM, and CORN.PROGRAM:

```
libname mylib 'SAS-data-library';

proc catalog cat=mylib.sample;
   copy out=feed;
      exclude corn.help barley corn / entrytype=program;
run;
```

SAVE Statement

SAVE *entry-list* </ ENTRYTYPE=*etype*>;

Use the SAVE statement to delete all but a few entries in a catalog. You can specify multiple entries in the statement. You may also use multiple SAVE statements in a RUN group. For example, the following statements delete everything in catalog MYLIB.CATS except MANX.PROGRAM, HIMALAYN.PROGRAM, CALICO.HELP, TABBY.HELP, PERSIAN.CBT, and PERSIAN.LIST:

```
libname mylib 'SAS-data-library';

proc catalog cat=mylib.cats;
   save manx himalayn / entrytype=program;
   save calico tabby / entrytype=help;
   save persian.cbt persian.list;
run;
```

The ENTRYTYPE= option in the SAVE statement specifies an entry type to make available for processing if the ENTRYTYPE= option is not used in the PROC CATALOG statement. See **Using the ENTRYTYPE= Option in Subordinate Statements** earlier in this chapter for information on how to use the ENTRYTYPE= option in this statement.

SELECT Statement

SELECT *entry-list* </ ENTRYTYPE=*etype*>;

Use the SELECT statement with the COPY statement to specify which entries to copy. The SELECT and EXCLUDE statements cannot be used at the same time within a single COPY statement RUN group, but one or the other can be used multiple times.

The ENTRYTYPE= option in the SELECT statement specifies an entry type to make available for processing if the ENTRYTYPE= option is not used in the PROC CATALOG statement. See **Using the ENTRYTYPE= Option in Subordinate Statements** earlier in this chapter for information on how to use the ENTRYTYPE= option in this statement.

The following example copies RYE.HELP, WHEAT.SCREEN, OATS.SCREEN, and CORN.SCREEN from MYLIB.SAMPLE to WORK.FEED:

```
libname mylib 'SAS-data-library';

proc catalog cat=mylib.sample;
   copy out=feed entrytype=screen;
      select rye.help wheat oats corn;
run;
```

DETAILS

Printed Output

In most cases, the CATALOG procedure writes the list of entries being processed to the SAS log. For example, the following statements change the name of one of the entries in a catalog. The log shows a record of the action as shown in **Output 8.1**.

```
libname mylib 'SAS-data-library';

proc catalog cat=mylib.cats;
   change persion.cbt=persian.cbt;
run;
```

Output 8.1 Log Showing PROC CATALOG Processing

```
6           proc catalog cat=mylib.cats;
7              change persion.cbt=persian.cbt;
8           run;

NOTE: Changing object PERSION.CBT to PERSIAN.CBT in catalog MYLIB.CATS.
```

If you use the CONTENTS statement without the FILE= or OUT= options, PROC CATALOG sends the output to the procedure output listing, as shown in the example below. The following statements produce **Output 8.2**.

```
libname mylib 'SAS-data-library';

proc catalog cat=mylib.cats;
   contents;
   title 'Output from CONTENTS Statement of PROC CATALOG';
run;
```

Output 8.2 Output from CONTENTS Statement of PROC CATALOG

```
                    Output from CONTENTS Statement of PROC CATALOG                          1

                              Contents of Catalog MYLIB.CATS

    # Name      Type      Date      Description

    1 PERSIAN   CBT       07/24/89  CBT Entry for Persians
    2 CALICO    HELP      04/05/89  CALICO.HELP
    3 TABBY     HELP      04/05/89  TABBY.HELP
    4 PERSIAN   LIST      04/17/89  List Entry for Persians
    5 HIMALAYN  PROGRAM   04/17/89  HIMALAYN.PROGRAM
    6 MANX      PROGRAM   04/05/89  MANX.PROGRAM
```

You can use the FILE= or OUT= options on the CONTENTS statement to redirect the list to a file.

The CHART Procedure

ABSTRACT

The CHART procedure produces vertical and horizontal bar charts (also called *histograms*), block charts, pie charts, and star charts. These charts are useful as a visual representation of the values of a single variable or several variables.

INTRODUCTION

You can control the appearance of charts you produce with the CHART procedure by specifying several factors:

- the type of chart
- the summary measures displayed for the variable whose values are charted
- the way values are grouped
- the line-size, page-size, and form-character options you use.

You request the type of chart in PROC CHART with the following statements:

- the VBAR statement for a vertical bar chart
- the HBAR statement for a horizontal bar chart
- the BLOCK statement for a block chart
- the PIE statement for a pie chart
- the STAR statement for a star chart.

In each case, the variable listed (the chart variable) determines the values that label the bars or sections. Options can be used to control the kind of statistics presented. For example, you can use the TYPE= option to choose a measure to compute and display:

- TYPE=FREQ for frequency counts
- TYPE=PCT for percentages
- TYPE=CFREQ for cumulative frequencies
- TYPE=CPCT for cumulative percentages
- TYPE=SUM for totals
- TYPE=MEAN for averages.

You can also use options to control any grouping you want to perform. Among the characteristics that determine how values are grouped is the type of variable charted, numeric or character. The following options control grouping:

- The DISCRETE option groups numeric variables as categorical variables.
- The GROUP= option groups variable values.
- The SUBGROUP= option determines subgrouping.
- The MIDPOINTS= option locates interval midpoints for continuous or character variables.
- The SUMVAR= option names the variable that collects summaries for means, sums, or frequencies.

PROC CHART produces charts for both numeric and character variables. Character variables and formats cannot exceed a length of 16. For continuous numeric variables, PROC CHART automatically selects display intervals, although you can explicitly define interval midpoints. For character variables and discrete numeric variables, which contain several distinct values rather than a continuous range, the data values themselves define the intervals.

Introductory Examples

To give you an idea of PROC CHART's capabilities, this section shows an example of each kind of chart that you can produce. If you have a specific chart in mind, glance through the following examples to find a similar chart. Then you can use options to alter the chart to your specifications.

The DATA step that creates the SAS data set STUDENTS used in many of the introductory examples is shown below:

```
libname intrchem 'SAS-data-library';

data intrchem.students;
   input name $ 1-14 sex $ 15 section $ 17-19 grade;
   cards;
Abdallah       F Mon 46
Anderson       M Wed 75
Aziz           F Wed 67
Bayer          M Wed 77
```

```
       Black        M Fri 79
       Blair        F Fri 70
       Blue         F Mon 63
       Brown        M Wed 58
       Bush         F Mon 63
       Chung        M Wed 85
       Davis        F Fri 89
       Drew         F Mon 49
       DuPont       M Mon 41
       Elliott      F Wed 85
       Farmer       F Wed 58
       Franklin     F Wed 59
       Freeman      F Mon 79
       Friedman     M Mon 58
       Gabriel      M Fri 75
       Grant        M Mon 79
       Harding      M Mon 49
       Hazelton     M Mon 55
       Hinton       M Fri 85
       Hope         F Fri 98
       Jackson      F Wed 64
       Janeway      F Wed 51
       Jones K      F Mon 39
       Jones M      M Mon 63
       Judson       F Fri 89
       Keller       F Mon 89
       LeBlanc      F Fri 70
       Lee          M Fri 48
       Litowski     M Fri 85
       Malloy       M Wed 79
       Meyer        F Fri 85
       Nichols      M Mon 58
       Oliver       F Mon 41
       Parker       F Mon 77
       Patton       M Wed 73
       Randleman    F Wed 46
       Robinson     M Fri 64
       Shien        M Wed 55
       Simonson     M Wed 62
       Smith N      M Wed 71
       Smith R      M Mon 79
       Sullivan     M Fri 77
       Swift        M Wed 63
       Wolfe        F Fri 79
       Wolfson      F Fri 89
       Zabriski     M Fri 89
       ;
       run;
```

Frequency Bar Charts

When you want to divide your data into groups based on the values of a variable, frequency bar charts are useful. For example, consider the data set STUDENTS, which contains information about students' grades in an introductory chemistry course. First you want to create a bar chart comparing the number of male students with the number of female students. This chart is a frequency chart: it shows the number of students of each sex. The following SAS code produces the vertical frequency chart shown in **Output 9.1**:

```
libname intrchem 'SAS-data-library';

proc chart data=intrchem.students;
   vbar sex;
run;
```

Output 9.1 Vertical Frequency Bar Chart of the Variable SEX

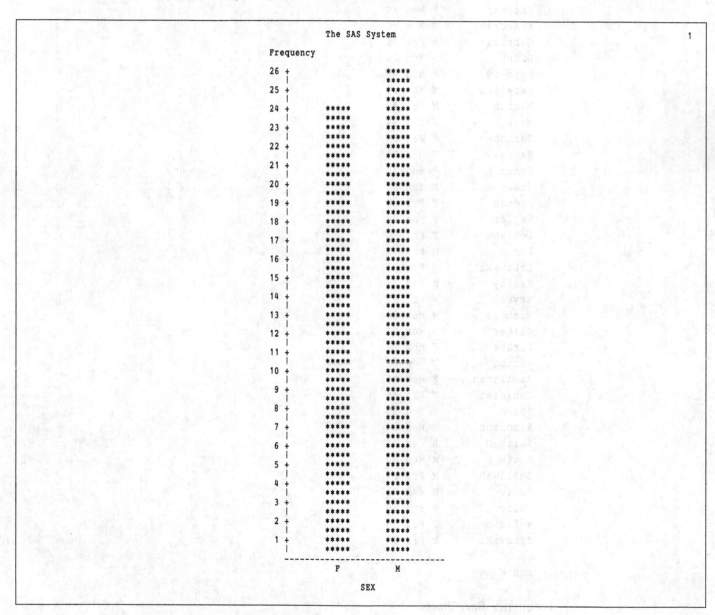

At the bottom of the chart are the two values of the variable SEX, **F** and **M**. The vertical axis represents the number of observations in the data set containing each value; 24 of the students are women and 26 are men.

If you prefer a horizontal bar chart, use the HBAR statement instead of the VBAR statement. You can substitute the HBAR statement in any of the examples that follow. Simply replace the keyword VBAR with HBAR. The statements below produce the horizontal frequency bar chart shown in **Output 9.2**:

```
proc chart data=intrchem.students;
   hbar sex;
run;
```

Output 9.2   Horizontal Frequency Bar Chart of the Variable SEX

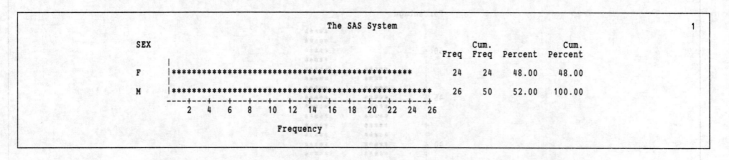

Output 9.2 shows the horizontal frequency bar chart. By default, PROC CHART prints the four statistics shown: frequency, cumulative frequency, percentage, and cumulative percentage. Here you see that 24 people, or 48%, in the class are women, and 26 people, or 52%, are men.

Percentage Bar Charts

These charts are useful for showing what percentage of the observations falls into different groups. For example, say you want to show the percentage of students of each sex. Specifying TYPE=PERCENT produces a percentage bar chart. The following statements produce the percentage bar chart shown in **Output 9.3**.

```
proc chart data=intrchem.students;
   vbar sex / type=percent;
run;
```

Output 9.3 Percentage Bar Chart of the Variable SEX

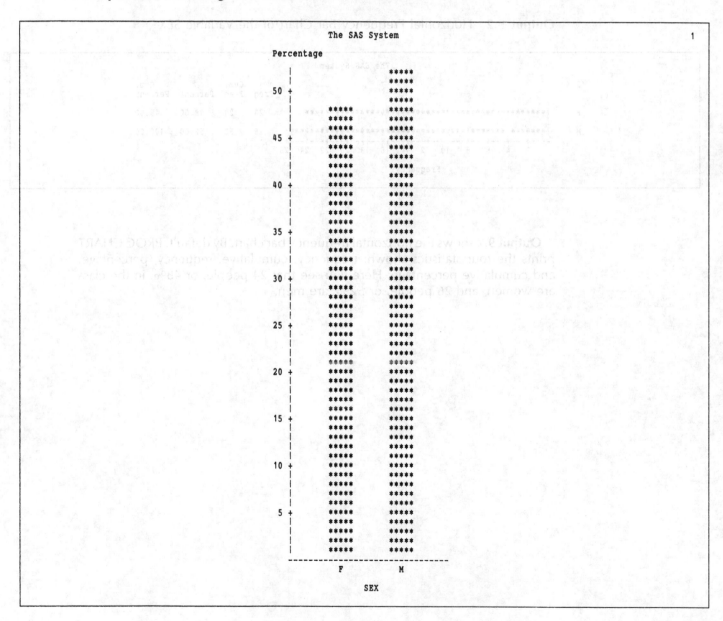

This chart shows that 48% of the students are female and 52% are male.

Cumulative Frequency Charts

Sometimes you want a cumulative frequency chart, where each bar represents the frequency of a given value plus the frequencies of all the values to its left in the chart. For example, using the data set containing student information, you may want to see how many students received a grade less than 75% on the first exam. The GRADE MIDPOINT of 70 in **Output 9.4** contains the grades ranging from 65 to <75. PROC CHART automatically produces a chart with seven bars. Note: If you are using a release earlier than Release 6.03, your chart has six bars with midpoints selected differently.

Use the MIDPOINTS= option if you want to specify the values to be included in each bar, for example, the statements

```
proc chart data=intrchem.students;
    vbar grade / type=freq midpoints=55 65 75 85 95;
run;
```

produce a bar chart with a bar for each of the following ranges:

Midpoint	Range of Values
55	$0 \leq$ Value < 59
65	$60 \leq$ Value < 69
75	$70 \leq$ Value < 79
85	$80 \leq$ Value < 89
95	$90 \leq$ Value < 99

Notice that the leftmost bar would contain a greater range of values than the other four. PROC CHART will place all values under 59 in this bar.

The TYPE=CFREQ option produces a cumulative frequency chart. The following statements produce the cumulative frequency bar chart shown in **Output 9.4**:

```
proc chart data=intrchem.students;
    vbar grade / type=cfreq;
run;
```

Output 9.4 Cumulative Frequency Bar Chart

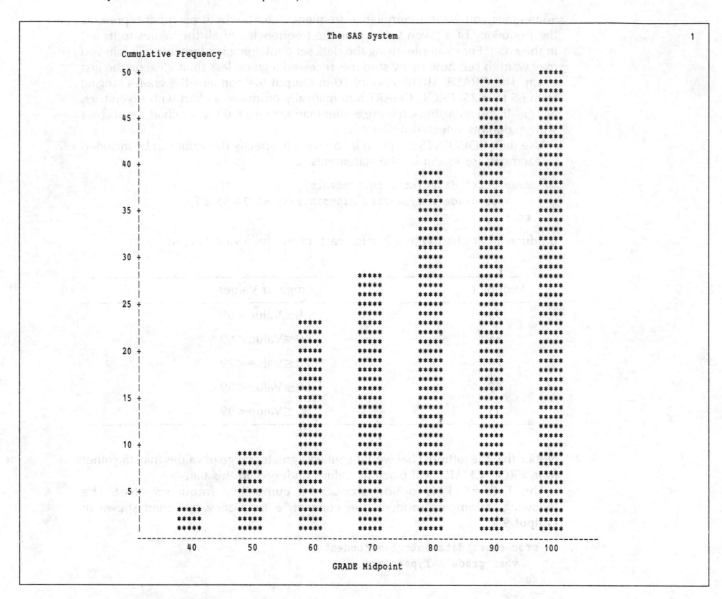

Output 9.4 shows that 28 students have a grade of 74% or below.

Cumulative Percentage Charts

The bars of a cumulative percentage chart represent the percentage of the observations having a given value plus the percentages of all the values appearing to the left in the chart.

For example, suppose you want to represent the grades of the students in terms of percentages rather than frequencies. The TYPE=CPERCENT option produces a cumulative percentage chart. The following statements produce the cumulative percentage bar chart shown in **Output 9.5**:

```
proc chart data=intrchem.students;
   vbar grade / type=cpercent;
run;
```

Output 9.5 Cumulative Percentage Bar Chart

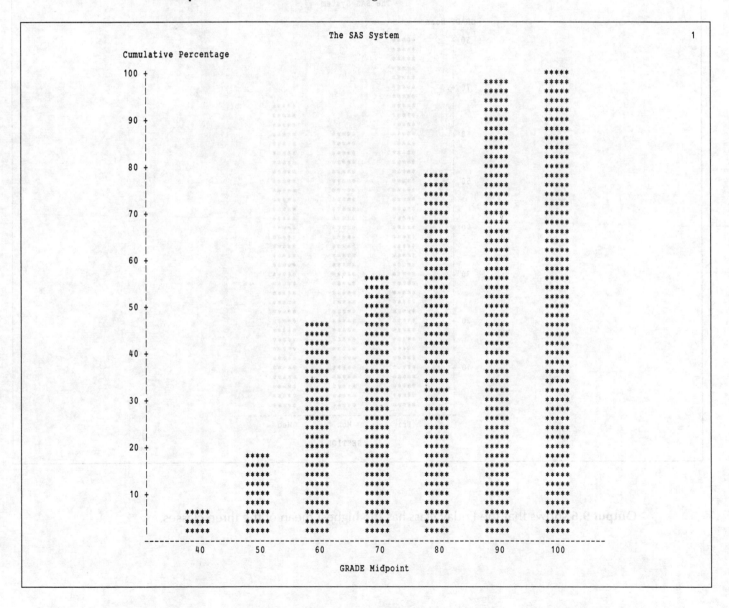

Output 9.5 shows that over 50% of the class received grades higher than 69%.

Bar Charts for Group Means

Bar charts of group means are like the bar charts of group totals shown in **Output 9.4** and **Output 9.5**. In bar charts of group means, the vertical axis represents the means of a variable rather than the sums. The statements below produce the bar chart for group means shown in **Output 9.6**:

```
proc chart data=intrchem.students;
   vbar section / type=mean sumvar=grade;
run;
```

Output 9.6　Bar Charts for Group Means

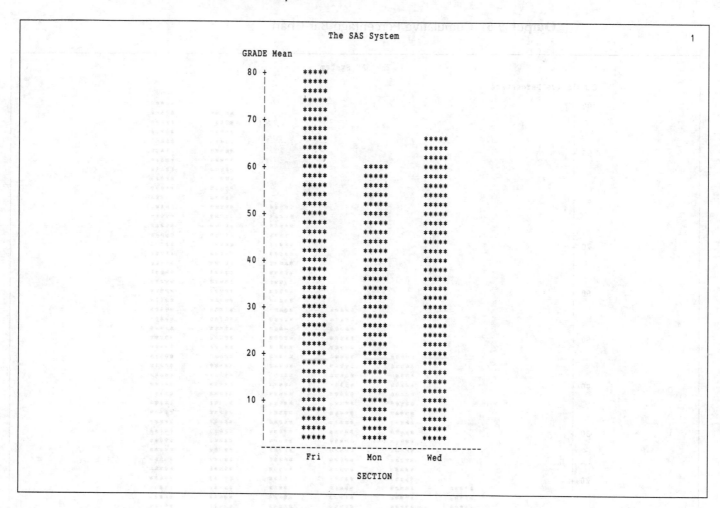

Output 9.6 shows that the Friday class has the highest mean of the three classes.

Subdividing the Bars

You can show the distribution of a second variable by using the first character of each value to print the bars. For example, say you want to compare the number of men and women in each of the three sections. The statements below cause PROC CHART to subdivide the bars using **F** and **M**.

```
proc chart data=intrchem.students;
   vbar section / subgroup=sex;
run;
```

Output 9.7   Subdividing a Frequency Bar Chart

```
                          The SAS System                                    1

         Frequency

            17 +                      MMMMM       MMMMM
               I                      MMMMM       MMMMM
            16 +           MMMMM      MMMMM       MMMMM
               I           MMMMM      MMMMM       MMMMM
            15 +           MMMMM      MMMMM       MMMMM
               I           MMMMM      MMMMM       MMMMM
            14 +           MMMMM      MMMMM       MMMMM
               I           MMMMM      MMMMM       MMMMM
            13 +           MMMMM      MMMMM       MMMMM
               I           MMMMM      MMMMM       MMMMM
            12 +           MMMMM      MMMMM       MMMMM
               I           MMMMM      MMMMM       MMMMM
            11 +           MMMMM      MMMMM       MMMMM
               I           MMMMM      MMMMM       MMMMM
            10 +           MMMMM      MMMMM       MMMMM
               I           MMMMM      MMMMM       MMMMM
             9 +           MMMMM      FFFFF       MMMMM
               I           MMMMM      FFFFF       MMMMM
             8 +           FFFFF      FFFFF       MMMMM
               I           FFFFF      FFFFF       MMMMM
             7 +           FFFFF      FFFFF       FFFFF
               I           FFFFF      FFFFF       FFFFF
             6 +           FFFFF      FFFFF       FFFFF
               I           FFFFF      FFFFF       FFFFF
             5 +           FFFFF      FFFFF       FFFFF
               I           FFFFF      FFFFF       FFFFF
             4 +           FFFFF      FFFFF       FFFFF
               I           FFFFF      FFFFF       FFFFF
             3 +           FFFFF      FFFFF       FFFFF
               I           FFFFF      FFFFF       FFFFF
             2 +           FFFFF      FFFFF       FFFFF
               I           FFFFF      FFFFF       FFFFF
             1 +           FFFFF      FFFFF       FFFFF
               I           FFFFF      FFFFF       FFFFF
               --------------------------------------------
                            Fri        Mon         Wed

                                   SECTION


               Symbol SEX    Symbol SEX

                 F   F          M   M
```

From **Output 9.7**, you can see that the Monday section contains more women than men, and the Wednesday section contains more men than women. Glancing at the bar representing Friday, you can see that the class is evenly divided, with eight women and eight men.

You can use other options in addition to SUBGROUP= to produce more informative charts. For example, say you want to compare the mean grade in each section. You also want an idea of how the men and women contributed to each section's mean. The statements below produce the chart shown in **Output 9.8**:

```
proc chart data=intrchem.students;
   vbar section / sumvar=grade type=mean subgroup=sex;
run;
```

Output 9.8   Subdividing a Bar Chart of Sums

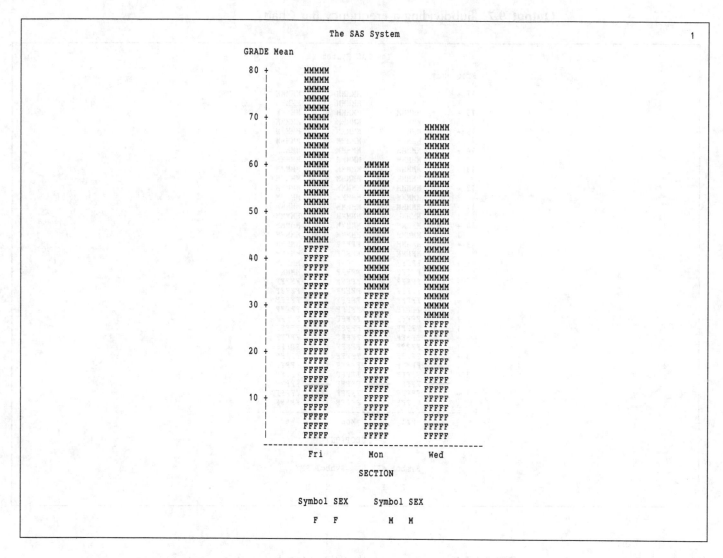

In **Output 9.6** you see the mean grade for each section (men and women combined). In **Output 9.7** you have a frequency chart with the bars subdivided using SUBGROUP=SEX. **Output 9.8** uses both SUBGROUP=SEX and TYPE=MEAN to approximate the way that men and women in each section contribute to the mean grade for that section. **Output 9.8** shows that men did better in the Wednesday section. In the next example, **Output 9.9** gives a more precise representation.

Side-by-Side Charts

Another way of comparing quantities is with side-by-side charts. You can compare information, such as mean scores for the three sections for men and women. The chart variable specified in the statements below is SECTION, as in the previous examples. The bars in **Output 9.9** are the class sections. The option GROUP=SEX produces a chart with SECTION subdivided by SEX. The option TYPE=MEAN is used so that the height of each bar represents the mean grade, as in **Output 9.8**. The following statements produce **Output 9.9**:

```
proc chart data=intrchem.students;
    vbar section / group=sex sumvar=grade type=mean;
run;
```

Output 9.9 Side-by-Side Charts

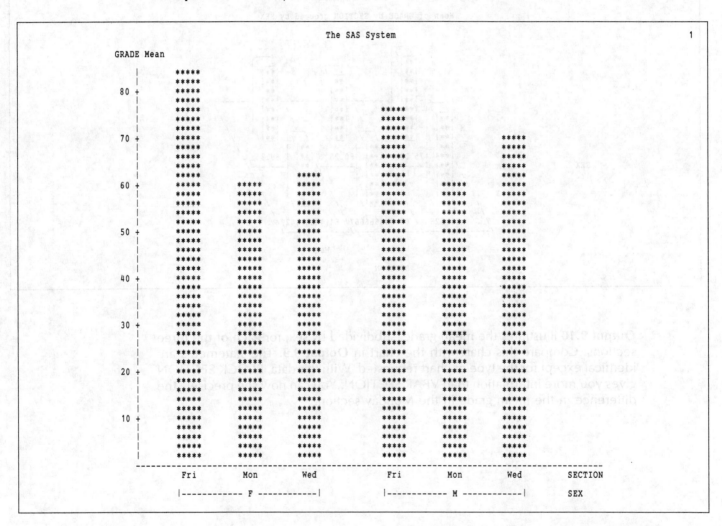

This chart gives more specific information than the chart produced in **Output 9.8**. Compare this chart with **Output 9.6** and **Output 9.8**. The GROUP= option, combined with options used in the earlier charts, allows you to see the exact mean grade for each sex in each section.

Block Charts

Another way you can show class information by section is to use a block chart. You can represent the frequency, mean, or sum by the height of the block. The statements below produce the block chart shown in **Output 9.10**, which displays the same grade information as the vertical bar chart presented in **Output 9.9**.

```
proc chart data=intrchem.students;
   block section/group=sex sumvar=grade type=mean;
run;
```

Output 9.10 Block Chart of Mean Grades

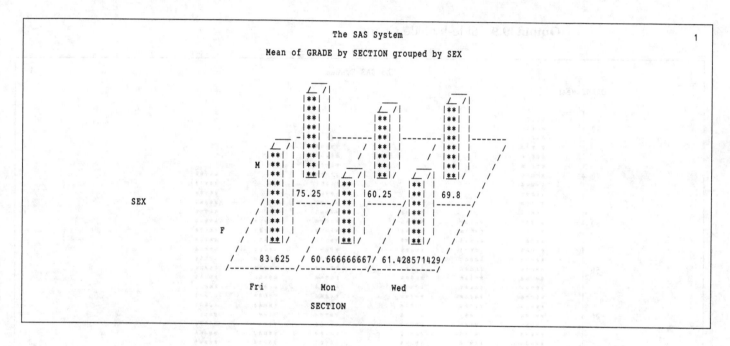

Output 9.10 illustrates the mean grade, subdivided by sex, for each of the three sections. Compare this chart with the chart in **Output 9.9**. The statements are identical except for the type of chart requested. With this data, BLOCK SECTION gives you more information than VBAR SECTION. You can now see precisely the difference in the mean grade in the Monday section.

Pie Charts

You can also use the CHART procedure to draw a pie chart representing the distribution of a variable's values. In the example below, a chemistry professor calculates the percentage of time devoted to professional activities during a month. The statements below produce the pie chart shown in **Output 9.11**:

```
data time;
   input activity $ hours @@;
   cards;
teach    6 meets  3 grades   4 research 20 counsel 5
teach    6 meets  2 grades   5 research 25 counsel 5
teach    6 meets  5 grades   2 research 28 counsel 3
teach    6 meets  1 grades   5 research 20 counsel 4
;
run;

proc chart;
   pie activity / sumvar=hours type=mean;
run;
```

Output 9.11   Mean Pie Chart of Monthly Activities

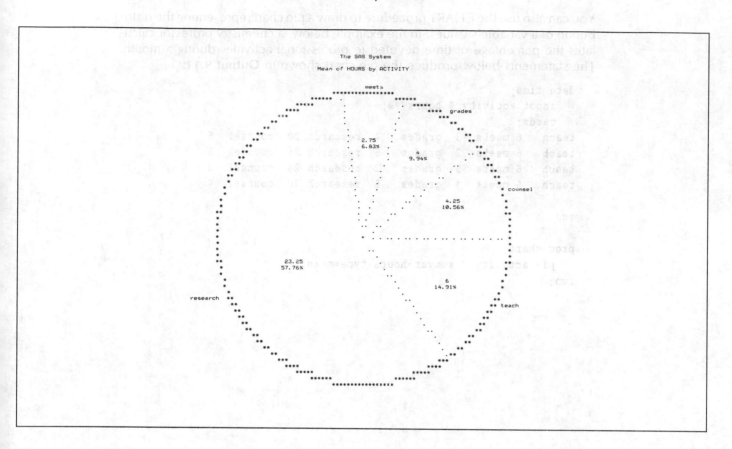

The pie chart in **Output 9.11** shows that 6.83% of the professor's time each month is devoted to meetings (MEETS). The TYPE=MEAN option shows that an average of 2.75 hours a week are devoted to meetings.

Star Charts

You can produce star charts showing group frequencies, totals, or means with PROC CHART. (The star chart that results is like a vertical bar chart, but the bars now radiate from a center point, like spokes in a wheel.) Star charts are appropriate for cyclical data, such as measures taken every month or every hour. The following statements produce the star chart shown in **Output 9.12** that shows monthly temperature averages:

```
proc format;
    value _mon 1='JAN'  2='FEB'  3='MAR'  4='APR'  5='MAY'  6='JUN'
               7='JUL'  8='AUG'  9='SEP' 10='OCT' 11='NOV' 12='DEC';
run;

data monthly;
    title 'St. Louis Monthly Mean Temperatures';
    do month=1 to 12;
        input temp @@;
        output;
    end;
    format month _mon.;
    cards;
31.3 35.1 43.3 56.5 65.8 74.9 78.6 77.2 69.6 59.1 45.0 34.6
;
run;

proc chart;
    star month / sumvar=temp discrete;
run;
```

Output 9.12 Star Chart of Temperatures Grouped by Month

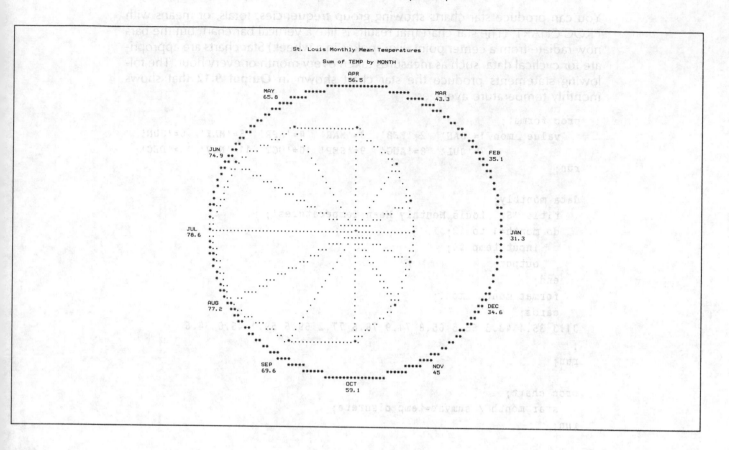

Output 9.12 shows the mean temperatures in St. Louis. July is the hottest month on this chart; January is the coldest.

SPECIFICATIONS

The CHART procedure is controlled by the following statements:

PROC CHART <option-list>;
   BY <variable-list>;
   VBAR variable-list </ <standard-option-list><VBAR-specific-option-list>>;
   HBAR variable-list </ <standard-option-list><HBAR-specific-option-list>>;
   BLOCK variable-list </ <standard-option-list><BLOCK-specific-option-list>>;
   PIE variable-list </ <standard-option-list><NOHEADER>>;
   STAR variable-list </ <standard-option-list><NOHEADER>>;

Any number of chart-request statements can follow a PROC CHART statement. The options in the *standard-option-list* can be used on any CHART procedure statement. These options are discussed in detail in **Standard and Statement-specific Options** later in this chapter. **Table 9.1** shows the options that can be specified in *standard-option-list*.

Table 9.1   Standard Options for the CHART Procedure

Function	Option
Group variables	DISCRETE
Collect summaries	SUMVAR=
Weight an observation	FREQ=
Locate interval midpoints	MIDPOINTS=
Locate chart midpoints	LEVELS=
Choose a measure to compute and display it	TYPE=
Control output	MISSING
	AXIS=

Table 9.2 shows the options that are available for specific types of charts.

Table 9.2   Summary of Statement-specific Options

Options Grouped by Function	HBAR	VBAR	BLOCK	PIE	STAR
Separate into groups					
GROUP=	X	X	X		
SUBGROUP=	X	X	X		
G100	X	X	X		
Request statistical analysis					
FREQ	X				
CFREQ	X				
PERCENT	X				
CPERCENT	X				
SUM	X				
MEAN	X				
Control output					
NOLEGEND	X	X	X		
NOSYMBOL	X	X	X		
SYMBOL=	X	X	X		
ASCENDING	X	X			
DESCENDING	X	X			
NOZEROS	X	X			
REF=	X	X			
NOSTATS	X				
NOSPACE		X			
NOHEADER				X	X	X

These options are listed again with the appropriate chart-request statement, and then each option is described in **Standard and Statement-specific Options** later in this chapter.

PROC CHART Statement

PROC CHART <option-list>;

The following options can be used in the PROC CHART statement:

DATA=*SAS-data-set*
  names the SAS data set to be used by PROC CHART. If the DATA= option is not specified, PROC CHART uses the most recently created SAS data set.

FORMCHAR<*index-list* > =*'formchar-string'*
  defines the characters used to construct the horizontal and vertical axes and the lower left corner, and defines the symbols used to create the bars, sections, or blocks in the PROC CHART output. The default value is a string six characters long composed of the horizontal and vertical lines, the lower left corner, the cross, the slash, and the asterisk. Any character or hexadecimal string can be used to customize table appearance. If you omit the FORMCHAR= option, the value supplied, if any, with the system option FORMCHAR= is used. You can set the

format characters using the SAS system option FORMCHAR= or the PROC CHART statement option FORMCHAR=. You can set all the format characters or only selected ones. See **Formatting Your Output Using the FORMCHAR= Option** later in this chapter for more information.

LPI=*number*

specifies the proportions of PIE and STAR charts. The LPI= value is determined by

$$(\text{lines per inch} / \text{columns per inch}) * 10$$

The default is LPI=6. For example, if you have a printer with 8 lines per inch and 12 columns per inch, specify LPI=6.6667.

BLOCK Statement

BLOCK *variable-list* </ *<standard-option-list>* *<BLOCK-specific-option-list>>*;

Table 9.3 shows the options that can be used in *standard-option-list* and *BLOCK-specific-option-list*.

Table 9.3 Options Available with the BLOCK statement

Specify Grouping	Control Printing	Standard Options
GROUP=	NOLEGEND	AXIS=
SUBGROUP=	NOSYMBOL	DISCRETE
G100	SYMBOL=	FREQ=
	NOHEADER	LEVELS=
		MIDPOINTS=
		MISSING
		SUMVAR=
		TYPE=

In the BLOCK statement, list the variables for which you want block charts. Since each block chart must fit on one output page, there are some restrictions on the number of bars of the BLOCK and GROUP= variables. For example, if you use

```
proc chart;
    block school / group=class;
run;
```

and there are three different values for SCHOOL and six different values (or groups) for CLASS in each school, you need to specify

```
option pagesize=66 linesize=76;
```

Table 9.4 shows the maximum number of bars of BLOCK variables for selected LINESIZE= (LS=) specifications that can be represented in a block chart using a 66-line page.

Table 9.4 Maximum Number of Bars of BLOCK Variables

GROUP= Value	LS=132	LS=120	LS=105	LS=90	LS=76	LS=64
0,1	9	8	7	6	5	4
2	8	8	7	6	5	4
3	8	7	6	5	4	3
4	7	7	6	5	4	3
5,6	7	6	5	4	3	2

If the value of any GROUP= level is longer than three characters, the maximum number of BLOCK levels that can be produced may be reduced by one. BLOCK level values are truncated to 12 characters. If these limits are exceeded, data are represented as a horizontal bar chart. See **Standard and Statement-specific Options** later in this chapter for details on available options.

BY Statement

BY *variable-list*;

A BY statement can be used with PROC CHART to obtain separate analyses on observations in groups defined by the BY variables. When a BY statement appears, PROC CHART expects the input data set to be sorted in order of the BY variables or to have an appropriate index. If your input data set is not sorted in ascending order or is not indexed, you can do one of the following:

- Use the SORT procedure with a similar BY statement to sort the data.
- If appropriate, use the BY statement options NOTSORTED or DESCENDING.
- Create an index on the BY variables you want to use. For more information on creating indexes and using the BY statement with indexed data sets, see Chapter 17, "The DATASETS Procedure."

HBAR Statement

HBAR *variable-list* </ *<standard-option-list>* *<HBAR-specific-option-list>*;

Table 9.5 shows the options that can be used in *standard-option-list* and *HBAR-specific-option-list*.

Table 9.5   Options Available with the HBAR Statement

Specify Grouping	Request Statistics	Control Printing	Standard Options
GROUP=	FREQ	NOLEGEND	AXIS=
SUBGROUP=	CFREQ	NOSYMBOL=	DISCRETE
G100	PERCENT	SYMBOL=	FREQ=
	CPERCENT	ASCENDING	LEVELS=
	SUM	DESCENDING	MIDPOINTS=
	MEAN	NOZEROS	MISSING
	NOSTATS	REF=	SUMVAR=
			TYPE=

The HBAR statement requests a horizontal bar chart for each variable listed. For example, the following statements produce three horizontal bar charts:

```
proc chart;
   hbar a x1 x2;
run;
```

Each chart occupies one or more output pages, depending on the number of bars; each bar occupies one line.

By default, for horizontal bar charts of TYPE=FREQ, CFREQ, PCT, or CPCT, the CHART procedure prints the following statistics: frequency, cumulative frequency, percentage, and cumulative percentage. If you use one or more of the statistics options, PROC CHART prints only the statistics you request. For example, using TYPE=MEAN, statistics include only frequency and mean. For TYPE=SUM, statistics printed are frequency and sum. See **Standard and Statement-specific Options** later in this chapter for details.

PIE Statement

PIE *variable-list* </ *<standard-option-list>* *<NOHEADER>*;

The following options can be used in *standard-option-list*:

AXIS=	MIDPOINTS=
DISCRETE	MISSING
FREQ=	SUMVAR=
LEVELS=	TYPE=

The PIE statement requests a pie chart for each variable listed. For example, the following statements produce three one-page pie charts:

```
proc chart;
    pie a x1 x2;
run;
```

PROC CHART determines the number of slices for the pie in the same way that it determines the number of bars for vertical bar charts. Any slices of the pie accounting for less than three print positions are grouped together into a slice called OTHER.

The pie's size is determined only by the LINESIZE= and PAGESIZE= system options. By default, the pie looks elliptical if your printer does not print 6 lines per inch and 10 columns per inch. To make a circular pie chart on a printer that does not print 6 lines and 10 columns per inch, use the LPI= option on the PROC CHART statement. For example, if your printer prints 8 lines per inch and 10 columns per inch, specify LPI=8 in the PROC CHART statement.

If a PIE chart is requested for a variable with over 50 levels, a horizontal bar chart is produced instead. See **Standard and Statement-specific Options** later in this chapter for descriptions of each option.

STAR Statement

STAR *variable-list* </ <*standard-option-list*> <NOHEADER>>;

The following options can be specified in *standard-option-list*:

AXIS=	MIDPOINTS=
DISCRETE	MISSING
FREQ=	SUMVAR=
LEVELS=	TYPE=

The STAR statement requests a star chart for each variable listed. For example, the following statements produce a one-page star chart for the variable Z:

```
proc chart;
    star z;
```

The number of points in the star is determined in the same way as the number of bars for vertical bar charts.

If all the data to be charted with a STAR statement are positive, the center of the star represents zero and the outside circle represents the maximum value. If negative values occur in the data, the center represents the minimum. See the AXIS= option for more information about how to specify maximum and minimum values. If a star chart is requested for a variable with over 24 levels, a horizontal bar chart is produced instead. See **Standard and Statement-specific Options** later in this chapter for descriptions of each option.

Note: If you want different variables to form the rays of the star, use an OUTPUT statement in a DATA step to create new observations having one variable with values equal to the variables you want represented by the rays; in other words, create another variable whose values are the original variable names.

VBAR Statement

VBAR *variable-list* `</` `<standard-option-list>` `<VBAR-specific-option-list>`;

Table 9.6 shows the options that can be specified in the VBAR statement.

Table 9.6 Options Available in the VBAR Statement

Specify Grouping	Control Printing	Standard Options
GROUP=	NOLEGEND	AXIS=
SUBGROUP=	NOSYMBOL	DISCRETE
G100	NOSPACE	FREQ=
	SYMBOL=	LEVELS=
	ASCENDING	MIDPOINTS=
	DESCENDING	MISSING
	NOZEROS	SUMVAR=
	REF=	TYPE=

In the VBAR statement, list the variables for which you want vertical bar charts. For example, if you list STUDENTS as a chart variable, then a vertical bar chart is produced with the values of STUDENTS underneath the bars.

The procedure prints one page per chart. Along the vertical axis, PROC CHART describes the chart frequency, the cumulative frequency, the chart percentage, the cumulative percentage, the sum, or the mean. At the bottom of each bar, PROC CHART prints a value according to the value of the TYPE= option, if specified. For character variables or discrete numeric variables, this value is the actual value represented by the bar. For continuous numeric variables, the value gives the midpoint of the interval represented by the bar.

PROC CHART can automatically scale the vertical axis, determine the bar width, and choose spacing between the bars. However, options allow you to choose bar intervals and the number of bars, include missing values in the chart, produce side-by-side charts, and subdivide the bars. If the number of characters per line (LINESIZE=) is not sufficient to display all vertical bars, PROC CHART will produce a horizontal bar chart instead.

Standard and Statement-specific Options

Each of the following options is either a standard option or an option that can be used only in some chart-request statements. The options are presented in alphabetic order.

You can use an option with any of the chart-request statements unless otherwise specified. You need to specify these options following a slash (/), for example,

```
proc chart;
   hbar year / <standard-option-list> <HBAR-specific-list>;
run;
```

ASCENDING | ASC
  prints the bars and any associated statistics in ascending order of size within groups. The ASCENDING option can only be used with the HBAR and VBAR statements.

AXIS=<*min-value*> *max-value*

allows you to specify the minimum and maximum values used in constructing the FREQ, PCT, CFREQ, CPCT, SUM, or MEAN axis. If you use the VBAR or HBAR statements and TYPE=SUM or TYPE=MEAN, and if any of the sums or means are less than zero, then a negative minimum value can also be specified in the AXIS= option. Otherwise, the default is a minimum value of zero. Counts or percentages outside the maximum (or minimum) override the AXIS= specification. If the AXIS= option is specified and a BY statement also appears, uniform axes are produced over BY groups. When the AXIS= option appears in a STAR statement, the first value specified is the center (minimum) of the star and the second value is the outside circle (maximum). If only one AXIS= value is specified in a STAR statement, PROC CHART assumes this value is the maximum and zero is the minimum. For example, the following statements produce a star chart for the sums of X classified by A and scaled from 100 at the center to 200 at the outside circle:

```
proc chart;
   star a / sumvar=x type=sum axis=100 200;
run;
```

CFREQ

prints the cumulative frequency. The CFREQ option can only be used with the HBAR statement.

CPERCENT

prints the cumulative percentages. The CPERCENT option can only be used with the HBAR statement.

DESCENDING | DESC

prints the bars and any associated statistics in descending order of size within groups. The DESCENDING option can only be used with the HBAR and VBAR statements.

DISCRETE

is used when the numeric chart variable specified is discrete rather than continuous. If the DISCRETE option is omitted, PROC CHART assumes that all numeric variables are continuous and automatically chooses intervals for them unless the MIDPOINTS= or LEVELS= options are used.

FREQ

prints the frequency of each bar to the side of the chart. The FREQ option can only be used with the HBAR statement.

FREQ=*variable*

is used when a variable in the data set represents a count (or weight) for each observation. Normally, each observation contributes a value of one to the frequency counts. When the FREQ= option appears, each observation contributes the FREQ= value. If the FREQ= values are not integers, they are truncated to integers. If the values are missing or negative, the contribution is zero. If the SUMVAR= option is specified, the sums are multiplied by the FREQ= value.

GROUP=*variable*

produces side-by-side charts, with each chart representing the observations having a given value of the GROUP= variable. The GROUP= variable can be character or numeric and is assumed to be discrete. For example, the following statement produces a frequency bar chart for men and women in each department:

```
vbar sex / group=dept;
```

Missing values for a GROUP= variable are treated as valid levels when a chart is produced. The GROUP= option can only be used with the HBAR, VBAR, and BLOCK statements.

G100

is used in conjunction with the GROUP= option to force the bars and statistics to add to 100% for each group. The G100 option can only be used with the HBAR, VBAR, and BLOCK statements.

LEVELS=*number-of-midpoints*

specifies the number of bars, blocks, or sections representing each chart variable when the variables given in the VBAR statement are continuous.

MEAN

prints the mean of the observations represented by each bar. The MEAN option can only be used with the HBAR statement.

MIDPOINTS=*midpoint-list* | OLD

defines the range of values each bar or section represents by specifying the range midpoints. For example, the following statement produces a chart with five bars: the first bar represents the range of data values with a midpoint of 10; the second bar represents the range of data values with a midpoint of 20; and so on.

```
vbar x / midpoints=10 20 30 40 50;
```

When the variables given in the VBAR statement are numeric, the midpoints must be given in ascending order, although they need not be uniformly distributed. For example, the following statement produces a chart of X with logarithmic intervals:

```
vbar x / midpoints=10 100 1000 10000;
```

A numeric *midpoint-list* of the form

```
midpoints=10 to 100 by 5
```

is also acceptable. For character variables, the MIDPOINTS= option can be specified in any order, which is useful in ordering the bars or in specifying a subset of the possible values. For example, you can give a list of the form

```
midpoints='JAN' 'FEB' 'MAR'
```

Without the MIDPOINTS= option, the values are displayed in sorted order.

If you don't use the MIDPOINTS= option to specify midpoints, PROC CHART uses its own internal algorithm to choose midpoints for continuous variables. In previous versions of the SAS System, this algorithm was based on the work of Nelder (1976); now an improved algorithm has been implemented based on the work of Terrell and Scott (1985). If you prefer the old algorithm, you can use it by specifying MIDPOINTS=OLD.

MISSING

specifies that missing values are to be considered as valid levels for the chart variable.

NOHEADER
NOHEADING

suppresses the default header line normally printed at the top of a chart. The NOHEADER option can only be used with the BLOCK, PIE, and STAR statements.

NOSTATS
NOSTAT

suppresses printing statistics on a horizontal bar chart. The NOSTATS option can only be used with the HBAR statement.

NOSYMBOL
NOLEGEND

is used in conjunction with the SUBGROUP= option to suppress printing of the subgroup legend or symbol table. Both the NOSYMBOL and NOLEGEND options can only be used with the HBAR, VBAR, and BLOCK statements.

NOZEROS

suppresses any bar with zero frequency. The NOZEROS option can only be used with the HBAR and VBAR statements.

PERCENT

prints the percentages of observations having a given value for the chart variable. The PERCENT option can only be used with the HBAR statement.

REF=*value*

draws a single reference line on the response axis. For TYPE=FREQ or TYPE=CFREQ, the REF= option should be a frequency; for TYPE=PCT or TYPE=CPCT, the REF= option should be a percent between 1 and 100. For TYPE=SUM or TYPE=MEAN, the REF= option should be a sum or mean. The REF= option can only be used with the HBAR and VBAR statements.

SUBGROUP=*variable*

subdivides each bar into characters that show the SUBGROUP= variable's contribution to the bar. For example, the following statement produces a chart with one bar for each department:

```
vbar dept / subgroup=sex;
```

The portion of each bar filled in with the character **M** represents those observations that have a SEX value of **M**. The SUBGROUP= option can only be used with the HBAR, VBAR, and BLOCK statements.

The first character of the value is used to fill in the portion of the bar corresponding to the value unless more than one value begins with the same first character. In that case, the letters A, B, C, and so on are used. If the variable is formatted, PROC CHART uses the first character of the formatted value. The subgroup symbols are ordered A through Z and 0 through 9 with the characters in ascending order. You will notice, for example, that **Output 9.7** shown earlier in this chapter has the value **F** at the lower part of the bar chart and **M** on the upper part. The characters used in the chart and the values they represent are given in a legend at the bottom of the chart.

Missing values for a SUBGROUP= variable are treated as valid levels when a chart is produced.

PROC CHART calculates the height of the bar for each subgroup individually and then rounds each bar's percentage of the total bar up or down. Thus, the total height of the bar may be higher or lower than the same bar without the SUBGROUP= option.

If you use both TYPE=MEAN and the SUBGROUP= option, PROC CHART first calculates the mean for each variable listed in the SUMVAR= option, then subdivides the bar into the percentages contributed by each subgroup.

SUM

prints the total number of observations that each bar represents.

SUMVAR=*variable*

names the variable to collect summaries for means, sums, or frequencies. The SUMVAR= option is useful for producing bar charts showing total expenditures for each department or showing means at each level of an experiment. For example, the following statement produces a chart showing the mean yield for each location:

```
vbar location / type=mean sumvar=yield;
```

The next example charts total expenditures by department:

```
vbar dept / sumvar=expend;
```

If the SUMVAR= option is specified but the TYPE= value is not MEAN or SUM, then TYPE=SUM overrides whatever TYPE= value is specified.

SYMBOL=*'character-list'*

is used, when the SUBGROUP= option is *not* used, to define the symbol or symbols in the bars or blocks of the chart. The default SYMBOL= value is the asterisk (*). If the SAS system option OVP is set and your printing device supports overprinting, you can specify up to three characters in *character-list* to produce overprinted charts. For example, the following statements produce a chart of very thick, dark horizontal bars:

```
options ovp;
proc chart;
    hbar dept / symbol='XOA';
run;
```

The SYMBOL= option can only be used with the HBAR, VBAR, and BLOCK statements.

TYPE=*type*

specifies what the bars or sections in the chart represent. If the TYPE= option is omitted, the default TYPE is FREQ. When the SUMVAR= option is specified, the default TYPE is SUM. You can specify one of the following keywords for *type*:

> CFREQ   makes each bar or section represent cumulative frequency, which is the frequency for the group plus all the frequencies that precede it.
>
> CPERCENT | CPCT
> makes each bar represent the cumulative percentage of observations of the chart variable, which is the percentage of the group plus the percentages of all the groups that precede it.
>
> FREQ   makes each bar or section represent the frequency with which a value or range occurs for the chart variable in the data.

MEAN　makes each bar or section represent the mean of the SUMVAR= variable for observations having the bar's value. For example, the following statement produces a chart showing the mean sales for each department:

```
vbar dept / sumvar=sales type=mean;
```

PERCENT | PCT

makes each bar or section represent the percentage of observations of the chart variable having a given value or falling into a given range.

SUM　makes each bar or section represent the sum of the SUMVAR= variable for observations having the bar's value. For example, the following statement produces a chart with one bar or section for each DEPT value:

```
vbar dept / sumvar=sales type=sum;
```

The bar height for a given DEPT corresponds to the total of the SALES values for observations having that DEPT value.

DETAILS

Missing Values

If you use the MISSING option, missing values are not considered as valid levels for the chart variable. The MISSING option is available in all chart-request statements.

Missing values for a GROUP= or SUBGROUP= variable are treated as valid levels when a chart is produced.

Formatting Your Output Using the FORMCHAR= Option

The SAS system option FORMCHAR= and the FORMCHAR= option in the PROC CHART statement both define the characters used to print charts. If you set the FORMCHAR= option in the PROC CHART statement, it affects only PROC CHART output; if you set the SAS system option FORMCHAR=, it affects the output of all procedures that use the FORMCHAR= option.

PROC CHART uses 6 of the 20 possible form characters. **Table 9.7** shows all format characters available in PROC CHART and gives appropriate definitions.

Table 9.7 Form Characters Used in PROC CHART

Position in FORMCHAR= String	Task Performed	Default Character
1	Draws the vertical axes of vertical and horizontal bar charts and of block charts, and draws sides of blocks in block charts	|
2	Draws the horizontal axes of vertical and horizontal bar charts and of block charts, and indicates width of cells in block charts	—
7	Draws tic marks in vertical and horizontal bar charts, and marks the center in pie and star charts	+
9	Marks the intersection of axes in vertical and horizontal bar charts	—
16	Draws the ends of blocks in block charts, and indicates the depth of cells in block charts	/
20	Draws the circles in pie and star charts, and is used in blocks of block charts	*

For example, specifying

```
formchar(1,2,7)='   '
```

where the space indicated by the quote marks equals three blanks, produces charts with no outlines or dividers.

EXAMPLE

The statements below produce charts of summary statistics for three variables: DEPT, YEAR, and SEX. All variables are discrete: DEPT can have one of three values, YEAR can have one of six values, and SEX can have one of two values. The statements below produce **Output 9.13**.

```
data sales;
   title 'Department Sales For The Years 1982-1987';
   input dept :$7. sex :$1. wt p82 p83 p84 p85 p86 p87;
   year=1982; sales=p82; output;
   year=1983; sales=p83; output;
   year=1984; sales=p84; output;
   year=1985; sales=p85; output;
   year=1986; sales=p86; output;
   year=1987; sales=p87; output;
   cards;
parts   f 17   3500  2500   800   900 1100 2340
parts   m 21   3651  5391  4500  2301 4360 2357
parts   m 21   2644  3500  3000  4500 3240 1789
tools   f 12   5672  6100  7400  6789 5432 3569
tools   m 45   1253  4698  9345  3489 2319 4298
repairs f  2   9050 12062 15931 12890 8290 9980
repairs m  8   8941  9432 16837 13489 8756 8990
repairs m 16   9550 10351 14810 15340 9877 9880
;
run;

proc chart data=sales;
   hbar year/ sumvar=sales group=dept discrete;
   block dept / group=sex sumvar=sales;
   pie dept / freq=sales;
   vbar year / discrete subgroup=dept sumvar=sales;
title 'Results of Sales Data';
run;
```

Output 9.13 A Report Using PROC CHART and Summary Statistics

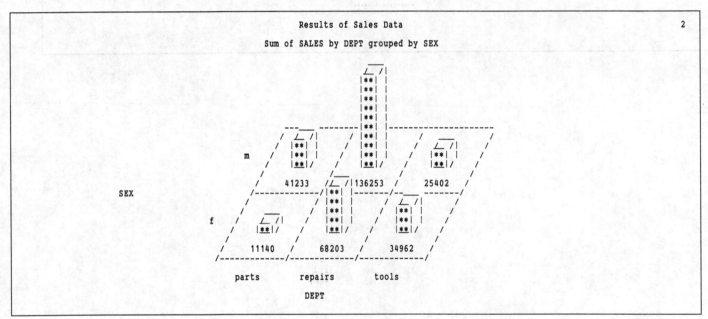

```
                              Results of Sales Data                                    1

DEPT    YEAR                                                            SALES
                                                               Freq       Sum
parts   1982   |********************                            3      9795.00
        1983   |************************                        3     11391.00
        1984   |*****************                               3      8300.00
        1985   |***************                                 3      7701.00
        1986   |******************                              3      8700.00
        1987   |*************                                   3      6486.00

repairs 1982   |********************************************************              3     27541.00
        1983   |*****************************************************************              3     31845.00
        1984   |*********************************************************************************************************              3     47578.00
        1985   |*********************************************************************************              3     41719.00
        1986   |******************************************************              3     26923.00
        1987   |**********************************************************              3     28850.00

tools   1982   |**************                                  2      6925.00
        1983   |**********************                          2     10798.00
        1984   |***********************************             2     16745.00
        1985   |*********************                           2     10278.00
        1986   |****************                                2      7751.00
        1987   |****************                                2      7867.00

        ---------+-------+-------+-------+-------+-------+-------+-------+-------+-------+-------+-------
             4000    8000   12000   16000   20000   24000   28000   32000   36000   40000   44000
                                        SALES Sum
```

Results of Sales Data   2

Sum of SALES by DEPT grouped by SEX

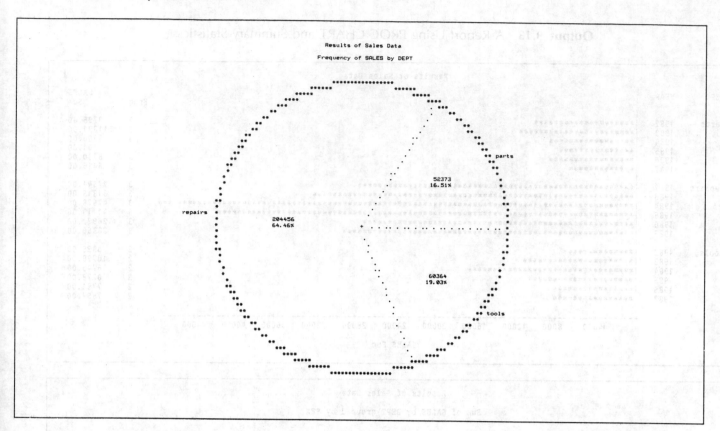

Results of Sales Data
Frequency of SALES by DEPT

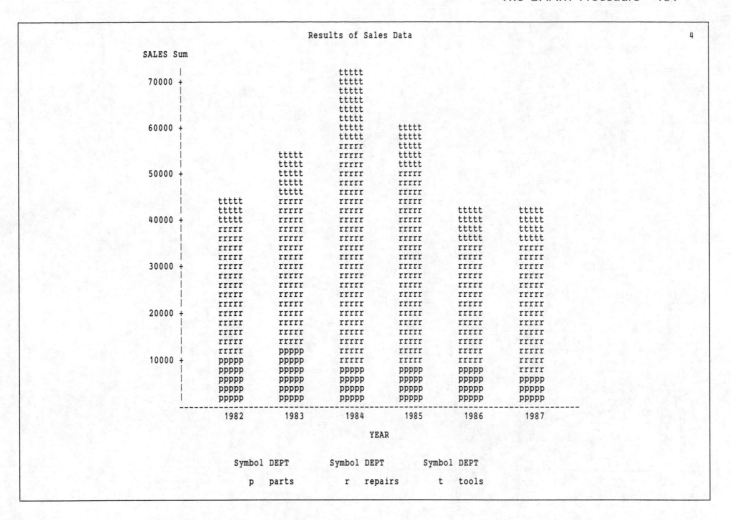

```
                          Results of Sales Data                              4

       SALES Sum
           |                                ttttt
     70000 +                                ttttt
           |                                ttttt
           |                                ttttt
           |                                ttttt
           |                                ttttt
     60000 +                                ttttt     ttttt
           |                                ttttt     ttttt
           |                                rrrrr     ttttt
           |                      ttttt     rrrrr     ttttt
           |                      ttttt     rrrrr     ttttt
     50000 +                      ttttt     rrrrr     rrrrr
           |                      ttttt     rrrrr     rrrrr
           |                      ttttt     rrrrr     rrrrr
           |            ttttt     rrrrr     rrrrr     rrrrr
           |            ttttt     rrrrr     rrrrr     rrrrr     ttttt     ttttt
     40000 +            ttttt     rrrrr     rrrrr     rrrrr     ttttt     ttttt
           |            rrrrr     rrrrr     rrrrr     rrrrr     ttttt     ttttt
           |            rrrrr     rrrrr     rrrrr     rrrrr     rrrrr     rrrrr
           |            rrrrr     rrrrr     rrrrr     rrrrr     rrrrr     rrrrr
           |            rrrrr     rrrrr     rrrrr     rrrrr     rrrrr     rrrrr
     30000 +            rrrrr     rrrrr     rrrrr     rrrrr     rrrrr     rrrrr
           |            rrrrr     rrrrr     rrrrr     rrrrr     rrrrr     rrrrr
           |            rrrrr     rrrrr     rrrrr     rrrrr     rrrrr     rrrrr
           |            rrrrr     rrrrr     rrrrr     rrrrr     rrrrr     rrrrr
           |            rrrrr     rrrrr     rrrrr     rrrrr     rrrrr     rrrrr
     20000 +            rrrrr     rrrrr     rrrrr     rrrrr     rrrrr     rrrrr
           |            rrrrr     rrrrr     rrrrr     rrrrr     rrrrr     rrrrr
           |            rrrrr     rrrrr     rrrrr     rrrrr     rrrrr     rrrrr
           |            rrrrr     rrrrr     rrrrr     rrrrr     rrrrr     rrrrr
           |            rrrrr     ppppp     rrrrr     rrrrr     rrrrr     rrrrr
     10000 +            ppppp     ppppp     rrrrr     rrrrr     rrrrr     rrrrr
           |            ppppp     ppppp     rrrrr     rrrrr     rrrrr     rrrrr
           |            ppppp     ppppp     ppppp     ppppp     ppppp     ppppp
           |            ppppp     ppppp     ppppp     ppppp     ppppp     ppppp
           |            ppppp     ppppp     ppppp     ppppp     ppppp     ppppp
           -----------------------------------------------------------------------
                         1982      1983      1984      1985      1986      1987

                                         YEAR


           Symbol DEPT       Symbol DEPT       Symbol DEPT

             p   parts         r   repairs       t   tools
```

The first chart in **Output 9.13** is a horizontal bar chart of sales data by department. The REPAIRS department has the highest sales. The second chart is a block chart of sales data, subdivided by department and by sex. The pie chart is another representation of sales data by department. The last chart is a vertical bar chart showing the annual sales by department.

REFERENCES

Nelder, J.A. (1976), "A Simple Algorithm for Scaling Graphs," *Applied Statistics*, Volume 25, Number 1, London: The Royal Statistical Society.

Terrell, G.R. and Scott, D.W. (1985), "Oversmoothed Nonparametric Density Estimates," *Journal of the American Statistical Association*, 80, 389, 209–214.

The CIMPORT Procedure

ABSTRACT

The CIMPORT procedure restores a transport file created by the CPORT procedure to its original form (a SAS data library, a SAS catalog, or a SAS data set) in the format appropriate to the host operating system. Coupled with the CPORT procedure, PROC CIMPORT allows you to move SAS catalogs and data sets from one operating system to another.

INTRODUCTION

This chapter uses the following terminology:

exporting
   is putting a SAS data library, a SAS catalog, or a SAS data set into
   transport format. The CPORT procedure exports catalogs and data sets,
   either singly or as a SAS data library.

importing
   is restoring a transport file to its original form (as a SAS data library, a
   SAS catalog, or a SAS data set) in the format appropriate to the host
   operating system. The CIMPORT procedure imports a transport file
   created by PROC CPORT.

a *transport file*

is a sequential file containing a SAS data library, a SAS catalog, or a SAS data set in transport format. The transport format written by PROC CPORT is the same for all operating systems and for many releases of the SAS System. Thus, Release 6.06 PROC CIMPORT running under any operating system can read a transport file created by Version 5, Release 6.03, or Release 6.06 PROC CPORT on any operating system. (See the definition of *converting* below for information on using the CPORT and CIMPORT procedures from different releases of the SAS System.)

Only PROC CIMPORT can read a transport file created by PROC CPORT. PROC CIMPORT can read only transport files created by PROC CPORT. For information on transport files created by the transport engine, refer to Chapter 6, "SAS Files," in *SAS Language: Reference, Version 6, First Edition.*

converting

a SAS file is changing its format from the format appropriate to one version of the SAS System to the format appropriate to another version running on the same operating system.

The CPORT and CIMPORT procedures are not primarily intended for converting files but for moving them from one operating system to another. You can use these procedures to move SAS catalogs and SAS data sets from an operating system running an earlier release of the SAS System to another operating system running a more recent release. In such a case, the CIMPORT procedure automatically converts the contents of the transport file as it imports it. However, because of the many enhancements in Release 6.06 of the SAS System, you cannot use the CPORT and CIMPORT procedures to move catalogs and data sets from an operating system running a newer release of the SAS System to an operating system running an older release.

Note: Although you can use the CPORT and CIMPORT procedures to convert some SAS files from Version 5 format to Version 6 format on the same operating system, it is simpler to use the V5TOV6 procedure (see Chapter 43, "The V5TOV6 Procedure.")

Some restrictions exist on the types of catalogs you can move from one operating system to another. See **DETAILS** for information on which SAS catalogs you can import.

To move Release 6.06 data sets and catalogs from one operating system to another, follow these steps:

1. Use PROC CPORT to export the SAS files you want to move.
2. Move the transport file to the new machine using either communications software or magnetic medium.

   Note: If you use communications software, be sure that it treats the transport file as a *binary* file and that it modifies neither the attributes nor the contents of the file.
3. Use PROC CIMPORT to translate the transport file into the format appropriate for the new host.

You can use a similar process to move catalogs and data sets from an operating system running Version 5 of the SAS System to an operating system running Release 6.06. However, keep in mind the following important points:

- You must use Version 5 PROC CPORT to export Version 5 catalogs.
- You cannot use Version 5 PROC CPORT to export data sets because in Version 5, PROC CPORT exports only catalogs. However, if the operating system running Version 5 is also running Release 6.06, you can create a transport file of data sets from a Version 5 library by using Release 6.06 PROC CPORT if you are accessing the Version 5 library with the Version 5 engine (see Chapter 6, "SAS Files," in *SAS Language: Reference*).

SPECIFICATIONS

The PROC CIMPORT statement is the only statement associated with the CIMPORT procedure.

PROC CIMPORT Statement

PROC CIMPORT *destination*=*libref*<*.member-name*> <*option-list*>;

where

destination   identifies the file or files in the transport file as a single catalog or as the members of a SAS data library. The *destination* argument can be one of the following:

CATALOG | CAT | C
LIBRARY | LIB | L

If the transport file was created by a version of PROC CPORT that can export SAS data sets (Release 6.03 or later), *destination* can also be

DATA | DS

libref<*.member-name*>

identifies a particular catalog, SAS data set, or SAS data library as the destination of the imported transport file. If the *destination* argument is CATALOG or DATA, specify both a libref and a member name. If the *destination* argument is LIBRARY, specify only a libref.

Table 10.1 summarizes the options you can use in the PROC CIMPORT statement. Descriptions of the options follow in alphabetic order.

Table 10.1 Summary of PROC CIMPORT Statement Options

Class	Option	Function
Options identifying the transport file	INFILE=	specifies the transport file to read
	TAPE	directs PROC CIMPORT to read from tape
Options selecting files to import	SELECT=	selects individual catalog entries to import
	EXCLUDE=	excludes individual catalog entries from the import process
Options affecting contents of the imported file	NOCOMPRESS	suppresses the compression of binary zeros and blanks in SAS catalogs and data sets created by PROC CIMPORT
Options for importing Version 5 SAS/AF PROGRAM entries	OPT	imports entries to optimized Version 6 programs
	NOOPT	imports entries without optimizing
	MODEV5	copies entries without modification

Some devices on some operating systems support options that specify the background color for Version 5 catalogs that you import. See the SAS documentation for your host system for details.

EXCLUDE=(entry-list)
:   excludes individual catalog entries from the import process. Each element of entry-list has the form

    entry.etype

    where entry is the name of the entry and etype is its entry type. Note that entry-list can be a single entry or a list of entries. If you specify a single entry, you do not need to enclose it in parentheses. (For information on entry types see SAS Language: Reference.)
    If the transport file contains more than one catalog in transport format, PROC CIMPORT searches all catalogs for entries named entry.etype.
    You cannot use the EXCLUDE= and SELECT= options in the same PROC CIMPORT step.

INFILE=fileref | 'filename'
:   specifies a previously defined fileref or the filename of the transport file to read. If you do not use the INFILE= option, the CIMPORT procedure reads from a file with the reserved fileref SASCAT.

Note: The behavior of the CIMPORT procedure when SASCAT is undefined varies from one operating system to another. See SAS documentation for your host system for details.

MODEV5

copies source of Version 5 SAS/AF PROGRAM entries without modification. You can neither compile nor execute the program under Version 6. This option is effective only when you are importing Version 5 catalogs.

If the program that created the entry you want to move contains an error, PROC CIMPORT may not be able to convert the entry to optimized Version 6 format. If it cannot make the conversion, the procedure invokes the NOOPT option. If it still cannot make the conversion, PROC CIMPORT invokes the MODEV5 option.

You may want to invoke the option if you want to

- save a copy of the Version 5 entry for an archive
- compare the Version 5 entry to its Version 6 counterpart.

For more information on this option, see SAS Technical Report P-195, *Transporting SAS Files between Host Systems.*

NOCOMPRESS

suppresses the compression of blanks and binary zeros in SAS catalogs and data sets created by PROC CIMPORT. PROC CIMPORT can compress these characters to save space. For instance, it can replace a string of 100 binary zeros with a shorter string that the SAS System recognizes as being equivalent to 100 binary zeros. The SAS System treats the compressed and noncompressed versions of a file identically. However, the compressed version may use considerably less storage space.

By default, the CIMPORT procedure imports each catalog and data set in the transport file in the form it originally had in the source file. If you use the NOCOMPRESS option on the PROC CIMPORT statement, the procedure imports each catalog and data set in the transport file as a noncompressed file.

NOOPT

imports source of Version 5 SAS/AF PROGRAM entries to Version 6 syntax without optimizing. This option is effective only when you are importing Version 5 catalogs.

If PROC CIMPORT cannot import the entry with the NOOPT option, it automatically invokes the MODEV5 option.

For more information on this option, see SAS Technical Report P-195.

OPT

imports source of Version 5 SAS/AF PROGRAM entries to optimized Version 6 programs. By default, PROC CIMPORT uses this option. If it cannot perform the optimization, it invokes the NOOPT option. This option is effective only when you are importing Version 5 catalogs.

For more information on this option, see SAS Technical Report P-195.

SELECT=(*entry-list*)

> selects individual catalog entries to import. Each element of *entry-list* has the following form:

> *entry.etype*

> where

> > *entry*   is the name of the entry or the name of a group of GRSEG entries

> > *etype*   is the entry type.

> Note that *entry-list* can be a single entry or a list of entries. If you specify a single entry, you do not need to enclose it in parentheses. (For information on entry types see *SAS Language: Reference*.)

> If the transport file contains more than one catalog in transport format, PROC CIMPORT searches all catalogs for entries named *entry.etype*.

> **Caution:** If an entry of the same name already exists at the destination, the new entry replaces the old one.

> You cannot use the SELECT= and EXCLUDE= options in the same PROC CIMPORT step.

TAPE

> directs PROC CIMPORT to read from tape. By default, the procedure reads from disk.

DETAILS

Characteristics of a Transport File

A transport file written by PROC CPORT always has a logical record length of 80 and, therefore, a fixed record format. However, the procedure cannot control the transport file's block size. On all operating systems except OS/2, for which block size has no meaning, you control the block size with a host-specific option on the FILENAME statement or with job control language. (See the SAS documentation for your host system for details.) While other block sizes may work, it is recommended that you always specify a block size of 8000 so that you do not have to determine the block size of each transport file before importing it.

If you have trouble importing a transport file, it may be because the block size or the logical record length is inappropriate. (You may need to execute a system utility to determine the block size and logical record length.)

If you always specify a block size of 8000 in the FILENAME statement or the job control language you use in conjunction with PROC CPORT, you should always be able to specify a block size of 8000 in the FILENAME statement or the job control language you use in conjunction with PROC CIMPORT. However, if the block size is not 8000, simply change the argument to the host-specific option in the FILENAME statement you use with PROC CIMPORT (or change your job control language) to reflect the actual block size. (See the SAS documentation for your host system for details.)

If the logical record length is not 80, it has changed since PROC CPORT created the transport file. PROC CIMPORT cannot read the file until you restore the logical record length to 80.

OS/2 is a registered trademark of International Business Machines Corporation.

Moving Version 5 SAS Catalogs to Release 6.06

You can use Version 5 PROC CPORT and Release 6.06 PROC CIMPORT to move the following types of Version 5 catalog entries to Release 6.06:

CBT	LETTER
CBTGO (AFGO in Version 6)	LIST
CBTSAVE (AFCBT in Version 6)	MENU
FORM	PROGRAM
HELP	SCREEN
KEYS	

The V5TOV6 procedure can convert additional types of catalog entries, but it cannot move the entries from one operating system to another.

For more information on moving Version 5 catalogs from one operating system to another, see SAS Technical Report P-195.

Moving Release 6.03 SAS Catalogs to Release 6.06

You can use Release 6.03 PROC CPORT and Release 6.06 PROC CIMPORT to move the following types of Release 6.03 catalog entries to Release 6.06:

AFCBT	DEVICE	HELP	MENU
AFGO	EDPARMS	LETTER	PROGRAM
AFMACRO	FORM	LIST	SCREEN
CBT			

Note: You cannot move KEYS entries from Release 6.03 to Release 6.06.

Moving Release 6.06 SAS Catalogs from One Operating System to Another

You can use the Release 6.06 CPORT and CIMPORT procedures to move the following types of Release 6.06 catalog entries from one operating system to another:

AFCBT	FORMAT	LIST
AFGO	FORMATC	LOG
AFMACRO	FORMULA	MENU
CBT	GRSEG	OUTPUT
CMAP	HELP	PMENU
DEVICE	INFMT	PROGRAM
EDPARMS	INFMTC	SCREEN
FONT	KEYS	SOURCE
FORM	LETTER	TEMPLATE

EXAMPLES

Because PROC CIMPORT does not write anything to SAS output, you can only tell if the procedure performs as you expect it to by looking at your SAS log. Always check your log when you are importing files.

Example 1: Importing an Entire Data Library

In the following example PROC CIMPORT reads from disk a transport file (TRAN-FILE) that PROC CPORT created from a SAS data library on another operating system. The procedure imports the transport file to a SAS data library (NEWLIBE) on the host operating system.

```
libname newlibe 'SAS-data-library';
filename tranfile 'transport-file-name'
                  host-option-for-block-size;

proc cimport library=newlibe infile=tranfile;
run;
```

Output 10.1 The Log Produced by Importing an Entire Data Library

```
NOTE: Libref NEWLIBE was successfully assigned as follows:
      Engine:        V606
      Physical Name: SAS-data-library
4
5            libname newlibe 'SAS-data-library';
6            filename tranfile 'transport-file-name' host-option-for-block-size;

7            proc cimport library=newlibe infile=tranfile;
8            run;
NOTE: Proc CIMPORT begins to create/update data set NEWLIBE.COTTON
NOTE: Data set contains 3 variables and 16 observations
      Logical record length is 24

NOTE: Proc CIMPORT begins to create/update data set NEWLIBE.DOW
NOTE: Data set contains 5 variables and 20 observations
      Logical record length is 40

NOTE: Proc CIMPORT begins to create/update data set NEWLIBE.GRADES
NOTE: Data set contains 4 variables and 50 observations
      Logical record length is 26

NOTE: Proc CIMPORT begins to create/update data set NEWLIBE.HIGHLOW
NOTE: Data set contains 5 variables and 34 observations
      Logical record length is 40

NOTE: Proc CIMPORT begins to create/update catalog NEWLIBE.PRECIP
NOTE: Importing entry RAIN    .PROGRAM
NOTE: Importing entry SLEET   .PROGRAM
NOTE: Importing entry SNOW    .PROGRAM
NOTE: Total number of entries processed: 3

NOTE: Proc CIMPORT begins to create/update catalog NEWLIBE.PROFILE
NOTE: Importing entry DMKEYS  .KEYS
NOTE: Total number of entries processed: 1

NOTE: Proc CIMPORT begins to create/update catalog NEWLIBE.TEMP
NOTE: Importing entry HIGH    .PROGRAM
NOTE: Importing entry LOW     .PROGRAM
NOTE: Total number of entries processed: 2
```

The log provides a record of the data sets and catalogs that the procedure imports.

Example 2:   Selecting Individual Catalog Entries

The following example selects the catalog entries RAIN.PROGRAM and SNOW.PROGRAM from the transport file OLDCATS, which was created from a single SAS catalog, and imports them to the SAS catalog CLIMATE.PRECIP.

```
libname climate 'SAS-data-library';
filename oldcats 'transport-file-name'
                  host-option-for-block-size;

proc cimport catalog=climate.precip infile=oldcats
             select=(rain.program snow.program);
run;
```

Output 10.2   The Log Produced by Importing Selected Catalog Entries

```
NOTE: Libref CLIMATE was successfully assigned as follows:
      Engine:        V606
      Physical Name: SAS-data-library
4
5          libname climate 'SAS-data-library';
6          filename oldcats 'transport-file-name' host-option-for-block-size;
7          proc cimport catalog=climate.precip infile=oldcats
8                       select=(rain.program snow.program);
9          run;

NOTE: Proc CIMPORT begins to create/update catalog CLIMATE.PRECIP
NOTE: Importing entry RAIN    .PROGRAM
NOTE: Importing entry SNOW    .PROGRAM
NOTE: Total number of entries processed: 2
```

The log shows that PROC CIMPORT imports only the catalog entries specified with the SELECT= option.

Example 3:   Moving a Single SAS Data Set

In this example PROC CIMPORT reads the transport file OLDDATA, which was created by PROC CPORT from a single SAS data set, and imports it to the data set NEWDATA.GRADES.

```
libname newdata 'SAS-data-library';
filename olddata 'transport-file-name'
                  host-option-for-block-size;

proc cimport data=newdata.grades infile=olddata;
run;
```

Output 10.3   The Log Produced by Importing a Single SAS Data Set

```
NOTE: Libref NEWDATA was successfully assigned as follows:
      Engine:        V606
      Physical Name: SAS-data-library
4
5           libname newdata 'SAS-data-library';
6           filename olddata 'transport-file-name' host-option-for-block-size;

7           proc cimport data=newdata.grades infile=olddata;
8           run;

NOTE: Proc CIMPORT begins to create/update data set NEWDATA.GRADES
NOTE: Data set contains 4 variables and 50 observations
      Logical record length is 26
```

Chapter 11

The COMPARE
Procedure

ABSTRACT

The COMPARE procedure compares the contents of two SAS data sets. You can also use PROC COMPARE to compare the values of different variables within a single data set. PROC COMPARE can produce a variety of reports on the comparisons it performs.

INTRODUCTION

The COMPARE procedure compares two SAS data sets: the *base data set* and the *comparison data set*. This chapter uses the following terminology:

matching variables
> are variables with the same name or variables that you explicitly pair by using the VAR and WITH statements.

matching observations
> are observations that have the same values for all ID variables you specify or, if you do not use the ID statement, that occur in the same position in the data sets. If you match observations by ID variables, both data sets must be sorted by all ID variables or have an appropriate index.

When the base data set and the comparison data set are different, PROC COMPARE first compares the following:

- data set attributes (set by the TYPE= and LABEL= options in the DATA statement)
- variables; that is, the COMPARE procedure checks each variable in one data set to determine whether it matches a variable in the other data set
- attributes (type, length, labels, formats, and informats) of matching variables
- observations; that is, the COMPARE procedure checks each observation in one data set to determine whether it matches an observation in the other data set.

After making these comparisons, PROC COMPARE compares the values in the parts of the data sets that match. See **Understanding a Simple Comparison** later in this chapter for an illustration of a simple comparison.

PROC COMPARE can report the results of its comparisons in any combination of the following four kinds of output:

- printed reports
- messages in the SAS log
- an output data set
- a numeric return code stored in the automatic macro variable &SYSINFO.

A wide selection of options enables you to control the kinds of output to produce, the kinds of comparisons to make, and the degree of detail to report.

Understanding a Simple Comparison

Consider the two data sets shown in **Figure 11.1**. For simplicity's sake assume that neither data set has a label or a type, and that variables with the same names have the same attributes.

Data Set 1

STUDENT	BIRTH	STATE
1000	1970	NC
1042	1971	MD
1204	1971	NC

Data Set 2

STUDENT	BIRTH	STATE	MAJOR
1000	1970	NC	MATH
1042	1971	MA	HISTORY

Figure 11.1   Data Sets to Compare

Assuming that STUDENT is the ID variable (the variable that determines which observations match), the data sets contain two matching variables: BIRTH and STATE. They also contain two matching observations, the observations with values of 1000 and 1042 for the ID variable, STUDENT.

Data Set 1 contains an observation (STUDENT=1204) for which Data Set 2 contains no matching observation. Similarly, no variable in Data Set 1 matches the variable MAJOR in Data Set 2.

Once PROC COMPARE has determined the matching variables and matching observations, it compares the values in the data sets. When it compares values, PROC COMPARE considers only values in the matching parts of the data sets (see **Figure 11.2**).

Data Set 1

STUDENT	BIRTH	STATE
1000	1970	NC
1042	1971	MD
1204	1971	NC

Data Set 2

STUDENT	BIRTH	STATE	MAJOR
1000	1970	NC	MATH
1042	1971	MA	HISTORY

Figure 11.2   PROC COMPARE Compares Only the Values Outlined

In this case the COMPARE procedure judges all values equal except the value of STATE in the observations with STUDENT=1042. PROC COMPARE reports this inequality as both

- a variable (STATE) with some observations unequal
- an observation (STUDENT=1042) with some compared variables unequal.

SPECIFICATIONS

The following statements control the COMPARE procedure:

> **PROC COMPARE** <*option-list*>;
>   **VAR** *variable-list*;
>   **WITH** *variable-list*;
>   **ID** <DESCENDING> *variable-1* <...<DESCENDING> *variable-n*>
>   <NOTSORTED>;
>   **BY** *variable-list*;

PROC COMPARE Statement

> **PROC COMPARE** <*option-list*>;

The COMPARE procedure supports a wide variety of options. Each option falls into one of five classes. **Table 11.1** summarizes the functions of the options. Descriptions of the options follow the table in alphabetic order.

Table 11.1 Summary of PROC COMPARE Statement Options

Specify Data Set Names	Specify Content of Output Data Set	Control Comparisons of Data Values	Control Detail in Printed Reports	Control Listing of Variables and Observations
BASE=	OUTALL	CRITERION=	ALLOBS	LISTALL
COMPARE=	OUTBASE	METHOD=	ALLSTATS	LISTBASE
OUT=	OUTCOMP	NOMISSBASE	ALLVARS	LISTBASEOBS
OUTSTATS=	OUTDIF	NOMISSCOMP	BRIEF	LISTBASEVAR
	OUTNOEQUAL	OUTNOEQUAL	FUZZ=	LISTCOMP
	OUTPERCENT		MAXPRINT=	LISTCOMPOBS
			NODATE	LISTCOMPVAR
			NOPRINT	LISTEQUALVAR
			NOSUMMARY	LISTOBS
			NOVALUES	LISTVAR
			PRINTALL	
			STATS	
			TRANSPOSE	

ALLOBS

includes in the report of value comparison results the values and, for numeric variables, the differences for all matching observations, whether or not they are judged equal. If you omit the ALLOBS option, PROC COMPARE prints values only for observations judged unequal.

When used with the TRANSPOSE option, the ALLOBS option invokes the ALLVARS option and displays the values for all matching observations and variables.

ALLSTATS

prints a table of summary statistics for all pairs of matching variables. See **The Summary Statistics Report** later in this chapter for information on the statistics produced.

ALLVARS

includes in the report of value comparison results the values and, for numeric variables, the differences for all pairs of matching variables, whether or not they are judged equal. If you omit the ALLVAR option, PROC COMPARE prints values only for variables judged unequal.

When used with the TRANSPOSE option, the ALLVARS option displays unequal values in context with the values for other matching variables. If you do not use the TRANSPOSE option, the ALLVARS option invokes the ALLOBS option and displays the values for all matching observations and variables.

BASE=*SAS-data-set*
DATA=*SAS-data-set*

name the data set to use as the base data set. If you omit the BASE= option, the COMPARE procedure uses the most recently created SAS data set.

Note: You can use the WHERE= data set option with the BASE= option to limit which observations are available for comparison. For example, the following statements consider all observations in the comparison data set, but only those observations from the base data set where STATE=NC:

```
proc compare base=one(where=(state=nc))
             compare=two;
run;
```

You can also use the WHERE statement in the PROC COMPARE step to limit the observations from both data sets. The following statements consider only those observations from both the base and comparison data sets where STATE=NC:

```
proc compare base=one
             compare=two;
  where state=nc;
run;
```

Refer to Chapter 9, "SAS Language Statements," and Chapter 15, "SAS Data Set Options," in *SAS Language: Reference, Version 6, First Edition* for more information on the WHERE statement and the WHERE= data set option.

BRIEFSUMMARY
BRIEF

produces a short comparison summary and suppresses the four default summary reports (data set summary report, variables summary report, observation summary report, and values comparison summary report).

Note: By default, a listing of value differences accompanies the summary reports. To suppress this listing, use the NOVALUES option.

COMPARE=*SAS-data-set*
COMP=*SAS-data-set*
C=*SAS-data-set*

names the data set to use as the comparison data set. If you omit the COMPARE= option, the comparison data set is the same as the base data set, and PROC COMPARE compares variables within the data set. If you omit the COMPARE= option, you must use the WITH statement.

You can use the WHERE= data set option with the COMPARE= option. For a discussion of the use of the WHERE= data set option and the WHERE statement, see the description of the BASE= option earlier in this chapter.

CRITERION=γ

specifies the criterion for judging the equality of numeric values. Normally, the value of γ is positive, in which case the number itself becomes the equality criterion. If you use a negative value for γ, PROC COMPARE uses an equality criterion proportional to the precision of the computer on which the SAS System is running. The default value for γ is 0.00001.

See **The Equality Criterion** later in this chapter for details.

ERROR

displays an error message in the SAS log when differences are found. This option overrides the WARNING option.

FUZZ=*number*

alters the display in the values comparison summary report of values with a magnitude less than *number*. The value of *number* must be between 0 and 1. The default value is 0.

PROC COMPARE prints a variable value whose magnitude is less than *number* as 0 and a difference or percent difference as a blank. A report containing many trivial differences is easier to read in this form.

LISTALL
LIST

lists all variables and observations found in only one data set. Using this option is equivalent to using the following four options: LISTBASEOBS, LISTCOMPOBS, LISTBASEVAR, and LISTCOMPVAR.

LISTBASE

lists all observations and variables found in the base data set but not in the comparison data set. Using this option is equivalent to using both the LISTBASEOBS and LISTBASEVAR options.

LISTBASEOBS

lists all observations found in the base data set but not in the comparison data set.

LISTBASEVAR

lists all variables found in the base data set but not in the comparison data set.

LISTCOMP

lists all observations and variables found in the comparison data set but not in the base data set. Using this option is equivalent to using both the LISTCOMPOBS and LISTCOMPVAR options.

LISTCOMPOBS

lists all observations found in the comparison data set but not in the base data set.

LISTCOMPVAR

lists all variables found in the comparison data set but not in the base data set.

LISTEQUALVAR

prints a list of variables whose values are judged equal at all observations in addition to the default list of variables whose values are judged unequal.

LISTOBS

lists all observations found in only one data set. Using this option is equivalent to using both the LISTBASEOBS and LISTCOMPOBS options.

LISTVAR

lists all variables found in only one data set. Using this option is equivalent to using both the LISTBASEVAR and LISTCOMPVAR options.

MAXPRINT=*total*
MAXPRINT=*(per-variable, total)*

specifies the maximum number of differences to print, where

> *total*   is the maximum total number of differences to print. The default value is 500 unless you use the ALLOBS option (or both the ALLVAR and TRANSPOSE options), in which case the default is 32000.

> *per-variable*
>
> is the maximum number of differences to print for each variable within a BY group. The default value is 50 unless you use the ALLOBS option (or both the ALLVAR and TRANSPOSE options), in which case the default is 1000.

The MAXPRINT= option prevents the output from becoming extremely large when data sets differ greatly.

METHOD=ABSOLUTE
    | EXACT
    | PERCENT
    | RELATIVE | RELATIVE(δ)

specifies the method for judging the equality of numeric values. The constant δ is a number between 0 and 1 that specifies a value to add to the denominator when calculating the equality measure. By default, δ is 0.

Unless you use the CRITERION= option, the default method is EXACT. If you use the CRITERION= option, the default method is RELATIVE(φ), where φ is a small number that depends on the numerical precision of the computer on which you are running the SAS System and on the value of the CRITERION= option.

See **The Equality Criterion** later in this chapter for details.

NODATE

suppresses the display in the data set summary report of the creation dates and the last modified dates of the base and comparison data sets.

NOMISSBASE

judges a missing value in the base data set equal to any value. (By default, a missing value is only equal to a missing value of the same kind, that is .=., .^=.A, .A=.A, .A^=.B, and so on.)

You can use this option to determine the changes that would be made to the observations in the comparison data set if it were used as the master data set and the base data set were used as the transaction data set in a DATA step UPDATE statement. For information on the UPDATE statement, see **Combining SAS Data Sets** in Chapter 4, "Rules of the SAS Language," in *SAS Language: Reference*.

NOMISSCOMP

judges a missing value in the comparison data set equal to any value. (By default, a missing value is only equal to a missing value of the same kind, that is .=., .^=.A, .A=.A, .A^=.B, and so on.)

You can use this option to determine the changes that would be made to the observations in the base data set if it were used as the master data set and the comparison data set were used as the transaction data set in a DATA step UPDATE statement. For information on the UPDATE statement, see **Combining SAS Data Sets** in Chapter 4 of *SAS Language: Reference*.

NOMISSING
NOMISS

judges missing values in both the base and comparison data sets equal to any value. (By default, a missing value is only equal to a missing value of the same kind, that is .=., .^=.A, .A=.A, .A^=.B, and so on.)

Using this option is equivalent to using both the NOMISSBASE and NOMISSCOMP options.

NOPRINT

suppresses all printed output. You may want to use this option when you are creating one or more output data sets.

NOSUMMARY

suppresses the data set, variable, observation, and values comparison summary reports.

NOTE

displays notes in the SAS log describing the results of the comparison, whether or not differences were found.

NOVALUES

suppresses the report of the value comparison results.

OUT=*SAS-data-set*

writes the differences between matching variables to the specified *SAS-data-set*.

OUTALL

writes an observation to the output data set for each observation in the base data set and for each observation in the comparison data set. The option also writes observations to the output data set containing the differences and percent differences between the values in matching observations. (See **Out= Data Set** later in this chapter.)

Using this option is equivalent to using the following four options: OUTBASE, OUTCOMP, OUTDIF, and OUTPERCENT.

OUTBASE

writes an observation to the output data set for each observation in the base data set, creating observations in which _TYPE_=BASE. (See **Out= Data Set** later in this chapter.)

OUTCOMP

> writes an observation to the output data set for each observation in the comparison data set, creating observations in which _TYPE_=COMP. (See **Out= Data Set** later in this chapter.)

OUTDIF

> writes an observation to the output data set for each pair of matching observations. The values in the observation include values for the differences between the values in the pair of observations. The value of _TYPE_ in each observation is DIF. (See **Out= Data Set** later in this chapter.)
>
> The OUTDIF option is the default unless you specify the OUTBASE, OUTCOMP, or OUTPERCENT option. If you use any of these options, you must explicitly invoke the OUTDIF option to create _TYPE_=DIF observations in the output data set.

OUTNOEQUAL

> suppresses the writing of an observation to the output data set when all values in the observation are judged equal. In addition, in observations containing values for some variables judged equal and others judged unequal, the OUTNOEQUAL option uses the special missing value ".E" to represent differences and percent differences for variables judged equal.

OUTPERCENT

> writes an observation to the output data set for each pair of matching observations. The values in the observation include values for the percent differences between the values in the pair of observations. The value of _TYPE_ in each observation is PERCENT. (See **Out= Data Set** later in this chapter.)

OUTSTATS=*SAS-data-set*

> writes summary statistics for all pairs of matching variables to the specified *SAS-data-set*. For a description of this data set, see **OUTSTATS= Data Set** and **The Summary Statistics Report** later in this chapter.
>
> Note: If you want to print a table of statistics in your SAS output, you must use the STATS or ALLSTATS option.

PRINTALL

> invokes the following options: ALLVARS, ALLOBS, ALLSTATS, LISTALL, and WARNING.

STATS

> prints a table of summary statistics for all pairs of matching numeric variables judged unequal. See **The Summary Statistics Report** later in this chapter for information on the statistics produced.

TRANSPOSE

> prints the reports of value differences by observation instead of by variable. If you also use the NOVALUES option, the TRANSPOSE option lists only the names of the variables whose values compare as unequal for each observation, not the values and differences.

WARNING

> displays a warning message in the SAS log when differences are found. The ERROR option overrides the WARNING option.

BY Statement

BY *variable-list*;

If you want to use a BY statement with PROC COMPARE, both the base and comparison data sets must be sorted by the BY variables or have an appropriate index. The nature of the comparison depends on whether all BY variables are in the comparison data set and, if they are, whether their attributes match those of the BY variables in the base data set. **Table 11.2** shows how PROC COMPARE behaves under different circumstances.

Table 11.2   BY Processing with PROC COMPARE

Condition	Behavior of PROC COMPARE
All BY variables are in the comparison data set and all attributes match exactly	Compares corresponding BY groups
None of the BY variables are in the comparison data set	Compares each BY group in the base data set with the entire comparison data set
Some BY variables are not in the comparison data set	Writes an error message to the SAS log and terminates
Some BY variables have different types in the two data sets	Writes an error message to the SAS log and terminates

ID Statement

ID <DESCENDING> *variable-1* <...<DESCENDING> *variable-n*> <NOTSORTED>;

The ID statement lists variables to use to match observations in the base data set with corresponding observations in the comparison data set. The ID variables also identify observations on the printed reports and in the output data set.

All ID variables must be in the base data set. If an ID variable is not found in the comparison data set, PROC COMPARE prints a warning on the SAS log and does not use that variable to match observations in the comparison data set (but does write it to the OUT= data set).

You should sort or index both data sets by the common ID variables (within the BY variables, if any) unless you specify the NOTSORTED option. The use of the DESCENDING option for ID variables must correspond to the use of the DESCENDING option in the BY statement or statements used to sort the data sets.

Note: If you use the DESCENDING option, you must sort the data sets. The SAS System does not use an index to process an ID statement with the DESCENDING option.

When you are comparing variables within a data set (by omitting the COMPARE= option), you do not need to sort or index the data set by the ID variables. If the data sets are neither sorted nor indexed by the common ID variables and you do not specify the NOTSORTED option, PROC COMPARE prints a warning message and continues to process the data sets as if you had specified the NOTSORTED option.

When the NOTSORTED option is specified, or if the ID statement is omitted, PROC COMPARE matches the observations one-to-one. That is, the COMPARE procedure matches the first observation in the base data set with the first observation in the comparison data set, the second with the second, and so on. When the ID statement is used with the NOTSORTED option, PROC COMPARE verifies that the ID values of corresponding observations are the same. If they are not, the COMPARE procedure prints an error message and terminates.

The observations in each data set should be uniquely labeled by the values of the ID variables. If PROC COMPARE finds two successive observations with the same ID values in a data set, it prints the warning "Duplicate Observations" for the first occurrence for that data set and prints the total number of duplicate observations found in the data set in the observation summary report. Note that when the data sets are not sorted, the COMPARE procedure detects only those duplicate observations that occur in succession.

VAR Statement

VAR *variable-list*;

The VAR statement restricts the comparison of the values of variables to those named in the VAR statement. If you do not use the VAR statement, PROC COMPARE compares the values of all matching variables except those appearing in BY and ID statements. If no variable in the comparison data set matches a variable in the VAR statement, PROC COMPARE writes a warning to the SAS log and ignores the variable.

Note: The VAR statement restricts only the comparison of values of matching variables. PROC COMPARE still reports on the total number of matching variables and compares their attributes. However, it produces neither error nor warning messages about these variables.

WITH Statement

WITH *variable-list*;

If you want to compare variables in the base data set with variables with different names in the comparison data set, specify the names of the variables in the base data set in the VAR statement and the names of the matching variables in the WITH statement. The first variable you list in the WITH statement corresponds to the first variable you list in the VAR statement, the second with the second, and so on. If the WITH statement list is shorter than the VAR statement list, PROC COMPARE assumes that the extra variables in the VAR statement have the same names in the comparison data set as they do in the base data set. If the WITH statement list is longer than the VAR statement list, PROC COMPARE ignores the extra variables.

A variable name can appear any number of times in the VAR statement or the WITH statement. By selecting VAR and WITH statement lists, you can compare the variables in any permutation.

If you omit the COMPARE= option, you must use the WITH statement. In this case the COMPARE procedure compares the values of variables with different names in the same data set.

You must use the VAR statement when you use the WITH statement.

DETAILS

OUT= Data Set

By default, the OUT= data set contains an observation for each pair of matching observations. The OUT= data set contains the following variables from the data sets you are comparing:

- all variables named in the BY statement
- all variables named in the ID statement
- all matching variables or, if you use the VAR statement, all variables listed in the VAR statement.

In addition, the data set contains two variables created by PROC COMPARE to identify the source of the values for the matching variables: _TYPE_ and _OBS_.

TYPE
: is a character variable of length 8. Its value indicates the source of the values for the matching (or VAR) variables in that observation. (For ID and BY variables, which are not compared, the values are the values from the original data sets.) The four possible values of this variable are as follows:

> BASE
> : The values in this observation are from an observation in the base data set. PROC COMPARE writes this type of observation to the OUT= data set when you specify the OUTBASE option.

> COMPARE
> : The values in this observation are from an observation in the comparison data set. PROC COMPARE writes this type of observation to the OUT= data set when you specify the OUTCOMP option.

> DIF
> : The values in this observation are the differences between the values in the base and comparison data sets. For character variables, PROC COMPARE uses a period (.) to represent equal characters and an X to represent unequal characters. PROC COMPARE writes this type of observation to the OUT= data set by default. However, if you request any other type of observation with the OUTBASE, OUTCOMP, or OUTPERCENT option, you must specify the OUTDIF option to generate observations of this type in the OUT= data set.

> PERCENT
> : The values in this observation are the percent differences between the values in the base and comparison data sets. For character variables the values in observations of type PERCENT are the same as the values in observations of type DIF.

OBS
: is a numeric variable containing a number further identifying the source of the OUT= observations.

For observations with _TYPE_ equal to BASE, _OBS_ is the number of the observation in the base data set from which the values of the VAR variables were copied. Similarly, for observations with _TYPE_ equal to COMPARE, _OBS_ is the number of the observation in the comparison data set from which the values of the VAR variables were copied.

For observations with _TYPE_ equal to **DIF** or **PERCENT**, _OBS_ is a sequence number that counts the matching observations in the BY group.

Output 11.1 shows an example of an OUT= data set.

Output 11.1   An OUT= Data Set

```
                              An OUT= Data Set                                 1

         OBS    _TYPE_     _OBS_     A     B     C

          1     BASE         1       1     2     cat
          2     COMPARE      1       1     2     bat
          3     DIF          1       0     0     X.......
          4     PERCENT      1       0     0     X.......
          5     BASE         2       3     4     mouse
          6     COMPARE      2       3     4     mountain
          7     DIF          2       0     0     ...XXXXX
          8     PERCENT      2       0     0     ...XXXXX
          9     BASE         3       5     6     duck
         10     COMPARE      3       5     6     gander
         11     DIF          3       0     0     XXXXXX..
         12     PERCENT      3       0     0     XXXXXX..
         13     BASE         4       7     8     goose
```

You can see from the variables in this OUT= data set that the COMPARE procedure compared the variables A, B, and C. Each observation in the OUT= data set relates to the values of these variables in the base and comparison data sets. For instance, in the sixth observation in the OUT= data set, the value of _TYPE_ is **COMPARE** and the value of _OBS_ is 2. These values indicate that the observation contains the values of A, B, and C from the second observation in the comparison data set. Similarly, the seventh observation contains the differences between the values of A, B, and C in the second observation of the base data set and their values in the second observation in the comparison data set.

The COMPARE procedure takes variable names and attributes for the OUT= data set from the base data set except for the lengths of ID and VAR variables, for which it uses the longer length regardless of which data set that length is from. This behavior has two important repercussions:

- If you use the VAR and WITH statements, the names of the variables in the OUT= data set come from the VAR statement. Thus, observations with _TYPE_ equal to **BASE** contain the values of the VAR variables, while observations with _TYPE_ equal to **COMPARE** contain the values of the WITH variables.
- If you include a variable more than once in the VAR statement in order to compare it with more than one variable, PROC COMPARE can include only the first comparison in the OUT= data set because each variable must have a unique name. Other comparisons produce warning messages.

OUTSTATS= Data Set

When you use the OUTSTATS= option, PROC COMPARE calculates the same summary statistics as the ALLSTATS option for each pair of numeric variables compared (see **The Summary Statistics Report**). The OUTSTATS= data set contains an observation for each summary statistic for each pair of variables. The data set also contains the BY variables used in the comparison and several variables created by PROC COMPARE. Descriptions of these variables follow.

VAR
> is a character variable containing the name of the variable from the base data set for which the statistic in the observation was calculated.

WITH
> is a character variable containing the name of the variable from the comparison data set for which the statistic in the observation was calculated. The _WITH_ variable is not included in the OUTSTATS= data set unless you use the WITH statement.

TYPE
> is a character variable containing the name of the statistic contained in the observation. Values of the _TYPE_ variable are N, MEAN, STD, MIN, MAX, STDERR, T, PROBT, NDIF, DIFMEANS, and R,RSQ.

BASE
> is a numeric variable containing the value of the statistic calculated from the values of the variable named by _VAR_ in the observations in the base data set with matching observations in the comparison data set.

COMP
> is a numeric variable containing the value of the statistic calculated from the values of the variable named by the _VAR_ variable (or by the _WITH_ variable if you use the WITH statement) in the observations in the comparison data set with matching observations in the base data set.

DIF
> is a numeric variable containing the value of the statistic calculated from the differences of the values of the variable named by the _VAR_ variable in the base data set and the matching variable (named by the _VAR_ or _WITH_ variable) in the comparison data set.

PCTDIF
> is a numeric variable containing the value of the statistic calculated from the percent differences of the values of the variable named by the _VAR_ variable in the base data set and the matching variable (named by the _VAR_ or _WITH_ variable) in the comparison data set.

For example, the following SAS statements produce an OUTSTATS= data set containing 11 observations. The value of the _VAR_ variable for all observations is X; the value of the _WITH_ variable for all observations is Y.

```
proc compare base=dataset1 outstats=tempout;
   var x;
   with y;
run;
```

The output in **Example 6** later in this chapter includes an OUTSTATS= data set.

The Equality Criterion

The COMPARE procedure judges numeric values unequal if the magnitude of their difference, as measured according to the METHOD= option, is greater than the value of the CRITERION= option. PROC COMPARE provides four methods for applying the CRITERION= option:

- The EXACT method tests for exact equality.
- The ABSOLUTE method compares the absolute difference to the value specified by the CRITERION= option.

- The RELATIVE method compares the absolute relative difference to the value specified by the CRITERION= option.
- The PERCENT method compares the absolute percent difference to the value specified by the CRITERION= option.

For a numeric variable compared, let x be its value in the base data set and let y be its value in the comparison data set. If both x and y are nonmissing, the values are judged unequal according to the value of the METHOD= option and the value of the CRITERION= option (γ) as described below.

- If METHOD=EXACT, the values are unequal if y does not equal x.
- If METHOD=ABSOLUTE, the values are unequal if

$$ABS(y - x) > \gamma$$

- If METHOD=RELATIVE, the values are unequal if

$$ABS(y - x) / ((ABS(x) + ABS(y)) / 2 + \delta) > \gamma$$

The values are equal if $x=y=0$.
- If METHOD=PERCENT, the values are unequal if

$$ABS(y - x) / ABS(x)*100 > \gamma \quad \text{for } x \neq 0$$

or

$$y \neq 0 \quad \text{for } x = 0 \quad .$$

If x or y is missing, then the comparison depends on the NOMISSING option. If the NOMISSING option is in effect, a missing value will always compare equal to anything. Otherwise, a missing value is judged equal only to a missing value of the same type, (that is, .=., .^=.A, .A=.A, .A^=.B, and so on).

If the value specified for the CRITERION= option is negative, the actual criterion used is made equal to the absolute value of γ times a very small number ε that depends on the numerical precision of the computer. This number ε is defined as the smallest positive floating-point value such that, using machine arithmetic, $1-\varepsilon<1<1+\varepsilon$. Round-off or truncation error in floating-point computations is typically a few orders of magnitude larger than ε. This means that CRITERION=-1000 often provides a reasonable test of the equality of computed results at the machine level of precision.

The value δ added to the denominator in the RELATIVE method is specified in parentheses after the method name: METHOD=RELATIVE(δ). If not specified in the METHOD= option, δ defaults to 0. The value of δ can be used to control the behavior of the error measure when both x and y are very close to 0. If δ is not given and x and y are very close to 0, any error produces a large relative error (in the limit, 2).

Specifying a value for δ avoids this extreme sensitivity of the RELATIVE method for small values. If you specify METHOD=RELATIVE(δ) CRITERION=γ when both x and y are much smaller than δ in absolute value, the comparison is as if you had specified METHOD=ABSOLUTE CRITERION=$\delta\gamma$. However, when either x or y is much larger than δ in absolute value, the comparison is like METHOD=RELATIVE CRITERION=γ. For moderate values of x and y, METHOD=RELATIVE(δ) CRITERION=γ is, in effect, a compromise between METHOD=ABSOLUTE CRITERION=$\delta\gamma$ and METHOD=RELATIVE CRITERION=γ.

For character variables, if one value has a greater length than the other, the shorter value is padded with blanks for the comparison. Nonblank character values are judged equal only if they agree at each character. If the NOMISSING option is in effect, blank character values compare equal to anything.

Definition of Difference and Percent Difference

In the reports of value comparisons and in the OUT= data set, PROC COMPARE displays difference and percent difference values for the numbers compared. These quantities are defined using the value from the base data set as the reference value. For a numeric variable compared, let x be its value in the base data set and let y be its value in the comparison data set. If x and y are both nonmissing, the difference and percent difference are defined as follows:

$$\text{Difference} = y - x$$

$$\text{Percent Difference} = (y - x) / x * 100 \quad \text{for } x \neq 0$$

$$= \text{missing} \quad \text{for } x = 0.$$

Macro Return Codes (&SYSINFO)

PROC COMPARE encodes in a numeric variable a summary of the kinds of differences it finds. It stores this number in the automatic macro variable &SYSINFO. By checking the value of &SYSINFO after PROC COMPARE has run and before any other step begins, SAS macros can use the results of a PROC COMPARE step to determine what action to take or what parts of a SAS program to execute.

Below is a key for interpreting the &SYSINFO return code from PROC COMPARE. For each of the conditions listed, the associated value is added to the return code if the condition is true. Thus, the &SYSINFO return code is the sum of the following codes for the applicable conditions:

Bit	Condition	Code	Hex	Description
1	DSLABEL	1	0001X	Data set LABEL= options differ
2	DSTYPE	2	0002X	Data set TYPE= options differ
3	INFORMAT	4	0004X	Variable has different informat
4	FORMAT	8	0008X	Variable has different format
5	LENGTH	16	0010X	Variable has different length
6	LABEL	32	0020X	Variable has different label
7	BASEOBS	64	0040X	Base data set has observation not in comparison
8	COMPOBS	128	0080X	Comparison data set has observation not in base
9	BASEBY	256	0100X	Base data set has BY group not in comparison
10	COMPBY	512	0200X	Comparison data set has BY group not in base
11	BASEVAR	1024	0400X	Base data set has variable not in comparison
12	COMPVAR	2048	0800X	Comparison data set has variable not in base
13	VALUE	4096	1000X	A value comparison was unequal
14	TYPE	8192	2000X	Conflicting variable types
15	BYVAR	16384	4000X	BY variables do not match
16	ERROR	32768	8000X	Fatal error: comparison not done

These codes are ordered and scaled to allow a simple check of the degree to which the data sets differ. For example, if you want to check that two data sets contain the same variables, observations, and values, but you do not care about differences in labels, formats, and so forth, you can use the following statements:

```
proc compare ...;
run;

%if &sysinfo >= 64 %then
   %do;
      handle error;
   %end;
```

You can examine individual bits in the &SYSINFO value by using DATA step bit-testing features to check for specific conditions. For example, to check for the presence of observations in the base data set that are not in the comparison data set, you can use the following statements:

```
proc compare ...;
run;

%let rc=&sysinfo;
data _null_;
   if &rc='1......'b then
      put 'Observations in Base but not in Comparison Data Set';
run;
```

Note that PROC COMPARE must run before you check &SYSINFO and that you must obtain the &SYSINFO value before another SAS step starts because every SAS step resets &SYSINFO.

Reports Printed

PROC COMPARE produces a variety of reports. These reports are described below and illustrated in the output shown in **EXAMPLES** later in this chapter. The format for most reports is very flexible. A variety of options suppresses and adds to the basic reports described here (see **Table 11.1** for a list of options affecting reports and **SPECIFICATIONS** for a description of each option, both earlier in this chapter).

The Data Set Summary Report

This report lists the attributes of the data sets being compared. These attributes include the following:

- the data set names
- the data set types (assigned with the TYPE= option in the DATA step), if any
- the data set labels (assigned with the LABEL= option in the DATA step), if any
- the dates created and last modified
- the number of variables in each data set
- the number of observations in each data set.

You can suppress the data set summary report with the NOSUMMARY or BRIEFSUMMARY options.

The Variables Summary Report

This report compares the variables in the two data sets (but not the values of the variables; see **The Values Comparison Summary Report** later in this chapter). The first part of the report lists the following:

- the number of variables the data sets have in common
- the number of variables in the base data set that are not in the comparison data set and vice versa
- the number of variables in both data sets that have different types
- the number of variables that differ on other attributes (length, label, format, or informat)
- the number of BY, ID, VAR, and WITH variables specified for the comparison.

The second part of the report lists matching variables with different attributes and shows how the attributes differ. (The COMPARE procedure omits variable labels if the line size is too small for them.)

You can suppress the variables summary report with the NOSUMMARY or BRIEFSUMMARY options.

The Observation Summary Report

This report provides information about observations in the base and comparison data sets. First of all, the report identifies the first and last observation in each data set, the first and last matching observations, and the first and last differing observations. Then, the report lists the following:

- the number of observations that the data sets have in common
- the number of observations in the base data set that are not in the comparison data set and vice versa
- the total number of observations in each data set
- the number of matching observations for which the COMPARE procedure judged some variables unequal
- the number of matching observations for which the COMPARE procedure judged all variables equal.

You can suppress the observation summary report with the NOSUMMARY or BRIEFSUMMARY options.

The Values Comparison Summary Report

This report consists of two parts. The first part lists the following:

- the number of variables compared with all observations equal
- the number of variables compared with some observations unequal
- the number of variables with differences involving missing values
- the total number of values judged unequal
- the maximum difference measure between unequal values for all pairs of matching variables (for differences not involving missing values).

The second part of the report is a table listing the variables for which some matching observations have unequal values. The table shows

- the name of the variable
- other variable attributes
- the number of times the COMPARE procedure judged the variable unequal

- the maximum difference measure found between values (for differences not involving missing values)
- the number of differences caused by comparison with missing values.

You can suppress the values comparison summary report with the NOSUMMARY or BRIEFSUMMARY options.

The Value Comparison Results

The value comparison results for variables (or for observations if you use the TRANSPOSE option) consist of a table for each pair of matching variables judged unequal at one or more observations. When comparing character values, PROC COMPARE displays only the first 12 characters. Each table shows

- the number of the observation or, if you use the ID statement, the values of the ID variables
- the value of the variable in the base data set
- the value of the variable in the comparison data set
- the difference between these two values (numeric variables only)
- the percent difference between these two values (numeric variables only).

If you use the TRANSPOSE option, PROC COMPARE prints the value comparison results by observation instead of by variable. In this case, the value comparison results precede the observation summary report. By default, the source of the values for each row of the table is indicated by the following label:

_OBS_1=number-1 _OBS_2=number-2

where *number-1* is the number of the observation in the base data set for which the value of the variable is shown, and *number-2* is the number of the observation in the comparison data set.

If you use an ID statement, the identifying label has the following form:

ID-1=ID-value-1...ID-n=ID-value-n

where *ID* is the name of an ID variable and *ID-value* is the value of the ID variable.

You can suppress the value comparison results with the NOVALUES option. If you use both the NOVALUES and TRANSPOSE options, PROC COMPARE lists for each observation the names of the variables with values judged unequal but does not display the values and differences.

The Summary Statistics Report

You can use the STATS or ALLSTATS option to request a table of summary statistics for the variables being compared. The STATS option generates these statistics for only the variable pairs whose values are judged unequal, while the ALLSTATS option generates statistics for all the variable pairs. The OUTSTATS= option writes these statistics to an output data set.

Note: In all cases PROC COMPARE calculates the summary statistics based on all matching observations that do not contain missing values, not just on those containing unequal values.

The statistics table consists of two parts. The first part shows the following summary statistics for base data set values, comparison data set values, differences, and percent differences:

N	the number of nonmissing values
MEAN	the mean, or average, of the values
STD	the standard deviation
MAX	the maximum value
MIN	the minimum value
STDERR	the standard error of the mean
T	the T ratio (MEAN/STDERR)
PROB > |T|	the probability of a greater absolute T value if the true population mean is 0.

The second part of the table contains these statistics:

NDIF	the number of matching observations judged unequal, and the percent of the matching observations that were judged unequal.
DIFMEANS	the difference between the mean of the base values and the mean of the comparison values. This line contains three numbers. The first is the mean expressed as a percentage of the base values mean. The second is the mean expressed as a percentage of the comparison values mean. The third is the difference in the two means (the comparison mean minus the base mean).
R	the correlation of the base and comparison values for matching observations that are nonmissing in both data sets.
RSQ	the square of the correlation of the base and comparison values for matching observations that are nonmissing in both data sets.

Note: For character variables PROC COMPARE calculates only NDIF.

EXAMPLES

Example 1:   Default Report of the Differences between Two Data Sets

This example creates and displays two similar data sets. Then, PROC COMPARE is used with no options specified to compare the data sets STUDENTS.ONE and STUDENTS.TWO. The COMPARE procedure generates the following reports (numbers correspond to the numbers in the output):

1. data set summary
2. variables summary
3. observation summary
4. values comparison summary
5. value comparison results for all variables judged unequal.

The following statements produce **Output 11.2**:

```
libname students 'SAS-data-library';

data students.one(label='First Data Set');
   input student year state $ grade1 grade2;
   label year='Year of Birth';
   format grade1 4.1;
   cards;
1000 1970 NC 85 87
1042 1971 MD 92 92
1095 1969 PA 78 72
1187 1970 MA 87 94
;
run;

data students.two(label='Second Data Set');
   input student $ year state $ grade1 grade2 major $;
   label state='Home State';
   format grade1 5.2;
   cards;
1000 1970 NC 84 87 Math
1042 1971 MA 92 92 History
1095 1969 PA 79 73 Physics
1187 1970 MD 87 74 Dance
1204 1971 NC 82 96 French
;
run;

proc print data=students.one;
   title 'The Data Set STUDENTS.ONE';
run;

proc print data=students.two;
   title 'The Data Set STUDENTS.TWO';
run;

proc compare base=students.one compare=students.two;
   title 'Comparing Two Data Sets: Default Report';
run;
```

Output 11.2   Comparing Two Data Sets with No Options in the
PROC COMPARE Statement

```
                    The Data Set STUDENTS.ONE                              1

         OBS    STUDENT    YEAR    STATE    GRADE1    GRADE2

          1      1000      1970     NC      85.0       87
          2      1042      1971     MD      92.0       92
          3      1095      1969     PA      78.0       72
          4      1187      1970     MA      87.0       94
```

```
                    The Data Set STUDENTS.TWO                              2

         OBS    STUDENT    YEAR    STATE    GRADE1    GRADE2    MAJOR

          1      1000      1970     NC      84.00       87     Math
          2      1042      1971     MA      92.00       92     History
          3      1095      1969     PA      79.00       73     Physics
          4      1187      1970     MD      87.00       74     Dance
          5      1204      1971     NC      82.00       96     French
```

```
               Comparing Two Data Sets: Default Report                    3

                          COMPARE Procedure
                 Comparison of STUDENTS.ONE with STUDENTS.TWO
                            (Method=EXACT)

                    ❶      Data Set Summary

Dataset              Created           Modified     NVar    NObs    Label

STUDENTS.ONE   12SEP89:10:39:52   12SEP89:10:39:52    5       4    First Data Set
STUDENTS.TWO   12SEP89:10:39:53   12SEP89:10:39:53    6       5    Second Data Set


                    ❷      Variables Summary

          Number of Variables in Common: 5.
          Number of Variables in STUDENTS.TWO but not in STUDENTS.ONE: 1.
          Number of Variables with Conflicting Types: 1.
          Number of Variables with Differing Attributes: 3.


          Listing of Common Variables with Conflicting Types

                Variable  Dataset        Type  Length

                STUDENT   STUDENTS.ONE   Num      8
                          STUDENTS.TWO   Char     8


          Listing of Common Variables with Differing Attributes

          Variable  Dataset        Type  Length  Format  Label

          YEAR      STUDENTS.ONE   Num      8             Year of Birth
                    STUDENTS.TWO   Num      8
          STATE     STUDENTS.ONE   Char     8
                    STUDENTS.TWO   Char     8             Home State
          GRADE1    STUDENTS.ONE   Num      8     4.1
                    STUDENTS.TWO   Num      8     5.2
```

(continued on next page)

(continued from previous page)

```
          ❸     Observation Summary

             Observation     Base   Compare

             First  Obs        1       1
             First  Unequal     1       1
             Last   Unequal     4       4
             Last   Match       4       4
             Last   Obs         .       5

Number of Observations in Common: 4.
Number of Observations in STUDENTS.TWO but not in STUDENTS.ONE: 1.
Total Number of Observations Read from STUDENTS.ONE: 4.
Total Number of Observations Read from STUDENTS.TWO: 5.

Number of Observations with Some Compared Variables Unequal: 4.
Number of Observations with All Compared Variables Equal: 0.
```

```
                    Comparing Two Data Sets: Default Report                    4

                           COMPARE Procedure
                 Comparison of STUDENTS.ONE with STUDENTS.TWO
                              (Method=EXACT)
          ❹     Values Comparison Summary

Number of Variables Compared with All Observations Equal: 1.
Number of Variables Compared with Some Observations Unequal: 3.
Total Number of Values which Compare Unequal: 6.
Maximum Difference: 20.


                       Variables with Unequal Values

        Variable  Type  Len   Compare Label   Ndif   MaxDif

        STATE     CHAR   8     Home State        2
        GRADE1    NUM    8                       2     1.000
        GRADE2    NUM    8                       2    20.000


          ❺     Value Comparison Results for Variables


                 ||  Home State
                 ||  Base Value       Compare Value
           Obs   ||  STATE            STATE
          _____||_____
                 ||
            2    ||  MD               MA
            4    ||  MA               MD
          _____


                 ||    Base     Compare
           Obs   ||   GRADE1    GRADE1      Diff.     % Diff
          _____||_____
                 ||
            1    ||    85.0      84.00    -1.0000    -1.1765
            3    ||    78.0      79.00     1.0000     1.2821
          _____


                 ||    Base     Compare
           Obs   ||   GRADE2    GRADE2      Diff.     % Diff
          _____||_____
                 ||
            3    ||  72.0000    73.0000    1.0000     1.3889
            4    ||  94.0000    74.0000  -20.0000   -21.2766
          _____
```

Example 2: Full Report of the Differences between Two Data Sets

This example compares the same data sets as the previous example, but it uses the PRINTALL option to display the full range of reports PROC COMPARE can produce. In addition to the reports shown in **Output 11.2**, this example includes a listing of variables found in one data set but not the other (numbered 6 in the output) and a similar listing of observations (numbered 7 in the output). The statements below produce **Output 11.3**.

```
libname students 'SAS-data-library';

proc compare base=students.one compare=students.two printall;
    title 'Comparing Two Data Sets: Full Report';
run;
```

Output 11.3 Producing a Full Report on the Differences between Two Data Sets

```
                        Comparing Two Data Sets: Full Report                        1

                                 COMPARE Procedure
                       Comparison of STUDENTS.ONE with STUDENTS.TWO
                                   (Method=EXACT)

                                  Data Set Summary

        Dataset          Created         Modified   NVar   NObs  Label

        STUDENTS.ONE  12SEP89:10:39:52  12SEP89:10:39:52    5      4  First Data Set
        STUDENTS.TWO  12SEP89:10:39:53  12SEP89:10:39:53    6      5  Second Data Set


                                  Variables Summary

                Number of Variables in Common: 5.
                Number of Variables in STUDENTS.TWO but not in STUDENTS.ONE: 1.
                Number of Variables with Conflicting Types: 1.
                Number of Variables with Differing Attributes: 3.

   ❻           Listing of Variables in STUDENTS.TWO but not in STUDENTS.ONE

                              Variable   Type   Length

                              MAJOR      Char       8


                    Listing of Common Variables with Conflicting Types

                        Variable  Dataset        Type  Length

                        STUDENT   STUDENTS.ONE   Num       8
                                  STUDENTS.TWO   Char      8


                    Listing of Common Variables with Differing Attributes

           Variable  Dataset        Type  Length  Format  Label

           YEAR      STUDENTS.ONE   Num       8                   Year of Birth
                     STUDENTS.TWO   Num       8
           STATE     STUDENTS.ONE   Char      8
                     STUDENTS.TWO   Char      8                   Home State
           GRADE1    STUDENTS.ONE   Num       8    4.1
                     STUDENTS.TWO   Num       8    5.2
```

```
                    Comparing Two Data Sets: Full Report                        2

                            COMPARE Procedure
                  Comparison of STUDENTS.ONE with STUDENTS.TWO
                              (Method=EXACT)
      ❼          Comparison Results for Observations

        Observation 5 in STUDENTS.TWO not found in STUDENTS.ONE.


                          Observation Summary

                   Observation      Base  Compare

                   First Obs           1        1
                   First Unequal       1        1
                   Last  Unequal       4        4
                   Last  Match         4        4
                   Last  Obs           .        5

        Number of Observations in Common: 4.
        Number of Observations in STUDENTS.TWO but not in STUDENTS.ONE: 1.
        Total Number of Observations Read from STUDENTS.ONE: 4.
        Total Number of Observations Read from STUDENTS.TWO: 5.

        Number of Observations with Some Compared Variables Unequal: 4.
        Number of Observations with All Compared Variables Equal: 0.


                        Values Comparison Summary

        Number of Variables Compared with All Observations Equal: 1.
        Number of Variables Compared with Some Observations Unequal: 3.
        Total Number of Values which Compare Unequal: 6.
        Maximum Difference: 20.


                        Variables with All Equal Values

                   Variable  Type  Len   Label

                   YEAR      NUM    8    Year of Birth

                        Variables with Unequal Values

           Variable  Type  Len   Compare Label  Ndif    MaxDif

              STATE   CHAR   8    Home State        2
              GRADE1  NUM    8                      2     1.000
              GRADE2  NUM    8                      2    20.000
```

Comparing Two Data Sets: Full Report　　　　　　　　3

COMPARE Procedure
Comparison of STUDENTS.ONE with STUDENTS.TWO
(Method=EXACT)

Value Comparison Results for Variables

Obs	Year of Birth Base YEAR	Compare YEAR	Diff.	% Diff	Home State Base Value STATE	Compare Value STATE
1	1970	1970	0	0	NC	NC
2	1971	1971	0	0	MD	MA
3	1969	1969	0	0	PA	PA
4	1970	1970	0	0	MA	MD
N	4	4	4	4		
Mean	1970	1970	0	0		
Std	0.8165	0.8165	0	0		
Max	1971	1971	0	0		
Min	1969	1969	0	0		
StdErr	0.4082	0.4082	0	0		
t	4825.4948	4825.4948	.	.		
Prob>|t|	0.0001	0.0001	.	.		
Ndif	0	0.000%			2	50.000%
DifMeans	0.000%	0.000%	0			
r, rsq	1.000	1.000				

Obs	Base GRADE1	Compare GRADE1	Diff.	% Diff	Base GRADE2	Compare GRADE2	Diff.	% Diff
1	85.0	84.00	-1.0000	-1.1765	87.0000	87.0000	0	0
2	92.0	92.00	0	0	92.0000	92.0000	0	0
3	78.0	79.00	1.0000	1.2821	72.0000	73.0000	1.0000	1.3889
4	87.0	87.00	0	0	94.0000	74.0000	-20.0000	-21.2766
N	4	4	4	4	4	4	4	4
Mean	85.5000	85.5000	0	0.0264	86.2500	81.5000	-4.7500	-4.9719
Std	5.8023	5.4467	0.8165	1.0042	9.9457	9.4692	10.1776	10.8895
Max	92.0000	92.0000	1.0000	1.2821	94.0000	92.0000	1.0000	1.3889
Min	78.0000	79.0000	-1.0000	-1.1765	72.0000	73.0000	-20.0000	-21.2766
StdErr	2.9011	2.7234	0.4082	0.5021	4.9728	4.7346	5.0888	5.4447
t	29.4711	31.3951	0.0000	0.0526	17.3442	17.2136	-0.9334	-0.9132
Prob>|t|	0.0001	0.0001	1.0000	0.9614	0.0004	0.0004	0.4195	0.4285
Ndif	2	50.000%			2	50.000%		
DifMeans	0.000%	0.000%	0		-5.507%	-5.828%	-4.7500	
r, rsq	0.991	0.983			0.451	0.204		

Example 3: Brief Report of the Differences between Two Data Sets

This example compares the data sets in the previous example, but it uses the BRIEFSUMMARY option to suppress the usual summary reports and produce a brief summary report (numbered 8 in the output). The following statements produce **Output 11.4**:

```
libname students 'SAS-data-library';

proc compare base=students.one compare=students.two briefsummary;
   title 'Comparing Two Data Sets: Brief Report';
run;
```

Output 11.4   Producing a Brief Report on the Differences between Two Data Sets

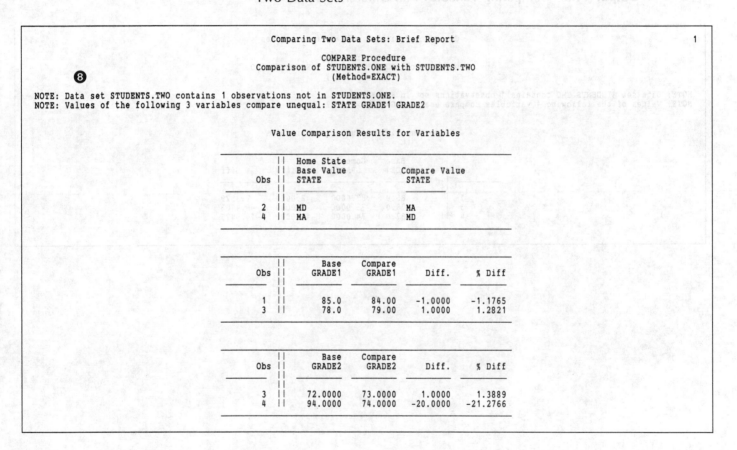

```
                    Comparing Two Data Sets: Brief Report                         1

                              COMPARE Procedure
                  Comparison of STUDENTS.ONE with STUDENTS.TWO
                              (Method=EXACT)

NOTE: Data set STUDENTS.TWO contains 1 observations not in STUDENTS.ONE.
NOTE: Values of the following 3 variables compare unequal: STATE GRADE1 GRADE2


                     Value Comparison Results for Variables


             ||  Home State
             ||  Base Value         Compare Value
        Obs  ||  STATE              STATE
        _____||_____
             ||
          2  ||  MD                 MA
          4  ||  MA                 MD
        _____



             ||    Base      Compare
        Obs  ||   GRADE1      GRADE1      Diff.       % Diff
        _____||_____
             ||
          1  ||     85.0      84.00     -1.0000      -1.1765
          3  ||     78.0      79.00      1.0000       1.2821
        _____



             ||    Base      Compare
        Obs  ||   GRADE2      GRADE2      Diff.       % Diff
        _____||_____
             ||
          3  ||   72.0000    73.0000     1.0000       1.3889
          4  ||   94.0000    74.0000   -20.0000     -21.2766
        _____
```

Example 4:   Comparing Variables with Different Names

This example compares the variable GRADE1 from the base data set with the variable GRADE2 in the comparison data set. The NOSUMMARY option suppresses the creation of all summary reports. The following statements produce **Output 11.5**:

```
libname students 'SAS-data-library';

proc compare base=students.one compare=students.two nosummary;
   var grade1;
   with grade2;
   title 'Comparing Variables with Different Names';
run;
```

Output 11.5   Comparing Variables with Different Names

```
                        Comparing Variables with Different Names                    1

                                  COMPARE Procedure
                     Comparison of STUDENTS.ONE with STUDENTS.TWO
                                  (Method=EXACT)

NOTE: Data set STUDENTS.TWO contains 1 observations not in STUDENTS.ONE.
NOTE: Values of the following 1 variables compare unequal: GRADE1¬=GRADE2


                       Value Comparison Results for Variables

                       ||    Base      Compare
                 Obs   ||   GRADE1      GRADE2      Diff.      % Diff
                       ||
                       ||
                   1   ||     85.0     87.0000     2.0000      2.3529
                   3   ||     78.0     73.0000    -5.0000     -6.4103
                   4   ||     87.0     74.0000   -13.0000    -14.9425
```

Example 5:   Comparing Variables within a Data Set

This example compares the variables GRADE1 and GRADE2 within the data set
STUDENTS.ONE. It differs from the previous example in not specifying a comparison data set. In addition, this example produces a table of summary statistics for
all pairs of matching variables instead of a table of differences and percent differences. The following statements produce **Output 11.6**:

```
libname students 'SAS-data-library';

proc compare base=students.one nosummary allstats novalues;
   var grade1;
   with grade2;
   title 'Comparing Variables within a Data Set';
run;
```

Output 11.6   Comparing Variables within a Data Set

```
                         Comparing Variables within a Data Set                       1

                                  COMPARE Procedure
                        Comparisons of variables in STUDENTS.ONE
                                   (Method=EXACT)

NOTE: Values of the following 1 variables compare unequal: GRADE1¬=GRADE2

                              Value Comparison Results for Variables


                   ||    Base     Compare
                   ||   GRADE1     GRADE2      Diff.      % Diff
                   ||
                   ||
           N       ||       4          4          4          4
        Mean       || 85.5000    86.2500     0.7500     0.6767
         Std       ||  5.8023     9.9457     5.3774     6.5221
         Max       || 92.0000    94.0000     7.0000     8.0460
         Min       || 78.0000    72.0000    -6.0000    -7.6923
      StdErr       ||  2.9011     4.9728     2.6887     3.2611
           t       || 29.4711    17.3442     0.2789     0.2075
     Prob>|t|      ||  0.0001     0.0004     0.7984     0.8489
                   ||
        Ndif       ||       3    75.000%
     DifMeans      ||  0.877%     0.870%     0.7500
      r, rsq       ||  0.898      0.807
```

Example 6: Using the OUTSTATS= Option

This example creates an output data set containing the statistics from the summary statistics report. The NOPRINT option suppresses output from PROC COMPARE. The PRINT procedure displays the data set. The data set contains 11 observations for each numeric variable judged unequal. The following statements produce **Output 11.7**:

```
libname students 'SAS-data-library';

proc compare base=students.one compare=students.two
        outstats=students.outstat noprint;
run;

proc print data=students.outstat;
   title 'The OUTSTAT= Data Set Created by PROC COMPARE';
run;
```

Output 11.7   The OUTSTATS= Data Set Created by PROC COMPARE

```
                    The OUTSTAT= Data Set Created by PROC COMPARE                        1

      OBS    _VAR_     _TYPE_      _BASE_      _COMP_       _DIF_      _PCTDIF_

        1    YEAR      N             4.00        4.00      4.0000      4.0000
        2    YEAR      MEAN       1970.00     1970.00      0.0000      0.0000
        3    YEAR      STD           0.82        0.82      0.0000      0.0000
        4    YEAR      MAX        1971.00     1971.00      0.0000      0.0000
        5    YEAR      MIN        1969.00     1969.00      0.0000      0.0000
        6    YEAR      STDERR        0.41        0.41      0.0000      0.0000
        7    YEAR      T          4825.49     4825.49         .           .
        8    YEAR      PROBT         0.00        0.00         .           .
        9    YEAR      NDIF          0.00        0.00         .           .
       10    YEAR      DIFMEANS      0.00        0.00      0.0000         .
       11    YEAR      R,RSQ         1.00        1.00         .           .
       12    GRADE1    N             4.00        4.00      4.0000      4.0000
       13    GRADE1    MEAN         85.50       85.50      0.0000      0.0264
       14    GRADE1    STD           5.80        5.45      0.8165      1.0042
       15    GRADE1    MAX          92.00       92.00      1.0000      1.2821
       16    GRADE1    MIN          78.00       79.00     -1.0000     -1.1765
       17    GRADE1    STDERR        2.90        2.72      0.4082      0.5021
       18    GRADE1    T            29.47       31.40      0.0000      0.0526
       19    GRADE1    PROBT         0.00        0.00      1.0000      0.9614
       20    GRADE1    NDIF          2.00       50.00         .           .
       21    GRADE1    DIFMEANS      0.00        0.00      0.0000         .
       22    GRADE1    R,RSQ         0.99        0.98         .           .
       23    GRADE2    N             4.00        4.00      4.0000      4.0000
       24    GRADE2    MEAN         86.25       81.50     -4.7500     -4.9719
       25    GRADE2    STD           9.95        9.47     10.1776     10.8895
       26    GRADE2    MAX          94.00       92.00      1.0000      1.3889
       27    GRADE2    MIN          72.00       73.00    -20.0000    -21.2766
       28    GRADE2    STDERR        4.97        4.73      5.0888      5.4447
       29    GRADE2    T            17.34       17.21     -0.9334     -0.9132
       30    GRADE2    PROBT         0.00        0.00      0.4195      0.4285
       31    GRADE2    NDIF          2.00       50.00         .           .
       32    GRADE2    DIFMEANS     -5.51       -5.83     -4.7500         .
       33    GRADE2    R,RSQ         0.45        0.20         .           .
```

The CONTENTS Procedure

ABSTRACT

The CONTENTS procedure prints descriptions of the contents of one or more files from a SAS data library.

INTRODUCTION

PROC CONTENTS provides information about a SAS data library or individual files in a SAS data library. It is particularly useful for documenting permanent SAS data sets.

   Specific information pertaining to the physical characteristics of a member depends on whether the file is a SAS data set or another type of SAS file. Refer to Chapter 6, "SAS Files," in *SAS Language: Reference, Version 6, First Edition* to familiarize yourself with the basic features of SAS data libraries and the types of files (or members) that can reside in them, or if you need help with the terminology used in this procedure description.

   The CONTENTS statement in the DATASETS procedure (described in Chapter 17) works in the same way the CONTENTS procedure does.

SPECIFICATIONS

The PROC CONTENTS statement is the only statement associated with the CONTENTS procedure.

PROC CONTENTS Statement

PROC CONTENTS <DATA=<*libref.*>*member*> <DIRECTORY>
<MEMTYPE=(*mtype-list*)> <NODS> <NOPRINT>
<OUT=*SAS-data-set*> <POSITION> <SHORT>;

Table 12.1 summarizes how to use the options on the PROC CONTENTS statement. These options are described in alphabetical order following the table.

Table 12.1 Summary of PROC CONTENTS Statement Options

Class	Option	Function
Options for input and output	DATA=	specifies the data set name or _ALL_ for all members of the library
	OUT=	produces a SAS data set that contains information similar to the printed output from PROC CONTENTS
Options to list members in a SAS data library	DIRECTORY	lists members in the library when used with DATA=*SAS-data-set*
	MEMTYPE=	specifies which member types to list
	NODS	suppresses listing the contents of data sets and prints a list of members in the SAS data library when used with DATA=<*libref.*>_ALL_
Options to change the default output	POSITION	lists variables in a SAS data set in order of their position in the data set
	SHORT	prints only a list of the variable names in a SAS data set
	NOPRINT	suppresses the printed output (useful only in combination with the OUT= option)

DATA=<*libref.*>*member*
specifies an entire library or a specific member within a library. If you use a two-level name, *libref* refers to the SAS data library, and *member* is either the name of a member in the library or the keyword _ALL_. If you use a one-level name, *member* is either the name of a member in the WORK library or the keyword _ALL_.

When you specify the name of a member, you get a report on that member. When you specify _ALL_, you get information about all members having the type or types specified by the MEMTYPE= option.

For example, to print a description of all the members of all types in the SAS data library referenced by the libref STUDY, use these statements:

```
libname study 'SAS-data-library';

proc contents data=study._all_ ;
run;
```

To obtain the contents of one member named HTWT of type DATA from the same library, use these statements:

```
libname study 'SAS-data-library';

proc contents data=study.htwt;
run;
```

If you do not specify the DATA= option, PROC CONTENTS describes the member created most recently in your job or session.

DIRECTORY
prints a list of all members in the specified SAS data library. This option is useful when you are printing the contents of just one file and you also want to see the directory for the library. (When _ALL_ is specified in the DATA= option, the directory is automatically printed.)

MEMTYPE=(mtype-list)
MTYPE=(mtype-list)
MT=(mtype-list)
specifies one or more types of members in the SAS data library. PROC CONTENTS lists information only for members of the type specified in the MEMTYPE= option. If mtype-list is a single member type, you can omit the parentheses. For example, the statements

```
libname study 'SAS-data-library';

proc contents data=study._all_ memtype=view;
run;
```

produce descriptions of all files of type VIEW in the library.
The following values can be specified in the MEMTYPE= option:

ACCESS	access files (created using SAS/ACCESS software)
ALL	all member types
CATALOG	catalogs
DATA	SAS data sets
PROGRAM	stored compiled SAS programs
VIEW	views created using the SQL procedure.

If the MEMTYPE= option is not specified, the default value is DATA or VIEW when you specify a single member name on the DATA= option. If you specify DATA=libref._ALL_ or DATA=_ALL_, the default is MEMTYPE= ALL.

NODS

suppresses printing the contents of individual files when _ALL_ is specified in the DATA= option. Only the SAS data library directory is printed.

NOPRINT

suppresses printing the output of the CONTENTS procedure. This option is only useful when used with the OUT= option.

OUT=*SAS-data-set*

gives the name of an output SAS data set. The output SAS data set contains information similar to that given in the variable description section in the printed output of PROC CONTENTS. See **OUT= SAS Data Set** later in this chapter for details. This option is for SAS data sets only.

Note: The OUT= option does not suppress the printed output from the procedure. If you want to suppress the printed output, you must specify the NOPRINT option.

POSITION

prints a second list of the variable names in the order of their position in the data set. By default, the variables are listed alphabetically. This option is for SAS data sets only.

SHORT

prints only the list of variable names in the SAS data set. This option is for SAS data sets only.

DETAILS

OUT= SAS Data Set

The output SAS data set produced by PROC CONTENTS when you specify the OUT= option contains information on the variables in the SAS data sets specified in the DATA= option. Each variable in each DATA= data set has one observation in the OUT= data set. Keep in mind that the OUT= option produces output only for SAS data sets.

The variables in the output data set are described below. Note that the values of some variables in the output data set are unique to each observation and the values of other variables are the same for all observations in a single DATA= data set.

CRDATE   date the data set was created.

DELOBS   number of observations marked for deletion in the data set. (Observations can be marked for deletion but not actually deleted when you use the FSEDIT procedure of SAS/FSP software.)

ENGINE   name of the method used to read from and write to the data set.

FORMAT   variable format (blank if none given).

FORMATD   number of decimals for format (0 if none given).

FORMATL   format width (0 if none given).

IDXCOUNT	number of indexes for the data set.
IDXUSAGE	use of the variable in indexes. Possible values are

	NONE	the variable is not indexed.
	SIMPLE	the variable is indexed. No other variables are included in the index.
	COMPOSITE	
		the variable is one of multiple variables included in an index.
	BOTH	the variable is indexed with a simple index and included in a composite index.

INFORMAT	variable informat (blank if none given).
INFORMD	number of decimals for informat (0 if none given).
INFORML	informat width (0 if none given).
JUST	justification (0=left, 1=right).
LABEL	variable label (blank if none given).
LENGTH	variable length.
LIBNAME	libref used for the data library.
MEMLABEL	label for this data set (blank if no label).
MEMNAME	member in which the variable is located.
MEMTYPE	library member type (DATA or VIEW).
MODATE	date the data set was last modified.
NAME	variable name.
NOBS	number of observations in the data set.
NPOS	relative position of the variable in the data set input buffer.
TYPE	type of the variable (1=numeric, 2=character).
TYPEMEM	special data set type (blank if no TYPE= value is specified).
VARNUM	variable number in the data set.

For each SAS data set reported (identified by MEMNAME), the variable names are sorted. Note that they are sorted so that the values X1, X2, and X10 are listed in that order, not in the true collating sequence of X1, X10, X2. Therefore, if you want to use a BY statement on MEMNAME in subsequent steps, you should run a PROC SORT on the output data set first or use the NOTSORTED option on the BY statement.

Printed Output

The amount and appearance of the output depend on the type of member being described and the options you specify in the PROC CONTENTS statement. For types other than DATA or VIEW, PROC CONTENTS gives only the name and type of the file.

For SAS data sets, PROC CONTENTS produces the information listed below. Refer to the circled numbers in **Output 12.1** for an illustration of each of these parts of the output. In addition, the circled numbers in **Output 12.2** indicate how the same, or comparable, information is included in the OUT= data set.

1. the LIBNAME used for the PROC CONTENTS step.
2. the name of the SAS data set.
3. the type of library member (DATA or VIEW).
4. the engine used to read from and write to the data set.
5. the date the data set was created.
6. the date the data set was last modified.
7. the special data set type (such as CORR, COV, SSPC, EST, or FACTOR), if any.
8. data set label, if one exists.
9. the number of observations in the data set.
10. the number of variables.
11. the number of indexes for the data set.
12. the length of the observation.
13. the number of observations marked for deletion. Note: Observations marked for deletion are not included in the count of observations (number 9 above).
14. an indicator of whether the data set is compressed. If the data set is compressed, an additional item, Reuse Space, (values of YES or NO) is printed to indicate whether space made available when observations are deleted should be reused.

For each variable, PROC CONTENTS produces the following information:

15. the position of the variable in the data set.
16. the variable's name. By default, variables are listed alphabetically.
    Note: Variable names that contain special characters and digits may appear in a nonstandard sort order. For example, P25 and P75 appear before P2_5.
17. the type of the variable, character or numeric. (In the OUT= data set, 1 means numeric and 2 means character.)
18. the variable's length.
19. the starting position of the variable in the observation.
20. the variable's format, if any. (In the OUT= data set, the format is described by three variables: FORMAT, FORMATL, and FORMATD.)
21. the variable's informat, if any. (In the OUT= data set, the informat is described by three variables: INFORMAT, INFORML, and INFORMD.)
22. the variable's label, if any.

Note: If none of the variables in the SAS data set has a format, informat, or label associated with it, the heading for that attribute (numbers 20, 21, or 22) is not printed.

If the data set has indexes associated with it, PROC CONTENTS produces the following information:

23. the name of the index.
24. an indicator of whether the index must have unique values (not shown). If the column contains YES, the combination of values of the index variables are unique for each observation.

25. an indicator of whether observations with missing values for all index variables are excluded from the index. If the column contains YES, observations with missing values for all index variables are not indexed.
26. a list of variables that make up a composite index.

In addition, PROC CONTENTS may include host-specific, as well as engine-specific, information at the end of the output. Refer to the SAS documentation for your host system for more information.

EXAMPLES

Example 1:   Printing the Contents of a Data Set

This example uses PROC CONTENTS to describe a SAS data set named WINTER in a library referenced by the libref SPORTS. The variables are listed alphabetically. The POSITION option produces a second list of the variables in the data set by their position in the data set. The statements below produce **Output 12.1**.

```
libname sports 'SAS-data-library';

proc contents data=sports.winter position;
   title 'Contents of a SAS Data Set';
run;
```

Output 12.1   Contents of a SAS Data Set

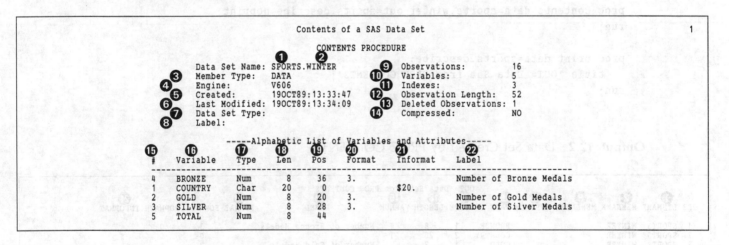

```
                              Contents of a SAS Data Set                              2
                                CONTENTS PROCEDURE
                          -----Variables Ordered by Position-----

            #   Variable   Type   Len   Pos   Format   Informat   Label
            --------------------------------------------------------------------------
            1   COUNTRY    Char   20    0              $20.
            2   GOLD       Num    8     20    3.                   Number of Gold Medals
            3   SILVER     Num    8     28    3.                   Number of Silver Medals
            4   BRONZE     Num    8     36    3.                   Number of Bronze Medals
            5   TOTAL      Num    8     44

                     -----Alphabetic List of Indexes and Attributes-----
                               ㉓            ㉕         ㉖
                                          Nomiss
                        #    Index        Option    Var1      Var2
                        -------------------------------------------
                        1    GOLD
                        2    TOTAL
                        3    TOTGOLD      YES       TOTAL     GOLD
```

Example 2:   Data Set Produced by PROC CONTENTS

This example creates a SAS data set, SPORTS.DESCRIBE, that contains the description of the SPORTS.WINTER data set. The PROC PRINT step displays the contents of the SPORTS.DESCRIBE data set. The statements below produce **Output 12.2**.

```
libname sports 'SAS-data-library';
options linesize=120;

proc contents data=sports.winter out=sports.describe noprint;
run;

proc print data=sports.describe;
   title 'OUT= Data Set from PROC CONTENTS';
run;
```

Output 12.2   Data Set Created by PROC CONTENTS

```
                              OUT= Data Set from PROC CONTENTS                                                      1
     ❶        ❷        ❽        ❼       ⓰      ⓱      ⓲       ⓯           ㉒              ⓴                   ㉑
OBS  LIBNAME  MEMNAME  MEMLABEL  TYPEMEM  NAME    TYPE  LENGTH  VARNUM      LABEL          FORMAT FORMATL FORMATD INFORMAT

1    SPORTS   WINTER                      BRONZE   1    8       4     Number of Bronze Medals      3      0
2    SPORTS   WINTER                      COUNTRY  2    20      1                                  0      0       $
3    SPORTS   WINTER                      GOLD     1    8       2     Number of Gold Medals        3      0
4    SPORTS   WINTER                      SILVER   1    8       3     Number of Silver Medals      3      0
5    SPORTS   WINTER                      TOTAL    1    8       5                                  0      0


                              ⓳     ❾                       ❺                      ❻          ⓭           ❸        ⓫
OBS  INFORML  INFORMD  JUST  NPOS  NOBS  ENGINE          CRDATE              MODATE      DELOBS  IDXUSAGE  MEMTYPE  IDXCOUNT

1    0        0        1     36    16    V606   19OCT89:13:33:47  19OCT89:13:34:09   1    NONE      DATA     3
2    20       0        0     0     16    V606   19OCT89:13:33:47  19OCT89:13:34:09   1    NONE      DATA     3
3    0        0        1     20    16    V606   19OCT89:13:33:47  19OCT89:13:34:09   1    BOTH      DATA     3
4    0        0        1     28    16    V606   19OCT89:13:33:47  19OCT89:13:34:09   1    NONE      DATA     3
5    0        0        1     44    16    V606   19OCT89:13:33:47  19OCT89:13:34:09   1    BOTH      DATA     3
```

Chapter 13
The CONVERT
Procedure

ABSTRACT

The CONVERT procedure converts BMDP, OSIRIS, and SPSS system files to SAS
data sets. This procedure is described in system-dependent documentation.

The COPY Procedure

ABSTRACT

The COPY procedure copies an entire SAS data library or selected members of the library. Optional features allow you to limit processing to specific types of library members.

INTRODUCTION

The COPY procedure is a general utility for copying SAS data libraries from one device to another or from one file to another. You can copy the entire library or you can select or exclude members of specific types. The COPY procedure also provides a simple method for transporting SAS data sets from one host system to another. The **EXAMPLES** section of this chapter illustrates how to use PROC COPY to create and read files in transport format. Note that you can use PROC COPY to transport only SAS data sets, not catalogs or other member types. Refer to Chapter 16, "The CPORT Procedure," and Chapter 10, "The CIMPORT Procedure," for information on transporting other member types.

The COPY statement in Chapter 17, "The DATASETS Procedure," works in the same way as the COPY procedure does.

Refer to *SAS Language: Reference, Version 6, First Edition* for a discussion of the different types of files (or members) that can reside in a SAS data library.

SPECIFICATIONS

PROC COPY IN=*libref* OUT=*libref* <MEMTYPE=(*mtype-list*)> <MOVE>;
EXCLUDE *member-list* </ MEMTYPE=*mtype*>;
SELECT *member-list* </ MEMTYPE=*mtype*>;

where *mtype* can be a single member type and *mtype-list* can be a single member
type or a list of member types enclosed in parentheses. You can omit the parentheses if *mtype-list* contains only one type. You can use either SELECT statements
or EXCLUDE statements in a PROC COPY step but not both.

PROC COPY Statement

PROC COPY IN=*libref* OUT=*libref* <MEMTYPE=(*mtype-list*)> <MOVE>;

Requirements

The following arguments are required in the PROC COPY statement:

IN=*libref*
INLIB=*libref*
INDD=*libref*
> refers to the SAS data library containing members to be copied. The
> input data library can be a Version 6 or Version 5 SAS data library.

OUT=*libref*
OUTLIB=*libref*
OUTDD=*libref*
> refers to the SAS data library into which members are copied.

Options

You can use the following options in the PROC COPY statement:

MEMTYPE=(*mtype-list*)
MTYPE=(*mtype-list*)
MT=(*mtype-list*)
> specifies one or more types of members that are to be copied or
> moved. Note that *mtype-list* can be a single member type or a list of
> member types enclosed in parentheses. If *mtype-list* is a single type, you
> can omit the parentheses. The following example illustrates specifying
> multiple member types:

```
proc copy in=ds1 out=ds2 memtype=(data catalog);
run;
```

> Valid member types are

ACCESS	access files (created by SAS/ACCESS software)
ALL	all member types
CATALOG	catalogs
DATA	SAS data sets
PROGRAM	stored compiled SAS programs
VIEW	views created by the SQL procedure.

> If the MEMTYPE= option is not specified, all types of members in the
> library are available for processing.

MOVE
   causes each member that is successfully copied to the output library
   (specified with the OUT= argument) to be deleted from the input
   library (specified with the IN= argument). For example, the following
   statements copy members of the SAS library referenced by OLD into the
   SAS library referenced by NEW and delete the members from the OLD
   library:

```
proc copy in=old out=new move;
run;
```

EXCLUDE Statement

If you want to copy most of the members in a library, use one or more EXCLUDE
statements to specify the names of those to be excluded from the copy operation.
Note: You can use either SELECT statements or EXCLUDE statements in a PROC
COPY step but not both.
   The general form of the EXCLUDE statement is

EXCLUDE *member-list* </ MEMTYPE=*mtype*>;

where *member-list* names one or more SAS files (or members) to be excluded
from the SAS library specified by the OUT= argument in the PROC COPY statement. See **Specifying Member Names** later in this chapter.
   You can specify the following option in the EXCLUDE statement:

MEMTYPE=*mtype*
MTYPE=*mtype*
MT=*mtype*
   specifies the type of the members that are to be excluded. Valid values
   for *mtype* are the same as those shown for the MEMTYPE= option in
   the PROC COPY statement. Note that *mtype* must be a single member
   type. Refer to **Using the MEMTYPE= Option** later in this chapter.

SELECT Statement

If you want to copy only selected members, use one or more SELECT statements
to list the names of the members to be copied. Note: You can use either SELECT
statements or EXCLUDE statements in a PROC COPY step but not both.
   The general form of the SELECT statement is

SELECT *member-list* </ MEMTYPE=*mtype*>;

where *member-list* names one or more SAS files from the SAS library specified
by the IN= argument in the PROC COPY statement. Refer to **Specifying Member
Names** later in this chapter.
   You can use the following option in the SELECT statement:

MEMTYPE=*mtype*
MTYPE=*mtype*
MT=*mtype*
   specifies the type of the members to be selected. Valid values are the
   same as those shown for the MEMTYPE= option in the PROC COPY
   statement. Note that *mtype* must be a single member type. Refer to
   Using the MEMTYPE= Option later in this chapter.

DETAILS

When you copy a data set, any indexes associated with the data set are re-created for the copied data set. Note that indexes are only re-created if the format of the output data set is for Release 6.06 or later of the SAS System.

Specifying Member Names

You can select or exclude one member by giving the name in the SELECT or EXCLUDE statement. You can select or exclude more than one member by giving a list of member names. You can also select or exclude an abbreviated list of members. For example, the following statement selects members TABS, TEST1, TEST2, and TEST3:

```
select tabs test1-test3;
```

Also, you can select a group of members whose names begin with the same letter or letters by entering the common letters followed by a colon (:). For example, you can select the four members shown in the previous example and all other members having names that begin with the letter T by specifying

```
select t:;
```

Remember that the MEMTYPE= option affects which types of members are available to be selected. Therefore, if MEMTYPE=ALL (the default) is in effect, this example selects all member types having names that begin with the letter T.

You specify members to exclude the same way that you specify those to select. That is, you can list individual member names, use an abbreviated list, or specify a common letter or letters followed by a colon (:). For example, the following statement excludes the members STATS, TEAMS1, TEAMS2, TEAMS3, TEAMS4, and all the members beginning with the letters RBI from the copy operation:

```
exclude stats teams1-teams4 rbi:;
```

Again, keep in mind that all types having the specified names are excluded if MEMTYPE=ALL is in effect.

Using the MEMTYPE= Option

If the MEMTYPE= option is not specified in the PROC COPY, SELECT, or EXCLUDE statements, MEMTYPE=ALL is in effect.

If you do not specify the MEMTYPE= option on the SELECT or EXCLUDE statement, those types specified with the MEMTYPE= option in the PROC COPY statement are processed. For example, the following statements copy the members MATH, LANG, and GEO of types DATA and CATALOG:

```
libname orig 'SAS-data-library';
libname new 'SAS-data-library';

proc copy in=orig out=new memtype=(data catalog);
   select math lang geo;
run;
```

If you specify the MEMTYPE= option in the PROC COPY statement and also in either the SELECT or EXCLUDE statement, the type specified in the SELECT or EXCLUDE statement overrides the type specified in the PROC COPY statement. For example, the following statements copy members named MATH, LANG, and GEO of type CATALOG:

```
libname orig 'SAS-data-library';
libname new 'SAS-data-library';

proc copy in=orig out=new memtype=data;
   select math lang geo / memtype=catalog;
run;
```

No other members are copied. The MEMTYPE= option on the PROC COPY statement is ignored.

For the EXCLUDE and SELECT statements, you can also specify the MEMTYPE= option, enclosed in parentheses, immediately after the name of a member. In parentheses, the MEMTYPE= option identifies the type of the member name just preceding it. When you use this form of the option, it overrides the MEMTYPE= option following the slash in the EXCLUDE or SELECT statement and the MEMTYPE= option in the PROC COPY statement. For example, the following statements copy all members except A.DATA, B.CATALOG, and C.DATA:

```
libname abc 'SAS-data-library';

proc copy in=abc out=work;
   exclude a b (memtype=catalog) c / memtype=data;
run;
```

Output

A note appears in the SAS log as each data set is successfully copied. No printed output is produced.

EXAMPLES

Example 1:   Copying a SAS Data Library

This example copies all members in the SAS data library referenced by the libref MISC to a library referenced by the libref NEW. Because the MEMTYPE= option is not specified, all types are copied.

```
libname misc 'SAS-data-library';
libname new 'SAS-data-library';

proc copy in=misc out=new;
run;
```

Example 2:   Moving Selected Members of a SAS Data Library

In this example, selected members in the SAS data library referenced by the libref MISC are moved to a library referenced by the libref NEW. Notice that only SAS data sets (DATA type) are initially available for processing.

```
libname misc 'SAS-data-library';
libname new 'SAS-data-library';

proc copy in=misc out=new move memtype=data;
   select mlist;
   select gtest: / memtype=catalog;
run;
```

The first SELECT statement moves the SAS data set MLIST from the MISC data library to the NEW data library. The second SELECT statement moves all catalogs with names beginning with letters GTEST from MISC to NEW.

Example 3:   Transporting SAS Data Sets to Another Host

In the first step of this example, all of the data sets in a SAS data library are copied to a transport file. Note the use of the XPORT engine name in the LIBNAME statement. This engine name indicates that the output from PROC COPY should be a transport file.

```
libname misc 'SAS-data-library';
libname alldata xport 'host1-filename';

proc copy in=misc out=alldata memtype=data;
run;
```

The *host1-filename* can now be sent to another host system via a network or tape. **Be sure to send the transport file in binary format to avoid ASCII to EBCDIC translation (or vice versa).** You can read the transport file into the second host system as shown here:

```
libname misc 'SAS-data-library';
libname alldata xport 'host2-filename';

proc copy in=alldata out=misc;
run;
```

As in the first step, you must specify the XPORT engine in the LIBNAME statement for the transport file to be able to read the file with PROC COPY and copy the SAS data sets to the new host.

For more information on engines and transport files, refer to Chapter 6, "SAS Files," in *SAS Language: Reference* and SAS Technical Report P-195, *Transporting SAS Files between Host Systems.*

ABSTRACT

The CORR procedure computes correlation coefficients between variables, including Pearson product-moment and weighted product-moment correlations. Three nonparametric measures of association (Spearman's rank-order correlation, Kendall's tau-b, and Hoeffding's measure of dependence, D) can also be produced. In addition, the CORR procedure computes partial correlations (Pearson's partial correlation, Spearman's partial rank-order correlation, and Kendall's partial tau-b) and Cronbach's coefficient alpha. Some univariate descriptive statistics are also generated.

INTRODUCTION

Correlation measures the strength of the linear relationship between two variables. If one variable x can be expressed exactly as a linear function of another variable y, then the correlation is 1 if the variables are directly related or −1 if the variables are inversely related. A correlation of 0 between two variables means that each variable has no linear predictive ability for the other. If the values are normally distributed, then a correlation of 0 means that the variables are independent of one another.

The true product-moment correlation (Pearson), denoted ρ_{xy}, is defined as follows:

$$\rho_{xy} = \frac{\text{cov}(x,y)}{\sqrt{\text{var}(x)\,\text{var}(y)}}$$

$$= \frac{E((x - Ex)(y - Ey))}{\sqrt{E(x - Ex)^2\, E(y - Ey)^2}}$$

The sample correlation estimates the true correlation. The correlation can be the Pearson product-moment or the weighted product-moment correlation. The Pearson product-moment correlation is computed as

$$r_{xy} = \frac{\sum (x_i - \bar{x})(y_i - \bar{y})}{\sqrt{\sum (x_i - \bar{x})^2 \sum (y_i - \bar{y})^2}}$$

where $\bar{x}$ and $\bar{y}$ are the sample means of x and y. The weighted Pearson product-moment correlation is computed as

$$r_{xy} = \frac{\sum w_i(x_i - \bar{x}_w)(y_i - \bar{y}_w)}{\sqrt{\sum w_i(x_i - \bar{x}_w)^2 \sum w_i(y_i - \bar{y}_w)^2}}$$

where $\bar{x}_w = \sum w_i x_i / \sum w_i$ and $\bar{y}_w = \sum w_i y_i / \sum w_i$ are weighted means of x and y and w_i is the weight.

The relationship between two variables can be depicted graphically. You may want to plot the relationship between these variables:

- the height and weight of a group of fitness club members
- the average length of time teachers are employed and the average salary for the location
- the sales of homes in your area and the interest rates.

In a scatterplot, each unit is represented by a point on the scatter diagram. **Table 15.1** illustrates several scatterplots.

Table 15.1   Interpreting Plots of r_{xy} Values

Scatterplot	Interpretation
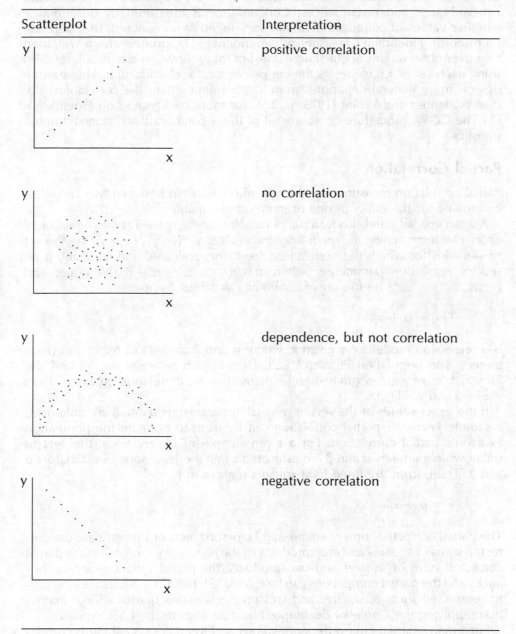	positive correlation
	no correlation
	dependence, but not correlation
	negative correlation

The plots illustrated in **Table 15.1** are ideal cases; the plots you produce may not be as easily interpretable.

Correlations among a set of variables contain information sufficient for computing regressions, partial correlations, canonical correlations, factor patterns, principal component coefficients, and many other statistics. Note that correlation does not imply causality because, in some cases, an underlying causal relationship may exist. For more information, consult an introductory statistics textbook such as Moore (1979), Ott (1977), or Snedecor and Cochran (1967).

In addition to Pearson correlations, several other statistics have been proposed to measure the association between two continuous variables. Spearman's rank-order correlation coefficient is a nonparametric measure that is calculated as the correlation of the ranks of the data. Kendall's tau-b is a measure calculated from concordances and discordances. Concordance is measured by determining whether values of paired observations vary together (in concord) or differently (in discord). Hoeffding's measure of dependence, D, approximates a weighted sum over observations of chi-square statistics for two-by-two classification tables using each set of x,y values as the cut points for the classification. This statistic detects more general departures from independence than the correlations do. (See Hollander and Wolfe (1973, p. 228) for more background on Hoeffding's D.) The CORR procedure computes all of these parametric and nonparametric statistics.

Partial Correlation

Partial correlation measures the strength of relationship between two variables, controlling for the effect of one or more other variables.

Pearson's partial correlation for a pair of variables may be defined as the correlation of errors after regression on the controlling variables. Let $\mathbf{y} = (y_1, y_2, \ldots, y_v)$ be the set of variables for which the correlations are to be evaluated and let α and β be sets of regression parameters, where $\alpha = (\alpha_1, \ldots, \alpha_v)$, β the slope, and $\mathbf{z} = (z_1, z_2, \ldots, z_p)$ be the set of controlling variables. Suppose

$$E(\mathbf{y}) = \alpha + \mathbf{z}\beta$$

is a regression model for $\mathbf{y}$ given $\mathbf{z}$, where α and β are sets of regression parameters. The population Pearson's partial correlation between the ith and the jth variables of $\mathbf{y}$ given $\mathbf{z}$ may then be defined as the correlation between errors $y_i - E(y_i)$ and $y_j - E(y_j)$.

If the exact values of the sets of regression parameters α and β are unknown, a sample Pearson's partial correlation can be used to estimate the population Pearson's partial correlation. For a given sample of observations, the sets of unknown parameters α and β are estimated using the least-squares estimators $\hat{\alpha}$ and $\hat{\beta}$. Then, from the fitted least-squares regression model

$$\hat{\mathbf{y}} = \hat{\alpha} + \mathbf{z}\hat{\beta}$$

The partial corrected sums of squares and crossproducts of $\mathbf{y}$ given $\mathbf{z}$ are the corrected sums of squares and crossproducts of the residuals $\mathbf{y} - \hat{\mathbf{y}}$. With these partial corrected sums of squares and crossproducts, the partial variances and covariances and the partial correlations can be calculated. PROC CORR derives the partial corrected sums of squares and crossproducts matrix (partial CSSCP matrix) from applying the Cholesky decomposition algorithm to the CSSCP matrix.

Spearman's partial rank-order correlations and Kendall's partial tau-b correlations are calculated by applying the Cholesky decomposition algorithm to the corresponding correlation matrix (see **Formulas** later in this chapter). The resulting partial tau-b, which has values in the range of -1 to 1, gives a sensible indication of partial correlation. However, the sampling distribution of this partial tau-b is unknown, and therefore the probability values are not available.

Cronbach's Coefficient Alpha

When a variable value is recorded, the observed value contains a certain degree of measurement error. Two sets of measurements on the same variable for the same individual may not have exactly the same value. However, repeated measurements of a series of individuals will show some consistency. Reliability is a measure of internal consistency from one set of measurements to another. An observed value Y is divided into two components, a true value T and a measurement error E. The measurement error is assumed to be independent of the true value, that is,

$$Y = T + E, \quad cov(T, E) = 0 \quad .$$

The reliability coefficient is defined as the squared correlation between the observed value Y and the true value T, that is,

$$\rho^2(Y,T) = cov(Y,T)^2 / (var(Y)\, var(T))$$
$$= var(T)^2 / (var(Y)\, var(T))$$
$$= var(T) / var(Y)$$

which is the proportion of the observed variance that is due to true differences among individuals in the sample. When a measurement consists of two or more separate parts from which a total score is obtained, var(T) can be estimated. Cronbach's coefficient alpha (Cronbach 1951), based on a lower bound for var(T), can be used to estimate the reliability coefficient (see **Formulas** later in this chapter for Cronbach's coefficient alpha).

SPECIFICATIONS

The CORR procedure is controlled by the following statements:

> **PROC CORR** <*option-list*>;
>   **BY** *variable-list*;
>   **FREQ** *variable*;
>   **PARTIAL** *variable-list*;
>   **VAR** *variable-list*;
>   **WEIGHT** *variable*;
>   **WITH** *variable-list*;

The PROC CORR statement invokes the procedure and is the only required statement. If you use only a PROC CORR statement, the CORR procedure calculates correlations between all the numeric variables in the input data set. Use the VAR and WITH statements to specify variables for the analysis. The WITH statement, used in conjunction with the VAR statement, allows you to produce correlations for specific combinations of variables. For example, the following statements give you the correlations for RUNTIME with HEIGHT, WEIGHT, and RESTPLSE:

```
proc corr data=school;
   var height weight restplse;
   with  runtime;
run;
```

The subordinate statements following the PROC CORR statement may appear in any order. In this chapter, they are described in alphabetic order following the PROC CORR statement.

PROC CORR Statement

PROC CORR <*option-list*>;

The options that can appear in the PROC CORR statement are given below. If you use only the following statements, the CORR procedure calculates Pearson product-moment correlations and significance probabilities for all numeric variables, as well as select univariate statistics (the mean, standard deviation, sum, minimum and maximum):

```
proc corr;
run;
```

If you want to create a permanent SAS data set containing statistics generated by PROC CORR, use the OUTP=, OUTH=, OUTK=, or OUTS= option and a two-level data set name. (See *SAS Language: Reference, Version 6, First Edition* for more information on permanent SAS data sets. Also, see **Output Data Sets** later in this chapter for a complete description of the data sets' structures.) The PROC CORR statement options are grouped by task in **Table 15.2**. Descriptions follow the table in alphabetic order.

Table 15.2 Options Available in the PROC CORR Statement

Task	Options
Select data sets	DATA= OUTP= OUTH= OUTK= OUTS=
Select types of correlations	HOEFFDING KENDALL PEARSON SPEARMAN
Exclude missing values	NOMISS
Specify variance divisor	VARDEF=
Specify singularity check	SINGULAR=
Specify Pearson Correlations	ALPHA COV CSSCP NOCORR SSCP
Select printing options	BEST= NOPRINT NOPROB NOSIMPLE RANK

ALPHA
  calculates and prints Cronbach's coefficient alpha. Separate coefficients are generated using the raw variables and the standardized variables (each variable is scaled to have unit variance). Only the variables in the

VAR statement are used. For each variable, PROC CORR calculates the correlation between the variable and the total of the remaining variables. It also calculates Cronbach's coefficient alpha using only the remaining variables. When a PARTIAL statement is also used, the coefficient alpha is calculated by using the variables after partialling. Requesting this option also activates the PEARSON option. If both the ALPHA and OUTP= options are specified, the output data set also contains the above coefficients and correlations (see **Output Data Sets** later in this chapter).

BEST=*number*

prints the *number* of correlations for each variable with the largest absolute values; the coefficients are printed in descending order.

COV

calculates and prints the covariances. If the COV and OUTP= options are both specified, the output data set also contains the covariance matrix. For the observations containing the covariance matrix, the _TYPE_ variable's value is COV. Specifying the COV option also activates the PEARSON option.

When a PARTIAL statement is used, the partial covariance matrix is printed. If, in addition, the OUTP= option is specified, the partial covariance matrix is added to the data set.

CSSCP

prints the corrected sums of squares and crossproducts (CSSCP). If both the CSSCP and OUTP= options are specified, the output data set also contains the CSSCP matrix. For the CSSCP observations, the _TYPE_ variable's value is CSSCP. Specifying the CSSCP option also activates the PEARSON option.

When a PARTIAL statement is used, both unpartialled and partialled CSSCP matrices are printed. When the OUTP= option is used, the partialled CSSCP matrix is placed in the output data set.

DATA=*SAS-data-set*

names the SAS data set used by PROC CORR. If the DATA= option is omitted, the most recently created SAS data set is used.

HOEFFDING

calculates and prints Hoeffding's D statistic. Note that the statistic calculated by the CORR procedure is 30 times the usual definition. (See **Formulas** later in this chapter for Hoeffding's statistic.) This scales the statistic to a range between -0.5 and 1, with only large positive values indicating dependence. The HOEFFDING option is not valid if either a WEIGHT or a PARTIAL statement is included.

KENDALL

calculates and prints Kendall's tau-b coefficients. Kendall's tau-b is based on the number of concordant and discordant pairs of observations and uses a correction for tied pairs (that is, pairs of observations that have equal values of X or equal values of Y). Kendall's tau-b has the range $-1 \leq \text{tau-b} \leq 1$. The KENDALL option is not valid if a WEIGHT statement is included. See **Formulas** later in this chapter for Kendall's tau-b.

NOCORR

supresses calculation and printing of Pearson correlations. If both the NOCORR and OUTP= options are specified, the output data set does not contain correlations but PROC CORR still makes the data set

TYPE=CORR. To change the data set type to COV, CSSCP, or SSCP, use the TYPE= option, for example,

```
proc corr nocorr cov outp=b(type=cov);
```

NOMISS

drops an observation with a missing value for any variable used in the analysis from all calculations. Otherwise, PROC CORR includes all observations that have nonmissing values for any pair of variables. Specifying NOMISS can be much faster and cheaper.

NOPRINT

suppresses all printed output. Specify this option when you use PROC CORR only to create an output data set containing correlations.

NOPROB

suppresses the printing of significance probabilities associated with the correlations.

NOSIMPLE

suppresses printing the simple descriptive statistics for each variable. However, when an output data set is requested, the simple descriptive statistics for each variable specified in the VAR statement are output to the specified data set.

OUTH=*SAS-data-set*

creates a new SAS data set containing the Hoeffding statistics. Requesting this data set activates the HOEFFDING option. The OUTH= option is similar in other respects to the OUTP= option.

OUTK=*SAS-data-set*

creates a new SAS data set containing Kendall correlations. Requesting this data set activates the KENDALL option. The OUTK= option is similar in other respects to the OUTP= option.

OUTP=*SAS-data-set*

creates a new SAS data set containing Pearson correlations. The new data set is TYPE=CORR and includes means, standard deviations, number of observations, and correlation coefficients. Requesting this data set activates the PEARSON option as well as the previously mentioned statistics.

OUTS=*SAS-data-set*

creates a new SAS data set containing Spearman correlations. Requesting this data set activates the SPEARMAN option. The OUTS= option is similar in other respects to the OUTP= option.

PEARSON

requests the usual Pearson product-moment correlations. Since these are the default statistics if no options are given, specify this option only if you are also requesting Spearman, Kendall, or Hoeffding statistics. The formula for the Pearson correlation is given in **Partial Correlation** earlier in this chapter.

RANK

prints the correlation coefficients for each variable in order from highest to lowest in absolute value. When the RANK option is omitted, the correlations are printed in a rectangular table defined by variable names at the top and side.

SINGULAR=*p*

specifies the criterion for determining the singularity of a variable when a PARTIAL statement is used, where $0<p<1$. The default is SINGULAR=1E-8.

For Pearson's partial correlations, a variable in the PARTIAL statement is considered singular if the R^2 for predicting this variable from the variables preceding it in the PARTIAL statement exceeds $1-p$. When a partial variable is singular, it is not used in the analysis. Similarly, a variable in the VAR or WITH statement is considered singular if the R^2 for predicting this variable from the variables in the PARTIAL statement exceeds $1-p$. When a variable is singular, its associated corrected sums of squares and crossproducts are set to zero.

For nonparametric partial correlations, the computations are the same as for Pearson correlations except that a matrix of nonparametric correlations is used. When a variable is singular, its associated correlations are set to missing (see **Formulas** later in this chapter).

SPEARMAN

calculates and prints the Spearman coefficients. These are the correlations of the ranks of the variables. The formula for Spearman's rank correlation is given under **Formulas** later in this chapter. Spearman coefficients have the range $-1 \leq r_s \leq 1$. The SPEARMAN option is not valid if you include a WEIGHT statement.

SSCP

prints the sums of squares and crossproducts (SSCP). If both the SSCP and OUTP= options are specified, the output data set also contains the SSCP matrix. For the SSCP observations, the _TYPE_ variable's value is SSCP. Specifying the SSCP option also activates the Pearson option.

When a PARTIAL statement is used, the unpartialled SSCP matrix is printed. If the OUTP= option is also specified, the output data set does not include the partial SSCP matrix.

VARDEF=DF
    | N
    | WDF
    | WEIGHT | WGT

specifies the divisor used in the calculation of variances and covariances. The default value is VARDEF=DF. The values and associated divisors are shown in the table below, where k is the number of partial variables specified in the PARTIAL statement.

Value	Divisor	Formula
DF	degrees of freedom	$n - k - 1$
N	number of observations	n
WEIGHT | WGT	sum of weights	$\Sigma_i w_i$
WDF	sum of weights DF	$(\Sigma_i w_i) - k - 1$

BY Statement

    BY *variable-list*;

A BY statement can be used with PROC CORR to obtain separate analyses on observations in groups defined by the BY variables.

When a BY statement appears, the procedure expects the input data set to be sorted in order of the BY variables or to have an appropriate index. If your input data set is not sorted in ascending order, you can do one of the following:

- Use the SORT procedure with a similar BY statement to sort the data.
- If appropriate, use the BY statement options NOTSORTED or DESCENDING.

- Create an index on the BY variables you want to use. For more information on creating indexes and using the BY statement with indexed data sets, see Chapter 17, "The DATASETS Procedure."

FREQ Statement

> **FREQ** *variable*;

When a FREQ statement is specified, each observation in the input data set is assumed to represent *n* observations, where *n* is the value of the FREQ variable for the observation. The total number of observations is considered equal to the sum of the FREQ variable.

If the value of the FREQ variable is missing or less than one, the observation is not used in the analysis. If the value is not an integer, the value is truncated to an integer.

WEIGHT and FREQ statements have similar effects except in the calculation of degrees of freedom. Also, unlike a WEIGHT variable, a FREQ variable can be specified for any correlation.

PARTIAL Statement

> **PARTIAL** *variable-list*;

To compute Pearson's partial correlation, Spearman's partial rank-order correlation, or Kendall's partial tau-b, give the names of the variables to be partialled in a PARTIAL statement.

When you use the PARTIAL statement with the PEARSON option, PROC CORR also prints the partial variance and standard deviation for each variable in the VAR or WITH statements.

The HOEFFDING option is not valid with a PARTIAL statement. Specifying the PARTIAL statement also activates the NOMISS option; only observations with all variables nonmissing are used in the analysis.

VAR Statement

> **VAR** *variable-list*;

The VAR statement lists the names of the variables for which correlations are to be evaluated. If the VAR statement is omitted, PROC CORR calculates correlations between all the numeric variables in the input data set that are not listed in other statements.

For example, the following statements produce correlation coefficients between three pairs of variables: A and B, A and C, and B and C:

```
proc corr;
   var a b c;
```

WEIGHT Statement

> **WEIGHT** *variable*;

To compute weighted product-moment correlation coefficients, give the name of the weighting variable in a WEIGHT statement. If the value of the WEIGHT variable is missing or less than zero, then a value of zero is used for the weight. You cannot use a WEIGHT statement to compute nonparametric measures of association; the SPEARMAN, KENDALL, and HOEFFDING options are not valid with a WEIGHT statement. A WEIGHT statement should be used only with Pearson correlations. See the formula in **Correlation** earlier in this chapter for details on the weighted product-moment correlation.

WITH Statement

   WITH *variable-list*;

To obtain correlations for specific combinations of variables, list the variables to appear on the top of the printed correlation matrix in the VAR statement, and list variables to appear on the side of the correlation matrix in the WITH statement.

   For example, the statements

```
proc corr;
   var a b;
   with x y z;
```

produce correlations for the following combinations:

X and A	X and B
Y and A	Y and B
Z and A	Z and B

DETAILS

Missing Values

The default method of handling missing values is to use all nonmissing pairs of values for each pair of variables. This means that some correlations are computed using more observations than others.

   An alternative method is available with the NOMISS option, which uses an observation only if none of the variables specified in the BY, FREQ, PARTIAL, VAR, WEIGHT and WITH statements are missing. There are two reasons for specifying the NOMISS option and avoiding the pairwise default method. First, specifying the NOMISS option is computationally more efficient. Second, if the correlations are used as input to regression or other statistical procedures, a pairwise-missing correlation matrix leads to several statistical difficulties. Pairwise correlation matrices may not be nonnegative definite, and the pattern of missing values may bias the results. However, when you use the PARTIAL statement, any observations with missing values are not used in the analysis.

Output Data Sets

Output data sets are requested by the OUTP=, OUTS=, OUTK=, and OUTH= options in the PROC CORR statement. The OUTP=, OUTS=, OUTK=, and OUTH= options produce SAS data sets with Pearson, Spearman, Kendall, and Hoeffding statistics, respectively. The data sets are designated as a special data set type, TYPE=CORR. This type of data set is recognized by many SAS/STAT procedures, including PROC REG and PROC FACTOR. See **Output 15.1 in Example 1** later in this chapter for an example of an output data set.

   The variables in these output data sets are

- BY variables, if a BY statement is used
- _TYPE_, identifying the type of observation
- _NAME_, identifying variable names
- INTERCEP, identifying variable sums, but only if the SSCP option is specified
- the variables listed in the VAR statement.

The observations, as identified by the _TYPE_ variable can be

- MEAN, the mean of each variable
- STD, the standard deviation of each variable
- N, the number of nonmissing observations for each variable
- SUMWGT, the sum of the weights for each variable, but only if a WEIGHT statement is used.

The following kinds of observations are further identified by the combination of the variables _TYPE_ and _NAME_. The _NAME_ variable identifies the variable with which a given row of the correlation matrix is associated. If you use the SSCP option, a row which specifies the intercept is added. The values of the _TYPE_ variable can be

- SSCP, the uncorrected sums of squares and crossproducts, but only if the SSCP option is given
- CSSCP, the corrected sums of squares and crossproducts, but only if the CSSCP option is given
- COV, the covariances, but only if the COV option is given
- CORR, a sequence of observations containing correlations.

When the ALPHA option is used, the output data set requested by the OUTP= option also includes the observations with the following _TYPE_ values:

- RAWALPHA, the Cronbach's coefficient alpha for raw variables
- STDALPHA, the Cronbach's coefficient alpha for standardized variables
- RAWALDEL, the Cronbach's coefficient alpha for raw variables with one variable being deleted
- STDALDEL, the Cronbach's coefficient alpha for standardized variables with one variable being deleted
- RAWCTDEL, the correlation between a raw variable and the total of the remaining raw variables
- STDCTDEL, the correlation between a standardized variable and the total of the remaining standardized variables.

When a PARTIAL statement is used, the statistics above are based on the variables after partialling. For the OUTP=, OUTK=, and OUTS= data sets when the PEARSON option is used, MEAN is set to zero and STD is the partial standard deviation associated with the partial variance. Without the PEARSON option, the statistics MEAN and STD are set to missing. See **Example 1** for use of the OUTP= data set.

Computational Methods

For the Spearman, Kendall, or Hoeffding correlations, the data are first ranked. The Spearman correlation is then computed on the ranks using the formula for the Pearson correlation. Averaged ranks are used in case of ties. The Kendall correlation is computed using a method similar to Knight (1966). Briefly, the method proceeds in this way: observations are ranked in order according to values of the first variable, the observations are then reranked according to values of the second variable, and the number of interchanges of the first variable is noted and used to compute Kendall's tau-b. The Q_i values needed to compute Hoeffding's D are also obtained from this double sorting.

Formulas

Spearman Correlation

The formula for the Spearman correlation is

$$\theta = \frac{\Sigma(R_i - \bar{R})(S_i - \bar{S})}{\sqrt{\Sigma(R_i - \bar{R})^2 \Sigma(S_i - \bar{S})^2}}$$

where R_i is the rank of the ith x value, S_i is the rank of the ith y value, and $\bar{R}$ and $\bar{S}$ are the means of the R_i and S_i values, respectively. Averaged ranks are used in the case of ties.

Kendall's tau-b

The formula for Kendall's tau-b is

$$\tau = \frac{\Sigma_{i<j} \, sgn(x_i - x_j) \, sgn(y_i - y_j)}{\sqrt{(T_0 - T_1)(T_0 - T_2)}}$$

where $T_0 = n(n-1)/2$, $T_1 = \Sigma t_i(t_i - 1)/2$, and $T_2 = \Sigma u_i(u_i - 1)/2$. The t_i (the u_i) are the number of tied x (respectively y) values in the ith group of tied x (respectively y) values, n is the number of observations, and $sgn(z) = 1$ if z is greater than 0, 0 if z is equal to 0, and -1 if z is less than 0.

Hoeffding's D Statistic

The formula for Hoeffding's D statistic (Hoeffding 1948) is

$$D = 30 \frac{(n-2)(n-3)D_1 + D_2 - 2(n-2)D_3}{n(n-1)(n-2)(n-3)(n-4)}$$

where $D_1 = \Sigma_i(Q_i - 1)(Q_i - 2)$, $D_2 = \Sigma_i(R_i - 1)(R_i - 2)(S_i - 1)(S_i - 2)$, and $D_3 = \Sigma_i(R_i - 2)(S_i - 2)(Q_i - 1)$. The R_i and S_i are the ranks of the x and y values as before, and the Q_i (sometimes called bivariate ranks) are one plus the number of points that have both x and y values less than the ith points. A point that is tied on its x value or y value, but not both, contributes $1/2$ to Q_i if the other value is less than the corresponding value for the ith point, and a point tied on both x and y contributes $1/4$ to Q_i.

When there are no ties among observations in a data set, the D statistic has values between -0.5 and 1, with 1 indicating complete dependence. However, when there are ties among observations in a data set, smaller values may result for the D statistics. That is, for a pair of variables with identical values, the Hoeffding's D statistic may be less than 1. With a large number of ties in a small data set, the D statistic may have values less than -0.5.

Partial Correlation

When you request the Pearson partial correlations, the CORR procedure derives the partial CSSCP matrix from applying the Cholesky decomposition algorithm to the CSSCP matrix. Let **S** be the partitioned CSSCP matrix between two sets of variables, $\mathbf{z}$ and $\mathbf{y}$:

$$S = \begin{bmatrix} S_{zz} & S_{zy} \\ S'_{zy} & S_{yy} \end{bmatrix}$$

Then $\mathbf{S}_{yy.z}$ is the partial CSSCP matrix of $\mathbf{y}$ after controlling for $\mathbf{z}$ and is calculated by applying the Cholesky decomposition algorithm sequentially on the rows associated with $\mathbf{z}$, the variables being partialled out.

After applying the Cholesky decomposition algorithm to each row associated with variables $\mathbf{z}$, all higher numbered diagonal elements associated with $\mathbf{z}$ are checked for singularity. A variable is considered singular if its corresponding diagonal element after Cholesky decomposition has a value less than p times the original unpartialled corrected sum of squares of that variable, where p is the singularity criterion specified in the SINGULAR= option. That is, a variable in the PARTIAL statement is considered singular if the R^2 for predicting this variable from the variables that already have been partialled out exceeds $1-p$. If this happens, the variable is not used in the analysis. Similarly, a variable in the VAR or WITH statement is considered singular if the R^2 for predicting this variable from the variables in the PARTIAL statement exceeds $1-p$. If this happens, its associated diagonal element and all higher numbered elements in this row or column are set to zero.

After completing the Cholesky decomposition algorithm on all rows associated with $\mathbf{z}$, the resulting matrix has the form

$$\begin{bmatrix} T_{zz} & T_{zy} \\ 0 & S_{yy.z} \end{bmatrix}$$

where $\mathbf{T}_{zz}$ is an upper triangular matrix with $\mathbf{T}'_{zz}\mathbf{T}_{zz}=\mathbf{S}_{zz}$, $\mathbf{T}'_{zz}\mathbf{T}_{zy}=\mathbf{S}_{zy}$, and $\mathbf{S}_{yy.z}=\mathbf{S}_{yy}-\mathbf{T}'_{zy}\mathbf{T}_{zy}$.

If $\mathbf{S}_{zz}$ is positive definite, then the partial CSSCP matrix $\mathbf{S}_{yy.z}$ derived from the CORR procedure is identical to the matrix derived from the formula

$$S_{yy.z} = S_{yy} - S'_{zy}\,S_{zz}^{-1}\,S_{zy}$$

By using the divisor evaluated from the VARDEF= option, the partial variance-covariance matrix can be calculated. Pearson's partial correlation matrix can be calculated by using the standard Pearson's correlation formula on the partial variance-covariance matrix. The Pearson's partial correlation can also be calculated by applying the Cholesky decomposition algorithm directly to the correlation matrix and then using the correlation formula on the resulting matrix.

The CORR procedure applies the Cholesky decomposition algorithm to Spearman's rank-order correlation matrix and Kendall's tau-b correlation matrix, and then it uses the correlation formula to derive the corresponding Spearman's partial rank-order correlations and Kendall's partial tau-b correlations.

When a correlation matrix (Pearson's correlation matrix, Spearman's rank-order correlation matrix, and Kendall's tau-b correlation matrix) is positive definite, the resulting partial correlation between variables x and y after adjusting for a single variable z from the CORR procedure is identical to that obtained from the first-order partial correlation formula

$$r_{xy.z} = \frac{r_{xy} - r_{xz}\,r_{yz}}{\sqrt{(1 - r_{xz}^2)(1 - r_{yz}^2)}}$$

where r_{xy}, r_{xz}, and r_{yz} are the appropriate correlations.

The formula for higher-order partial correlations is a straightforward extension of the first-order formula above. For example, when the correlation matrix is positive definite, the partial correlation between x and y controlling for both z_1 and z_2 derived from the CORR procedure is identical to the second-order partial correlation formula

$$r_{xy.z_1 z_2} = \frac{r_{xy.z_1} - r_{xz_2.z_1}\,r_{yz_2.z_1}}{\sqrt{(1 - r_{xz_2.z_1}^2)(1 - r_{yz_2.z_1}^2)}}$$

where $r_{xy.z_1}$, $r_{xz_2.z_1}$, and $r_{yz_2.z_1}$ are the first-order partial correlations among variables x, y, and z_2 given z_1.

Cronbach's Coefficient Alpha

The reliability coefficient of a measurement test is defined as the squared correlation between the observed value Y and the true value T

$$\rho^2(Y,T) = \frac{\mathrm{var}(T)}{\mathrm{var}(Y)}$$

where the measurement error $E = Y - T$ is independent of T.

The var(T) can be estimated if Y is the sum of several observed variables with the same feature. Suppose p variables are used with $Y_j = T_j + E_j$ for $j = 1, \ldots, p$, where Y_j is the observed value, T_j is the true value, and E_j is the measurement error. The measurement errors (E_j) are independent of the true values (T_j) and are also independent of each other.

Let $Y_0 = \Sigma Y_j$ be the total observed score and $T_0 = \Sigma T_j$ be the total true score. Since $(p - 1)\,\Sigma \mathrm{var}(T_j) \geq \Sigma_{i \neq j}\,\mathrm{cov}(T_i, T_j)$, a lower bound for var($T_0$) is given by

$$\left(\frac{p}{p-1}\right) \Sigma_{i \neq j}\,\mathrm{cov}(T_i, T_j) \quad.$$

With $\mathrm{cov}(Y_i, Y_j) = \mathrm{cov}(T_i, T_j)$ for $i \neq j$, a lower bound for the reliability coefficient is then given by the Cronbach's coefficient alpha:

$$\alpha = \left(\frac{p}{p-1}\right) \frac{\Sigma_{i \neq j}\,\mathrm{cov}(Y_i, Y_j)}{\mathrm{var}(Y_0)}$$

$$= \left(\frac{p}{p-1}\right)\left(1 - \frac{\Sigma_j\,\mathrm{var}(Y_j)}{\mathrm{var}(Y_0)}\right) \quad.$$

The coefficient alpha has a maximum value of one when the correlation between each pair of variables is one. With negative correlations between some variables, the coefficient alpha can have a value less than zero.

Similarly, the Cronbach's coefficient alpha from all variables except the kth variable is given by

$$\alpha_k = \left(\frac{p-1}{p-2} \right)\left(1 - \frac{\Sigma_{i \neq k}\, var(Y_i)}{var(\Sigma_{i \neq k}\, Y_i)} \right)$$

Probability Values

Probability values for the Pearson and Spearman correlations are obtained by treating $(n-2)^{1/2}\, r/(1-r^2)^{1/2}$ as coming from a t distribution with $n-2$ degrees of freedom, where r is the appropriate correlation. When a PARTIAL statement is used, probability values for the Pearson and Spearman partial correlations are obtained by treating $(n-k-2)^{1/2} r/(1-r^2)^{1/2}$ as coming from a t distribution with $n-k-2$ degrees of freedom, where r is the appropriate partial correlation and k is the number of variables being partialled out.

Probability values for Kendall correlations are obtained by treating $s/\sqrt{var(s)}$ as coming from a normal distribution where

$$s = \Sigma_{i<j}\, sgn(x_i - x_j)\, sgn(y_i - y_j)$$

and where x_i are the values of the first variable, y_i are the values of the second variable, and $sgn(z)=1$ if z is greater than 0, 0 if z is equal to 0, and -1 if z is less than 0. The variance of s, $var(s)$, is computed as

$$var(s) = \frac{v_0 - v_t - v_u}{18} + \frac{v_1}{2n(n-1)} + \frac{v_2}{9n(n-1)(n-2)}$$

where

$$v_0 = n(n-1)(2n+5)$$
$$v_t = \Sigma\, t_i(t_i - 1)\, (2t_i + 5)$$
$$v_u = \Sigma\, u_i\, (u_i - 1)(2u_i + 5)$$

$$v_1 = (\Sigma t_i\, (t_i - 1))(\Sigma u_i(u_i - 1))$$
$$v_2 = (\Sigma t_i\, (t_i - 1)(t_i - 2))(\Sigma u_i\, (u_i - 1)(u_i - 2))$$

The sums are over tied groups of values, t_i is the number of tied x values, and u_i is the number of tied y values (Noether 1967).

When a PARTIAL statement is used, the probability values for Kendall's partial tau-b are not available.

The probability values for Hoeffding's D statistic are computed using the asymptotic distribution computed by Blum, Keifer, and Rosenblatt (1961). The statistic

$$\frac{(n-1)\pi^4}{60} D + \frac{\pi^4}{72}$$

is computed and treated as coming from the asymptotic distribution. Tables for the distribution of D for sample sizes less than ten are available in Hollander and Wolfe (1973).

Computer Resources

Let

- N   be the number of observations
- C   be the number of types of correlations requested
- V   be the number of variables in the VAR list
- W   be the number of variables in the WITH list
- P   be the number of variables in the PARTIAL list.

Then

$$T = V + W + P$$

$$K = V * W \quad \text{if a WITH statement is used}$$

$$= V * (V+1) / 2 \quad \text{if a WITH statement is not used}$$

$$L = T * (T+1) / 2 \quad \text{if a PARTIAL statement is used}$$

$$= K \quad \text{if a PARTIAL statement is not used.}$$

If N is large, the CPU time required varies as $K*N$ when only Pearson correlations are requested. If Spearman correlations are requested, the CPU time varies as $T*N*\log N$. If Kendall or Hoeffding statistics are requested, the CPU time varies as $K*N*\log N$. If N is small and K is large, the CPU time required varies as K for all types of correlations. CPU time is much less if the NOMISS option is specified. Without the NOMISS option, processing is much faster if most of the observations have no missing values.

The amount of temporary storage required depends on the options specified and the statements used. The only factor limiting the number of variables used by PROC CORR is the available computer resources.

For Pearson's correlations alone, if both the NOMISS and NOSIMPLE options are specified, the minimum temporary storage needed in bytes to process the data is $M=40*T+16*L$. Without the NOMISS option, an additional $56*K$ bytes of memory for temporary storage is needed. If the NOSIMPLE option is not specified, the temporary storage must be increased by $56*T$ bytes. With a PARTIAL statement, PROC CORR requires an additional temporary memory of $12*T$ bytes. When the ALPHA option is specified, the temporary storage must be increased by $32*V+16$ bytes. In the following example, the NOMISS option is activated by the PARTIAL statement, so the minimum temporary storage needed in bytes is $M=40*T+16*L+56*T+12*T=984$:

```
proc corr;
   var x1 x2;
   with y1 y2 y3;
   partial z1;
```

With nonparametric options (SPEARMAN, KENDALL, or HOEFFDING) additional temporary storage is needed for each observation. For the most time-efficient processing, the amount of temporary storage needed in bytes is

$$M = 40*T + 8*K + 8*L*C + 12*T*N + 28*N + QS + QP + QK$$

where

QS	= 0	if the NOSIMPLE option is specified
	= 68 * T	otherwise
QP	= 56 * K	if the PEARSON option without the NOMISS option is specified
	= 0	otherwise
QK	= 32 * N	if the KENDALL or HOEFFDING option is specified
	= 0	otherwise.

For example, in the PROC statement

```
proc corr kendall;
  var x1 x2 x3;
```

the amount of temporary storage needed in bytes is M=96*N+420.

If M bytes are not available, PROC CORR must pass through the data several times to compute all the statistics. The minimum temporary storage then needed to process the data can be reduced by 12*(T−2)*N bytes. In this case, PROC CORR prints a note suggesting a larger memory region.

Printed Output

For each variable, the CORR procedure prints the following simple descriptive statistics:

1. the variable name
2. the number of observations having nonmissing values of the variable
3. the mean
4. the standard deviation
5. the median, if the SPEARMAN, KENDALL, or HOEFFDING option is specified
6. the sum, if only Pearson product-moment correlations are calculated
7. the minimum value
8. the maximum value.

When a PARTIAL statement is used and the PEARSON option is specified, PROC CORR also prints the following simple statistics after partialling for each variable in the VAR or WITH statement:

9. the partial variance
10. the partial standard deviation based on the partial variance.

For each pair of variables, PROC CORR prints

11. the Spearman, Kendall, Hoeffding, and Pearson coefficients requested.
12. N, the number of observations used to calculate the coefficient. If a FREQ statement is used, this number is the sum of the frequency variable.
13. Prob> | R | or Prob>D, the significance probability of the correlation or of Hoeffding's D under the null hypothesis that the statistic is zero. This probability is approximate for Spearman, Kendall, and Hoeffding statistics.

If requested, PROC CORR prints

14. SSCP (not shown), CSSCP, and COV matrices
15. partialled CORR (not shown), CSSCP, and COV matrices

16. SSCP, CSSCP, COV, and CORR matrices for specific combinations of variables (the WITH statement)
17. partialled CSSCP, COV, and CORR matrices for specific combinations of variables (the WITH statement)
18. the correlations for each variable in descending order of their absolute values (the RANK or BEST= options) (not shown).

When the input data set contains observations with missing values and the NOMISS option is not specified, the following statistics for each pair of variables can be printed. The statistics are calculated from observations with nonmissing row and column variable values.

19. SSCP('W','V'), the uncorrected sum-of-squares and crossproducts (not shown)
20. USS('W'), the uncorrected sum-of-squares for the row variable (not shown)
21. USS('V'), the uncorrected sum-of-squares for the column variable (not shown)
22. CSSCP('W','V'), the corrected sum-of-squares and crossproducts
23. CSS('W'), the corrected sum-of-squares for the row variable
24. CSS('V'), the corrected sum-of-squares for the column variable
25. COV ('W','V'), the covariance
26. VAR ('W'), the variance for the row variable
27. VAR ('V'), the variance for the column variable
28. DF('W','V'), the divisor used to calculate the covariance and variances.

When the ALPHA option is specified, then for each variable specified in the VAR statement, PROC CORR prints the following statistics for both the raw variables and the standardized variables:

29. the Cronbach Coefficient Alpha
30. the correlation between the variable and the total of the remaining variables
31. Cronbach's Coefficient Alpha, using the remaining variables.

EXAMPLES

Example 1:   Skin Data

In the following example PROC CORR is used three times to show

- all four kinds of measures of association
- a Pearson's partial correlation matrix
- Cronbach's coefficient alpha.

It also generates a TYPE=CORR output data set with covariances as well as correlations. The results are shown in **Output 15.1** through **Output 15.3**.

```
        /*  Data Courtesy A.C. Linnerud, N.C.State Univ. */
    data skinfold;
       input chest abdomen arm @@;
       cards;
    09.0 12.0 3.0  20.0 20.0 7.5  10.0 23.0 6.0  12.0  6.0 5.0
    08.5 15.0 3.0  12.0 17.0 4.0  11.0 13.0 6.0  05.0 14.0 3.0
    13.0 19.0 3.0  22.0 20.0 6.0  10.5 12.0 3.5  17.0 15.0 4.5
    10.0  7.0 4.0  17.0 28.0 5.5  15.0 15.5 3.0  16.0 11.0 3.0
    07.0 13.0 2.5  16.0 18.0 3.0  09.0 12.5 5.0  17.5 18.0 3.0
    15.5 28.5 5.0  21.0 27.5 6.0  23.0 24.0 6.5  11.5 15.0 3.0
```

```
22.5 20.0 4.5   13.0 14.0 4.0   14.0 21.0 2.5   04.0  3.0 2.0
05.5  8.5 3.0   21.0 13.0 9.0   16.0 11.0 3.0   17.5 15.0 4.5
25.0 35.0 6.5   21.0  6.0 3.5   16.5 17.0 4.0   09.5 11.5 2.5
15.0 19.0 4.0   13.5  6.5 3.5   16.0 15.0 3.0   26.0 38.0 4.0
12.5 20.0 3.0   05.0  7.5 3.5   12.0 15.0 3.5   15.0 13.0 4.5
17.0 19.5 5.0   16.0 20.0 5.5   09.0  4.0 2.0   19.0 12.0 3.0
16.0 17.5 6.0   14.5 14.5 4.0
;
run;

proc corr data=skinfold pearson spearman kendall hoeffding;
   var chest abdomen arm;
   title 'Spearman''s rho, Kendall''s tau-b, Pearson''s & Hoeffding';
run;

proc corr data=skinfold csscp cov;
   var chest abdomen;
   partial arm;
   title 'Partial Correlation Matrix';
run;

proc corr data=skinfold cov alpha outp=corrout;
   var chest abdomen arm;
   title 'Covariances and Correlations';
run;

proc print data=corrout;
   title2 'Output Data Set from PROC CORR';
run;
```

Output 15.1   Four Measures of Association

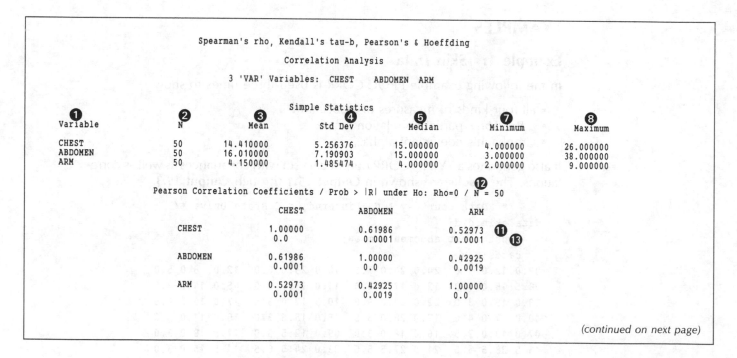

(continued on next page)

(continued from previous page)

```
          Spearman Correlation Coefficients / Prob > |R| under Ho: Rho=0 / N = 50

                          CHEST          ABDOMEN            ARM

          CHEST         1.00000          0.54825          0.51761  ⓫  ⓭
                        0.0              0.0001           0.0001

          ABDOMEN       0.54825          1.00000          0.45687
                        0.0001           0.0              0.0009

          ARM           0.51761          0.45687          1.00000
                        0.0001           0.0009           0.0


          Kendall Tau b Correlation Coefficients / Prob > |R| under Ho: Rho=0 / N = 50

                          CHEST          ABDOMEN            ARM

          CHEST         1.00000          0.41246          0.38974  ⓫  ⓭
                        0.0              0.0001           0.0002

          ABDOMEN       0.41246          1.00000          0.33048
                        0.0001           0.0              0.0015

          ARM           0.38974          0.33048          1.00000
                        0.0002           0.0015           0.0

              Spearman's rho, Kendall's tau-b, Pearson's & Hoeffding

                              Correlation Analysis

          Hoeffding Dependence Coefficients / Prob > D under Ho: D=0 / N = 50

                          CHEST          ABDOMEN            ARM

          CHEST         0.91768          0.09636          0.06797
                        0.0001           0.0001           0.0006

          ABDOMEN       0.09636          0.89934          0.04966
                        0.0001           0.0001           0.0030

          ARM           0.06797          0.04966          0.69550
                        0.0006           0.0030           0.0001
```

Output 15.2   Producing a Partial Correlation Matrix

```
                          Partial Correlation Matrix

                              Correlation Analysis

                  1 'PARTIAL' Variables:  ARM
                  2 'VAR'     Variables:  CHEST    ABDOMEN


                  Corrected Sum-of-Squares and Crossproducts

                          ARM             CHEST           ABDOMEN

        ⓮   ARM       108.125000      202.675000       224.675000
            CHEST     202.675000     1353.845000      1148.045000
            ABDOMEN   224.675000     1148.045000      2533.745000
```

(continued on next page)

(continued from previous page)

```
                   Partial Corrected Sum-of-Squares and Crossproducts

                                    CHEST           ABDOMEN

                   CHEST         973.940671        726.902751
                   ABDOMEN       726.902751       2066.888532

           ⑮            Partial Covariance Matrix    DF = 48

                                    CHEST           ABDOMEN

                   CHEST          20.29043064      15.14380732
                   ABDOMEN        15.14380732      43.06017775

                               Simple Statistics              ⑨           ⑩
                                          ⑥                  Partial      Partial
Variable      N       Mean     Std Dev     Sum      Minimum    Maximum    Variance     Std Dev

ARM          50     4.150000   1.485474   207.500000   2.000000    9.000000      .            .
CHEST        50    14.410000   5.256376   720.500000   4.000000   26.000000   20.290431   4.504490
ABDOMEN      50    16.010000   7.190903   800.500000   3.000000   38.000000   43.060178   6.562025


        Pearson Partial Correlation Coefficients / Prob > |R| under Ho: Partial Rho=0 / N = 50

                                    CHEST           ABDOMEN

                   CHEST          1.00000          0.51233
                                  0.0              0.0002

                   ABDOMEN        0.51233          1.00000
                                  0.0002           0.0
```

Output 15.3   Producing an Output Data Set with Covariances and
Correlations

```
                              Correlation Analysis

                   3 'VAR' Variables:  CHEST    ABDOMEN  ARM

                          Covariance Matrix    DF = 49

                            CHEST          ABDOMEN           ARM

            CHEST        27.62948980      23.42948980      4.13622449
            ABDOMEN      23.42948980      51.70908163      4.58520408
            ARM           4.13622449       4.58520408      2.20663265

                             Simple Statistics

Variable      N       Mean     Std Dev      Sum        Minimum      Maximum

CHEST        50    14.410000   5.256376   720.500000   4.000000    26.000000
ABDOMEN      50    16.010000   7.190903   800.500000   3.000000    38.000000
ARM          50     4.150000   1.485474   207.500000   2.000000     9.000000
```

(continued on next page)

(continued from previous page)

```
                        Covariances and Correlations

                          Correlation Analysis

                       Cronbach Coefficient Alpha
  29
              for RAW variables         :  0.661328
              for STANDARDIZED variables:  0.769205


                        Raw Variables          Std. Variables
                    30              31      30              31
        Deleted   Correlation             Correlation
        Variable  with Total      Alpha   with Total      Alpha
        -----------------------------------------------------------------
        CHEST       0.660261    0.290727    0.679943     0.600665
        ABDOMEN     0.631090    0.434152    0.599789     0.692578
        ARM         0.522633    0.742629    0.532788     0.765325


    Pearson Correlation Coefficients / Prob > |R| under Ho: Rho=0 / N = 50

                          CHEST          ABDOMEN            ARM

         CHEST          1.00000          0.61986          0.52973
                        0.0              0.0001           0.0001

         ABDOMEN        0.61986          1.00000          0.42925
                        0.0001           0.0              0.0019

         ARM            0.52973          0.42925          1.00000
                        0.0001           0.0019           0.0
```

```
                        Covariances and Correlations
                        Output Dataset from PROC CORR

         OBS   _TYPE_    _NAME_     CHEST     ABDOMEN      ARM

          1    COV       CHEST     27.6295    23.4295     4.1362
          2    COV       ABDOMEN   23.4295    51.7091     4.5852
          3    COV       ARM        4.1362     4.5852     2.2066
          4    MEAN                14.4100    16.0100     4.1500
          5    STD                  5.2564     7.1909     1.4855
          6    N                   50.0000    50.0000    50.0000
          7    RAWALPHA             0.6613     0.6613     0.6613
          8    STDALPHA             0.7692     0.7692     0.7692
          9    RAWALDEL             0.2907     0.4342     0.7426
         10    STDALDEL             0.6007     0.6926     0.7653
         11    RAWCTDEL             0.6603     0.6311     0.5226
         12    STDCTDEL             0.6799     0.5998     0.5328
         13    CORR      CHEST      1.0000     0.6199     0.5297
         14    CORR      ABDOMEN    0.6199     1.0000     0.4292
         15    CORR      ARM        0.5297     0.4292     1.0000
```

Example 2: Iris Setosa Data

The sepal length, sepal width, petal length, and petal width are measured in millimeters in the iris data published by Fisher (1936). Fifty iris specimens from the species *Iris setosa* are used in the example. Three missing values are used to illustrate output with missing values.

In the following example, the CORR procedure is used to show

- rectangular COV and CORR matrices
- CSSCP and COV matrices from a data set with missing values.

These statements produce **Output 15.4** and **Output 15.5**:

```
data setosa;
   title 'Fisher (1936) Iris Setosa Data';
   input sepallen sepalwid petallen petalwid @@;
   label sepallen='Sepal Length in mm.'
         sepalwid='Sepal Width  in mm.'
         petallen='Petal Length in mm.'
         petalwid='Petal Width  in mm.';
   cards;
50 33 14 02    46 34 14 03    46 36 .  02
51 33 17 05    55 35 13 02    48 31 16 02
52 34 14 02    49 36 14 01    44 32 13 02
50 35 16 06    44 30 13 02    47 32 16 02
48 30 14 03    51 38 16 02    48 34 19 02
50 30 16 02    50 32 12 02    43 30 11 .
58 40 12 02    51 38 19 04    49 30 14 02
51 35 14 02    50 34 16 04    46 32 14 02
57 44 15 04    50 36 14 02    54 34 15 04
52 41 15 .     55 42 14 02    49 31 15 02
54 39 17 04    50 34 15 02    44 29 14 02
47 32 13 02    46 31 15 02    51 34 15 02
50 35 13 03    49 31 15 01    54 37 15 02
54 39 13 04    51 35 14 03    48 34 16 02
48 30 14 01    45 23 13 03    57 38 17 03
51 38 15 03    54 34 17 02    51 37 15 04
52 35 15 02    53 37 15 02
;
run;

proc corr data=setosa nomiss nosimple cov;
   var sepallen sepalwid;
   with petallen petalwid;
   title2 'Rectangular COV and CORR Matrices';
run;

proc corr data=setosa csscp nosimple cov;
   title2 'CSSCP and COV Matrices from Data Set with Missing Values';
run;
```

Output 15.4   Producing a Rectangular Correlation Matrix

```
                    Fisher (1936) Iris Setosa Data
                   Rectangular COV and CORR Matrices

                        Correlation Analysis

                  2 'WITH' Variables:  PETALLEN PETALWID
                  2 'VAR'  Variables:  SEPALLEN SEPALWID


                     Covariance Matrix    DF = 46

                       SEPALLEN          SEPALWID

        PETALLEN      0.729417206       1.041628122   Petal Length in mm.
        PETALWID      0.882978723       1.091581869   Petal Width  in mm.


   Pearson Correlation Coefficients / Prob > |R| under Ho: Rho=0 / N = 47

                       SEPALLEN          SEPALWID

          PETALLEN      0.13690           0.17945
          Petal Length in mm.   0.3588           0.2275

          PETALWID      0.24863           0.28214
          Petal Width in mm.    0.0919           0.0547
```

Output 15.5   Producing CSSCP and COV Matrices with Missing Values

```
                    Fisher (1936) Iris Setosa Data
           CSSCP and COV Matrices from Data Set with Missing Values

                        Correlation Analysis

            4 'VAR' Variables:  SEPALLEN SEPALWID PETALLEN PETALWID


                Corrected Sum-of-Squares and Crossproducts
                  CSSCP('W','V') / CSS('W') / CSS('V')

 'W'/'V'              SEPALLEN        SEPALWID        PETALLEN        PETALWID

SEPALLEN          ㉒ 608.8200000    486.1600000     61.0000000      42.8333333
Sepal Length in mm. ㉓ 608.8200000    608.8200000     592.0000000     554.6666667
                  ㉔ 608.8200000    704.0800000     126.0000000     49.9791667

SEPALWID             486.1600000     704.0800000     65.4285714      49.2708333
Sepal Width  in mm.  704.0800000     704.0800000     701.0612245     640.4791667
                     608.8200000     704.0800000     126.0000000     49.9791667

PETALLEN             61.0000000      65.4285714      126.0000000     22.3191489
Petal Length in mm.  126.0000000     126.0000000     126.0000000     111.8723404
                     592.0000000     701.0612245     126.0000000     49.7021277

PETALWID             42.8333333      49.2708333      22.3191489      49.9791667
Petal Width  in mm.  49.9791667      49.9791667      49.7021277      49.9791667
                     554.6666667     640.4791667     111.8723404     49.9791667
```

(continued on next page)

(continued from previous page)

```
                              Variances and Covariances
                    COV('W','V') / VAR('W') / VAR('V') / DF('W','V')

       'W'/'V'              SEPALLEN        SEPALWID        PETALLEN        PETALWID

       SEPALLEN         25  12.42489796     9.92163265      1.27083333      0.91134752
       Sepal Length in mm. 26  12.42489796  12.42489796    12.33333333     11.80141844
                        27  12.42489796    14.36897959      2.62500000      1.06338652
                            28  49          49              48              47

       SEPALWID             9.92163265     14.36897959      1.36309524      1.04831560
       Sepal Width  in mm. 14.36897959     14.36897959     14.60544218     13.62721631
                           12.42489796     14.36897959      2.62500000      1.06338652
                            49             49               48              47

       PETALLEN             1.27083333      1.36309524      2.62500000      0.48519889
       Petal Length in mm.  2.62500000      2.62500000      2.62500000      2.43200740
                           12.33333333     14.60544218      2.62500000      1.08048104
                            48              48               48              46

       PETALWID             0.91134752      1.04831560      0.48519889      1.06338652
       Petal Width  in mm.  1.06338652      1.06338652      1.08048104      1.06338652
                           11.80141844     13.62721631      2.43200740      1.06338652
                            47              47               46              47
```

```
                         Fisher (1936) Iris Setosa Data
              CSSCP and COV Matrices from Data Set with Missing Values

                              Correlation Analysis

       Pearson Correlation Coefficients / Prob > |R| under Ho: Rho=0 / Number of Observations

                            SEPALLEN        SEPALWID        PETALLEN        PETALWID

       SEPALLEN             1.00000         0.74255         0.22335         0.25726
       Sepal Length in mm.  0.0             0.0001          0.1229          0.0775
                            50              50              49              48

       SEPALWID             0.74255         1.00000         0.22014         0.27539
       Sepal Width  in mm.  0.0001          0.0             0.1285          0.0582
                            50              50              49              48

       PETALLEN             0.22335         0.22014         1.00000         0.29932
       Petal Length in mm.  0.1229          0.1285          0.0             0.0410
                            49              49              49              47

       PETALWID             0.25726         0.27539         0.29932         1.00000
       Petal Width  in mm.  0.0775          0.0582          0.0410          0.0
                            48              48              47              48
```

REFERENCES

Blum, J.R., Kiefer, J., and Rosenblatt, M. (1961), "Distribution Free Tests of Independence Based on the Sample Distribution Function," *Annals of Mathematical Statistics*, 32, 485–498.

Conover, W.J. (1980), *Practical Nonparametric Statistics*, Second Edition, New York: John Wiley & Sons, Inc.

Cronbach, L.J. (1951), "Coefficient Alpha and the Internal Structure of Tests," *Psychometrika*, 16, 297–334.

Fisher, R.A. (1936), "The Use of Multiple Measurements in Taxonomic Problems," *Annals of Eugenics*, 7, 179–188.

Hoeffding, W. (1948), "A Non-Parametric Test of Independence," *Annals of Mathematical Statistics*, 19, 546–557.

Hollander, M. and Wolfe, D. (1973), *Nonparametric Statistical Methods*, New York: John Wiley & Sons, Inc.

Knight, W.E. (1966), "A Computer Method for Calculating Kendall's Tau with Ungrouped Data," *Journal of the American Statistical Association*, 61, 436–439.

Moore, D.S. (1979), *Statistics: Concepts and Controversies*, San Francisco: W.H. Freeman and Company.

Noether, G.E. (1967), *Elements of Nonparametric Statistics*, New York: John Wiley & Sons, Inc.

Novick, M.R. (1967), "Coefficient Alpha and the Reliability of Composite Measurements," *Psychometrika*, 32, 1–13.

Ott, L. (1977), *An Introduction to Statistical Methods and Data Analysis*, North Scituate, Mass.: Duxbury Press.

Snedecor, G.W. and Cochran, W.C. (1967), *Statistical Methods*, 6th Edition, Ames, Iowa: Iowa State University Press.

The CPORT
Procedure

ABSTRACT

The CPORT procedure writes SAS data sets and catalogs into a special format in a transport file. Coupled with the CIMPORT procedure, PROC CPORT allows you to move SAS catalogs and data sets from one operating system or host to another.

INTRODUCTION

This chapter uses the following terminology:

exporting
> is putting a SAS data library, a SAS catalog, or a SAS data set into transport format. The CPORT procedure exports catalogs and data sets, either singly or as a SAS data library.

importing
> is restoring a transport file to its original form (as a SAS data library, a SAS catalog, or a SAS data set) in the format appropriate to the host operating system. The CIMPORT procedure imports a transport file created by PROC CPORT.

a *transport file*
> is a sequential file containing a SAS data library, a SAS catalog, or a SAS data set in transport format. The transport format written by PROC CPORT is the same for all operating systems and many releases of the SAS System. Thus, Release 6.06 PROC CIMPORT running under any operating system can read a transport file created by Version 5, Release 6.03, or Release 6.06 PROC CPORT on any operating system. (See the following definition of *converting* for information on using the CPORT and CIMPORT procedures from different releases of the SAS System.)

Only PROC CIMPORT can read a transport file created by PROC CPORT. PROC CIMPORT can read only transport files created by PROC CPORT. For information on transport files created by the transport engine, refer to Chapter 6, "SAS Files," in SAS Language: Reference, Version 6, First Edition.

converting

a SAS file is changing its format from the format appropriate to one version of the SAS System to the format appropriate to another version running on the same operating system.

The CPORT and CIMPORT procedures are not primarily intended for converting files but for moving them from one operating system to another. You can use these procedures to move SAS catalogs and SAS data sets from an operating system running an earlier release of the SAS System to another operating system running a more recent release. In such a case, the CIMPORT procedure automatically converts the contents of the transport file as it imports it. However, because of the many enhancements in Release 6.06 of the SAS System, you cannot use the CPORT and CIMPORT procedures to move catalogs and data sets from an operating system running a newer release of the SAS System to an operating system running an older release.

Note: Although you can use the CPORT and CIMPORT procedures to convert some SAS files from Version 5 format to Version 6 format on the same operating system, it is simpler to use the V5TOV6 procedure. (See Chapter 43, "The V5TOV6 Procedure.")

Some restrictions exist on the types of catalog entries you can move from one operating system to another. See **DETAILS** later in this chapter for information on which catalog entries you can export.

To move Release 6.06 data sets and catalogs from one operating system to another, follow these steps:

1. Use PROC CPORT to export the SAS files you want to move.
2. Move the transport file to the new machine using either communications software or magnetic medium.
   Note: If you use communications software, be sure that it treats the transport file as a *binary* file and that it modifies neither the attributes nor the contents of the file.
3. Use PROC CIMPORT to translate the transport file into the format appropriate for the new host.

You can use a similar process to move catalogs and data sets from an operating system running Version 5 of the SAS System to an operating system running Release 6.06. However, keep in mind the following important points:

- You must use Version 5 PROC CPORT to export Version 5 catalogs.
- You cannot use Version 5 PROC CPORT to export Version 5 data sets because in Version 5, PROC CPORT exports only catalogs. However, if the operating system running Version 5 is also running Release 6.06, you can create a transport file of data sets from a Version 5 data library by using Release 6.06 PROC CPORT if you are accessing the Version 5 data library with the Version 5 engine. (See Chapter 6, "SAS Files," in SAS Language: Reference.)

SPECIFICATIONS

The PROC CPORT statement is the only statement associated with the CPORT procedure.

PROC CPORT Statement

PROC CPORT *source-type*=*libref*<.*member-name*> <*option-list*>;

where

source-type   identifies the file or files to export as a single catalog, as a single SAS data set, or as the members of a SAS data library. The *source-type* argument can be one of the following:

CATALOG | CAT | C
DATA | DS
LIBRARY | LIB | L

libref<.*member-name*>

identifies the particular catalog, SAS data set, or SAS data library to export. If the *source-type* argument is CATALOG or DATA, specify both a libref and a member name. If the *source-type* argument is LIBRARY, specify only a libref.

If you specify a data library, the CPORT procedure exports only data sets and catalogs from that library. You cannot export other types of files.

Table 16.1 summarizes the options you can use in the PROC CPORT statement. Descriptions of the options follow in alphabetic order.

Table 16.1 Summary of PROC CPORT Statement Options

Class	Option	Function
Options identifying the transport file	FILE=	specifies the transport file to write to
	TAPE	directs the output to tape
Options selecting files to export	SELECT=	selects individual catalog entries for the transport file
	EXCLUDE=	excludes individual catalog entries from the transport file
	MEMTYPE=	limits the type of SAS file PROC CPORT writes to the transport file
Options affecting contents of the transport file	ASIS	suppresses the conversion of displayed character data to transport format
	OUTTYPE= UPCASE	writes all alphabetic characters to the transport file in uppercase

(continued)

Table 16.1 Summary of PROC CPORT Statement Options (*continued*)

Class	Option	Function
	NOCOMPRESS	suppresses the compression of binary zeros and blanks in the transport file
	TRANSLATE=	translates specified characters from one ASCII or EBCDIC value to another
Options for files with DBCS data	INTYPE=	specifies the type of DBCS data stored in the SAS files you are exporting
	OUTTYPE= DBCS-type	specifies the type of DBCS data to use in the transport file
	OUTLIB=	specifies a libref associated with a SAS data library (PROC CPORT automatically recreates the input data library, data set, or catalog in the specified library)

ASIS
  suppresses the conversion of displayed character data to transport format. Use this option when you are moving files containing DBCS (double-byte character set) data from one machine to another if both machines use the same type of DBCS data. (Use the INTYPE= and OUTTYPE= options if the machines use different types of DBCS data.)
  The ASIS option invokes the NOCOMPRESS option.
  You cannot use both the ASIS option and the INTYPE= or OUTTYPE= options in the same PROC CPORT step.

EXCLUDE=(*entry-list*)
  excludes individual catalog entries from the transport file. Each element of *entry-list* has the following form:

  entry.etype

  where *entry* is the name of the entry and *etype* is its entry type. Note that *entry-list* can be a single entry or a list of entries. If you specify a single entry, you do not need to enclose it in parentheses. (For information on entry types, see *SAS Language: Reference*.)
  You cannot use the EXCLUDE= and the SELECT= options in the same PROC CPORT step.

FILE=*fileref* | '*filename*'
  specifies a previously defined fileref or the filename of the transport file to write to. If you do not use the FILE= option, the CPORT procedure writes to a file with the reserved fileref SASCAT.
  Note: The behavior of PROC CPORT when SASCAT is undefined varies from one operating system to another. Refer to the SAS documentation for your host system for details.

INTYPE=*DBCS-type*
  specifies the type of DBCS data stored in the SAS files you are exporting. If you do not use the INTYPE= option, *DBCS-type* defaults to the value of the DBCSTYPE= option. You must set the DBCSTYPE= option when you start your SAS session. You can set the option in your configuration file.

Valid values for *DBCS-type* can be the following:

IBM | HITAC | FACOM	(for MVS)
IBM	(for CMS and VSE)
DEC | SJIS	(for VAX™)
DG | SJIS	(for DG)
PRIME | SJIS	(for PRIME)
PCIBM | SJIS	(for OS/2)

Use the INTYPE= option in conjunction with the OUTTYPE=*DBCS-type* option to change from one type of DBCS data to another.

The INTYPE= option invokes the NOCOMPRESS option.

You cannot use the INTYPE= option and the ASIS option in the same PROC CPORT step.

MEMTYPE=CATALOG | DATA

limits the type of SAS file PROC CPORT writes to the transport file. When you specify MEMTYPE=CATALOG, the procedure writes only SAS catalogs to the transport file; when you specify MEMTYPE=DATA, it writes only SAS data sets.

NOCOMPRESS

suppresses the compression of binary zeros and blanks in the transport file. By default, the CPORT procedure compresses these characters to save space. For instance, it replaces a string of 100 binary zeros with a shorter string that the SAS System recognizes as being equivalent to 100 binary zeros. The SAS System treats the compressed and noncompressed versions of a file identically. However, the compressed version may use considerably less storage space.

Note: Compression of the transport file does not alter the flag in each catalog and data set that indicates whether the original file was compressed.

Use this option if you intend to work directly with the transport file. The ASIS, INTYPE=, and OUTTYPE= options invoke the NOCOMPRESS option.

OUTLIB=*libref*

OUT=*libref*

specifies a libref associated with a SAS data library. If you specify the OUTLIB= option, PROC CPORT automatically re-creates the input data library, data set, or catalog in the specified library. You do not need to use PROC CIMPORT. This option is useful for changing SAS files from one type of DBCS data to another on the same system while maintaining the original data intact.

PROC CPORT also creates the usual transport file.

OUTTYPE=*DBCS-type* | UPCASE

defines the format of DBCS and alphabetic characters in the transport file, where

DBCS-type   specifies the type of DBCS data to use in the transport file. If you omit the OUTTYPE= option, the value defaults to the value of the DBCSTYPE= option. You must set the DBCSTYPE= option when you start your SAS session. You can set the option in your configuration file.

VAX is a trademark of Digital Equipment Corporation.

Use OUTTYPE=*DBCS-type* in conjunction with the INTYPE= option to change from one type of DBCS data to another. See the INTYPE= option for a list of valid DBCS types.

UPCASE   writes all displayed alphabetic characters to the transport file and to the OUTLIB= file in uppercase.

You cannot use the OUTTYPE=UPCASE and the INTYPE= option in the same PROC CPORT step.

You cannot use the OUTTYPE= option and the ASIS option in the same PROC CPORT step.

SELECT=(*entry-list*)

selects individual catalog entries for the transport file. Each element of *entry-list* has the following form:

entry.etype

where

entry   is the name of the entry or the name of a group of GRSEG entries.

etype   is the entry type.

Note that *entry-list* can be a single entry or a list of entries. If you specify a single entry, you do not need to enclose it in parentheses. (For information on entry types, see *SAS Language: Reference*.)

You cannot use the SELECT= and EXCLUDE= options in the same PROC CPORT step.

TAPE

directs the output from PROC CPORT to tape. By default, output goes to disk.

TRANSLATE=(*translation-list*)

translates the specified characters from one ASCII or EBCDIC value to another. Each element of *translation-list* has the following form:

ASCII-value-1 TO *ASCII-value-2*

EBCDIC-value-1 TO *EBCDIC-value-2*

You can use either hexadecimal or decimal representations for ASCII values. If you use the hexadecimal representation, values must begin with a digit and end with an *x*. Use a leading zero if the hexadecimal number begins with an alphabetic character.

For example, to translate all left brackets to left braces, specify the option as follows (for ASCII characters):

```
translate=(5bx to 7bx)
```

The next example translates all left brackets to left braces and all right brackets to right braces:

```
translate=(5bx to 7bx 5dx to 7dx)
```

DETAILS

Characteristics of a Transport File

A transport file written by PROC CPORT always has a logical record length of 80 and, therefore, a fixed record format. However, the procedure cannot control the transport file's block size. On all operating systems except OS/2, for which block size has no meaning, you control the block size with a host-specific option in a FILENAME statement or with job control language (see the SAS documentation for your host system for details). While other block sizes may work, it is recommended that you always specify a block size of 8000 so that you do not have to determine the block size of each transport file before importing it.

Moving Release 6.06 SAS Catalogs from One Operating System to Another

The CPORT procedure can export the following types of Release 6.06 catalog entries:

AFCBT	FORMAT	LIST
AFGO	FORMATC	LOG
AFMACRO	FORMULA	MENU
CBT	GRSEG	OUTPUT
CMAP	HELP	PMENU
DEVICE	INFMT	PROGRAM
EDPARMS	INFMTC	SCREEN
FONT	KEYS	SOURCE
FORM	LETTER	TEMPLATE

EXAMPLES

These examples illustrate the use of PROC CPORT in Release 6.06 of the SAS System.

Because PROC CPORT does not write anything to SAS output, you can only tell if the procedure performed as you expected by looking at your SAS log. Always check your log when you are exporting files.

Example 1:   Selecting Members from a SAS Data Library

In the following example, PROC CPORT writes a transport file to the disk file referenced by TRANFILE. The file contains all the catalogs from the SAS data library SOURCE (selected by the MEMTYPE= option). In addition, all left brackets from the source file appear in the transport file as left braces and all right brackets as right braces. The log describing the export of the SAS data library SOURCE appears in **Output 16.1**.

```
libname source 'SAS-data-library';
filename tranfile 'transport-file-name'
                  host-option-for-block-size;

proc cport library=source file=tranfile memtype=catalog
           translate=(5bx to 7bx 5dx to 7dx);
run;
```

Output 16.1   Log Produced by Selecting Catalogs for Export with the
TRANSLATE= Option

```
NOTE: Libref SOURCE was successfully assigned as follows:
      Engine:       V606
      Physical Name: SAS-data-library
4
5         libname source 'SAS-data-library';
6         filename tranfile 'transport-file-name' host-option-for-block-size;
7
8         proc cport library=source file=tranfile memtype=catalog
9                   translate=(5bx to 7bx 5dx to 7dx);
10        run;

NOTE: Proc CPORT begins to transport catalog SOURCE.PRECIP
NOTE: The catalog has 3 entries and its maximum logical record length is 176
NOTE: Transporting entry RAIN     .PROGRAM
NOTE: Transporting entry SLEET    .PROGRAM
NOTE: Transporting entry SNOW     .PROGRAM

NOTE: Proc CPORT begins to transport catalog SOURCE.PROFILE
NOTE: The catalog has 1 entries and its maximum logical record length is 13
NOTE: Transporting entry DMKEYS   .KEYS

NOTE: Proc CPORT begins to transport catalog SOURCE.TEMP
NOTE: The catalog has 2 entries and its maximum logical record length is 176
NOTE: Transporting entry HIGH     .PROGRAM
NOTE: Transporting entry LOW      .PROGRAM
```

Example 2:   Exporting Individual Catalog Entries

The following example selects the catalog entries RAIN.PROGRAM and
SNOW.PROGRAM from the SAS catalog CLIMATE.PRECIP and writes them to
the transport file TRANFILE. The SAS log produced by these statements appears
in **Output 16.2**.

```
libname climate 'SAS-data-library';
filename tranfile 'transport-file-name'
                  host-option-for-block-size;

proc cport catalog=climate.precip file=tranfile
           select=(rain.program snow.program);
run;
```

Output 16.2   Log Produced by Exporting Individual Catalog Entries

```
NOTE: Libref CLIMATE was successfully assigned as follows:
      Engine:       V606
      Physical Name: SAS-data-library
4
5         libname climate 'SAS-data-library';
6         filename tranfile 'transport-file-name' host-option-for-block-size;
7
8         proc cport catalog=climate.precip file=tranfile
9                   select=(rain.program snow.program);
10        run;

NOTE: Proc CPORT begins to transport catalog CLIMATE.PRECIP
NOTE: The catalog has 3 entries and its maximum logical record length is 176
NOTE: Transporting entry RAIN    .PROGRAM
NOTE: Transporting entry SNOW    .PROGRAM
```

You can see from the log that the catalog CLIMATE.PRECIP contains three entries. However, the procedure exports only the two entries specified by the SELECT= option.

Example 3:   Changing DBCS Format

In this example PROC CPORT writes the contents of the SAS data library DBCSIBM to the transport file TRANFILE in transport format. The DBCS data in the transport file are written in DEC format. PROC CPORT also writes the contents of DBCSIBM to the SAS data library DBCSDEC, converting the DBCS data from IBM to DEC format.

```
libname dbcsibm 'SAS-data-library-1';
libname dbcsdec 'SAS-data-library-2';
filename tranfile 'transport-file-name'
                    host-option-for-block-size;

proc cport library=dbcsibm outlib=dbcsdec file=tranfile
            intype=ibm outtype=dec;
run;
```

Output 16.3   Log Produced by Exporting SAS Files Containing DBCS Data

```
NOTE: Libref DBCSIBM was successfully assigned as follows:
      Engine:       V606
      Physical Name: SAS-data-library-1
4
5          libname dbcsibm 'SAS-data-library-1';
6          filename tranfile 'transport-file-name' host-option-for-block-size;
7          libname dbcsdec 'SAS-data-library-2';
NOTE: Libref DBCSDEC was successfully assigned as follows:
      Engine:       V606
      Physical Name: SAS-data-library-2
10
11         proc cport library=dbcsibm outlib=dbcsdec file=tranfile
12                   intype=ibm outtype=dec;
13         run;


NOTE: Proc CPORT begins to transport catalog DBCSIBM.FIRST
NOTE: The catalog has 1 entries and its maximum logical record length is 176
NOTE: Transporting entry COPYRITE.HELP

NOTE: Proc CPORT begins to transport catalog DBCSIBM.SECOND
NOTE: The catalog has 6 entries and its maximum logical record length is 176
NOTE: Transporting entry CBT     .HELP
NOTE: Transporting entry HELP    .HELP
NOTE: Transporting entry MENU    .HELP
NOTE: Transporting entry PROGRAM .HELP
NOTE: Transporting entry CBT     .KEYS
NOTE: Transporting entry DISPLAY .KEYS
NOTE: Proc CIMPORT begins to create/update catalog DBCSDEC.FIRST
NOTE: Importing entry COPYRITE.HELP
NOTE: Total number of entries processed: 1

NOTE: Proc CIMPORT begins to create/update catalog DBCSDEC.SECOND
NOTE: Importing entry CBT     .HELP
NOTE: Importing entry HELP    .HELP
NOTE: Importing entry MENU    .HELP
NOTE: Importing entry PROGRAM .HELP
NOTE: Importing entry CBT     .KEYS
NOTE: Importing entry DISPLAY .KEYS
NOTE: Total number of entries processed: 6
```

The DATASETS Procedure

ABSTRACT

Use the DATASETS procedure to list, copy, rename, and delete SAS files and to manage indexes for and append SAS data sets in a SAS data library. Note that for your convenience, the DATASETS procedure now provides all the capabilities of the APPEND, CONTENTS, and COPY procedures, as well as the customary PROC DATASETS capabilities. The APPEND, CONTENTS, and COPY procedures continue to be supported, so existing SAS programs that use these procedures do not require modifications.

INTRODUCTION

Use the DATASETS procedure to manage a SAS data library. With PROC DATASETS you can list, copy, rename, and delete SAS files in a SAS data library. For SAS data sets, PROC DATASETS can append the contents of one data set to another; change variable names and related variable information, such as informats, formats, or labels; and create, delete, and repair indexes.

The APPEND, CONTENTS, and COPY statements enable you to perform these utility functions within the DATASETS procedure rather than using the APPEND, CONTENTS, and COPY procedures in separate PROC steps.

You specify changes to library members with the subordinate procedure statements: AGE, CHANGE, DELETE, EXCHANGE, and SAVE.

Although the DATASETS procedure can perform some operations on catalogs, generally you should use the CATALOG procedure or the CATALOG window in display manager instead when you are working with catalogs. They enable you to manage entries within catalogs as well as manage entire catalogs. See Chapter 6, "SAS Files," in *SAS Language: Reference, Version 6, First Edition* for information about SAS data libraries, especially the types of files (or members) that can reside in a SAS data library.

PROCEDURE EXECUTION

The DATASETS procedure is an interactive procedure. It remains active after a RUN statement is executed. Once you start the DATASETS procedure, you can continue to manipulate files within a library until you have finished all the tasks you planned. This capability can save time and resources when you plan a number of tasks for one session. The DATASETS procedure behaves in other ways that make it different from all other SAS procedures. The following paragraphs describe some of the differences that are important for you to remember:

- The input library is specified in the PROC DATASETS statement. When you start the DATASETS procedure, you specify the input library. If you do not specify an input library, the SAS System uses the temporary library WORK as the source of files. To specify a new input library, you must start the DATASETS procedure again.
- Statements execute in the order they are written. If you write a program that does several things to the same library, the SAS System completes those tasks in the order they appear in the program. For example, if you want to see the contents of a data set, copy in a data set from another library, and then compare the contents of the second data set with the first, the statements that perform those tasks must be written in that order (that is, CONTENTS, COPY, CONTENTS) so they execute correctly.

- Groups of statements can execute without a RUN statement. Like other SAS procedures, PROC DATASETS statements are executed when you submit a RUN statement. However, for the DATASETS procedure *only*, the SAS System also recognizes the primary PROC DATASETS statements as implied RUN statements as long as no syntax errors occur. Refer to **Error Handling** below for information on what occurs when the SAS System detects syntax errors in a PROC DATASETS step.

  The SAS System reads the program statements associated with one task until it reaches a RUN statement or a statement that functions as an implied RUN statement. It executes all of the preceding statements immediately, then continues reading until it reaches another of these statements. To execute the last task, you must still include a RUN statement.

  In addition, the PROC DATASETS statement executes as soon as it is submitted. You do not need to enter a RUN statement or any other statement to execute the PROC DATASETS statement.

  Note: If you are running in interactive line mode, this feature means you can receive messages that statements have already executed before you submit a RUN statement. You should plan your tasks carefully if you are using this environment for running PROC DATASETS.

- Some statements are dependent on other statements. The SELECT and EXCLUDE statements can only be used immediately after a COPY statement. The following statements can only be used immediately after a MODIFY statement:

FORMAT	INFORMAT
INDEX CREATE	LABEL
INDEX DELETE	RENAME

  These dependent statements execute immediately.

- The DATASETS procedure remains active until you submit a statement to stop it. To stop the DATASETS procedure, you must issue a QUIT statement, a RUN CANCEL statement, a new PROC statement, or a DATA statement. Submitting a QUIT statement executes any statements that have not executed and ends the procedure. Submitting a RUN CANCEL statement cancels any statements that have not executed and ends the procedure. If you are using display manager and leave the procedure without issuing one of the statements listed above, you receive a message asking you to verify that you want to stop.

Error Handling

If a syntax error is encountered, the RUN group containing the error is not executed. Run groups preceding or following the one containing the syntax error are processed normally. Note that if the first word of the statement (the statement name) is in error and cannot be recognized by the SAS System, the statement is treated as part of the preceding RUN group.

For example, suppose the following statements are submitted as a group:

```
libname drink 'SAS-data-library';
libname misc 'SAS-data-library';

proc datasets library=misc memtype=data;
   copy out=drink;
      select coffee tea;
   del georgia;
   change gdpstats=economic;
   modify cars(label='Cars Rated on Six Scales');
      rename noise=quiet;
run;
quit;
```

The DELETE statement is misspelled (DEL), so neither it nor the COPY and SELECT statements are executed. The misspelled statement is treated as part of the same RUN group as the COPY and SELECT statements. However, the CHANGE and MODIFY statements are executed because they are in a separate RUN group.

SPECIFICATIONS

The DATASETS procedure is controlled by the following statements:

PROC DATASETS <LIBRARY=*libref*> <MEMTYPE=(*mtype-list*)> <KILL>
<FORCE> <NOLIST> <NOWARN>;
AGE *current-name related-member-list* </ MEMTYPE=*mtype*>;
APPEND BASE=*SAS-data-set* <DATA=*SAS-data-set*> <FORCE>;
CHANGE *old-name-1=new-name-1* <...*old-name-n=new-name-n*>
</ MEMTYPE=*mtype*>;
CONTENTS <DATA=<*libref.*>*member*> <DIRECTORY>
<MEMTYPE=(*mtype-list*)> <NODS> <NOPRINT>
<OUT=*SAS-data-set*> <POSITION> <SHORT>;
COPY OUT=*libref* <IN=*libref*> <MEMTYPE=(*mtype-list*)> <MOVE>;
   EXCLUDE *member-list* </ MEMTYPE=*mtype*>;
   SELECT *member-list* </ MEMTYPE=*mtype*>;
DELETE *member-list* </ MEMTYPE=*mtype*>;
EXCHANGE *name-1=other-name-1* <...*name-n=other-name-n*>
</ MEMTYPE=*mtype*>;
MODIFY *member-name* <(<LABEL='*data-set-label*'> <TYPE=*special-type*>)>;
   FORMAT *variable-list-1 format-1* <...*variable-list-n format-n*>;
   INDEX CREATE *index-1<=(variable-list-1)>* <...*index-n<=(variable-list-n)>*>
</ <UNIQUE> <NOMISS>>;
   INDEX DELETE *index-list*;
   INFORMAT *variable-list-1 informat-1* <...*variable-list-n informat-n*>;
   LABEL *variable-1='variable-label-1'* <...*variable-n='variable-label-n'*>;
   RENAME *variable-1=new-name-1* <...*variable-n=new-name-n*>;
REPAIR *member-name* <(MEMTYPE=*mtype*)>;
SAVE *member-list* </ MEMTYPE=*mtype*>;

The *mtype* in all of the above statements must be a single member type, *mtype-list* can be one or more member types, and *SAS-data-set* can be a one- or two-level data set name. If *SAS-data-set* is a one-level name, the libref defaults to the libref specified in the PROC DATASETS statement or to the default library, which is usually WORK.

Table 17.1 summarizes how to use the statements in the DATASETS procedure.

Table 17.1 Summary of PROC DATASETS Functions

Function	Statements	Options
Produce list of members in a SAS data library	PROC DATASETS, CONTENTS	MEMTYPE=, DATA=_ALL_, DIRECTORY, NODS
List contents of a SAS data set	CONTENTS	DATA=, SHORT, POSITION
Send contents of a SAS data set to another data set	CONTENTS	DATA=, OUT=, NOPRINT
Change the names of members of a SAS data library	CHANGE, AGE	
Exchange the names of two members of a SAS data library that have the same member type	EXCHANGE	
Copy or move an entire SAS data library or selected members of a library to another SAS data library	COPY, SELECT, EXCLUDE	MOVE
Delete all members of a SAS data library	PROC DATASETS	KILL
Delete selected members of a SAS data library	DELETE, SAVE	MEMTYPE=
Concatenate two SAS data sets	APPEND	FORCE
Change data set attributes	MODIFY	LABEL=, TYPE=
Change variable attributes	MODIFY, LABEL, FORMAT, INFORMAT, RENAME	
Create, delete, and repair indexes	MODIFY, INDEX CREATE, INDEX DELETE, REPAIR	

PROC DATASETS Statement

PROC DATASETS <LIBRARY=*libref*> <MEMTYPE=(*mtype-list*)> <KILL>
<FORCE> <NOLIST> <NOWARN>;

By default, the PROC DATASETS statement lists in the SAS log all members in
the SAS data library that match the member type specified in the PROC
DATASETS statement. If no member type is specified, all members are listed. This
statement executes immediately, without a RUN statement.

Options

The following options can be used in the PROC DATASETS statement:

FORCE
> specifies a default action for all APPEND statements included in the
> PROC DATASETS step. If the FORCE option is specified, all APPEND
> statements are forced to concatenate two data sets when the variables in
> the data sets are not exactly the same. Refer to **Concatenating Data Sets
> with Different Descriptions** in Chapter 5, "The APPEND Procedure," for
> more information on how the FORCE option works.

KILL
> deletes *all* members in the SAS data library.
>
> **Caution:**   Be careful when submitting the KILL option. This option
> deletes all members of the library immediately after the statement is
> submitted.

LIBRARY=*libref*
> refers to the SAS data library to be processed. If LIBRARY= is not
> specified, the current default SAS data library (usually the WORK library)
> is processed.

MEMTYPE=(*mtype-list*)
MTYPE=(*mtype-list*)
MT=(*mtype-list*)
> specifies one or more member types that are available for processing. If
> *mtype-list* is a single member type, you can omit the parentheses. Valid
> member types are described in **Valid values for the MEMTYPE= option**
> later in this chapter.
>
> In the PROC DATASETS statement, the MEMTYPE= option limits the
> procedure processing to those types specified. For example, if the library
> being processed contains SAS data sets and catalogs, you can limit
> processing to SAS data sets with the MEMTYPE= option, as follows:
>
> ```
> libname ref1 'SAS-data-library';
> proc datasets library=ref1 memtype=data;
> ```
>
> For more information on types of members that can reside in a SAS
> data library, see Chapter 6 in *SAS Language: Reference*.
>
> You can also specify the MEMTYPE= option in most subordinate
> statements to the DATASETS procedure. For details on how the options
> interact when used in both the PROC DATASETS statement and other
> statements, refer to **Using the MEMTYPE= Option in Subordinate
> Statements** later in this chapter.

NOLIST
> suppresses listing the members that are available for processing in the
> SAS log.

NOWARN

suppresses the error processing that occurs when a member specified in a SAVE, CHANGE, EXCHANGE, or COPY statement or listed as the first member in an AGE statement is not in the SAS data library currently being processed. When an error occurs and you have not specified the NOWARN option, PROC DATASETS issues an error message and stops processing statements until the next RUN statement.

Using the MEMTYPE= Option in Subordinate Statements

Using the MEMTYPE= option in the PROC DATASETS statement limits what member types can be specified in most other statements used in the PROC DATASETS step. That is, if you specify a member type or several member types in the PROC DATASETS statement, in most subsequent statements in the PROC DATASETS step (the CONTENTS and COPY statements are exceptions to this rule), you can specify only a subset of the list of member types included in the PROC DATASETS statement.

Consider this example:

```
libname daily 'SAS-data-library';

proc datasets library=daily memtype=(data catalog);

    /* valid subset of member types */
  change day1=first / memtype=data;
run;

    /* incorrect subset of member types */
  change day1view=firstvs / memtype=view;
run;
```

If the MEMTYPE= option is not specified in the PROC DATASETS statement, or you want to limit the member types in a specific statement, you can specify the MEMTYPE= option in the AGE, CHANGE, DELETE, EXCHANGE, EXCLUDE, SAVE, and SELECT statements. The MEMTYPE= option works slightly differently for the CONTENTS and COPY statements. Refer to the description of these statements later in this chapter for more information.

For the AGE, CHANGE, DELETE, EXCHANGE, EXCLUDE, SAVE, and SELECT statements, use the following forms:

(MEMTYPE=mtype)
(MTYPE=mtype)
(MT=mtype)

in parentheses, the MEMTYPE= option identifies the type of the member name just preceding it. For example, the following statements delete A.DATA, B.CATALOG, and C.DATA because the default member type for the DELETE statement is DATA. (Refer to **Table 17.2** for the default types for each statement.)

```
libname abc 'SAS-data-library';

proc datasets lib=abc;
    delete a b (memtype=catalog) c;
run;
```

/ MEMTYPE=*mtype*
/ MTYPE=*mtype*
/ MT=*mtype*

after a slash, the MEMTYPE= option identifies the type of all member names preceding it.

If you specify the MEMTYPE= option after a slash and a preceding member is followed by (MEMTYPE=*mtype*), that member takes on the type specified immediately after the member. For example, these statements delete A.CATALOG, B.DATA, and C.CATALOG:

```
libname abc 'SAS-data-library';

proc datasets lib=abc;
    delete a b (memtype=data) c / memtype=catalog;
run;
```

Valid values for the MEMTYPE= option   For the AGE, CHANGE, CONTENTS, COPY, DELETE, EXCHANGE, EXCLUDE, SAVE, and SELECT statements, the possible member types specified in any MEMTYPE= option are

ACCESS	access files (created by SAS/ACCESS software)
ALL	all member types
CATALOG	catalogs
DATA	SAS data sets
PROGRAM	stored compiled SAS programs
VIEW	views created by the SQL procedure.

You cannot specify the MEMTYPE= option in the APPEND or MODIFY statements.

The default member types for each statement when you do not specify the MEMTYPE= option in the PROC DATASETS statement are shown in **Table 17.2**.

Table 17.2 Default Member Types for Statements in DATASETS Procedure

Statement	Default Member Type	Comment
AGE	DATA	
APPEND	DATA	
CHANGE	ALL	
CONTENTS	DATA	when DATA=_ALL_ then default is ALL
COPY	ALL	
DELETE	DATA	
EXCHANGE	ALL	
MODIFY	DATA	no other member type permitted
REPAIR	ALL	only DATA and CATALOG are included in ALL
SAVE	ALL	

AGE Statement

> **AGE** *current-name related-member-list* </ MEMTYPE=*mtype*>;

where *mtype* is a single member type. You can use the AGE statement to rename a group of related members in a library so that programs can then access the latest addition to the group using one name that does not change.

When an AGE statement is used, the member named *current-name* is renamed to the first name in the *related-member-list*, the second member (which is the first member name in *related-member-list*) is renamed to the second name in *related-member-list*, and so on until the name of the next-to-last member is changed to the last name. The last member is then deleted.

For example, each day you run a SAS program that creates the SAS data set TODAY. You keep that SAS data set in a SAS data library with seven other members. Each time you want to create a new SAS data set, the oldest SAS data set must be deleted and the remaining members renamed, leaving the name TODAY available for the new SAS data set. You can delete and rename the members using PROC DATASETS with the AGE statement:

```
libname daily 'SAS-data-library';

proc datasets library=daily;
   age today day1-day7 / memtype=data;
run;
```

After PROC DATASETS executes, the SAS data set originally named TODAY is renamed DAY1, the SAS data set originally named DAY1 is renamed DAY2, and so on. The SAS data set originally named DAY6 is renamed DAY7, and the SAS data set originally named DAY7 is deleted. Since there is no longer a member named TODAY, the name TODAY is available for the new SAS data set. Notice that this example uses an abbreviated SAS data set list, DAY1-DAY7.

If the first member named in the AGE statement does not exist in the SAS data library, PROC DATASETS stops processing the RUN group containing the AGE statement and issues an error message. To override this behavior, specify the NOWARN option in the PROC DATASETS statement. If other members listed are not present, the SAS System prints a message in the log and renames all the members that are present.

If the MEMTYPE= option is not specified in the PROC DATASETS statement or the AGE statement, the default type is DATA. Refer to **Using the MEMTYPE= Option in Subordinate Statements** earlier in this chapter for more information.

If you age a data set that has an index, the index is also aged so that it continues to correspond with the data set.

APPEND Statement

> **APPEND** BASE=*SAS-data-set* <DATA=*SAS-data-set*> <FORCE>;

where *SAS-data-set* can be a one- or two-level name. If *SAS-data-set* is a one-level name, the libref defaults to the libref specified in the PROC DATASETS statement.

Use the APPEND statement to append observations from one SAS data set to another. This statement can be used only with SAS data sets.

You can append compressed SAS data sets, but some restrictions apply. Refer to **Concatenating Compressed Data Sets** in Chapter 5 for more information.

The APPEND statement performs the same functions as those performed by the APPEND procedure (described in Chapter 5).

Requirements

The following argument is required in the APPEND statement:

> BASE=*SAS-data-set*
> OUT=*SAS-data-set*
>> name the SAS data set to which you want to add observations. If the APPEND statement cannot find an existing data set with this name, it creates a new data set. In other words, you can use the APPEND statement to create a data set by specifying a new data set name in the BASE= argument. The OUT= argument is equivalent to the BASE= argument. Either the BASE= or the OUT= argument must be specified.

Options

The following options can be specified in the APPEND statement:

> DATA=*SAS-data-set*
> NEW=*SAS-data-set*
>> name the SAS data set containing observations you want to add to the end of the SAS data set specified by the BASE= argument. If the DATA= option is omitted, the member created most recently in this job or session is used. The NEW= argument is equivalent to the DATA= option.
>>
>>   Note: You can use the WHERE= data set option or a WHERE statement with the APPEND statement to limit which observations from the DATA= data set are added to the BASE= data set, as shown in this example:

```
proc datasets;
   append base=test1 data=test2(where=(x=2));
run;
```

Refer to Chapter 9, "SAS Language Statements," and Chapter 15, "SAS Data Set Options," in *SAS Language: Reference* for more information on the WHERE statement and the WHERE= data set option.

FORCE
   forces the APPEND statement to concatenate data sets when the DATA= data set contains variables that
   - are not in the BASE= data set
   - do not have the same type as the variables in the BASE= data set
   - are longer than the variables in the BASE= data set.

Refer to **Concatenating Data Sets with Different Descriptions** in Chapter 5 for more information on how the FORCE option works.

CHANGE Statement

> **CHANGE** *old-name-1=new-name-1* <...*old-name-n=new-name-n*> </ MEMTYPE=*mtype*>;

where *mtype* is a single member type. Use the CHANGE statement to rename one or more members. Specify the old member name on the left side of the equal sign and the new member name on the right side. For example, these statements change the name of the SAS data set PERSIA to IRAN and RUSSIA to USSR:

```
libname oil 'SAS-data-library';


proc datasets library=oil memtype=data;
   change persia=iran russia=ussr;
run;
```

PROC DATASETS performs the changes in the order that the *old-names* occur in the directory listing, not in the order that the changes are listed in the CHANGE statement. If the *old-name* member does not exist in the SAS data library, PROC DATASETS stops processing the RUN group containing the CHANGE statement and issues an error message. To override this behavior, specify the NOWARN option in the PROC DATASETS statement.

When you change the name of a data set, any indexes associated with the data set are also changed so that they will be associated with the new name.

If the MEMTYPE= option is not specified in the PROC DATASETS statement or the CHANGE statement, the default value is ALL. Refer to **Using the MEMTYPE= Option in Subordinate Statements** earlier in this chapter for more information on the MEMTYPE= option.

CONTENTS Statement

> **CONTENTS** <DATA=<*libref.*>*member*> <DIRECTORY> <MEMTYPE=(*mtype-list*)> <NODS> <NOPRINT> <OUT=*SAS-data-set*> <POSITION> <SHORT>;

Use the CONTENTS statement to describe one or more members of a SAS data library. The CONTENTS statement performs the same functions as those performed by the CONTENTS procedure. Refer to Chapter 12, "The CONTENTS Procedure," for a description of the output produced by the CONTENTS statement.

Options

The following options can be specified in the CONTENTS statement:

DATA=<*libref.*>*member*
> specifies an entire library or a specific member within a library. If you use a two-level name, *libref* refers to the SAS data library, and *member* is either the name of a member in the library or the keyword _ALL_. If you use a one-level name, *member* is either the name of a member in the library specified in the PROC DATASETS statement or the keyword _ALL_.
>
> When you specify the name of a member, you get a report on that member. When you specify _ALL_, you get information about all members having the type or types specified by the MEMTYPE= option.
>
> If you do not specify the DATA= option, the CONTENTS statement describes the member created most recently in this job or session.

DIRECTORY
> prints the list of members contained in the specified SAS data library. This option is useful when you are printing the contents of just one file and when you also want to see the directory for the library. (When _ALL_ is specified in the DATA= option, the directory is automatically printed.)

MEMTYPE=(*mtype-list*)
MTYPE=(*mtype-list*)
MT=(*mtype-list*)
> prints a list of members of the specified types that are in the SAS data library. Note that *mtype-list* can be one or more member types. If *mtype-list* is a single member type, you can omit the parentheses. Valid member types are described in **Valid values for the MEMTYPE= option** earlier in this chapter.
>
> The MEMTYPE= option in the CONTENTS statement differs from the MEMTYPE= option in other statements in PROC DATASETS in several ways:
>
> - The option is not preceded by a slash.
> - The MEMTYPE= option cannot be enclosed in parentheses to limit its effect to only the member immediately preceding it. Note that you can enclose a list of member types in parentheses but not the MEMTYPE= option.
> - If you specify a data set name in the DATA= option, the contents operation is not affected by the MEMTYPE= option specified in the PROC DATASETS statement. The MEMTYPE= option in the PROC DATASETS statement only limits the processing for the _ALL_ value.
>
> If the MEMTYPE= option is not specified in either the PROC DATASETS statement or the CONTENTS statement, the default value is DATA when you specify a single member name in the DATA= option. If you specify DATA=*libref.*_ALL_ or DATA=_ALL_, the default MEMTYPE= value is ALL.

NODS
> suppresses printing the contents of individual files when _ALL_ is specified in the DATA= option. Only the SAS data library directory is printed.
>
> Using the CONTENTS statement with the NODS option produces the same information as using the PROC DATASETS statement alone, but

the CONTENTS statement routes the output to the procedure output
listing, not the log.

```
libname misc 'SAS-data-library';

    /* library information printed on log */
proc datasets lib=misc;

        /* same information printed on procedure output listing */
    contents data=misc._all_ nods;
    run;
```

NOPRINT
specifies that you do not want the CONTENTS output to be printed.
The NOPRINT option is useful only when used with the OUT= option.
The NOPRINT option is for SAS data sets only.

OUT=*SAS-data-set*
gives the name of an output SAS data set. The *SAS-data-set* can be a
one- or two-level name. If *SAS-data-set* is a one-level name, the libref
defaults to the libref specified in the PROC DATASETS statement.

The output SAS data set contains information similar to that given in
the variable description section in the printed output of the CONTENTS
statement or procedure. See **OUT= SAS Data Set** in Chapter 12 for
more details.

Note: The OUT= option does not suppress the printed output from
the statement. If you want to suppress the printed output, you must
specify the NOPRINT option.

POSITION
prints a second list of the variable names in the order of their position in
the data set. By default, the variables are listed in alphabetic order. This
option produces output for SAS data sets only.

SHORT
prints only the list of variable names in the SAS data set. This option
produces output for SAS data sets only.

COPY Statement

COPY OUT=*libref* <IN=*libref*> <MEMTYPE=(*mtype-list*)> <MOVE>;

where *mtype-list* can be one or more member types. If *mtype-list* is a single member type, you can omit the parentheses.

Use the COPY statement and options when you want to copy members
from one library to another. You can use the SELECT and EXCLUDE statements
with the COPY statement to limit which members of the library are copied. However, using the SELECT and EXCLUDE statements simultaneously within the
COPY statement will cause an error, and the COPY statement will not take effect.

When you copy a data set, any indexes associated with the data set are re-
created for the copied data set if the format of the output data set is for Release
6.06 or later of the SAS System.

The COPY statement performs the same functions as those performed by the
COPY procedure. See Chapter 14, "The COPY Procedure," for more information.

Requirements

The following argument is required in the COPY statement:

OUT=*libref*
> specifies the output library into which members are copied.
> **Caution:** During processing, the SAS System automatically writes the member from the input library into a member with the same name in the output library. You do not receive a warning message if there are duplicate data set names before copying starts.

Options

The following options can be specified in the COPY statement:

IN=*libref*
> specifies an alternate input library. For example, the following program copies all of the members from the WORK library into the TEST library:

```
libname test 'SAS-data-library';

proc datasets library=test;
   copy in=work out=test;
run;
```

> If you do not specify the IN= option, the library referenced by the LIBRARY= option in the PROC DATASETS statement is used as the input library.

MEMTYPE=*(mtype-list)*
MTYPE=*(mtype-list)*
MT=*(mtype-list)*
> specifies one or more types of members to be copied or moved. If *mtype-list* is a single member type, you can omit the parentheses. Valid member types are described in **Valid values for the MEMTYPE= option** earlier in this chapter.
> The MEMTYPE= option in the COPY statement differs from the MEMTYPE= option in other statements in PROC DATASETS in several ways:
> - The option is not preceded by a slash.
> - The MEMTYPE= option cannot be enclosed in parentheses to limit its effect to only the member immediately preceding it. Note that you can enclose a list of member types in parentheses but not the MEMTYPE= option. For example, use the following form of the MEMTYPE= option to copy both data sets and catalogs:

```
libname lib1 'SAS-data-library';
libname lib2 'SAS-data-library';

proc datasets library=lib1;
   copy out=lib2 memtype=(data catalog);
run;
```

> - The behavior of the MEMTYPE= option in the COPY statement is affected by the SELECT and EXCLUDE statements and the IN= option as follows:
>   1. If you specify a SELECT or EXCLUDE statement, the member types specified in those statements take precedence over the MEMTYPE= option in the COPY statement. In this example,

only APPLES.CATALOG is copied; the MEMTYPE= value in
the COPY statement is ignored because a different
MEMTYPE= value is specified in the SELECT statement.

```
libname mylib 'SAS-data-library';

proc datasets lib=mylib;
   copy out=work memtype=data;
      select apples / memtype=catalog;
run;
```

2. If you do not use the IN= option, the copy operation is
   limited to the MEMTYPE= values specified in the PROC
   DATASETS statement. The order of precedence described in
   rule 1 is used to further subset the members to be copied. In
   this example, no members are copied; instead, you receive
   an error message because the MEMTYPE= value specified in
   the SELECT statement is not one of the types listed in the
   PROC DATASETS statement.

```
libname mylib 'SAS-data-library';

proc datasets lib=mylib memtype=(data program);
   copy out=work;

           /* incorrect use of MEMTYPE= option */
           /* on SELECT statement */
      select apples / memtype=catalog;
run;
```

3. If you specify the IN= option, the copy operation is not
   affected by the MEMTYPE= option in the PROC DATASETS
   statement. The order of precedence described in rule 1 is
   used to determine which types of members are copied. In
   this example, ORANGES.DATA is copied because the library
   specified in the IN= option in the COPY statement is not
   affected by the MEMTYPE= option in the PROC DATASETS
   statement.

```
libname mylib 'SAS-data-library';
libname othrlib 'SAS-data-library';

proc datasets lib=mylib memtype=catalog;
   copy in=othrlib out=work;
      select oranges / memtype=data;
run;
```

If you do not specify the MEMTYPE= option in any of the
PROC DATASETS, COPY, EXCLUDE, or SELECT statements, the
default member type is ALL.

MOVE
    causes each member successfully copied to the output library (specified
    in the OUT= option) to be deleted from the input library (specified in
    the IN= option in the COPY statement or the LIB= option in the PROC
    DATASETS statement). For example, these statements copy

members of the SAS library referenced by OLD into the SAS library referenced by NEW and delete the members from the OLD library:

```
libname old 'SAS-data-library';
libname new 'SAS-data-library';

proc datasets library=old;
   copy out=new move;
run;
```

Caution: Be careful when you are moving libraries and data sets. The MOVE option deletes all or part of the input library immediately after the statements are submitted.

DELETE Statement

DELETE *member-list* </ MEMTYPE=*mtype*>;

where *mtype* can be a single member type.

Use the DELETE statement to specify members to be deleted from the SAS data library.

Caution: The SAS System immediately deletes libraries and library members when a RUN group is submitted. You are not asked to verify the delete operation before it begins.

If you attempt to delete a member that does not exist in the SAS data library, PROC DATASETS issues a message and continues processing.

The following example illustrates the DELETE statement:

```
libname digit 'SAS-data-library';

proc datasets library=digit;
   delete one two;
run;
```

This program deletes the members ONE and TWO from the SAS data library referenced by the libref DIGIT.

Use the MEMTYPE= option in the DELETE statement to restrict processing to one type. Refer to **Using the MEMTYPE= Option in Subordinate Statements** earlier in this chapter for detailed information on the MEMTYPE= option.

If MEMTYPE= is specified in the PROC DATASETS statement, use the MEMTYPE= option in the DELETE statement to further restrict processing to one of those previously specified types. For example, the MEMTYPE= option is used in both the PROC DATASETS statement and the DELETE statement in the following program:

```
libname food 'SAS-data-library';

proc datasets library=food memtype=(data catalog);
   delete meats dairy / memtype=catalog;
run;
```

When this program executes, only MEATS and DAIRY of type CATALOG are deleted. If the MEMTYPE= option had not been specified in the DELETE statement, SAS data sets and CATALOG members named MEATS and DAIRY would have been deleted.

If the MEMTYPE= option is not specified in the DELETE statement or the PROC DATASETS statement, the default value is DATA.

When you delete a data set that has indexes associated with it, the indexes are deleted as well.

EXCHANGE Statement

EXCHANGE *name-1=other-name-1 <...name-n=other-name-n>*
               </ MEMTYPE=mtype>;

where *mtype* can be a single member type. Use the EXCHANGE statement to exchange the names of two members in a SAS data library. More than one pair of member names can be changed with one EXCHANGE statement. PROC DATASETS performs the changes in the order that the *name* members occur in the directory listing, not in the order that the changes are listed in the EXCHANGE statement.

If the *name* member does not exist in the SAS data library, PROC DATASETS stops processing the RUN group containing the EXCHANGE statement and issues an error message. To override this behavior, specify the NOWARN option in the PROC DATASETS statement.

The following example exchanges the name of the member originally called A to Z and the name of the member Z to A:

```
libname mylib 'SAS-data-library';


proc datasets library=mylib;
   exchange a=z;
run;
```

Use the MEMTYPE= option to restrict name exchanges to one type of member. If the MEMTYPE= option is not specified in the EXCHANGE statement or the PROC DATASETS statement, ALL is the default value. Refer to **Using the MEMTYPE= Option in Subordinate Statements** earlier in this chapter for more information on the MEMTYPE= option.

If you exchange the name of a data set that has indexes associated with it, the indexes are also exchanged so that they will be associated with the new name.

EXCLUDE Statement

The EXCLUDE statement can be used only after a COPY statement. The general form of the EXCLUDE statement is

EXCLUDE *member-list </ MEMTYPE=mtype>;*

The EXCLUDE statement names one or more SAS files (or members) that should not be copied to the output library.

For example, the following program copies all of the files (members) from the library referenced by STUDY to the library referenced by CONTROL except GROUP1, GROUP2, and GROUP 3:

```
libname study 'SAS-data-library';
libname control 'SAS-data-library';


proc datasets library=study;
   copy out=control;
      exclude group1-group3;
run;
```

Refer to **Using the MEMTYPE= Option in Subordinate Statements** earlier in this chapter for information on the MEMTYPE= option. Note: If you specify the MEMTYPE= option in both the COPY statement and the EXCLUDE statement, the value you specify in the EXCLUDE statement takes precedence.

FORMAT Statement

The FORMAT statement can be used only after a MODIFY statement. The general form of the FORMAT statement is:

FORMAT *variable-list-1 format-1 <...variable-list-n format-n>*;

Variable formats in the SAS data set specified by the MODIFY statement can be changed or removed with the FORMAT statement. To change a format, specify the name of the variable and then the new format. When the variable name is given but there is no accompanying format, the old format is removed and not replaced. Multiple variables can be used, and abbreviated variable lists, such as X1-X5, can be used where appropriate. You can change as many formats as you want with one FORMAT statement. The following example assigns the variables X1, X2, and X3 the 4.1 format; the variable TIME is assigned the HHMM2.2 format; and the format of the variable AGE is removed:

```
libname study 'SAS-data-library';

proc datasets library=study;
  modify group1;
      format x1-x3 4.1 time hhmm2.2 age;
run;
```

Any variables whose formats are to be removed must be listed last in the FORMAT statement; otherwise, they are assigned the first format that follows. For example, if you write the FORMAT statement shown above as follows,

```
format x1-x3 4.1 age time hhmm2.2;
```

the variable AGE would have its format changed to HHMM2.2, rather than removed.

INDEX CREATE Statement

The INDEX CREATE statement can be used only after a MODIFY statement. The general form of the INDEX CREATE statement is

INDEX CREATE *index-1<=(variable-list-1)>*
                    <...index-n<=(variable-list-n)>> </ <UNIQUE> <NOMISS>>;

The INDEX CREATE statement creates simple or composite indexes on the data set named in the MODIFY statement. You can create indexes for a SAS data set from Release 6.06 or later. An *index* is a SAS file that can be used to efficiently locate observations in a SAS data set. A *simple index* is an index that locates observations based on the value of a single variable. A *composite index* is an index that locates observations based on the values of two or more variables.

To create a simple index, use the INDEX CREATE statement as follows:

INDEX CREATE *variable*;

This form of the statement creates a simple index on the variable named in the statement.

To create a composite index, use the INDEX CREATE statement as follows:

INDEX CREATE *index=(variable-1...variable-n)*;

This form of the statement creates a composite index named *index* that is based on the variables *variable-1* to *variable-n*. The name for *index* must be unique within the SAS data set; it cannot be the same as any variable name or any other composite index name. Refer to Chapter 6 in *SAS Language: Reference* for more information on indexes.

Options

For either form of index, you can use the options listed below. Note that these options apply to all indexes created in a single INDEX CREATE statement.

NOMISS
> excludes from the index all observations with missing values for all index variables.
>
> > Note: Indexes created with this option are not used by the BY statement. If you specify a BY statement with the same variables as those in the index and the data set is not sorted in that order, you receive a message indicating that the data set is not in sorted order. The PROC or DATA step containing the BY statement does not attempt to use the index.
>
> When you create an index with the NOMISS option, the index is used only for WHERE processing and only when missing values fail to satisfy the WHERE clause. For example, if you have indexed the variable DEPT with the NOMISS option and use this WHERE statement

```
where dept eq '01';
```

> the index can be used to search the data set. However, if you use this WHERE statement

```
where dept ne '01';
```

> the SAS System does not use the index because missing values satisfy the WHERE clause. Refer to Chapter 9 and Chapter 15 in *SAS Language: Reference* for more information on the WHERE statement and the WHERE= data set option.

UNIQUE
> specifies that the combination of values of the index variables must be unique. If you specify UNIQUE and multiple observations have the same values for the index variables, the index is not created.

Using Indexes

Indexes are separate files in SAS data libraries, but in general, they are treated as an extension of the data set. Therefore, if you copy, delete, move, or perform some other data management task on the data set, the index is treated in the same manner so that it continues to be associated with the data set.

Indexing a data set enables you to use BY statements in DATA and PROC steps without first sorting the data set. Simply specify in the BY statement the variable or list of variables that have been indexed. Do not use the name of a composite index in a BY statement; instead use the list of variables that make up the index. Note that you must use the same list of variables in the same order in the BY statement that you specified in the INDEX CREATE statement. You can, however, use only the first part of a list of variables that make up a composite index. That is, if you have an index based on the variables A, B, and C, you can specify a BY statement with only A and B.

INDEX DELETE Statement

The INDEX DELETE statement can be used only after a MODIFY statement. The general form of the INDEX DELETE statement is

INDEX DELETE *index-list*;

The INDEX DELETE statement deletes one or more indexes associated with the data set named in the MODIFY statement. You can delete both simple and composite indexes.

Note: You can use the CONTENTS statement to produce a list of all indexes on a data set.

INFORMAT Statement

The INFORMAT statement can be used only after a MODIFY statement. The general form of the INFORMAT statement is

INFORMAT *variable-list-1 informat-1* <*...variable-list-n informat-n*>;

Informats in the SAS data set specified by the MODIFY statement can be changed or removed using the INFORMAT statement. To change an informat, specify the name of the variable and then the new informat. When a variable name is specified without an accompanying informat, the old informat is removed.

Multiple variables and abbreviated variable lists can be used. For example, in the SAS data set GROUP1, the variables A, B, and X1-X3 are assigned new informats and the variable C has its informat removed with the following statements:

```
libname study 'SAS-data-library';

proc datasets library=study;
   modify group1;
      informat a b 2. x1-x3 4.1 c;
run;
```

Any variables whose informats are to be removed must be listed last in the INFORMAT statement; otherwise, they are assigned the first informat that follows.

LABEL Statement

The LABEL statement can be used only after a MODIFY statement. The general form of the LABEL statement is

LABEL *variable-1='variable-label-1'* <*...variable-n='variable-label-n'*>;

The LABEL statement changes or removes variable labels in the SAS data set specified by the MODIFY statement. You can use as many variables as you want in the LABEL statement, as long as each variable name is followed by an equal sign. To specify a new label, follow the equal sign with a new label. To remove a label, you must specify a blank enclosed in single quotes. If the new label includes a right parenthesis, equal sign, or semicolon, it must be enclosed in single quotes. If a single quote appears in the label, it must be written as two single quotes in the LABEL statement. The new label can be up to 40 characters long. The following statements change the labels for variables X1 and X2 and remove the label for variable A in the SAS data set GROUP1:

```
libname study 'SAS-data-library';

proc datasets library=study;
   modify group1;
      label x1='Score 1=' x2='Score 2=' a=' ';
run;
```

MODIFY Statement

MODIFY *member-name* <(<LABEL=*'data-set-label'*> <TYPE=*special-type*>)>;

where *member-name* must be a member of type DATA in the data library specified in the PROC DATASETS statement.

Use the MODIFY statement and options when you want to change attributes in the specified SAS data set. You can specify only one SAS data set name in each MODIFY statement. If the *member-name* does not exist in the SAS data library, PROC DATASETS stops processing the RUN group containing the MODIFY statement and issues an error message.

The MODIFY statement is used with the following statements to change variable names, labels, informats, or formats in the specified SAS data set or to create or delete indexes:

- FORMAT
- INDEX CREATE
- INDEX DELETE
- INFORMAT
- LABEL
- RENAME

Each of these statements is described in detail in this chapter.

Options

The following options can be specified in the MODIFY statement. Note that options must be enclosed in parentheses.

LABEL=*'data-set-label'*
LABEL=*' '*

specifies a data set label or removes a label for the SAS data set named in the MODIFY statement. A new label cannot be longer than 40 characters and must be enclosed in single quotes.

If you specify the LABEL= option with one blank, the old label is removed. In the following example, the first MODIFY statement removes the label of the SAS data set TEST.EXP1, and the second MODIFY statement changes the label of TEST.EXP2:

```
libname test 'SAS-data-library';

proc datasets library=test;
   modify exp1 (label=' ');
   modify exp2 (label='Tests on Three Year Olds');
run;
```

TYPE=*special-type*

assigns or changes the special data set type of a SAS data set. Most SAS data sets have no special type. However, a number of special SAS data sets can be created by certain SAS procedures (for example, the CORR and FACTOR procedures) or in a DATA step.

Valid *special-type* values are

CORR
COV
EST
FACTOR
SSCP

See Appendix 1 in *SAS/STAT User's Guide, Version 6, Fourth Edition, Volume 2* for a discussion of special SAS data sets.

Note: Do not confuse the TYPE= option with the MEMTYPE=
option. The TYPE= option specifies a type of special SAS data set. The
MEMTYPE= option specifies one or more types of members in a SAS
data library.

You must be sure that the specified value of the TYPE= option
corresponds to the actual SAS data set type. The SAS data set type
specified by the TYPE= option is not validated by the SAS System
(except to check if it has a length of eight characters or fewer). The
SAS System does not verify that the SAS data set's structure is
appropriate for the type you have designated or even that you have
specified a valid special type.

When you specify both the LABEL= and TYPE= options, separate them with
one blank and enclose them in parentheses, for example,

```
modify exp3 (label='Tests For All Ages' type=corr);
```

RENAME Statement

The RENAME statement can be used only after a MODIFY statement. The general
form of the RENAME statement is

RENAME *variable-1=new-name-1* <...*variable-n=new-name-n*>;

Variables from the SAS data set specified in the MODIFY statement can be
assigned new names using the RENAME statement. The new name must be a valid
SAS name. The number of variables that you can rename in one statement is
unlimited. The following example changes the name of two variables:

```
rename day1=time1 day2=time2;
```

PROC DATASETS performs the changes in the order that they are listed in the
RENAME statement. If the *variable* does not exist in the SAS data set or *new-name*
already exists, PROC DATASETS stops processing the RUN group containing the
RENAME statement and issues an error message.

When you change the name of a variable for which there is a simple index,
the index is also renamed. If the variable is used in a composite index, the composite index references the new variable name. However, if you attempt to
change the name of a variable to a name that has already been used for a composite index, the following error message occurs:

```
The name name conflicts with an index name on file libref.member.
```

For example, if you have a data set with a variable named TEMP and a composite
index for the same data set named OLD, you cannot change the variable TEMP
to OLD, even if the TEMP variable has no index.

REPAIR Statement

REPAIR *member-name* <(MEMTYPE=*mtype*)>;

where *member-name* must be a SAS data set or catalog in the data library specified in the PROC DATASETS statement and *member-type* can be DATA,
CATALOG, or ALL.

The REPAIR statement attempts to restore damaged SAS data sets or catalogs
to a usable condition. The most common situations that require the REPAIR statement are

- a system failure occurs while you are updating a SAS data set or catalog.
- the device on which a SAS data set or an associated index resides is
  damaged. In this case, the damaged data set or index can be restored
  from a backup device, but the data set and index no longer match.

- the disk where the SAS data set or catalog is stored becomes full before the file is completely written to disk.
- an I/O error occurs while writing a SAS data set or catalog entry.

When you use the REPAIR statement for SAS data sets, it re-creates all simple indexes for the data set. It also attempts to restore the data set to a usable condition, but the restored data set may not include the last several updates that occurred before the system failed.

Note: You cannot use the REPAIR statement to re-create indexes that were destroyed by using the FORCE option in a SORT procedure step.

When you use the REPAIR statement for a catalog, it checks the catalog to see which entries are potentially damaged and attempts to restore those entries. You receive a message stating whether the entry is restored for each entry that was potentially damaged. In some situations where the catalog is damaged, for example when a system failure occurs, the entire catalog is potentially damaged. The REPAIR statement then attempts to restore all the entries in the catalog. In other situations, for example when a single entry is being updated and a disk-full condition occurs, on most systems only the entry that is open when the problem occurs is potentially damaged. In this case, the REPAIR statement attempts to repair only that entry.

The REPAIR statement restores a catalog as much as possible. However, some entries within the restored catalog may not include the last updates that occurred before a system crash or an I/O error. The REPAIR statement issues warning messages for entries that may have truncated data.

SAVE Statement

SAVE *member-list* </ MEMTYPE=*mtype*>;

where *member-list* specifies the members that should not be deleted and *mtype* specifies a single member type.

Use the SAVE statement to delete all the members in a library except the ones listed in the SAVE statement.

Caution: The SAS System immediately deletes libraries and library members when the RUN group is submitted. You are not asked to verify the delete operation before it begins. Because the SAVE statement deletes many members in one operation, be sure that you understand how the MEMTYPE= option affects which member types are saved and which types are deleted.

If one of the members in the *member-list* does not exist in the SAS data library, PROC DATASETS stops processing the RUN group containing the SAVE statement and issues an error message. To override this behavior, specify the NOWARN option in the PROC DATASETS statement.

The MEMTYPE= option in the SAVE statement specifies the type of members to be saved. Refer to **Using the MEMTYPE= Option in Subordinate Statements** earlier in this chapter for more information on the MEMTYPE= option.

The following program deletes all members except APPLES.DATA, ORANGES.CATALOG, and PEARS.DATA:

```
libname fruit 'SAS-data-library';

proc datasets library=fruit;
   save apples oranges (memtype=catalog) pears / memtype=data;
run;
```

If you do not specify the MEMTYPE= option in the PROC DATASETS statement or the SAVE statement, MEMTYPE=ALL is in effect. For example, the following program deletes all members in the library (referenced by FRUIT) except those named APPLES, ORANGES, and PEARS:

```
libname fruit 'SAS-data-library';

proc datasets library=fruit;
   save apples oranges pears;
run;
```

If you specify the MEMTYPE= option in the PROC DATASETS statement, the MEMTYPE= value in the SAVE statement must be one of those previously specified types. For example, these statements

```
libname fruit 'SAS-data-library';

proc datasets library=fruit memtype=(data catalog);
   save apples oranges pears (memtype=catalog);
run;
```

delete all members except the following:

- APPLES.DATA
- APPLES.CATALOG
- ORANGES.DATA
- ORANGES.CATALOG
- PEARS.CATALOG

If MEMTYPE=CATALOG had not been specified in the SAVE statement in this example, all members of CATALOG type except APPLES, ORANGES, and PEARS, and all members of DATA type except APPLES, ORANGES, and PEARS would have been deleted.

Abbreviated member lists (for example, STUDY1-STUDY10) can be used with the SAVE statement.

If you delete a data set by not including it in the SAVE statement, any indexes associated with it are deleted as well.

SELECT Statement

The SELECT statement can be used only after a COPY statement. The general form of the SELECT statement is

SELECT *member-list* </ MEMTYPE=*mtype*>;

Use the SELECT statement to name one or more SAS files (or members) to be copied from the input library to the output library. For example, the following program copies all SAS files named GROUP1, GROUP2, or GROUP3 from the SAS data library referenced by STUDY to the SAS data library referenced by CONTROL:

```
libname study 'SAS-data-library';
libname control 'SAS-data-library';

proc datasets library=study;
   copy out=control;
      select group1-group3;
run;
```

Refer to **Using the MEMTYPE= Option in Subordinate Statements** earlier in this chapter for information on the MEMTYPE= option. Note: If you specify the

MEMTYPE= option in both the COPY statement and the SELECT statement, the value you specify in the SELECT statement takes precedence.

OUTPUT

The DATASETS procedure lists the members in the SAS data library before the library is updated unless the NOLIST option is specified. The list is written in the SAS log. If the MEMTYPE= option is used, only specified types are listed.

The information produced by the CONTENTS statement is written to the procedure output listing, not the SAS log.

EXAMPLES

Example 1: Managing SAS Data Sets

This program processes a SAS data library referenced by libref TOTALLIB. Since the MEMTYPE= option is specified in the PROC DATASETS statement, only DATA types are available for processing.

First, PROC DATASETS produces a list of SAS data sets in the SAS log. Then, the DATASETS procedure deletes a SAS data set named A and changes a SAS data set name from OLYMPICS to CALGARY. The PROC DATASETS step then modifies the characteristics of two SAS data sets (HSSPORTS and VOTING) and creates two simple indexes and one composite index for the renamed CALGARY data set. The contents of the modified data set named CALGARY are listed in the procedure output listing (see **Output 17.2**), and the data sets CALGARY and HSSPORTS are copied to the library SPORTS. Note that the indexes for the CALGARY data set are re-created in the SPORTS library. The following statements produce **Output 17.1**:

```
libname totallib 'SAS-data-library-1';
libname sports 'SAS-data-library-2';

proc datasets lib=totallib memtype=data;
   delete a;
   change olympics=calgary;
   modify hssports;
      rename number=players;
      format players comma7.;
   modify voting;
      label votepct='% of Voting Age Population';
   modify calgary;
      index create total;
      index create gold;
      index create totgold=(total gold) / nomiss;
   contents data=calgary;
   copy out=sports;
      select hssports calgary;
run;
```

Output 17.1 Log of PROC DATASETS Activity

```
6          libname totallib 'SAS-data-library-1';
NOTE: Libref TOTALLIB was successfully assigned as follows:
      Engine:        V606
      Physical Name: SAS-data-library-1
7          libname sports 'SAS-data-library-2';
NOTE: Libref SPORTS was successfully assigned as follows:
      Engine:        V606
      Physical Name: SAS-data-library-2
8          proc datasets lib=totallib;

                                        -----Directory-----

                         Libref:        TOTALLIB
                         Engine:        V606
                         Physical Name: SAS-data-library-1

                         #  Name     Memtype  Indexes
                         ----------------------------
                         1  A        DATA
                         2  CARS     DATA
                         3  COFFEE   DATA
                         4  GDPSTATS DATA
                         5  GEORGIA  DATA
                         6  HSSPORTS DATA
                         7  OLYMPICS DATA
                         8  TEA      DATA
                         9  VOTING   DATA

9          delete a;
10         change olympics=calgary;
NOTE: Deleting TOTALLIB.A (memtype=DATA).
NOTE: Changing the name TOTALLIB.OLYMPICS to TOTALLIB.CALGARY (memtype=DATA).
11         modify hssports;
12            rename number=players;
NOTE: Renaming variable NUMBER to PLAYERS.
13            format players comma7.;
14         modify voting;
15            label votepct='% of Voting Age Population';
16         modify calgary;
17            index create total;
NOTE: Single index TOTAL defined.
18            index create gold;
NOTE: Single index GOLD defined.
19            index create totgold=(total gold) / nomiss;
NOTE: Composite index TOTGOLD defined.
20         contents data=calgary;
21         copy out=sports;
22            select hssports calgary;
23      run;

NOTE: Copying TOTALLIB.HSSPORTS to SPORTS.HSSPORTS (MEMTYPE=DATA).
NOTE: The data set SPORTS.HSSPORTS has 20 observations and 3 variables.
NOTE: Copying TOTALLIB.CALGARY to SPORTS.CALGARY (MEMTYPE=DATA).
NOTE: Composite index TOTGOLD defined.
NOTE: Single index GOLD defined.
NOTE: Single index TOTAL defined.
NOTE: The data set SPORTS.CALGARY has 16 observations and 5 variables.
```

Example 2:   Printing Contents of SAS Data Sets

This example demonstrates the CONTENTS statement of PROC DATASETS. Refer to Chapter 12 for a detailed description of output from the CONTENTS statement. The following statements produce **Output 17.2**:

```
libname totallib 'SAS-data-library';

proc datasets lib=totallib;
   contents data=calgary;
   title 'Printing Contents of SAS Data Sets';
run;
```

Output 17.2   Output from CONTENTS Statement of PROC DATASETS

```
                    Printing Contents of SAS Data Sets                      1
                           DATASETS PROCEDURE

    Data Set Name: TOTALLIB.CALGARY       Observations:          16
    Member Type:   DATA                   Variables:             5
    Engine:        V606                   Indexes:               3
    Created:       19OCT89:13:33:47       Observation Length:    52
    Last Modified: 19OCT89:13:34:09       Deleted Observations:  0
    Data Set Type:                        Compressed:            NO
    Label:

            -----Alphabetic List of Variables and Attributes-----

                  #    Variable   Type   Len   Pos
                  ------------------------------------
                  4    BRONZE     Num     8    36
                  1    COUNTRY    Char   20     0
                  2    GOLD       Num     8    20
                  3    SILVER     Num     8    28
                  5    TOTAL      Num     8    44

            -----Alphabetic List of Indexes and Attributes-----

                             Nomiss
               #    Index     Option   Var1    Var2
               ------------------------------------------
               1    GOLD
               2    TOTAL
               3    TOTGOLD    YES      TOTAL   GOLD
```

The FORMAT Procedure

ABSTRACT

Use the FORMAT procedure to define your own informats and formats for character or numeric variables. Options for the FORMAT procedure print the contents of a format library, create a control data set for writing other informats and formats, or read a control data set to create informats or formats.

INTRODUCTION

Informats and formats give the SAS System information about data that is to be read or written. Informats and formats tell the SAS System the data's type (character or numeric) and form (such as how many bytes it occupies, decimal placement for numbers, how to handle leading, trailing, or embedded blanks and zeros, and so forth).

The SAS System provides standard informats and formats for reading and writing character, numeric, and datetime values. In addition, you can define your own informats and formats with the FORMAT procedure.

A word immediately followed by a period indicates a format or an informat name. Formats and informats can have an optional width specification before the period (for example, DOLLAR10.). SAS numeric formats and informats can also have an optional decimal specification immediately after the period (for example, DOLLAR10.2).*

Formats

Standard SAS formats write variable values in a predefined way. For example, you can choose SAS formats to write a numeric value in floating-point representation, scientific notation, hexadecimal representation, or monetary units. There are SAS formats for character variables that write values with embedded blanks, hexadecimal values, and varying-length values. Formats for writing character variable values begin with a dollar sign ($).

User-defined formats convert a value to a different form for output. For instance, you can

- convert a number to a character string (for example, write the data value 1 as **YES**)
- convert one character string to another character string (for example, write the data value **YES** as **1** or **YES** as **OUI**)
- specify a template to format the way a numeric value is printed (for example, format a string of numbers to the pattern for telephone numbers).

User-defined formats always associate variable values with character values. Therefore, formatted numeric output values are character numbers. If you attempt arithmetic operations on user-formatted numeric values, the SAS System uses the unformatted values.

Both standard SAS formats and user-written formats can be associated with variables in

- DATA step PUT, ATTRIB, and FORMAT statements and the PUT function
- a PROC step with a FORMAT statement.

In general, the format name follows the variable in the PUT and FORMAT statements. The format name is specified after the variable with the FORMAT= option in the ATTRIB statement. The general form of the PUT function is

PUT(*variable,format*);

If you use a format in a PROC step, the procedure uses the format to print the variable's values.

---

*Do not specify decimal places in formats and informats that you define with PROC FORMAT because user-defined formats and informats match variable values with different values or pictures. Decimals have no meaning in character values. Decimal points for picture formats are specified in the picture.

For general information about how formats are used with the SAS System, see Chapter 3, "Components of the SAS Language," Chapter 14, "SAS Formats," and discussions of the ATTRIB statement and the FORMAT statement in Chapter 9, "SAS Language Statements," in *SAS Language: Reference, Version 6, First Edition*.

Informats

Standard SAS informats read variable values in predefined ways. For example, you can choose SAS informats to read numeric values in floating-point representation, scientific notation, hexadecimal representation, or monetary units. There are SAS informats for reading character values with embedded blanks, varying-length values, and hexadecimal characters. Informats for reading character variable values begin with a dollar sign ($).

User-defined informats convert character input values into a different form. For instance, you can

- convert a character number to a character string (for example, read the data value **1** as **YES**)
- convert a character string to a number (for example, read the data value **YES** as 1)
- convert a character string to a different character string (for example, read **YES** as **OUI**).

Note that user-defined informats read only character data. They can convert character values into real numeric values, but they cannot convert real numbers into characters.

Both standard SAS informats and user-written informats can be associated with variables in

- DATA step INPUT, ATTRIB, and INFORMAT statements and the INPUT function
- a PROC step with an INFORMAT statement.

In general, the informat name follows the variable in the INPUT and INFORMAT statements. The informat name is specified after the variable with the INFORMAT= option in the ATTRIB statement. The general form of the INPUT function is

INPUT(*variable,informat*);

Procedures do not often use informats because the data values have already been read into SAS variables. However, informats can be very useful in certain procedures that allow you to enter new data values, such as the FSEDIT procedure in SAS/FSP software or the BUILD procedure in SAS/AF software.

For general information on how informats are used with the SAS System, see Chapter 3, "Components of the SAS Language," Chapter 13, "SAS Informats," and discussion of the ATTRIB statement and the INFORMAT statement in Chapter 9 in *SAS Language: Reference*.

User-defined Formats

The FORMAT procedure creates two kinds of formats:

- value formats that convert output values into a different form: numeric to character, or character string to a different character string. The VALUE statement generates value formats.

    For example, the VALUE statement below defines a format named SEX. that converts numeric variable values to character values. Variable values written with the SEX. format are stored as numbers (1 or 2) but formatted as character values (**MALE** or **FEMALE**):

    ```
    value sex 1='MALE' 2='FEMALE';
    ```

- picture formats that specify templates for printing numbers, giving specifics such as leading zeros, decimal and comma punctuation, fill characters, prefixes, and negative-number representation. Only numeric variables can have picture formats.

For example, the PICTURE statement in the example below defines a picture format named PHONENUM. that specifies a template for printing phone numbers and a FAX. format that specifies a picture for printing FAX numbers. The PRINT procedure uses the formats when it prints the variables.

```
proc format;
   picture phonenum other='000/000-0000';
   picture fax other='0999)999-9999' (prefix='(');
run;

data a;
   input phone fx;
   put phone phonenum.;
   format fx fax.;
   cards;
9196778000 3332211111
9195551212 5556677777
;
run;
```

The PUT statement writes the values for PHONE according to the PHONENUM. format, as shown in **Output 18.1**.

Output 18.1   Log Showing Formats Associated with a SAS Data Set

```
5          proc format;
6             picture phonenum other='000/000-0000';
NOTE: Format PHONENUM has been output.
7             picture fax other='0999)999-9999' (prefix='(');
NOTE: Format FAX has been output.
8          run;


9
10         data a;
11            input phone fx;
12            put phone phonenum.;
13            format fx fax.;
14            cards;
919/677-8000
919/555-1212
NOTE: The data set WORK.A has 2 observations and 2 variables.

17         ;
18         run;
```

The FORMAT statement in the following PROC PRINT step indicates that the procedure is to use the PHONENUM. picture format to print PHONE values. Because the FAX. format is associated with the FX variable by a FORMAT statement within a DATA step, the association is permanent. The PRINT procedure uses the FAX. format even though it doesn't appear in the FORMAT statement because the FAX. format is permanently associated with the FX variable in the data set.

```
proc print data=a;
    format phone phonenum.;
    title 'Formatting in the PROC PRINT Step';
run;
```

Note, however, that the PROC PRINT step must have a FORMAT statement to associate the PHONENUM. format with the PHONE variable. The output from the PRINT procedure appears in **Output 18.2**.

Output 18.2 Using the FORMAT statement with PROC PRINT

```
                        Formatting in the PROC PRINT Step                          1

                    OBS        PHONE            FX

                     1      919/677-8000    (333)221-1111
                     2      919/555-1212    (555)667-7777
```

The PHONE values are printed in the pattern specified by PHONENUM. However, the PHONENUM. format is not permanently associated with PHONE the way FAX. is associated with FX. To permanently associate the PHONENUM. format with the PHONE variable, change the FORMAT statement in the DATA step to the following:

```
format fx fax. phone phonenum.;
```

User-defined Informats

The FORMAT procedure produces informats that convert input values into a different form. Value informats read variables and transform them into another value: characters to numbers or one character string to a different character string. The INVALUE statement generates value informats.

The INVALUE statement below defines an informat named SEX. that transforms a character variable's value to a numeric value. For instance, when the value of the variable read with the SEX. informat is **MALE**, the variable's value is converted to 1:

```
invalue sex 'MALE'=1 'FEMALE'=2;
```

The INVALUE statement below defines an informat that substitutes one character string for another. For instance, when the value of the variable read with the $FRENCH. informat is **OUI**, the variable's value is transformed to **YES**:

```
invalue $french 'OUI'='YES' 'NON'='NO';
```

Informats are especially useful when you want to transform the input data into more meaningful values. The following example illustrates an application that translates input data into another form; the letter grades for three courses are transformed into numbers for computing grade point averages. The statements below produce **Output 18.3**.

```
proc format;
   invalue grade 'A'=4 'B'=3 'C'=2 'D'=1 'F'=0;

data grades;
   input name $ (course1-course3) (: grade.);
   gpa = mean(of course1-course3);
   cards;
BILL   A B A
JIM    A B B
RICK   B C D
ROBERT D . F
;

proc print data=grades;
   title 'Reading Data with an Informat';
run;
```

Output 18.3   Data Transformed by Using an Informat

```
                        Reading Data with an Informat
            OBS    NAME      COURSE1     COURSE2     COURSE3     GPA

             1     BILL         4           3           4       3.66667
             2     JIM          4           3           3       3.33333
             3     RICK         3           2           1       2.00000
             4     ROBERT       1           .           0       0.50000
```

Using Formats and Informats

When used in the DATA step that creates a SAS data set, the FORMAT, INFORMAT, and ATTRIB statements permanently associate the format or informat with a variable. When used in a PROC step, the FORMAT, INFORMAT, and ATTRIB statements associate the format with a variable only for the duration of that step.*

   Note: Permanently associating a format or an informat with a variable does not permanently store the format or informat. Serious complications arise if you do not save the format or informat for a permanent data set variable. Be sure you permanently store all formats and informats associated with permanent SAS data set variables. See **Temporary and Permanent Formats and Informats** later in this chapter for more information.

Storing Formats and Informats

User-written formats and informats are stored in a type of SAS file called a *catalog*. A catalog containing formats or informats has FORMATS as its second-level SAS name. You can have only one catalog containing formats and informats in a SAS data library.

---

* Do not confuse the FORMAT procedure with the FORMAT statement. PROC FORMAT creates user-defined formats or informats. The FORMAT and INFORMAT statements associate an existing format or informat (either standard SAS or user-defined) with one or more variables.

A catalog is composed of entries; an informat or format can be an entry. The format or informat entries in a catalog are identified by the informat or format name that is assigned with an INVALUE statement for informats and either a PICTURE or VALUE statement for formats.

User-written informats and formats are either temporary or permanent, depending on whether they are stored in a temporary or permanent catalog. You can use temporary informats and formats only in the same SAS job or session in which they are created. Permanent informats and formats can be used in the program that creates them and in subsequent SAS jobs or sessions. For more information on storing and using informats and formats, see **Temporary and Permanent Formats and Informats** later in this chapter.

SPECIFICATIONS

The FORMAT procedure is controlled by the following statements:

PROC FORMAT <*option-list*>;
    VALUE *name* <*(format-option-list)*> *range-1*='*formatted-value-1*'
        <...*range-n*='*formatted-value-n*'>;
    INVALUE *name* <*(informat-option-list)*> '*range-1*'=*informatted-value-1*
        <...'*range-n*'=*informatted-value-n*>;
    PICTURE *name* <*(format-option-list)*>
        range-1='*picture-1*' <*(picture-option-list)*>
        <...*range-n*='*picture-n*' <*(picture-option-list)*>>;
    SELECT *entry-list*;
    EXCLUDE *entry-list*;

The VALUE statement defines a value format. The PICTURE statement defines a picture format for numeric variables. The INVALUE statement defines a value informat. You can specify as many formats or informats as you want in a PROC FORMAT step, with one format per VALUE or PICTURE statement and one informat per INVALUE statement.

The SELECT statement selects entries from a catalog containing formats and informats for processing. (Each format and informat is an entry in a catalog.) The selected entries are printed, or if you specify the CNTLOUT= option in the PROC FORMAT statement, the selected entries are written as observations (range and value pairs) in an output control data set. If you want to print the selected entries as well as write the entries to an output control data set, you must use both the CNTLOUT= option and the FMTLIB option in the PROC FORMAT statement.

The EXCLUDE statement is used like the SELECT statement, but the entries listed in the EXCLUDE statement are the only ones not included in the processing.

You can use only one SELECT or one EXCLUDE statement in a PROC FORMAT step; you cannot use both in the same step.

Table 18.1 summarizes how to use the statements of the FORMAT procedure. The options in the right-hand column go with the corresponding statements in the center column.

Table 18.1 Summary of PROC FORMAT Functions

Function	Statements	Options
Permanently store a format or informat	PROC FORMAT	LIB=
Create a format to convert output values into a different form	VALUE	
Create a template for printing numbers	PICTURE	
Create an informat for converting input values into a different form	INVALUE	
Print the contents of the FORMATS catalog in a SAS data library	PROC FORMAT	FMTLIB, PAGE
Store information in a SAS data set on the contents of the FORMATS catalog of a SAS data library	PROC FORMAT SELECT, EXCLUDE	CNTLOUT=
Create a format or informat from information stored in a SAS data set	PROC FORMAT	CNTLIN=

PROC FORMAT Statement

PROC FORMAT <option-list>;

Options

The options available in the PROC FORMAT statement are described below.

CNTLIN=SAS-data-set

specifies an input control data set. A *control data set* is a SAS data set that the FORMAT procedure can use to construct formats and informats. The CNTLIN= option provides a way to build formats and informats without specifying all the information in VALUE, PICTURE, or INVALUE statements. If you specify a one-level name, the input control data set is a temporary file in the WORK library. An input control data set is used only when the CNTLIN= option is specified.

Common sources for an input control data set are the output from the CNTLOUT= option of another PROC FORMAT step or from the Version 5 SUGI supplemental procedure FMTLIB. The input data set could also be a codebook file, that is, a file that matches values with character strings. See **Output and Input Control Data Sets** later in this chapter for more information.

CNTLOUT=SAS-data-set

specifies an output control data set. A *control data set* is a SAS data set that contains information about formats and informats that you create in the PROC FORMAT step. The FORMAT procedure can use the control data set to construct formats and informats. If you specify the LIBRARY= option, the output control data set contains information on the formats and informats in the FORMATS catalog of the specified data library. If you do not specify the LIBRARY= option, the output control data set contains information on the formats and informats in the default FORMATS catalog in the WORK library.

If you specify a one-level name, the output control data set is a temporary file in the WORK library. An output control data set is created only when the CNTLOUT= option is specified.

You can use an output control data set as an input control data set to a later execution of the FORMAT procedure. See **Output and Input Control Data Sets** later in this chapter for more information.

FMTLIB

prints the contents of the catalog containing formats or informats. See **Printed Output** later in this chapter for details.

LIBRARY=*libref*

specifies the libref for a SAS data library containing a permanent catalog that contains formats or informats. (If the library does not already contain such a catalog, the SAS System automatically creates one.) When you specify a libref with the LIBRARY= option, all formats and informats you create in the PROC FORMAT step are permanent.

Before you invoke PROC FORMAT, use a LIBNAME statement to associate a libref with the SAS data library that contains the catalog where you want to store the formats and informats. It is recommended, but not necessary, that you use LIBRARY as the libref. In the PROC FORMAT step, you can specify a different libref with the LIBRARY= option, but subsequent PROC or DATA steps that need to access the permanently stored formats can find them only if they are in a library associated with the LIBRARY libref.

PAGE

prints information about each format and informat (that is, each entry) in the catalog on a separate page. The PAGE option is meaningful only when you print the contents of the catalog containing informats and formats; using the PAGE option activates the FMTLIB option. See **Printed Output** later in this chapter for an illustration.

EXCLUDE Statement

EXCLUDE *entry-list*;

Use the EXCLUDE statement to subset a catalog containing formats and informats for processing. (Each format and informat is an entry in a catalog.) The formats and informats listed in the EXCLUDE statement are not printed from the format catalog, and if you have specified the CNTLOUT= option, they are not written to the output control data set.

Entry-list is the list of formats and informats to be excluded. The three forms for *entry-list* are

A	entry A is excluded.
A:	all entries starting with A are excluded.
AB-AQ	all entries alphabetically between AB and AQ inclusive are excluded. Nothing after AQ is excluded. For example, AQA would be included, rather than excluded.

You can use any combination of these forms in an entry list, but you can use only one EXCLUDE statement per PROC FORMAT step. You cannot use both a SELECT and an EXCLUDE statement within the same step.

INVALUE Statement

INVALUE *name* <*(informat-option-list)*> *'range-1'=informatted-value-1*
        <*...'range-n'=informatted-value-n*>;

The INVALUE statement defines an informat that converts a variable's value into a different value. The elements of the INVALUE statement are listed below.

name

names the informat being created. You must specify a name in the INVALUE statement. The name must be a valid SAS name up to seven characters long, not ending in a number. The informat name for character variables must have a dollar sign ($) as the first character and no more than six additional characters. A user-defined informat name cannot be a standard SAS informat name. Refer to the informat later by using the name followed by a period. (Do not put a period after the informat name in the INVALUE statement.)

Note: Messages printed by the SAS System referring to a user-written informat show an at sign (@) prefixing the name of the informat. You do not need to specify the at sign when you create the informat or when you use it in a DATA step. When the informat is stored, the at sign is prefixed to the one- to seven-character name you specify for the informat, which is why you are limited to only seven characters in the name.

informat-option-list

is enclosed in parentheses and follows the informat name. Valid options are MAX=, MIN=, DEFAULT=, JUST, and UPCASE. You can specify any combination of these options separated by spaces. Each of these options is described in the next section, **Informat Options for the INVALUE Statement**.

range

specifies one or more values, a range of values, or a list of ranges that a variable read with the informat can have. You must specify one or more ranges in the INVALUE statement.

If the variable can have more than one value, the range specification determines what the input value is converted to. That is, the appropriate informatted result is the one associated with the range in which the variable's value falls.

Range values are always character strings enclosed in quotes, except for special ranges indicated by the keywords LOW, HIGH, and OTHER.

For example, the INVALUE statement below defines a SURNAME. informat that converts three ranges of character variable values into three corresponding numeric values. Note that the range values are enclosed in quotes, except for the special range value OTHER:

```
invalue surname 'A'-<'M'  =1
                'M'- 'Z'  =2
                     other=3;
```

In this example, the first range includes any names beginning with the letters A through L inclusive. The next range includes any names beginning with M through Z inclusive. The keyword OTHER indicates a special range of all values not given in any other range specification for the informat. In this example, OTHER includes non-alphabetic values or missing values.

informatted-value

specifies the value to which the informat converts the variable values. The *informatted-value* is associated with all variable values specified by *range* on the left side of the equal sign.

Informatted values are numeric unless the informat name begins with a dollar sign ($). Informatted values for character variables can be up to 40 characters and can be numbers, that is, character numerics. Character numerics are usually enclosed in single quotes; if you do not put quotes around them, the FORMAT procedure assumes the quotes to be there. For example, these two informats are equivalent:

```
invalue $charno 'one'=1 'two'=2 'three'=3;
invalue $charno 'one'='1' 'two'='2' 'three'='3';
```

If you do not give a range value for a variable's value, the action taken depends on whether the informat is character or numeric. For character informats, any data value not defined in a *range* is stored as read; that is, it is not converted to any other value. For numeric informats, if a value is not defined in a *range*, the SAS System tries to convert it to a numeric value. If this is not possible, the SAS System assigns a missing value and issues a message that the data is invalid. For example, the statements

```
proc format;
    invalue abc 'A'=1 'B'=2;
data a;
    input value abc.;
    put value;
    cards;
A
B
1
X
;
```

produce the lines

```
1
2
1
```

```
NOTE: Invalid data for VALUE in line nn 1-1.
```

You can also use two special values for informats: _SAME_ and _ERROR_. The _SAME_ informatted value causes the SAS System to store the data values in the range without change. If the informat is numeric, the SAS System tries to read the data values as numbers and, if that is not possible, assigns a missing value and issues an invalid data message. Note that this is the default action for any data value not specified in a *range*; the primary reason for using _SAME_ is that it enables you to request the default action for a specific range of values. Thus, you can exclude certain values from the OTHER category without having to define formats for those values. For example, the GROUP. informat below reads values 01 through 20 and assigns the numbers 1 through 20 as the result. All other values are assigned a missing value.

```
invalue group '01' - '20' = _same_
               other       = .;
```

The __ERROR__ informatted value treats data values in the designated range as invalid data. The SAS System assigns a missing value to the variable, prints the data line in the SAS log, and issues a warning message.

The __ERROR__ specification is useful in combination with __SAME__ for performing data validation. For example, the CHECK. informat below allows values of 1 through 4 and 99. All other values are invalid.

```
invalue check '1'-'4'=_same_
               '99'=.
               other=_error_;
```

Informat Options for the INVALUE Statement

INVALUE statement options are stored with width information. You can use the DEFAULT=, MAX=, and MIN= options to change the default width attributes. You can also use the JUST and UPCASE options to transform data as they are read. Specify these options immediately after the name of the informat, enclosed in parentheses.

DEFAULT=*n*

   specifies the default width if the informat does not have a width specification. If you do not specify the DEFAULT= option, the default width is the length of the longest informatted value.

JUST

   left-justifies all input strings before they are compared to the possible ranges. In the example below, the first and second input strings will match the ranges of the informat because they are left-justified before they are compared to the ranges. If the JUST option had not been specified, the first two input strings would not match any value of the informat.

```
proc format;
   invalue abc (just) 'one'=1 'two'=2 'three'=3;
run;

data _null_;
   input x abc.;
   put x=;
   cards;
 one
  two
three
one
two
;
```

Be careful that the input length of the data value is long enough to read the entire value, or the data will be truncated before it is left-justified. For example, the value **one** in the following example has three leading blanks, which makes the total length of the data six characters:

```
data _null_;
   input x abc.;
   cards;
three
   one
two
;
```

The DATA step reads only the first five characters (the length of the value **three**), so for the second value, it reads **on** and left-justifies that value.

Note: When you use the JUST option, the values specified for the ranges of the informat must be left-justified. Otherwise, nothing can ever match the informat ranges.

MAX=n

specifies a maximum width for the format. The maximum value allowed is MAX=40. The default maximum width for informat values if you do not specify the MAX= option is the length of the longest label.

MIN=n

specifies a minimum width for the informat. If you do not specify the MIN= option, the minimum default width is 1.

UPCASE

converts all input strings to uppercase before they are compared to the possible ranges. In the example below, all input strings will match the ranges in the informat because they are translated to uppercase before they are compared to the ranges. If the UPCASE option had not been specified, only the last input string would have matched the informat ranges.

```
proc format;
    invalue def (upcase) 'ONE'=1 'TWO'=2 'THREE'=3;
run;

data _null_;
    input x def.;
    put x=;
    cards;
one
Two
THree
ONE
;
```

Note that the JUST and UPCASE options can be used in combination, as in this example:

```
proc format;
    invalue abcdef (just upcase) 'ONE'=1 'TWO'=2 'THREE'=3;
run;
```

PICTURE Statement

PICTURE name <(format-option-list)>
　　　　range-1='picture-1' <(picture-option-list)>
　　　　<...range-n='picture-n' <(picture-option-list)>>;

The PICTURE statement defines a picture format, which is a template for printing numbers. The picture format gives specifics such as leading zeros, decimal and comma punctuation, fill characters, prefixes, and negative number representation.

The elements of the PICTURE statement are listed below:

name
> names the picture format being created. You must specify a name in the PICTURE statement. The name must be a valid SAS name up to eight characters long, not ending in a number. Refer to the format later by using the name followed by a period. (Do not put a period after the format name in the PICTURE statement.)

format-option-list
> is enclosed in parentheses and follows the format name. Valid options are MAX=, MIN=, and DEFAULT=. You can specify any combination of these options. They are described in detail in the next section, **Format Options for the PICTURE Statement**.

range
> specifies one or more values, a range of values, or a list of ranges that the numeric variable can have. You must specify one or more ranges in the PICTURE statement. If the variable can have more than one picture, the appropriate picture is the one associated with the range in which the variable's value falls. For example, in the statements

```
picture fm low-<0='99999-'
             0-high='99999+';
```

> the −<0 indicates that the LOW range is not to include zero.

picture
> specifies a template for printing numbers. The picture is a sequence of characters in single quotes. The maximum length for a picture is 40 characters. Pictures are specified with two types of characters: digit selectors and message characters. You can have a maximum of 15 digit selectors in a *picture*.

> *Digit selectors* are numeric characters (0 through 9) that define positions for numeric values. A picture format with nonzero digit selectors prints any leading zeros in variable values; picture digit selectors of 0 do not print leading zeros in variable values. If the picture format contains digit selectors, the digit selectors must appear at the beginning of the format before any message characters.

> *Message characters* are nonnumeric characters that print as specified in the picture. They are inserted into the picture after the numeric digits are formatted.

> The following PICTURE statement defines a DAYS. format to write values for days of the month without leading zeros:

```
picture days 01-31='00';
```

For example, with the output values of 11, 02, and 10, the value 02 prints without the leading zero:

```
11
 2
10
```

The following PICTURE statement contains both digit selectors (99) and message characters (`illegal day value`). Because the DAYS. format has nonzero digit selectors, values are printed with leading zeros. The special range OTHER prints the message characters for any values that do not fall into the valid value range (1 through 31).

```
picture days 01-31='99'
             other='99-illegal day value';
```

For example, the values 02 and 67 print as

```
02
67-illegal day value
```

picture-option-list

is enclosed in parentheses and specifies optional fill characters, prefix characters, and multipliers, as described in detail in **Picture Options** later in this chapter.

Format Options for the PICTURE Statement

Picture formats are stored with width attribute information. You can use the following options to change the default width attributes for all ranges of a picture format. Specify these options immediately after the name of the picture, enclosed in parentheses.

DEFAULT=*n*

specifies the default width if the format does not have a width specification. If you do not specify the DEFAULT= option, the default width is the length of the longest picture or formatted value.

MAX=*n*

specifies a maximum width for the format. The maximum value allowed is MAX=40. The default maximum width for pictures if you do not specify the MAX= option is also 40. Because fill characters pad on the left, the MAX= value for picture formats can be greater than the picture.

MIN=*n*

specifies a minimum width for the format. If you do not specify the MIN= option, the minimum default width is 1.

Picture Options

Picture options modify the picture for a single range of a picture format. These options can be specified in parentheses after each picture in a picture format. You can specify any combination of these options.

FILL='*character*'

specifies a fill character. This character replaces the leading blanks of the picture until a significant digit is encountered. The default is FILL=' ' (a blank). The specified character must be enclosed in quotes. One use of the FILL= option is to prevent a number with leading blanks from being altered, for example, on a check. (See the example following the description of the PREFIX= option later in this section.)

In most cases, this option is ignored if you specify all 9s (or other nonzero numbers) for the digit selectors in the picture. However, if the DEFAULT= option specifies a width that is larger than *picture*, the leading blanks are replaced by the fill character.

MULTIPLIER=*n*

MULT=*n*

specifies a number that the variable's value is to be multiplied by before it is formatted by the picture. The MULT= option is used to get data values with a decimal point into a form that will fit into the picture template because decimal points are specified in the picture. For example, the following PICTURE statement with the PREFIX= and MULT= options formats the variable value 1600000 as $1.6M:

```
picture million low-high='00.0M'
   (prefix='$' mult=.00001);
```

If you do not specify a value for the MULT= option, the FORMAT procedure uses a default value of 10^n, where n is the number of digits after the first decimal point in the picture. For example, suppose your data contain a value 123.456 and you want to print it using a picture of '999.999'. The FORMAT procedure multiplies 123.456 by 10^3 to obtain a value of 123456 and then fits this value into the picture template to produce 123.456.

NOEDIT

forces the format to treat the picture as a value format, or label, rather than as a picture specification. This means that numbers are message characters rather than digit selectors; that is, the numbers in the picture are printed as they appear. For example, these statements produce the output shown in **Output 18.4**.

```
proc format;
   picture miles 1-99='000000'
             100-high='>100 MILES' (noedit);

data temp;
   input name $ distance 3.;
   cards;
JOHN 300
MARY 600
DAVID 27
ANN 2
;

proc print data=temp;
   format distance miles.;
   title 'NOEDIT Option';
run;
```

Output 18.4 Effect of NOEDIT Option

```
                        NOEDIT Option

           OBS    NAME      DISTANCE

            1     JOHN     >100 MILES
            2     MARY     >100 MILES
            3     DAVID           27
            4     ANN              2
```

PREFIX='*character-list*'

specifies a one- or two-character prefix to place in front of the value's first significant digit. The default is no prefix. The *character-list* must be enclosed in single quotes. The prefix occupies positions within the picture, not additional positions. Thus, if the picture is not wide enough to contain both the value and the prefix, the prefix is truncated or omitted. The PREFIX= option is often used for leading dollar signs and minus signs. For example, the PICTURE statement

```
picture pay other='00,000,009.99'
     (fill='*' prefix='$');
```

prints the value 25500 as

```
***$25,500.00
```

SELECT Statement

SELECT *entry-list*;

Use the SELECT statement to subset a catalog containing formats and informats for processing. (Each format and informat is an entry in a catalog.) The entries selected are printed and, if you have specified the CNTLOUT= option in the PROC FORMAT statement, written to the control output data set.

Entry-list is the list of formats and informats to be selected. The syntax for *entry-list* is

A   entry A is selected.

A: all entries starting with A are selected.

AB-AQ   all entries alphabetically between AB and AQ inclusive are selected. Nothing after AQ is selected. For example, AQA would be excluded, rather than selected.

You can use any combination of these forms in an entry list, but you can use only one SELECT statement per PROC FORMAT step. You cannot use both a SELECT and an EXCLUDE statement within the same step.

VALUE Statement

VALUE *name* <(*format-option-list*)> *range-1*='*formatted-value-1*'
     <...*range-n*='*formatted-value-n*'>;

The VALUE statement defines a format that writes a variable's value as a different value. The elements of the VALUE statement are described below.

name
names the format being created. You must specify a name in the VALUE statement. The name must be a valid SAS name up to eight characters long, not ending in a number. The format name for character variables must have a dollar sign ($) as the first character and no more than seven additional characters. A user-defined format cannot have a standard SAS format name. Refer to the format later by using the name followed by a period. (Do not put a period after the format name in the VALUE statement.)

format-option-list
is enclosed in parentheses and follows the format name. Valid options are MAX=, MIN=, DEFAULT—, and FUZZ=. You can specify any combination of these options. These options are described in detail in the next section, **Format Options for the VALUE Statement**.

range
specifies one or more values, a range of values, or a list of ranges that the variable can have. You must specify one or more ranges in the VALUE statement. If the variable can have more than one formatted

output value, the appropriate formatted result is the one associated with the range in which the variable's value falls.

Character values in ranges must be enclosed in single quotes, except for special ranges indicated by the keywords LOW, HIGH, and OTHER.

The following VALUE statement defines an ABC. format that transforms numeric variable values into character values by associating three single-value numeric ranges with appropriate formatted character output values:

```
value abc 1='A' 2='B' 3='C';
```

The VALUE statement below defines an AGEFMT. format that transforms numeric variable values into character labels by associating three numeric ranges with appropriate formatted character output values:

```
value agefmt low-12='child'
             13-19='teen'
            20-high='adult';
```

The range LOW-12 refers to all values from the lowest value of the variable to 12. However, the LOW keyword does not include missing values. The range 20-HIGH refers to all values from 20 through the largest value of the variable.

The next VALUE statement defines a SEXFMT. format that transforms numeric variable values into character labels by associating a combination of single numeric variable values and a range of values with appropriate formatted character output values.

```
value sexfmt 1='female'
             2='male'
           0,3-9='miscoded';
```

The range for the `miscoded` label could also be specified as

```
other='miscoded';
```

to mean that all values other than 1 and 2 are to have the `miscoded` label.

formatted-value
is the output value to which the format converts the variable value. The formatted value is a label associated with all variable values specified by the range on the left side of the equal sign. Formatted values are always character strings and can be up to 40 characters. Some procedures, however, use only the first 8 or 16 characters of a formatted value. All formatted values should be enclosed in quotes.

For example, the following VALUE statement defines an ANSWER. format that converts numeric variable values of 1 and 2 to the character values **yes** and **no**, respectively:

```
value answer 1='yes' 2='no';
```

The VALUE statement below defines a format that substitutes one character string for another. Note that the $MENU. format starts with $ because it is for character variables, and that both ranges and labels are enclosed in single quotes.

```
value $menu 'A'='Good' 'B'='Bad';
```

If a label contains a single quote, write it as two separate single quotes:

```
value sect 1='Smith''s class'
            2='Doe''s class';
```

If a VALUE statement does not specify ranges that include all possible values for the variable, only those in the VALUE statement are formatted with the specified format. All other values for the variable are formatted with a default format. For example, the statements

```
proc format;
    value temp 98.6='NORMAL';


data a;
    input t;
    put t temp.;
    cards;
98.4
98.6
101.2
;
```

produce the lines

```
 98.4
NORMAL
101.2
```

Note: A numeric value with a default format is right-aligned in a field with a width equal to that given in the PUT statement. If you do not give a width in the format, the default width is used. If the format does not have a range defined for a variable value, the SAS System uses the BEST*w*. format, where *w* is the width of the longest formatted value defined for the format. Character values printed with a default format are left-aligned.

Format Options for the VALUE Statement

Formats are stored with width attribute information. You can use the following options to change the default width attributes for a format or to specify a fuzz factor for matching values to a range. These options are specified immediately after the name of the format and are enclosed in parentheses.

DEFAULT=*n*
specifies the default width if the format does not have a width specification. If you do not specify the DEFAULT= option, the default width is the length of the longest formatted value.

FUZZ=*fuzz-factor*
specifies a fuzz factor for matching values to a range. If a number does not match a value or fall in a range exactly but comes within the fuzz value, it is considered a match. For example, in the following statements

```
proc format;
    value abc (fuzz=.4) 1='A' 2='B' 3='C';
```

FUZZ=.4 means that if a variable value falls within 0.4 of a value specified in the VALUE statement, the corresponding label is used to print the value. So the ABC. format formats the value 1.2 as **A**, the value 1.7 as **B**, and the value 2.8 as **C**.

Do not use a FUZZ= value that is ambiguous, that is, a value that is exactly midway between two ranges. The default FUZZ= value is 1E−12.

MAX=*n*

specifies a maximum width for the format. The maximum value allowed is MAX=40. The default maximum width for format values if you do not specify the MAX= option is the length of the longest label.

MIN=*n*

specifies a minimum width for the format. If you do not specify the MIN= option, the minimum default width is 1.

DETAILS

Range Specifications in Statements

The purpose of the INVALUE, VALUE, and PICTURE statements is to associate one or more variable values with a specified informatted or formatted value.

The values of a variable that are to be converted to a particular formatted or informatted result are specified by the range. A *range* is a single value, a list of values, a range of values, or a list of ranges that the variable can have. At least one range specification is required in INVALUE, VALUE, and PICTURE statements. If the variable can have more than one value, the range specification determines what the variable value is converted to, that is, the appropriate informatted or formatted result. The informatted or formatted result is the one that is associated with the range in which the variable's value falls.

The general forms for *range* are given in the table below.

Form	Meaning	Example
value	a single value	12
value, . . . ,*value*	a list of values	12,24,68
value-value	a range of values	12–68
range, . . . ,*range*	a list of ranges	12–24,34–68

Each value in a range specification can be up to 16 characters. If a range specification has more than 16 characters, the procedure truncates the value and processes only the first 16 characters. This truncation causes an error message if the truncated values result in identical ranges. For example, the following range specifications generate an error message because the truncated values are identical:

```
proc format;
   value $long   'abcdefghijklmnopq'-
                 'abcdefghijklmnopqr'    ='1'
                 'abcdefghijklmnopqrs'-
                 'abcdefghijklmnopqrst' ='2';
run;
```

Range specifications can include the keywords LOW and HIGH to represent the smallest and largest values of character variables. For picture formats and numeric formats, LOW and HIGH represent the largest negative and positive numbers, respectively. The keyword OTHER represents a special range of all values not included in any other range. Missing values are represented with a period (.). The LOW keyword does not include missing values.

The informatted and formatted values (specified to the right of the equal sign) in INVALUE and VALUE statements can have a maximum of 40 characters.

You can use the following notation to specify noninclusive ranges so that values in ranges do not overlap. Specifying this VALUE statement indicates that the first value is not part of the range:

```
value1<-value2
```

Specifying the following VALUE statement indicates that the second value is not part of the range:

```
value1-<value2
```

You should not overlap values in ranges. For example, the statement

```
invalue xxx 'X1'-'X2'=1 'X2'-'X3'=2;
```

is confusing because the value X2 can be part of the first or second range. (See the note at the end of this section.) The following INVALUE statement clarifies the overlapping ranges with noninclusive notation:

```
invalue xxx 'X1'-<'X2'=1 'X2'-'X3'=2;
```

The second value of the first range is excluded; if the input values are X1, X2, and X3, only the input value of X1 is converted to the informatted value 1.
   In the statement

```
invalue xxx 'X1'-'X2'=1 'X2'<-'X3'=2;
```

the first value of the second range is excluded; if the input values are X1, X2, and X3, only the input value of X3 is converted to the informatted value 2.
   Note: The FORMAT procedure automatically changes overlapping range values to be noninclusive, the first occurrence is included and the second occurrence is excluded.

Temporary and Permanent Formats and Informats

Formats and informats are temporary when you do not specify the LIBRARY= option in the PROC FORMAT statement. They are stored in a temporary catalog named WORK.FORMATS. To retrieve a temporary format or informat for writing a variable value, simply include the name of the format or informat in the appropriate SAS statement. The SAS System automatically looks for the format or informat in the WORK.FORMATS catalog. You can retrieve temporary formats and informats only in the same SAS session or job in which they are created.
   If you want to be able to use a format or informat created in one SAS job or session in a subsequent job or session, you must permanently store the format or informat in a SAS catalog.* To create permanent formats and informats, you must perform the following steps:

1. Choose a SAS data library in which to store the permanent catalog, if you do not already have a permanent catalog for formats and informats.
2. Use a LIBNAME statement to associate a libref with that SAS data library. At this point, it is recommended, but not required, that you use the word LIBRARY as the libref. In DATA or PROC steps following the PROC FORMAT step, the SAS System looks for permanent formats and informats only in the SAS data library that has been assigned the LIBRARY libref.

---

* In some host environments, formats can also be stored in external files. If this capability was available in your host environment in Version 5 of the SAS System, refer to the SAS documentation for your host system for information on how to continue to use external files for storing formats.

3. Specify the LIBRARY= option in the PROC FORMAT statement. If you assign LIBRARY as the libref, your PROC statement is

```
proc format library=library;
```

When you follow these steps, any formats and informats you create in the same PROC FORMAT step are stored in a permanent format catalog called LIBRARY.FORMATS.

To use permanent formats and informats in a later program, you must first issue a LIBNAME statement assigning the libref LIBRARY to the SAS data library in which you stored the formats. At this point, the LIBRARY libref is required.

If you do not specify LIBRARY as the libref, the SAS System cannot find the formats and informats because it looks in only two places for user-written formats and informats. The SAS System first looks in the temporary WORK library's catalog. If the formats and informats are not in WORK.FORMATS, the SAS System then looks in the FORMATS catalog located in a SAS data library that has been assigned the LIBRARY libref.

For example, suppose you create a permanent format named ANSWER. and store it in the FORMATS catalog in a SAS data library. Later, when you want to use the ANSWER. format with the PRINT procedure, you need to issue a LIBNAME statement before the PROC PRINT step, as shown in the following example:

```
libname library 'SAS-data-library';

proc print data=tvsurvey;
   var id week q1 q2 q3;
   format q1 q2 q3 answer.;
run;
```

When the SAS System processes the FORMAT statement, it first looks for the ANSWER. format in the current WORK library's format catalog. If the format is not there, the SAS System then looks for it in the library associated with the LIBRARY libref.

Note that because the libref must be LIBRARY to retrieve formats and informats stored in a permanent catalog, you cannot use formats and informats from more than one permanent catalog in a given DATA or PROC step. If you want to create new formats and informats in one catalog and write values with formats retrieved from another catalog, use LIBRARY as the libref for the catalog containing the formats needed for writing values. Assign a libref other than LIBRARY to the catalog in which you are planning to store the new formats and informats created with PROC FORMAT.

When you create a permanent SAS data set and assign user-written formats and informats to any of its variables, be sure to store them permanently. Serious complications arise if you do not save formats and informats for permanent data set variables. The data set directory marks variables as having formats, informats, or both, but when the variables are referenced in later jobs, the SAS System cannot find the formats and informats if they have not been saved. When this occurs, the SAS System issues an error message and stops processing unless the NOFMTERR system option is in effect. When the NOFMTERR system option is in effect, the values for variables with formats that cannot be found are printed using the *w.* or $*w.* default format. Refer to Chapter 16, "SAS System Options," in *SAS Language: Reference* for more information on the FMTERR system option.

Rules for Applying Pictures to Values

The following rules describe how data values appear when you apply a user-written picture format to the values:

- All data values are treated as positive values; the sign is ignored when the picture is applied.
- If the picture has no decimal places and the MULT= option is not specified, all decimal places of input data are ignored. Note: Decimal places are truncated, not rounded.

  For example, when the data value 23456.78 is printed with the PICTURE statement

  ```
  picture nodecs low-high = '000000';
  ```

  the result is 23456.
- When the picture value has decimal places but the MULT= option is not specified, the decimals of the data values and the picture are simply aligned.

  For example, when the data value 23456.78 is printed with the PICTURE statement

  ```
  picture decs low-high = '00000.0';
  ```

  the result is 23456.7.
- When the MULT= option is specified, the following steps occur:
  1. The data values are multiplied by the MULT= value. For example, when MULT=.1, a data value of 123.45 is transformed to 12.345.
  2. All decimal places from the result of step 1 are truncated. Thus, the example data value in step 1 becomes 12.
  3. The value from step 2 is mapped to the digit selectors in the picture from right to left. If the picture for the example data value from step 2 is 000.0, the value is printed as 1.2.

  The following code illustrates the rules for the MULT= option in more detail. This example includes data values with decimals and MULT= values with decimals.

  ```
  data test;
     a=123.45;
     b=123.45;
     c=12345;
     d=12345;
  run;

  proc format;
     picture mwdec low-high='00000.0' (mult=.1);
     picture mnodec low-high='00000.0'  (mult=10);
  run;
  ```

  When you print A and C with the MWDEC. format and B and D with the MNODEC. format, the results appear as follows:

A	B	C	D
1.2	123.4	123.4	12345.0

- If the picture you specify does not include enough digits to the left of the decimal to print the entire data value, the digits on the far left of the data value are truncated until the value fits into the picture.

An inappropriate picture can cause serious misrepresentations of data values. For example, when the data value 23456.78 is printed with the PICTURE statement

```
picture short low-high = '000.0';
```

the result is 456.7.

- When you specify digits to the right of a decimal point in a picture, additional digits may change the value that is printed by an order of 10. In the simplest case, adding more decimal places to the picture does not cause a problem; it simply produces printed values with greater precision. For example, if the data value is 12.34, the picture can change from 0000.0 to 0000.00 and only change the printed value from 12.3 to 12.34. However, if the picture includes the MULT= option, adding digits to the right of the decimal changes the value entirely. For example, if you print the data value 12.34 using the two PICTURE statements shown below, the first picture produces the value 12.3, but the second picture produces the value 1.23:

```
picture onedec low-high='0000.0' (mult=10);
picture twodec low-high='0000.00' (mult=10);
```

- If you specify a picture that uses only 0 digit selectors and the picture includes decimal places, you may produce serious misrepresentations of data if the actual value should be less than 0. That is, if the data value is 123 and the picture is 0.00 (MULT=.01), the printed value is 1 instead of .01 because the leading zeros are suppressed by the 0 digit selector. If you change the picture to 9.99 (MULT=.01), the printed value becomes 0.01.

Note that these rules discuss MULT= values of less than 1 in some detail because these situations can be confusing. A possible application for setting the MULT= option to a decimal value is to represent values of dollars and cents as whole dollar amounts, as in the following example:

```
data temp;
   input cents;
   cards;
4123
2130
7250
5379
;

proc format;
   picture dolls low-high='009' (mult=.01);
   run;

proc print;
   format cents dolls.;
   run;
```

This code prints these values: 41, 21, 72, and 53.

The following example illustrates a MULT= value that is not a power of 10. This is useful for currency conversions.

```
proc format;
   picture feet other='000000009' (mult=5280);
run;
```

```
data feet;
   input miles @@;
   format miles feet.;
   cards;
1   1.5   2
;
run;

proc print;
run;
```

This code prints these values: 5280, 7920, and 10560.

Table 18.2 summarizes the examples shown in this section.

Table 18.2 Summary of Picture Rules

Data Value	Picture	Printed Result	Comments
23456.78	000000	23456	Decimal portions of input data are ignored because the picture has no decimals.
23456.78	00000.0	23456.7	Decimal portions of the input data are aligned with decimal portions of the picture.
123.45	00000.0 (MULT=.1)	1.2	Data value changed by MULT= value to 12. This value is then mapped right to left to the picture.
123.45	00000.0 (MULT=10)	123.4	Data value changed by MULT= value to 1234. This value is then mapped right to left to the picture.
12345	00000.0 (MULT=.1)	123.4	Data value changed by MULT= value to 1234. This value is then mapped right to left to the picture.
12345	00000.0 (MULT=10)	12345.0	Data value changed by MULT= value to 123450. This value is then mapped right to left to the picture.
123456.78	000.0	456.7	Data value truncated by inappropriate picture.
12.34	00.0	12.3	Decimal points aligned because MULT= option is not used.

continued on next page

Table 18.2   *continued*

Data Value	Picture	Printed Result	Comments
12.34	00.00	12.34	Adding decimal places to previous example simply increases precision because MULT= option not used.
1234	00.0 (MULT=.1)	12.3	MULT= option changes data value to 123. This value is then mapped right to left to the picture.
1234	00.00 (MULT=.1)	1.23	Adding decimal places to previous example changes the value because the MULT= option is used.
123	0.00 (MULT=.01)	1	Using the digit selector 0 in this picture produces a misrepresentation of the data because leading zeros and the decimal point are suppressed.
123	9.99 (MULT=.01)	.01	Using the digit selector 9 in this picture ensures that any leading zeros and the decimal point are printed.

Output and Input Control Data Sets

A control data set is a SAS data set that contains information about formats and informats. You specify an input control data set in the CNTLIN= option to process a control data set as input to the FORMAT procedure. An input control data set can be a codebook file that matches variable values to character strings; it can also be the output control data set produced from a previous FORMAT procedure execution. The FORMAT procedure uses the data in the input control data set to construct formats and informats.

The CNTLOUT= option enables you to produce an output control data set from the FORMAT procedure. The output control data set contains information about the informats and formats in the FORMATS catalog of the library specified by the LIBRARY= option. If no LIBRARY= option is specified, the output control data set contains information on the formats in the WORK library.

Because an input control data set can be a subset of an output control data set, the latter is described first.

Output Control Data Set

The output control data set consists of variables that give either global information about each format and informat created in the PROC FORMAT step or specific information about each range and value. An observation consists of a range (START and optionally END) and value (LABEL) pair associated with a format or informat name (FMTNAME). That is, there is an observation for each range defined for the format or informat.

The variables in the output control data set are shown in **Table 18.3**.

Table 18.3   Output Control Data Set Variables

Global Information For Each Format and Informat		
Name	Type	Description
FMTNAME	Char	Format or informat name
TYPE	Char	Type of format: C=character format, N=numeric format, P=picture format, I=numeric informat, J=character informat
DEFAULT	Num	Default length for format or informat
MIN	Num	MIN= option value (or default)
MAX	Num	MAX= option value (or default)
LENGTH	Num	LENGTH= option value (or default)
FUZZ	Num	FUZZ= option value (or default)

Range and Value Information		
Name	Type	Description
START	Char	Range starting value
SEXCL	Char	Y if range start value is excluded; N if not
END	Char	Range ending value
EEXCL	Char	Y if range end value is excluded; N if not
HLO	Char	O, L, H, or LH when the special values OTHER, LOW, HIGH, or LOW-HIGH occur in the range; blank otherwise.
LABEL	Char	Label: informatted or formatted value
PREFIX	Char	PREFIX= option characters
MULT	Num	MULT= option value
FILL	Char	FILL= option value
NOEDIT	Char	1 if NOEDIT option specified; 0 if not

Input Control Data Set

An input control data set contains information that the FORMAT procedure can use to construct formats and informats. You can create formats and informats without having to write VALUE and INVALUE statements by altering your input to conform to the input control data set specifications. Although the input control data set usually comes from a previous invocation of the FORMAT procedure, it can come from any source, as long as the FMTNAME, START, and LABEL variables are created as described for the output control data set. The remaining variables are not required.

Another source for an input control data set is codebook data derived from data entry or from an existing database. (Codebook files match values with corresponding character strings.)

You can give specifications in the VALUE, PICTURE, or INVALUE statements in addition to the information provided in an input control data set. You might do this to augment or change information in the input control data set. The control data set information is processed before the information given in the statements.

If the input control data set does not have a TYPE variable value, a value format is assumed. In other words, if the input control data set contains picture or character formats, there must be a TYPE variable value with **P** for picture or **C** for character formats.

If the input data set contains informats, there must be a TYPE variable value with **I** for numeric informats or **J** for character informats. The START and END variables can be either numeric or character for formats.

If range values are to be noninclusive, the input control data set must have the variables SEXCL and EEXCL with **Y** values. Inclusion is the default.

Printed Output

The FORMAT procedure prints output only when you specify the FMTLIB option or the PAGE option in the PROC FORMAT statement. The printed output is a table for each format or informat entry in the catalog. The output also contains global information and the specifics of each range and value (LABEL) pair defined for the format or informat.

Output 18.5 shows the output produced by the FMTLIB option for a format named ZIPNE.*

1. FORMAT NAME is the name. The name begins with an at sign (@) for informats.
2. LENGTH is the length of the longest value in the LABEL field.
3. NUMBER OF VALUES specifies the number of ranges associated with the format.
4. MIN LENGTH is the minimum length of a value specified in the LABEL field. The value for MIN LENGTH is 1 unless a different minimum length was specified with the MIN= format option.
5. MAX LENGTH is the length of the longest value in the label field, unless a different maximum length was specified with the MAX= format option.
6. DEFAULT LENGTH is the length of the longest value in the label field.
7. START is the beginning value of a range specification.
8. END is the ending value of a range specification.
9. LABEL is the formatted value to which the variable is converted. This is called INVALUE for informats. The version of the SAS System and the date on which the format or informat was created is in parentheses after the LABEL field.

---

* This output is produced from a subset of the format values shown in **Example 1**.

Output 18.5 Output Produced by the FMTLIB Option for a Value Format

```
                              FMTLIB Option

                            ❶          ❷             ❸
--------------------------------------------------------------------
|      FORMAT NAME: ZIPNE   LENGTH:   13   NUMBER OF VALUES:   10   |
|   MIN LENGTH:   1 MAX LENGTH:  13 DEFAULT LENGTH  13 FUZZ: STD    |
|        ❹              ❺                    ❻                       |
--------------------------------------------------------------------
|START  ❼        |END ❽         |LABEL❾(VER. 6.06   12APR89:13:46:05)|
--------------------------------------------------------------------
|          1000|          2799|Massachusetts                        |
|          2800|          2999|Rhode Island                         |
|          3000|          3899|New Hampshire                        |
|          3900|          4999|Maine                                |
|          5000|          5999|Vermont                              |
|          6000|          6999|Connecticut                          |
|          7000|          8999|New Jersey                           |
|          9000|         14999|New York                             |
|         15000|         19699|Pennsylvania                         |
|         19700|         19999|Delaware                             |
--------------------------------------------------------------------
```

Output 18.6 shows the printed output produced by the PAGE option in the PROC FORMAT statement for picture formats that include the PREFIX=, FILL=, MULT=, and NOEDIT options.*

1. The hyphen after the P in the picture specification is the prefix character.
2. The digits after the M are the MULT= option digits.
3. The < after the 0 in the END field indicates that the value is excluded in the range.
4. The asterisk (*) after the F is the fill character.

The P, F, or M field is blank if you did not specify the corresponding option when you created the format.

Output 18.6 Printed Output for Picture Formats

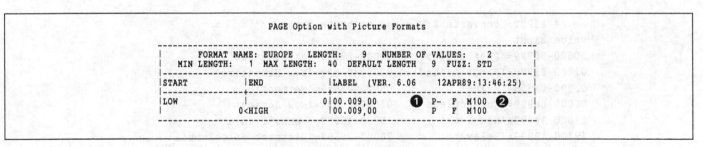

```
                     PAGE Option with Picture Formats

--------------------------------------------------------------------
|      FORMAT NAME: EUROPE  LENGTH:   9   NUMBER OF VALUES:   2     |
|   MIN LENGTH:   1 MAX LENGTH:  40 DEFAULT LENGTH  9 FUZZ: STD     |
--------------------------------------------------------------------
|START           |END          |LABEL  (VER. 6.06   12APR89:13:46:25) |
--------------------------------------------------------------------
|LOW    |        0|00.009,00   ❶  P-    F  M100 ❷        |
|       0<HIGH    |00.009,00      P     F  M100             |
--------------------------------------------------------------------
```

```
                     PAGE Option with Picture Formats

--------------------------------------------------------------------
|      FORMAT NAME: PROT    LENGTH:  10   NUMBER OF VALUES:   4     |
|   MIN LENGTH:   1 MAX LENGTH:  40 DEFAULT LENGTH  10 FUZZ: STD    |
--------------------------------------------------------------------
|START           |END          |LABEL  (VER. 6.06   12APR89:13:46:24) |
--------------------------------------------------------------------
|LOW    |         -100000|-OVERFLOW     N P   F  M1         |
|  -99999.99|      0<000,009.99    P-    F* M100             |
|          0|  999999.99|000,009.99    P     F* M100          |
|    1000000|HIGH      |OVERFLOW      N P   F  M1            |
--------------------------------------------------------------------
                                        ❹
```

---

* This output is produced from the PROT. and EUROPE. formats shown in **Example 2.**

The FORMCHAR= option is used to determine the characters for the table. You can change these characters to alter the appearance of the table to your specifications. See Chapter 16 in *SAS Language: Reference* for more information on the FORMCHAR= system option.

EXAMPLES

Example 1:   PROC FORMAT with the VALUE Statement

The three format definitions shown in this example are useful for transforming state codes or abbreviations into state names. The ZIPST. format corresponds to the ZIPNAME function, $STATE. to STNAME, and STATE. to FIPNAME. These formats are useful because you can access them in a PROC step, whereas you must use a DATA step to use the state functions. In addition, you can use these formats with the PUT function in the DATA step to create variables. For example, after you create the formats shown later in this example, you could use them in this DATA step. In this case, ZIPST, CSTATE, and NSTATE all have a value of **North Carolina**. This DATA step is repeated at the end of the PROC FORMAT step, and a PROC PRINT step prints the results in **Output 18.7**.

```
data new;
   input zip abbrev $ censusbu;
   zipst=put(zip,zipst.);
   cstate=put(abbrev,$state.);
   nstate=put(censusbu,state.);
   cards;
27512 NC 37
;
```

The following PROC FORMAT step creates the formats used by this DATA step above. See **Output 18.7** for the results of using these formats produced by PROC FORMAT in a PROC PRINT step.

```
proc format;

      /* ZIPST: converts ZIP codes to state names */
   value zipst
   00600-00999='Puerto Rico'      01000-02799='Massachusetts'
   02800-02999='Rhode Island'     03000-03899='New Hampshire'
   03900-04999='Maine'            05000-05999='Vermont'
   06000-06999='Connecticut'      07000-08999='New Jersey'
   09000-14999='New York'         15000-19699='Pennsylvania'
   19700-19999='Delaware'         20000-20599='District of Columbia'
   20600-21999='Maryland'         22000-24699='Virginia'
   24700-26899='West Virginia'    27000-28999='North Carolina'
   29000-29999='South Carolina'   30000-31999='Georgia'
   32000-34999='Florida'          35000-36999='Alabama'
   37000-38599='Tennessee'        38600-39799='Mississippi'
   40000-42799='Kentucky'         43000-45899='Ohio'
   46000-47999='Indiana'          48000-49999='Michigan'
   50000-52899='Iowa'             53000-54999='Wisconsin'
   55000-56799='Minnesota'        57000-57799='South Dakota'
   58000-58899='North Dakota'     59000-59999='Montana'
   60000-62999='Illinois'         63000-65899='Missouri'
   66000-67999='Kansas'           68000-69399='Nebraska'
   70000-71499='Louisiana'        71600-72999='Arkansas'
```

```
73000-74999='Oklahoma'      75000-79999='Texas'
80000-81699='Colorado'      82000-83199='Wyoming'
83200-83899='Idaho'         84000-84799='Utah'
85000-86599='Arizona'       87000-88499='New Mexico'
89000-89899='Nevada'        90000-96699='California'
96700-96899='Hawaii'        96900-96999='Guam'
97000-97999='Oregon'        98000-99499='Washington'
99500-99999='Alaska'
;

   /* STATE: converts state abbrev. to state names */
value $state
'AL'='Alabama'              'NB'='Nebraska'
'AK'='Alaska'               'NV'='Nevada'
'AZ'='Arizona'              'NH'='New Hampshire'
'AR'='Arkansas'             'NJ'='New Jersey'
'CA'='California'           'NM'='New Mexico'
'CO'='Colorado'             'NY'='New York'
'CT'='Connecticut'          'NC'='North Carolina'
'DE'='Delaware'             'ND'='North Dakota'
'DC'='District of Columbia' 'OH'='Ohio'
'FL'='Florida'              'OK'='Oklahoma'
'GA'='Georgia'              'OR'='Oregon'
'HI'='Hawaii'               'PA'='Pennsylvania'
'ID'='Idaho'                'RI'='Rhode Island'
'IL'='Illinois'             'SC'='South Carolina'
'IN'='Indiana'              'SD'='South Dakota'
'IA'='Iowa'                 'TN'='Tennessee'
'KS'='Kansas'               'TX'='Texas'
'KY'='Kentucky'             'UT'='Utah'
'LA'='Louisiana'            'VT'='Vermont'
'ME'='Maine'                'VA'='Virginia'
'MD'='Maryland'             'WA'='Washington'
'MA'='Massachusetts'        'WV'='West Virginia'
'MI'='Michigan'             'WI'='Wisconsin'
'MN'='Minnesota'            'WY'='Wyoming'
'MS'='Mississippi'          'RQ'='Puerto Rico'
'MO'='Missouri'             'GQ'='Guam'
'MT'='Montana'              '99'='Foreign'
;

   /* STATE: official census bureau codes for state */
value state
01='Alabama'        30='Montana'
02='Alaska'         31='Nebraska'
04='Arizona'        32='Nevada'
05='Arkansas'       33='New Hampshire'
06='California'     34='New Jersey'
08='Colorado'       35='New Mexico'
09='Connecticut'    36='New York'
10='Delaware'       37='North Carolina'
11='D.C.'           38='North Dakota'
12='Florida'        39='Ohio'
13='Georgia'        40='Oklahoma'
15='Hawaii'         41='Oregon'
```

```
        16='Idaho'        42='Pennsylvania'
        17='Illinois'     44='Rhode Island'
        18='Indiana'      45='South Carolina'
        19='Iowa'         46='South Dakota'
        20='Kansas'       47='Tennessee'
        21='Kentucky'     48='Texas'
        22='Louisiana'    49='Utah'
        23='Maine'        50='Vermont'
        24='Maryland'     51='Virginia'
        25='Massachusetts' 53='Washington'
        26='Michigan'     54='West Virginia'
        27='Minnesota'    55='Wisconsin'
        28='Mississippi'  56='Wyoming'
        29='Missouri'
        ;

data new;
   input zip abbrev $ censusbu;
   zipst=put(zip,zipst.);
   cstate=put(abbrev,$state.);
   nstate=put(censusbu,state.);
   cards;
27512 NC 37
;

proc print;
   var zip zipst abbrev cstate censusbu nstate;
   title 'Formatted State Codes and Abbreviations';
run;
```

Output 18.7   State Code and Abbreviation Formats

```
                    Formatted State Codes and Abbreviations
     OBS    ZIP       ZIPST        ABBREV     CSTATE      CENSUSBU     NSTATE

      1    27512   North Carolina    NC     North Carolina    37     North Carolina
```

Example 2:   PROC FORMAT with the PICTURE Statement

The ten formats in this example illustrate several picture format features. Note especially the specifications of the format PROT., which establish error ranges so that numbers that do not fit the picture are flagged with an error message. The last value in the example shows that most of the formats produce a misleading value for an overflowed field. See **Output 18.8** for the picture formats created with the following PROC FORMAT step.

```
proc format;
   picture acct     low-<0='000,009.99)' (prefix='(')
                    0-high='000,009.99ꞌ;
```

```
         picture prot     low- -1E5='-OVERFLOW'      (noedit)
                      -99999.99-<0='000,009.99' (prefix='-' fill='*')
                      0-999999.99='000,009.99' (fill='*')
                           1E6-high='OVERFLOW'     (noedit);

         picture dol      low-<0='000,009.99' (prefix='$-')
                          0-high='000,009.99' (prefix='$');

         picture rsign    low-<0='000,009.99-'
                          0-high='000,009.00+';

         picture credit   low-<0='00,009.99DR'
                          0-high='00,009.99CR';

         picture europe   low-<0='00.009,00' (prefix='-' mult=100)
                          0-high='00.009,00'  (mult=100);

         picture blank    low-<0='000 009.99' (prefix='-')
                          0-high='000 009.99';

         picture thous    0-high='00,009K'       (mult=.001);

         picture phone    other='000/000-0000';
      run;

      data a;
         input x phone;
         acct=x; prot=x; dol=x; rsign=x; credit=x; europe=x; blank=x; thou=x;
         format acct acct.  prot prot.  dol dol.  rsign rsign.
         credit credit. europe europe. blank blank. thou thous.
         phone phone.  X 12.2;
         cards;
      12345   9196778000
      0       6778000
      -12345  .
      -187.65 9196778000
      187.65  .
      .23     .
      101.23  .
      1.1E6   .
      ;

      proc print data=a;
         id x;
         var acct prot dol rsign credit europe blank thou phone;
         title 'Print the Formats Created with PROC FORMAT';
      run;
```

Output 18.8 Picture Formats Created with PROC FORMAT

```
                        Print the Formats Created with PROC FORMAT                                    1

        X          ACCT         PROT          DOL        RSIGN       CREDIT      EUROPE        BLANK     THOU        PHONE
   12345.00     12,345.00    *12,345.00   $12,345.00   12,345.00+  12,345.00CR  12.345,00  12 345.00     12K   919/677-8000
       0.00          0.00   ******0.00        $0.00        0.00+       0.00CR      0,00        0.00       0K       677-8000
  -12345.00    (12,345.00)  -12,345.00   -12,345.00   12,345.00-  12,345.00DR  12.345,00  -12 345.00  -12345             .
    -187.65       (187.65)  ***-187.65    $-187.65      187.65-     187.65DR     -187,65    -187.65   -187.65  919/677-8000
     187.65        187.65   ****187.65     $187.65      187.65+     187.65CR     187,65     187.65       0K             .
       0.23          0.23   ******0.23       $0.23        0.23+       0.23CR       0,23       0.23       0K             .
     101.23        101.23   ****101.23     $101.23      101.23+     101.23CR     101,23     101.23       0K             .
 1100000.00     100,000.00  OVERFLOW    100,000.00   100,000.00+     0.00CR       0,00    100 000.00   1,100K            .
```

Example 3: PROC FORMAT with the INVALUE Statement

The following example uses the FORMAT procedure to create informats named GRADE. and SEX.. The GRADE. informat converts letter grades into numbers by defining 14 single value ranges. The SEX. informat converts the values **M** and **F** to the numbers 1 and 2, respectively.

The first DATA step creates the data set STUDENTS and uses the SEX. informat to convert the character value for the SEX variable to either 1 or 2.

After the SORT procedure arranges the STUDENTS data sets in order of the ID variable value, the second DATA step creates the data set GRADES by reading the ID and NCLASSES variables, and uses the GRADE. informat to convert the letter grades into numbers. As each informat is created, the SAS System writes a message that the informat name has been output.

```
    /*-----Create informats for grade scales and for sex-----*/
proc format;
    invalue grade 'A+'=4.0 'A'=3.5 'A-'=3.2
                  'B+'=3.0 'B'=2.5 'B-'=2.2
                  'C+'=2.0 'C'=1.5 'C-'=1.2
                  'D+'=1.0 'D'=0.5 'D-'=0.2
                  'F'=0 'I'=.;
    invalue sex 'M'=1 'F'=2;
run;

    /*-----Read in the student name data-----*/
data students;
   input id sex : sex. name $;
   cards;
003 F Jane
005 F Mary
001 M John
002 F Robin
004 M Rick
;

    /*-----Sort to be in order by ID-----*/
proc sort data=students;
   by id;
run;
```

```
     /*-----Input the grade information-----*/
  data grades;
     input id nclasses @;
     do i=1 to nclasses;
        input grade: grade. @;
        output;
     end;
     keep id grade;
     cards;
003 5 A B+ B C+ A-
002 5 B+ I C C F
001 4 A B C- B-
005 5 A A A A+ A-
004 4 B- D F C
;
```

After the SORT procedure arranges the GRADES data set in order according to the ID variable, use the MEANS procedure to compute the GPA and write the results to the data set FINAL.

```
     /*-----Sort to be in order by ID-----*/
  proc sort data=grades;
     by id;
  run;


     /*-----Determine the GPAs for the students-----*/
  proc means data=grades noprint;
     by id;
     var grade;
     output out=final(drop=_type_) mean=gpa;
  run;
```

The final DATA step merges the STUDENTS data set with the FINAL data set that the MEANS procedure produced. Both data sets have been sorted by their common BY variable, ID. Note that when you process with a BY statement, the BY variables with formats are classified according to formatted values rather than internal values.

```
     /*-----Merge GPA into student info-----*/
  data students;
    merge students final;
    by id;
  run;
```

The merged STUDENTS data set is now sorted by SEX and then printed with the PRINT procedure.

```
     /*-----Sort to print by SEX-----*/
  proc sort data=students;
    by sex;


     /*-----Print the final results-----*/
  proc print data=students;
    by sex;
    title 'Students'' Names and GPAs';
  run;
```

The output that the PRINT procedure produces is shown in **Output 18.9**.

Output 18.9   Data Values Read with Informats Created by PROC FORMAT

```
                              Students' Names and GPAs
------------------------------------ SEX=1 -----------------------------------------

                    OBS    ID    NAME    _FREQ_    GPA

                     1      1    John       4      2.35
                     2      4    Rick       4      1.05


------------------------------------ SEX=2 -----------------------------------------

                    OBS    ID    NAME    _FREQ_    GPA

                     3      2    Robin      5      1.50
                     4      3    Jane       5      2.84
                     5      5    Mary       5      3.54
```

Example 4:   PROC FORMAT with the CNTLIN= Option

An existing SAS data set contains account codes and corresponding customer names. There is one observation per account number. Using the data in this data set, you want to create a format that converts an account code into a name. The observations in the data set have the following structure:

ACCTNUM	NAME	OPENDATE
5008074	John Smith	01JAN87
5008075	Bill Jones	10JAN87
5009766	Benjamin Estes	18OCT86
more account observations		

You need to create the required START, LABEL, and FMTNAME variables for the input control data set that creates the format for converting the account number to the customer's name. The DATA step below uses the RENAME= data set option to convert the ACCTNUM variable to START and the NAME variable to LABEL. The assignment statement creates the FMTNAME variable by giving it the value of ACCOUNT.

```
    /*-----First create an input control data set-----*/
libname in 'SAS-data-library';
data in.cntlacct(rename=(acctnum=start name=label));
   set in.acctinfo(keep=acctnum name);
   fmtname='account';
run;


proc print data=in.cntlacct;
   title 'Input Control Data Set';
run;
```

The data in the input control data set is shown in **Output 18.10**.

Output 18.10   Contents of the Input Control Data Set

```
                      Input Control Data Set

          OBS    START        LABEL          FMTNAME

           1    5008074    John Smith        account
           2    5008075    Bill Jones        account
           3    5009766    Benjamin Estes    account
           4    7089477    Mary Wilson       account
```

The following PROC FORMAT statement uses the CNTLACCT data set created
above as an input control data set and creates the format ACCOUNT. The DATA
step then reads the ACCTNUM and TRANSAMT variables and writes ACCTNUM
with the ACCOUNT. format created in the PROC FORMAT step.

```
    /*-----Read the control data set into PROC FORMAT-----*/
proc format cntlin=in.cntlacct;
run;


    /*-----The format is now created and ready to use-----*/
data charges;
   input acctnum transamt;
   put acctnum account. ' account charged ' transamt dollar10.2;
   cards;
5008074 127.86
7089477 100.00
5009766  50.00
;
```

The output generated is shown in **Output 18.11**.

Output 18.11   Log Showing a Format Created from a CNTLIN= Data Set

```
5         libname in 'SAS-data-library';
6            /*-----Read the control data set into PROC FORMAT-----*/
7         proc format cntlin=in.cntlacct;
NOTE: Format ACCOUNT has been output.
8         run;


9
10           /*-----The format is now created and ready to use-----*/
11        data charges;
12           input acctnum transamt;
13           put acctnum account. ' account charged ' transamt dollar10.2;
14           cards;

John Smith      account charged    $127.86
Mary Wilson     account charged    $100.00
Benjamin Estes  account charged     $50.00
NOTE: The data set WORK.CHARGES has 3 observations and 2 variables.
```

Example 5:   PROC FORMAT with the CNTLOUT= Option

The program statements that follow create a picture format and five informats.
The CNTLOUT= option in the PROC FORMAT statement causes the information
about the format and informats created in the step to be output to an output con-

trol data set. The PROC PRINT step prints the output control data set variables and the values in the SAS print file, as shown in **Output 18.12**.

```
proc format cntlout=outdata;
  picture phonenum other='000/000-0000';
  invalue grade 'a'=4 'b'=3 'c'=2 'd'=1 'e'=0;
run;

proc print data=outdata;
  title 'Output Control Data Set';
run;
```

Output 18.12 Contents of an Output Control Data Set

```
                                 Output Control Data Set                                          1

OBS FMTNAME  START END   LABEL         MIN MAX DEFAULT LENGTH  FUZZ  PREFIX MULT FILL NOEDIT TYPE SEXCL EEXCL HLO

 1  PHONENUM OTHER OTHER 000/000-0000    1  40    12     12   1E-12    1         0      P    N     N    O
 2  GRADE    a     a                   4  1   1     1      1   1E-12          0         0      I    N     N
 3  GRADE    b     b                   3  1   1     1      1   1E-12          0         0      I    N     N
 4  GRADE    c     c                   2  1   1     1      1   1E-12          0         0      I    N     N
 5  GRADE    d     d                   1  1   1     1      1   1E-12          0         0      I    N     N
 6  GRADE    e     e                   0  1   1     1      1   1E-12          0         0      I    N     N
```

The FORMS Procedure

ABSTRACT

The FORMS procedure can produce labels for envelopes, mailing labels, external tape labels, file cards, and any other printer forms that have a regular pattern.

INTRODUCTION

For each observation in the input SAS data set, PROC FORMS prints data in a rectangular block called a *form unit*. For example, a mailing label is a form unit. The results can be routed to a specified external file or printed in the SAS print file. For external files, carriage controls can be used or suppressed.

Form Layout

The size and spacing of the forms are controlled by options as illustrated in **Figure 19.1**. The keyword options for the PROC FORMS statement are shown with their abbreviations in uppercase.

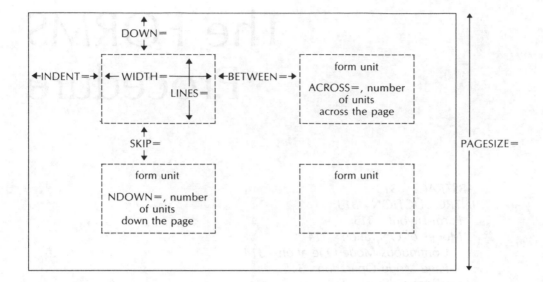

Figure 19.1 Sample PROC FORMS Placement

The values of the variables specified in LINE statements are formatted into a form unit that is WIDTH= columns wide and LINES= lines long. Values that do not fit into WIDTH= columns are truncated. ACROSS= form units are printed across the page, with BETWEEN= spaces between adjacent form units. The forms are indented INDENT= spaces from the left margin. SKIP= blank lines are printed between form units down the page.

Modes of Operation

PROC FORMS has two modes of operation: continuous mode and page mode. The procedure operates in page mode if you use either the NDOWN= or the PAGESIZE= option, or if you write to the SAS print file rather than an external file specified with the FILE= option.

Continuous-Mode Operation

For continuous-mode operation, the procedure first skips DOWN= lines, then alternately prints LINES= print lines and SKIP= blank lines until all the data are printed. No carriage-control characters are used to skip to the top of the form. However, you can use the CC option in continuous mode to put a top-of-form character at the beginning of the first page.

Continuous-mode operation is suitable for most forms unless the distance between form units changes between pages.

Page-Mode Operation

First, PROC FORMS goes to the start of a new page, then skips DOWN= lines (see **Carriage Control** below). Next, the procedure prints NDOWN= form units down the page. If you do not use the NDOWN= option, PROC FORMS prints the maximum number of form units allowed by the PAGESIZE= value specified or assumed.

If the SAS print file is used (which occurs if the FILE= option is not specified), all the page calculations are done with respect to the lines remaining on the page after the title lines are printed.

Carriage Control

When you write to the SAS print file, the FORMS procedure automatically sends carriage-control characters to the file. However, when you route the forms to an external file specified by the FILE= option, you must choose whether to use carriage-control characters. A carriage control is an extra character prefixed to each record that controls the printer for line spacing and top-of-form ejection. If you want PROC FORMS to use carriage controls, you must choose the CC option in the PROC FORMS statement and an appropriate specification for the record format of the print file. If you do not use carriage controls, PROC FORMS prints blank lines to align form units correctly on the page.

If you are using page-mode printing with the CC option, PROC FORMS uses the top-of-form carriage control to start each page. For page-mode operation without the CC option, the PAGESIZE= option must be correct since PROC FORMS uses it to calculate the number of blank lines to print at the bottom of a page before starting the next page.

Multiple Copies

Three features in PROC FORMS provide for multiple copies of forms. If you want the whole list repeated as a unit, use the SETS= option. (See **Output 19.2** in **EXAMPLES** at the end of this chapter.) If you want each observation repeated in adjacent form units, use the COPIES= option. (See **Output 19.3**.) If you want a variable number of copies depending on a variable in a data set, use the FREQ statement. You can use these two options and the statement separately or together.

SPECIFICATIONS

The statements used to control PROC FORMS are

> **PROC FORMS** <*option-list*>;
> **LINE** *line-number variable-list* </ *option-list*>;
> **FREQ** *variable*;
> **BY** *variable-list*;

You must use at least one LINE statement with the PROC FORMS statement to tell the procedure which variables to print on which lines. You can use multiple LINE statements.

PROC FORMS Statement

PROC FORMS <*option-list*>;

Table 19.1 summarizes the options supported by the PROC FORMS statement. Detailed descriptions follow in alphabetic order.

Table 19.1 Summary of PROC FORMS Statement Options

Class	Option	Function
Specifying input and output	DATA=	names the input data set
	FILE=	specifies an external file to write to
Controlling placement of form units	WIDTH=	specifies the number of columns across the form unit
	LINES=	specifies the number of lines in a form unit
	DOWN=	specifies the number of lines to skip on a page before printing the first form unit
	INDENT=	specifies the number of spaces to indent before printing the first form unit of each row
	SKIP=	specifies the number of lines to skip between form units
	ACROSS=	specifies the number of form units across the page
	NDOWN=	specifies the number of form units down the page
	BETWEEN=	specifies the number of spaces between form units
	PAGESIZE=	specifies the number of lines on a form page
Controlling the number of form units	COPIES=	specifies the number of copies to produce for each observation in the data set (all copies of an observation appear together)
	SETS=	specifies the number of sets of forms to produce
Carriage control	CC	adds carriage-control characters to the beginning of each line
Printer alignment	ALIGN	specifies the number of form units consisting solely of Xs to print

ACROSS=*form-units-per-line*
A=*form-units-per-line*
specifies the number of form units across the page. The minimum is 1, the maximum is 200, and the default is 1.

ALIGN=*number*
specifies the number of form units consisting solely of Xs to print so that the printer can be aligned. If you specify the FILE= option, the default is 8; otherwise it is 0.

BETWEEN=*spaces-between-form-units*
B=*spaces-between-form-units*
specifies the number of spaces between form units. The minimum is 0, the maximum is 200, and the default is 1.

CC
adds carriage-control characters to the beginning of each line. This option is relevant only if you use the FILE= option.

COPIES=*number*
C=*number*
specifies the number of form units to produce for each observation in each set of form units. All copies of an observation appear together. (See **Output 19.3** in **EXAMPLES** at the end of this chapter.)
If you use the FREQ statement, the number of form units for each observation in a set of form units is the product of the value of the COPIES= option and the value of the FREQ variable for that observation.

DATA=*SAS-data-set*
names the input data set for PROC FORMS. If you omit the DATA= option, PROC FORMS uses the most recently created SAS data set.

DOWN=*top-margin*
D=*top-margin*
specifies the number of lines to skip on a page before printing the first form unit. The minimum is 0, the maximum is 200, and the default is 0.
Note: When PROC FORMS writes to the SAS print file, it always reserves the first line for a title and leaves the second line blank. Counting for the top margin begins at the third line. Thus, if you specify DOWN=5, the FORMS procedure begins printing the first form unit on line 8.

FILE=*fileref*
DDNAME=*fileref*
DD=*fileref*
specifies an external file where PROC FORMS writes the forms. Use the FILENAME statement to associate an external file with a fileref. (See *SAS Language: Reference, Version 6, First Edition* for information on using the FILENAME statement.)
If you do not use the FILE= option, PROC FORMS uses the SAS print file.

INDENT=*left-margin*
I=*left-margin*
specifies the number of spaces to indent before printing the first form unit in each row. The minimum is 0, the maximum is 200, and the default is 0.

LINES=*form-unit-length*
L=*form-unit-length*
> specifies the number of lines in a form unit. The minimum is 1, the maximum is 200, and the default is the maximum LINE statement number.

NDOWN=*form-units-per-page*
ND=*form-units-per-page*
> specifies the number of form units printed down the page. This option triggers page-mode operation. The default is

$$FLOOR((PAGESIZE - DOWN + SKIP)/(LINES + SKIP))$$

> where FLOOR is a SAS function that returns the largest integer less than or equal to the value of the argument.

PAGESIZE=*lines-per-page*
P=*lines-per-page*
> specifies the number of lines on a form page. This information is needed for page-mode operation only. The minimum is DOWN+LINES, the maximum is 255, and the default is the value of the PAGESIZE= system option if FILE= is specified. Otherwise PROC FORMS infers the number of lines from SAS print file characteristics and titling information. This option triggers page-mode operation.
>
> Note: The PAGESIZE= option used with the PROC FORMS statement is different from the PAGESIZE= system option. Setting the PAGESIZE= option in PROC FORMS has no effect outside that PROC step.

SETS=*number*
> specifies the number of sets of forms to produce. (See **Output 19.2** in **EXAMPLES** at the end of this chapter.) For page-mode operation, PROC FORMS skips to a new page to start each set. This option is different from COPIES=, which prints multiples copies of the form unit for each observation in adjacent positions within one set of forms.

SKIP=*lines-between-form-units*
S=*lines-between-form-units*
> specifies the number of lines to skip between form units. The minimum is 0, the maximum is 200, and the default is 1.

WIDTH=*form-unit-width*
W=*form-unit-width*
> specifies the number of columns across the form unit. The minimum is 1, the maximum is 255, and the default is the width of the widest line.

BY Statement

> **BY** *variable-list*;

A BY statement can be used with PROC FORMS to force new pages to be started (in page-mode operation) when the BY values change. When a BY statement appears, the procedure expects the input data set to be sorted in order of the BY variables or to have an appropriate index. If your input data set is not sorted in ascending order, you can do one of the following:

- Use the SORT procedure with a similar BY statement to sort the data.
- If appropriate, use the BY statement option NOTSORTED or DESCENDING.

- Create an index on the BY variables you want to use. For more information on creating indexes and using the BY statement with indexed data sets, see Chapter 17, "The DATASETS Procedure."

For more information on the BY statement see *SAS Language: Reference*.

FREQ Statement

FREQ *variable*;

When a FREQ statement is included, the value of the frequency variable determines the number of form units printed for each observation.

The variable given in the FREQ statement must be numeric. If the value is not an integer, the integer portion of the value determines the number of form units printed for a given observation. If the value of the FREQ variable is less than 1 or is missing, PROC FORMS treats it as 0 and does not print any form units for that observation.

The actual number of copies produced in adjacent form units is the product of the FREQ variable multiplied by the value of the COPIES= option. For example, if the FREQ variable is 3 and the COPIES= value is 2, then 6 copies are printed.

LINE Statement

LINE *line-number variable-list </ option-list>*;

LINE statements specify the information to print on each line of the form unit. The *line-number* identifies the number of the line. It must be an integer from 1 to the value of the LINES= option specified in the PROC FORMS statement. You can specify lines in any order. You do not need to specify a line statement for a blank line; if you do not define a line with a LINE statement, PROC FORMS leaves that line blank.

Values of the *variables* specified in the LINE statement are printed on the specified line of the form unit. The FORMS procedure inserts one space between each value. By default, PROC FORMS places each variable in a field whose length is determined by the length of that variable in the data set. If the length of all values in a line is longer than the WIDTH= value specified in the PROC FORMS statement, the values are truncated to fit the WIDTH= value.

The PACK option, which eliminates extra spaces from a field, may allow you to fit more fields onto a small form unit. However, if you must squeeze fields onto a form unit, it is better to use a FORMAT statement to truncate each field individually, rather than risk losing an entire field. For example, the following statement sets the field widths of the variables CITY and STATE to 20 and 2 columns, respectively:

```
format city $20. state $2.;
```

The following options can appear in LINE statements after a slash (/):

INDENT=*margin-within-form-unit*
I=*margin-within-form-unit*
    indents the line within the form unit, where *margin-within-form-unit* is the number of spaces to indent. This indent is done within the form unit (in contrast to the indent specified by the INDENT= option in the PROC FORMS statement).

LASTNAME
L
    looks for a comma in a character variable and rotates the words after the comma if it finds one. For example, a variable NAME might have the value **SMITH, JAMES P.**. If the LASTNAME option is given, the value is printed **JAMES P. SMITH**.

PACK
P

removes extra blanks from the line so that all the values are separated by one space. For example, if a variable NAME has a length of 20 and the value of NAME is SMITH, the PACK option removes the extra 15 blanks. As usual, PROC FORMS inserts one space between values.

REMOVE
R

deletes the entire line if the values of the variables are all blanks or missing values.

DETAILS

Compatibility Features

PROC FORMS is similar to an earlier FORMS procedure in the SUGI supplemental library. The following options are still maintained to ensure compatibility: NACROSS= and NA= for ACROSS=, NSKIP= and NS= for SKIP=, NBETWEEN= and NB= for BETWEEN=, NCOPIES= and N= for COPIES=. The former PROC FORMS options BURST, TRUNCATE, NOALIGN, and EIGHTLPI have been replaced by more efficient options.

EXAMPLES

Example 1:   Printing a List of Names and Addresses

This example creates a SAS data set containing names and addresses, sorts it by ZIP code, and uses PROC FORMS to print one set of mailing labels consisting of one copy of the form unit for each observation. The following statements produce **Output 19.1**.

```
libname mailing 'SAS-data-library';

data mailing.list;
   input name &$20. street &$20. city &$15. state :$2. zip :$5.;
   cards;
John Smith         202 Main St.        Anytown     IN  22432
Joe Williams       101 Broadway        Gotham      NY  32334
Alice Gordon       55 Hazel Way        Atlanta     GA  68549
George Hayes       2132 Goodview       Muncie      IN  54345
Penelope Peters    543 Peanut Circle   Columbia    MD  53455
Harrison Harrison  898 7th St.         Big Rock    AK  98733
Bill Smith         123 State           Rockford    IL  81522
Will Red           544 Hillside Ave.   Rocquefort  KY  98783
Ann Anderson       5456 Pleasant Blvd. Seattle     WA  49747
Aristotle Johnson  234 Peace           Phoenix     AZ  77898
Gary Miller        7 Gray Drive        St. Louis   MO  26578
Winston Martin     34 Red Road         Newton      MA  34678
Allison Towson     44 Mars Hill Dr.    Redwood     CA  23432
Mathew Mackem      78 Highview Ct.     Virgil      VA  87373
;
run;
```

```
proc sort data=mailing.list;
   by zip;
run;

proc forms data=mailing.list
            width=25 lines=3 down=2 skip=2 across=3;
   line 1 name;
   line 2 street;
   line 3 city state zip / pack;
run;
```

Output 19.1   A Single Set of Mailing Labels

```
                                    The SAS System                                                    1

John Smith              Allison Towson         Gary Miller
202 Main St.            44 Mars Hill Dr.       7 Gray Drive
Anytown IN 22432        Redwood CA 23432       St. Louis MO 26578


Joe Williams            Winston Martin         Ann Anderson
101 Broadway            34 Red Road            5456 Pleasant Blvd.
Gotham NY 32334         Newton MA 34678        Seattle WA 49747


Penelope Peters         George Hayes           Alice Gordon
543 Peanut Circle       2132 Goodview          55 Hazel Way
Columbia MD 53455       Muncie IN 54345        Atlanta GA 68549


Aristotle Johnson       Bill Smith             Mathew Mackem
234 Peace               123 State              78 Highview Ct.
Phoenix AZ 77898        Rockford IL 81522      Virgil VA 87373


Harrison Harrison       Will Red
898 7th St.             544 Hillside Ave.
Big Rock AK 98733       Rocquefort KY 98783
```

Example 2:   Printing Multiple Sets of Mailing Labels

This example uses the SETS= option to produce two sets of mailing labels from the same data set used in the previous example. The following statements produce **Output 19.2**.

```
libname mailing 'SAS-data-library';

proc forms data=mailing.list
            width=25 lines=3 down=2 skip=2 across=3
            sets=2;
   line 1 name;
   line 2 street;
   line 3 city state zip / pack;
run;
```

Output 19.2   Two Sets of Mailing Labels

```
                                        The SAS System                                        1


John Smith            Allison Towson        Gary Miller
202 Main St.          44 Mars Hill Dr.      7 Gray Drive
Anytown IN 22432      Redwood CA 23432      St. Louis MO 26578


Joe Williams          Winston Martin        Ann Anderson
101 Broadway          34 Red Road           5456 Pleasant Blvd.
Gotham NY 32334       Newton MA 34678       Seattle WA 49747


Penelope Peters       George Hayes          Alice Gordon
543 Peanut Circle     2132 Goodview         55 Hazel Way
Columbia MD 53455     Muncie IN 54345       Atlanta GA 68549


Aristotle Johnson     Bill Smith            Mathew Mackem
234 Peace             123 State             78 Highview Ct.
Phoenix AZ 77898      Rockford IL 81522     Virgil VA 87373


Harrison Harrison     Will Red
898 7th St.           544 Hillside Ave.
Big Rock AK 98733     Rocquefort KY 98783
```

```
                                        The SAS System                                        2


John Smith            Allison Towson        Gary Miller
202 Main St.          44 Mars Hill Dr.      7 Gray Drive
Anytown IN 22432      Redwood CA 23432      St. Louis MO 26578


Joe Williams          Winston Martin        Ann Anderson
101 Broadway          34 Red Road           5456 Pleasant Blvd.
Gotham NY 32334       Newton MA 34678       Seattle WA 49747


Penelope Peters       George Hayes          Alice Gordon
543 Peanut Circle     2132 Goodview         55 Hazel Way
Columbia MD 53455     Muncie IN 54345       Atlanta GA 68549


Aristotle Johnson     Bill Smith            Mathew Mackem
234 Peace             123 State             78 Highview Ct.
Phoenix AZ 77898      Rockford IL 81522     Virgil VA 87373


Harrison Harrison     Will Red
898 7th St.           544 Hillside Ave.
Big Rock AK 98733     Rocquefort KY 98783
```

Example 3:   Printing Multiple Copies of Each Form Unit

This example uses the COPIES= option to produce one set of mailing labels containing two copies of each form unit. The following statements produce **Output 19.3**.

```
libname mailing 'SAS-data-library';

proc forms data=mailing.list
           width=25 lines=3 down=2 skip=2 across=3
           copies=2;
    line 1 name;
    line 2 street;
    line 3 city state zip / pack;
run;
```

Output 19.3   One Set of Mailing Labels Consisting of Two Copies of Each Form Unit

```
                                        The SAS System                                              1

John Smith             John Smith             Allison Towson
202 Main St.           202 Main St.           44 Mars Hill Dr.
Anytown IN 22432       Anytown IN 22432       Redwood CA 23432


Allison Towson         Gary Miller            Gary Miller
44 Mars Hill Dr.       7 Gray Drive           7 Gray Drive
Redwood CA 23432       St. Louis MO 26578     St. Louis MO 26578


Joe Williams           Joe Williams           Winston Martin
101 Broadway           101 Broadway           34 Red Road
Gotham NY 32334        Gotham NY 32334        Newton MA 34678


Winston Martin         Ann Anderson           Ann Anderson
34 Red Road            5456 Pleasant Blvd.    5456 Pleasant Blvd.
Newton MA 34678        Seattle WA 49747       Seattle WA 49747


Penelope Peters        Penelope Peters        George Hayes
543 Peanut Circle      543 Peanut Circle      2132 Goodview
Columbia MD 53455      Columbia MD 53455      Muncie IN 54345


George Hayes           Alice Gordon           Alice Gordon
2132 Goodview          55 Hazel Way           55 Hazel Way
Muncie IN 54345        Atlanta GA 68549       Atlanta GA 68549


Aristotle Johnson      Aristotle Johnson      Bill Smith
234 Peace              234 Peace              123 State
Phoenix AZ 77898       Phoenix AZ 77898       Rockford IL 81522


Bill Smith             Mathew Mackem          Mathew Mackem
123 State              78 Highview Ct.        78 Highview Ct.
Rockford IL 81522      Virgil VA 87373        Virgil VA 87373


Harrison Harrison      Harrison Harrison      Will Red
898 7th St.            898 7th St.            544 Hillside Ave.
Big Rock AK 98733      Big Rock AK 98733      Rocquefort KY 98783


Will Red
544 Hillside Ave.
Rocquefort KY 98783
```

The FREQ Procedure

ABSTRACT

The FREQ procedure produces one-way to n-way frequency and crosstabulation tables. For two-way tables, PROC FREQ computes tests and measures of association. For n-way tables, PROC FREQ does stratified analysis, computing statistics within, as well as across, strata. Frequencies can also be output to a SAS data set.

INTRODUCTION

PROC FREQ is a procedure that serves two purposes. It is a descriptive procedure in the sense that it produces frequency counts and crosstabulation tables, allowing you to describe your data in a concise way. PROC FREQ is also a statistical procedure: the numerous statistics produced allow you to analyze the relationships among variables.

Frequency tables show the distribution of variable values. For example, if a variable A has six possible values, a frequency table for A shows how many observations in the data set have the first value of A, how many have the second value, and so on.

Crosstabulation tables show combined frequency distributions for two or more variables. For example, a crosstabulation table for the variables SEX and EMPLOY shows the number of working females, the number of nonworking females, the number of working males, and the number of nonworking males.

This chapter contains detailed information about both the descriptive and statistical uses of PROC FREQ. If you are interested only in the descriptive aspects, you can ignore the section **Statistical Analysis** later in this introductory section, the subsections **Tests and Measures of Association** and **Summary Statistics** in **DETAILS** later in this chapter, and **Example 2** through **Example 5**.

One-Way Frequency Tables

If you want a one-way frequency table for a variable, simply name the variable in a TABLES statement. The values of the variable can be either character or numeric. For example, in a survey of small-scale farm owners, 90 farm operators were asked questions regarding farming practices. VAR18 asks "Did you farm any land you did not own?" with "YES" coded as 1 and "NO" coded as 2. Adding the following statement to the DATA step clarifies the printed output:

```
label var18='Did you farm any land you did not own?';
```

The statements below produce the one-way frequency table giving the values of VAR18 and the frequency of each value shown in **Output 20.1**. The majority of farmers in this survey farmed land that they did not own.

```
proc freq;
    tables var18;
run;
```

Output 20.1 One-Way Frequency Table

```
                          The SAS System

                 Did you farm any land you did not own?

                                    Cumulative Cumulative
        VAR18  Frequency   Percent   Frequency   Percent
        ---------------------------------------------------
          1       70       77.8         70        77.8
          2       20       22.2         90       100.0
```

Two-Way Crosstabulation Tables

If you want a crosstabulation table for two variables, give the variable names separated by an asterisk. Values of the first variable form the rows of the table, and values of the second variable form the columns. For example, using the small-farm survey, VAR86 asks "Do you have an off-farm job?" As before, "YES" is coded as 1 and "NO" is coded as 2, and labels are used in the DATA step to identify the variables. PROC FORMAT is used to format the variable values. PROC FREQ is used to create a two-way crosstabulation table. The following statements produce **Output 20.2**:

```
proc freq;
    tables var18*var86;
    format var18 var86 rsp.;
    title 'Small-Scale Farm Survey';
run;
```

Output 20.2   Two-Way Crosstabulation Table

```
                    Small-Scale Farm Survey
                    TABLE OF VAR18 BY VAR86

          VAR18(Did you farm any land you did not own?)
                VAR86(Did you have an off-farm job?)
          Frequency|
          Percent  |
          Row Pct  |
          Col Pct  |yes     |no      |  Total
          ---------+--------+--------+
          yes      |    37  |    33  |     70
                   | 41.11  | 36.67  |  77.78
                   | 52.86  | 47.14  |
                   | 75.51  | 80.49  |
          ---------+--------+--------+
          no       |    12  |     8  |     20
                   | 13.33  |  8.89  |  22.22
                   | 60.00  | 40.00  |
                   | 24.49  | 19.51  |
          ---------+--------+--------+
          Total        49       41        90
                     54.44    45.56    100.00
```

The values of VAR18 are listed down the side and values of VAR86 are listed across the top. Of the farmers surveyed, 41.11 percent farm land that they do not own, as well as work off-farm.

n-Way Crosstabulation Tables

If you want a three-way (or n-way) crosstabulation table, give the three (or n) variable names separated by asterisks in the TABLES statement. Values of the last variable form the columns of a contingency table; values of the next-to-last variable form the rows. Each level (or combination of levels) of the other variables form one stratum, and a separate contingency table is produced for each stratum. For example, the following statements produce k tables, where k is the number of different combinations of values for the variables A and B:

```
proc freq;
   tables a*b*c*d ;
run;
```

Each table lists the values of C down the side and the values of D across the top.

Multi-way tables can generate a great deal of printed output. For example, if the variables A, B, C, D, and E each have ten levels, five-way tables of A*B*C*D*E could generate 4000 or more pages of output.

Statistical Analysis

For some pairs of variables, you may want information about the existence or the strength of any association between the variables. With respect to the existence of an association, PROC FREQ computes statistics that test the null hypothesis of no association. With respect to the strength of an association, PROC FREQ computes measures of association that tend to be close to zero when there is no association and close to the maximum (or minimum) value when there is perfect association. You can request the computation and printing of these statistics by specifying one or more options in the TABLES statement. For information on specific statistics computed by PROC FREQ, see **Tests and Measures of Association** later in this chapter.

In choosing measures of association to use in analyzing a two-way table, you should consider the study design (which indicates whether the row and column variables are dependent or independent), the measurement scale of the variables (nominal, ordinal, or interval), the type of association that each measure is designed to detect, and any assumptions required for valid interpretation of a measure. You should exercise care in selecting measures that are appropriate for your data. For more information to guide you in choosing measures of association for a specific set of data, see Hayes (1963) and Garson (1971). For an advanced treatment, refer to Goodman and Kruskal (1979) or Bishop, Fienberg, and Holland (1975, Chapter 11).

Similar comments apply to the choice and interpretation of the test statistics. For example, the Mantel-Haenszel chi-square statistic requires an ordinal scale for both variables and is designed to detect a linear association. The Pearson chi-square, on the other hand, is appropriate for all variables and can detect any kind of association, but it is less powerful for detecting a linear association because its power is dispersed over a greater number of degrees of freedom (except for 2×2 tables).

For *n-way* crosstabulation tables, consider the following example:

```
proc freq;
    tables a*b*c*d / cmh;
run;
```

The CMH option in the TABLES statement gives a stratified statistical analysis of the relationship between C and D, after controlling for A and B. The stratified analysis provides a convenient way to adjust for the possible confounding effects of A and B without being forced to estimate parameters for them. The analysis produces Cochran-Mantel-Haenszel statistics, and for 2×2 tables, it includes estimation of the common relative risk (case-control and cohort studies) and Breslow's test for homogeneity of the odds ratios. See **Summary Statistics** later in this chapter for details of the stratified analysis.

PROC FREQ Contrasted with Other SAS Procedures

Many other SAS procedures can collect .requency counts. PROC FREQ is distinguished by its ability to compute chi-square tests and measures of association for two-way and *n*-way tables. Other procedures to consider for counting are the following: PROC TABULATE for more general table layouts, PROC SUMMARY for output data sets, and PROC CHART for bar charts and other graphical representations. The FREQ option in PROC UNIVARIATE provides one-way frequency tables. PROC CATMOD can be used for general linear model analysis of categorical data.

SPECIFICATIONS

The FREQ procedure is controlled by the following statements:

PROC FREQ <options>;
  BY variables;
  TABLES requests</ options>;
  WEIGHT variable;

If you specify
```
proc freq;
run;
```

a one-way frequency table is output for each variable in your data set. The BY, TABLES, and WEIGHT statements are described in alphabetical order after the PROC FREQ statement.

PROC FREQ Statement

PROC FREQ <*options*>;

The PROC FREQ statement starts the procedure. You can use the following options in the PROC FREQ statement:

DATA=*SAS-data-set*
    specifies the data set to be used by PROC FREQ. If you omit the DATA= option, PROC FREQ uses the most recently created data set.

FORMCHAR (1,2,7)='*formchar-string*'
    defines the characters to be used for constructing the outlines and dividers for the cells of contingency tables. The string should be three characters long. The characters are used to denote (1) vertical divider, (2) horizontal divider, (7) vertical-horizontal intersection. Any character or hexadecimal string can be used to customize table appearance.
    Specifying three blanks produces tables with no outlines or dividers:

```
formchar (1,2,7)='   ' (3 blanks)
```

    If you do not specify the FORMCHAR= option, PROC FREQ uses the default

```
formchar (1,2,7)='|-+'
```

    See the CALENDAR, PLOT, and TABULATE procedures in base SAS documentation for further information on form characters.

ORDER=DATA
       | FORMATTED
       | FREQ
       | INTERNAL
specifies the order in which the variable levels are to be reported, as shown in the following table:

Value of ORDER=	Sorted by
DATA	order of appearance in the input data set provided they have nonzero weights
FORMATTED	formatted value
FREQ	descending frequency count; levels with the most observations appear first
INTERNAL	unformatted value

By default, ORDER=INTERNAL. For FORMATTED and INTERNAL, the sort order is machine-dependent. The ORDER= option does not apply to missing values, which are always ordered first.

PAGE
    prints only one table per page. Otherwise, PROC FREQ prints multiple tables per page as space permits.

BY Statement

BY *variables*;

A BY statement can be used with PROC FREQ to obtain separate analyses for the groups defined by the BY variables. When a BY statement appears, the procedure expects the input data set to be sorted in order of the BY variables or to have an appropriate index. If your input data set is not sorted, you can do one of the following:

- Use the SORT procedure with a similar BY statement to sort the data.
- If appropriate, use the BY statement options NOTSORTED or DESCENDING. As a cautionary note, the NOTSORTED option does not mean that the data are unsorted, but rather means that the data are arranged in groups (according to values of the BY variables) and that these groups are not necessarily in alphabetic or increasing numeric order.
- Create an index on the BY variables you want to use. For more information on creating indexes and using the BY statement with indexed data sets, see "SAS Files" in *SAS Language: Reference, Version 6, First Edition*.

TABLES Statement

TABLES *requests* </ *options*>;

For each frequency or crosstabulation table that you want, put a table request in the TABLES statement, where *requests* are composed of one or more variable names joined by asterisks. A one-way frequency is generated by a single name. Two-way crosstabulations are generated by two variables joined with an asterisk. Any number of variables can be joined for a multi-way table. For two- to multi-way tables, the last variable is the column variable, and the next-to-last variable is the row variable. A grouping syntax is also available to make the specifications of many tables easier. Several variables can be put in parentheses and joined to other effects. For example, the statements below illustrate several ways to specify requests:

`tables a*(b c);`	is equivalent to	`tables a*b a*c;`
`tables (a b)*(c d);`	is equivalent to	`tables a*c b*c a*d b*d;`
`tables (a b c)*d;`	is equivalent to	`tables a*d b*d c*d;`
`tables a--c;`	is equivalent to	`tables a b c;`
`tables (a--c)*d;`	is equivalent to	`tables a*d b*d c*d;`

Any number of requests can be given in one TABLES statement, and any number of TABLES statements can be included in one execution of PROC FREQ. If you do not use a TABLES statement, PROC FREQ does one-way frequencies for all of the variables in the data set.

If you request a one-way frequency table for a variable and do not specify any options, the FREQ procedure produces frequencies, cumulative frequencies, percentages of the total frequency, and cumulative percentages for each level of the variable.

If you request a two-way or *n*-way crosstabulation table and do not specify any options, PROC FREQ produces crosstabulation tables that include cell frequencies, cell percentages of the total frequency, cell percentages of row frequencies, and cell percentages of column frequencies. Missing levels of each variable are excluded from the table, but the total frequency of missing subjects is printed below each table.

If you request four or more tables using a single PROC FREQ statement, a table of contents is printed on the SAS log, provided that you are running under display manager or in batch mode or some other noninteractive mode. This table of contents lists each table specification and the page on which it can be found in the output.

The table below groups TABLE statement options into categories. Each option is described in detail in alphabetic order immediately following the table.

Table 20.1 TABLE Statement Options in PROC FREQ

Task	Options
Specify statistical analysis	ALL
	ALPHA=
	CHISQ
	CMH1
	CMH
	CMH2
	EXACT
	MEASURES
	SCORES=
Request further information	CELLCHI2
	CUMCOL
	DEVIATION
	EXPECTED
	MISSPRINT
	MISSING
	OUT=
	SPARSE
Control output	LIST
	NOCOL
	NOCUM
	NOFREQ
	NOPERCENT
	NOPRINT
	NOROW

General Option List

ALL
> requests all of the tests and measures given by the CHISQ, MEASURES, and CMH options. The number of CMH statistics computed can be controlled by CMH1 and CMH2.

ALPHA=p
> specifies that confidence intervals are to be $100(1-p)$ percent confidence intervals, where $0.0001 < p < 0.9999$. By default, PROC FREQ uses ALPHA=0.05. If the specified ALPHA= value is between 0 and 1 but is outside the limits, the closest limit is used. For example, if you specify ALPHA=0.000001, an ALPHA= value of 0.0001 is used. If the

specified ALPHA= value is less than 0 or greater than 1, PROC FREQ prints an error message.

CELLCHI2

prints each cell's contribution to the total χ^2 statistic. This is computed as $(frequency - expected)^2/expected$.

CHISQ

performs chi-square (χ^2) tests of homogeneity or independence for each stratum, and computes measures of association based on chi-square. The tests include Pearson chi-square, likelihood ratio chi-square, and Mantel-Haenszel chi-square. The measures include the phi coefficient, the contingency coefficient, and Cramer's V. For 2×2 tables, Fisher's exact test is also included. The formulas for these tests and measures are given in **Tests and Measures of Association** later in this chapter.

CMH

computes Cochran-Mantel-Haenszel statistics, which test for association between the row variable and the column variable after adjusting for all other variables in the TABLES statement. In addition, for 2×2 tables, PROC FREQ gives the estimate of the common relative risk for both case-control and cohort studies and the corresponding confidence intervals. Breslow's test for homogeneity of the odds ratios is also given for the 2×2 case. The formulas for these statistics are given in **Tests and Measures of Association** later in this chapter.

CMH1

requests the same summary information as the CMH option, except that the only Cochran-Mantel-Haenszel statistic requested is the first one, which is the correlation statistic with one degree of freedom. Except for 2×2 tables, this request requires less memory than the CMH option, which can require an enormous amount for large tables.

CMH2

requests the same summary information as the CMH option, except that the only Cochran-Mantel-Haenszel statistics requested are the first two, which are the correlation and the mean score (*ANOVA*) statistics. Except for tables with two columns, this request requires less memory than the CMH option, which can require an enormous amount for large tables.

CUMCOL

prints the cumulative column percentages in the cells.

DEVIATION

for each cell, prints the deviation of the cell frequency from the expected value.

EXACT

performs Fisher's exact test for tables that are larger than 2×2. The computational algorithm is the network algorithm given by Mehta and Patel (1983). Although the computational algorithm is faster than previous algorithms by orders of magnitude, the computational time can still be prohibitive, depending on the size of the table and the sample size. The test is generally not practical (in terms of CPU time and memory usage) when

$$\frac{n}{(r-1)(c-1)} > 5$$

where n is the sample size of the table, r is the number of rows, and c is the number of columns. The practicality increases as the sample size per degree of freedom decreases toward zero. This option is not requested when you use the ALL option.

EXPECTED

prints the expected cell frequencies under the hypothesis of independence (or homogeneity). If both the EXPECTED and LIST options are used, expected cell frequencies are not printed.

LIST

prints two-way to n-way tables in a list format rather than as crosstabulation tables. The LIST option cannot be used when statistical tests or measures of association are requested. Expected cell frequencies are not printed when the LIST option is specified, even if the EXPECTED option is specified.

MEASURES

requests a basic set of measures of association and their asymptotic standard errors (ASE). The measures include Pearson and Spearman correlation coefficients, gamma, Kendall's tau-b, Stuart's tau-c, Somers' D, lambda (symmetric and asymmetric), uncertainty coefficients (symmetric and asymmetric), and for 2×2 tables, odds ratios, risk ratios, and the corresponding confidence intervals. The formulas for these measures are given in **Tests and Measures of Association** later in this chapter.

MISSING

interprets missing values as nonmissing and includes them in calculations of percentages and other statistics.

MISSPRINT

prints missing value frequencies for two-way to n-way tables, even though the frequencies are not used in the calculation of statistics.

NOCOL

suppresses printing of the column percentages in cells of a crosstabulation.

NOCUM

suppresses printing of the cumulative frequencies and cumulative percentages for one-way frequencies and for frequencies in list format.

NOFREQ

suppresses printing of the cell frequencies for a crosstabulation. This also suppresses frequencies for row totals.

NOPERCENT

suppresses printing of cell percentages for a crosstabulation. This also suppresses printing of percentages for row totals and column totals in a crosstabulation. For one-way frequencies and frequencies in list format, the NOPERCENT option supresses printing of percentages and cumulative percentages.

NOPRINT

suppresses printing of the tables, but allows printing of the statistics specified by the CHISQ, MEASURES, CMH, EXACT, and ALL options.

NOROW

suppresses printing of the row percentages in cells of a crosstabulation.

OUT=*SAS-data-set*

creates an output SAS data set containing variable values and frequency counts. If more than one table request appears in the TABLES statement, the contents of the data set correspond to the last table request in the TABLES statement. For details on the output data set created by PROC FREQ, see **Output Data Set** later in this chapter. If you want to create a permanent SAS data set, you must specify a two-level name. See "SAS Files" in *SAS Language: Reference* and "Introduction to DATA Step Processing" in *SAS Language and Procedures: Usage, Version 6, First Edition* for more information on permanent SAS data sets.

SCORES=MODRIDIT

| RANK

| RIDIT

| TABLE

specifies the type of row and column scores to be used by the Mantel-Haenszel chi-square, the Cochran-Mantel-Haenszel statistics, and the Pearson correlation. For numeric variables, TABLE scores are the values of the numeric row and column headings. For character variables, TABLE scores are defined by the row and column numbers (for example, 1 for the first row, 2 for the second row, and so on). The other scores yield nonparametric analyses. If no scores are specified, PROC FREQ uses TABLE scores. See **Scores** later in this chapter for further details.

SPARSE

prints information about all possible combinations of levels of the variables in the table request, even when some combinations of levels do not occur in the data. This option affects printed output produced under the LIST option and output data sets.

WEIGHT Statement

WEIGHT *variable*;

Normally, each observation contributes a value of 1 to the frequency counts. (In other words, each observation represents one subject.) However, when you use a WEIGHT statement, each observation contributes the weighting variable's value for that observation. (For example, a weight of 3 means that the observation represents three subjects.) The weight values need not be integers.

If the value of the weight variable is missing or zero, the corresponding observation is ignored. If the value of the weight variable is negative, the frequencies (as measured by the weighted values) are printed, but the computation and printing of percentages and other statistics are suppressed. If an output data set is created, the variable PERCENT is created and assigned a value of missing for each observation.

The FREQ procedure uses double-precision floating-point arithmetic to accumulate the counts or weights. Values are summed and then printed with decimal places, if appropriate.

Only one WEIGHT statement can be used, and that statement applies to counts collected for all tables.

For example, suppose a data set contains variables RACE, SEX, and HRSWORK. The following statements produce a table showing how many nonwhite females, nonwhite males, white females, and white males are present:

```
proc freq;
   tables race*sex;
run;
```

The statements below produce a table showing the number of hours worked by nonwhite females, by nonwhite males, and so on:

```
proc freq;
   tables race*sex;
   weight hrswork;
run;
```

DETAILS

Missing Values

By default, missing value frequencies do not appear in contingency tables or frequency tables, but the total frequency of missing subjects is given below each table. Also by default, the statistics do not include missing values.

Missing value frequencies can be printed by specifying the MISSPRINT option in the TABLES statement; they can be included in the computation of statistics by specifying the MISSING option.

Output Data Set

The OUT= data set produced by PROC FREQ contains one observation for each combination of the variable values in the last table request. Each observation contains these variables plus two new variables, COUNT and PERCENT, which give the frequency and cell percentage, respectively, for the combination of variable values.

For example, consider the statements

```
proc freq;
   tables a a*b / out=d;
run;
```

The output data set D corresponds to the rightmost table request, A*B. If A has two values (1 and 2) and B has three values (1, 2, and 3), the output data set D can have up to six observations, one for each combination of the A and B values. In observation 1, A=1 and B=1; in observation 2, A=1 and B=2; and so on. The data set also contains the variables COUNT and PERCENT. COUNT's value in each observation is the number of subjects that have the given combination of A and B values; PERCENT's value is the percent of the total number of subjects having that A and B combination.

When the FREQ procedure collects different class values into the same formatted level, it saves the smallest internal value to output in the output data set.

Limitations

Any number of TABLES statements can be included after the PROC FREQ statement. Since PROC FREQ builds all the tables requested in all TABLES statements in one pass of the data, there is essentially no loss of efficiency when you use multiple TABLES statements.

A TABLES statement can contain any number of table requests, and each request can include any number of variables. The maximum number of levels allowed for any one variable is 32,767. If you have a variable with more than 32,767 levels, use the SUMMARY procedure or reduce the number of levels by using the FORMAT statement.

The FREQ procedure stores each combination of values in memory. When PROC FREQ is compiling and developing multi-way tables or when some variables have many levels, you may run out of memory. If increasing the available memory is impractical, use the SORT procedure to sort the data set by one or more of the variables and then use PROC FREQ with a BY statement that includes the sorted variables.

The FREQ procedure handles both internal and formatted values up to length 16 on both the printed output and the output data set. Longer data values are truncated to 16 characters, and a warning message is printed on the SAS log.

Frequency values with more than seven significant digits may be printed in scientific notation (E format), in which case only the first few significant digits of the mantissa are printed. If you need more significant digits than PROC FREQ prints, you can specify an output data set with the OUT= option. Then use the PRINT procedure and the BEST. format to print the data set. The variable COUNT, containing the frequency values, is then printed with additional significant digits. For more information on formats, see "Components of the SAS Language," in *SAS Language: Reference*.

Computational Resources

For each variable, PROC FREQ stores all of the levels in memory, requiring about 72 bytes for each formatted level. If PROC FREQ runs out of memory, it stops collecting levels on the variable with the most levels and returns the memory so that counting can continue. The procedure then builds the tables that do not contain the disabled variables.

For two-way and *n*-way tables, PROC FREQ uses a utility file to store frequencies when it runs out of memory. Nevertheless, for any single contingency table requested, PROC FREQ builds the entire table in memory, regardless of whether the cells of the table have zero frequencies. Thus, if variables A, B, and C each have 10 levels, then a table request for A*B*C requires

1000 cells * 8 bytes per cell = 8000 bytes

even though there may be only 10 observations. This is in addition to the 2160 bytes required to store the variable levels:

3 variables * 10 levels per variable * 72 bytes per level

Grouping with Formats

When you use PROC FREQ, remember that it groups a variable's values according to their format. If you assign a format to a variable with a FORMAT statement, the variable's values are formatted for printing before PROC FREQ divides the observations into groups for the frequency counts.

For example, suppose a variable X has the values 1.3, 1.7, and 2.0. Each of these values appears as a level in the frequency table. If you want each value rounded to a single digit, you include the statement

```
format x 1.;
```

after the PROC FREQ statement. The frequency table levels are then 1 and 2.

Formatted character variables are treated in the same way: the formatted values are used to divide the observations into groups. For character variables, formatted or not, only the first 16 characters are used to determine the groups.

If you use formats to put missing and nonmissing values into one group, PROC FREQ treats that entire group of formatted values as missing.

You can also use the FORMAT statement to assign formats created by PROC FORMAT to variables. Formats created by PROC FORMAT can serve two purposes: they can define the levels, and they can label the levels. You can use the same data with different formats to collect counts on different partitions of the class values.

In frequency tables, values of both character and numeric variables appear in ascending order by the original (unformatted) values unless you specify otherwise with the ORDER= option.

Tests and Measures of Association

Definitions and Notation

Suppose a two-way table represents the crosstabulation of variables X and Y. Let the rows of the table be labeled by the values X_i, $i = 1, 2, \ldots, R$, and the columns by Y_j, $j = 1, 2, \ldots, C$. Let ln denote natural logarithm (base e), let the cell frequency in the ith row and the jth column be denoted n_{ij}, and define the following:

$$n_{\bullet j} = \Sigma_i\, n_{ij} \quad \text{(column totals)}$$

$$n_{i\bullet} = \Sigma_j\, n_{ij} \quad \text{(row totals)}$$

$$n = \Sigma_i\Sigma_j\, n_{ij} \quad \text{(overall total)}$$

$$A_{ij} = \Sigma_{k>i}\Sigma_{l>j}\, n_{kl} + \Sigma_{k<i}\Sigma_{l<j}\, n_{kl}$$

$$D_{ij} = \Sigma_{k>i}\Sigma_{l<j}\, n_{kl} + \Sigma_{k<i}\Sigma_{l>j}\, n_{kl}$$

$$P = \Sigma_i\Sigma_j\, n_{ij}A_{ij} \quad \text{(twice the number of concordances)}$$

$$Q = \Sigma_i\Sigma_j\, n_{ij}\, D_{ij} \quad \text{(twice the number of discordances)}.$$

Statistics Produced for Each Two-Way Table

All of the test statistics in this section test the null hypothesis of no association between the row variable and the column variable. When n is large, the chi-square statistics are distributed approximately as χ^2 when the null hypothesis is true. Throughout this section, let *var* denote the asymptotic variance of the most recently defined estimator. Its square root, the asymptotic standard error (ASE), is included in the printed output.

If the sample size is large enough, then the estimator (denoted by Est) is distributed approximately normally, so that Est ± 1.96 (ASE) can be used as an asymptotic 95 percent confidence interval. To test H_0: Est=0, the best asymptotic method is to use the chi-square tests, since they incorporate ASEs that are conditional on the truth of H_0.

The following subsections give the formulas that PROC FREQ uses to compute statistics for two-way tables. For further information on the formulas and on the applicability and interpretation of each statistic, consult the cited references or those listed in **INTRODUCTION** earlier in this chapter.

Chi-square (Q_P) The Pearson chi-square statistic involves the differences between the observed and expected frequencies. This test can also be thought of as a test of difference between two proportions. The alternative hypothesis for this statistic is one of general association. The chi-square distribution has $(R-1)(C-1)$ degrees of freedom (df) and is determined as

$$Q_P = \Sigma_i \Sigma_j \, (n_{ij} - m_{ij})^2 / m_{ij}$$

where

$$m_{ij} = n_{i\bullet} n_{\bullet j} / n \quad.$$

See Fienberg (1977, p. 9).

Continuity-adjusted chi-square (Q_C) The adjusted chi-square statistic for 2×2 tables is similar to the Pearson chi-square, except that it is adjusted for the continuity of the χ^2 distribution. The continuity-adjusted chi-square is most useful for small sample sizes. The use of the continuity adjustment is controversial; the chi-square test is more conservative, and more like Fisher's exact test, when your sample size is small. As the sample size increases, the statistic becomes more and more like the Pearson chi-square. It has $(R-1)(C-1)$ df and is determined as

$$Q_C = \Sigma_i \Sigma_j \, [\max{(0, \, | \, n_{ij} - m_{ij} \, | \, - 0.5)}]^2 / m_{ij} \quad.$$

See Fienberg (1977, p. 21).

Likelihood-ratio chi-square (G^2) The likelihood-ratio chi-square statistic involves the ratios between the observed and expected frequencies. The alternative hypothesis for this statistic is one of general association. The χ^2 distribution has $(R-1)(C-1)$ df and is determined as

$$G^2 = 2 \, \Sigma_i \Sigma_j \, n_{ij} \ln(n_{ij} / m_{ij}) \quad.$$

See Fienberg (1977, p. 36).

Mantel-Haenszel chi-square (Q_{MH}) The Mantel-Haenszel chi-square statistic tests the alternative hypothesis that there is a linear association between the row variable and the column variable. The χ^2 distribution has 1 df and is determined as

$$Q_{MH} = (n - 1)r^2$$

where r^2 is the Pearson correlation between the row variable and the column variable. Both the MH statistic and the Pearson correlation use the scores specified with the SCORES option. The Mantel-Haenszel chi-square statistic is appropriate only when both variables lie on an ordinal scale.

See Mantel and Haenszel (1959) and Landis, Heyman, and Koch (1978).

Fisher's exact test For 2×2 tables, Fisher's exact test yields the probability of observing a table that gives at least as much evidence of association as the one actually observed, given that the null hypothesis is true. The row and column margins are assumed fixed. The hypergeometric probability, p, of every possible table is computed, and the p-value is defined as

$$PROB = \Sigma_A p \quad.$$

For two-tailed tests, A is the set of tables with p less than or equal to the probability of the observed table. For left-tailed (right-tailed) tests, A is the set of tables where the frequency in the (1,1) cell is less than (greater than) or equal to that of the observed table.

For general $r \times c$ tables, the two-tailed p-value is defined the same way as it is for 2×2 tables. Since the alternative hypothesis in the $r \times c$ case is defined only in terms of general, and not linear, association, no right-tailed or left-tailed tests are given. The computational algorithm is the network algorithm given by Mehta and Patel (1983). See the EXACT option in **TABLES Statement** earlier in this chapter for guidelines on the practicality of this test.

See Kendall and Stuart (1979, pp. 580–585) and Mehta and Patel (1983).

Phi coefficient (φ)   The phi coefficient is derived from the chi-square statistic. It has the range $-1 \leq \varphi \leq 1$ for the 2 x 2 case and $0 \leq \varphi \leq 1$ otherwise, although the attainable upper bound may be less than 1, depending on the marginal distributions. The phi coefficient is determined as

$$\varphi = (n_{11}n_{22} - n_{12}n_{21}) / \sqrt{n_{1\bullet}n_{2\bullet}n_{\bullet1}n_{\bullet2}} \quad \text{for } 2 \times 2 \text{ tables}$$

$$\varphi = \sqrt{Q_P / n} \quad \text{otherwise.}$$

See Fleiss (1981, pp. 59–60).

Contingency coefficient (P)   The contingency coefficient is also derived from chi-square. It has the range $0 \leq P \leq 1$, although the attainable upper bound may be less than 1, depending on the marginal distributions. The contingency coefficient is

$$P = \sqrt{Q_P / (Q_P + n)} \quad .$$

See Kendall and Stuart (1979, pp. 587–588).

Cramer's V   A third measure of association derived from chi-square is Cramer's V, designed so that the attainable upper bound is always 1. It has the range $-1 \leq V \leq 1$. For 2×2 tables, $V = \varphi$; otherwise,

$$V = \sqrt{(Q_P / n) / \min (R - 1, C - 1)} \quad .$$

See Kendall and Stuart (1979, p. 588).

Gamma (γ)   The estimator of gamma is based only on the number of concordant and discordant pairs of observations. It ignores tied pairs (that is, pairs of observations that have equal values of X or equal values of Y). If the two variables are independent, then the estimator of gamma tends to be close to zero. Gamma is appropriate only when both variables lie on an ordinal scale. It has the range $-1 \leq \gamma \leq 1$. Gamma is estimated by

$$G = (P - Q) / (P + Q)$$

with

$$var = 16 \, \Sigma n_{ij} (QA_{ij} - PD_{ij})^2 / (P + Q)^4 \quad .$$

See Goodman and Kruskal (1963; 1972).

Kendall's tau-b (τ_b)   Kendall's tau-b is similar to gamma except that tau-b uses a correction for ties. Tau-b is appropriate only when both variables lie on an ordinal scale. Tau-b has the range $-1 \leq \tau_b \leq 1$. It is estimated by

$$t_b = (P - Q) / w = (P - Q) / \sqrt{w_r w_c}$$

with

$$var = [\Sigma_i \Sigma_j \, n_{ij} \, (2wd_{ij} + t_b v_{ij})^2 - n^3 t_b^2 (w_r + w_c)^2] / w^4$$

where

$$w_r = n^2 - \Sigma_i \, n_{i\bullet}^2$$

$$w_c = n^2 - \Sigma_j \, n_{\bullet j}^2$$

$$d_{ij} = A_{ij} - D_{ij}$$

$$v_{ij} = n_{i\bullet} w_c + n_{\bullet j} w_r \quad .$$

See Goodman and Kruskal (1972).

Stuart's tau-c (τ_c)   Stuart's tau-c makes an adjustment for table size in addition to a correction for ties. Tau-c is appropriate only when both variables lie on an ordinal scale. Tau-c has the range $-1 \leq \tau_c \leq 1$. It is estimated by

$$t_c = (P - Q) / [n^2 \, (m - 1) / m]$$

with

$$var = 4m^2 [\Sigma_i \Sigma_j \, n_{ij} d_{ij}^2 - (P - Q)^2 / n] / (m - 1)^2 n^4$$

where

$$m = \min(R, C)$$

$$d_{ij} = A_{ij} - D_{ij} \quad .$$

See Brown and Benedetti (1977).

Somers' D (C | R)   Somers' D is an asymmetric modification of tau-b. C | R denotes that the row variable X is regarded as an independent variable, while the column variable Y is regarded as dependent. Somers' D differs from tau-b in that it uses a correction only for pairs that are tied on the independent variable. Somers' D is appropriate only when both variables lie on an ordinal scale. It has the range $-1 \leq D \leq 1$. Formulas for Somers' D(R | C) are obtained by interchanging the indices:

$$D(C \mid R) = (P - Q) / w_r$$

with

$$var = 4\Sigma_i \Sigma_j \, n_{ij} [w_r d_{ij} - (P - Q)(n - n_{i\bullet})]^2 / w_r^4$$

where

$$w_r = n^2 - \Sigma_i\, n_{i\bullet}^2$$

$$d_{ij} = A_{ij} - D_{ij} \quad.$$

See Somers (1962) and Goodman and Kruskal (1972).

Pearson correlation coefficient (r)   The Pearson correlation coefficient is computed by using the scores specified in the SCORES= option. It is appropriate only when both variables lie on an ordinal scale. It has the range $-1 \leq r \leq 1$. The Pearson correlation coefficient is computed as

$$r = v\,/\,w = ss_{rc}\,/\,\sqrt{ss_r ss_c}$$

with

$$var = \Sigma_i\Sigma_j\, n_{ij}[w(r_i - \bar{r})(c_j - \bar{c}) - b_{ij}v\,/\,2w]^2\,/\,w^4$$

where the r_i are the row scores, the c_j are the column scores, and

$$\bar{r} = \Sigma_i\Sigma_j\, n_{ij}r_i\,/\,n$$

$$\bar{c} = \Sigma_i\Sigma_j\, n_{ij}c_j\,/\,n$$

$$ss_r = \Sigma_i\Sigma_j\, n_{ij}(r_i - \bar{r})^2$$

$$ss_c = \Sigma_i\Sigma_j\, n_{ij}(c_j - \bar{c})^2$$

$$ss_{rc} = \Sigma_i\Sigma_j\, n_{ij}(r_i - \bar{r})(c_j - \bar{c})$$

$$b_{ij} = (r_i - \bar{r})^2 ss_c + (c_j - \bar{c})^2 ss_r$$

$$v \;= ss_{rc}$$

$$w \;= \sqrt{ss_r ss_c} \quad.$$

See Snedecor and Cochran (1980, p. 175) and Brown and Benedetti (1977).

Spearman rank correlation coefficient (r$_s$)   The Spearman correlation coefficient is computed by using rank scores $r1_i$ and $c1_j$, defined in **Scores** later in this chapter. It is appropriate only when both variables lie on an ordinal scale. It has the range $-1 \leq r_s \leq 1$. The Spearman correlation coefficient is computed as

$$r_s = \frac{v}{w}$$

with

$$var = \frac{1}{n^2 w^4}\Sigma_i\Sigma_j n_{ij}(z_{ij} - \bar{z})^2$$

where

$$v = \Sigma_i \Sigma_j n_{ij} R(i) C(j)$$

$$w = \frac{1}{12} \sqrt{F^*G}$$

$$F = n^3 - \Sigma_i n_{i\bullet}^3$$

$$G = n^3 - \Sigma_j n_{\bullet j}^3$$

$$R(i) = r1_i - \frac{n}{2}$$

$$C(j) = c1_j - \frac{n}{2}$$

and

$$\bar{z} = \frac{1}{n} \Sigma_i \Sigma_j \, n_{ij} z_{ij}$$

$$z_{ij} = w v_{ij} - v w_{ij}$$

$$v_{ij} = n[R(i)C(j) \; + \frac{1}{2} \; \Sigma_l n_{il} C(l) + \frac{1}{2} \Sigma_k n_{kj} R(k)$$

$$\qquad + \Sigma_l \Sigma_{k > i} \, n_{kl} C(l) + \Sigma_k \Sigma_{l > j} n_{kl} R(k) \;]$$

$$w_{ij} = \frac{-n}{96w} \; \{ \; F n_{\bullet j}^2 + G n_{i\bullet}^{\;2} \} \; .$$

See Snedecor and Cochran (1980, p. 192) and Brown and Benedetti (1977).

Lambda asymmetric C | R   Asymmetric lambda, ($\lambda[C \mid R]$), is interpreted as the probable improvement in predicting the column variable Y given that one has knowledge of the row variable X. Asymetric lambda has the range $0 \leq \lambda[C \mid R] \leq 1$. It is computed as

$$\lambda[C \mid R] = (\Sigma_i \, r_i - r) \, / \, (n - r)$$

with

$$var = (n - \Sigma_i \, r_i)[\Sigma_i \, r_i + r - 2 \Sigma_i \; (r_i \mid l_i = l)] \, / \, (n - r)^3$$

where

$$r_i = \max_j (n_{ij})$$

$$r = \max_j (n_{\bullet j}) \quad .$$

Also, let l_i be the unique value of j such that $r_i = n_{ij}$, and let l be the unique value of j such that $r = n_{\bullet j}$.

Because of the uniqueness assumptions, ties in the frequencies or in the marginal totals must be broken in an arbitrary but consistent manner. In case of ties, l is defined here as the smallest value of j such that $r = n_{\bullet j}$. For a given i, if there is at least one value j such that $n_{ij} = r_i = c_j$, then l_i is defined here to be the smallest such value of j. Otherwise, if $n_{il} = r_i$, then l_i is defined to be equal to l. If neither condition is true, then l_i is taken to be the smallest value of j such that $n_{ij}=r_i$. The formulas for lambda asymmetric R | C can be obtained by interchanging the indices.

See Goodman and Kruskal (1963).

Lambda symmetric (λ)   The two asymmetric lambdas are averaged to obtain the nondirectional lambda. Lambda symmetric has range $0 \leq \lambda \leq 1$. Lambda symmetric is defined as

$$\lambda = (\Sigma_i r_i + \Sigma_j c_j - r - c) / (2n - r - c) = (w - v) / w$$

with

$$var = \{wvy - 2w^2[1 - \Sigma_i\Sigma_j (n_{ij} | j = l_i, i = k_j)] - 2v^2(1 - n_{kl})\} / w^4$$

where

$$w = 2n - r - c$$

$$v = 2n - \Sigma_i r_i - \Sigma_j c_j$$

$$x = \Sigma_i [r_i | l_i = l] + \Sigma_j [c_j | k_j = k] + r_k + c_l$$

$$y = 8n - w - v - 2x \quad .$$

See Goodman and Kruskal (1963).

Uncertainty coefficient C | R   The uncertainty coefficient, U[C | R], is the proportion of uncertainty (entropy) in the column variable Y that is explained by the row variable X. It has the range $0 \leq U[C | R] \leq 1$. The formulas for U[R | C] can be obtained by interchanging the indices:

$$U[C | R] = [H(X) + H(Y) - H(XY)] / H(Y) = v / w$$

with

$$var = \Sigma_i\Sigma_j\, n_{ij}\{H(Y)\, \ln(n_{ij} / n_{i\bullet}) + [H(X) - H(XY)]\ln(n_{\bullet j} / n)\}^2 / n^2 w^4$$

where

$$v = H(X) + H(Y) - H(XY)$$

$$w = H(Y)$$

$$H(X) = -\Sigma_i (n_{i\bullet} / n) \ln (n_{i\bullet} / n)$$

$$H(Y) = -\Sigma_j (n_{\bullet j} / n) \ln (n_{\bullet j} / n)$$

$$H(XY) = -\Sigma_i\Sigma_j (n_{ij} / n) \ln (n_{ij} / n) \quad .$$

See Theil (1972, pp. 115–120) and Goodman and Kruskal (1972).

Uncertainty coefficient (U)   The uncertainty coefficient, U, is the symmetric version of the two asymmetric coefficients. It has the range $0 \leq U \leq 1$. It is defined as

$$U = 2[H(X) + H(Y) - H(XY)] / [H(X) + H(Y)]$$

with

$$var = 4 \; \Sigma_i \Sigma_j \; n_{ij} \; \{H(XY) \ln (n_{i\bullet} n_{\bullet j} / n^2)$$

$$-[H(X) + H(Y)] \ln (n_{ij} / n)\}^2 / n^2 [H(X) + H(Y)]^4 \; .$$

See Goodman and Kruskal (1972).

Relative risk estimates For two dichotomous variables, disease (D) and exposure (E) to a risk factor, the relative risk of disease is defined as

$$RR = \text{Prob} (D = yes \mid E = yes) / \text{Prob} (D = yes \mid E = no) \; .$$

Relative risk estimates are computed only for 2×2 tables, in which case the table is presumed to be set up with E as the row variable and D as the column variable. Throughout this section, z is the $100(1-\alpha/2)$ percent point of the standard normal distribution. The estimation of the relative risk depends on the study design:

1. Case-control (retrospective) studies It is assumed that the (E=yes, D=yes) cell is on the main diagonal. The estimate of the relative risk is the odds ratio,

$$OR = n_{11} n_{22} / n_{12} n_{21} \; .$$

The $100(1-\alpha)$ percent confidence interval for OR is obtained as

$$\left(OR \exp \left[-z \sqrt{v} \right], \; OR \exp \left[z \sqrt{v} \right] \right)$$

where

$$v = var (\ln OR) = \frac{1}{n_{11}} + \frac{1}{n_{12}} + \frac{1}{n_{21}} + \frac{1}{n_{22}} \; .$$

If any of the four cell frequencies are zero, the estimates are not computed.

2. Cohort (prospective) studies It is assumed that (E=yes) is the first row of the contingency table. If (D=yes) is the first column, then use the estimates labeled COL1 RISK. Otherwise, use the estimates labeled COL2 RISK. Define

$$p_1 = n_{11} / n_{1\bullet}$$
$$p_2 = n_{21} / n_{2\bullet} \; .$$

The COL1 relative risk is estimated by

$$RR = p_1 / p_2$$

and the corresponding $100(1-\alpha)$ percent confidence interval is

$$\left(RR \exp \left[-z \sqrt{v} \right], \; RR \exp \left[z \sqrt{v} \right] \right)$$

where

$$v = var (\ln RR) = (1 - p_1) / n_{11} + (1 - p_2) / n_{21} \; .$$

If either n_{11} or n_{21} is zero, the estimates are not computed. The COL2 relative risk estimates are computed similarly.

See Kleinbaum, Kupper, and Morgenstern (1982, p. 299).

Summary Statistics

Suppose there are q strata, indexed by $h=1, 2, \ldots, q$, and within each stratum is a contingency table with X as the row variable and Y as the column variable. For table h, let the cell frequency in the ith row and jth column be denoted by n_{hij}, with corresponding marginal totals denoted by $n_{hi\bullet}$ and $n_{h\bullet j}$ and with overall total N_h. The CMH summary statistics use row and column scores, for which there are several choices.

Scores

For numeric variables, TABLE scores are the values of numeric row and column headings. If the row or column variables are formatted, then the TABLE score is the internal numeric value corresponding to that category. If two or more numeric values have been classified into the same formatted category, then the internal numeric value for that category is the smallest of these values. For character variables, TABLE scores are defined as the row numbers and column numbers (for example, 1 for the first row, 2 for the second row, and so on). TABLE scores are the same for each of the q tables and are used by PROC FREQ if no choice of scores is specified with the SCORES option.

RANK scores, which can be used to obtain nonparametric analyses, are defined by

Row scores: $r1_{hi} = \Sigma_{k<i}\, n_{hk\bullet} + (n_{hi\bullet} + 1) / 2 \qquad i = 1, 2, \ldots, R$

Col scores: $c1_{hj} = \Sigma_{l<j}\, n_{h\bullet l} + (n_{h\bullet j} + 1) / 2 \qquad j = 1, 2, \ldots, C$.

RIDIT scores (Bross 1958; Mack and Skillings 1980) also yield nonparametric analyses, but they are standardized by the stratum sample size. RIDIT scores are derived from RANK scores as

$r2_{hi} = r1_{hi} / N_h$

$c2_{hj} = c1_{hj} / N_h$.

Modified ridit (MODRIDIT) scores (van Elteren 1960; Lehmann 1975), which also yield nonparametric analyses, represent the expected values of the within-stratum order statistics for the uniform distribution on (0,1). Modified ridit scores are derived from rank scores as

$r3_{hi} = r1_{hi} / (N_h + 1)$

$c3_{hj} = c1_{hj} / (N_h + 1)$.

The specified scores are used not only for Cochran-Mantel-Haenszel Statistics, but for Pearson correlation and Mantel-Haenszel chi-square as well.

Cochran-Mantel-Haenszel (CMH) Statistics

Since the formulas for CMH statistics are more easily defined in terms of matrices, the following notation is used. Vectors are presumed to be column vectors unless they are transposed ($'$).

$$\mathbf{n}_{hi}' = (n_{hi1}, n_{hi2}, \ldots, n_{hiC}) \qquad (1 \times C)$$

$$\mathbf{n}_h' = (\mathbf{n}_{h1}', \mathbf{n}_{h2}', \ldots, \mathbf{n}_{hR}') \qquad (1 \times RC)$$

$$P_{hi\bullet} = n_{hi\bullet} / N_h \qquad (1 \times 1)$$

$$P_{h\bullet j} = n_{h\bullet j} / N_h \qquad (1 \times 1)$$

$$\mathbf{P}_{h\star\bullet}' = (P_{h1\bullet}, P_{h2\bullet}, \ldots, P_{hR\bullet}) \qquad (1 \times R)$$

$$\mathbf{P}_{h\bullet\star}' = (P_{h\bullet1}, P_{h\bullet2}, \ldots, P_{h\bullet C}) \qquad (1 \times C).$$

Assume that the strata are independent and that the marginal totals of each stratum are fixed. The null hypothesis, H_0, is that there is no association between X and Y in any of the strata. The corresponding model is the multiple hypergeometric, which implies that under H_0, the expected value and covariance matrix of the frequencies are, respectively,

$$\mathbf{m}_h = \mathbf{E}[\mathbf{n}_h \mid H_0] = N_h(\mathbf{P}_{h\bullet\star} \otimes \mathbf{P}_{h\star\bullet})$$

and

$$\mathbf{Var}\,[\mathbf{n}_h \mid H_0] = c[(\mathbf{D}_{\mathbf{P}_{h\bullet\star}} - \mathbf{P}_{h\bullet\star}\mathbf{P}_{h\bullet\star}') \otimes (\mathbf{D}_{\mathbf{P}_{h\star\bullet}} - \mathbf{P}_{h\star\bullet}\mathbf{P}_{h\star\bullet}')]$$

where

$$c = N_h^2 / (N_h - 1)$$

and where $\otimes$ denotes Kronecker product multiplication and $\mathbf{D}_a$ is a diagonal matrix with elements of $\mathbf{a}$ on the main diagonal.

The generalized CMH statistic (Landis, Heyman, and Koch 1978) is defined as

$$Q_{CMH} = \mathbf{G}'\mathbf{V}_{\mathbf{G}}^{-1}\mathbf{G}$$

where

$$\mathbf{G} = \Sigma_h\,\mathbf{B}_h(\mathbf{n}_h - \mathbf{m}_h)$$

$$\mathbf{V}_{\mathbf{G}} = \Sigma_h\,\mathbf{B}_h[\mathbf{Var}(\mathbf{n}_h \mid H_0)]\mathbf{B}_h'$$

and where

$$\mathbf{B}_h = \mathbf{C}_h \otimes \mathbf{R}_h$$

is a matrix of fixed constants based on column scores $\mathbf{C}_h$ and row scores $\mathbf{R}_h$. When the null hypothesis is true, the CMH statistic is approximately distributed as chi-square with degrees of freedom equal to the rank of $\mathbf{B}_h$. If $\mathbf{V}_{\mathbf{G}}$ is found to be singular, PROC FREQ prints a message and sets the value of the CMH statistic to missing.

A word of caution is necessary. CMH statistics have low power for detecting an association in which the patterns of association for some of the strata are in the opposite direction of the patterns displayed by other strata. Thus, a nonsignificant CMH statistic suggests either that there is no association or that no pattern of association had enough strength or consistency to dominate any other pattern. The types of CMH statistics that the FREQ procedure computes are described in the sections that follow.

The correlation statistic (df = 1) The correlation statistic, with one degree of freedom, was popularized by Mantel and Haenszel (1959) and Mantel (1963) and is therefore known as the Mantel-Haenszel statistic.

The alternative hypothesis in this case is that there is a linear association between X and Y in at least one stratum. If either X or Y does not lie on an ordinal (or interval) scale, then this statistic is meaningless.

The matrix $\mathbf{C}_h$ has dimension $1 \times C$, and the scores, one for each column, are specified in the SCORES= option. Similarly, the matrix $\mathbf{R}_h$ has dimension $1 \times R$, and these scores, one for each row, are also controlled by the SCORES= option.

When there is only one stratum, this CMH statistic reduces to $(N-1)r^2$, where r is the correlation coefficient between X and Y. When nonparametric (RANK or RIDIT) scores are specified, then the statistic reduces to $(N-1)r_s^2$, where r_s is the Spearman rank correlation coefficient between X and Y. When there is more than one stratum, then the CMH statistic becomes a stratum-adjusted correlation statistic.

The *ANOVA* statistic (df = R − 1) The *ANOVA* statistic can be used only when the column variable Y lies on an ordinal (or interval) scale so that the mean score of Y is a meaningful notion. In that case, the mean score is computed for each row of the table, and the alternative hypothesis is that, for at least one stratum, the mean scores of the R rows are unequal. In other words, the statistic is sensitive to location differences among the R distributions of Y.

The matrix $\mathbf{C}_h$ has dimension $1 \times C$, and the scores, one for each column, are specified in the SCORES option. The matrix $\mathbf{R}_h$ has dimension $(R-1) \times R$ and is created internally by PROC FREQ as

$$\mathbf{R}_h = [\mathbf{I}_{R-1}, - \mathbf{J}_{R-1}]$$

where $\mathbf{I}_{R-1}$ is an identity matrix of rank $R-1$, and $\mathbf{J}_{R-1}$ is an $(R-1) \times 1$ vector of ones. This matrix has the effect of forming $R-1$ independent contrasts of the R mean scores.

When there is only one stratum, this CMH statistic is essentially an analysis-of-variance (*ANOVA*) statistic in the sense that it is a function of the variance ratio F statistic that would be obtained from a one-way *ANOVA* on the dependent variable Y. If nonparametric scores are specified in this case, then the *ANOVA* statistic is a Kruskal-Wallis test.

If there is more than one stratum, then the CMH statistic corresponds to a stratum-adjusted *ANOVA* or Kruskal-Wallis test. In the special case where there is one subject per row and one subject per column in the contingency table of each stratum, this CMH statistic is identical to Friedman's chi-square. See **Example 5** for an illustration.

The general association statistic (df = (R − 1)(C − 1)) The general association statistic is always interpretable because it does not require an ordinal scale for either X or Y. The alternative hypothesis is that, for at least one stratum, there is some kind of association between X and Y.

The matrix R_h is the same as the one used for the *ANOVA* statistic. The matrix C_h is defined similarly as

$$C_h = [I_{C-1}, -J_{C-1}] \quad .$$

Both score matrices are generated internally by PROC FREQ.

When there is only one stratum, then the general association CMH statistic reduces to $[(N-1)/N]Q_P$, where Q_P is the Pearson chi-square statistic. When there is more than one stratum, then the CMH statistic becomes a stratum-adjusted Pearson chi-square statistic. Note that a similar adjustment can be made by summing the Pearson chi-squares across the strata. However, the latter statistic requires a large sample size in each stratum to support the resulting chi-square distribution with $q(R-1)(C-1)$ df. The CMH statistic requires only a large overall sample size since it has only $(R-1)(C-1)$ df.

See Cochran (1954); Mantel and Haenszel (1959); Mantel (1963); Birch (1965); and Landis, Heyman, and Koch (1978).

Adjusted Relative Risk Estimates

The notation and definitions from **Relative risk estimates** earlier in this chapter are also used in this section. If you would like RR estimates of E, which are adjusted for confounding variables A and B, specify

```
proc freq;
    tables a*b*e*d / all;
run;
```

As before, E must be the row variable, D must be the column variable, and RR estimates are computed only when E and D each have two levels. Throughout this section, z is the $100(1-\alpha/2)$ percent point of the standard normal distribution, and Q is the general association CMH statistic. (Note that the value of the general association statistic is independent of the scores that are specified.) Tables with a zero row or column are not included in any of the summary relative risk computations. The estimation procedure depends on the study design.

Case-control (Retrospective) studies   It is assumed that the (E=yes, D=yes) cell is on the main diagonal of the matrix in each stratum. Two sets of estimators are given for case-control studies:

1. Mantel-Haenszel estimate and test-based confidence interval The adjusted odds ratio estimator is given by

$$OR_{MH} = [\Sigma_h \, n_{h11}n_{h22} \, / \, N_h] \, / \, [\Sigma_h \, n_{h12}n_{h21} \, / \, N_h]$$

and is always computed unless the denominator is zero. The corresponding $100(1-\alpha)$ percent test-based confidence interval is given by

$$\left(OR_{MH}^{1-z/\sqrt{Q}}, OR_{MH}^{1+z/\sqrt{Q}} \right)$$

if $OR_{MH} > 1$. Otherwise, the lower and upper limits are reversed. The confidence interval is computed unless $Q=0$ or OR_{MH} is undefined.

2. Logit estimator with precision-based confidence interval This odds ratio estimator (Woolf 1955) is given by

$$OR_L = \exp\left[\left(\Sigma_h w_h \ln OR_h\right) / \Sigma w_h\right]$$

and the corresponding $100(1-\alpha)$ percent confidence interval is

$$\left(OR_L \exp\left[-z / \sqrt{\Sigma_h w_h}\right], OR_L \exp\left[z / \sqrt{\Sigma_h w_h}\right]\right)$$

where OR_h is the odds ratio for stratum h, and

$$w_h = 1 / \mathrm{var}\,(\ln OR_h)\,.$$

If any cell frequency in a stratum h is zero, then 1/2 is added to each cell of the stratum before OR_h and w_h are computed (Haldane 1955), and a warning is printed.

Cohort (Prospective) studies   It is assumed that (E=yes) is the first row of the contingency tables. If (D=yes) is the first column, then use the estimates labeled COL1 RISK. Otherwise, use the estimates labeled COL2 RISK. The COL1 estimators are given in this section; the COL2 estimators have corresponding definitions. Two sets of estimators are given for cohort studies:

1. Mantel-Haenszel estimate and test-based confidence interval The adjusted relative risk estimator is given by

$$RR_{MH} = \left[\Sigma_h n_{h11} n_{h2\bullet} / N_h\right] / \left[\Sigma_h n_{h21} n_{h1\bullet} / N_h\right]$$

and is always computed unless the denominator is zero. The corresponding $100(1-\alpha)$ percent test-based confidence interval is given by

$$\left(RR_{MH}^{1 - z/\sqrt{Q}},\ RR_{MH}^{1 + z/\sqrt{Q}}\right)$$

if $RR_{MH} > 1$. Otherwise, the lower and upper limits are reversed. The confidence interval is computed unless $Q=0$ or RR_{MH} is undefined.

2. Logit estimator with precision-based confidence interval This relative risk estimator is given by

$$RR_L = \exp\left[\left(\Sigma_h w_h \ln RR_h\right) / \Sigma w_h\right]$$

and the corresponding $100(1-\alpha)$ percent confidence interval is

$$\left(RR_L \exp\left[-z / \sqrt{\Sigma_h w_h}\right],\ RR_L \exp\left[z / \sqrt{\Sigma_h w_h}\right]\right)$$

where RR_h is the relative risk estimator for stratum h, and

$$w_h = 1 / \mathrm{var}\,(\ln RR_h)\,.$$

If n_{h11} or n_{h21} is zero, then 1/2 is added to each cell of the stratum before RR_h and w_h are computed, and a warning is printed.

See Kleinbaum, Kupper, and Morgenstern (1982, Sections 17.4, 17.5).

Breslow-Day Test for Homogeneity of the Odds Ratios

This statistic (computed only for the stratified analysis of 2×2 tables) tests the hypothesis that the odds ratios from the q strata are all equal. When the hypothesis is true, the statistic is distributed approximately as chi-square with $q-1$ degrees of freedom. The statistic is defined as

$$Q_{BD} = \Sigma_h \left[n_{h11} - E\left(n_{h11} \mid OR_{MH} \right) \right]^2 / Var\left(n_{h11} \mid OR_{MH} \right)$$

where E and Var denote expected value and variance, respectively. If $OR_{MH}=0$ or if it is undefined, then PROC FREQ does not compute the statistic, and a warning message is printed. The summation does not include any tables with a zero row or column.

A note of caution is appropriate here. Unlike the Cochran-Mantel-Haenszel statistics, the Breslow-Day test requires a large sample size within each stratum, and this limits its usefulness. In addition, the validity of the CMH tests does not depend on any assumption of homogeneity of the odds ratios, and therefore, the Breslow-Day test should never be used as such an indicator of validity.

See Breslow and Day (1980, p. 142).

Sample Size Summary

The total sample size and the frequency of missing subjects are printed. The effective sample size is the frequency of nonmissing subjects.

Printed Output

For a one-way table showing the frequency distribution of a single variable, PROC FREQ prints these items:

1. the name of the variable and its values
2. Frequency counts, giving the number of subjects that have each value
3. percentages, labeled Percent, giving the percent of the total number of subjects represented by that value
4. Cumulative Frequency counts, giving the sum of the frequency counts of that value and all other values listed above it in the table (the total number of nonmissing subjects is the last cumulative frequency)
5. Cumulative Percent values, giving the percent of the total number of subjects represented by that value and all others previously listed in the table.

Two-way tables can be printed either as crosstabulation tables (the default) or as lists (when the LIST option is specified). Each cell of a crosstabulation table may contain items 6 through 12:

6. Frequency counts, giving the number of subjects that have the indicated values of the two variables.
7. Percent, the percentage of the total frequency count represented by that cell.
8. Row Pct, or the row percentage, the percent of the total frequency count for that row represented by the cell.
9. Col Pct, or column percent, the percent of the total frequency count for that column represented by the cell.
10. if the EXPECTED option is specified, the expected cell frequency under the hypothesis of independence (not shown).
11. if the DEVIATION option is specified, the deviation of the cell frequency from the expected value (not shown).

12. if the CELLCHI2 option is specified, the cell's contribution to the total chi-square statistic (not shown).

13. If the CHISQ option is specified, the following statistics are printed for the two-way table in each stratum: Pearson Chi-Square, Likelihood-Ratio Chi-Square, Continuity-Adjusted Chi-Square, Mantel-Haenszel Chi-Square, Fisher's Exact Test (for 2×2 tables), the Phi Coefficient, the Contingency Coefficient, Cramer's V, the Sample Size, and the Frequency Missing. For each test statistic, its degrees of freedom (DF) and its probability value (Prob) are also printed.

14. If the EXACT option is specified, the two-tailed p-value from Fisher's exact test is printed, regardless of the size of the table. In addition, all of the statistics requested by the CHISQ option are also printed.

15. If the MEASURES option is specified, the following statistics and their asymptotic standard errors (ASE) are printed for the two-way table in each stratum: Gamma, Kendall's Tau-b, Stuart's Tau-c, Somers' D, Pearson Correlation, Spearman Correlation, Lambda Asymmetric, Lambda Symmetric, and the Uncertainty Coefficient (Symmetric and Asymmetric). Also printed are Sample Size, Frequency Missing, and (for 2×2 tables) Estimates of the Relative Risk for Case-Control and Cohort studies, together with their Confidence Bounds.

16. If the CMH option is specified, the following statistics are printed: Total Sample Size, Total Frequency Missing, and three Cochran-Mantel-Haenszel summary statistics (the correlation statistic, the *ANOVA* statistic, and the general association statistic), with corresponding degrees of freedom (DF) and significance probabilities (Prob). For 2×2 tables, the additional statistics printed are stratum-adjusted estimates (both Mantel-Haenszel and logit estimates) of the common relative risk for case-control and cohort studies, together with their confidence intervals, and the Breslow-Day test for homogeneity of the odds ratios.

17. If the ALL option is specified, all of the statistics requested by the CHISQ, MEASURES, and CMH options are printed (not shown).

18. If two contingency tables can fit on a page, one table above the other, then the tables are printed in that manner. Similarly, a table and its corresponding statistics are printed on the same page, provided that they fit (not shown).

EXAMPLES

Example 1: Options Available Using PROC FREQ

The following example demonstrates various options in the PROC FREQ and TABLES statements. These statements produce the output shown in **Output 20.3**.

```
data new;
  input a b @@;
  cards;
1 2    2 1    . 2   . .    1 1    2 1
;

proc freq;
  title 'NO TABLES STATEMENT';
run;
```

```
proc freq;
   tables a / missprint;
   title '1-WAY FREQUENCY TABLE WITH MISSPRINT OPTION';
run;

proc freq;
   tables a*b;
   title '2-WAY CONTINGENCY TABLE';
run;

proc freq;
   tables a*b / missprint;
   title '2-WAY CONTINGENCY TABLE WITH MISSPRINT OPTION';
run;

proc freq;
   tables a*b / missing;
   title '2-WAY CONTINGENCY TABLE WITH MISSING OPTION';
run;

proc freq;
   tables a*b / list;
   title '2-WAY FREQUENCY TABLE';
run;

proc freq;
   tables a*b / list missing;
   title '2-WAY FREQUENCY TABLE WITH MISSING OPTION';
run;

proc freq;
   tables a*b / list sparse;
   title '2-WAY FREQUENCY TABLE WITH SPARSE OPTION';
run;

proc freq order=data;
   tables a*b / list;
   title '2-WAY FREQUENCY TABLE, ORDER=DATA';
run;
```

Output 20.3 Options Available Using PROC FREQ

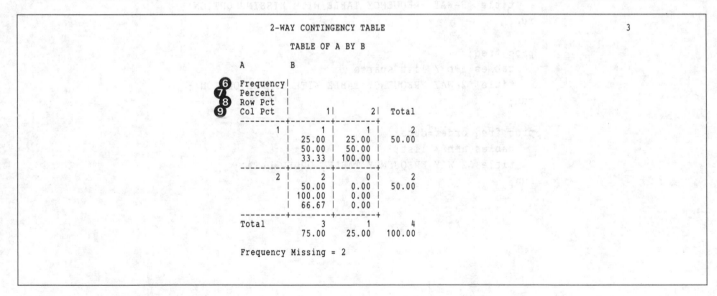

```
                              NO TABLES STATEMENT                                    1
   ❶       ❷         ❸         ❹         ❺
                            Cumulative  Cumulative
   A    Frequency   Percent   Frequency   Percent
   --------------------------------------------------
   1        2        50.0        2        50.0
   2        2        50.0        4       100.0

                Frequency Missing = 2



                            Cumulative  Cumulative
   B    Frequency   Percent   Frequency   Percent
   --------------------------------------------------
   1        3        60.0        3        60.0
   2        2        40.0        5       100.0

                Frequency Missing = 1
```

```
              1-WAY FREQUENCY TABLE WITH MISSPRINT OPTION                           2
                            Cumulative  Cumulative
   A    Frequency   Percent   Frequency   Percent
   --------------------------------------------------
   .        2         .          .          .
   1        2        50.0        2        50.0
   2        2        50.0        4       100.0

                Frequency Missing = 2
```

```
                        2-WAY CONTINGENCY TABLE                                      3

                          TABLE OF A BY B

              A           B

       ❻  Frequency|
       ❼  Percent   |
       ❽  Row Pct   |
       ❾  Col Pct   |      1|      2|  Total
          ---------+-------+-------+
              1 |     1 |     1 |     2
                | 25.00 | 25.00 | 50.00
                | 50.00 | 50.00 |
                | 33.33 |100.00 |
          ---------+-------+-------+
              2 |     2 |     0 |     2
                | 50.00 |  0.00 | 50.00
                |100.00 |  0.00 |
                | 66.67 |  0.00 |
          ---------+-------+-------+
          Total        3       1      4
                    75.00   25.00 100.00

                Frequency Missing = 2
```

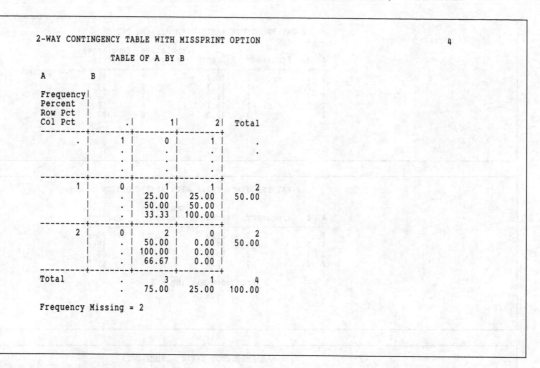

```
2-WAY CONTINGENCY TABLE WITH MISSPRINT OPTION                          4

                    TABLE OF A BY B

        A          B

        Frequency|
        Percent  |
        Row Pct  |
        Col Pct  |     .|      1|      2| Total
        ---------+-------+-------+-------+
              .  |    1  |    0  |    1  |    .
                 |    .  |    .  |    .  |
                 |    .  |    .  |    .  |
                 |    .  |    .  |    .  |
        ---------+-------+-------+-------+
              1  |    0  |    1  |    1  |    2
                 |    .  | 25.00 | 25.00 | 50.00
                 |    .  | 50.00 | 50.00 |
                 |    .  | 33.33 |100.00 |
        ---------+-------+-------+-------+
              2  |    0  |    2  |    0  |    2
                 |    .  | 50.00 |  0.00 | 50.00
                 |    .  |100.00 |  0.00 |
                 |    .  | 66.67 |  0.00 |
        ---------+-------+-------+-------+
        Total         .       3       1       4
                      .    75.00   25.00  100.00

        Frequency Missing = 2
```

```
2-WAY CONTINGENCY TABLE WITH MISSING OPTION                            5

                    TABLE OF A BY B

        A          B

        Frequency|
        Percent  |
        Row Pct  |
        Col Pct  |     .|      1|      2| Total
        ---------+-------+-------+-------+
              .  |    1  |    0  |    1  |    2
                 | 16.67 |  0.00 | 16.67 | 33.33
                 | 50.00 |  0.00 | 50.00 |
                 |100.00 |  0.00 | 50.00 |
        ---------+-------+-------+-------+
              1  |    0  |    1  |    1  |    2
                 |  0.00 | 16.67 | 16.67 | 33.33
                 |  0.00 | 50.00 | 50.00 |
                 |  0.00 | 33.33 | 50.00 |
        ---------+-------+-------+-------+
              2  |    0  |    2  |    0  |    2
                 |  0.00 | 33.33 |  0.00 | 33.33
                 |  0.00 |100.00 |  0.00 |
                 |  0.00 | 66.67 |  0.00 |
        ---------+-------+-------+-------+
        Total         1       3       2       6
                  16.67   50.00   33.33  100.00
```

```
2-WAY FREQUENCY TABLE                                                  6

                              Cumulative  Cumulative
        A B  Frequency  Percent  Frequency   Percent
        ---------------------------------------------
        1 1      1       25.0        1        25.0
        1 2      1       25.0        2        50.0
        2 1      2       50.0        4       100.0

               Frequency Missing = 2
```

```
                    2-WAY FREQUENCY TABLE WITH MISSING OPTION                    7

                                          Cumulative  Cumulative
                A  B  Frequency  Percent   Frequency    Percent
                -----------------------------------------------------
                .  .      1       16.7         1         16.7
                .  2      1       16.7         2         33.3
                1  1      1       16.7         3         50.0
                1  2      1       16.7         4         66.7
                2  1      2       33.3         6        100.0
```

```
                    2-WAY FREQUENCY TABLE WITH SPARSE OPTION                     8

                                          Cumulative  Cumulative
                A  B  Frequency  Percent   Frequency    Percent
                -----------------------------------------------------
                1  1      1       25.0         1         25.0
                1  2      1       25.0         2         50.0
                2  1      2       50.0         4        100.0
                2  2      0        0.0         4        100.0

                          Frequency Missing = 2
```

```
                       2-WAY FREQUENCY TABLE, ORDER=DATA                         9

                                          Cumulative  Cumulative
                A  B  Frequency  Percent   Frequency    Percent
                -----------------------------------------------------
                1  2      1       25.0         1         25.0
                1  1      1       25.0         2         50.0
                2  1      2       50.0         4        100.0

                          Frequency Missing = 2
```

Example 2:   Fisher's Exact Test for a 3×6 Table

When the sample size is small relative to the size of a contingency table, chi-square may not be a valid test. In that case, Fisher's exact test is a more appropriate test of no association. In the following table, the sample size is 9, and the number of degrees of freedom for the chi-square statistic is 10. Since the sample size per degree of freedom is much less than 5 and the sample size is small, Fisher's exact test is likely to be feasible in this situation. The test is requested by the EXACT option in the TABLES statement. The output shows that the chi-square statistic and Fisher's exact test yield somewhat different results. The following statements produce **Output 20.4**:

```
data;
   do a=1 to 3;
      do b=1 to 6;
         input wt @@;
         output;
      end;
   end;
cards;
2 0 0 0 0 0
0 1 2 0 0 0
0 0 0 1 2 1
;
```

```
proc freq;
   weight wt;
   tables a*b / exact;
   title 'Fisher''s Exact Test for 3 by 6 Table';
run;
```

Output 20.4   Fisher's Exact Test for a 3×6 Table

```
                    Fisher's Exact Test for 3 by 6 Table                      1
                            TABLE OF A BY B

  A          B

  Frequency|
  Percent  |
  Row Pct  |
  Col Pct  |      1|      2|      3|      4|      5|      6|  Total
  ---------+-------+-------+-------+-------+-------+-------+
         1 |     2 |     0 |     0 |     0 |     0 |     0 |     2
           | 22.22 |  0.00 |  0.00 |  0.00 |  0.00 |  0.00 | 22.22
           |100.00 |  0.00 |  0.00 |  0.00 |  0.00 |  0.00 |
           |100.00 |  0.00 |  0.00 |  0.00 |  0.00 |  0.00 |
  ---------+-------+-------+-------+-------+-------+-------+
         2 |     0 |     1 |     2 |     0 |     0 |     0 |     3
           |  0.00 | 11.11 | 22.22 |  0.00 |  0.00 |  0.00 | 33.33
           |  0.00 | 33.33 | 66.67 |  0.00 |  0.00 |  0.00 |
           |  0.00 |100.00 |100.00 |  0.00 |  0.00 |  0.00 |
  ---------+-------+-------+-------+-------+-------+-------+
         3 |     0 |     0 |     0 |     1 |     2 |     1 |     4
           |  0.00 |  0.00 |  0.00 | 11.11 | 22.22 | 11.11 | 44.44
           |  0.00 |  0.00 |  0.00 | 25.00 | 50.00 | 25.00 |
           |  0.00 |  0.00 |  0.00 |100.00 |100.00 |100.00 |
  ---------+-------+-------+-------+-------+-------+-------+
  Total          2       1       2       1       2       1       9
             22.22   11.11   22.22   11.11   22.22   11.11  100.00


               STATISTICS FOR TABLE OF A BY B

      Statistic                   DF     Value      Prob
      -------------------------------------------------------
      Chi-Square                  10    18.000     0.055
      Likelihood Ratio Chi-Square 10    19.095     0.039
      Mantel-Haenszel Chi-Square   1     7.114     0.008
  ⑭  Fisher's Exact Test (2-Tail)                  0.024
      Phi Coefficient                    1.414
      Contingency Coefficient            0.816
      Cramer's V                         1.000

      Sample Size = 9
      WARNING: 100% of the cells have expected counts less
               than 5. Chi-Square may not be a valid test.
```

Example 3:   Analysis of a 2×2 Table

The following example illustrates the analysis of a single 2×2 table. Fisher's exact test includes left- and right-tailed *p*-values, as well as the two-tailed *p*-value. The results indicate substantial evidence of a moderately strong negative association. The following statements produce **Output 20.5**:

```
data;
   do a=1 to 2;
      do b=1 to 2;
         input wt @@;
         output;
         end;
      end;
   cards;
3  11  6  2
;

proc freq;
   weight wt;
   tables a*b / chisq measures;
   title 'Analysis of 2 by 2 Table';
run;
```

Output 20.5   Analysis of a 2×2 Table

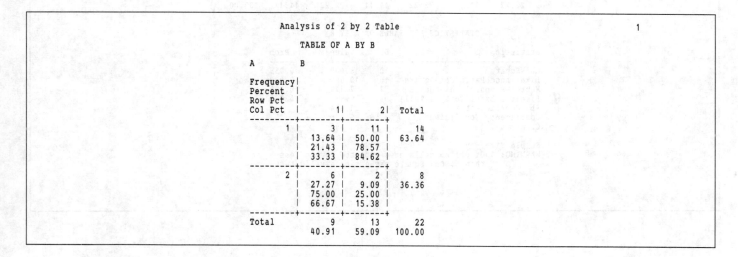

```
                        Analysis of 2 by 2 Table                      2
                      STATISTICS FOR TABLE OF A BY B
```

⑬
Statistic	DF	Value	Prob
Chi-Square	1	6.044	0.014
Likelihood Ratio Chi-Square	1	6.222	0.013
Continuity Adj. Chi-Square	1	4.031	0.045
Mantel-Haenszel Chi-Square	1	5.769	0.016
Fisher's Exact Test (Left)			0.022
(Right)			0.999
(2-Tail)			0.026
Phi Coefficient		-0.524	
Contingency Coefficient		0.464	
Cramer's V		-0.524	

⑮
Statistic	Value	ASE
Gamma	-0.833	0.160
Kendall's Tau-b	-0.524	0.185
Stuart's Tau-c	-0.496	0.184
Somers' D C|R	-0.536	0.188
Somers' D R|C	-0.513	0.186
Pearson Correlation	-0.524	0.185
Spearman Correlation	-0.524	0.185
Lambda Asymmetric C|R	0.444	0.234
Lambda Asymmetric R|C	0.375	0.296
Lambda Symmetric	0.412	0.251
Uncertainty Coefficient C|R	0.209	0.156
Uncertainty Coefficient R|C	0.216	0.159
Uncertainty Coefficient Symmetric	0.212	0.157

```
                 Estimates of the Relative Risk (Row1/Row2)
```

		95%	
Type of Study	Value	Confidence Bounds	
Case-Control	0.091	0.012	0.704
Cohort (Col1 Risk)	0.286	0.097	0.841
Cohort (Col2 Risk)	3.143	0.918	10.763

```
Sample Size = 22
WARNING:  50% of the cells have expected counts less
          than 5. Chi-Square may not be a valid test.
```

Example 4:   Evans County Study

Data for the following example are from the Evans County cohort study of coronary heart disease. Data for the variable CAT, however, are hypothetical. The data are given in Table 17.7 and used in Examples 17.2 and 17.9 of Kleinbaum, Kupper, and Morgenstern (1982).

The purpose of the analysis is to evaluate the association between serum catecholamine (CAT) and coronary heart disease (CHD) after controlling for AGE and electrocardiogram abnormality (ECG). The summary statistics show that the association is significant ($p=0.04$) and that subjects with high serum catecholamine are about 1.7 times more likely to develop coronary heart disease than those subjects with low serum catecholamine. The NOPRINT option suppresses printing of the contingency tables. The CHISQ and MEASURES options are excluded in order to suppress the computation and printing of statistics on the individual tables. The following statements produce **Output 20.6**:

```
data chd;
   input age $ ecg $ chd $ cat $ wt;
   cards;
<55  0  yes  yes    1
<55  0  yes  no    17
<55  0  no   yes    7
<55  0  no   no   257
<55  1  yes  yes    3
<55  1  yes  no     7
<55  1  no   yes   14
<55  1  no   no    52
55+  0  yes  yes    9
55+  0  yes  no    15
55+  0  no   yes   30
55+  0  no   no   107
55+  1  yes  yes   14
55+  1  yes  no     5
55+  1  no   yes   44
55+  1  no   no    27
;

proc freq order=data;
   weight wt;
   tables age*ecg*cat*chd / noprint cmh;
   title 'Example 17.9 from Kleinbaum, et al. , p. 353';
run;
```

Output 20.6   Evans County Study of Heart Disease

```
             Example 17.9 from Kleinbaum, et al. , p. 353                    1

                    SUMMARY STATISTICS FOR CAT BY CHD
                     CONTROLLING FOR AGE AND ECG


    🔟 Cochran-Mantel-Haenszel Statistics (Based on Table Scores)

      Statistic  Alternative Hypothesis   DF    Value    Prob
      ---------------------------------------------------------------
          1      Nonzero Correlation       1    4.153    0.042
          2      Row Mean Scores Differ    1    4.153    0.042
          3      General Association       1    4.153    0.042



            Estimates of the Common Relative Risk (Row1/Row2)
                                                    95%
      Type of Study   Method        Value   Confidence Bounds
      ---------------------------------------------------------------
      Case-Control    Mantel-Haenszel  1.891   1.025   3.490
       (Odds Ratio)   Logit            1.906   1.030   3.526

      Cohort          Mantel-Haenszel  1.696   1.020   2.818
       (Col1 Risk)    Logit            1.712   1.032   2.840

      Cohort          Mantel-Haenszel  0.900   0.814   0.996
       (Col2 Risk)    Logit            0.904   0.811   1.008

      The confidence bounds for the M-H estimates are test-based.
```

(continued on next page)

(continued from previous page)

```
                    Breslow-Day Test for Homogeneity of the Odds Ratios

          Chi-Square =   0.164          DF =   3          Prob = 0.983

          Total Sample Size = 609
```

Example 5:   Friedman's Chi-Square

Eight subjects were asked to display certain emotions while under hypnosis (Lehmann 1975, 264). The null hypothesis is that hypnosis has the same effect on skin potential for each of the following four emotions: fear, happiness (joy), depression (sadness), and calmness. Skin potential was measured in millivolts, and the four measurements were then ranked within each subject. Since there are no tied ranks within a subject, the analysis of variance CMH statistic is Friedman's chi-square ($Q=6.45$, $p=0.09$). The NOPRINT option is used to suppress printing of the contingency tables. These statements produce **Output 20.7**:

```
data hypnosis;
   input subject emotion $ ranking @@;
   cards;
1 fear 4    1 joy 3    1 sadness 1    1 calmness 2
2 fear 4    2 joy 2    2 sadness 3    2 calmness 1
3 fear 3    3 joy 2    3 sadness 4    3 calmness 1
4 fear 4    4 joy 1    4 sadness 2    4 calmness 3
5 fear 1    5 joy 4    5 sadness 3    5 calmness 2
6 fear 4    6 joy 3    6 sadness 2    6 calmness 1
7 fear 4    7 joy 1    7 sadness 2    7 calmness 3
8 fear 3    8 joy 4    8 sadness 2    8 calmness 1
;

proc freq;
   tables subject*emotion*ranking / noprint cmh;
   title 'Friedman''s Chi-Square';
run;
```

Output 20.7   Friedman's Chi-Square

```
                        Friedman's Chi-Square                              1

                 SUMMARY STATISTICS FOR EMOTION BY RANKING
                          CONTROLLING FOR SUBJECT


            Cochran-Mantel-Haenszel Statistics (Based on Table Scores)

            Statistic  Alternative Hypothesis   DF    Value    Prob
            ----------------------------------------------------------
                1       Nonzero Correlation       1    0.240   0.624
                2       Row Mean Scores Differ     3    6.450   0.092
                3       General Association        9   10.500   0.312


       Total Sample Size = 32
```

REFERENCES

Birch, M.W. (1965), "The Detection of Partial Association, II: The General Case," *Journal of the Royal Statistical Society, B,* 27, 111–124.

Bishop, Y., Fienberg, S.E., and Holland, P.W. (1975), *Discrete Multivariate Analysis: Theory and Practice,* Cambridge, MA: MIT Press.

Blalock, H.M., Jr. (1960), *Social Statistics,* New York: McGraw-Hill Book Co.

Breslow, N.E. and Day, N.E. (1980), *Statistical Methods in Cancer Research, Volume 1: The Analysis of Case-Control Studies,* Lyon: International Agency for Research on Cancer.

Bross, I.D.J. (1958), "How to Use Ridit Analysis," *Biometrics,* 14, 18–38.

Brown, M.B. and Benedetti, J.K. (1977) "Sampling Behavior of Tests for Correlation in Two-Way Contingency Tables," *Journal of the American Statistical Association* 72, 309–315.

Cochran, W.G. (1954), "Some Methods for Strengthening the Common χ^2 Tests," *Biometrics,* 10, 417–451.

van Elteren, P.H. (1960), "On the Combination of Independent Two-Sample Tests of Wilcoxon," *Bulletin of the International Statistical Institute,* 37, 351–361.

Fienberg, S.E. (1977), *The Analysis of Cross-Classified Data,* Cambridge, MA: MIT Press.

Fleiss, J.L. (1981), *Statistical Methods for Rates and Proportions,* 2d Edition, New York: John Wiley & Sons, Inc.

Garson, G.D. (1971), *Handbook of Political Science Methods,* Boston, MA: Holbrook Press, Inc.

Goodman, L.A. and Kruskal, W.H. (1954, 1959, 1963, 1972), "Measures of Association for Cross-Classification I, II, III, and IV," *Journal of the American Statistical Association,* 49, 732–764; 54, 123–163; 58, 310–364; 67, 415–421.

Goodman, L.A. and Kruskal, W.H. (1979), *Measures of Association for Cross Classification,* New York: Springer-Verlag (reprint of JASA articles above).

Haldane, J.B.S. (1955), "The Estimation and Significance of the Logarithm of a Ratio of Frequencies," *Annals of Human Genetics,* 20, 309–314.

Hayes, W.L. (1963), *Psychological Statistics,* New York: Holt, Rinehart and Winston, Inc.

Kendall, M. and Stuart, A. (1979), *The Advanced Theory of Statistics, Volume 2,* New York: Macmillan Publishing Company, Inc.

Kleinbaum, D.G., Kupper, L.L., and Morgenstern, H. (1982) *Epidemiologic Research: Principles and Quantitative Methods,* Belmont, CA: Wadsworth, Inc.

Landis, R.J. , Heyman, E.R. , and Koch, G.G. (1978), "Average Partial Association in Three-way Contingency Tables: A Review and Discussion of Alternative Tests," *International Statistical Review*, 46, 237–254.

Lehmann, E.L. (1975), *Nonparametrics: Statistical Methods Based on Ranks*, San Francisco: Holden-Day.

Mack, G.A. and Skillings, J.H. (1980), "A Friedman-Type Rank Test for Main Effects in a Two-Factor ANOVA," *Journal of the American Statistical Association*, 75, 947–951.

Mantel, N. (1963), "Chi-square Tests with One Degree of Freedom: Extensions of the Mantel-Haenszel Procedure," *Journal of the American Statistical Association*, 58, 690–700.

Mantel, N. and Haenszel, W. (1959), "Statistical Aspects of the Analysis of Data from Retrospective Studies of Disease," *Journal of the National Cancer Institute*, 22, 719–748.

Mehta, C.R. and Patel, N.R. (1983), "A Network Algorithm for Performing Fisher's Exact Test in $r \times c$ Contingency Tables," *Journal of the American Statistical Association, 78*, 427–434.

Snedecor, G.W. and Cochran, W.G. (1980), *Statistical Methods*, 7th Edition, Ames, IA: Iowa State University Press.

Somers, R.H. (1962), "A New Asymmetric Measure of Association for Ordinal Variables," *American Sociological Review*, 27, 799–811.

Theil, H. (1972), *Statistical Decomposition Analysis*, Amsterdam: North-Holland Publishing Company.

Woolf, B. (1955), "On Estimating the Relationship between Blood Group and Disease," *Annals of Human Genetics*, 19, 251–253.

The MEANS Procedure

ABSTRACT

The MEANS procedure produces simple univariate descriptive statistics for numeric variables. You can use the OUTPUT statement to request that MEANS output statistics to a SAS data set.

INTRODUCTION

PROC MEANS computes statistics for an entire SAS data set or for groups of observations in the data set. PROC MEANS is nearly identical to PROC SUMMARY. A major difference between the MEANS and SUMMARY procedures is that, by default, PROC SUMMARY produces no printed output; PROC MEANS does.

If you use the CLASS statement, PROC MEANS calculates descriptive statistics separately for groups of observations. If you want to subdivide your data into groups, use the CLASS statement. Your input data set does not need to be sorted by the class variables. If you have a large data set, you may have to use the BY statement to subdivide your data. However, the BY statement requires that the input data set be sorted according to the BY variables or have an appropriate index. No such restriction is imposed by the CLASS statement.

The MEANS procedure can optionally create one or more SAS data sets containing the statistics calculated. If you want descriptive statistics in a data set and do not require printed output, use the NOPRINT option in the PROC MEANS statement.

Other SAS procedures also compute univariate statistics. Although PROC MEANS is the easiest and most direct descriptive procedure, other procedures provide additional features. See Chapter 1, "SAS Elementary Statistics Procedures," for an overview of statistics procedures contained in this book.

Note: In this discussion, names of statistics refer to the sample estimates of the true parameters. Thus, the term *mean* refers to the sample mean, *variance* refers to the sample variance, and so forth.

SPECIFICATIONS

The MEANS procedure is controlled by the following statements:

PROC MEANS <*option-list*> <*statistic-keyword-list*>;
  VAR *variable-list*;
  CLASS *variable-list*;
  FREQ *variable*;
  WEIGHT *variable*;
  ID *variable-list*;
  BY *variable-list*;
  OUTPUT <OUT=*SAS-data-set*> <*output-statistic-list*>
        <MAXID <(var-1<(id-list-1)> <...var-n<(id-list-n)>>)>=*name-list*>
        <MINID <(var-1<(id-list-1)> <...var-n<(id-list-n)>>)>=*name-list*>;

There is no limit to the number of OUTPUT statements that can accompany a PROC MEANS statement. The options given in **PROC MEANS Statement** also apply to the PROC SUMMARY statement, and the statements that follow can also be used with the SUMMARY procedure.

PROC MEANS Statement

  PROC MEANS <*option-list*> <*statistic-keyword-list*>;

The PROC MEANS statement starts the procedure. The options shown in **Table 21.1** can be specified in the PROC MEANS statement. The options are described in alphabetic order following the table.

Table 21.1 PROC MEANS Statement Options

Task	Options
Specify input data set	DATA=
Select printing options	DESCENDING
	FW=
	MAXDEC=
	NOPRINT
	PRINT
Specify the minimum ID value	IDMIN
Treat missing values as valid	MISSING
Indicate order	ORDER=
	DESCENDING
Output statistics with highest _TYPE_ value	NWAY
Specify variance divisor	VARDEF=

DATA=*SAS-data-set*
   names the SAS data set to be analyzed by PROC MEANS. If the DATA= option is omitted, the most recently created SAS data set is used.

DESCENDING
   orders the output data set by descending _TYPE_ value (ASCENDING is the default). This causes the overall totals (_TYPE_=0) to be placed at the end of each BY group. This option has no effect if the NWAY option is also specified.

FW=*field-width*
   specifies the field width for PROC MEANS to use in printing each statistic. The default is FW=12.

IDMIN
   specifies that the value of the ID variable should be its minimum (rather than its maximum) value for the corresponding observations of the input data set.

MAXDEC=*number*
   gives the maximum number of decimal places (0 to 8) for PROC MEANS to use in printing results. The default is the BEST. width for columnar format, typically about 7. This applies to all statistics except PROBT (labeled Prob>|T| on the printed output), which is determined by the PROBSIG SAS system option.

MISSING
   requests that PROC MEANS treat missing values as valid subgroup values for the CLASS variables.

NOPRINT
   suppresses printing of all the descriptive statistics. Use the NOPRINT option when the only purpose of using the procedure is to create a new SAS data set.

NWAY

> specifies that statistics be output for only the observation with the highest _TYPE_ value (highest level of interaction among CLASS variables).

ORDER=DATA
> | EXTERNAL | FORMATTED
> | FREQ
> | INTERNAL

specifies the sorting order for the levels of the classification variables (specified in the CLASS statement). The table below shows how PROC MEANS interprets values of the ORDER= option.

Value of ORDER=	Levels Sorted By
DATA	order of appearance in the input data set
EXTERNAL | FORMATTED	external formatted value
FREQ	descending frequency count; levels with the most observations come first
INTERNAL	unformatted value

> By default, ORDER=INTERNAL. For FORMATTED and INTERNAL, the sort order is machine-dependent. The ORDER= option does not apply to missing values, which are always ordered first.

PRINT

> use with PROC SUMMARY to print any of the descriptive statistics. By default, PROC SUMMARY produces no printed output.

VARDEF=DF
> | N
> | WDF
> | WEIGHT | WGT

specifies the divisor to be used in the calculation of variances and covariances. The default value is VARDEF=DF. The values and associated divisors are shown below.

Value	Divisor	Formula
DF	degrees of freedom	$n - 1$
N	number of observations	n
WDF	sum of weights minus one	$(\sum_i w_i) - 1$
WEIGHT | WGT	sum of weights	$\sum_i w_i$

Statistic Keywords Available in the PROC MEANS Statement

You can request the statistics below by giving their keywords in a PROC MEANS statement. These keywords are also used in the OUTPUT statement, described later in this chapter. The statistics are defined and formulas are given in Chapter 1, "SAS Elementary Statistics Procedures."

The valid keywords and the statistics they represent are as follows:

N	the number of observations in the subgroup having nonmissing values for the variable
NMISS	the number of observations in the subgroup having missing values for the variable
MIN	the minimum value
MAX	the maximum value
RANGE	the range
SUM	the sum
SUMWGT	the sum of the WEIGHT variable values
MEAN	the mean
CSS	the corrected sum of squares
USS	the uncorrected sum of squares
VAR	the variance
STD	the standard deviation
STDERR	the standard error of the mean
CV	the coefficient of variation
SKEWNESS	skewness
KURTOSIS	kurtosis
T	Student's t for testing the hypothesis that the population mean is 0
PRT	the probability of a greater absolute value for the t-value above.

If no statistics are specifically requested, PROC MEANS prints the variable name, N, MEAN, STD, MIN, and MAX.

An additional statistic, N Obs, is printed when you use PROC MEANS with the CLASS statement or PROC SUMMARY with the PRINT option. The N Obs statistic is the total number of observations in a given group or subgroup. N Obs is the sum of N and NMISS. The statements below produce **Output 21.1**.

```
data gains;
   input name $  team $  age ;
   cards;
   Alfred  blue    6
   Alicia  red     5
   Barbara .       5
   Bennett red     .
   Carol   blue    5
   Carlos  blue    6
   ;
run;

proc means nmiss n;
   class team;
run;
```

Output 21.1 The N Obs Statistic

```
                              The SAS System                                    1
                        Analysis Variable : AGE

                  TEAM      N Obs  N  Nmiss
                  -------------------------
                  blue        3    3      0

                  red         2    1      1
                  -------------------------
```

PROC MEANS needs the CLASS statement to activate the N Obs statistic; PROC SUMMARY does not. In PROC SUMMARY, N Obs is activated by the PRINT option.

BY Statement

BY *variable-list*;

A BY statement can be used with PROC MEANS to obtain separate analyses on observations in groups defined by the BY variables. When you use a BY statement, PROC MEANS expects your input data set to be sorted according to the BY variables, or to have an appropriate index. If your input data set is not sorted, you can do one of the following:

- Use the SORT procedure with a similar BY statement to sort the data.
- If appropriate, use the BY statement options NOTSORTED or DESCENDING.
- Use the DATASETS procedure to create an index on the BY variables you want to use. For more information on using the BY statement with indexed data sets, see Chapter 17, "The DATASETS Procedure."

CLASS Statement

CLASS *variable-list*;

The CLASS statement assigns the variables used to form subgroups. Class variables may be either numeric or character, but normally each variable has a small number of discrete values or unique levels. The class variable used to produce **Output 21.1** is an example. The CLASS statement has an effect on the statistics computed similar to the effect of the BY statement. The differences are in the format of the printed output and in the BY statement sorting requirement.

You can do analysis on larger data sets using the BY statement because PROC MEANS need not hold all the groups in memory. **Example 1** illustrates the differences in printed output. You can use both the CLASS and BY statements together, each defining a different set of variables.

FREQ Statement

FREQ *variable*;

When a FREQ statement appears with PROC MEANS, each observation in the input data set is assumed to represent *n* observations in the calculation of statistics, where *n* is the value of the FREQ variable. If the value of the FREQ variable is less than 1 or is missing, the observation is not used in the calculations. If the value is not an integer, only the integer portion is used.

ID Statement

ID *variable-list*;

An ID statement can be used with PROC MEANS to include additional variables in the output data set. If your ID statement names only one variable, the value of the ID variable for a given observation in the output data set is the maximum value it has in the corresponding observations of the input data set, unless the IDMIN option is specified in the PROC MEANS statement. When your ID statement includes two or more variables, the maximum value is chosen as if the values of the ID variables were concatenated into one value for each observation. Thus, the maximum value comes from only one of the corresponding observations in the input data set.

OUTPUT Statement

OUTPUT <OUT=*SAS-data-set*> <*output-statistic-list*>
       <MAXID<(*var-1*<(*id-list-1*)> <...*var-n*<(*id-list-n*)>>)>=*name-list*>
       <MINID<(*var-1*<(*id-list-1*)> <...*var-n*<(*id-list-n*)>>)>=*name-list*>;

The OUTPUT statement requests that PROC MEANS output statistics to a new SAS data set. There is no limit to the number of OUTPUT statements you can use in a single PROC MEANS step. One SAS data set is created for each valid OUTPUT statement. Use options in the OUTPUT statement to name the data set and to include specific variables.

The following options can be specified in the OUTPUT statement:

MAXID<(*var-1*<(*id-list-1*)> <...*var-n*<(*id-list-n*)>>)>=*name-list*
MINID<(*var-1*<(*id-list-1*)> <...*var-n*<(*id-list-n*)>>)>=*name-list*
   allow you to associate lists of identifying variables with the maximum or minimum of different analysis variables, where

              var   is a variable to be minimized or maximized.

           id-list is the identifying variable for the minima or maxima.

   Here is an example of a valid specification:

```
minid (height (name) ) = shortest
```

   If you use an ID statement, you do not need to specifically identify the *id-list* variables. For example, the specification

```
minid=shortest
```

   is sufficient.

   For a full description of specifying these options, see the next section, **Using the MAXID and MINID Options**.

OUT=*SAS-data-set*
   specifies the name of an output data set. If you want to create a permanent SAS data set, you must specify a two-level name (see *SAS*

Language: Reference for more information on permanent data sets). If the OUT= option is omitted, the new data set is named using the DATA*n* naming convention.

output-statistic-list

specifies the statistics you want in the new data set and also names the variable or variables to contain these statistics. Any of the statistics available in the PROC MEANS statement can be output by using the keyword for that statistic in the OUTPUT statement. The keywords are listed below. Their definitions are listed in **Statistic Keywords Available in the PROC MEANS Statement** earlier in this chapter, and detailed descriptions are given in Chapter 1, "SAS Elementary Statistics Procedures."

N	SUMWGT	STDERR
NMISS	MEAN	CV
MIN	USS	SKEWNESS
MAX	CSS	KURTOSIS
RANGE	VAR	T
SUM	STD	PRT

The form of the output request determines the name of the new variable containing the statistic. There are three forms for specifying statistics for the output data set. Either the MAXID or MINID option can be used with any of the following forms. The various forms are described below.

statistic-keyword=;

supplies one (and only one) statistic to be output to the data set. The statistic in the new data set has the same name as the corresponding variable in the input data set if you simply follow the keyword with an equal sign and a semicolon.

For example, say you want the output data set to contain means for the variables PRE and POST, and the variables containing the means are also to be called PRE and POST. You can specify the following:

```
proc means;
   class teacher;
   var pre post;
   output out=results mean=;
run;
```

You cannot use this form for more than one statistic keyword in the OUTPUT statement. Requests for multiple statistics using this form cause the output data set to contain two or more variables with the same name, which is not allowed.

statistic-keyword=name-list;

requests names that differ from the original variable names. These names are used for the variables in the new data set that contain the statistics.

The first variable name following the equal sign is given to the corresponding statistic for the first variable in the VAR statement; the second name is given to the statistic for the second variable in the VAR statement; and so on.

For example, suppose that you still want to calculate means for the variables PRE and POST, but this time you want to use different names for the variables in the output data set. This time you want to list the values as MEANEX1 and MEANEX2, referring to the first exam and second exam. In the output data set named RESULTS, the variable containing the PRE mean is MEANEX1; the variable containing the POST mean is MEANEX2.

```
proc means;
    class teacher;
    var pre post;
    output out=results mean=meanex1 meanex2;
run;
```

statistic-keyword(variable-list)=name-list;

requests a statistic for only certain variables in the VAR statement, and gives those statistics new names in the output data set. After the keyword, list in parentheses the variables for which you want the statistic. Then place the names you assign to the variables in the new data set after the equal sign.

For example, suppose you want to output standard deviations for only the POST variable, but you want means for both the PRE and POST variables. The following statements do this:

```
proc means;
    class teacher;
    var pre post;
    output out=results mean=premean postmean
        std(post)=stdpost;
run;
```

Caution: When no new variable names follow the equal sign, the statistics will have the same names as the original variables, as shown in the first example, *statistic-keyword=;* .

Again, omitting the *name-list* for more than one statistic per variable causes duplicate variable names and is not allowed.

The statements in the following example assign new names to the standard deviations for PRE and POST, name the mimimum for POST MINPOST, and leave the mean for PRE named PRE.

```
proc means;
    var pre post;
    output out=results mean(pre)=
                        std=stdpre stdpost
                        min(post)=minpost;
run;
```

Using the MAXID and MINID Options

The MAXID and MINID options allow you to associate lists of identifying variables with the maximum or minimum of different analysis variables. For example, you could rewrite the example from the previous section as

```
proc means;
    class teacher;
    var pre post;
    output out=results mean=
        maxid(pre(student))=hipre   minid(post(student))=lopost;
run;
```

You do not have to specify an ID statement to specify an *id-list*, and the variables in *id-list* can be different from the variables in an ID statement. However, if you omit the *id-list* variables, PROC MEANS uses all the variables specified in the ID statement.

The *name-list* is the list of output variable names for all the associated IDs defined by the different *var* and *id-list* combinations.

Names from the *name-list* are assigned to variables in the order in which they appear in the *id-list*. If there are fewer names in the *name-list* than there are variables defined (implicitly or explicitly) by the different *var* and *id-list* combinations, the remaining output variables use the corresponding names from the input file once the *name-list* is exhausted. If, for example, you specify the *name-list* but do not specify a *var* and *id-list* combination, such as

```
minid=(name-list)
```

then PROC MEANS associates all the variables in the ID statement with each analysis variable. Thus, for each analysis variable, the number of variables defined for the output data set is the same as the number of variables mentioned in the ID statement.

Caution: The flexibility of the syntax makes it possible to mistakenly create several output variables with the same name. If this occurs, only the first of these variables is accessible in the output data set.

Example   Suppose you have a data set containing the WEIGHT and HEIGHT of a group of middle school students. You want to find the largest value for HEIGHT and WEIGHT, the name of the person who is the tallest, and the name of the person who is the heaviest. The complete data set is given in **Example 1** later in this chapter. The statements below produce **Output 21.2**.

```
proc means data=gains;
   var height weight;
   class sex;
   output out=test
         max=maxht maxwght
         maxid(height(name) weight(name))=tallest heaviest;
run;


proc print data=test;
run;
```

Output 21.2   Using PROC MEANS with the MAXID Option

				The SAS System				1
SEX	N Obs	Variable	N	Mean	Std Dev	Minimum	Maximum	
F	14	HEIGHT	14	63.9642857	3.8509953	56.5000000	69.5000000	
		WEIGHT	14	97.8642857	9.6857236	84.0000000	114.9000000	
M	24	HEIGHT	23	65.0391304	5.4584996	51.3000000	71.0000000	
		WEIGHT	22	101.1681818	21.8181966	50.5000000	130.5000000	

```
                                The SAS System                                2

          OBS    SEX    _TYPE_    _FREQ_    MAXHT    MAXWGHT    TALLEST    HEAVIEST

           1              0        38       71.0     130.5      Alfred     Alfred
           2      F       1        14       69.5     114.9      Marie      Marie
           3      M       1        24       71.0     130.5      Alfred     Alfred
```

In this example, the output data set has one observation for each sex and the new variables MAXHT (the maximum height), MAXWGT (the maximum weight), TALLEST (the name of the tallest person), and HEAVIEST (the name of the heaviest person). Note that only one name is saved for each sex. If multiple observations have the maximum height or weight, only the first one found is saved.

VAR Statement

VAR *variable-list*;

Statistics are calculated for each numeric variable listed in the VAR statement. If a VAR statement is not used, all numeric variables in the input data set, except for those listed in BY, CLASS, FREQ, ID, or WEIGHT statements, are analyzed. The results are printed in the order of the variables in the VAR statement.

   Note: If you omit the VAR statement with PROC SUMMARY, a simple count of observations is produced.

WEIGHT Statement

WEIGHT *variable*;

The WEIGHT statement specifies a numeric variable in the input SAS data set whose values are used to weight each observation. Only one variable can be specified. Both the FREQ and WEIGHT statements can be used. When a WEIGHT statement is specified, PROC MEANS uses the value of the WEIGHT variable, w_i, to calculate a weighted mean $\bar{x}_w$, a weighted variance s_w^2, and a weighted sum $\Sigma w_i x_i$. The sample mean and sample variance are then represented as

$$\bar{x}_w = \Sigma_i \, w_i x_i \, / \, \Sigma_i \, w_i$$

and

$$s_w^2 = \Sigma_i \, w_i (x_i - \bar{x}_w)^2 \, / \, d$$

where the x_i values are the variable values and the divisor d is controlled by the VARDEF= option. The divisor can be $n-1$ (when VARDEF=DF), Σw_i (when VARDEF=WEIGHT), n (when VARDEF=N), or $\Sigma w_i - 1$ (when VARDEF=WDF), where n is the number of values. VARDEF=DF is the default.

   The WEIGHT variable values can be nonintegers. If the value of the WEIGHT variable is less than zero or is missing, a value of zero is assumed for the weight. If you use more than one WEIGHT statement, only the last one specified is used.

DETAILS

Missing Values

The MEANS and SUMMARY procedures exclude missing analysis variable values before calculating statistics. Each variable is treated individually; a missing value in one variable does not affect the calculations for other variables. If any class variable has a missing value for an observation, that observation is not used in the calculations unless the MISSING option is specified in the PROC MEANS statement. Missing values for a BY variable form a separate BY group and are treated in the same way as BY groups with nonmissing values. If the FREQ variable value is missing, a value of zero is assumed. If the WEIGHT variable value is missing, the observation's weight is zero.

Computer Resources

Theoretically, the maximum number of combinations of class levels allowed is 200 million. Realistically, it becomes a machine dependent estimate limited solely by the amount of computer memory available. The maximum number of class variables allowed is 30. Sorting by one of the class variables and using it as a BY variable saves considerable memory, since each BY group is loaded into memory separately.

Output Data Set

Using the OUTPUT statement and the OUT= option, the MEANS and SUMMARY procedures can create one or more output SAS data sets. The output data set's record contents are described below.

Variables

The following variables can be in the output data set:

- the BY variables, if a BY statement is used.
- the ID variables, if an ID statement is used.
- the class variables, if a CLASS statement is used. When formats combine several internal values into one formatted value, the lowest internal value is output.
- a variable created by the MEANS and SUMMARY procedures named _TYPE_ that contains information about the class variables that define each subgroup, if a CLASS statement is used.
- a variable created by the MEANS and SUMMARY procedures named _FREQ_ that gives the number of observations (whether the analysis variables values are missing or not) for the current subgroup.
- the variables containing the subgroup statistics requested by the keywords in the OUTPUT statement.
- a variable called _STATS_ if no statistic keywords are specified. See **Creating the Default _STAT_ Data Set** for details.

For example, consider the data set created by PROC MEANS with these statements:

```
proc means;
   class tmt;
   var x y;
   output out=stats mean=mx my n=nx ny;
   run;
```

The output data set STATS contains the variables TMT, _TYPE_, _FREQ_, MX, MY, NX, and NY.

Observations

The number of observations in the output data set produced by the MEANS procedure depends on the number of distinct values or levels of the class variables. To illustrate this concept, imagine a data set where the class variables are SCHOOL, AGE, and SEX, (or A, B, and C in **Table 21.2**). The number of levels of these variables is as follows: SCHOOL has 2, AGE has 5, and SEX has 2 (a, b, and c in **Table 21.2**). There may be categories without observations, for instance, one junior high school without a sixth grade may not have any students in the 11- to 12-year-old level. **Table 21.2** examines these possibilities for a general case. The table uses binary representation: the 0 means that a variable is not taken into account; a 1 means that it is taken into account. This formula gives the maximum number of combinations possible, assuming that all combinations are present.

Observations in the data set produced by PROC MEANS are identified by the variable named _TYPE_. Values of _TYPE_ indicate which subgroup (defined by values of the class variables) produced the summary statistics in that observation in the output data set.

Table 21.2 shows how values of _TYPE_ are determined for one class variable (A), two class variables (A and B), and three class variables (A, B, and C). The same logic can be extended to analyses by PROC MEANS with more than three class variables. The table assumes that all combinations of class levels occur in the data.

Table 21.2 Observations in PROC MEANS Output Data Set

C	B	A	_TYPE_	Subgroup Defined By	Number of Observations of this _TYPE_ in the Data Set	Total Number of Observations in the Data Set
0	0	0	0	Total	1	
0	0	1	1	A	a	1+a
0	1	0	2	B	b	
0	1	1	3	A*B	a*b	1+a+b+a*b
1	0	0	4	C	c	
1	0	1	5	A*C	a*c	
1	1	0	6	B*C	b*c	1+a+b+a*b+c
1	1	1	7	A*B*C	a*b*c	+a*c+b*c+a*b*c
Binary equivalent of _TYPE_ value				A ,B ,C=CLASS variables	a, b, c=number of levels of A, B, C respectively	

For a CLASS statement with one class variable,

```
class A;
```

the output data set contains one observation for totals (_TYPE_=0) and an observation for each level of A (_TYPE_=1).

For a CLASS statement with two class variables,

```
class B A;
```

an observation for each level of B (_TYPE_=2) and an observation for each level of A*B (_TYPE_=3) are added.

For a CLASS statement with three class variables,

```
class C B A;
```

observations for levels of C (_TYPE_=4), levels of A*C (_TYPE_=5), B*C (_TYPE_=6), and A*B*C (_TYPE_=7) are added.

You can extend the table to an n-way analysis by adding columns to the table on the left. A value of 1 is entered in a column if that class variable is involved in defining the subgroup, a 0 otherwise. Note that the 1s and 0s in the class variable columns form binary numbers across the row for each subgroup.

The decimal equivalent of one of these binary numbers for a subgroup is the _TYPE_ value for that subgroup. There are 2^n different values of _TYPE_ produced by PROC MEANS for a given analysis, where n is the number of class variables. The number of observations of each _TYPE_ in the output data set depends on the number of levels of the class variables, as shown in the table above.

Consider the case where the CLASS statement contains two variables, AGE and HOMEOWN. The variable AGE has two values, 1 and 2 (where "under thirty" is coded as 1, and "over thirty" is coded as 2); the variable HOMEOWN has two values, Y and N. The observations in the output data set are determined as in **Table 21.3**.

Table 21.3 Two CLASS Variables

Homeown	Age	_TYPE_	Subgroup Defined By	Number of Observations of this _TYPE_ in the Data Set	Total Number of Observations in the Data Set
0	0	0	Total	1	
0	1	1	Age	2	
1	0	2	Homeown	2	
1	1	3	Age * Homeown	4	9

The SAS statements below produce **Output 21.3** and **Output 21.4** using two CLASS variables. The output illustrates the concepts shown in **Table 21.3**.

```
data homes;
   input name $ homeown $ age income ;
   cards;
rodrick    n  1    30000
smith      n  2    25400
freiss     y  1    42000
garcia     y  1    18000
williams   n  2    14000
mason      n  2    20000
lopez      n  2    18500
gregory    n  1    30000
reid       n  1    27000
schulman   y  1    35000
garrett    y  1    32000
zingraff   y  2    35000
;
run;

proc means;
   class age homeown;
   var income;
   output out=stats mean=incmean;
run;

proc print data=stats;
run;
```

Output 21.3   The _TYPE_ and _FREQ_ Variables

```
                                    The SAS System                                        1
Analysis Variable : INCOME

    AGE HOMEOWN  N Obs   N      Mean      Std Dev     Minimum      Maximum
    -----------------------------------------------------------------------
     1    n        3    3    29000.00     1732.05    27000.00     30000.00
          y        4    4    31750.00    10078.86    18000.00     42000.00
     2    n        4    4    19475.00     4701.33    14000.00     25400.00
          y        1    1    35000.00         .      35000.00     35000.00
    -----------------------------------------------------------------------
```

```
                                 The SAS System                                    2
          OBS    AGE    HOMEOWN    _TYPE_    _FREQ_    INCMEAN

           1      .                   0        12      27241.67
           2      .        n          1         7      23557.14
           3      .        y          1         5      32400.00
           4      1                   2         7      30571.43
           5      2                   2         5      22580.00
           6      1        n          3         3      29000.00
           7      1        y          3         4      31750.00
           8      2        n          3         4      19475.00
           9      2        y          3         1      35000.00
```

In **Output 21.3**, the columns of interest are HOMEOWN, AGE, _TYPE_ and _FREQ_. The analysis variable is the variable upon which the statistic, mean income, was computed (in this case INCOME). You could substitute any statistical keyword available to MEANS and SUMMARY.

Notice the _TYPE_ variable in the fourth column of **Output 21.3**, page 2. The _TYPE_=0 observation contains data from all observations in the data set. The _TYPE_ variable is an indicator of the class variable interactions in a particular group. The HOMEOWN and AGE values for this output observation are missing. The value of _FREQ_ is 12 because 12 observations were used to form this group.

The _TYPE_=1 observations are formed from values of the rightmost variable in the CLASS statement, in this case HOMEOWN. The first of these incorporates data from the seven observations having a value of **N** for HOMEOWN; the second incorporates data from the five observations having the value of **Y** for HOMEOWN.

The _TYPE_=2 observations use data from the two groups of observations defined by the AGE values.

The _TYPE_=3 observations present the subgroups defined by the combinations of the AGE and HOMEOWN values. For example, the first observation in this set combines the data for the three observations having an AGE value of 1 and a HOMEOWN value of **N**.

Creating the Default _STAT_ Data Set

If you use a CLASS statement and the OUTPUT statement but omit the statistic keywords, PROC MEANS creates a special SAS data set in which five records are generated for each subgroup defined by the class variables in each BY group. The five records contain the following statistics : N, MIN, MAX, MEAN, and STD which are values of the variable _STAT_. This is shown in **Output 21.4** below.

```
data gains;
   input name $ height weight teacher $ school $;
   cards;
Alfred  69.0   122.5 Burke   Central
Alicia  56.5    84.0 Vargas  Clinton
Barbara 65.3    98.0 Vargas  Clinton
Bennett 63.2    96.2 Burke   Central
Carol   62.8   102.5 Burke   Central
Carlos  63.7   102.9 Vargas  Clinton
 ;
run;
```

```
proc means noprint;
   class teacher;
   output out=results;
run;

proc print data=results;
run;
```

Output 21.4   The Default _STAT_ Data Set

```
                              The SAS System                                 1

    OBS    TEACHER    _TYPE_    _FREQ_    _STAT_    HEIGHT     WEIGHT

     1                   0         6       N        6.0000      6.000
     2                   0         6       MIN     56.5000     84.000
     3                   0         6       MAX     69.0000    122.500
     4                   0         6       MEAN    63.4167    101.017
     5                   0         6       STD      4.0760     12.563
     6      Burke         1         3       N        3.0000      3.000
     7      Burke         1         3       MIN     62.8000     96.200
     8      Burke         1         3       MAX     69.0000    122.500
     9      Burke         1         3       MEAN    65.0000    107.067
    10      Burke         1         3       STD      3.4699     13.732
    11      Vargas        1         3       N        3.0000      3.000
    12      Vargas        1         3       MIN     56.5000     84.000
    13      Vargas        1         3       MAX     65.3000    102.900
    14      Vargas        1         3       MEAN    61.8333     94.967
    15      Vargas        1         3       STD      4.6876      9.808
```

If you use the WEIGHT statement, a sixth record containing the sum of weights (SUMWGT) is also output. Note that the statistic N here refers to the number of observations on which calculations are based.

Usage Note: SAS Bit-Testing Feature

The _TYPE_ variable is a good candidate for use with the SAS bit-testing feature. For example, say that you want to print a report using just the observations from the previous example with the TEACHER and SCHOOL combinations:

```
proc means data=gains;
   class name teacher school;
   var height weight;
   output out=stats mean=;
run;

data select;
   set stats;
   if _type_='011'b;
proc print data=select;
   title 'teacher * school';
run;
```

The IF statement could also be written

```
if _type_=3;
```

Printed Output

If you do not specifically request statistics in the PROC MEANS statement, the MEANS procedure prints the following statistics for each variable in the VAR statement:

1. N, the number of observations with no missing data in the CLASS group for the given BY group
2. N Obs, the number of observations in the CLASS group
3. the name of the variable
4. the minimum value of the variable
5. the maximum value of the variable
6. the mean or average of the variable
7. the standard deviation of the variable.

If you request specific statistics in the PROC MEANS statement, only those statistics are printed. The following is a list of additional statistics that PROC MEANS can print if requested:

8. the standard error of the mean
9. the sum of all the values for a variable
10. the variance of each variable
11. C.V., or the coefficient of variation expressed as a percentage
12. the number of missing values for each variable
13. the range of each variable
14. USS, the raw sum of squares (not adjusted for the mean)
15. CSS, the sum of squares adjusted for the mean
16. T, Student's t for testing the hypothesis that the population mean is zero
17. Prob > $|T|$, the probability of a greater absolute value for Student's t under the hypothesis that the mean is zero
18. the sum of the WEIGHT variable values
19. SKEWNESS, the measure of sidedness
20. KURTOSIS, the measure of the heaviness of tails.

If you use a WEIGHT statement, SKEWNESS and KURTOSIS cannot be computed.

If a statistic cannot be computed because of insufficient or inappropriate data, the statistic is reported as missing. See Chapter 1, "SAS Elementary Statistics Procedures."

If a BY statement is included, a line is drawn to separate the statistics for each BY group.

EXAMPLES

Example 1: Univariate Statistics

The following example uses the data set GAINS, with the data from two middle school classes. Physical education instructors took students' weight and height measurements for two time periods, fall and spring. The example requests univariate statistics for two variables, HEIGHT and WEIGHT. The first PROC MEANS statement asks for statistics on all numeric variables (including TIME) for all observations.

The second PROC MEANS statement asks for the statistics that must be specifically requested.

The third PROC MEANS statement requests statistics for each combination of values of the variables SCHOOL and TIME with the CLASS statement. MAXDEC=3 requests that only three decimal places be used to print the results. FW=10 limits the field width to ten positions.

The fourth PROC MEANS statement shows that exactly the same statistics as those of the previous statement can be obtained using the BY statement instead of the CLASS statement. However, note the use of the SORT procedure prior to invoking PROC MEANS. PROC MEANS creates an output data set that includes the means and standard errors of the means for the two variables. The PRINT procedure is used to print the new data set. The statements below produce **Output 21.5**.

```
data gains;
   input name $ sex $ height  weight  school $ time;
   cards;
Alfred  M 69.0 122.5 AJH  1
Alfred  M 71.0 130.5 AJH  2
Alicia  F 56.5  84.0 BJH  1
Alicia  F 60.5  86.9 BJH  2
Benicia F 65.3  98.0 BJH  1
Benicia F 69.3  99.1 BJH  2
Bennett F 63.2  96.2 AJH  1
Bennett F 69.2  98.2 AJH  2
Carol   F 62.8 102.5 BJH  1
Carol   F 65.3 105.4 BJH  2
Carlos  M 63.7 102.9 AJH  1
Carlos  M 70.3 106.9 AJH  2
Henry   M 63.5 102.5 AJH  1
Henry   M 68.9 108.6 AJH  2
Jaime   M 57.3  86.0 BJH  1
Jaime   M 62.9  90.0 BJH  2
Janet   F 59.8  84.5 AJH  1
Janet   F 62.5  86.5 AJH  2
Jean    M 68.2 113.4 AJH  1
Jean    M 70.3 116.0 AJH  2
Joyce   M 51.3  50.5 BJH  1
Joyce   M 55.5  53.5 BJH  2
Luc     M 66.3  77.0 AJH  1
Luc     M 69.3  82.9 AJH  2
Marie   F 66.5 112.0 BJH  1
Marie   F 69.5 114.9 BJH  2
Medford M 64.9 114.0 AJH  1
Medford M  .     .   .    .
Philip  M 69.0 115.0 AJH  1
Philip  M 70.0 118.0 AJH  2
Robert  M 64.8 128.0 BJH  1
Robert  M 68.3   .   BJH  2
Thomas  M 57.5  85.0 AJH  1
Thomas  M 59.1  92.3 AJH  2
Wakana  F 61.3  99.0 AJH  1
Wakana  F 63.8 102.9 AJH  2
William M 66.5 112.0 BJH  1
William M 68.3 118.2 BJH  2
;

proc means;
   title 'Statistics For All Numeric Variables';
run;
```

```
proc means data=gains maxdec=3 nmiss range
            uss css t prt sumwgt skewness kurtosis;
   var height weight;
   title 'Requesting Assorted Statistics';
run;

proc format;
   value timepr 1='Fall'
                2='Spring';

proc means maxdec=3 fw=10;
   class school time;
   var height weight;
   format time timepr.;
   title 'Statistics With Two Class Variables';
run;

proc sort;
   by school time;
run;

proc means maxdec=3 fw=10;
   by school time;
   var height weight;
   output out=new mean=hmean wmean stderr=hse wse;
   format time timepr.;
   title 'Statistics With Two By Variables';
run;

proc print;
   title 'New Data Set';
   format time timepr.;
run;
```

Output 21.5 Several Kinds of PROC MEANS Output

```
                 Statistics For All Numeric Variables                    1

       Variable   N      Mean      Std Dev      Minimum      Maximum
       ----------------------------------------------------------------
       HEIGHT    37   64.6324324   4.8829098   51.3000000   71.0000000
       WEIGHT    36   99.8833333  17.9759125   50.5000000  130.5000000
       TIME      37    1.4864865   0.5067117    1.0000000    2.0000000
       ----------------------------------------------------------------
```

```
                        Requesting Assorted Statistics                            2

Variable  Nmiss    Range     Sumwgt       CSS        USS        T    Prob>|T|  Skewness  Kurtosis
-------------------------------------------------------------------------------------------------
HEIGHT      1     19.700    37.000     858.341  155420.340   80.514   0.0001    -0.819    0.107
WEIGHT      2     80.000    36.000   11309.670  370470.160   33.339   0.0001    -0.839    1.108
-------------------------------------------------------------------------------------------------
```

```
                       Statistics With Two Class Variables                        3

SCHOOL    TIME   N Obs  Variable    N       Mean     Std Dev    Minimum    Maximum
-----------------------------------------------------------------------------------
AJH      Fall     11    HEIGHT     11      64.218      3.760     57.500     69.000
                        WEIGHT     11     101.091     14.554     77.000    122.500

         Spring   10    HEIGHT     10      67.440      4.103     59.100     71.000
                        WEIGHT     10     104.280     14.886     82.900    130.500

BJH      Fall      8    HEIGHT      8      61.375      5.651     51.300     66.500
                        WEIGHT      8      96.625     23.584     50.500    128.000

         Spring    8    HEIGHT      8      64.950      5.007     55.500     69.500
                        WEIGHT      7      95.429     21.874     53.500    118.200
-----------------------------------------------------------------------------------
```

```
                        Statistics With Two By Variables                          4
---------------------------------- SCHOOL=' ' TIME=. -------------------------------

         Variable    N       Mean     Std Dev    Minimum    Maximum
         ------------------------------------------------------------
         HEIGHT      0         .          .          .          .
         WEIGHT      0         .          .          .          .
         ------------------------------------------------------------

----------------------------------- SCHOOL=AJH TIME=Fall ---------------------------

         Variable    N       Mean     Std Dev    Minimum    Maximum
         ------------------------------------------------------------
         HEIGHT     11      64.218      3.760     57.500     69.000
         WEIGHT     11     101.091     14.554     77.000    122.500
         ------------------------------------------------------------

---------------------------------- SCHOOL=AJH TIME=Spring --------------------------

         Variable    N       Mean     Std Dev    Minimum    Maximum
         ------------------------------------------------------------
         HEIGHT     10      67.440      4.103     59.100     71.000
         WEIGHT     10     104.280     14.886     82.900    130.500
         ------------------------------------------------------------

----------------------------------- SCHOOL=BJH TIME=Fall ---------------------------

         Variable    N       Mean     Std Dev    Minimum    Maximum
         ------------------------------------------------------------
         HEIGHT      8      61.375      5.651     51.300     66.500
         WEIGHT      8      96.625     23.584     50.500    128.000
         ------------------------------------------------------------

---------------------------------- SCHOOL=BJH TIME=Spring --------------------------

         Variable    N       Mean     Std Dev    Minimum    Maximum
         ------------------------------------------------------------
         HEIGHT      8      64.950      5.007     55.500     69.500
         WEIGHT      7      95.429     21.874     53.500    118.200
         ------------------------------------------------------------
```

```
                                  New Data Set                                    5

OBS   SCHOOL   TIME   _TYPE_   _FREQ_    HMEAN     WMEAN      HSE       WSE
 1                       0        1        .          .        .          .
 2     AJH     Fall      0       11     64.2182   101.091   1.13368    4.38807
 3     AJH     Spring    0       10     67.4400   104.280   1.29736    4.70725
 4     BJH     Fall      0        8     61.3750    96.625   1.99810    8.33814
 5     BJH     Spring    0        8     64.9500    95.429   1.77029    8.26754
```

PROC MEANS is used with the CLASS, VAR, BY, and OUTPUT statements to illustrate the procedure's capabilities. The final page of the output displays the summarized data.

Example 2:   Comparison of MEANS and SUMMARY Output

This example uses data from a swim team to illustrate PROC MEANS with the NOPRINT option and an OUTPUT statement. The PRINT option is used with PROC SUMMARY. The statistical keyword used in both instances is MIN, and the minimum swim times for the four strokes are output.

```
data relay;
   input name $ sex $ back breast fly free;
   cards;
Sue      F 35.1 36.7 28.3 36.1
Karen    F 34.6 32.6 26.9 26.2
Jan      F 31.3 33.9 27.1 31.2
Andrea   F 28.6 34.1 29.1 30.3
Carol    F 32.9 32.2 26.6 24.0
Ellen    F 27.8 32.5 27.8 27.0
Jim      M 26.3 27.6 23.5 22.4
Mike     M 29.0 24.0 27.9 25.4
Sam      M 27.2 33.8 25.2 24.1
Clayton  M 27.0 29.2 23.0 21.9
;
run;

proc means data=relay noprint;
   var back breast fly free;
   class sex;
   output out=newmeans min=;
run;

proc print data=newmeans;
   title 'Using PROC PRINT with PROC MEANS';
run;

proc summary data=relay print min;
   var back breast fly free;
   class sex;
   output out=newsumm min=;
   title 'Using  PROC SUMMARY with the PRINT option';
run;

proc print data=newsumm;
   title 'Using PROC PRINT with PROC SUMMARY';
run;
```

Output 21.6   Output from PROC MEANS and PROC SUMMARY

```
                      Using PROC PRINT with PROC MEANS                            1

         OBS   SEX   _TYPE_   _FREQ_   BACK    BREAST    FLY    FREE

          1             0       10     26.3     24.0    23.0    21.9
          2     F       1        6     27.8     32.2    26.6    24.0
          3     M       1        4     26.3     24.0    23.0    21.9
```

```
                    Using  PROC SUMMARY with the PRINT option                          2

                    SEX    N Obs  Variable      Minimum
                    -------------------------------------------
                    F        6    BACK        27.8000000
                                  BREAST      32.2000000
                                  FLY         26.6000000
                                  FREE        24.0000000

                    M        4    BACK        26.3000000
                                  BREAST      24.0000000
                                  FLY         23.0000000
                                  FREE        21.9000000
                    -------------------------------------------
```

```
                    Using PROC PRINT with PROC SUMMARY                                 3

           OBS    SEX    _TYPE_    _FREQ_    BACK    BREAST    FLY    FREE
            1             0         10      26.3    24.0     23.0   21.9
            2      F      1          6      27.8    32.2     26.6   24.0
            3      M      1          4      26.3    24.0     23.0   21.9
```

PROC SUMMARY is used with the PRINT option to produce printed output.
The OUTPUT statement, used with both the MEANS and SUMMARY procedures,
produces identical output.

The OPTIONS Procedure

ABSTRACT

The OPTIONS procedure lists the current values of all SAS system options.

INTRODUCTION

SAS system options are used by the SAS System to control processing of SAS data sets, format and content of output, and so on. The values assigned to SAS system options are specified in the SAS command, in a configuration or autoexec file, in an OPTIONS statement, or through the display manager OPTIONS window. Values for system options are effective throughout a SAS program or session, not just for one step or data set. Refer to Chapter 16, "SAS System Options," in *SAS Language: Reference, Version 6, First Edition* for more details on SAS system options.

If you want to check the current setting of any system option, you can use the OPTIONS procedure to produce a listing of all the SAS system options and their values. The OPTIONS procedure is especially useful if you are executing an interactive line-mode SAS session or a noninteractive SAS program. If you are running a display manager session, you can check most system option settings with the OPTIONS window, but host-dependent options are displayed only by PROC OPTIONS. See Chapter 7, "SAS Display Manager System," in *SAS Language: Reference* for a description of the OPTIONS window.

SPECIFICATIONS

The only statement used with the OPTIONS procedure is the PROC OPTIONS statement.

PROC OPTIONS Statement

PROC OPTIONS <SHORT | LONG>;

The following option can be used in the PROC OPTIONS statement:

SHORT | LONG
> specifies the format in which you want the options printed. If you specify SHORT, the system produces a compressed listing of the system options. If you specify LONG or omit the option, each option is listed on a separate line and is followed by an explanation. Refer to **EXAMPLES** below for an illustration of each form.

DETAILS

Printed Output

The OPTIONS procedure produces a list of all SAS system options and their current settings. Note that the form of the options in the output corresponds to the form used in the OPTIONS statement, not the form in which they are displayed in the OPTIONS window. Thus, options that take character or numeric strings as arguments are listed with the equal sign. Positive/negative options are listed as *option* or NO*option*.

The OPTIONS procedure lists three types of SAS system options:

SESSION
> can be changed during the SAS job or session. Options included in this category are available on all operating systems.

CONFIGURATION
> must be specified at invocation. These options can be included in the SAS command line, or they can be specified in a configuration file. They cannot be changed in the middle of a SAS session or job. Options included in this category are available on all operating systems.

HOST
> are specific to the environment in which the SAS System is running.

If you execute the OPTIONS procedure from display manager, the options list is written to the LOG window, not the OUTPUT window. If you execute the OPTIONS procedure in a batch program, the listing is written to the log file, not the procedure output file.

EXAMPLES

Example 1:   Full Options Listing

This example shows the default output from PROC OPTIONS. In addition to the output illustrated here, PROC OPTIONS produces additional output specific to the environment in which you are running the SAS System. Refer to the SAS documentation for your host system for more information on additional output from PROC OPTIONS and for descriptions of host-specific options.

Note: The values of the system options shown in **Output 22.1** may vary on different host systems.

```
proc options;
run;
```

Output 22.1 Log Showing Long Form of Output Produced by PROC OPTIONS

```
6           proc options;
7           run;

    SAS (r) Software Release 6.06

SESSION OPTIONS:

  BUFNO=1          Number of buffers to use for each SAS data set
  BUFSIZE=0        Size of internal I/O buffer
  NOCAPS           Translate quoted strings and titles to upper case?
  CARDIMAGE        SAS source lines are processed as 80-byte cards
  CENTER           Center SAS output?
  NOCHARCODE       Represent special symbols with alternate characters?
  CLEANUP          Try to recover from an out-of-resource condition ?
  COMPRESS=NO      Compress observations in created datasets ?
  NODATE           Date printed in title?
  NODBCS           Support Japanese, Chinese, Korean and other languages that use double-byte character sets?
  DBCSLANG=        Double byte character set language
  DBCSTYPE=        Double byte character set collating sequence
  DEVICE=          Graphics device name
  DSNFERR          Treat data set not found as an error or set ds to _NULL_?
  NOERRORABEND     Abend on error conditions ?
  ERRORS=20        Maximum number of observations with error messages
  FIRSTOBS=1       First observation of each data set to be processed
  FMTERR           Treat missing format or informat as an error?
  FORMCHAR=|----|+|---+=|-/\<>*
                   Specifies the formatting characters for the print device
  FORMDLIM=        Delimiter character for page separation
  FORMS=DEFAULT    Default form for PRINT command
  GWINDOW          Graphics output put in a DMS window ?
  NOIMPLMAC        SAS statements scanned for implicit invocation of a 'STMT' macro?
  INVALIDDATA=     Missing value for invalid data
  LABEL            Allow procedures to use variable labels?
  LINESIZE=132     Line size for printed output
  MAPS=MAPS        Libref of map datasets
  MAUTOSOURCE      Allow SAS macro automatic call from source library?
  MERROR           Treat apparent undefined macro references as an error?
  MISSING=.        Character printed to represent numeric missing values
  NOMLOGIC         Trace macro execution?
  NOMPRINT         Print macro facility results in a synthetic compressed form?
  NOMRECALL        Attempt to look up autocall macros which were not found previously?
  MSGLEVEL=N       Print informatory messages ? Valid values are I and N
  NOTES            Print SAS notes on log?
  NUMBER           Print page number on each page of SAS output?
  OBS=MAX          Number of last observation to be processed
  OVP              Allow SAS printed output lines to be overprinted?
  PAGENO=1         Resets the current page number on the print file
  PAGESIZE=60      Number of lines printed per page of output
  PARM=            Parm for external programs
  PARMCARDS=FT15F001
                   Logical name for PARMCARDS
  PROBSIG=0        Number of significant figures guaranteed when printing P-values
  REMOTE=          Target access method for Micro-to-Host link
  REPLACE          Allow replacement of permanent SAS data sets?
  REUSE=NO         Reuse Space when adding records to a compressed SAS Data Set ?
  S=0              Source statement length
  S2=0             %INCLUDE statement length
  SASAUTOS=SASAUTOS Filename of automatic call library for source macros
  SEQ=8            Number of numeric digits in sequence numbers
  SERROR           Consider undefined macro variable references an error ?
  SOURCE           List SAS source statements on log?
  NOSOURCE2        List included SAS source statements on log?
  SPOOL            Spool SAS statements entered at terminal to utility file ?
  NOSYMBOLGEN      Print symbolic replacement text?
  SYSPARM=         Value return by the SYSPARM() function
  TAPECLOSE=REREAD Close disposition (volume positioning) for tape data libraries
  USER=            Default libname for all one-level SAS data set names
  VNFERR           Treat variable not found on _NULL_ data set as error ?
  WORKTERM         Erase WORK library at SAS termination time
  YEARCUTOFF=1900  Cutoff year for DATE7. informat
  _LAST_=_NULL_    Last data set created


CONFIGURATION OPTIONS:

  BATCH            Use batch mode default system options
  CATCACHE=        Requested number of cached SAS catalogs
  NODMS            Invoke the Display Manager?
  NODMR            Invoke the Display Manager on remote host?
  NOECHOAUTO       Echo AUTOEXEC input to log ?
  ENGINE=          Default access method for SAS libraries
  FS               Procedures to operate in full screen mode?
```

(continued on next page)

```
(continued from previous page)

GRAPH              SAS/GRAPH supervisor required ?
INITSTMT=          Initial statement(s) executed before SYSIN
MACRO              Perform macro processing?
NEWS=(system-specific pathname)
                   Specifies where news come from
SASHELP=(system-specific pathname)
                   Libref of SAS system catalog library
SASMSG=(system-specific pathname)
                   Filename for message library
SASUSER=(system-specific pathname)
                   Libname for SAS data library containing user profile catalog
NOSETINIT          Update site validation data via proc setinit or setinit window ?
SITEINFO=(system-specific pathname)
                   Filename of site information
NOTERMINAL         Is a terminal available ?
WORK=(system-specific pathname)
                   Logical file name for WORK library
WORKINIT           Erase WORK library at SAS invocation ?
```

Example 2:   Short Form of Options Listing

This example shows the output from PROC OPTIONS when you specify the
SHORT option. Note: The values of the system options shown in **Output 22.2**
may vary on different host systems.

```
proc options short;
run;
```

Output 22.2   Log Showing Short Form of Output Produced by PROC
OPTIONS

```
7         proc options short;
8         run;

    SAS (r) Software Release 6.06

SESSION OPTIONS:

 BUFNO=1 BUFSIZE=0 NOCAPS CARDIMAGE CENTER NOCHARCODE CLEANUP COMPRESS=NO NODATE NODBCS DBCSLANG= DBCSTYPE= DEVICE= DSNFERR
 NOERRORABEND ERRORS=20 FIRSTOBS=1 FMTERR FORMCHAR=|----|+|---+=|-/\<>* FORMDLIM= FORMS=DEFAULT GWINDOW NOIMPLMAC INVALIDDATA= LABEL
 LINESIZE=132 MAPS=MAPS MAUTOSOURCE MERROR MISSING=. NOMLOGIC NOMPRINT NOMRECALL MSGLEVEL=N NOTES NUMBER OBS=MAX OVP PAGENO=1
 PAGESIZE=60 PARM= PARMCARDS=FT15F001 PROBSIG=0 REMOTE= REPLACE REUSE=NO S=0 S2=0 SASAUTOS=SASAUTOS SEQ=8 SERROR SOURCE NOSOURCE2
 SPOOL NOSYMBOLGEN SYSPARM= TAPECLOSE=REREAD USER= VNFERR WORKTERM YEARCUTOFF=1900 _LAST_=_NULL_

CONFIGURATION OPTIONS:

 BATCH CATCACHE= NODMS NODMR NOECHOAUTO ENGINE= FS GRAPH INITSTMT= MACRO NEWS=(system-specific pathname) SASHELP=(system-specific
 pathname) SASMSG=(system-specific pathname) SASUSER=(system-specific pathname) NOSETINIT SITEINFO=(system-specific pathname)
 NOTERMINAL WORK=(system-specific pathname) WORKINIT
```

Chapter 23
The PDS Procedure

ABSTRACT

The PDS procedure lists, deletes, and renames the members of a partitioned data set. This procedure is described in system-dependent documentation.

Chapter 24

The PDSCOPY Procedure

ABSTRACT

The PDSCOPY procedure copies partitioned data sets from disk to tape, disk to disk, tape to tape, or tape to disk. This procedure is described in system-dependent documentation.

The PLOT Procedure

ABSTRACT

The PLOT procedure graphs one variable against another, producing a printer plot. The coordinates of each point on the plot correspond to the two variables' values in one or more observations of the input data set.

INTRODUCTION

The PLOT procedure plots the values of two variables for each observation in an input SAS data set. All you need to do to produce a plot is to tell the procedure which variables to plot. The examples in this section all use data about the high and low values of the Dow Jones Industrial Average between 1954 and 1987.

For example, the following statements produce the simple plot shown in
Output 25.1:

```
libname stocks 'SAS-data-library';

data stocks.highlow;
   input year @7 hdate date7. high @24 ldate date7. low;
   format hdate ldate date7.;
   cards;
1954   31DEC54   404.39   11JAN54   279.87
1955   30DEC55   488.40   17JAN55   388.20
1956   06APR56   521.05   23JAN56   462.35
1957   12JUL57   520.77   22OCT57   419.79
1958   31DEC58   583.65   25FEB58   436.89
1959   31DEC59   679.36   09FEB59   574.46
1960   05JAN60   685.47   25OCT60   568.05
1961   13DEC61   734.91   03JAN61   610.25
1962   03JAN62   726.01   26JUN62   535.76
1963   18DEC63   767.21   02JAN63   646.79
1964   18NOV64   891.71   02JAN64   768.08
1965   31DEC65   969.26   28JUN65   840.59
1966   09FEB66   995.15   07OCT66   744.32
1967   25SEP67   943.08   03JAN67   786.41
1968   03DEC68   985.21   21MAR68   825.13
1969   14MAY69   968.85   17DEC69   769.93
1970   29DEC70   842.00   06MAY70   631.16
1971   28APR71   950.82   23NOV71   797.97
1972   11DEC72  1036.27   26JAN72   889.15
1973   11JAN73  1051.70   05DEC73   788.31
1974   13MAR74   891.66   06DEC74   577.60
1975   15JUL75   881.81   02JAN75   632.04
1976   21SEP76  1014.79   02JAN76   858.71
1977   03JAN77   999.75   02NOV77   800.85
1978   08SEP78   907.74   28FEB78   742.12
1979   05OCT79   897.61   07NOV79   796.67
1980   20NOV80  1000.17   21APR80   759.13
1981   27APR81  1024.05   25SEP81   824.01
1982   27DEC82  1070.55   12AUG82   776.92
1983   29NOV83  1287.20   03JAN83  1027.04
1984   06JAN84  1286.64   24JUL84  1086.57
1985   16DEC85  1553.10   04JAN85  1184.96
1986   02DEC86  1955.57   22JAN86  1502.29
1987   25AUG87  2722.42   19OCT87  1738.74
;
run;

proc plot data=stocks.highlow;
   plot high*year;
run;
```

Output 25.1 Producing a Simple Plot of the High Value of the Dow Jones Industrial Average from 1954 to 1987

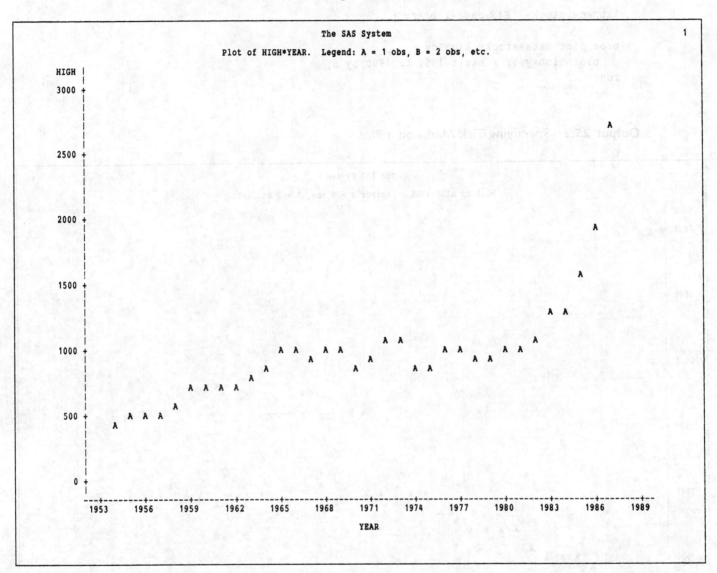

Note that PROC PLOT automatically scales the values of X and Y on the plot.

Or, you can specify the tick marks (the lines on the axis marking values). For example, the following statements produce the output shown in **Output 25.2**:

```
libname stocks 'SAS-data-library';

proc plot data=stocks.highlow;
   plot high*year / haxis=1950 to 1990 by 5;
run;
```

Output 25.2   Specifying Tick Marks on a Plot

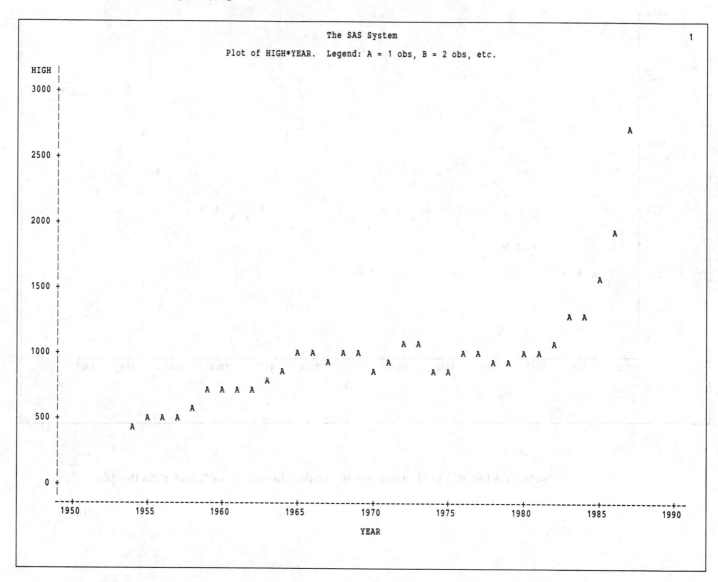

In this example, PROC PLOT uses the plotting symbol A to indicate that one observation occurs at each point. If two observations coincide, PROC PLOT uses the plotting symbol B; if three coincide, the symbol C, and so forth. The plotting symbol Z represents 26 or more coinciding observations.

The next example illustrates how you can specify another symbol, like the asterisk (*), as the plotting symbol. The following statements produce **Output 25.3**:

```
libname stocks 'SAS-data-library';

proc plot data=stocks.highlow;
   plot high*year='*' / haxis=1950 to 1990 by 5;
run;
```

Output 25.3   Specifying Other Plotting Symbols

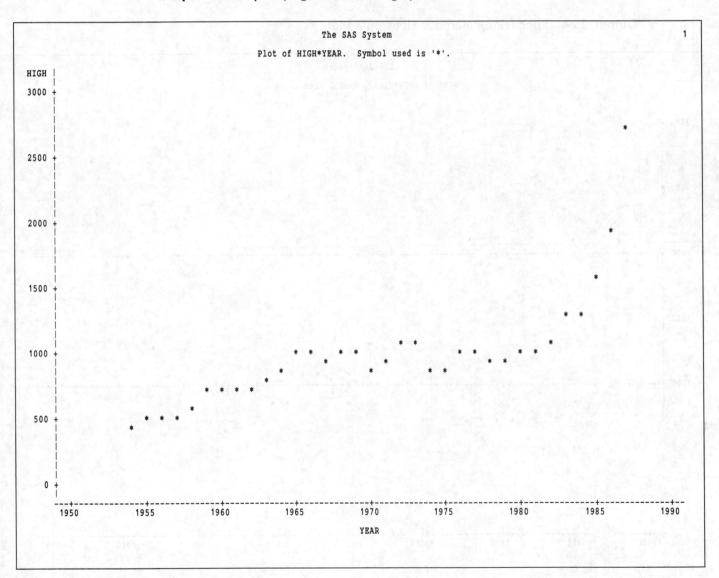

Another way to enhance the information contained in the plot is to use reference lines at specific values. For example, to draw reference lines perpendicular to the vertical axis at values of 1000 and 2000, use these statements, which produce **Output 25.4**:

```
libname stocks 'SAS-data-library';

proc plot data=stocks.highlow;
   plot high*year='*' / haxis=1950 to 1990 by 5
                        vref=1000 2000;
run;
```

Output 25.4   Specifying Reference Lines on a Plot

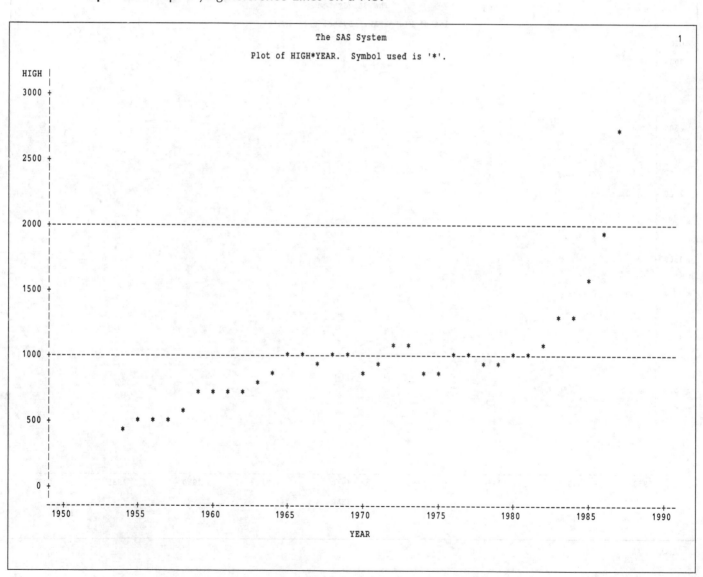

Output 25.5 shows that you can also superimpose two or more plots on the same axes. The BOX option causes PROC PLOT to draw a box all the way around the plot.

```
libname stocks 'SAS-data-library';

proc plot data=stocks.highlow;
   plot high*year='*' low*year='o' / overlay box;
run;
```

Output 25.5   Superimposing Two or More Plots on the Same Axes

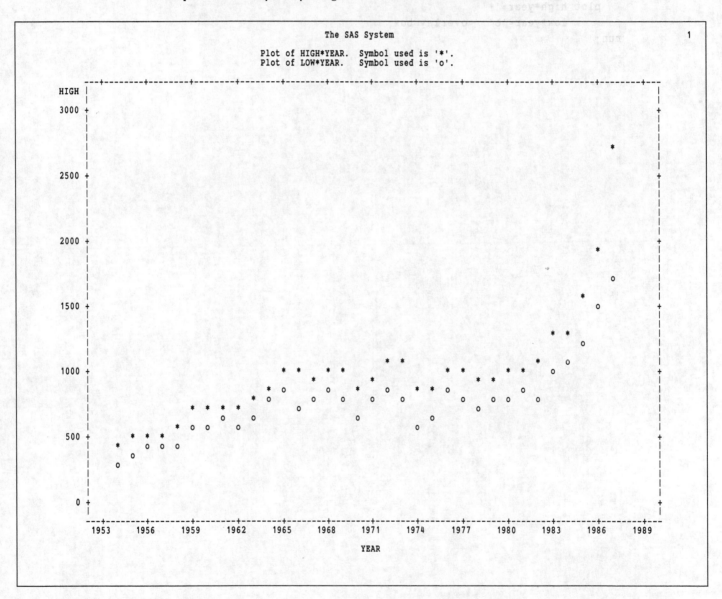

You can also print multiple plots per page with PROC PLOT. For example, **Output 25.6** shows all five of the preceding plots on the same page. It was produced with the following statements:

```
libname stocks 'SAS-data-library';

proc plot data=stocks.highlow hpercent=50 vpercent=33;
   title 'Multiple Plots per Page';
   plot high*year;
   plot high*year      / haxis=1950 to 1990 by 5;
   plot high*year='*' / haxis=1950 to 1990 by 5;
   plot high*year='*' / haxis=1950 to 1990 by 5
                         vref=1000 2000;
   plot high*year='*'
        low*year='o' / overlay box;
run;
```

Output 25.6 Multiple Plots per Page

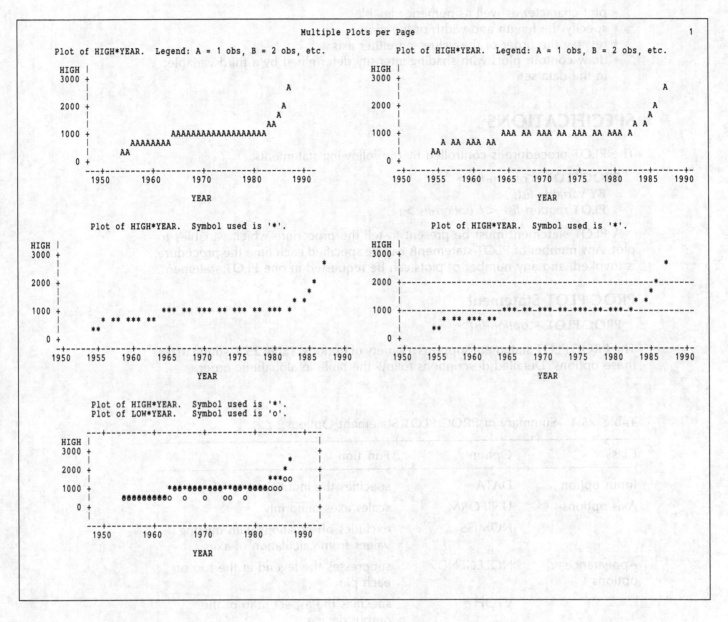

You can also use the PLOT procedure to

- plot character as well as numeric variables
- specify the length and width of the plot
- reverse the order of the values on either axis
- draw contour plots with shading intensity determined by a third variable in the data set.

SPECIFICATIONS

The PLOT procedure is controlled by the following statements:

PROC PLOT <*option-list*>;
   BY *variable-list*;
   PLOT *request-list* </ *option-list*>;

A PLOT statement must be present to tell the procedure which variables to plot. Any number of PLOT statements can be specified each time the procedure is invoked, and any number of plots can be requested in one PLOT statement.

PROC PLOT Statement

   PROC PLOT <*option-list*>;

The PROC PLOT statement supports a variety of options. **Table 25.1** summarizes these options. Detailed descriptions follow the table in alphabetic order.

Table 25.1 Summary of PROC PLOT Statement Options

Class	Option	Function
Input option	DATA=	specifies the input data set
Axis options	UNIFORM	scales axes uniformly
	NOMISS	excludes observations with missing values from calculation of axes
Appearance options	NOLEGEND	suppresses the legend at the top of each plot
	VTOH=	specifies the aspect ratio of the output device
	FORMCHAR=	specifies the characters to use to construct the borders of the plot
Sizing options	HPERCENT=	specifies the percentage of the horizontal page to use for each plot
	VPERCENT=	specifies the percentage of the vertical page to use for each plot

DATA=*SAS-data-set*
   names the input SAS data set to use. If you do not specify the DATA= option, PROC PLOT uses the most recently created SAS data set.

FORMCHAR <(*index-list*)>='*formchar-string*'
: specifies the characters to use to construct the borders of the plot. The *formchar-string* is a string up to 11 characters long defining the 2 bar characters, vertical and horizontal, and the 9 corner characters: upper left, upper middle, upper right, middle left, middle middle (cross), middle right, lower left, lower middle, and lower right. Of these, PROC PLOT uses only the horizontal and vertical bars, the four corners, and the cross. If the FORMCHAR= option in the PROC PLOT statement is not given, the procedure uses the *formchar-string* supplied with the FORMCHAR= system option. The default for the system option is FORMCHAR=' | ---- | + | ---'.

You can use any character string or a string of hexadecimal constants to customize the plot's appearance. Use an *index-list* to specify which default form character each supplied character replaces, or replace the entire default string by specifying the full 11-character replacement string with no index list. For example, change the four corners to asterisks by using

```
formchar(3 5 9 11)='****'
```

Specifying eleven blanks, as follows, produces plots with no borders:

```
formchar='           '
```

PROC PLOT uses only the following FORMCHAR characters:

Character	Position	Default
vertical bar	1	|
horizontal bar	2	-
upper left corner	3	-
upper right corner	5	-
cross (for tick marks)	7	+
lower left corner	9	-
lower right corner	11	-

HPERCENT=*percent-list*
HPCT=*percent-list*
: specifies the percentage of the horizontal page to use for each plot. By default, the PLOT procedure uses one page for each plot. After reaching the end of the *percent-list*, PROC PLOT cycles back to the beginning of the list. When you use the HPERCENT= option, the procedure tries to fit as many plots as possible on a page. For example, this option specification prints three plots per page horizontally:

```
hpercent=33
```

Each plot is one-third of a page wide.

The next option specification also prints three plots per page, but the first one is twice as big as the other two:

```
hpercent=50 25 25
```

By specifying a zero in the list, you can force PROC PLOT to go to a new page even though it could fit the next plot on the same page.

For example, this option specification produces plots that are only one-third of a page wide, but each plot is on a separate page:

```
hpercent=33 0
```

You can use the HPERCENT= option to print very wide plots. For example, this example produces plots three pages wide:

```
hpercent=300
```

At the beginning of every BY group and after each RUN statement, PROC PLOT returns to the beginning of the *percent-list* and starts printing a new page.

NOLEGEND
suppresses the legend at the top of each plot. The legend lists the names of the variables being plotted and the plotting symbols used in the plot.

NOMISS
excludes observations for which either variable is missing from the calculation of the axes. Normally, PROC PLOT draws an axis based on all the values of the variable being plotted, including points for which the other variable is missing. The HAXIS= option overrides the effect of the NOMISS option on the horizontal axis; the VAXIS= option overrides the effect on the vertical axis.

UNIFORM
uniformly scales axes across BY groups. Uniform scaling allows you to directly compare the plots for different values of the BY variables.

VPERCENT=*percent-list*
VPCT=*percent-list*
specifies the percentage of the vertical page to use for each plot, just as HPERCENT= specifies the horizontal percentage. If you use a percentage greater than 100, the PLOT procedure prints sections of the plot on successive pages.

VTOH=*character-height/character-width*
specifies the aspect ratio (vertical to horizontal) of the characters on the output device. If you use the VTOH= option, PROC PLOT spaces tick marks so that the distance between horizontal tick marks is nearly equal to the distance between vertical tick marks. The VTOH= option has no effect if you use the HSPACE= and the VSPACE= options in the PLOT statement.

BY Statement

BY *variable-list*;

A BY statement can be used with PROC PLOT to obtain separate plots on observations in groups defined by the BY variables.

When a BY statement appears, the procedure expects the input data set to be sorted in order of the BY variables or to have an appropriate index. If your input data set is not sorted in ascending order, you can do one of the following:

- Use the SORT procedure with a similar BY statement to sort the data.
- If appropriate, use the BY statement option NOTSORTED or DESCENDING.
- Create an index on the BY variables you want to use. For more information on creating indexes and using the BY statement with indexed data sets, see Chapter 17, "The DATASETS Procedure."

PROC PLOT produces a new page each time the value of the BY variable changes.

PLOT Statement

PLOT *request-list* </ *option-list*>;

The PLOT statement requests the plots to be produced by PROC PLOT. You must use at least one PLOT statement. You can include many PLOT statements, and you can specify many plot requests in one PLOT statement.

Each element of the *request-list* in the PLOT statement specifies the variables (vertical and horizontal) to plot and the plotting symbol to use to mark the points on the plot. The request can take the following forms:

vertical*horizontal

> names the variable to plot on the vertical axis and the variable to plot on the horizontal axis.
>
> For example, the following statements request a plot of Y by X:

```
proc plot;
   plot y*x;
run;
```

> Y appears on the vertical axis, X on the horizontal axis.
>
> This form of the plot request uses the default method of choosing a plotting symbol to mark plot points. When a point on the plot represents the values of one observation in the data set, PROC PLOT puts the character A at that point. When a point represents the values of two observations, the character B appears. When a point represents values of three observations, the character C appears, and so on through the alphabet. The character Z is used for the occurrence of 26 or more observations at the same printing position.

vertical*horizontal='character'

> names the variables to plot on the vertical and horizontal axes and specifies a plotting symbol to mark each point on the plot. A single character is used to represent values from one or more observations.
>
> For example, the following statements request a plot of Y by X, with each point on the plot represented by a plus sign (+):

```
proc plot;
   plot y*x='+';
run;
```

vertical*horizontal=variable

> names the variables to plot on the vertical and horizontal axes and specifies a variable whose values are to mark each point on the plot. The variable can be either numeric or character. The first (left-most) nonblank character in the formatted value of the variable is used as the plotting symbol. When more than one observation maps to the same plotting position, the value from the first observation marks the point. For example, in the following statements SEX is a character variable with values of **FEMALE** and **MALE**: the values F and M mark each observation on the plot.

```
proc plot;
   plot height*weight=sex;
run;
```

Note: The plotting symbol is the first nonblank character of each value even if more than one value starts with the same letter.

To request two or more plots, write one request after another:

```
proc plot;
   plot a*b r*s;
run;
```

If you want to plot all the combinations of one set of variables with another, you can use a grouping specification. Enclose each set of variables in parentheses, joining them with an asterisk (*). For example, the following PLOT statements are equivalent:

```
plot (y x)*(a b);
```

```
plot y*a y*b x*a x*b;
```

You can also abbreviate a variable list to request a number of plots:

```
plot y*(a--z);
```

For more information on variable lists, refer to Chapter 4, "Rules of the SAS Language," in *SAS Language: Reference, Version 6, First Edition*.

If both the vertical and horizontal specifications request more than one variable and a variable appears in both lists, it will not be plotted against itself. For example, the following statement plots all combinations of the variables A, B, and C with B, C, and D, but it does not plot B*B and C*C:

```
plot (a b c)*(b c d);
```

To plot all unique combinations of a list of variables, simply omit the second list. Thus, the following two statements are equivalent:

```
plot (a b c);
```

```
plot a*b a*c b*c;
```

Table 25.2 summarizes the options you can use in the PLOT statement. A slash (/) separates these options from the plot requests. No slash is needed if no options are specified. Detailed descriptions of the options follow the table in alphabetic order.

Table 25.2   Summary of PLOT Statement Options

Class	Option	Function
Axis options	HAXIS=	specifies values for tick marks on the horizontal axis
	VAXIS=	specifies values for tick marks on the vertical axis
	HZERO	assigns a value of 0 to the first tick mark on the horizontal axis
	VZERO	assigns a value of 0 to the first tick mark on the vertical axis

(continued)

Table 25.2   Summary of PLOT Statement Options (*continued*)

Class	Option	Function
	HREVERSE	reverses the order of the values on the horizontal axis
	VREVERSE	reverses the order of the values on the vertical axis
	HEXPAND	expands the horizontal axis to minimize the margins at the sides of the plot
	VEXPAND	expands the vertical axis to minimize the margins above and below the plot
	HSPACE=	specifies the number of print positions between tick marks on the horizontal axis
	VSPACE=	specifies the number of print positions between tick marks on the vertical axis
Reference line options	HREF=	draws lines on the plot perpendicular to the specified values on the horizontal axis
	VREF=	draws lines on the plot perpendicular to the specified values on the vertical axis
	HREFCHAR=	specifies the character to use to draw reference HREF= reference lines
	VREFCHAR=	specifies the character to use to draw reference VREF= reference lines
Appearance option	BOX	draws a border around the entire plot
Sizing options	HPOS=	specifies the number of print positions on the horizontal axis
	VPOS=	specifies the number of print positions on the vertical axis
Overlaying option	OVERLAY	overlays all plots specified in the PLOT statement on one set of axes
Contour options	CONTOUR	draws a contour plot using plotting symbols with varying degrees of shading
	S<*level*>=	specifies the plotting symbol to use for specified contour level
	SLIST=	specifies plotting symbols for multiple contour levels

BOX

    draws a border around the entire plot, rather than just on the left side and bottom.

CONTOUR<=*number-of-levels*>

    draws a contour plot using plotting symbols with varying degrees of shading where *number-of-levels* is the number of levels for dividing the range of the response variable. The plot request must be of the form *vertical*horizontal=variable* where *variable* is a numeric variable in the data set. The intensity of shading is determined by the values of this variable. The value of *number-of-levels* can range from 1 to 10. If you specify simply CONTOUR, the default value is 10. For example, these statements request a plot whose points vary in darkness depending on the value of Z:

```
proc plot;
   plot a*b=z / contour=10;
```

PROC PLOT uses 10 darkness levels, as specified by the CONTOUR option.

    Overprinting, if it is allowed, is used to produce the shading. Otherwise, single characters varying in darkness are used. The CONTOUR option is most effective when the plot is dense.

HAXIS=*tick-value-list*

    specifies the tick-mark values to space equally along the horizontal axis. When the variable is numeric, you must give HAXIS= values in either ascending or descending order.

    The following statements ask for a plot of Y by X, with tick marks at 10, 15, 20, and so on up to 100 on the horizontal axis:

```
proc plot;
   plot y*x / haxis=10 to 100 by 5;
run;
```

Numeric values need not be uniformly distributed; a specification of the following form is valid and produces a logarithmic plot:

```
haxis=10 100 1000 10000
```

If PROC PLOT cannot determine the function implied by the axis specification, it uses simple linear interpolation between the points.

    To determine whether PLOT correctly interpolates a function you wish to use, you can generate data with the DATA step that determines the function and see whether it appears linear when plotted. For example, the following statements produce a linear plot:

```
data test;
   do y=1 to 3 by .1;
      x=10**y;
      output;
   end;
run;

proc plot data=test;
   plot y*x / haxis=10 100 1000 10000;
run;
```

You can list the values of character variables in any order.

In addition, the following HAXIS= specifications are valid:

```
haxis='01JAN85'd to '01JAN86'd by month
```

or

```
haxis='01JAN85'd to '01JAN86'd by qtr
```

In these examples, the FROM and TO values can be any of the valid SAS date, time, or datetime values described for the SAS functions INTCK and INTNX. (See Chapter 11, "SAS Functions," in *SAS Language: Reference*.) The BY value can be any of the valid values listed for the *interval* argument in the SAS functions INTCK and INTNX. You must use a FORMAT statement to print the tick-mark values in an understandable form.

HEXPAND

expands the horizontal axis to minimize the margins at the sides of the plot and to maximize the distance between tick marks, if possible.

Normally, PROC PLOT looks at the minimum difference between each pair of the five lowest ordered values of each variable (the *delta*) and ensures that there is no more than one of these intervals per print position on the final scaled axis, if possible. If there is not enough room to do this, and if PROC PLOT guesses that the data were artificially generated, it puts a fixed number of deltas in each print position. Otherwise it ignores the value.

HPOS=*axis-length*

specifies the number of print positions on the horizontal axis. The maximum value of *axis-length* that allows a plot to fit on one page is three positions less than the value of the LINESIZE= system option because you must allow room for the procedure to print information next to the vertical axis. The exact maximum depends on the number of characters in the vertical variable's values. If *axis-length* is too large to fit on a line, PROC PLOT ignores the option.

HREF=*value-list*

draws lines on the plot perpendicular to the specified values on the horizontal axis. PROC PLOT includes the values you specify with the HREF= option on the horizontal axis unless you specify otherwise with the HAXIS= option.

For example, the following statements request a plot of Y by X with a line perpendicular to the value 5 on the horizontal axis:

```
proc plot,
   plot y*x / href=5;
```

The following statements draw a plot with reference lines intersecting the horizontal axis at 10, 20, 30, and so on up to 100:

```
proc plot;
   plot y*x / href=10 to 100 by 10;
```

HREFCHAR=*'character'*

specifies the character to use to draw the HREF= reference lines. If you do not specify a character with the HREFCHAR= option, PROC PLOT uses the vertical bar character (|) by default. (See the FORMCHAR= option earlier in **PROC PLOT Statement**.)

HREVERSE

reverses the order of the values on the horizontal axis.

HSPACE=*number-of-print-positions*

specifies the number of print positions between tick marks on the horizontal axis.

HZERO

assigns a value of zero to the first tick mark on the horizontal axis. PROC PLOT ignores the HZERO option if the horizontal variable has negative values or if the HAXIS= option specifies a range that does not begin with zero.

OVERLAY

overlays all plots specified in the PLOT statement on one set of axes. The variables (or labels of variables if specified in the PROC step) from the first plot label the axes. Unless you use the HAXIS= or the VAXIS= option, PROC PLOT automatically scales the axes in the way that best fits all the variables.

When the SAS system option OVP is in effect and overprinting is allowed, the plots are superimposed; otherwise, when NOOVP is in effect, PROC PLOT uses the plotting symbol from the first plot to represent points appearing in more than one plot. In such a case, the output includes a message telling you how many observations are hidden.

S<*contour-level*>='*character-list*'

specifies the plotting symbol to use for a single contour level. You can use this option repeatedly. When PROC PLOT produces contour plots, it automatically chooses the symbols to use for each level of intensity. You can use the S option to override these symbols and specify your own. The *contour-level* is a whole number between 1 and the highest contour level (determined by the CONTOUR option). You can include up to three characters in *character-list*. If overprinting is not allowed, PROC PLOT uses only the first character.

For example, to specify three levels of shading for the Z variable, use the following statements:

```
proc plot;
   plot y*x=z / contour=3
                s1='A' s2='+' s3='X0A';
run;
```

You can also specify the plotting symbols as hexadecimal constants:

```
proc plot;
   plot y*x=z / contour=3
                s1='7A'x  s2='7F'x s3='A6'x;
run;
```

This feature was designed especially for printers where the hex constants can represent grey-scale fill characters.

See the SLIST= option for an alternate way to specify plotting symbols for a contour plot.

SLIST='*character-list-1*' <...'*character-list-n*'>

specifies plotting symbols for multiple contour levels. Each *character-list* specifies the plotting symbol for one contour level: the first *character-list* for the first level, the second *character-list* for the second level, and so on.

For example, the following statements are equivalent:

```
plot y*x=z / contour=5   s1='.' s2=':' s3='!' s4='=' s5='+0';

plot y*x=z / contour=5   slist='.' ':' '!' '=' '+0';
```

If you do not specify a plotting symbol for each contour level, PROC PLOT uses the default symbols for the remaining levels. By default, PROC PLOT uses the equivalent of

```
slist='.' ',' '-' '=' '+' 'O' 'X' 'W' '*' '#'
```

This sequence is normally satisfactory for contour plots because the symbols appear as lightest (.) to darkest (#); however, you can change any of these symbols using the S= option. For example, some printers print the asterisk (*) as a very light symbol. If this is the case with your printer, you can substitute another, darker, symbol for the asterisk (the ninth symbol in the list) by specifying, for example, the following statement in the PROC PLOT statement:

```
s9='&'
```

VAXIS=*tick-value-list*
specifies the tick-mark values to space equally along the vertical axis. The VAXIS= option follows the same rules as the HAXIS= option, described earlier.

VEXPAND
expands the vertical axis to minimize the margins above and below the plot and to maximize the space between vertical tick marks, if possible. The behavior of the VEXPAND option is the same as that of the HEXPAND option, described earlier.

VPOS=*axis-length*
specifies the number of print positions on the vertical axis. The maximum value for *axis-length* that allows a plot to fit on one page is 8 lines less than the value of the PAGESIZE= system option because you must allow room for the procedure to print information under the horizontal axis. The exact maximum depends on the titles used, whether or not plots are overlayed, and whether or not CONTOUR is specified. If the value of *axis-length* specifies a plot that cannot fit on one page, the plot spans multiple pages.

VREF=*value-list*
draws lines on the plot perpendicular to the specified values on the vertical axis. The VREF= option behaves like the HREF= option, described earlier.

VREFCHAR=*'character'*
specifies the character to use to draw the VREF= reference lines. If you do not specify a character with the VREFCHAR= option, PROC PLOT uses the horizontal bar character (-) by default. (See the FORMCHAR= option earlier in **PROC PLOT Statement**.)

VREVERSE
reverses the order of the values on the vertical axis.

VSPACE=*number-of-lines*
specifies the number of print lines between tick marks on the vertical axis.

VZERO
assigns a value of zero to the first tick mark on the vertical axis. PROC PLOT ignores the VZERO option if the vertical variable has negative values or if the VAXIS= option specifies a range that does not begin with zero.

DETAILS

Missing Values

If values on either of the plotting variables are missing, PROC PLOT does not include the observation in the plot. However, in a plot of Y*X, values of X with corresponding missing values of Y are included in scaling the X axis, unless the NOMISS option is specified in the PROC PLOT statement.

Hidden Observations

By default, PROC PLOT uses different plotting symbols (A, B, C, and so on) to represent observations whose values coincide on a plot. However, if you specify your own plotting symbol or if you use the OVERLAY option, you may not be able to recognize coinciding values.

If you specify a plotting symbol, PROC PLOT uses the same symbol regardless of the number of observations whose values coincide. If you use the OVERLAY option and overprinting is not in effect, PROC PLOT uses the symbol from the first plot request. In both cases, the output includes a message telling you how many observations are hidden.

RUN Groups

The PLOT procedure is an interactive procedure. It conserves time and resources by remaining active after a RUN statement is executed. (Usually, the SAS System terminates a procedure after executing a RUN statement.) Once you start the procedure, you can continue to submit any valid statements without resubmitting the PROC PLOT statement. Thus, you can easily and quickly experiment with changing labels, values of tick marks, and so forth. Any options submitted in the PROC PLOT statement remain in effect until you submit another PLOT statement.

When you submit a RUN statement, the PLOT procedure executes all the statements submitted since the last PROC PLOT or RUN statement. Each group of statements is called a *RUN group*. With each RUN group, PROC PLOT begins a new page and begins with the first item in the VPERCENT= and HPERCENT= lists, if any.

When you are ready to terminate the procedure, submit a QUIT statement, a DATA statement, or a PROC statement. Like the RUN statement, each of these statements completes a RUN group. However, they also terminate the procedure. If you do not want to execute the statements in the RUN group, use the RUN CANCEL statement, which terminates the procedure immediately.

You can use the BY statement interactively. The BY statement remains in effect until you submit another BY statement or terminate the procedure.

Generating Data with Program Statements

When you generate data to be plotted, a good rule is to generate fewer observations than the number of positions on the horizontal axis. The PLOT procedure then uses the increment of the horizontal variable as the interval between tick marks.

Because the PLOT procedure prints one character for each observation, using SAS program statements to generate the data set for PROC PLOT can enhance the effectiveness of continuous plots (see **Example 3**) and contour plots (see **Example 5**).

For example, suppose that you want to generate data in order to plot the following equation, for x ranging from 0 to 100:

$$y = 2.54 + 3.83 * x \ .$$

You can submit these statements:

```
options linesize=80;

data generate;
   do x=0 to 100 by 2;
      y=2.54+3.83*x;
      output;
   end;
run;

proc plot data=generate;
   plot y*x;
run;
```

If the plot is printed with a LINESIZE= value of 80, about 75 positions are available on the horizontal axis for the X values. Thus, 2 is a good increment: 51 observations are generated, which is less than 75.

However, if the plot is printed with a LINESIZE= value of 132, an increment of 2 produces a plot with a space between each plotting symbol. For a smoother line, a better increment is 1, since 101 observations are generated.

Printed Output

Each plot uses one full page unless the plot's size is changed by the VPOS= and HPOS= options in the PLOT statement, the VPERCENT= or HPERCENT= options in the PROC PLOT statement, or the PAGESIZE= and LINESIZE= system options. Titles, legends, and variable labels are printed at the top of each page. Each axis is labeled with the variable name or the variable label, if one is specified. Normally, PROC PLOT begins a new plot on a new page. However, the VPERCENT= and HPERCENT= options enable you to print more than one plot on a page. (See the VPERCENT= and HPERCENT= options earlier in **PROC PLOT Statement**.)

The PLOT procedure always begins a new page after a RUN statement and at the beginning of a BY group.

EXAMPLES

Example 1: Plotting Observed Data

This example plots the two variables RATED and ACTUAL against each other. PROC PLOT uses an increment of 10 for tick marks on the vertical axis; tick marks on the horizontal axis have an increment of 4. Since two observations have a RATED value of 118 and an ACTUAL value of 121, PROC PLOT uses a B to represent the point corresponding to RATED=118 and ACTUAL=121. Other points are represented by A's. The following statements produce **Output 25.7**:

```
data speed;
   input rated actual;
   label rated='Rated Speed'  actual='Actual Speed';
   cards;
 75  85
110 112
 75  81
105 108
112 115
 75  77
 90  89
 70  73
118 121
103 100
118 121
;
run;

proc plot data=speed;
   plot rated*actual;
   title 'Rated Speed Versus Actual Speed';
run;
```

Output 25.7 Plotting Observed Data

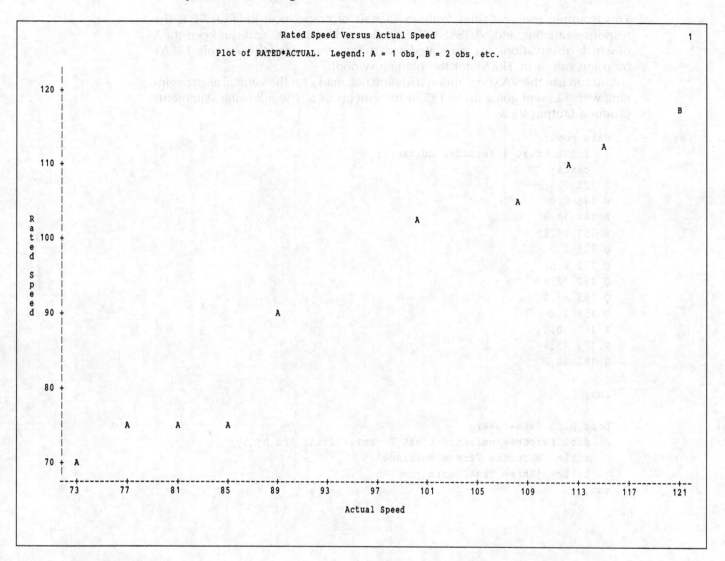

```
                        Rated Speed Versus Actual Speed                              1
                  Plot of RATED*ACTUAL.  Legend: A = 1 obs, B = 2 obs, etc.

         |
     120 +
         |
         |
         |                                                                      B
         |
     110 +                                                              A
         |                                                          A
R        |
a        |                                                  A
t    100 +
e        |
d        |
         |                                        A
S        |
p     90 +                            A
e        |
e        |
d        |
         |
      80 +
         |
         |
         |             A         A         A
         |
      70 + A
         ---+---------+---------+---------+---------+---------+---------+---------+---------+---------+---------+---------+---------+--
           73        77        81        85        89        93        97       101       105       109       113       117       121
                                                     Actual Speed
```

Example 2:   Using a Plot Character and Defining Tick Marks

This example uses variables from an analysis of covariance: RESPONSE is the response variable, and NUISANCE is a presumed covariate. You can keep track of which observations are associated with different values of the variable TREAT by using values of TREAT for the plotting symbols.

You can use the VAXIS= option to define tick marks for the vertical axis, beginning with 125 and going up to 185 by increments of 5. The following statements produce **Output 25.8**:

```
data covar;
   input treat $ response nuisance;
   cards;
P 125 3.1
P 135 9.0
P 144 14.9
P 153 20.2
Q 136 2.0
Q 152 8.5
Q 160 12.6
Q 165 17.1
R 154 3.2
R 164 10.5
R 173 15.4
R 183 20.7
;
run;

proc plot data=covar;
   plot response*nuisance=treat / vaxis=125 to 185 by 5;
   title 'Response Versus Nuisance';
   title2 'Three Treatments';
run;
```

Output 25.8   Using a Plot Character and Defining Tick Marks

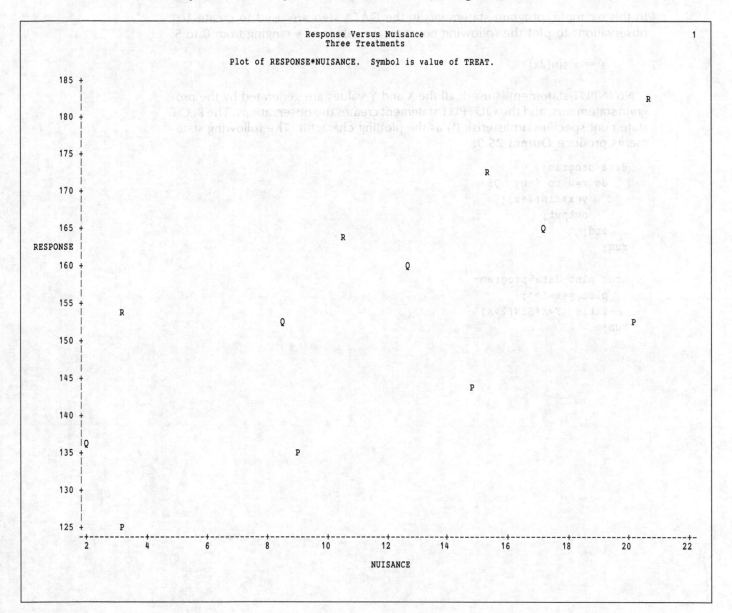

Example 3:   Plotting the Graph of an Equation

In this example, program statements in the DATA step are used to create 101 observations to plot the following equation for values of x ranging from 0 to 5:

$$y = x \sin(2x) \quad .$$

No INPUT statement is used; all the X and Y values are generated by the program statements, and the OUTPUT statement creates the observations. The PLOT statement specifies an asterisk (*) as the plotting character. The following statements produce **Output 25.9**:

```
data program;
   do x=0 to 5 by .05;
      y=x*sin(2*x);
      output;
   end;
run;

proc plot data=program;
   plot y*x='*';
   title 'Y=X*SIN(2*X)';
run;
```

Output 25.9   Plotting the Graph of an Equation

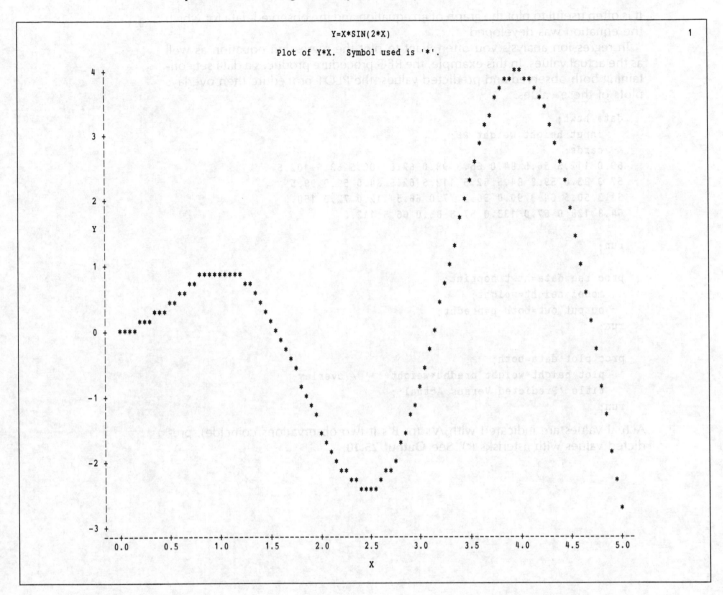

Example 4:   Plotting Predicted versus Actual Values

It is often useful to plot the graph of an equation and the observed data for which the equation was developed.

In regression analysis you often want to plot the regression equation as well as the actual values. In this example, the REG procedure produces a data set containing both observed and predicted values; the PLOT procedure then overlays plots of these values.

```
data htwt;
   input height weight aa;
   cards;
69.0 112.5 56.5 84.0 65.3 98.0 62.8 102.5 63.5 102.5
57.3 83.0 59.8 84.5 62.5 112.5 62.5 84.0 59.0 99.5
51.3 50.5 64.3 90.0 56.3 77.0 66.5 112.0 72.0 150.0
64.8 128.0 67.0 133.0 57.5 85.0 66.5 112.0
;
run;

proc reg data=htwt noprint;
   model height=weight;
   output out=both p=predht;
run;

proc plot data=both;
   plot height*weight predht*weight='*' / overlay;
   title 'Predicted Versus Actual';
run;
```

Actual values are indicated with A's (or B's if two observations coincide), predicted values with asterisks (*). See **Output 25.10**.

Output 25.10   Plotting Predicted versus Actual Values

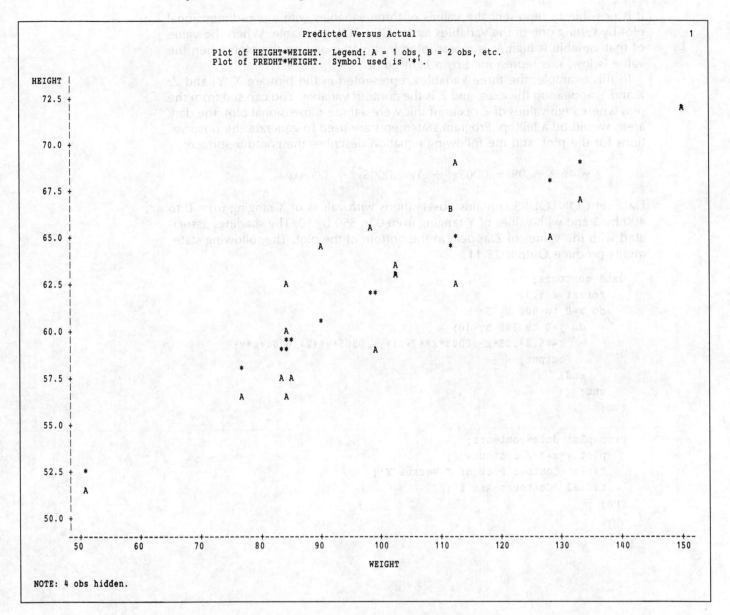

NOTE: 4 obs hidden.

Example 5:   Contour Plotting

It is possible to represent the values of three variables with a two-dimensional plot by setting one of the variables as the CONTOUR variable. When the value of that variable is high, it is represented by a dark point on the plot; when the value is low, it is represented by a light point.

In this example, the three variables represented in the plot are X, Y, and Z: X and Y appear on the axes, and Z is the contour variable. You can see from the plot where high values of Z occur: if this were a three-dimensional plot, the dark areas would be a hilltop. Program statements are used to generate the observations for the plot, and the following equation describes the contour surface:

$$z = 46.2 + .09x - .0005x^2 + .1y - .0005y^2 + .0004xy \quad .$$

Data set CONTOURS contains observations with values of X ranging from 0 to 400 by 5 and with values of Y ranging from 0 to 350 by 10. The shadings associated with the values of Z appear at the bottom of the plot. The following statements produce **Output 25.11**.

```
data contours;
   format z 5.1;
   do x=0 to 400 by 5;
      do y=0 to 350 by 10;
         z=46.2+.09*x-.0005*x**2+.1*y-.0005*y**2+.0004*x*y;
         output;
      end;
   end;
run;

proc plot data=contours;
   plot y*x=z / contour=10;
   title 'Contour Plot of X Versus Y';
   title2 'Contours Are Z';
run;
```

Output 25.11   Contour Plotting

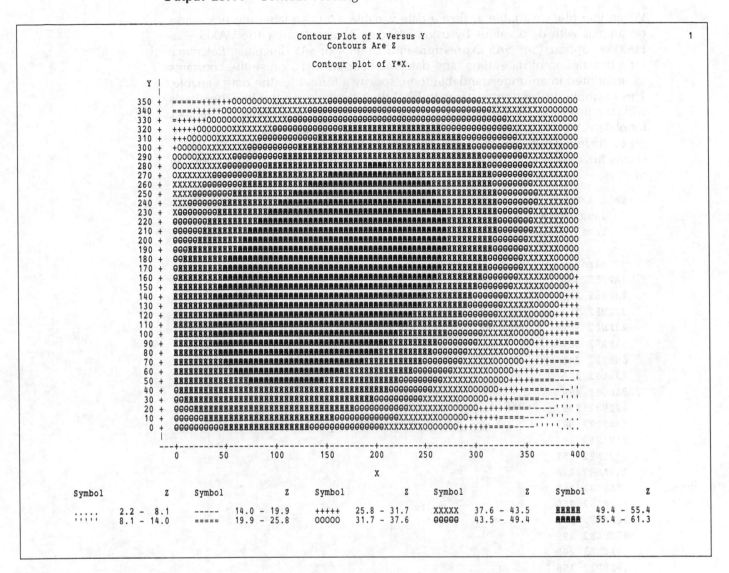

Example 6:   Labeling an Axis with Date Values

When you plot a variable against a date variable, you can label the tick marks on an axis with date values by using SAS date constants after the VAXIS= or HAXIS= option. (See **SAS Expressions** in Chapter 4 of *SAS Language: Reference* for a description of date, time, and datetime constants.) To cause the constants to be printed in an understandable form, specify a format for the date variable. This example uses date constants to label the tick marks on the horizontal axis with the first day of each month. Note that in order to have room on the axis for observations in the month of December, you must specify a tick mark for January of the following year. The following statements produce **Output 25.12** , which shows how many calls the emergency service operators handled on a sampling of days:

```
data sample;
   input date : date7. calls;
   label date='Date'
         calls='Number of Calls';
   cards;
1APR82 134
2MAR82 289
3JUN82 184
4JAN82 179
5APR82 360
6MAY82 245
7JUL82 280
8AUG82 494
9SEP82 309
11APR82 384
21MAR82 201
13JUN82 152
14JAN82 128
15APR82 350
15DEC82 150
16MAY82 240
17JUL82 499
18AUG82 248
19SEP82 356
10OCT82 222
11NOV82 294
2DEC82  511
22DEC82 413
13FEB82 488
14MAR82 460
30APR82 356
16JUN82 480
24JUL82 388
17NOV82 328
25AUG82 280
26SEP82 394
23NOV82 590
24FEB82 201
25MAR82 183
26APR82 412
27MAY82 292
28JUN82 309
```

```
29JUL82 330
30AUG82 321
;
run;

proc plot data=sample;
    plot calls*date / haxis='1JAN82'd '1FEB82'd '1MAR82'd '1APR82'd
                              '1MAY82'd '1JUN82'd '1JUL82'd '1AUG82'd
                              '1SEP82'd '1OCT82'd '1NOV82'd '1DEC82'd
                              '1JAN83'd;
    format date date7.;
    title 'Calls to City Emergency Services Number';
    title2 'Sample of Days for 1982';
run;
```

Output 25.12   Labeling an Axis with Date Values

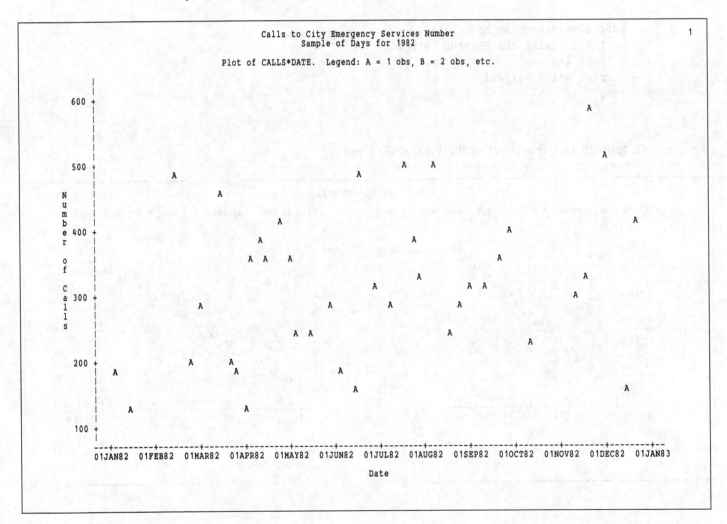

Example 7:　The Effect of the HEXPAND Option

The HEXPAND option causes the PLOT procedure to ignore information about the spacing of the data. Plots produced with this option waste less space but may obscure the nature of the relationship between the variables. For instance, the following example plots a variable against itself both with and without the HEXPAND option. Without the HEXPAND option, the one-to-one relationship of the data is obvious; however, the plot does not fill as much space as it could. With the HEXPAND option, the plot uses more of the space available; however, the one-to-one relationship of the data is obscured. The following statements produce **Output 25.13**:

```
options pagesize=30;

data even;
   do a=1 to 30;
      output;
   end;
run;

proc plot data=even hpercent=50;
   title 'Using the HEXPAND Option';
   plot a*a;
   plot a*a / hexpand;
run;
```

Output 25.13　The Effect of the HEXPAND Option

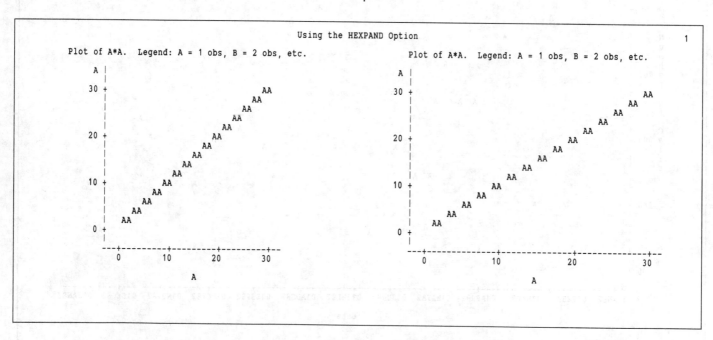

Example 8:   The Effect of the NOMISS Option

This example shows the effect of the NOMISS option. The data show sales for a firm over a 15-year period. Since part of the period lies in the future, the SALES data are missing for those years. They are plotted once with NOMISS and once without it. The following statements produce the plots shown in **Output 25.14**:

```
options pagesize=40;

data firm;
   input year sales;
   cards;
1974  3825
1975  4000
1976  4578
1977  5103
1978  5732
1979  6295
1980  6728
1981  2917
1982  2898
1983  3745
1984  4207
1985  .
1986  .
1987  .
1988  .
;
run;

proc plot data=firm;
   title 'Plot with Missing Values Included';
   plot sales*year;
run;

proc plot data=firm nomiss;
   title 'Plot with Missing Values Excluded';
   plot sales*year;
run;
```

Output 25.14 The Effect of the NOMISS Option

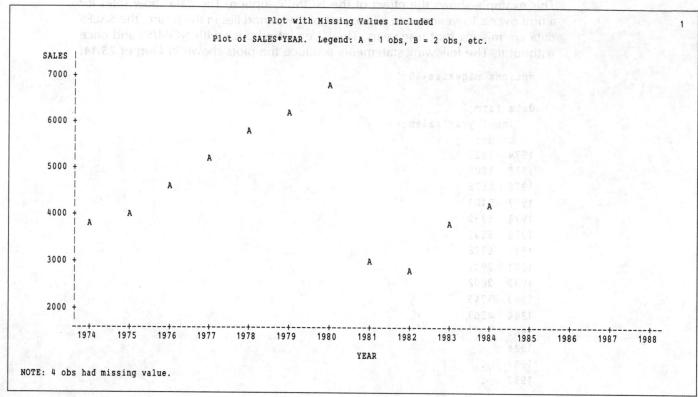

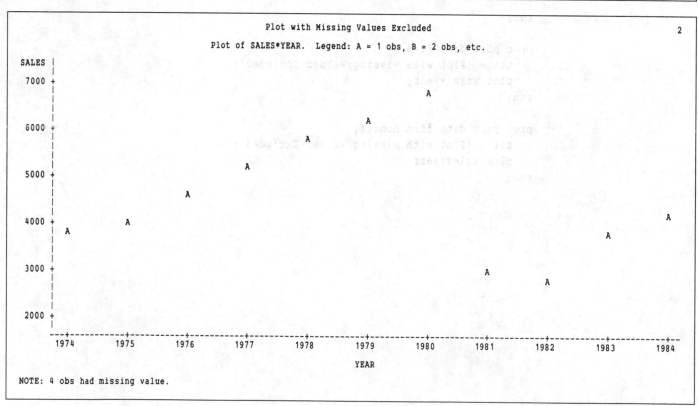

Chapter 26

The PMENU
Procedure

ABSTRACT

The PMENU procedure defines PMENU facilities for windows created by using the WINDOW statement in base SAS software, the %WINDOW macro statement, the BUILD procedure of SAS/AF software, or the Screen Control Language (SCL) PMENU function with SAS/AF and SAS/FSP software.

INTRODUCTION

The PMENU Facility

The *PMENU facility* is a menuing system that replaces the command line as a way to execute commands. It is the default at some sites and an option at others. To activate the PMENU facility if it is not the default at your site, issue the PMENU command from any command line. When the PMENU facility is active, each active window has an *action bar*, which lists items you can select. To make a selection, position your cursor on the item and press ENTER (or point and click with a mouse). Depending upon which item you select, the system either processes a command, displays information, displays another list of selections (this time in a column format called a *pull-down menu*), or requests that you complete information in a *dialog box*. The *dialog box* is simply a box of questions or choices that require answers before an action can be performed. **Figure 26.1** illustrates an action bar, a pull-down menu, and a dialog box.

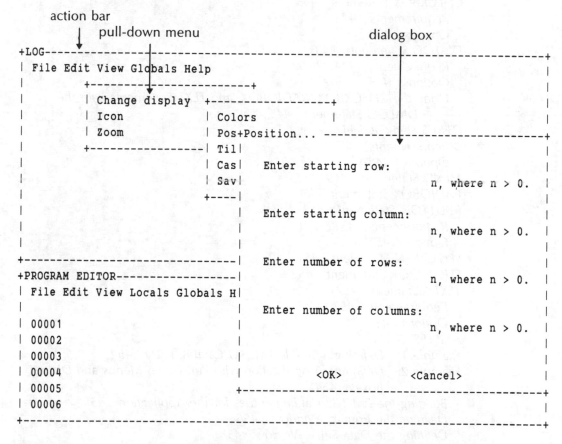

Figure 26.1 Action Bar, Pull-Down Menu, and Dialog Box on LOG Window

Using Dialog Boxes

A dialog box can request information in three ways:

- You may be asked to fill in a field. For example, you might need to provide a filename. Fields that accept this type of information are called *text fields*.
- You may have to select one choice from a list of mutually exclusive choices. For example, you could choose a single color for the background of a window. A group of selections of this type is called a *radio box*, and each individual selection is called a *radio button*.
- You may be asked to indicate whether you want to select other independent choices. For example, you could choose to use various options by selecting any or all of the listed selections. A selection of this type is called a *check box*.

Figure 26.2 illustrates each of these methods of entering information in a dialog box.

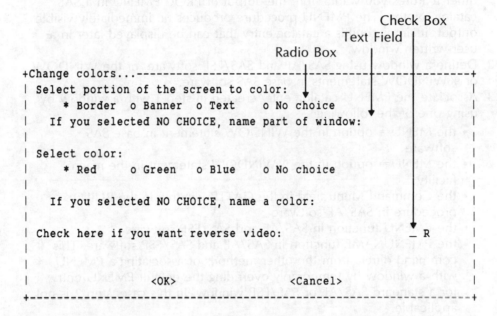

```
                                                    Check Box
                                          Text Field
                               Radio Box
+Change colors...---------------------------------------------------------+
| Select portion of the screen to color:   |
|     * Border   o Banner   o Text     o No choice                        |
|   If you selected NO CHOICE, name part of window:                       |
|                                                                         |
| Select color:                                                           |
|     * Red      o Green    o Blue     o No choice                        |
|                                                                         |
|   If you selected NO CHOICE, name a color:                              |
|                                                                         |
| Check here if you want reverse video:                         _ R       |
|                                                                         |
|                                                                         |
|               <OK>                      <Cancel>                        |
+-------------------------------------------------------------------------+
```

Figure 26.2   Text Field, Radio Box, and Check Box in Dialog Box

Special Features of Dialog Boxes

Figure 26.2 illustrates some special features of dialog boxes. Note that the name of the item that is associated with the dialog box appears in the corner of the dialog box with an ellipsis appended to it (for example, Change colors...).

In addition, dialog boxes have two or more *push buttons*, such as OK and Cancel, automatically built into the box.* A *push button* causes an action to occur. Select the OK push button to complete the actions defined in the dialog box; select the Cancel push button to cancel the actions in the dialog box.

In this chapter, radio buttons within a radio box are prefixed by a lowercase o. The radio button that has been selected, by default or by the user's action, is indicated by an asterisk. For example, **Figure 26.2** shows that Border is the

---

* The actual names of the push buttons vary in different windowing environments.

selected value, and Banner, Text, and No choice are additional buttons in the same radio box.

A check box appears as an underscore before the name of the check box or as an uppercase X when the box has been selected. In **Figure 26.2**, the R check box is prefixed by an underscore indicating that the reverse video option has not been selected.

Using PROC PMENU to Create PMENU Catalog Entries

Steps Required to Build and Use PMENU Catalog Entries

The SAS System supplies the PMENU facility for all windows included in the system. With PROC PMENU, you can create action bars, pull-down menus, and dialog boxes for windows you define. In most cases, building and using PMENU entries requires the following steps:

1. Use PROC PMENU to define the action bars, pull-down menus and other features you want. Store the output of PROC PMENU in a SAS catalog. Note: The PMENU procedure produces no immediately visible output; it simply builds a catalog entry that can be displayed later in a user-written window.

2. Define a window using SAS/AF and SAS/FSP software, or the WINDOW or %WINDOW statements in base SAS software.

3. Associate the PMENU catalog entry created in step 1 with a window by using one of the following:

   - the MENU= option in the WINDOW statement in base SAS software
   - the MENU= option in the %WINDOW statement in the macro facility
   - the Command Menu field in the GATTR window in the BUILD procedure in SAS/AF software
   - the PMENU function in SAS/AF and SAS/FSP software
   - the PMENUNAME function in SAS/AF and SAS/FSP software. This command differs from the other methods of associating a PMENU with a window by temporarily overriding the default PMENU entry for a standard SAS/AF or SAS/FSP window. In this case, step 2 is not applicable.

4. Activate the window you have created with the PMENU facility on in the SAS Display Manager System. The action bar appears at the top of the window when the window is displayed.

This chapter describes how to create PMENU catalog entries. **Example 2** at the end of this chapter illustrates how to build a PMENU catalog entry and how to create a window and associate the PMENU entry with the window. For detailed information on how to create windows, refer to *SAS Language: Reference, Version 6, First Edition*; *SAS/AF Software: Usage and Reference, Version 6, First Edition*; or *SAS/FSP Software: Usage and Reference, Version 6, First Edition*.

How to Use Statements in the PMENU Procedure

The PROC PMENU statement invokes the PMENU procedure and specifies the SAS catalog in which you want to store the PMENU catalog entries created in the step. The following paragraphs explain the relationships among the other statements in the PMENU procedure:

1. The first MENU statement in a set of statements begins the definition of the action bar that is associated with a window and assigns the name of the PMENU catalog entry.

```
     /* incomplete example */
proc pmenu cat=mylib.mycat;
   menu simple;
```

In these statements, the PROC PMENU statement specifies that the PMENU catalog entry should be stored in the MYCAT catalog. The name of the PMENU catalog entry is SIMPLE, as defined in the MENU statement.

2. Immediately after the MENU statement, you must specify one or more ITEM statements to identify what items are to be listed on the action bar. You must list all ITEM statements before any other statements. If you want an item to be a simple display manager command that is invoked when the user selects the item, use the simplest form of the ITEM statement as illustrated here:

```
libname mylib 'SAS-data-library';
```

```
proc pmenu cat=mylib.mycat;
   menu simple;
      item end;
   run;
```

These statements create the action bar with only one item, shown in **Figure 26.3**.

```
┌─────────────────────────────────────────────┐
│                                             │
│  END                                        │
│                                             │
└─────────────────────────────────────────────┘
```

Figure 26.3 Action Bar with One Item

Keep in mind, however, that the action bar is not displayed immediately when you submit the PROC PMENU step. The PMENU procedure simply stores a PMENU catalog entry. The action bar is displayed only when it is associated with a user-written window and you activate that window with the PMENU facility on.

3. If you want to create an item on an action bar that performs more than a simple display manager command-line command, use the SELECTION= option in the ITEM statement and include a SELECTION statement in the same RUN group. (RUN groups are described in **Procedure Execution** later in this chapter.) The SELECTION statement is similar to the ITEM statement because both statements can submit commands without any input from the user. The difference between these statements is that what appears in the ITEM command is also displayed as an item on the action bar; if you want to submit a different command than what appears as an item on the action bar, use the SELECTION= option in the ITEM statement, and specify the actual command in the SELECTION statement.

The SELECTION statement is useful if you have built an application using SAS/AF software and you want to enable users to invoke the application simply. For example, you can include an item on the action bar that represents the application you have built, such as Run Reports.

The actual command that gets processed when the user selects this item is the AF command to display the application. The following statements illustrate this process:

```
libname mylib 'SAS-data-library';

proc pmenu cat=mylib.mycat;
   menu selects;
   item end;
   item 'Run Reports' selection=reports;
   selection reports 'af catalog=mylib.mycat.mypgm.program';
run;
```

The two ITEM statements create an action bar with the items shown in **Figure 26.4**.

```
END    Run Reports
```

Figure 26.4   Action Bar Item for SELECTION= Option

When you have developed a window and associated with it the PMENU catalog entry built by these statements, the user can select one of two items:

- END simply submits the END command.
- Run Reports submits the commands defined in the SELECTION statement.

4. To produce a dialog box when the user selects an item from the action bar, specify the DIALOG= option in the ITEM statement and include a DIALOG statement in the same RUN group. The ITEM statement defines the item that appears on the action bar; the DIALOG statement defines a dialog box that is displayed when a user selects the action bar item associated with this DIALOG statement.

The DIALOG statement has two main parts: the primary command that is executed when the user selects the item and the information that the user provides, which is added to the primary command. For example, you can define a dialog box that enables the user to change the color of parts of the display. The dialog box asks the user to select the part of the display and the color. Those two pieces of information are then added to the COLOR command, and the complete command is executed. The following statements show the relationship of the MENU, ITEM, and DIALOG statements for this example:

```
   /* incomplete code */
 proc pmenu cat=mylib.mycat;
   menu dbox;
   item 'Change colors' dialog=dboxcolr;
   dialog dboxcolr 'color %1 %2';
   more statements to gather information
 run;
```

To build a dialog box, you need to include (in addition to the ITEM and DIALOG statements) TEXT statements to define the text that appears in the dialog box and to create fields in which the user enters the appropriate information. In addition, you can use CHECKBOX, RADIOBOX, and RBUTTON statements to enable the user to make selections instead of entering in values. The following example shows all the statements needed to build a dialog box that enables the user to select colors for portions of a window:

```
libname mylib 'SAS-data-library';

proc pmenu cat=mylib.mycat;
   menu dbox;
   item 'Change colors' dialog=dboxcolr;
   dialog dboxcolr 'color %1 %2';
      text #1 @1 'Select portion of the screen to color';
      radiobox  default=1;
         rbutton #3 @3 'Border';
         rbutton #4 @3 'Banner';
      text #6 @1 'Select color';
      radiobox  default=1;
         rbutton #8 @3 'Red';
         rbutton #9 @3 'Green';
   run;
```

These statements create the dialog box illustrated in **Figure 26.5**. This dialog box is displayed when the user selects the item Change colors... from the action bar. In this figure, the asterisk indicates the default selections (specified by the DEFAULT= option in the RADIOBOX statement) for each of the choices the user can make.

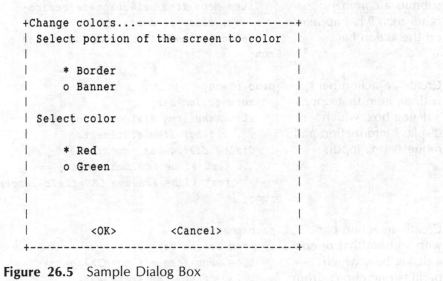

```
+Change colors...------------------------+
| Select portion of the screen to color  |
|                                         |
|                                         |
|      * Border                           |
|      o Banner                           |
|                                         |
| Select color                            |
|                                         |
|      * Red                              |
|      o Green                            |
|                                         |
|                                         |
|                                         |
|       <OK>           <Cancel>           |
+-----------------------------------------+
```

Figure 26.5 Sample Dialog Box

5. To display a pull-down menu when the user selects an item on the action bar, use the MENU= option in the ITEM statement and include another MENU statement to define the pull-down menu. You use the MENU statement for a pull-down menu the same way you use it to define the action bar for the window. As with the primary MENU statement, you can specify multiple ITEM statements, SELECTION statements, and DIALOG statements to define the items on the pull-down menu.

Note: You must include the MENU statement and other statements that define a pull-down menu in the same RUN group as the ITEM statement for the pull-down menu.

Table 26.1 summarizes how to use the statements in the PMENU procedure. Refer to descriptions of the statements later in this chapter for more information.

Table 26.1 Coding Templates for Using PROC PMENU

Function	Statements to Use
Build a simple action bar. All items on the action bar are display manager commands.	```proc pmenu; menu action-bar; item command; . . . other item statements run;```
Create an action bar with an item that produces a pull-down menu.	```proc pmenu; menu action-bar; item menu-item menu=pull-down-menu; . . . other item statements for action bar menu pull-down-menu; . . . item statements for pull-down menu run;```
Create an action bar with an item that submits a command other than what appears on the action bar.	```proc pmenu; menu action-bar; item menu-item selection=selection; . . . other item statements selection selection 'command-string'; run;```
Create an action bar with an item that opens a dialog box, which displays information and requests text input.	```proc pmenu; menu action-bar; item menu-item dialog=dialog-box; . . . other item statements dialog dialog-box 'command @1'; text #line @column 'text'; text #line @column LEN=field-length; run;```
Create an action bar with an item that opens a dialog box, which permits one choice from a list of possible values.	```proc pmenu; menu action-bar; item menu-item dialog=dialog-box; . . . other item statements dialog dialog-box 'command %1'; text #line @column 'text'; radiobox default=button-number; rbutton #line @column 'text-for-selection'; . . . more rbutton statements run;```

(continued)

Table 26.1   Coding Templates for Using PROC PMENU (*continued*)

Function	Statements to Use

Create an action bar with an item that opens a dialog box, which permits several independent choices.	`proc pmenu;`
	`  menu ` *action-bar*`;`
	`    item ` *menu-item* `dialog=`*dialog-box*`;`
	`    . . . other item statements`
	`    dialog ` *dialog-box* ` 'command &1';`
	`      text #`*line* `@`*column* ` 'text';`
	`      checkbox #`*line* `@`*column* ` 'text';`
	`      . . . more checkbox statements`
	`run;`

Procedure Execution

The PMENU procedure is interactive. You can define multiple action bars by sep-arating their definitions with RUN statements. A group of statements that ends with a RUN statement is called a *RUN group*. You must completely define a PMENU catalog entry before issuing a RUN statement; that is, in addition to the first MENU statement that defines the action bar, you must include all ITEM state-ments and any SELECTION, MENU, and DIALOG statements as well as state-ments associated with the DIALOG statement within the same RUN group. For example, the following series of statements defines two separate PMENU catalog entries. Both are stored in the same catalog, but each PMENU catalog entry is independent of the other. In the following example, both PMENU catalog entries create action bars that simply list display manager commands the user can select and execute:

```
libname mylib 'SAS-data-library';

proc pmenu cat=mylib.mycat;
   menu menu1;
   item end;
   item bye;
 run;

   menu menu2;
   item end;
   item pgm;
   item log;
   item output;
run;
```

When you submit these statements, you receive a message that says the PMENU entries have been created. To display one of these action bars, you must associate the PMENU catalog entry with a window and then activate the window with the PMENU facility on, as described earlier in **Steps Required to Build and Use PMENU Catalog Entries**.

To stop the PMENU procedure, you must issue a QUIT statement, a RUN CANCEL statement, a new PROC statement, or a DATA statement. Submitting a QUIT, DATA, or new PROC statement executes any statements that have not executed and ends the PMENU procedure. Submitting a RUN CANCEL statement cancels any statements that have not executed and ends the PMENU procedure.

SPECIFICATIONS

PROC PMENU <CATALOG=<*libref.*>*catalog*> <DESC '*entry-description*'>;
    MENU *action-bar* | *pull-down-menu*;
    ITEM *command* | '*menu-item*' <*action-option*> <GRAY>
        <ACCELERATE='*name-of-key*'> <MNEMONIC='*character*'>;
    SEPARATOR;
    SELECTION *selection   command* | '*command-string*';
    DIALOG *dialog-box* '*command-string* <@1...@n> <%1...%n>
        <&1...&n>' <HELP='*libref.catalog.entry*'>;
    CHECKBOX <ON> #*line* @*column* '*text-for-selection*'
        <COLOR=*color*>;
    RADIOBOX DEFAULT=*button-number*;
      RBUTTON <NONE> #*line* @*column* '*text-for-selection*'
        <COLOR=*color*>;
    TEXT #*line* @*column* *field-description* <ATTR=*attribute*>
        <COLOR=*color*>;

To define a PMENU catalog entry, you must use at least one MENU statement followed by at least one ITEM statement. If you use a DIALOG statement, you must follow it with at least one TEXT statement.

PROC PMENU Statement

PROC PMENU <CATALOG=<*libref.*>*catalog*> <DESC '*entry-description*'>;

The PROC PMENU statement invokes the PMENU procedure and specifies where to store all PMENU catalog entries created with the PMENU procedure step.

Options

The following options are available in the PROC PMENU statement:

CATALOG=<*libref.*>*catalog*
    names the catalog in which you want to store PMENU entries. If you omit the *libref*, the PMENU entries are stored in a catalog in the WORK SAS data library. In most cases, this is a temporary library. To reuse the PMENU entries in later display manager sessions, you must permanently store the entries. If you omit the CATALOG= option, the PMENU catalog entries are stored in your SASUSER library.

DESC '*entry-description*'
    provides a description for the PMENU catalog entries created in the step. Use this option if you want to override the default description for the catalog entry, Menu description. Note: These descriptions are displayed when you use the CATALOG window in display manager or the CONTENTS statement in the CATALOG procedure.

CHECKBOX Statement

CHECKBOX <ON> *#line @column 'text-for-selection'* <COLOR=*color*>;

The CHECKBOX statement is used after a DIALOG statement to define choices that a user can make within a dialog box.

Each CHECKBOX statement defines a single item that the user can select independent of other selections. That is, if you define five choices with five CHECKBOX statements, the user can select any combination of these choices. When the user selects choices, the *text-for-selection* values associated with the selections are inserted into the command string of the previous DIALOG statement at field locations prefixed by an & (ampersand). Refer to **Using the CHECKBOX, RADIOBOX, and TEXT Statements with the DIALOG Statement** later in this chapter for more information and an example of how to use the CHECKBOX statement.

Requirements

The following arguments are required in the CHECKBOX statement:

#line @column
> defines the location within a dialog box of the check box and text for the selection.

'text-for-selection'
> defines the text that describes this check box. This text appears in the window and is also inserted into the command in the DIALOG statement preceding the CHECKBOX statement when the user selects the check box.

Options

The following options are available in the CHECKBOX statement:

COLOR=*color*
> defines the color of the check box and the text that describes it.

ON
> indicates that by default this check box is on. If you use this option, you must specify it immediately after the CHECKBOX keyword.

DIALOG Statement

DIALOG *dialog-box 'command-string* <@1...@n> <%1...%n> <&1...&n>' <HELP='*libref.catalog.entry*'>;

The DIALOG statement describes a dialog box associated with an item on a menu. Before you can use the DIALOG statement, you must specify an ITEM statement with the DIALOG= option. The ITEM statement creates an entry on an action bar or pull-down menu, and the DIALOG= option specifies which DIALOG statement describes the dialog box. The DIALOG statement must be followed by at least one TEXT statement. In addition, you can use CHECKBOX, RADIOBOX, and RBUTTON statements to define the contents of the dialog box.

Requirements

The following arguments are required in the DIALOG statement:

command-string
   is the command or partial command that is invoked when the item is selected. Note: To specify a literal @ (at sign), % (percent sign), or & (ampersand) in the *command-string*, use a double character: @@ (at signs), %% (percent signs), or && (ampersands).

dialog-box
   is the same name specified for the DIALOG= option in a previous ITEM statement.

Options

The following options are available in the DIALOG statement. Note: You can embed the field numbers, for example @1, %1, or &1, in the command string and mix different types of field numbers within a command string. The numeric portion of the field number corresponds to the relative position of TEXT, RADIOBOX, and CHECKBOX statements, not to any actual number in these statements.

@1...@n
   are optional TEXT statement numbers that can add information to the command before it is submitted. Numbers preceded by an at sign (@) correspond to TEXT statements that use the LEN= option to define input fields.

%1...%n
   are optional RADIOBOX statement numbers that can add information to the command before it is submitted. Numbers preceded by a percent sign (%) correspond to RADIOBOX statements following the DIALOG statement. Note: Keep in mind that the numbers correspond to RADIOBOX statements, not RBUTTON statements.

&1...&n
   are optional CHECKBOX statement numbers that can add information to the command before it is submitted. Numbers preceded by an ampersand (&) correspond to CHECKBOX statements following the DIALOG statement.

HELP='*libref.catalog.entry*'
   defines the catalog entry that contains a help description for this dialog box. Note: This option is not available in all host environments. If you include this option and it is not available on your host, the option is ignored. Refer to the SAS documentation for your host system for more information.

Using the CHECKBOX, RADIOBOX, and TEXT Statements with the DIALOG Statement

When you include field numbers, preceded by either &, %, or @, in the command string of the DIALOG statement, you must define one or more CHECKBOX, RADIOBOX, or TEXT statements to gather the information to substitute for the field numbers. The following example illustrates how to use all of these statements together:

```
libname mylib 'SAS-data-library';

proc pmenu cat=mylib.mycat;
   menu cbox;
   item 'Change colors' dialog=dboxcolr;
❶  item pmenu;

      /* COLOR command has five possible input fields in this */
      /* order: radiobox, text, radiobox, text, checkbox      */
❷  dialog dboxcolr 'color %1 @1 %2 @2 &1';

      /* define the first set of radiobox choices */
      /* corresponds to %1 in DIALOG statement     */
   text #1 @1 'Select portion of the screen to color:';
❸  radiobox  default=1;
      rbutton #2 @3 'Border';
❹      rbutton #2 @13 'Banner';
      rbutton #2 @23 'Text';
      rbutton none #2 @33 'No choice';

      /* define the first input text field         */
      /* corresponds to @1 in DIALOG statement     */
   text #4 @3 'If you selected NO CHOICE, name part of window:';
❺   text #4 @55 len=9;

      /* define the second set of radiobox choices */
      /* corresponds to %2 in DIALOG statement     */
   text #6 @1 'Select color:';
❸  radiobox  default=1;
      rbutton #7 @3 'Red' color=red;
      rbutton #7 @13 'Green' color=green;
❹      rbutton #7 @23 'Blue' color=blue;
      rbutton none #7 @33 'No choice';

      /* define the second input text field    */
      /* corresponds to @2 in DIALOG statement */
   text #9 @3 'If you selected NO CHOICE, name a color:';
❺   text #9 @55 len=7;

      /* define the checkbox selection         */
      /* corresponds to &1 in DIALOG statement */
   text #11 @1 'Check here if you want reverse video:';
❻   checkbox #11 @55 'R' color=yellow;
 run;
```

There are several things to notice about these statements:

1. All ITEM statements for a menu must appear immediately after the MENU statement and before any DIALOG, SELECTION, or other MENU statement. In the following example, there are two ITEM statements. The first one defines the action bar item for the dialog box; the second one simply defines the PMENU command, which enables the user to turn the PMENU facility off.
2. The DIALOG statement contains input field numbers that correspond to RADIOBOX, TEXT, and CHECKBOX statements in the same RUN group.
    The input field numbers begin at 1 for each type of statement. That is, the first TEXT statement with an input field corresponds to @1, the first RADIOBOX statement corresponds to %1, and the first CHECKBOX statement corresponds to &1.
    The RADIOBOX, TEXT, and CHECKBOX statements must follow a DIALOG statement.
3. The RADIOBOX statement defines the beginning of a set of mutually exclusive choices, which are described by RBUTTON statements. You must indicate a default RBUTTON statement with the DEFAULT= option.
4. The RADIOBOX statement must be followed by RBUTTON statements to define all possible choices for a group. The user can select only one of the choices defined in a group.
5. TEXT statements can define text that appears on the display or input fields in which the user enters text. Both of the numbered text statements define input fields. The unnumbered TEXT statements in this example simply display text in the dialog box.
6. The CHECKBOX statements define independent items that can be selected without regard to other selections.

All information gathered from RADIOBOX, TEXT, and CHECKBOX statements is combined with the command string in the DIALOG statement to build a complete command that is submitted when the user selects the OK push button at the bottom of the dialog box.

These statements produce the dialog box illustrated in **Figure 26.6** when the user selects Change colors... from the action bar.

```
+Change colors...-----------------------------------------------+
| Select portion of the screen to color:                        |
|     * Border   o Banner  o Text     o No choice                |
|                                                                |
|   If you selected NO CHOICE, name part of window:              |
|                                                                |
| Select color:                                                  |
|     * Red      o Green   o Blue     o No choice                |
|                                                                |
|   If you selected NO CHOICE, name a color:                     |
|                                                                |
| Check here if you want reverse video:              _ R         |
|                                                                |
|                                                                |
|              <OK>                    <Cancel>                  |
+----------------------------------------------------------------+
```

Figure 26.6   Dialog Box with Three Kinds of Input

If you press the OK push button with the selections indicated in **Figure 26.6**, the following command is built by appending your selections to the COLOR command in the DIALOG statement (see ❷ in the previous example):

```
color Border Red
```

Note that values are appended for the %1 and %2 fields in the DIALOG statement, but the @1, @2, and &1 fields are empty.

ITEM Statement

ITEM *command* | *'menu-item'* <*action-option*> <GRAY>
        <ACCELERATE=*'name-of-key'*> <MNEMONIC=*'character'*>;

The *action-option* can be one of the following:

DIALOG=*dialog-box*
MENU=*pull-down-menu*
SELECTION=*selection*

The ITEM statement identifies an item to be listed on an action bar. You must use ITEM statements to name all the items that appear on an action bar. You also use the ITEM statement to name the items that appear on any pull-down menus. The items you specify in the ITEM statement can be simple display manager commands that are invoked when the user selects the item, or they can be descriptions of other actions that are performed by associated DIALOG, SELECTION, or MENU statements.

All ITEM statements for a menu must be placed immediately after the MENU statement and before any DIALOG, SELECTION, or other MENU statements. In some host environments, you can insert SEPARATOR statements between ITEM statements to produce lines separating groups of items on a pull-down menu. Refer to **SEPARATOR Statement** later in this chapter.

Requirements

One of the following arguments is required in the ITEM statement:

command
   is a single word, adhering to SAS naming conventions, that describes the action that occurs when the user selects this item. In many cases, the *command* is a display manager command. The *command* is displayed in uppercase letters on the action bar.

'menu-item'
   is a word or text string, enclosed in quotes, that describes the action that occurs when the user selects this item. Use this form if the item to appear on the action bar or pull-down menu does not adhere to standard SAS naming conventions or if you want to create an item that contains lowercase letters. For example, if you define these two items,

```
item pmenu;
item 'pmenu';
```

the action bar appears as follows:

```
PMENU  pmenu
```

Figure 26.7 Action Bar with Upper- and Lowercase Items

Options

The following options are available in the ITEM statement. If no DIALOG=, SELECTION=, or MENU= option is specified, the *command* or *menu-item* text string is submitted as a command-line command when the user selects the item.

ACCELERATE='*name-of-key*'
> defines a key that can be used instead of selecting an item. When the user presses the key named in this option, it has the same effect as selecting the item from the action bar or pull-down menu. Note: This option is not available in all host environments. If you include this option and it is not available on your host, the option is ignored. Refer to the SAS documentation for your host system for more information.

DIALOG=*dialog-box*
> is the name of an associated DIALOG statement, which displays a dialog box when the user selects this item.

GRAY
> indicates that the item is not an active choice in this window. This option is useful when you want to define standard lists of items for many windows, but not all items are valid in all windows. In some host environments, items that have the GRAY option set appear different from items that do not have this option. In all systems, when this option is set and the user selects the item, no action occurs.

MENU=*pull-down-menu*
> is the name of an associated MENU statement, which displays a pull-down menu when the user selects this item.

MNEMONIC='*character*'
> defines a single character that can be typed instead of selecting an item. When the user types the character named in this option, it has the same effect as selecting the item from the action bar or pull-down menu. Note: This option is not available in all host environments. If you include this option and it is not available on your host, the option is ignored. Refer to the SAS documentation for your host system for more information.

SELECTION=*selection*
> is the name of an associated SELECTION statement, which submits a command when the user selects this item.

MENU Statement

MENU *action-bar* | *pull-down-menu*;

where

action-bar
    names the catalog entry for this action-bar.

pull-down-menu
    names the pull-down menu that appears when the user selects an
    item on the action bar. The value of *pull-down-menu* must match the
    pull-down-menu name specified in the MENU= option in a previous
    ITEM statement.

The MENU statement is used in two ways in PROC PMENU. The first MENU statement after the PROC PMENU statement or a RUN statement defines an action
bar. The name specified in the MENU statement becomes the name of the catalog
entry in which the action bar is stored. Use this name when you associate a
PMENU entry with a window you have created.

The MENU statement can also be used to define a pull-down menu. When
used in this way, the MENU statement must follow an ITEM statement that specifies the MENU= option. Both the ITEM statement and the MENU statement for
the pull-down menu must be in the same RUN group as the MENU statement
that defines the action bar for the PMENU catalog entry.

For both action bars and pull-down menus, you must follow the MENU statement with ITEM statements that define each of the items that appear on the
menu. All ITEM statements for a menu must be grouped together. For example,
the statements below create one catalog entry, WINDOWS, which produces an
action bar with two items, Primary windows and Other windows. When you
select one of these items, a pull-down menu is displayed.

```
libname mylib 'SAS-data-library';

proc pmenu cat=mylib.mycat;

       /* create catalog entry */
   menu windows;
   item 'Primary windows' menu=prime;
   item 'Other windows' menu=other;

       /* create first pull-down menu */
   menu prime;
   item output;
   item manager;
   item log;
   item pgm;

       /* create second pull-down menu */
   menu other;
   item keys;
   item help;
   item pmenu;
   item bye;

       /* end of run group */
   run;
```

Figure 26.8 illustrates the action bar for the WINDOWS catalog entry.

```
 ┌─────────────────────────────────────────────────┐
 │                                                 │
 │   Primary windows   Other windows               │
 │                                                 │
 └─────────────────────────────────────────────────┘
```

Figure 26.8 WINDOWS Action Bar

Figure 26.9 illustrates the pull-down menu named PRIME.

```
 ┌───────────┐
 │           │
 │  OUTPUT   │
 │  MANAGER  │
 │  LOG      │
 │  PGM      │
 │           │
 └───────────┘
```

Figure 26.9 PRIME Pull-Down Menu

Figure 26.10 illustrates the pull-down menu named OTHER.

```
 ┌───────────┐
 │           │
 │  KEYS     │
 │  HELP     │
 │  PMENU    │
 │  BYE      │
 │           │
 └───────────┘
```

Figure 26.10 OTHER Pull-Down Menu

RADIOBOX Statement

RADIOBOX DEFAULT=*button-number*;

where

DEFAULT=*button-number*
indicates which of the following RBUTTON statements supplies the
default value. A value of 1 indicates that the value defined by the first
RBUTTON statement is checked by default.

The RADIOBOX statement is used after a DIALOG statement to define a list of
mutually exclusive choices within a dialog box. The RADIOBOX statement must
be followed by one or more RBUTTON statements.

The RADIOBOX statement indicates the beginning of a list of selections. Immediately after the RADIOBOX statement, you must list an RBUTTON statement
for each of the selections the user can make. The user must choose one of the
selections. When the user makes a choice, the text value associated with the
selection is inserted into the command string of the previous DIALOG statement
at field locations prefixed by a % (percent sign). Refer to **Using the CHECKBOX,
RADIOBOX, and TEXT Statements with the DIALOG Statement** earlier in this
chapter for more information and an example of how to use the RADIOBOX
statement.

RBUTTON Statement

RBUTTON <NONE> #*line* @*column* '*text-for-selection*' <COLOR=*color*>;

The RBUTTON statement is used after a RADIOBOX statement to define each of the choices in a list of mutually exclusive choices within a dialog box. Refer to **Using the CHECKBOX, RADIOBOX, and TEXT Statements with the DIALOG Statement** earlier in this chapter for more information and an example of how to use the RBUTTON statement.

Requirements

The following arguments are required in the RBUTTON statement:

#line @column
   defines the location within a dialog box where the radio button and text are placed.

'text-for-selection'
   defines the text that appears in the dialog box and the text inserted into the command in the preceding DIALOG statement.

Options

The following options are available with the RBUTTON statement:

COLOR=*color*
   defines the color of the radio button and the text that describes the button.

NONE
   defines a button that indicates none of the other choices. Defining this button enables the user to ignore any of the other choices. In effect, blanks are inserted into the command string built by the DIALOG statement. If you use this option, it must occur immediately after the RBUTTON keyword.

SELECTION Statement

SELECTION *selection command* | '*command-string*';

where

selection
   is the same name specified for the SELECTION= option in a previous ITEM statement.

command
   is a single-word command that is invoked when the item is selected.

command-string
   is a text string, enclosed in quotes, that is submitted as a command-line command when the user selects this item.

The SELECTION statement is used with an ITEM statement to define a command that is submitted when a user selects an item from an action bar or pull-down menu. You define the name of the item in the ITEM statement and specify the SELECTION= option to associate the item with a subsequent SELECTION statement. The SELECTION statement then defines the actual command that is submitted when the user chooses the item on the action bar or pull-down menu.

In general, you are likely to use the SELECTION statement to define a command string. You create a simple alias using the ITEM statement, which invokes a longer command string defined in the SELECTION statement. For example, you could include an item on the action bar that invokes a WINDOW statement to allow data entry. The actual commands that get processed when the user selects this item are the commands to include and submit the application. The following statements illustrate this process:

```
libname mylib 'SAS-data-library';
filename window 'external-file';
proc pmenu cat=mylib.mycat;
   menu select;
   item 'DATA_ENTRY' selection=de;
   selection de 'include window;submit';
run;
```

The simple term DATA_ENTRY appears on the action bar. When the user selects that item, the following more complicated command string is submitted:

```
include window;submit
```

The INCLUDE command includes a DATA step stored in the external file into the PROGRAM EDITOR window, and the SUBMIT statement submits the included program. In this example, the included program contains statements that define the window for data entry. Note: **Example 2** later in this chapter illustrates one method of building a window for data entry.

SEPARATOR Statement

SEPARATOR;

The SEPARATOR statement can be used after an ITEM statement to draw a separating line between items in a pull-down menu. This statement allows you to visually group items in a pull-down menu. Note: This statement is not available in all host environments. If you include this statement and it is not available on your host, the statement is ignored. Refer to the SAS documentation for your host system for more information.

TEXT Statement

TEXT #*line* @*column field-description* <ATTR=*attribute*>
    <COLOR=*color*>;

where *field-description* can be one of the following:

LEN=*field-length*
'*text*'

The TEXT statement can be used only after a DIALOG statement. The TEXT statement defines both the descriptive text that appears in a dialog box and the input fields in which the user enters information. When the LEN= argument is specified, information entered by the user is added to the command defined in the DIALOG statement at the location specified by the field numbers in the DIALOG statement.

Each dialog box requires at least one TEXT statement. Refer to **Using the CHECKBOX, RADIOBOX, and TEXT Statements with the DIALOG Statement** earlier in this chapter for more information and an example of how to use the TEXT statement.

Requirements

The following arguments are required in the TEXT statement:

field-description
> defines how the TEXT statement is used. The *field-description* can be one of the following:
>
> LEN=*field-length*
>> is the length of an input field in which the user can enter information. If the LEN= argument is used, the information entered in the field is inserted into the command string of the previous DIALOG statement at field locations prefixed by an @ (at sign).
>
> *text*
>> is the text string that appears inside the dialog box at the location defined by *line* and *column*.

#*line* @*column*
> defines the location within a dialog box where the text or input field is located.

Options

The following options can be used in the TEXT statement:

ATTR=*attribute*
> defines the attribute for the text or input field. Valid attribute values are
>
> - BLINK
> - HIGHLIGH
> - REV_VIDE
> - UNDERLIN.
>
> Note that your hardware may not support all of these attributes.

COLOR=*color*
> defines the color for the text or input field characters. Valid color values are

BLACK	GRAY	PINK
BLUE	GREEN	RED
BROWN	MAGENTA	WHITE
CYAN	ORANGE	YELLOW

Note that your hardware may not support all of these colors.

EXAMPLES

Example 1: Defining a Simple PMENU Catalog Entry

The following statements define an action bar that lists simple display manager commands to invoke various windows and the BYE and PMENU commands. Note that what appears on the action bar as an item is exactly what is submitted to the system when the user selects the item.

```
libname mylib 'SAS-data-library';

proc pmenu cat=mylib.mycat;
   menu general;
   item output;
   item manager;
   item log;
   item pgm;
   item keys;
   item help;
   item pmenu;
   item bye;
run;
quit;
```

Example 2: Defining an Application with Pull-Down Menus and Dialog Boxes

The following example shows how to define an action bar, a pull-down menu, and a dialog box for a sample application developed using the WINDOW statement. This example requires the following steps:

1. Build the PMENU entries needed for all windows.
2. Define all windows and other SAS programs needed by the application; store these SAS programs in an external file.
3. Create an operating system command file to invoke the application you have built.

This example defines an application that enables the user to enter human resources data for various departments and to request reports from the data sets created by the data entry.

Building the PMENU Catalog Entries for the Application

The following statements define the PMENU entries that are used in the windows. The circled numbers correspond to the numbered list following the statements.

```
❶ libname hr 'SAS-data-library';
  filename pmenex08 'external-file';
  filename pmenex09 'external-file';
❷ proc pmenu cat=hr.menus;

              /* define action bar */
❸   menu select;
❹   item 'Data_Entry' menu=deptsde;
    item 'Print_Report' menu=deptsprt;
❺   item 'End';
    item 'Bye';

              /* define pull-down menu */
❻   menu deptsde;
❼     item 'For Dept01' selection=de1;
      item 'For Dept02' selection=de2;
❾     item 'Other Departments' dialog=deother;
❽     selection de1 'end;pgm;include pmenex08;change xx 01;submit';
      selection de2 'end;pgm;include pmenex08;change xx 02;submit';
❿     dialog deother 'end;pgm;include pmenex08;c deptxx @1;submit';
        text #1 @1 'Enter department name';
⓫       text #2 @3 'in the form DEPT99:';
⓬       text #2 @25 len=7;

              /* define second pull-down menu */
    menu deptsprt;
      item 'For Dept01' selection=prt1;
      item 'For Dept02' selection=prt2;
      item 'Other Departments' dialog=prother;
      selection prt1 'end;pgm;include pmenex09;change xx 01;submit';
⓭     selection prt2 'end;pgm;include pmenex09;change xx 02;submit';
      dialog prother 'end;pgm;include pmenex09;c deptxx @1;submit';
        text #1 @1 'Enter department name';
        text #2 @3 'in the form DEPT99:';
        text #2 @25 len=7;
  run;

              /* define second action bar */
⓮   menu entrdata;
      item stop;
      item end;
  run;
⓯ quit;
```

1. The LIBNAME statement defines the SAS data library in which the PMENU entries are stored. The FILENAME statements define the external files in which the programs to create the windows are stored.
2. The PROC PMENU statement specifies the catalog in the library in which the PMENU entries are stored.
3. The first MENU statement in a PROC PMENU step (as well as the first MENU statement after a RUN statement) defines the name of the

PMENU entry in the catalog. These MENU statements produce action bars when the PMENU entry is associated with a window.

4. This ITEM statement illustrates the use of the MENU= option. When the user selects this item, a pull-down menu (defined by the MENU DEPTSDE statement) appears. See number 6.

5. This statement and the next statement are simple ITEM statements; that is, neither one has any options. Therefore, the item listed in this statement not only appears on the action bar; it is also the command that is executed when the user selects this item.

6. As mentioned in number 4, this MENU statement defines the pull-down menu that appears when the user selects the Data_Entry item. The ITEM statements following this MENU statement describe the items that are listed in the pull-down menu.

7. This ITEM statement uses the SELECTION= option so that the command executed when the user selects this item can have a meaningful alias. That is, For Dept01 appears as the item on the pull-down menu, but the string of commands that are actually executed are defined in the SELECTION DE1 statement (number 8).

8. As described in number 7, the string of commands listed in this SELECTION statement are submitted when the user selects For Dept01. These commands

   - end the current window and return to the PROGRAM EDITOR window so further commands can be submitted
   - include the SAS statements that create the data entry window
   - modify the DATA statement in the included program so it creates the correct data set
   - submit the program so the user simply sees the data entry window.

9. This ITEM statement uses the DIALOG= option to invoke a dialog box in which the user can enter the name of another department. See number 10 also.

10. The DIALOG statement works much like the SELECTION statement described in number 8, but the DIALOG statement also modifies the command string so the name of the department entered by the user is used to change the name of the data set in the DATA statement. Refer to number 12 for more information.

11. The first two TEXT statements simply describe the text that appears in the dialog box.

12. The last TEXT statement defines an input field. This is the area in which the user enters the name of the department. The name entered in this field is substituted for the @1 in the DIALOG statement. Therefore, if the user enters DEPT05, the command string becomes

    ```
    end;include pmenex08;c deptxx dept05;submit
    ```

13. These SELECTION and DIALOG statements parallel the structure of the statements numbered 8 and 10, but they invoke different SAS programs. These statements include and modify a program that prints a report.

14. This MENU statement also defines an action bar (and a separate catalog entry) because it follows a RUN statement. Note that this menu, which appears on the data entry screen, is very simple. Only two items appear on the action bar, and they are simple display manager commands.

15. The QUIT statement ends the PROC PMENU step.

Defining the Primary Window

The following statements define the primary window for the application. Note that the MENU= option in the WINDOW statement associates the

HR.MENUS.SELECT PMENU entry, defined in the previous example, with this window.

```
  /* stored in the file referenced by pmenex07 */
libname hr 'SAS-data-library';

data _null_;

     /* define window */
  window hrselect menu=hr.menus.select
     #4  @10 'This application allows you to'
     #6  @13 '- Enter human resources data for'
     #7  @15 'one department at a time.'
     #9  @13 '- Print reports on human resources data for'
     #10 @15 'one department at a time.'
     #12 @13 '- End the application and return to the PGM window.'
     #14 @13 '- Exit from the SAS System.'
     #19 @10 'You must have the PMENU facility ON.'
     #20 @10 'Select DATA_ENTRY, PRINT_REPORT, END or BYE.';

     /* display window */
  display hrselect;
run;
```

The window produced by these statements appears in **Display 26.1**. The window shows both the pull-down menu that is displayed when the user selects Data_Entry and the dialog box that is displayed when the user then selects Other Departments... .

Display 26.1   Primary Window in Human Resources Application

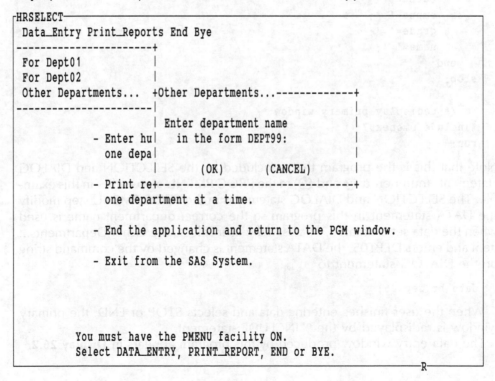

Defining the Data Entry Window

If the user selects the Data_Entry item from the action bar of the primary menu, a pull-down menu is displayed. When the user selects one of the listed departments or chooses to enter a different department, the following statements are invoked:

```
      /* stored in the file referenced by pmenex08 */
    libname hr 'SAS-data-library';
    filename pmenex07 'external-file';

    data hr.deptxx;

        /* define window */
      window hrdata menu=hr.menus.entrdata
        #5  @10 'Employee'
            @20 'Salary'
            @30 'Employee'
        #6  @10 ' Number '
            @20 ' Grade'
            @30 '  Name  '
        #8  @10 empno $8.
            @20 grade $4.
            @30 name $30.
        #19 @10 'Press ENTER to add an observation.  '
        #20 @10 'Press STOP to end data entry.';

        /* display window until STOP */
      do while (upcase(_cmd_) ne 'STOP');
        display hrdata;
        output;
        empno=' ';
        grade=' ';
        name=' ';
      end;
    stop;

      /* redisplay primary window */
    %include pmenex07;
    run;
```

Note that this is the program that is included by the SELECTION and DIALOG statements (numbered ❽ and ❿) in the PROC PMENU step earlier in this example. The SELECTION and DIALOG statements in the PROC PMENU step modify the DATA statement in this program so the correct department name is used when the data set is created. That is, if the user selects the Other Departments... item and enters DEPT05, the DATA statement is changed by the command string on the DIALOG statement to

```
    data hr.dept05;
```

When the user finishes entering data and selects STOP or END, the primary window is redisplayed by the %INCLUDE statement.

The data entry window produced by this program appears in **Display 26.2**.

Display 26.2   Data Entry Window in Human Resources Application

```
┌HRDATA────────────────────────────────────────────────────┐
│ STOP END                                                  │
│                                                           │
│                                                           │
│                                                           │
│                                                           │
│                                                           │
│         Employee  Salary   Employee                       │
│         Number    Grade    Name                           │
│                                                           │
│                                                           │
│                                                           │
│                                                           │
│                                                           │
│                                                           │
│                                                           │
│                                                           │
│                                                           │
│         Press ENTER to add an observation.                │
│         Press STOP to end data entry.                     │
│                                                         R │
└───────────────────────────────────────────────────────────┘
```

Defining the Step to Print Reports

If the user selects the Print_Report item from the action bar of the primary menu, a pull-down menu is displayed. When the user selects one of the listed departments or chooses to enter a different department, the following statements are invoked:

```
    /* stored in the file referenced by pmenex09 */
libname hr 'SAS-data-library';
filename pmenex07 'external-file';

    /* route output to print file */
proc printto file='your.list.file' new;
run;

    /* print report */
proc print data=hr.deptxx;
run;

    /* restore default output destination */
proc printto;
run;

    /* redisplay primary window */
%include pmenex07;
run;
```

Like the DATA step described previously, this program is modified by the SELECTION or DIALOG statement that invokes it, so the name of the data set is changed from DEPTXX to the correct name. Thus, if the user selects For Dept01, the PROC PRINT statement is modified to the following:

```
proc print data=hr.dept01;
```

Note: This program does not produce a different window; it simply redisplays the primary menu when the file has been printed.

Creating a Simple User Interface

Finally, to make the application easy for users to access, you can build an operating system command file that automatically runs the SAS program that displays the primary window. The primary requirements are that the command file

- use operating-system commands to define a fileref for the file in which you have stored the SAS statements that generate the main window
- specify the SAS command with the AUTOEXEC= option to execute the statements for which you just defined a fileref.

The user can invoke the application by calling the command file.

Chapter 27

The PRINT Procedure

ABSTRACT

The PRINT procedure prints the observations in a SAS data set, using all or some of the variables. PROC PRINT can also print totals and subtotals for numeric variables.

INTRODUCTION

The PRINT procedure prints a listing of the values of some or all of the variables in a SAS data set. You can produce customized reports using procedure options and statements; for example, when you use a BY statement, PROC PRINT separates observations into groups defined by the BY variables. The PRINT procedure prints totals of the values of numeric variables when you use the SUM statement.

SPECIFICATIONS

The following statements control the PRINT procedure:

PROC PRINT <*option-list*>;
   VAR *variable-list*;
   ID *variable-list*;
   BY *variable-list*;
     PAGEBY *BY-variable*;
     SUMBY *BY-variable*;
   SUM *variable-list*;

PROC PRINT Statement

   PROC PRINT <*option-list*>;

Table 27.1 summarizes the options supported by the PROC PRINT statement. Detailed explanations follow the table in alphabetic order:

Table 27.1 Summary of PROC PRINT Statement Options

Class	Option	Function
Specifying data set	DATA=	names the SAS data set to print
Formatting output	DOUBLE	double-spaces the printed output
	NOOBS	suppresses the observation number in the output
	UNIFORM	formats all pages uniformly
	LABEL	uses variables' labels as column headings
	SPLIT=	splits labels used as column headings across multiple lines
	N	prints the number of observations in the data set, in each BY group, or both
	ROUND	rounds values to the number of decimal places specified for a variable in a FORMAT statement or, if you do not specify a format, to two decimal places

DATA=*SAS-data-set*
   names the SAS data set to print. If you do not use the DATA= option, PROC PRINT uses the most recently created data set.

DOUBLE
D
   double-spaces the printed output.

LABEL
L

uses variables' labels as column headings. You can specify labels in
LABEL statements either in the DATA step that creates the data set or in
the PROC PRINT step. See *SAS Language: Reference, Version 6, First
Edition* for a description of the LABEL statement.

If you do not specify the LABEL option, or if a variable does not have
a label, PROC PRINT uses the variable's name as the column heading. If
you specify the LABEL option and at least one variable has a label,
PROC PRINT prints all column headings horizontally. Therefore, using
the LABEL option may increase the number of pages of output.

PROC PRINT splits labels if necessary in order to conserve space. Use
the SPLIT= option to control where these splits occur.

The PRINT procedure uses labels for BY variables in the header it
prints above each BY group, but it uses the variables' names when
identifying subtotals and totals (see **Output 27.9**).

N

prints the number of observations in the data set at the end of the
printed output.

If you use a BY statement with the N option, PROC PRINT displays
the number of observations in each BY group but not the total number
of observations in the data set. However, if you use a BY statement and
a SUM statement with the N option, PROC PRINT displays the number
of observations in each BY group and the total number of observations
in the data set.

NOOBS

suppresses the observation number in the output. Use the NOOBS
option when you do not use an ID statement but do not want to print
the observation numbers. (The ID statement also suppresses the printing
of observation numbers).

ROUND
R

rounds values to the number of decimal places specified for a variable in
a FORMAT statement or, if you do not specify a format, to two decimal
places. If you specify the ROUND option, the PRINT procedure rounds
variables before summing them.

SPLIT='*split-character*'
S='*split-character*'

splits labels used as column headings across multiple lines where the
split character appears. PROC PRINT does not print the split character.

You do not need to use both the LABEL and SPLIT= options because
the SPLIT= option implies that labels are to be used. For example, the
statements

```
proc print data=class split='*';
   label x='This Is*a Label';
run;
```

print this label for X:

```
This Is
a Label
```

You can use blanks in a label, and you can use multiple split characters within a label. For example, the following statements produce **Output 27.1**:

```
data test;
   input x $ @@;
   cards;
aaa bbb ccc ddd
;
run;

proc print data=test split='*';
   label x='This *Is*a* Label';
   title 'Using Multiple Split Characters and Blanks in a Label';
run;
```

Output 27.1   Using Multiple Split Characters in a Label

```
                   Using Multiple Split Characters and Blanks in a Label                        1
                                            This
                                             Is
                                              a
                                   OBS       Label
                                    1         aaa
                                    2         bbb
                                    3         ccc
                                    4         ddd
```

To print a column with no heading, use the split character as the variable's label. For example, these statements produce **Output 27.2**:

```
data test;
   input x $ @@;
   cards;
AAA BBB CCC DDD
;
run;

proc print data=test split='*';
   label x='*';
   title 'Printing a Column without a Heading';
run;
```

Output 27.2   Printing a Column without a Heading

```
                         Printing a Column without a Heading                                    1
                                     OBS
                                      1          AAA
                                      2          BBB
                                      3          CCC
                                      4          DDD
```

Note: PROC PRINT does not split labels of BY variables in the header preceding each BY group even if you specify the SPLIT= option. Instead, PROC PRINT uses the split character as part of the label.

UNIFORM
U

formats all pages uniformly. When you specify the UNIFORM option, PROC PRINT normally reads the data set twice. The first time PROC PRINT reads the data set, it determines the width of the data so that it can print the data with a suitable field width. The PRINT procedure prints the data as it reads them the second time. However, if all the variables in the data set have formats that explicitly specify a field width (for example, BEST12., but not BEST.), PROC PRINT reads the data set only once.

BY Statement

BY *variable-list*;

When you use a BY statement with the PRINT procedure, the procedure prints a separate analysis for each BY group.

When a BY statement appears, the PRINT procedure expects the input data set to be sorted in order of the BY variables or to have an appropriate index. If your input data set is not sorted in ascending order, you can do one of the following:

- Use the SORT procedure with a similar BY statement to sort the data.
- If appropriate, use the BY statement option NOTSORTED or DESCENDING.
- Create an index on the BY variables you want to use. For more information on creating indexes and using the BY statement with indexed data sets, see Chapter 17, "The DATASETS Procedure."

The LABEL and SPLIT= options have no effect on BY variables when PROC PRINT places them in headers above each BY group. However, if the list of ID variables exactly matches the list of BY variables, PROC PRINT produces a specially formatted report, illustrated in **Output 27.11**. In this case, PROC PRINT honors the LABEL and SPLIT= options with BY variables because the same variables are also ID variables.

ID Statement

ID *variable-list*;

When you use an ID statement, the PRINT procedure uses the formatted values of the ID variables instead of observation numbers to identify observations in the output.

When an observation is too long to print on one line, the PRINT procedure prints the values of the ID variables at the beginning of every line containing data values for the observation. The ID list is too large if it does not allow enough room to print at least one variable that is not in the ID list.

If the list of ID variables exactly matches the list of BY variables, PROC PRINT produces a specially formatted report, illustrated in **Output 27.11**.

PAGEBY Statement

PAGEBY *BY-variable;*

The PAGEBY statement begins printing a new page whenever the value of the specified BY variable changes or whenever the value of any BY variable listed before it in the BY statement changes.

The PAGEBY variable is one of the BY variables appearing in the BY statement in the PROC PRINT step. You must use a BY statement when you use the PAGEBY statement.

For example, the following SAS statements print a new page whenever the value of either X or Y changes, but not when the value of Z changes:

```
proc print;
   by x y z;
   pageby y;
run;
```

See **Example 3** and **Example 5** for illustrations of the use of the PAGEBY option.

SUM Statement

SUM *variable-list;*

The SUM statement specifies variables whose values are to be totaled.

If you specify in a SUM statement a variable that is not listed in the VAR statement, PROC PRINT adds the variable to the VAR list.

When you use a BY statement and a SUM statement in the same PROC PRINT step, the PRINT procedure subtotals the SUM variables for each BY group containing more than one observation and totals them over all BY groups. Consider this example, which uses only one BY variable, X:

```
libname test 'SAS-data-library';

data test.a;
   input x y z;
   cards;
1 1 1
2 1 1
2 1 2
3 1 1
3 1 2
3 3 1
3 3 2
3 4 1
3 4 2
4 1 1
;
run;

proc print data=test.a;
   by x;
   sum z;
   title 'Sum Variable Z Whenever X Changes Value';
run;
```

These SAS statements create and print the data set TEST.A shown in **Output 27.3**. Notice the following features in the output:

1. The BY statement groups the data separately for each value of the BY variable, X, and prints a header for each BY group.
2. The combination of the BY statement and the SUM statement sums the values of the SUM variable, Z, for each BY group containing more than one observation.
3. The SUM statement sums the values of Z for the entire data set.

You do not need to sort the data set because the observations are already sorted by the values of X and Y.

Output 27.3 Subtotaling the SUM Variable for Each BY Group

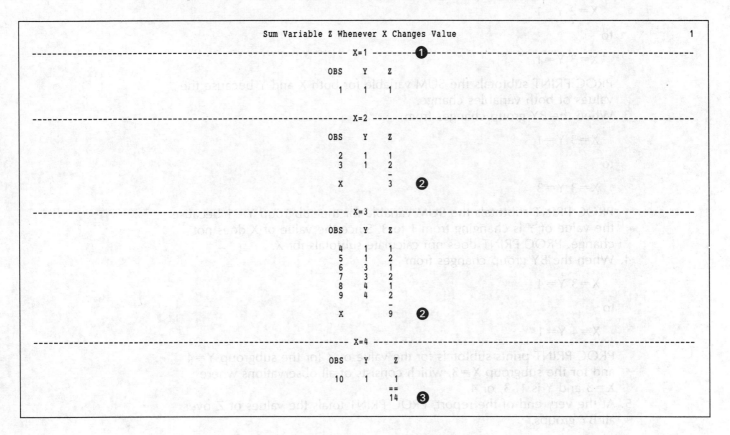

When you use a BY statement with multiple BY variables, PROC PRINT subtotals the SUM variables for each BY group containing more than one observation, just as it does if you use only one BY variable. However, it subtotals only those BY variables whose values change when the BY group changes.

Note: When the value of a BY variable changes, the SAS System considers that the values of all variables to its right in the BY statement change also.

Consider the following example, which uses two BY variables, X and Y:

```
libname test 'SAS-data-library';

proc print data=test.a;
   by x y;
   sum z;
   title 'Using the SUM statement with Multiple BY Variables';
run;
```

The output produced by these statements appears in **Output 27.4**. Notice the following features in the output:

1. The first and last subgroups in the report generate no subtotals because they contain only one observation.
2. When the BY group changes from

    X=2 Y=1

    to

    X=3 Y=1

    PROC PRINT subtotals the SUM variable for both X and Y because the values of both variables change.
3. When the BY group changes from

    X=3 Y=1

    to

    X=3 Y=3

    PROC PRINT subtotals the SUM variable for the subgroup Y=1 because the value of Y is changing from 1 to 3. Since the value of X does not change, PROC PRINT does not calculate subtotals for X.
4. When the BY group changes from

    X=3 Y=4

    to

    X=4 Y=1

    PROC PRINT prints subtotals for the value of Z for the subgroup Y=4 and for the subgroup X=3, which consists of all observations where X=3 and Y is 1, 3, or 4.
5. At the very end of the report, PROC PRINT totals the values of Z over all BY groups.

Output 27.4   Subtotaling the SUM Variable with Multiple BY Variables

```
                    Using the SUM statement with Multiple BY Variables                    1
--------------------------------------- X=1 Y=1 ---------------------------------------

                                        OBS    Z

                                         1     1          ❶

--------------------------------------- X=2 Y=1 ---------------------------------------

                                        OBS    Z

                                         2     1
                                         3     2
                                         Y     -
                                               3          ❷
                                         X     3

--------------------------------------- X=3 Y=1 ---------------------------------------

                                        OBS    Z

                                         4     1
                                         5     2
                                         Y     -
                                               3          ❸

--------------------------------------- X=3 Y=3 ---------------------------------------

                                        OBS    Z

                                         6     1
                                         7     2
                                         Y     -
                                               3

--------------------------------------- X=3 Y=4 ---------------------------------------

                                        OBS    Z

                                         8     1
                                         9     2
                                         Y     -
                                               3          ❹
                                         X     9

--------------------------------------- X=4 Y=1 ---------------------------------------

                                        OBS    Z

                                         10    1          ❶
                                               ==
                                               14         ❺
```

For another example of using the SUM statement with multiple BY variables, see **Example 5**.

SUMBY Statement

SUMBY *BY-variable*;

The SUMBY statement prints subtotals for the specified BY variable whenever its value changes or whenever the value of any BY variable listed before it in the BY statement changes.

The SUMBY variable is a numeric variable appearing in the BY statement in the PROC PRINT step. You must use a BY statement when you use the SUMBY statement.

The SUMBY statement limits the printing of subtotals for BY groups. PROC PRINT still groups the data by all BY variables but prints subtotals only when the SUMBY variable changes. Without the SUMBY variable, the PRINT procedure prints subtotals for each BY group containing more than one observation.

If you do not use a SUM statement, PROC PRINT subtotals all the numeric variables in the data set except those listed in the ID and BY statements. If you do use a SUM statement, the PRINT procedure subtotals only the variables listed in that statement.

For example, the following SAS statements subtotal the variables A, B, and C when either X or Y changes value, but not when Z changes value:

```
proc print;
   sum a b c;
   by x y z;
   sumby y;
run;
```

See **Example 6** for an illustration of the use of the SUMBY statement.

VAR Statement

VAR *variable-list*;

The VAR statement names the variables to print.

PROC PRINT prints the variables in the order you list them in the VAR statement. If you do not use the VAR statement, the PRINT procedure prints all variables in the data set.

DETAILS

Page Format

PROC PRINT uses an identical format for all observations on a page of output. First, it attempts to print observations on a single line. If it cannot do so, it splits the observations into two or more sections and prints the observation number or the ID variables at the beginning of each line. By default, spacing dictates whether the PRINT procedure prints column headings horizontally or vertically. If you use the LABEL option, the PRINT procedure prints all column headings horizontally, breaking up the report into additional sections if necessary.

The data width of an unformatted character variable is its length or the page size minus the length of the ID variable, whichever is less. The width of an unformatted numeric variable is 12.

Printed Output

The printed output for PROC PRINT includes:

1. OBS, the number of each observation in the data set, in the leftmost column of the output. (OBS is not a variable in the data set; it is only used by the PRINT procedure to identify observations when the ID statement is not used or when the NOOBS option is not used.) If an ID variable is used, ID values, rather than observation numbers, are printed, and the column is headed with the name or label of the ID variable.
2. the names or labels of all variables that are printed.
3. the names or labels of BY variables, if any, and their current values above each section.
4. totals for the specified variables.
5. subtotals for the specified variables for BY groups containing more than one observation.

EXAMPLES

Example 1:   Printing a Simple Report

This example creates, sorts, and prints a SAS data set containing a company's sales and expense reports for four regions of the United States. The example uses the simplest form of the PROC PRINT statement. The following statements produce **Output 27.5**:

```
libname branch 'SAS-data-library';

data branch.rawdata;
   input region $ state $ month monyy5.
         headcnt expenses revenue;
   format month monyy5.;
   cards;
Eastern  VA FEB78 10  7800 15500
Southern FL MAR78  9  9800 13500
Southern GA JAN78  5  2000  8000
Northern MA MAR78  3  1500  1000
Southern FL FEB78 10  8500 11000
Northern NY MAR78  5  6000  5000
Eastern  VA MAR78 11  8200 16600
Plains   NM MAR78  2  1350   500
Southern FL JAN78 10  8000 10000
Northern NY FEB78  4  3000  4000
Southern GA FEB78  7  1200  6000
;
run;
```

```
proc sort data=branch.rawdata out=branch.sorted;
   by region state month;
run;

proc print;
   title 'PROC PRINT Provides a Listing of BRANCH.SORTED';
run;
```

Output 27.5   The Data Set BRANCH.SORTED

```
                      PROC PRINT Provides a Listing of BRANCH.SORTED                    1
     ❶      ❷
     OBS    REGION     STATE    MONTH    HEADCNT    EXPENSES    REVENUE

      1     Eastern     VA      FEB78       10        7800       15500
      2     Eastern     VA      MAR78       11        8200       16600
      3     Northern    MA      MAR78        3        1500        1000
      4     Northern    NY      FEB78        4        3000        4000
      5     Northern    NY      MAR78        5        6000        5000
      6     Plains      NM      MAR78        2        1350         500
      7     Southern    FL      JAN78       10        8000       10000
      8     Southern    FL      FEB78       10        8500       11000
      9     Southern    FL      MAR78        9        9800       13500
     10     Southern    GA      JAN78        5        2000        8000
     11     Southern    GA      FEB78        7        1200        6000
```

Because the PROC PRINT statement does not include the DATA= option, PROC PRINT prints the most recently created SAS data set, BRANCH.SORTED. The PRINT procedure prints all variables in the data set and identifies each observation by number.

Example 2: Using the BY Statement

This example uses the BY statement to print a report that presents the data in BRANCH.SORTED for each sales region. The LABEL statement associates a label with each variable for the duration of the PROC PRINT step. The FORMAT statement associates a format with the variables HEADCNT, REVENUE, and EXPENSES for the duration of the step. The SPLIT= option assigns the asterisk as the split character so that PROC PRINT splits the label for HEADCNT over two lines. The following statements produce **Output 27.6**:

```
libname branch 'SAS-data-library';

proc print data=branch.sorted split='*';
   by region;
   label region='Sales Region'
          state='State'
          month='Month'
        headcnt='Sales*Personnel'
       expenses='Expenses'
        revenue='Revenue';
   format headcnt 3. revenue expenses comma10.;
   title 'Using the BY Statement to Group the Data by Sales Region';
run;
```

Output 27.6 Using the BY Statement to Group the Data by Sales Region

```
                    Using the BY Statement to Group the Data by Sales Region                                      1
-----------------------------❸----------- Sales Region=Eastern ------------------------------------------------

                                     Sales
           OBS    State    Month    Personnel         Expenses        Revenue

            1      VA       FEB78       10              7,800          15,500
            2      VA       MAR78       11              8,200          16,600


----------------------------------------- Sales Region=Northern -----------------------------------------------

                                     Sales
           OBS    State    Month    Personnel         Expenses        Revenue

            3      MA       MAR78        3              1,500           1,000
            4      NY       FEB78        4              3,000           4,000
            5      NY       MAR78        5              6,000           5,000


------------------------------------------- Sales Region=Plains -----------------------------------------------

                                     Sales
           OBS    State    Month    Personnel         Expenses        Revenue

            6      NM       MAR78        2              1,350            500


----------------------------------------- Sales Region=Southern -----------------------------------------------

                                     Sales
           OBS    State    Month    Personnel         Expenses        Revenue

            7      FL       JAN78       10              8,000          10,000
            8      FL       FEB78       10              8,500          11,000
            9      FL       MAR78        9              9,800          13,500
           10      GA       JAN78        5              2,000           8,000
           11      GA       FEB78        7              1,200           6,000
```

Example 3:   Using the PAGEBY Statement

This example uses the PAGEBY statement to produce a report in which PROC PRINT begins a new page each time the value of STATE or REGION changes. The following statements produce **Output 27.7**:

```
libname branch 'SAS-data-library';

proc print data=branch.sorted split='*';
     /* Group the data by REGION and STATE */
   by region state;
     /* Start a new page each time the value of */
     /* STATE or REGION changes                 */
   pageby state;
   label region='Sales Region'
         state='State'
         month='Month'
       headcnt='Sales*Personnel'
      expenses='Expenses'
       revenue='Revenue';
   format headcnt 3. revenue expenses comma10.;
   title 'Using the PAGEBY Statement to Start a New Page';
   title2 'Each Time the Value of STATE or REGION Changes';
run;
```

Output 27.7   Using the PAGEBY Statement

```
                    Using the PAGEBY Statement to Start a New Page                                 1
                    Each Time the Value of STATE or REGION Changes

------------------------------------- Sales Region=Eastern State=VA -----------------------------------

                                    Sales
                 OBS    Month    Personnel      Expenses        Revenue

                   1    FEB78       10            7,800          15,500
                   2    MAR78       11            8,200          16,600
```

```
                    Using the PAGEBY Statement to Start a New Page                                 2
                    Each Time the Value of STATE or REGION Changes

------------------------------------- Sales Region=Northern State=MA ----------------------------------

                                    Sales
                 OBS    Month    Personnel      Expenses        Revenue

                   3    MAR78        3            1,500          1,000
```

```
                          Using the PAGEBY Statement to Start a New Page                    3
                          Each Time the Value of STATE or REGION Changes

-------------------------------------------- Sales Region=Northern State=NY --------------------------------------------

                                    Sales
              OBS    Month      Personnel        Expenses          Revenue

               4     FEB78          4              3,000            4,000
               5     MAR78          5              6,000            5,000
```

```
                          Using the PAGEBY Statement to Start a New Page                    4
                          Each Time the Value of STATE or REGION Changes

-------------------------------------------- Sales Region=Plains State=NM --------------------------------------------

                                    Sales
              OBS    Month      Personnel        Expenses          Revenue

               6     MAR78          2              1,350             500
```

```
                          Using the PAGEBY Statement to Start a New Page                    5
                          Each Time the Value of STATE or REGION Changes

-------------------------------------------- Sales Region=Southern State=FL --------------------------------------------

                                    Sales
              OBS    Month      Personnel        Expenses          Revenue

               7     JAN78         10              8,000           10,000
               8     FEB78         10              8,500           11,000
               9     MAR78          9              9,800           13,500
```

```
                          Using the PAGEBY Statement to Start a New Page                    6
                          Each Time the Value of STATE or REGION Changes

-------------------------------------------- Sales Region=Southern State=GA --------------------------------------------

                                    Sales
              OBS    Month      Personnel        Expenses          Revenue

              10     JAN78          5              2,000            8,000
              11     FEB78          7              1,200            6,000
```

Example 4:   Using the SUM Statement

In this example, the SUM statement totals the values of the SUM variables, EXPENSES and REVENUE, at the end of the report. The example uses no BY processing (see **Example 5** for an illustration of using the SUM statement with the BY statement). The following statements produce **Output 27.8**:

```
libname branch 'SAS-data-library';

proc print data=branch.sorted split='*';
    /* Sum the values for REVENUE and EXPENSES at the */
    /* end of the report.                             */
  sum revenue expenses;
  label  region='Sales Region'
       headcnt='Sales*Personnel'
         state='State'
       revenue='Revenue'
      expenses='Expenses'
         month='Month';
  format headcnt 3. revenue expenses comma10.;
  title 'Revenue and Expense Totals';
run;
```

Output 27.8   Using the SUM Statement

```
                              Revenue and Expense Totals                              1

            Sales                       Sales
    OBS     Region    State   Month   Personnel      Expenses        Revenue

      1     Eastern     VA    FEB78      10             7,800         15,500
      2     Eastern     VA    MAR78      11             8,200         16,600
      3     Northern    MA    MAR78       3             1,500          1,000
      4     Northern    NY    FEB78       4             3,000          4,000
      5     Northern    NY    MAR78       5             6,000          5,000
      6     Plains      NM    MAR78       2             1,350            500
      7     Southern    FL    JAN78      10             8,000         10,000
      8     Southern    FL    FEB78      10             8,500         11,000
      9     Southern    FL    MAR78       9             9,800         13,500
     10     Southern    GA    JAN78       5             2,000          8,000
     11     Southern    GA    FEB78       7             1,200          6,000
                                                    ==========     ==========
                                                       57,350         91,100   ❹
```

Example 5:   Using the SUM Statement with a BY Statement

This example creates a report that totals revenues and expenses for each state and each region for which more than one observation exists. The last line of the report shows the grand total of revenues and expenses for all states and sales regions. The PAGEBY statement starts a new page each time the value of REGION changes, making the report easier to read. The following statements produce **Output 27.9**:

```
libname branch 'SAS-data-library';

proc print data=branch.sorted split='*';
     /* Group the data by REGION and STATE */
  by region state;
     /* Sum the values for REVENUE and EXPENSES for each   */
     /* BY group containing more than one observation.     */
     /* Also show the grand totals for all BY groups.      */
  sum revenue expenses;
     /* Start a new page when the value of REGION changes. */
  pageby region;
  label  region='Sales Region'
        headcnt='Sales*Personnel'
          state='State'
        revenue='Revenue'
       expenses='Expenses'
          month='Month';
  format headcnt 3. revenue expenses comma10.;
  title 'Revenue and Expense Totals';
run;
```

Output 27.9   Totaling REVENUE and EXPENSES

```
                        Revenue and Expense Totals                                          1
-------------------------------- Sales Region=Eastern State=VA -------------------------------

                              Sales
              OBS   Month   Personnel     Expenses     Revenue

               1    FEB78       10           7,800      15,500
               2    MAR78       11           8,200      16,600
                                          ----------  ----------
             STATE                           16,000      32,100     ❺
            REGION                           16,000      32,100
```

```
                               Revenue and Expense Totals                                    2
-------------------------------- Sales Region=Northern State=MA ---------------------------------
                            Sales
             OBS   Month   Personnel       Expenses       Revenue

              3    MAR78       3              1,500         1,000

-------------------------------- Sales Region=Northern State=NY ---------------------------------
                            Sales
             OBS   Month   Personnel       Expenses       Revenue

              4    FEB78       4              3,000         4,000
              5    MAR78       5              6,000         5,000
                                            ----------    ----------
            STATE                            9,000         9,000
            REGION                          10,500        10,000
```

```
                               Revenue and Expense Totals                                    3
-------------------------------- Sales Region=Plains State=NM -----------------------------------
                            Sales
             OBS   Month   Personnel       Expenses       Revenue

              6    MAR78       2              1,350          500
```

```
                               Revenue and Expense Totals                                    4
-------------------------------- Sales Region=Southern State=FL ---------------------------------
                            Sales
             OBS   Month   Personnel       Expenses       Revenue

              7    JAN78      10              8,000        10,000
              8    FEB78      10              8,500        11,000
              9    MAR78       9              9,800        13,500
                                            ----------    ----------
            STATE                           26,300        34,500

-------------------------------- Sales Region=Southern State=GA ---------------------------------
                            Sales
             OBS   Month   Personnel       Expenses       Revenue

             10    JAN78       5              2,000         8,000
             11    FEB78       7              1,200         6,000
                                            ----------    ----------
            STATE                            3,200        14,000
            REGION                          29,500        48,500
                                            ==========    ==========
                                            57,350        91,100
```

The SUM statement, in combination with the BY statement, sums REVENUE and EXPENSES for each BY group of REGION and STATE that contains more than one observation. If only the value of STATE changes from one BY group to the next, the PRINT procedure sums the variables only for STATE. If both STATE and REGION change, the PRINT procedure sums the variables for both STATE and REGION.

Example 6:   Using the SUMBY Statement

This example uses the SUMBY statement to produce a report in which PROC PRINT prints subtotals for REVENUE and EXPENSES each time the value of REGION changes.

```
libname branch 'SAS-data-library';

proc print data=branch.sorted split='*';
    /* Group the data by REGION and STATE */
  by region state;
    /* Sum the SUM variables when the value of REGION changes */
  sumby region;
  sum revenue expenses;
    /* Start a new page when the value of REGION changes. */
  pageby region;
  label region='Sales Region'
        state='State'
        month='Month'
      headcnt='Sales*Personnel'
     expenses='Expenses'
      revenue='Revenue';
  format headcnt 3. revenue expenses comma10.;
  title 'Using the SUMBY Statement to Sum the SUM Variables';
  title2 'Each Time the Value of REGION Changes';
run;
```

The output from these statements appears in **Output 27.10**. Compare this output with **Output 27.9**, which was produced by the same SAS statements without the SUMBY statement and, therefore, shows subtotals whenever STATE or REGION changes. Adding the SUMBY statement enables you to continue grouping the data by both BY variables but restricts the printing of subtotals to the cases where the value of the SUMBY variable changes.

Output 27.10   Using the SUMBY Statement to Sum the SUM Variables Each Time the Value of REGION Changes

```
                 Using the SUMBY Statement to Sum the SUM Variables                                    1
                        Each Time the Value of REGION Changes

------------------------------------------ Sales Region=Eastern State=VA ------------------------------------------

                          Sales
          OBS   Month   Personnel      Expenses      Revenue

            1   FEB78       10            7,800        15,500
            2   MAR78       11            8,200        16,600
                                       ----------    ----------
        REGION                            16,000       32,100
```

```
                Using the SUMBY Statement to Sum the SUM Variables                    2
                    Each Time the Value of REGION Changes
----------------------------------- Sales Region=Northern State=MA -----------------------------------

                                Sales
        OBS    Month       Personnel        Expenses       Revenue

         3     MAR78           3              1,500          1,000


----------------------------------- Sales Region=Northern State=NY -----------------------------------

                                Sales
        OBS    Month       Personnel        Expenses       Revenue

         4     FEB78           4              3,000          4,000
         5     MAR78           5              6,000          5,000
                                             ----------     ----------
     REGION                                  10,500         10,000
```

```
                Using the SUMBY Statement to Sum the SUM Variables                    3
                    Each Time the Value of REGION Changes
----------------------------------- Sales Region=Plains State=NM -----------------------------------

                                Sales
        OBS    Month       Personnel        Expenses       Revenue

         6     MAR78           2              1,350           500
```

```
                Using the SUMBY Statement to Sum the SUM Variables                    4
                    Each Time the Value of REGION Changes
----------------------------------- Sales Region=Southern State=FL -----------------------------------

                                Sales
        OBS    Month       Personnel        Expenses       Revenue

         7     JAN78          10              8,000         10,000
         8     FEB78          10              8,500         11,000
         9     MAR78           9              9,800         13,500


----------------------------------- Sales Region=Southern State=GA -----------------------------------

                                Sales
        OBS    Month       Personnel        Expenses       Revenue

        10     JAN78           5              2,000          8,000
        11     FEB78           7              1,200          6,000
                                             ----------     ----------
     REGION                                  29,500         48,500
                                             ==========     ==========
                                             57,350         91,100
```

Example 7:   Using Identical BY and ID Statements

PROC PRINT prepares a different type of summary report when the list of ID variables exactly matches the list of BY variables, as in the following example. The following statements produce **Output 27.11**:

```
libname branch 'SAS-data-library';

proc print data=branch.sorted split='*';
     /* Group the data by REGION and STATE */
   by region state;

     /* ID variables exactly match BY variables */
   id region state;
   sum revenue expenses;
   label region='Sales Region'
        headcnt='Sales*Personnel'
          state='State'
        revenue='Revenue'
       expenses='Expenses'
          month='Month';
   format headcnt 3. revenue expenses comma10.;
   title 'Format when ID and BY Variables Match';
run;
```

Output 27.11   Format of a Report when ID and BY Variables Match

```
                    Format when ID and BY Variables Match                          1

    Sales                          Sales
    Region      State    Month    Personnel      Expenses         Revenue

    Eastern      VA      FEB78        10            7,800          15,500
                         MAR78        11            8,200          16,600
    --------    -----                           ----------      ----------
    Eastern      VA                              16,000          32,100
    Eastern                                      16,000          32,100

    Northern     MA      MAR78         3           1,500           1,000

    Northern     NY      FEB78         4           3,000           4,000
                         MAR78         5           6,000           5,000
    --------    -----                           ----------      ----------
    Northern     NY                               9,000           9,000
    Northern                                     10,500          10,000

    Plains       NM      MAR78         2           1,350             500

    Southern     FL      JAN78        10           8,000          10,000
                         FEB78        10           8,500          11,000
                         MAR78         9           9,800          13,500
    --------    -----                           ----------      ----------
    Southern     FL                              26,300          34,500

    Southern     GA      JAN78         5           2,000           8,000
                         FEB78         7           1,200           6,000
    --------    -----                           ----------      ----------
    Southern     GA                               3,200          14,000
    Southern                                     29,500          48,500
                                                ==========      ==========
                                                57,350          91,100
```

Because the ID and BY variables match, PROC PRINT dispenses with the usual headings above each BY group. Instead, the labels for the ID variables identify the BY groups. In addition, PROC PRINT identifies subtotals by the value of the BY variables (for instance, **Eastern** and **VA**) rather than by their names (compare **Output 27.9**, which identifies subtotals by STATE and REGION).

Chapter 28

The PRINTTO
Procedure

ABSTRACT

The PRINTTO procedure defines destinations for SAS procedure output and for the SAS log.

INTRODUCTION

By default, SAS procedure output is routed to the default procedure output file for your execution mode. The SAS log is routed to the default SAS log file for your execution mode. (Refer to Chapter 5, "SAS Output," in *SAS Language: Reference, Version 6, First Edition* for information on default output destinations.) With PROC PRINTTO, you can specify a fileref, a filename, or a logical name as the destination for printed output or the SAS log.

  You can use PROC PRINTTO to

- choose a destination for procedure output
- choose a destination for the SAS log
- suppress SAS output selectively
- route the print file to a permanent file
- use SAS output as input data within the same job. (This requires additional programming.)

SPECIFICATIONS

The PROC PRINTTO statement is the only statement necessary. If no options are specified, PROC PRINTTO returns both the SAS log and the SAS procedure output to their default destinations.

PROC PRINTTO Statement

PROC PRINTTO <*option-list*>;

You can use the following options in the PROC PRINTTO statement:

LOG=*fileref* | '*filename*'
routes the SAS log to a file specified by either a fileref or a filename. For example, the statements

```
proc printto log='log-filename';
run;
```

route the SAS log to the specified file until the log is redirected to a new destination. You can also use the following statements to do the same thing:

```
filename newlog 'log-filename';

proc printto log=newlog;
run;
```

To route the SAS log back to its default destination, specify

```
proc printto log=log;
run;
```

NEW
clears any information that exists in a file and prepares the file to receive output. If you do not use the NEW option, the output is appended to the file.

If you use the NEW option on a PROC PRINTTO statement that redirects both the procedure output and the SAS log, both files referenced are cleared. For example, suppose the procedure output and the SAS log are currently routed to their standard print files. The statements

```
filename newlog 'log-filename';
filename newout 'output-filename';

proc printto log=newlog print=newout new;
run;
```

clear the files referenced by NEWLOG and NEWOUT and route the SAS log and the procedure output to these files. The statements

```
proc printto;
run;
```

route both the SAS log and the procedure output back to their default destinations. If later you want to add more information to the same files, use the PROC PRINTTO statement without the NEW option to append data to them:

```
proc printto log=newlog print=newout;
run;
```

Output from this point on is appended to the earlier output.

PRINT=*fileref* | '*filename*'
FILE=*fileref* | '*filename*'
NAME=*fileref* | '*filename*'

direct output to the file identified by the fileref previously created with a FILENAME statement or to the file designated by the filename. For example, the statements

```
proc printto print='output-filename';
run;
```

route the output to the specified file until the output is directed to a new destination. You can also use the following statements to do the same thing:

```
filename newout 'output-filename';

proc printto print=newout;
run;
```

To route the procedure output back to its default destination, specify

```
proc printto print=print;
run;
```

UNIT=*nn*

directs the output to the file identified by the fileref FT*nn*F001, where *nn* is an integer between 1 and 99. You can define this fileref yourself; however, some operating systems predefine certain filerefs of this form.

DETAILS

Output

The PRINTTO procedure does not produce an output data set or printed output.

Usage Notes

PROC PRINTTO is useful when you want to route output from different steps of a SAS job to different files. When the SAS system option NUMBER is in effect, there is a single page-numbering sequence for all output from the job. Alternatively, you can use the SAS system option PAGENO= in an OPTIONS statement to specify a beginning page number for the output you are currently producing. If the NUMBER option is not in effect, numbers do not appear on output pages.

When routing the SAS log, enter a RUN statement after the PROC PRINTTO statement. If you omit the RUN statement, the first line of the following DATA or PROC step is not routed to the new file. (This occurs because the PRINTTO procedure is not executed until after the next PROC, DATA, or RUN statement is encountered.)

EXAMPLES

Example 1: Changing the Print Destination and Switching Back

Suppose that you want to route the output of a certain procedure to a text file so that you can look at the information later, but you want all the other output generated by your SAS program to be routed to its default destination. You need to execute PROC PRINTTO twice. In this example, the first PRINTTO procedure routes the output to the file referenced by NEWOUT. The second PRINTTO procedure routes the output back to the standard SAS print file.

```
filename newout 'output-filename';

data numbers;
   input x y z;
   cards;
14.2    25.2    96.8
10.8    51.6    96.8
 9.5    34.2   138.2
 8.8    27.6    83.2
11.5    49.4   287.0
 6.3    42.0   170.7
;
run;


   /* Route output to NEWOUT. */
proc printto new print=newout;
run;

proc print data=numbers;
   title 'PROC PRINT Output Routed to NEWOUT';
run;

   /* Route output back to standard output file. */
proc printto;
run;

proc chart data=numbers;
   vbar x / sumvar=y;
   title 'PROC CHART Output Routed to Standard Output File';
run;
```

The procedure output is shown in **Output 28.1** and **Output 28.2**.

Output 28.1 Output Routed to NEWOUT

```
                        PROC PRINT Output Routed to NEWOUT                      1

                         OBS      X        Y        Z

                          1     14.2     25.2     96.8
                          2     10.8     51.6     96.8
                          3      9.5     34.2    138.2
                          4      8.8     27.6     83.2
                          5     11.5     49.4    287.0
                          6      6.3     42.0    170.7
```

Output 28.2   Output Routed to the Standard Print File

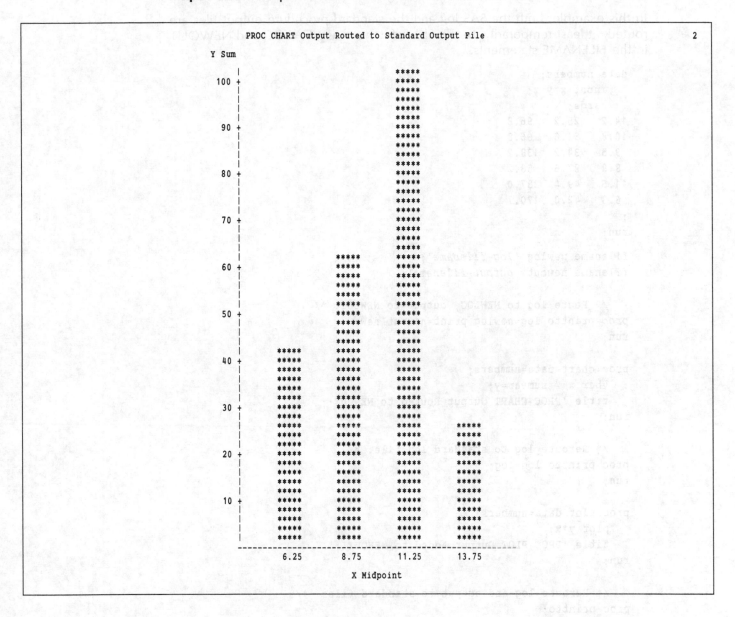

Example 2:   Rerouting the SAS Log and Procedure Output Files

In this example, both the SAS log and the standard procedure output files are routed, at least temporarily, to the files referenced as NEWLOG and NEWOUT in the FILENAME statements.

```
data numbers;
   input x y z;
   cards;
14.2   25.2    96.8
10.8   51.6    96.8
 9.5   34.2   138.2
 8.8   27.6    83.2
11.5   49.4   287.0
 6.3   42.0   170.7
;
run;

filename newlog 'log-filename';
filename newout 'output-filename';

   /* Route log to NEWLOG, output to NEWOUT. */
proc printto log=newlog print=newout new;
run;

proc chart data=numbers;
   vbar x / sumvar=y;
   title 'PROC CHART Output Routed to NEWOUT';
run;

   /* Reroute log to standard log file. */
proc printto log=log;
run;

proc plot data=numbers;
   plot y*x;
   title 'PROC PLOT Output Added to NEWOUT';
run;

   /* Reroute log and output to standard files. */
proc printto;
run;

proc print data=numbers;
   title 'PROC PRINT Output Routed to Standard Output File';
run;
```

The first PRINTTO procedure routes the SAS log to NEWLOG and the procedure output to NEWOUT. Thus, the SAS System writes the log for the CHART procedure to NEWLOG, the output to NEWOUT (see **Output 28.3** and **Output 28.4**).

The second PRINTTO procedure uses LOG=LOG to return the SAS log to its default output file. However, because the procedure output is still being routed to NEWOUT, the SAS System appends the output from the PLOT procedure to the alternate output file, NEWOUT (see **Output 28.4**).

Output 28.3   SAS Log Routed to Alternate Log File

```
19
20          proc chart data=numbers;
21             vbar x / sumvar=y;
22              title 'PROC CHART Output Routed to NEWOUT';
23          run;

NOTE: The PROCEDURE CHART printed page 1.

24
25             /* Reroute log to standard log file. */
26          proc printto log=log;
27          run;
```

Output 28.4   Output for PROC CHART and PROC PLOT Routed to Alternate Output File

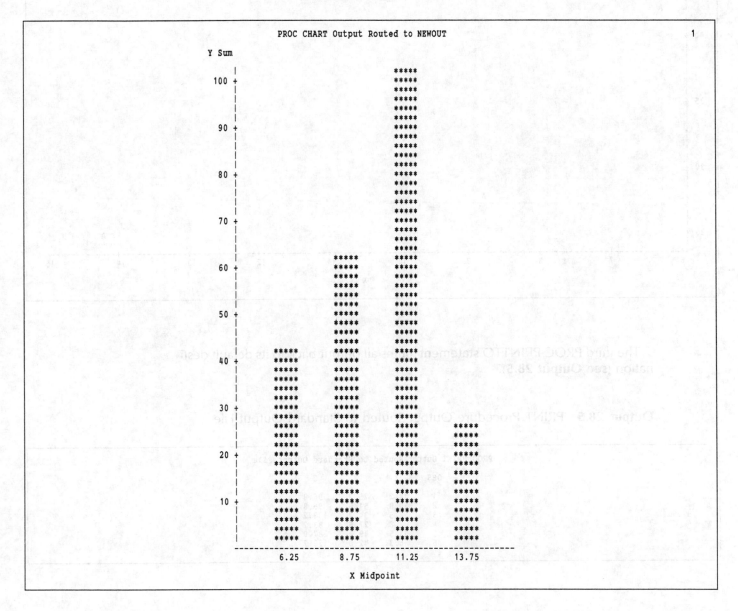

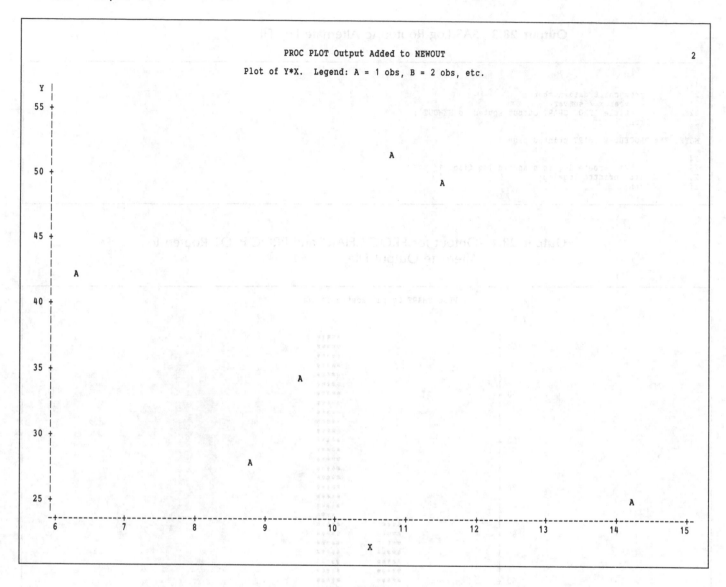

PROC PLOT Output Added to NEWOUT

Plot of Y*X. Legend: A = 1 obs, B = 2 obs, etc.

The third PROC PRINTTO statement routes all output back to its default destination (see **Output 28.5**).

Output 28.5   PRINT Procedure Output Routed to Standard Output File

```
            PROC PRINT Output Routed to Standard Output File           3

                 OBS      X       Y       Z

                  1     14.2    25.2     96.8
                  2     10.8    51.6     96.8
                  3      9.5    34.2    138.2
                  4      8.8    27.6     83.2
                  5     11.5    49.4    287.0
                  6      6.3    42.0    170.7
```

Example 3:   Routing Output to a File and Using that File for Input

This example routes output from the FREQ procedure to the file associated with the fileref ROUTED. It then uses that file for input, selecting from it the value for the chi-square statistic and its associated probability, and writing them to the data set PROB. (PROC FREQ can create an output data set itself, but that data set does not contain these statistics.)

```
filename routed 'output-filename';

data a;
   do n=1 to 1000;
      x=int(ranuni(77777)*7);
      y=int(ranuni(77777)*5);
      output;
   end;
run;

   /* Redirect output to the specified file.*/
proc printto print=routed new;
run;

   /* Output from PROC FREQ goes to the file specified   */
   /* in the PROC PRINTTO statement.                     */
proc freq;
   tables x*y / chisq;
   title 'PROC FREQ Output';
run;

   /* Reroute output to the default.*/
proc printto;
run;

   /* Use the output file for input. Read the first word on a   */
   /* line. If the first 8 characters of that word are          */
   /* "Chi-Squa", read the next three items in the line into the */
   /* variables DF, CHISQ, and PROB. Keep the variables CHISQ    */
   /* and PROB and output them to the data set PROB.             */
data prob;
   infile routed;
   input word1 $ a;
   if word1='Chi-Squa' then
      do;
         input df chisq prob;
         keep chisq prob;
         output;
      end;
run;

   /* Print the output to the default location. */
proc print data=prob;
   title 'The Data Set Created from the Output from PROC FREQ';
run;
```

The table produced by the CHISQ option on the PROC FREQ statement appears in **Output 28.6**. (The procedure also produces four frequency tables, which are not shown.) The output from the PROC PRINT step, which shows the variables selected by the DATA step, is in **Output 28.7**.

Output 28.6   Output from PROC FREQ Routed to the Alternate File. The output shows only the table generated by the CHISQ option, not the complete output from PROC FREQ.

```
                              PROC FREQ Output                                    1

                       STATISTICS FOR TABLE OF X BY Y

         Statistic                    DF    Value      Prob
         ------------------------------------------------------
         Chi-Square                   24    27.297     0.291
         Likelihood Ratio Chi-Square  24    28.183     0.252
         Mantel-Haenszel Chi-Square    1     0.615     0.433
         Phi Coefficient                     0.165
         Contingency Coefficient             0.163
         Cramer's V                          0.083

         Sample Size = 1000
```

Output 28.7   Output Showing the Two Variables Selected by the DATA Step

```
            The Data Set Created from the Output from PROC FREQ              3

                   OBS     CHISQ     PROB

                    1     27.297    0.291
```

The RANK Procedure

ABSTRACT

By default, the RANK procedure computes ranks for one or more numeric variables across the observations of a SAS data set. The ranks are output to a new SAS data set. Alternatively, PROC RANK produces normal scores or other rank scores.

INTRODUCTION

The RANK procedure ranks values from smallest to largest, assigning the rank 1 to the smallest number, 2 to the next largest, and so on up to rank n, the number of nonmissing observations. Tied values are given averaged ranks. Several options are available to request other ranking and tie-handling rules.

   Many nonparametric statistical methods use ranks rather than the original values of a variable. For example, a set of data can be passed through PROC RANK to obtain the ranks for a response variable that could then be fit to an analysis-of-variance model using the ANOVA or GLM procedures.

   Ranks are also useful for investigating the distribution of values for a variable. The ranks divided by n or $n+1$ form values in the range 0 to 1, and these values estimate the cumulative distribution function. Inverse cumulative distribution functions can be applied to these fractional ranks to obtain probability quantile scores, which can be compared to the original values to judge the fit to the distribution. For example, if a set of data has a normal distribution, the normal scores should be a linear function of the original values, and a plot of scores versus original values should be a straight line.

PROC RANK is also useful for grouping continuous data into ranges. The GROUPS= option can break a population into approximately equal-sized groups.

SPECIFICATIONS

The RANK procedure is controlled by the following statements:

PROC RANK <option-list>;
    BY variable-list;
    RANKS new-variable-list;
    VAR variable-list;

PROC RANK Statement

PROC RANK <option-list>;

The options listed in **Table 29.1** can appear in the PROC RANK statement. They are described in alphabetic order following the table.

Table 29.1 PROC RANK Statement Options

Task	Options
Specify data sets	DATA= OUT=
Select ranking method	FRACTION GROUPS= NORMAL= NPLUS1 PERCENT SAVAGE
Reverse ranking	DESCENDING
Report tied values	TIES=

The PROC RANK statement starts the procedure. You may specify *only one* ranking method (FRACTION, GROUPS=, NORMAL=, NPLUS1, PERCENT, or SAVAGE) in a given execution of PROC RANK. If you request more than one of these options on the same PROC RANK statement, you will get the following message:

```
ERROR:  More than one method has been specified.  No ranks will
be computed.
```

You can specify the following options in the PROC RANK statement:

DATA=*SAS-data-set*
    names the SAS data set to be used by PROC RANK. If the DATA= option is omitted, the most recently created SAS data set is used.

DESCENDING

reverses the ranking to be from largest to smallest. The largest value is given a rank of 1, the next smallest a rank of 2, and so on. When the DESCENDING option is omitted, values are ranked from smallest to largest.

FRACTION

F

requests fractional ranks. The RANK procedure divides each rank by the number of observations having nonmissing values of the ranking variable and expresses the ranks as fractions. If you use the FRACTION option and have tied values, TIES=HIGH is the default. If the TIES= option is omitted or if TIES=HIGH is specified, these fractional ranks can be considered values of a right-continuous empirical cumulative distribution function.

GROUPS=n

requests grouping scores, where n is the number of groups. The grouping scores are the integers 0 to $(n-1)$. In the absence of ties, the groups have equal or nearly equal numbers of observations. The lowest values are in the first group; the highest values are in the last group. The following are common specifications:

GROUPS=100   produces percentile ranks.

GROUPS=10   produces deciles.

GROUPS=4   produces quartiles.

For example, if you specify GROUPS=4, then PROC RANK separates the values of the ranking variable into four groups according to size. The values in the group containing the smallest values receive a quartile value of 0, the values in the next group receive a value of 1, the values in the next group receive a value of 2, and the largest values receive the value 3.

The formula used to calculate the quantile rank of a value is

$$\text{FLOOR} (rank*k / (n + 1))$$

where FLOOR is the floor function, $rank$ is the value's rank, k is the number of groups specified with the GROUPS= option, and n is the number of observations having nonmissing values of the ranking variable. Use the GROUP= option only once with a single PROC RANK statement.

NORMAL=BLOM | TUKEY | VW

requests normal scores to be computed from the ranks. The resulting variables appear normally distributed. The formulas are as follows:

BLOM $y_i = \Phi^{-1}(r_i - 3/8) / (n + 1/4)$

TUKEY $y_i = \Phi^{-1}(r_i - 1/3) / (n + 1/3)$

VW $y_i = \Phi^{-1}(r_i) / (n + 1)$

where Φ^{-1} is the inverse cumulative normal (PROBIT) function, r_i is the rank, of the ith observation, and n is the number of nonmissing observations for the ranking variable. VW stands for van der Waerden, whose scores are used for a nonparametric location test.

These three normal scores are approximations to the exact expected order statistics for the normal distribution, also called *normal scores*. The BLOM version appears to fit slightly better than the others (Blom 1958; Tukey 1962).

NPLUS1
FN1
N1

requests fractional ranks where the denominator is $n+1$ rather than n (as in the FRACTION option), where n is the number of observations having nonmissing values of the ranking variable.

OUT=*SAS-data-set*

names the output data set that will contain the resulting ranks. If you do not specify the OUT= option, the data set is named using the DATA*n* naming convention. If you want to create a permanent SAS data set, you must specify a two-level name (see Chapter 6, "SAS Files," in *SAS Language: Reference, Version 6, First Edition* for more information on permanent SAS data sets). For details on the data set created by PROC RANK, see **Output Data Set** later in this chapter.

PERCENT
P

asks the RANK procedure to divide each rank by the number of observations having nonmissing values of the ranking variable and then to multiply the result by 100 to get a percentage. Like the FRACTION option, the PERCENT option implies TIES=HIGH unless another TIES= value is specified.

  Note: The PERCENT option does not give what are usually called *percentile ranks*. These are produced by specifying GROUPS=100.

SAVAGE

requests Savage (or exponential) scores be computed from the ranks. The scores are computed by this formula (Lehman 1975):

$$y_i = \left[\Sigma_{j=n-r_i+1}^{n} (1/j) \right] - 1 \quad .$$

TIES=MEAN | HIGH | LOW

specifies which rank to report for tied values. TIES=MEAN requests that tied values receive the mean of the corresponding ranks (midranks). The specification TIES=HIGH requests that the largest of the corresponding ranks be used. TIES=LOW requests that the smallest of the corresponding ranks be used. The default is TIES=MEAN.

Table 29.2 illustrates the three options available for handling tied values. Consider the values of the variable WEIGHT and the ranks that are assigned for each TIES value.

Table 29.2   Options Available for Handling Tied Values

WEIGHT	TIES=MEAN	TIES=HIGH	TIES=LOW
107	1	1	1
110	2.5	3	2
110	2.5	3	2
121	4	4	4
125	6	7	5
125	6	7	5
125	6	7	5
132	8	8	8

BY Statement

BY *variable-list*;

A BY statement can be used with PROC RANK to obtain separate analyses on observations in groups defined by the BY variables. When a BY statement appears, the procedure expects the input data set to be sorted in order of the BY variables or to have an appropriate index. If your input data set is not sorted in ascending order, you can do one of the following:

- Use the SORT procedure with a similar BY statement to sort the data.
- If appropriate, use the BY statement options NOTSORTED or DESCENDING.
- Use the DATASETS procedure to create an index on the BY variables you want to use. For more information on using the BY statement with indexed data sets, see Chapter 17, "The DATASETS Procedure."

RANKS Statement

RANKS *new-variable-list*;

If you want the original variables included in the output data set in addition to the ranks, use the RANKS statement to assign variable names to the ranks. First, name the rank corresponding to the first variable in the VAR statement, next name the rank corresponding to the second variable in the VAR statement, and so on. If the RANKS statement is omitted, the rank values replace the original variable values in the output data set. See **Example 1** for an example using the RANKS statement and **Example 2** for an example without a RANKS statement.

VAR Statement

   VAR *variable-list*;

The RANK procedure computes ranks for the variables given in the VAR statement. These variables must be numeric. If the VAR statement is omitted, ranks
are computed for all numeric variables in the data set. The VAR statement must
be included if a RANKS statement is used.

DETAILS

Missing Values

Missing values are not ranked and are left missing when ranks or rank scores
replace the other values of the ranking variable.

Output Data Set

The RANK procedure creates a new SAS data set containing the ranks or rank
scores but does not create any printed output.

   The new output data set contains all the variables from the input data set plus
the variables named in the RANKS statement, if one is specified. If a RANKS statement is used, a VAR statement must also be included. If you do not use the
RANKS statement, the procedure stores the ranks in the output data set using
the names of the original variables, changing the values to rankings. See **Example
2** for an illustration. If no VAR statement is included, the procedure ranks all
numeric variables.

Nonparametric Statistics

Many nonparametric methods are based on taking the ranks of a variable and
analyzing these ranks instead of the original values:

   - A two-sample *t*-test applied to the ranks is equivalent to a Wilcoxon rank
     sum test using the *t* approximation for the significance level. If the *t*-test
     is applied to the normal scores rather than to the ranks, the test becomes
     equivalent to the van der Waerden test. If the *t*-test is applied to median
     scores (GROUPS=2), the test becomes the median test.
   - A one-way analysis of variance applied to ranks is equivalent to the
     Kruskal-Wallis *k*-sample test; the *F* test generated by the parametric
     procedure applied to the ranks is often better than the χ^2 approximation
     used by Kruskal-Wallis. This test can be extended to other rank scores
     (Quade 1966).
   - Friedman's two-way analysis for block designs can be obtained by ranking
     within blocks (using a BY statement with PROC RANK) and then
     performing a main-effects analysis of variance on these ranks (Conover
     1980).
   - Regression relationships can be investigated using rank transformations
     with a method described by Iman and Conover (1979).

EXAMPLES

Example 1:   Ranking of Gain Values

This example uses PROC RANK to compute the ranks of the variable GAIN. The RANKS statement assigns the name RANKGAIN to the variable in the output data set containing the ranks. Since the OUT= option is not specified in the first execution of PROC RANK, a new data set is created using the DATA*n* naming convention. The PRINT procedure prints the contents of the output data set. The second execution of PROC RANK uses a BY variable and specifies an output data set.

The following statements produce **Output 29.1**:

```
data a;
   input location gain;
   cards;
1 7.2
1 7.9
1 7.6
1 6.3
1 8.4
1 8.1
2 8.1
2 7.3
2 7.7
2 7.7
;
run;

proc rank data=a;
   var gain;
   ranks rankgain;
run;

proc print data=a;
   title 'Rank the Gain Values';
run;

proc rank data=a out=b;
   by location;
   ranks rgain;
   var gain;
run;

proc print data=b;
   by location;
   title 'Rankings Within Locations';
run;
```

Output 29.1   Data Sets Generated with PROC RANK and Printed Using
PROC PRINT

```
                         Rank the Gain Values                          1
                        OBS   LOCATION   GAIN
                         1       1       7.2
                         2       1       7.9
                         3       1       7.6
                         4       1       6.3
                         5       1       8.4
                         6       1       8.1
                         7       2       8.1
                         8       2       7.3
                         9       2       7.7
                        10       2       7.7
```

```
                      Rankings Within Locations                        2
----------------------------------- LOCATION=1 -----------------------------------
                      OBS    GAIN    RGAIN
                       1     7.2       2
                       2     7.9       4
                       3     7.6       3
                       4     6.3       1
                       5     8.4       6
                       6     8.1       5

----------------------------------- LOCATION=2 -----------------------------------
                      OBS    GAIN    RGAIN
                       7     8.1      4.0
                       8     7.3      1.0
                       9     7.7      2.5
                      10     7.7      2.5
```

Example 2:   Ranking of Swim Scores

A swim coach needs to select swim team members to swim in a local competition.
The swimmers best times are stored in a SAS data set. This example uses PROC
RANK with a BY variable to get the rankings of swim scores by the variable SEX.
Because the RANKS statement is omitted, only the rankings of the swim times
appear in the output. If both the swim times and the rankings were desired, you
could add the following RANKS statement:

```
var back breast fly free;
ranks rback rbreast rfly rfree;
```

The PROC RANK output shows who has the best ranking for a given stroke. The following statements produce **Output 29.2**:

```
title 'Ranking Times Using the BY Statement';

data relay;
   input name $ sex $ back breast fly free;
   cards;
Sue     F 35.1 36.7 28.3 36.1
Karen   F 34.6 32.6 26.9 26.2
Jan     F 31.3 33.9 27.1 31.2
Andrea  F 28.6 34.1 29.1 30.3
Carol   F 32.9 32.2 26.6 24.0
Ellen   F 27.8 32.5 27.8 27.0
Jim     M 26.3 27.6 23.5 22.4
Mike    M 29.0 24.0 27.9 25.4
Sam     M 27.2 33.8 25.2 24.1
Clayton M 27.0 29.2 23.0 21.9
;
run;

proc rank data=relay out=fast;
   var back breast fly free;
   by sex;
run;

proc print data=fast;
   by sex;
run;
```

Output 29.2   Using PROC RANK to Rank Swim Times

```
                          Ranking Times Using the BY Statement                                  1
------------------------------------------- SEX=F -----------------------------------------------

            OBS     NAME      BACK     BREAST     FLY     FREE

             1      Sue        6         6         5       6
             2      Karen      5         3         2       2
             3      Jan        3         4         3       5
             4      Andrea     2         5         6       4
             5      Carol      4         1         1       1
             6      Ellen      1         2         4       3


------------------------------------------- SEX=M -----------------------------------------------

            OBS     NAME      BACK     BREAST     FLY     FREE

             7      Jim        1         2         2       2
             8      Mike       4         1         4       4
             9      Sam        3         4         3       3
            10      Clayton    2         3         1       1
```

REFERENCES

Blom, G. (1958), *Statistical Estimates and Transformed Beta Variables*, New York: John Wiley & Sons, Inc.

Conover, W.J. (1980), *Practical Nonparametric Statistics*, Second Edition, New York: John Wiley & Sons, Inc.

Conover, W.J. and Iman, R.L. (1976), "On Some Alternative Procedures Using Ranks for the Analysis of Experimental Designs," *Communications in Statistics*, A5, 14, 1348–1368.

Conover, W.J. and Iman, R.L. (1981) "Rank Transformations as a Bridge between Parametric and Nonparametric Statistics," *The American Statistician*, 35, 124–129.

Iman, R.L. and Conover, W.J. (1979), "The Use of the Rank Transform in Regression," *Technometrics*, 21, 499–509.

Lehman, E.L. (1975), *Nonparametrics: Statistical Methods Based on Ranks*, San Francisco: Holden-Day.

Quade, D. (1966), "On Analysis of Variance for the *k*-Sample Problem," *Annals of Mathematical Statistics*, 37, 1747–1758.

Tukey, John W. (1962), "The Future of Data Analysis," *Annals of Mathematical Statistics*, 33, 22.

Chapter 30
The RELEASE Procedure

ABSTRACT

The RELEASE procedure releases unused space at the end of a disk data set in an MVS environment. This procedure is described in system-dependent documentation.

The SORT Procedure

ABSTRACT

The SORT procedure sorts observations in a SAS data set by one or more variables, storing the resulting sorted observations in a new SAS data set or replacing the original data set.

INTRODUCTION

PROC SORT is used most often for sorting a data set so that other SAS procedures can process it in subsets using BY statements. Data sets must also be sorted before they can be match-merged or updated.

Note: If you have an appropriate index for a data set, you do not need to sort the data set to use a BY statement in a DATA or PROC step. For more information on using the BY statement with indexed data sets, see Chapter 17, "The DATASETS Procedure."

PROC SORT rearranges the observations in the data set according to the values of the variables in the BY statement, which must accompany the PROC SORT statement (see **BY Statement** later in this chapter). Suppose you want to sort a data set by an ID value that occurs in every observation. PROC SORT rearranges the data set so that the observation with the lowest ID value is first, the observation with the second lowest ID value is second, and so on. PROC SORT can also arrange observations in descending order.

When you want to sort by two or more variables, PROC SORT first arranges the data set in the order of the first BY variable. Then PROC SORT arranges the observations having the lowest value of the first variable (if several observations have the same value) in the order of the second variable. This continues for every BY variable specified. For example, if you sort a data set containing state and city information by state and then by city, PROC SORT first arranges the data so that Alabama's observations are first, then Alaska's, and so on. Next, the SORT procedure arranges Alabama's observations by the city value, so that Birmingham's observations are followed by Dothan's, and so on.

Note: The sorting capabilities described in this chapter are available on all host systems. In addition, if you set the SORTPGM= system option to HOST, you might be able to use other sorting options available only in your host environment. Refer to the SAS documentation for your host system for information on other sorting capabilities available when you specify SORTPGM=HOST. Refer to Chapter 16, "SAS System Options," in *SAS Language: Reference, Version 6, First Edition* for more information on the SORTPGM= system option.

SORTING ORDERS

For numeric variables, the smallest-to-largest comparison sequence is

1. SAS System missing value (shown as a period or special missing value)
2. negative numeric values
3. zero
4. positive numeric values.

PROC SORT uses either the EBCDIC or the ASCII collating sequence when it compares character values, depending on the environment under which the procedure is running.

EBCDIC Order

The operating systems that use the EBCDIC collating sequence include

CMS
MVS
VSE

From the smallest to largest displayable character, the English-language EBCDIC sequence is

blank ¢ . < (+ | & ! $ *) ; ¬ - / ¦ , % _ > ? ` : # @ ' = "
a b c d e f g h i j k l m n o p q r ~ s t u v w x y z
{ A B C D E F G H I } J K L M N O P Q R \ S T U V W X Y Z
0 1 2 3 4 5 6 7 8 9

The main features of the EBCDIC sequence are that lowercase letters are smaller than uppercase ones and uppercase letters are smaller than digits. Note also that some special characters interrupt the alphabetic sequences. The blank is the smallest displayable character.

ASCII Order

The operating systems that use the ASCII collating sequence include

AOS/VS
MS-DOS®
OS/2
PC DOS
PRIMOS®
UNIX® and its derivatives
VMS™

From the smallest to largest displayable character, the English-language ASCII sequence is

blank ! " # $ % & ' ( ) * + , - . / 0 1 2 3 4 5 6 7 8 9 : ; < = > ? @
A B C D E F G H I J K L M N O P Q R S T U V W X Y Z [\ ] ^ _ `
a b c d e f g h i j k l m n o p q r s t u v w x y z { | } ~

The main features of the ASCII sequence are that digits are smaller than uppercase letters and uppercase letters are smaller than lowercase ones. The blank is the smallest displayable character.

SPECIFICATIONS

The SORT procedure is controlled by the following statements:

PROC SORT <option-list> <collating-sequence-option>;
   BY <DESCENDING> variable-1 <...<DESCENDING> variable-n>;

The BY statement is required.

Table 31.1 summarizes the options that can be used in the SORT procedure. The options listed in the last column are used in the statement listed in the middle column.

Table 31.1   Summary of PROC SORT Options

Function	Statement	Options
Specify data sets	PROC SORT	DATA=, OUT=
Eliminate duplication	PROC SORT	NODUPLICATES, NODUPKEY
Modify sort order	PROC SORT	EQUALS, REVERSE
Change default behavior	PROC SORT	FORCE
	BY	DESCENDING
Change collating sequence	PROC SORT	ASCII, EBCDIC, DANISH, NORWEGIAN, FINNISH, SWEDISH, NATIONAL, SORTSEQ=

PROC SORT Statement

PROC SORT <*option-list*> <*collating-sequence-option*>;

The *collating-sequence-option* is used to specify a collating sequence other than the standard ASCII or EBCDIC sequence native to your host environment. You can use only one *collating-sequence-option* in a PROC SORT step. **Table 31.1** lists the options that can be used to change the collating sequence.

The following section describes the options available on all hosts, including the collating sequence options, that can be specified in the PROC SORT statement.

ASCII

> sorts character variables using the ASCII collating sequence. This option needs to be specified only when you are running PROC SORT on a system where EBCDIC is the native collating sequence and you want to sort in ASCII order. Both of these collating sequences are listed in **SORTING ORDERS** earlier in this chapter.

DANISH
NORWEGIAN

> sort character variables using the alternate collating sequence matching the Danish and Norwegian National Use Differences standard.
>
> In the Danish and Norwegian National Use Differences alternate collating sequence, the standard graphics shown in **Table 31.2** are redefined.
>
> Thus, the Danish and Norwegian collating sequence for EBCDIC operating systems is (in part):
>
> a b c . . . x y z æ ø å A B C . . . X Y Z Æ Ø Å

Table 31.2 Danish and Norwegian National Use Differences (EBCDIC)

	UPPERCASE				LOWERCASE		
HEX	Standard Graphic	Alternate Collating Sequence	National Use Graphic	HEX	Standard Graphic	Alternate Collating Sequence	National Use Graphic
7B	#	EA	Æ	C0	{	AA	æ
7C	@	EB	Ø	6A	¦	AB	ø
5B	$	EC	Å	D0	}	AC	å

DATA=*SAS-data-set*

> names the SAS data set that you want to sort. If the DATA= option is omitted, the most recently created SAS data set is used.

EBCDIC

sorts character variables using the EBCDIC collating sequence. This option needs to be specified only when you are running PROC SORT on a system where ASCII is the native collating sequence and you want to sort in EBCDIC order. Both of these collating sequences are listed in **INTRODUCTION** earlier in this chapter.

EQUALS
NOEQUALS

specify the order of the observations in the output data set. The EQUALS option specifies that observations with identical BY-variable values are to retain the same relative positions in the output data set as in the input data set. The NOEQUALS option specifies that this restriction is not necessary.

FINNISH
SWEDISH

sort character variables using an alternate collating sequence matching the Finnish and Swedish National Use Differences standard.

In the Finnish and Swedish National Use Differences alternate collating sequence, the standard graphics shown in **Table 31.3** are redefined.

Table 31.3 Finnish and Swedish National Use Differences (EBCDIC)

	UPPERCASE				LOWERCASE		
HEX	Standard Graphic	Alternate Collating Sequence	National Use Graphic	HEX	Standard Graphic	Alternate Collating Sequence	National Use Graphic
5B	$	EA	Å	D0	}	AA	å
7B	#	EB	Ä	C0	{	AB	ä
7C	@	EC	Ö	6A	¦	AC	ö

Thus, the Finnish and Swedish collating sequence for EBCDIC operating systems is (in part):

a b c . . . x y z å ä ö A B C . . . X Y Z Å Ä Ö

FORCE

sorts and replaces an indexed or subsetted data set when no OUT= option is specified. If you do not specify the FORCE option, PROC SORT does not sort and replace an indexed data set because sorting destroys indexes for the data set. If you specify the FORCE option, the data set is sorted and replaced, and all indexes for the data set are destroyed.

If you specify any of the following with a PROC SORT step and do not specify an OUT= data set, you must use the FORCE option:

- the OBS= system option
- the FIRSTOBS= system option
- a WHERE= data set option on the DATA= data set
- a WHERE statement in the PROC SORT step.

If you use any of these methods to subset the data set while sorting the data, the resulting data set contains only the subsetted observations.

NATIONAL
sorts character variables using an alternate collating sequence, as defined by your installation, to reflect a country's National Use Differences (see the examples under the DANISH and FINNISH options). For you to use this option, your installation must have a customized national sort sequence defined. Check with the SAS Software Representative at your site to determine if a customized national sort sequence is available.

NODUPKEY
checks for and eliminates observations with duplicate BY values. This option causes PROC SORT to compare all BY values for each observation to those for the previous observation written to the output data set. If an exact match is found, the observation is not written to the output data set.
Note: This option differs from the NODUPLICATES option because the NODUPKEY option compares only the BY values, not the entire observation.

NODUPLICATES
NODUPREC
NODUP
checks for and eliminates adjacent duplicate observations after the sort.
Note: This option differs from the NODUPKEY option because the NODUPLICATES option compares the entire observation, not just the BY values.

OUT=SAS-data-set
specifies a name for the output data set. If the OUT= option is omitted, the DATA= data set is sorted and the sorted version replaces the original data set. If you want the OUT= data set to be permanent, specify a two-level name (see Chapter 6, "SAS Files," in SAS Language: Reference).

REVERSE
sorts character variables using a collating sequence that is reversed from the normal collating sequence.
This option is similar to the BY statement DESCENDING option; the difference is that the DESCENDING option can be used with both character and numeric variables.

SORTSEQ=*collating-sequence*
sorts character variables using the collating sequence specified in the option. Valid values for *collating-sequence* are as follows:

ASCII
DANISH
EBCDIC
FINNISH
NATIONAL
NORWEGIAN
SWEDISH

This option has the same effect as specifying one of the other collating-sequence options.

BY Statement

BY <DESCENDING> *variable* <...<DESCENDING> *variable*>;

Any number of variables can be specified in the BY statement. A BY statement must be used with PROC SORT.

As described in the **INTRODUCTION**, PROC SORT first arranges the observations in the order of the first variable in the BY statement; then it sorts observations with a given value of the first variable by the second variable, and so on. Note that PROC SORT retains the same relative positions of observations with identical BY variable values unless you specify the NOEQUALS option.

The following option can be specified in the BY statement:

DESCENDING
sorts variables in descending order. Use the keyword DESCENDING before the name of each variable in the BY statement whose values you want sorted in descending order. For example, these statements sort the RANDOM data set first by descending order of SIZE values, then by ascending order of AGE values:

```
proc sort data=random;
   by descending size age;
run;
```

To sort by descending AGE values, the DESCENDING keyword would also have to precede the AGE variable name.

DETAILS

Output Data Set

If an OUT= option appears in the PROC SORT statement, a new data set is created containing the sorted observations. Otherwise, the original data set is sorted, and the sorted observations replace the original values after the SORT procedure executes without errors. Even when a data set is replaced, there must be space in the data library to hold a second copy of the data set to be sorted.

You can sort compressed data sets like any other SAS data set. If you omit the OUT= option, the DATA= data set is sorted and continues to be compressed. If you specify an OUT= data set, the resulting data set is compressed only if you specify the COMPRESS=YES data set option. Refer to Chapter 15, "SAS Data Set Options," in *SAS Language: Reference* for more information on the COMPRESS= data set option.

Note: If the NOREPLACE SAS system option is on, you cannot replace the original data set with the sorted version. You must either use the OUT= option or specify the REPLACE SAS system option in an OPTIONS statement.

Multiple Sorts

When you know that you need to sort a data set for several purposes, you can sometimes plan ahead and reduce the number of sorts needed. For example, suppose you want to run a procedure for the same data set twice, once with the BY statement

```
by state;
```

and again with the BY statement

```
by state city;
```

You can sort the data set once and use it for both these runs if you use the statements

```
proc sort;
   by state city;
run;
```

It does not matter for the BY STATE run that the data set is sorted by both state and city. If the first statement above were BY CITY, you would need to sort the data twice.

EXAMPLE

Sorting Information

In the following example, a list of names, telephone extensions, and room numbers is sorted two different ways. PROC SORT first sorts the data alphabetically by name, then by room number and name, as shown in **Output 31.1**.

```
data phones;
   input name $ phone room;
   cards;
Rebeccah 424 112
Carol 450 112
Louise 409 110 .
Gina 474 110
Mimi 410 109
Alice 411 106
Brenda 414 105
David 438 141
Betty 464 141
Holly 466 140
Gretel 465 140
;
run;
```

```
proc sort data=phones out=list1;
   by name;
run;

proc print data=list1;
   title 'Name Order';
run;

proc sort data=phones out=list2;
   by room name;
run;

proc print data=list2;
   title 'Room Number and Name Order';
   var room name phone;
run;
```

Output 31.1   Data Set Sorted in Two Different Orders

```
                            Name Order                                         1

                 OBS    NAME      PHONE    ROOM

                   1    Alice      411      106
                   2    Betty      464      141
                   3    Brenda     414      105
                   4    Carol      450      112
                   5    David      438      141
                   6    Gina       474      110
                   7    Gretel     465      140
                   8    Holly      466      140
                   9    Louise     409      110
                  10    Mimi       410      109
                  11    Rebeccah   424      112
```

```
                  Room Number and Name Order                                   2

                 OBS    ROOM    NAME      PHONE

                   1    105     Brenda     414
                   2    106     Alice      411
                   3    109     Mimi       410
                   4    110     Gina       474
                   5    110     Louise     409
                   6    112     Carol      450
                   7    112     Rebeccah   424
                   8    140     Gretel     465
                   9    140     Holly      466
                  10    141     Betty      464
                  11    141     David      438
```

Chapter 32

The SOURCE
Procedure

ABSTRACT

The SOURCE procedure provides an easy way to back up and process library data sets. This procedure is described in system-dependent documentation.

Chapter 33

The SPELL Procedure

ABSTRACT

The SPELL procedure checks the spelling in an external file or in SAS catalog entries of type HELP or CBT. It also maintains dictionaries.

INTRODUCTION

The SPELL procedure has three functions:

- verifying the spelling in an external file or in SAS catalog entries of type HELP or CBT
- creating new dictionaries
- updating existing dictionaries.

By default, when the SPELL procedure checks spelling, it uses the master dictionary SASHELP.BASE.MASTER.DICTNARY. However, you can specify other dictionaries to use in place of or in addition to the master dictionary.

The SPELL command, which you can use in any window that allows text editing, is similar to PROC SPELL. (See **The SPELL Command** in Chapter 19, "SAS Text Editor Commands," in *SAS Language: Reference, Version 6, First Edition.*)

SPECIFICATIONS

The PROC SPELL statement is the only statement associated with the SPELL procedure.

PROC SPELL Statement

PROC SPELL WORDLIST=*file-to-process* <*option-list*>;

Requirements

You must specify the WORDLIST= (alias IN=) argument when you use PROC SPELL:

WORDLIST=*file-to-process*
IN=*file-to-process*

where *file-to-process* is a file that contains one of the following:

- a list of words for creating or updating a dictionary. This chapter uses the WORDLIST= argument in such cases.
- text to check for spelling errors. In these cases, this chapter uses the IN= argument.

If the file is a list of words for creating or updating a dictionary (called a *word list*), it must have a special format. (See **Formatting a Word List for Creating or Updating a Dictionary** later in this chapter.)
The file can be one of the following:

- an external file
- a SAS catalog
- a particular entry in a SAS catalog.

Specify an external file as follows:

IN=*fileref* | '*external-file*'

where

    fileref   is a fileref identifying an external file. Use the FILENAME statement to associate a fileref with an external file (see *SAS Language: Reference*).

    external-file   is the operating system's name for an external file. You must enclose this name in single or double quotes.

When you are checking the spelling of a file, you can specify an entire catalog. To do so, use the following form:

IN=*libref.catalog*

where

    libref   identifies a SAS data library. Use the LIBNAME statement to associate a libref with a library (see *SAS Language: Reference*).

    catalog   is the name of a catalog in the library.

If you specify an entire catalog, PROC SPELL processes all entries of type HELP and CBT in the catalog.

To specify a specific entry within a catalog, use the following form:

IN=*libref.catalog.entry.etype*

where

libref	identifies a SAS data library. Use the LIBNAME statement to associate a libref with a library (see *SAS Language: Reference*).
catalog	is the name of a catalog in the library.
entry	is the name of an entry in the catalog.
etype	is either HELP or CBT.

Options

Table 33.1 summarizes the options available with the PROC SPELL statement. Descriptions of the options follow the table in alphabetic order.

Table 33.1 Summary of PROC SPELL Statement Options

Class	Option	Function
Verifying spelling	VERIFY	verifies the spelling in the specified file
	SUGGEST	writes suggestions for unrecognized words to the SAS output
	NOMASTER	suppresses the use of the master dictionary
Creating a dictionary	CREATE	creates a dictionary
	SIZE=	specifies the size of a new dictionary
Updating a dictionary	UPDATE	updates the specified dictionary
Specifying a dictionary	DICTIONARY=	names the dictionary to create or update, or specifies one or more dictionaries to use to verify spelling

CREATE
> uses the words in the word list to create a new dictionary. You specify the name of the dictionary with the DICTIONARY= option. If a dictionary with the same name already exists, PROC SPELL deletes it without warning.
>
> If you use the CREATE option, you cannot use the UPDATE or VERIFY option.

DICTIONARY=(*dictionary-list*)

names the dictionary to create or update, or specifies one or more dictionaries to use to verify spelling. Each element of *dictionary-list* has the form

libref. catalog. dictionary

where

libref	identifies a SAS data library. Use the LIBNAME statement to associate a libref with a library (see *SAS Language: Reference*).
catalog	is the name of a catalog in the library.
dictionary	is the name of the catalog entry that contains the dictionary. PROC SPELL assigns a type DICTNARY to this entry.

If you name only one dictionary, you may omit the parentheses.

If you are creating or updating a dictionary, you can specify only one dictionary. However, if you are verifying the spelling in a file (the default action), you can specify a list of dictionaries. The list must be in parentheses as in the following statements:

```
proc spell in=testfile
          dictionary=(lib.cat.dict1 lib.cat.dict2);
run;
```

You do not need to specify the master dictionary. PROC SPELL uses it to verify spelling unless you specify the NOMASTER option.

NOMASTER

suppresses the use of SASHELP.BASE.MASTER.DICTNARY, the master dictionary.

SIZE=*number-of-bytes*

specifies the number of bytes in the dictionary you are creating. If you do not use this option, the size of the dictionary is the same as the size of the master dictionary, approximately 86K. (The dictionary contains approximately 50,000 words.) Most auxiliary dictionaries do not need to be this large. For more information, see **Specifying the Size of a Dictionary** later in this chapter.

SUGGEST

writes suggestions for unrecognized words to the SAS output. This option has no effect unless the VERIFY option is in effect.

UPDATE

updates the dictionary specified in the DICTIONARY= option with the words in the word list.

If you use the UPDATE option, you cannot use the CREATE or VERIFY options.

VERIFY

uses the specified dictionary or dictionaries to verify the spelling in the file specified in the IN= option. In this case, the file does not have to conform to the format for a word list. In fact, in most cases the file is a document such as a letter or memo.

If you use the VERIFY option, you cannot use the CREATE or UPDATE options. If you specify none of these options, the VERIFY option is the default.

DETAILS

Defining and Verifying Words

When verifying the spelling in a file, the SPELL procedure first identifies strings of characters as potential words. It then checks to see if these words are in the dictionaries it is using.

PROC SPELL uses the following steps to identify and verify the spelling of potential words:

1. The SPELL procedure scans the file, discarding characters until it finds an alphabetic character preceded by a blank, a special character, or a new-line character. That character is the first character of a potential word. *Special characters* are

   - a single quote (')
   - a double quote (")
   - a left parenthesis (()
   - a left square bracket ([)
   - a left brace ({)
   - a left angle bracket (or less-than sign) (<).

2. The SPELL procedure scans the characters until it reaches a character that is not valid in a word. A valid character is

   - any alphabetic character
   - a hyphen, if followed by an alphabetic character
   - an apostrophe (or single quote), if followed by an alphabetic character.

   The characters between the first character of the potential word and the last valid character form a potential word.

   Following these rules, PROC SPELL interprets the following character strings as potential words:

   ```
   doesn't
   copy-edit
   xxyy'zz
   ```

   The SPELL procedure treats the following character string as three potential words: *embedded, nested,* and *quotation*:

   ```
   "'embedded (nested) quotation'"
   ```

3. PROC SPELL looks for the word in the dictionaries it is using.
4. After determining whether the word is in the dictionaries, PROC SPELL begins to scan for another word. The SPELL procedure repeats steps 1, 2, and 3 until it reaches the end of the file.

Formatting a Word List for Creating or Updating a Dictionary

Each line of a word list used to create or update a dictionary must contain only one word. You can use two forms of abbreviated notation to reduce the number of separate entries you need:

- Encode words that can have a suffix of **s** by placing the character string /s at the end of the word.
- Encode words that can have a suffix of *s, ed,* or *ing* by placing the character string /* at the end of the word.

Table 33.2 shows a section of the word list used to construct the master dictionary and the words it represents.

Table 33.2 Using Special Notation in a Word List

Entry in Word List	Words Represented
`affable`	affable
`affably`	affably
`affair/s`	affair, affairs
`affect/*`	affect, affects, affected, affecting
`affectation/s`	affectation, affectations

Note: PROC SPELL imposes no restrictions on the characters in the words in a word list. Therefore, a word list can contain a word that PROC SPELL does not recognize as a valid word. When the SPELL procedure scans the file for potential words, it does not recognize such a word (or more importantly, some possible misspellings of the word) as a potential word. For example, you can enter the string **2x4** in a word list, but PROC SPELL does not recognize that string or some of the likely misspellings, such as **2x5** and **2xr**, as potential words. It cannot, therefore, catch these errors.

Specifying the Size of a Dictionary

By default, PROC SPELL creates a dictionary that is the same size as the master dictionary, approximately 86K. Many auxiliary dictionaries can be much smaller than this, perhaps as small as 2K.

When you use the SIZE= option to specify the size of a dictionary, you must balance two factors:

- You want the dictionary to be small enough so that it does not waste space.
- You want the dictionary to be large enough to minimize the chance that PROC SPELL accepts a word that is not in the dictionary. (The SPELL procedure never rejects a word that is in the dictionary.)

The probability of the SPELL procedure accepting a word that is not in the dictionary is a function of the number of words in the dictionary and the dictionary's size. When you create a dictionary, PROC SPELL writes a note to the SAS log telling you what the estimated chance of accepting a word not in the word list is. If this number is unacceptably high, re-create the dictionary using a larger value for the SIZE= option.

The estimated chance that the SPELL procedure will accept a word that is not in the master dictionary when it is using only the master dictionary is 0.0017 percent (about 1 in 60,000).

Saving Your Word Lists

Once you have created a dictionary, you may be tempted to save space by deleting your word lists. However, it is recommended that you save these lists for the following reasons:

- The dictionary does not actually contain the words. Therefore, you cannot look at the dictionary to see what words are in it. Your only recourse is to look at the word list or to run the SPELL procedure against a file containing the words in question.
- You cannot move a dictionary from one operating system to another. If you want to do so, you must move the word list and re-create the dictionary on the new host system.

Existing Auxiliary Dictionaries

The following four dictionaries are in the catalog SASHELP.BASE:

NAMES	contains common English first names.
CITIES	contains the names of cities in the United States.
CNTRIES	contains the names of countries.
STATES	contains the names of states and other entities identified by United States Post Office FIPS codes.

PRINTED OUTPUT

Creating or Updating a Dictionary

When you create or update a dictionary, PROC SPELL writes a message to the SAS log indicating the probability of accepting a word that is not in the dictionary.

Verifying a File

If PROC SPELL finds any spelling errors in the input file, it writes the following items to the standard output:

1. the unrecognized word
2. the number of times the word occurs in the document
3. the number of the line or lines on which the unrecognized word appears.

If you specify the SUGGEST option, the output also includes

4. suggestions for what word you may have intended to use.

EXAMPLES

Example 1:   Checking a File against the Master Dictionary

The following SAS statements check the file SPELLDOC against the master dictionary for spelling errors. SPELLDOC contains the text of this chapter as it was when the examples were written. The statements below produce **Output 33.1**:

```
filename spelldoc 'external-file';

proc spell in=spelldoc verify;
   title 'Checking a File Against the Master Dictionary';
run;
```

Output 33.1   Verifying a File against the Master Dictionary

```
                        Checking a File Against the Master Dictionary                        1

  File: "SPELLDOC"

❶ Unrecognized word      ❷  Freq      Line(s) ❸

  SAS                       12       10, 48, 50, 61, 77, 80, 99,
                                     102, 137, 140, 178, 333
  CBT                        3       11, 88, 114
  SASHELP                    2       20, 163
  PROC                      14       24, 27, 87, 118, 124, 149, 159,
                                     241, 268, 279, 287, 311, 324,
                                     332
  WORDLIST                   2       27, 192
  fileref                    2       56, 58
  FILENAME                   1       58
  libref                    10       71, 76, 78, 93, 98, 100, 130,
                                     131, 136, 138
  LIBNAME                    3       78, 100, 138
  DICTNARY                   1       149
  NOMASTER                   2       160, 161
  K                          2       169, 312
  auxilliary                 2       173, 313
  s                          2       207, 210
  ed                         1       210
  ing                        1       211
  xx                         4       215, 218, 275 (2)
  l                          3       217, 219, 220
  xxyy'zz                    1       284
  facors                     1       317
```

Example 2:   Creating an Auxiliary Dictionary

The output from **Example 1** includes a number of words used in SAS documentation that are not in the master dictionary. The following example uses these words to create an auxiliary dictionary, WRITE.SPELL.SASWORDS. The word list used to create the dictionary is in the file referenced by AUXWORDS. It has the following format:

```
SAS
CBT
SASHELP
PROC
fileref/s
FILENAME
libref/s
LIBNAME
DICTNARY
NOMASTER
```

Note: You can use the output from PROC SPELL to create a word list. If you are using the SAS System interactively, save your output. Then edit that file to produce a word list. If you are using the SAS System noninteractively or in batch mode, simply edit the output directly.

To create a dictionary from the list of words above, use the following SAS statements:

```
filename auxlist 'external-file';
libname write 'SAS-data-library';

proc spell dictionary=write.spell.saswords wordlist=auxlist
          create size=4096;
    title 'Creating an Auxiliary Dictionary';
run;
```

The SAS log, which appears in **Output 33.2**, shows the message indicating that the chance of the SPELL procedure incorrectly identifying a word as correct is 1.624239E-33%. Note that this form of the procedure does not produce printed output.

Output 33.2   Creating an Auxiliary Dictionary

```
NOTE: Libref WRITE was successfully assigned as follows:
      Engine:        V606
      Physical Name: SAS-data-library
4
5          libname write 'SAS-data-library';
6          filename auxlist 'external-file';
7
8          proc spell dictionary=write.spell.saswords wordlist=auxlist
9                    create size=4096;
10           title 'Creating an Auxiliary Dictionary';
11         run;

NOTE: Estimated chance of accepting a word not in SASWORDS using SASWORDS is 1.624239E-33%.
```

Example 3: Checking a File against the Master Dictionary and an Auxiliary Dictionary

The following example verifies the document SPELLDOC against both the master dictionary and the auxiliary dictionary created in **Example 2**. The SUGGEST option generates suggestions for unrecognized words. The statements below produce **Output 33.3**.

```
filename test 'external-file';
libname write 'SAS-data-library';

proc spell in=test dictionary=write.spell.saswords
        verify suggest;
   title1 'Checking a File against the Master Dictionary';
   title2 'and an Auxiliary Dictionary';
run;
```

Output 33.3   Verifying a File against the Master Dictionary and an Auxiliary Dictionary

```
                       Checking a File against the Master Dictionary                          1
                                 and an Auxiliary Dictionary

File: "TEST"

Unrecognized word          Freq    Line(s)

WORDLIST                    2       27, 192

K                          2       169, 312
❹       Suggestions: A, I, OK

auxilliary                 2       173, 313
        Suggestions: auxiliary

s                          2       207, 210
        Suggestions: a, i, as, is, us, so

ed                         1       210
        Suggestions: ad, id, eg, et, bed, fed, led, red, wed, end

ing                        1       211
        Suggestions: in, ink, inn, ins, ding, king, ping, ring, sing,
                     wing, zing

xx                         4       215, 218, 275 (2)
        Suggestions: ax, ox

l                          3       217, 219, 220
        Suggestions: a, i, lo

xxyy'zz                    1       284

facors                     1       317
        Suggestions: favors, factors
```

Example 4:   Updating a Dictionary

In this example, PROC SPELL adds the names of the SAS trigonometric functions to the existing dictionary of SAS words created in **Example 2**. The word list used to update the dictionary is in the file referenced by TRIGWRDS. It has the following format:

```
arcos
arsin
atan
cos
cosh
sin
sinh
tan
tanh
```

Use the following statements to add these words to the dictionary. **Output 33.4** shows the SAS log produced by these statements. Note that this form of the procedure does not produce printed output.

```
libname write SAS-data-library;
filename trigwrds 'external-file';

proc spell wordlist=trigwrds dictionary=write.spell.saswords update;
    title 'Updating a Dictionary';
run;
```

Output 33.4   Log Produced by Adding Words to an Auxiliary Dictionary

```
NOTE: Libref WRITE was successfully assigned as follows:
      Engine:      V606
      Physical Name: SAS-data-library
4
5          libname write 'SAS-data-library';
6          filename trigwrds 'external-file';
7
8          proc spell wordlist=trigwrds dictionary=write.spell.saswords update;
9              title 'Updating a Dictionary';
10         run;

NOTE: Estimated chance of accepting a word not in SASWORDS using SASWORDS is 2.103864E-29%.
```

INTRODUCTION

The SQL procedure implements the Structured Query Language (SQL) for Version 6 of the SAS System. SQL is a standardized, widely used language that retrieves and updates data in tables and views based on those tables. In this chapter, a table is a SAS data file, and a view is derived from one or more tables or views.*

The SAS System's SQL procedure gives you control over your data on three levels:

- You can retrieve and manipulate data stored in tables, views, and SAS/ACCESS views using the SELECT statement; a SELECT statement is also called a *query*. You can use the VALIDATE statement to check the accuracy of your SELECT statement's syntax without actually executing it. You can also simply display a PROC SQL view definition using the DESCRIBE statement.
- You can create tables, views, and indexes on columns in tables using the CREATE statement; these tables and views can be stored permanently in SAS data libraries and referred to using librefs. Or, you can delete tables, views, and indexes using the DROP statement.
- You can add or modify the data values in a table's columns using the UPDATE statement or insert and delete rows with the INSERT and DELETE statements. You can also modify the table itself by adding, modifying, or dropping columns with the ALTER statement.

Finally, the PROC SQL statement also allows a number of options, which can be added, changed, or removed with the RESET statement.

This chapter describes the SQL procedure and its options and statements. The Structured Query Language is a modular type of language, in that statements are composed of smaller building blocks called *components*. This chapter lists the options available for the PROC SQL and RESET statements. It then describes the other SQL procedure statements and lists the components that constitute these statements. The SQL procedure is fully described in the *SAS Guide to the SQL Procedure: Usage and Reference, Version 6, First Edition*.

---

* In this chapter, a view refers to a PROC SQL view; SAS/ACCESS views (or view descriptors) are distinguished from PROC SQL views.

SPECIFICATIONS

The SQL procedure includes several statements, two of which can take options:

PROC SQL <*option-list*>;
ALTER TABLE *alter-statement*;
CREATE *create-statement*;
DELETE *delete-statement*;
DESCRIBE *describe-statement*;
DROP *drop-statement*;
INSERT *insert-statement*;
RESET <*option-list*>;
SELECT *select-statement*;
UPDATE *update-statement*;
VALIDATE *validate-statement*;

SQL Procedure Coding Conventions

Because the SQL procedure implements the Structured Query Language, it works somewhat differently from other base SAS procedures, as described here:

- You do not need to repeat the PROC SQL statement with each SQL statement. You only need to repeat the PROC SQL statement if you process a DATA step or another SAS procedure between statements.
- SQL procedure statements are divided into clauses. For example, the most basic SELECT statement contains the SELECT and FROM clauses. Items within clauses are separated with commas in SQL, not blanks as in the SAS System. For example, if you list three columns in the SELECT clause, the columns are separated with commas.
- The SELECT statement, used to retrieve data, also outputs the data automatically unless you specify the NOPRINT option in the PROC SQL statement. Thus, you can display your output or send it to a list file without specifying the PRINT procedure.
- The SELECT and CREATE VIEW statements can each include an ORDER BY clause that enables you to sort data by columns, so you do not need to use the SORT procedure with your PROC SQL programs. SAS data sets do not need to be presorted by a variable for use in the SQL procedure.
- A PROC SQL statement runs when you submit it, without your specifying a RUN statement. If you follow a PROC SQL statement with a RUN statement, the SAS System ignores the RUN statement and submits the statements as usual.

See the descriptions and examples of each SQL procedure statement for more information.

PROC SQL and RESET Statements

PROC SQL <*option-list*>;
RESET <*option-list*>;

The following options can appear in the PROC SQL statement or the RESET statement. Used in the PROC SQL statement, they specify the initial state of an option. Options can be added, removed, or changed between PROC SQL statements with the RESET statement. An option remains in effect until its NO (or opposite) version is specified (for example, NOEXEC) or until it is reset.

ERRORSTOP | NOERRORSTOP
    specifies whether the SAS System should stop processing if an error is encountered. If the EXEC option is in effect, the SAS System always

checks the PROC SQL syntax for accuracy and, if no error occurs, executes the SQL statement.

Specifying the ERRORSTOP option instructs the SAS System to continue checking the syntax once it has encountered an error in processing a PROC SQL statement in a batch or noninteractive job. However, it stops executing the SQL procedure statements after the error. The ERRORSTOP option only has an effect when the SAS System is running in the batch or noninteractive execution mode.

The NOERRORSTOP option is the default in an interactive SAS session, but it works with all the execution modes. Resetting the NOERRORSTOP option to ERRORSTOP during an interactive session works only if you also reset the EXEC option to NOEXEC. See also the description of the EXEC option.

Specifying the NOERRORSTOP option instructs the SAS System to continue checking the syntax of SQL statements after an error occurs. It continues to try to execute the statements if the EXEC option is in effect. The NOERRORSTOP option is useful if you want a batch job to continue processing SQL procedure statements after an error is encountered.

EXEC | NOEXEC

specifies whether a statement should be executed after its syntax is checked for accuracy. The EXEC option is the default. See the ERRORSTOP option for the ways in which the two options interact.

The NOEXEC option is the only option that controls SQL statements that are run during an interactive SAS session. The NOEXEC option is useful if you want to check only the syntax of your SQL statements without executing the statements.

FEEDBACK | NOFEEDBACK

specifies whether the SQL procedure should display the statement after it expands view references or makes certain transformations on the statement. The NOFEEDBACK option is the default.

This option expands any use of an asterisk (for example, **SELECT** *) into the list of qualified columns it represents. Any PROC SQL view is expanded into the underlying query, and all expressions are fully parenthesized to further indicate their order of evaluation. See **DESCRIBE Statement** for more information on this option.

INOBS=n

restricts the number of rows (observations) that PROC SQL processes from any single source. For example, if you specify INOBS=10 and join two tables without using a WHERE clause, you get 100 rows in the output. This option is useful for debugging queries on large tables.

LOOPS=n

restricts the SQL procedure to n iterations through its inner loop. You can use the number of iterations reported in the SQLOOPS macro variable (after each SQL statement is executed) to gauge this value. Setting a limit prevents queries from consuming excessive computer resources. For example, joining three large tables without meeting the join-matching conditions could create a huge internal table that would be inefficient to process; using the LOOPS= option can prevent this error.

NUMBER | NONUMBER

specifies whether the SELECT statement should include a column called ROW, which is the row (or observation) number of the data as they are retrieved. This option works like the OBS | NOOBS option in the PRINT procedure. The NONUMBER option is the default.

OUTOBS=*n*

restricts the number of rows (or observations) that the SQL procedure processes as the target of an SQL statement. For example, if you specify OUTOBS=10 and insert values into a table using a query-expression, the SQL procedure inserts a maximum of 10 rows.

PRINT | NOPRINT

specifies whether a SELECT statement's results are printed (that is, displayed) in the SAS OUTPUT window or written to a list file. The PRINT option is the default. The NOPRINT option is useful when you are selecting values from a table into macro variables and do not want anything to be displayed.

SORTSEQ=*sort-table*

specifies the collating sequence to use when a query contains an ORDER BY clause. Use this option only if you want a collating sequence other than your system's or installation's default collating sequence. For more information, see the SORTSEQ= option in Chapter 31, "The SORT Procedure."

STIMER | NOSTIMER

specifies whether the SQL procedure writes timing information to the SAS log for each statement, rather than as a cumulative value for the entire procedure. For this option to work, you must also specify the SAS system option STIMER; some host systems require that you specify this system option when you invoke the SAS System. If you use the system option alone, you receive timing information for the entire SQL procedure, not on a statement-by-statement basis. The NOSTIMER option is the default.

SQL Procedure and SAS Data Set Options

The SQL procedure can apply any of the SAS data set options, such as KEEP= and DROP=, to tables or SAS/ACCESS views. In the SQL procedure, SAS data set options (separated by spaces) are enclosed in parentheses and follow immediately after the table or SAS/ACCESS view name, as in this example:

```
proc sql;
create table sql.hirange(label='High Range Salaries') as
select lastname, fname, ssnumber
   from sql.salaries
   where salary>4000;
```

You can also use SAS data set options on tables or SAS/ACCESS views listed in the FROM clause of a query. See **Creating Tables with the SQL Procedure** later in this chapter for a complete description of the CREATE TABLE statement.

You cannot associate SAS data set options with PROC SQL view names because the options are only valid on a view's underlying tables. For example, when you create a PROC SQL view, you cannot list SAS data set options after the view name. However, you can list data set options after the table name(s) in a view's FROM clause, provided those tables are not based on other PROC SQL views. See **Creating Views with the SQL Procedure** later in this chapter for more information on creating and using views.

When columns and their attributes are defined in a parenthesized list in the CREATE TABLE and CREATE INDEX statements, SAS data set options can be added to that list (without repeating the parentheses) as long as the options are separated from the columns by commas.

See *SAS Language: Reference, Version 6, First Edition* for a list and description of the SAS data set options.

STATEMENTS IN THE SQL PROCEDURE

This section describes the SQL procedure's statements. The components referenced in the syntax for these statements are defined in **Components of the SQL Procedure Statements** later in this chapter. See these component descriptions for more detailed information. Because the statements are in alphabetic order, some terms are referred to before they are defined.

ALTER Statement

> **ALTER TABLE** *table-name*
>   <**ADD** *column-definition* <*,column-definition*>...>
>   <**MODIFY** *column-definition* <*,column-definition*>...>
>   <**DROP** *column-name* <*,column-name*>...>;

The ALTER statement adds columns to or drops columns from an existing table. It is also used to change column attributes in an existing table. The ALTER statement cannot reference PROC SQL or SAS/ACCESS views (that is, view descriptors).

When the ALTER statement adds a column to the table, it initializes the column's values to missing in all rows of the table. You can then use the UPDATE statement to add values to the new column(s).

If a column is already in the table, you can change the following column (variable) attributes using the MODIFY clause: length, informat, format, and label. The values in a table are truncated or padded with blanks (if character data) as necessary to meet the specified length attribute.

To change a column's name, you must use the SAS data set option RENAME=. You cannot change this attribute with the ALTER statement. You also cannot change a column's data type; that is, you cannot change a character column to numeric and vice versa. To change a column's data type, you have to drop the column and then add it (and its data) again.

If you want to drop a column and all its values from a table, specify the column's name in the DROP clause. If you drop a column, be sure to remove all references to it in other statements.

When you alter the attributes of a column and an index has been defined for that column, the values in the altered column continue to have the index defined for them. If you drop a column with the ALTER statement, all the indexes (simple and composite) that the column participates in are also dropped. See **CREATE Statement** later in this chapter for more information on creating and using indexes.

Example

This example adds a column to the SQL.ALTERTAB table, which is a table based on the SQL.SALARIES table created in **Creating Tables with the SQL Procedure.** The name SQL.ALTERTAB is used here so that the chapter's sample table is not altered. The following statements produce **Output 34.1**:

```
libname sql 'SAS-data-library';

proc sql;
create table sql.altertab as
select * from sql.salaries;

alter table sql.altertab
   add gender char(1);
```

```
title 'Altertab Table';
select * from sql.altertab;
```

Output 34.1   SQL.ALTERTAB Table

```
                                  Altertab Table                                    1

                                                    Monthly    Annual
      LASTNAME     FNAME        SSNUMBER            Salary     Salary  GENDER
      ----------------------------------------------------------------------
      Conway       Kathryn      224-22-3312        $4,325.00  $51,900.00
      Schneyer     Samantha     321-53-8796        $1,275.00  $15,300.00
      Stein        Joel         323-09-3467        $3,211.00  $38,532.00
      Rodriguez    Jose         123-99-4563        $3,356.00  $40,272.00
      Johnston     Lois         276-11-6745        $2,444.00  $29,328.00
      Wong         William      321-68-4532        $1,798.00  $21,576.00
```

The example in **UPDATE Statement** adds values to the new GENDER column and displays the completed table. See this section for more information on updating data values.

CREATE Statement

The CREATE statement enables you to create tables, views that are based on tables or other views, and indexes on columns in tables. Each use is described separately.

Creating Tables with the SQL Procedure

The SQL procedure has three ways of creating tables (or SAS data files):

CREATE TABLE *table-name* (*column-definition* <,*column-definition*>...);
CREATE TABLE *table-name* **AS** *query-expression*;
CREATE TABLE *table-name* **LIKE** *table-name*;

The *first form* of the CREATE TABLE statement creates tables that automatically map SQL data types to those supported by the SAS System. Use this form when you want to create a new table with columns that are not present in existing tables. This form is also useful if you are running SQL statements from an SQL application in an SQL-based database.

This first form creates a new table without rows. You can use an INSERT statement to add rows to the table or the ALTER statement to modify column attributes or to add or drop columns.

You can use the *second form* of the CREATE TABLE statement to store the results of any query-expression in a table, instead of displaying the query results in SAS output. It is a convenient way of setting up temporary tables that are subsets or supersets of other tables.

Using this second form, a table is physically created as the statement is executed. If the underlying tables (in the query-expression) are changed after execution, the change(s) do not appear in the newly created table. If you want the change(s) reflected, you should create a view, which is evaluated each time it is referenced and therefore reflects the most current data and formats in its underlying tables. See **Creating Views with the SQL Procedure** later in this chapter.

The *third form* of the CREATE TABLE statement uses a LIKE clause to create a table that has the same column names and column attributes as another table. If you want to drop any columns in the new table, you can specify the DROP=

SAS data set option in the CREATE TABLE statement. The specified column(s) are dropped when the table is created.

This third form also creates a new table without rows. You can use an INSERT statement to add rows or an ALTER statement to modify column attributes or to add or drop columns.

Librefs and stored tables If you want to create a permanently stored table, you must specify the SAS data library (using a libref) in which the table will be stored. For example, for the two-level name SQL.EMPLOYEE, SQL is a libref pointing to the data library and EMPLOYEE is the name of the table. If you create a temporarily stored table, you may omit the libref; in this case, the default temporary library, WORK, is assumed.

Example This example creates the SQL.SALARIES table, which is used in the examples throughout this chapter. It represents the first form of the CREATE TABLE statement. Since the table is created without rows, the INSERT statement is used to supply the data.

```
libname sql 'SAS-data-library';


proc sql;
create table sql.salaries(type=data label='Salaries Table',
            lastname char(14),
            fname char(10),
            ssnumber num format=SSN11.,
            salary num label='Monthly Salary' format=dollar10.2,
            annsal num label='Annual Salary' format=dollar10.2);

insert into sql.salaries
   values('Conway','Kathryn',224223312,4325,51900)
   values('Schneyer','Samantha',321538796,1275,15300)
   values('Stein','Joel',323093467,3211,38532)
   values('Rodriguez','Jose',123994563,3356,40272)
   values('Johnston','Lois',276116745,2444,29328)
   values('Wong','William',321684532,1798,21576)
   ;

title 'Salaries Table';
select * from sql.salaries;
```

The SELECT statement retrieves and displays the SQL.SALARIES table, shown in **Output 34.2**. To select all the columns from a table, substitute an asterisk (*) for the column names. The order of the columns displayed matches the order of the columns in the table.

Output 34.2 SQL.SALARIES Table

```
                              Salaries Table                                    1

                                             Monthly      Annual
    LASTNAME       FNAME       SSNUMBER        Salary      Salary
    ----------------------------------------------------------------
    Conway         Kathryn     224-22-3312   $4,325.00  $51,900.00
    Schneyer       Samantha    321-53-8796   $1,275.00  $15,300.00
    Stein          Joel        323-09-3467   $3,211.00  $38,532.00
    Rodriguez      Jose        123-99-4563   $3,356.00  $40,272.00
    Johnston       Lois        276-11-6745   $2,444.00  $29,328.00
    Wong           William     321-68-4532   $1,798.00  $21,576.00
```

An example of the second form of the CREATE TABLE statement is included in **DROP Statement** later in this chapter.

Creating Views with the SQL Procedure

CREATE VIEW *viewname* **AS** *query-expression*
   <**ORDER BY** *order-by-item* <,*order-by-item*>...>;

A PROC SQL view is a query-expression that is given a name and stored for later use. You can refer to views in queries as if they were tables, but a view is not the same as a table. A table is stored data while a view is a stored query-expression, that is, a description or definition of a virtual table. When you define a view and submit it, the view derives its data from the tables, views, or SAS/ACCESS views listed in its FROM clause. The data accessed by a view are a subset or superset of the data in its underlying table(s), view(s), or SAS/ACCESS view(s).

When you refer to a view in a query-expression's FROM clause, the SQL procedure executes the view and builds a virtual, internal table. The SQL procedure then processes this internal table as if it were any table (SAS data file). For example, a view's columns can be joined with columns in other tables, views, or SAS/ACCESS views; summary functions and arithmetic calculations can be performed on a column's values; or a view's columns can be renamed with aliases or labels.

Because a PROC SQL view is a stored query-expression and contains no data, you cannot update it as you would a table. A PROC SQL view is a read-only object. In Release 6.06 of the SAS System, you cannot use a view to update the data in that view's underlying tables. That is, you cannot use the INSERT, DELETE, UPDATE, or ALTER statement when referencing a PROC SQL view. You also cannot update the data accessed by a view using a SAS procedure such as the FSEDIT procedure.

You can update the underlying data described by a SAS/ACCESS view using the SQL procedure, if the SAS/ACCESS view is created so that it can be updated. See the following sections later in this chapter for more information: **DELETE Statement**, **INSERT Statement**, and **UPDATE Statement**.

Unlike many SQL databases, the SQL procedure allows you to specify the ORDER BY clause in the CREATE VIEW statement. Each time a view is accessed, its data are sorted and displayed as specified by the ORDER BY clause. This sorting on every access has certain performance costs, especially if the view's underlying tables are large. You may want to omit the ORDER BY clause when creating the view and specify it as needed when referencing the view in queries.

When you access a PROC SQL or SAS/ACCESS view using the SQL procedure or any other SAS procedure, the view is evaluated against the current state of its underlying data. Therefore, accessing data through a view gives you the most up-to-date information. A stored subset of a table, for example, is current only at the time the data are stored—the data may be out-of-date by the time you use them.

Librefs and stored views   Storing tables using first-level names (librefs) and second-level names (table names) is described in **Creating Tables with the SQL Procedure** earlier in this chapter. Using a second-level name alone in the SAS System usually indicates a temporarily stored table, except in the case of PROC SQL views. If a table and a view are in the same data library, you can refer to a table name alone (without the libref) in the FROM clause of a CREATE VIEW statement.

Example   This example defines a temporarily stored view based on the SQL.SALARIES table created in **Creating Tables with the SQL Procedure** earlier in this chapter.

```
libname sql 'SAS-data-library';

proc sql;
create view midrange as
select lastname, fname, ssnumber
  from sql.salaries
  where salary>2000 and salary<3999.99;

title 'Middle-Range Salaries View';
select * from midrange;
```

A message is written to the SAS log indicating that the view has been defined. The SELECT statement retrieves and displays the view, as shown in **Output 34.3**.

Output 34.3   WORK.MIDRANGE View Based on the SQL.SALARIES Table

```
                        Middle-Range Salaries View                          1

         LASTNAME          FNAME          SSNUMBER
         -------------------------------------------------
         Stein             Joel           323-09-3467
         Rodriguez         Jose           123-99-4563
         Johnston          Lois           276-11-6745
```

Creating Indexes with the SQL Procedure

CREATE <UNIQUE> INDEX *indexname*
   ON *table-name (column-name <,column-name>...);*

An index stores both the values of a table's columns and a system of directions that enable access to rows (in that table) by index value. Defining an index on a column or set of columns enables the SAS System, under certain circumstances, to locate rows in a table more quickly and efficiently. In particular, indexes allow the SQL procedure to process the following classes of queries more efficiently:

- comparisons against a column that is indexed
- IN subquery where the column in the inner subquery is indexed
- correlated subqueries, where the column being compared with the correlated reference is indexed

- join-queries, where the join-expression is an equals comparison and all the columns involved in the join-expression are indexed in one of the tables being joined.

Indexes are maintained by the SAS System for all changes to the table, whether the changes originate from the SQL procedure or some other source. Therefore, if you alter a column's definition or update its values, the same index continues to be defined for it. However, if an indexed column in a table is dropped, the index on it is also dropped.

You can create simple or composite indexes. A *simple index* is created on one column in a table. The V606 engine requires that a simple index have the same name as that column. See *SAS Language: Reference* for more information on the V606 engine.

A *composite index* is one index name that is defined for two or more columns. The columns can be specified in any order, and they can have different data types. A composite index name cannot match the name of one of the columns. If you drop a composite index, the index is dropped for all the columns named in that composite index. See the second example in the next section for more information on composite indexes.

The UNIQUE keyword causes the SAS System to reject any change to a table that would cause more than one row to have the same index value. Unique indexes guarantee that data in one column, or a composite group of columns, remain unique for every value in a table. For this reason, a unique index should not be defined for a column that could include NULL or missing values. In a personnel table, for example, each employee's Social Security number should be unique, so you can create a unique index on that column.

You can use the CONTENTS procedure to display a table's index names and the columns for which they are defined.

Creating, managing, and deleting indexes are also described in Chapter 17, "The DATASETS Procedure." *SAS Language: Reference* describes when to use indexes and how they affect SAS statements that handle BY-group processing.

Examples   This example defines an index on the SSNUMBER column of the SQL.SALARIES table created in **Creating Tables with the SQL Procedure** earlier in this chapter. The note is written to the SAS log indicating that the index has been defined.

```
libname sql 'SAS-data-library';


proc sql;
create unique index ssnumber on sql.salaries (ssnumber);
```

NOTE: Simple index SSNUMBER has been defined.

The following example combines employees' first and last names into a composite index called BOTHNAME:

```
create index bothname on sql.salaries (lastname,fname);
```

NOTE: Composite index BOTHNAME has been defined.

DELETE Statement

DELETE
   FROM *table-name* | <*libref.*>*sas-access-view* <**AS** *alias*>
   <**WHERE** *sql-expression*>;

The DELETE statement removes all the rows from the table or DBMS table described by a SAS/ACCESS view specified in the FROM clause, for which the

WHERE expression is true. This statement cannot reference PROC SQL views in its FROM clause.

If the WHERE clause is not specified, the DELETE statement *deletes all the rows from the table or DBMS table* described by a SAS/ACCESS view. Therefore, use this statement cautiously.

Using SAS/ACCESS Views in the DELETE Statement

You can refer to a SAS/ACCESS view (or view descriptor) in the FROM clause of a DELETE statement in the following cases:

- You have been granted the appropriate authorization by the external database management system (for example, DB2) to delete rows from a table.
- The SAS/ACCESS view accesses data from an external database table (such as a DB2 table). The DELETE statement removes rows from the external database table.
- The SAS/ACCESS view accesses data from an external database view (such as a DB2 view) that is based on a single database table. The DELETE statement removes rows from the single database table.

   You cannot use the DELETE statement when referencing a SAS/ACCESS view that accesses data from an external database view that is based on multiple database tables or database views.

See the SAS/ACCESS interface guide for your database system for more information.

Example

This example deletes employees from the table who earn less than $20,000 annually. A temporary table WORK.SALTEMP, based on the SQL.SALARIES table, is created here so that the SQL.SALARIES table is not altered.

```
libname sql 'SAS-data-library';

proc sql;
create table saltemp as
select * from sql.salaries;

delete from saltemp
   where annsal < 20000;

title 'Temporary Saltemp Table';
select * from saltemp;
```

Output 34.4   WORK.SALTEMP Table

```
                          Temporary Saltemp Table                             1
                                              Monthly      Annual
         LASTNAME     FNAME        SSNUMBER    Salary       Salary
         ---------------------------------------------------------------
         Conway       Kathryn      224-22-3312  $4,325.00  $51,900.00
         Stein        Joel         323-09-3467  $3,211.00  $38,532.00
         Rodriguez    Jose         123-99-4563  $3,356.00  $40,272.00
         Johnston     Lois         276-11-6745  $2,444.00  $29,328.00
         Wong         William      321-68-4532  $1,798.00  $21,576.00
```

DESCRIBE Statement

DESCRIBE VIEW *viewname* ;

The DESCRIBE statement writes the definition of an SQL procedure view to the SAS log. This statement is helpful for reminding the user how a view is defined.

If a view is based on or derived from another view, you may want to use the FEEDBACK option in the PROC SQL statement. This option displays (in the SAS log) how the underlying view is defined and expands any expressions used in this view definition. The CONTENTS or DATASETS procedure can also be used with a view to find out more information.

The DESCRIBE statement can only be specified for PROC SQL views. To find out more information on a table, use the FEEDBACK option or the CONTENTS procedure.

Example

This example describes the WORK.MIDRANGE view, as defined in **Creating Views with the SQL Procedure** earlier in this chapter. Its output is written to the SAS log, as shown in **Display 34.1**.

```
proc sql;
describe view midrange;
```

Display 34.1   DESCRIBE Statement: Definition of an SQL View in the SAS Log

```
SAS LOG
COMMAND ===>
...
70      proc sql;
71      describe view midrange;
NOTE: SQL view WORK.MIDRANGE is defined as:

     select LASTNAME, FNAME, SSNUMBER
       from SQL.SALARIES
       where (SALARY>2000) and (SALARY<3999.99);
```

DROP Statement

> **DROP TABLE** *table-name* <,*table-name*>...;
> **DROP VIEW** *viewname* <,*viewname*>...;
> **DROP INDEX** *indexname* <,*indexname*>... **FROM** *table-name*;

The DROP statement deletes the entire table, PROC SQL view, or index requested. If a table or view has been stored permanently, you must qualify the name with its libref. If you drop a table that is referenced in a view definition and try to execute the view, an error message is written to the SAS log stating that the table does not exist. Therefore, remove references in queries and views to any table(s) and view(s) that you drop.

If you drop a table with indexed columns, all the indexes are automatically dropped. If you drop a composite index, the index is dropped for all the columns named in that index.

You cannot use the DROP statement to drop a table or view in an external database that is described by a SAS/ACCESS view.

Example

This example drops the composite index BOTHNAME from the SQL.SALARIES table. A note is written to the SAS log indicating that the index has been dropped.

```
libname sql 'SAS-data-library';

proc sql;
drop index bothname from sql.salaries;
```

```
NOTE:  Index BOTHNAME has been deleted.
```

INSERT Statement

> **INSERT INTO** *table-name* | <*libref.*>*sas-access-view*
>   <(*column-name* <,*column-name*>...)>
>   **SET** *column-name*=*sql-expression* <,*column-name*=*sql-expression*>...
>   <**SET** *column-name*=*sql-expression* <,*column-name*=*sql-expression*>...>;

> **INSERT INTO** *table-name* | <*libref.*>*sas-access-view*
>   <(*column-name* <,*column-name*>...)>
>   **VALUES** (*value* <,*value*>...)
>   <**VALUES** (*value* <,*value*>...)>...;

> **INSERT INTO** *table-name* | <*libref.*>*sas-access-view*
>   <(*column-name* <,*column-name*>...)>
>   *query-expression*;

The INSERT statement adds new rows to a new or existing table, setting the values of the columns in one of three ways. This statement can only be used with tables and SAS/ACCESS views.* If the INSERT statement includes an optional list of column names, only those columns are given values by the statement; columns in the table, but not listed, are given missing values.

The *first form* of the INSERT statement uses the SET clause, which sets or alters the values of a column. You can use more than one SET clause per INSERT statement, and each SET clause can set more than one column. Notice in the syntax

---

* For simplicity, *table* is used in the rest of this description to mean *table* or *SAS/ACCESS view*.

that multiple SET clauses are not separated by commas. If you specify an optional list of columns, you can only set a value for a column that is specified in the list of columns to be inserted.

The *second form* of the INSERT statement uses the VALUES clause. This clause can be used to insert lists of values into a table. You can either give a value for each column in the table or give values just for the columns specified in the list of column names. One row is inserted for each VALUES clause. Notice in the syntax that multiple VALUES clauses are not separated by commas. The order of the values in the VALUES clause matches the order of the column names in the INSERT column list or, if no list was specified, the order of the columns in the table.

The *third form* of the INSERT statement inserts the results of a query-expression into a table. The order of the values in the query-expression matches the order of the column names in the INSERT column list or, if no list was specified, the order of the columns in the table.

If an index is defined on a column and you insert a new row into the table, that value is added to the index. You can display a table's definition using the CONTENTS procedure; index names and the columns for which they are defined are also listed. See **CREATE Statement** earlier in this chapter for more information on creating and using indexes.

Using SAS/ACCESS Views in the INSERT Statement

You can refer to a SAS/ACCESS view (or view descriptor) in the INTO clause of an INSERT statement in the following cases:

- You have been granted the appropriate authorization by the external database management system (for example, DB2) to insert rows into a table.
- The SAS/ACCESS view accesses data from an external database table (such as a DB2 table). The INSERT statement adds rows to the external database table.
- The SAS/ACCESS view accesses data from an external database view (such as a DB2 view) that is based on a single database table. The INSERT statement adds rows to the single database table.

    You cannot use the INSERT statement when referencing a SAS/ACCESS view that accesses data from an external database view that is based on multiple database tables or database views.

See the SAS/ACCESS interface guide for your database system for more information.

Example

See the example using the second form of the INSERT statement in **Creating Tables with the SQL Procedure** earlier in this chapter.

SELECT Statement

> *query-expression*
>   <**ORDER BY** *order-by-item* <,*order-by-item*>...>;

The SELECT statement evaluates the query, formats the rows selected into a report, and prints it in the SAS OUTPUT window (or to a list file). The SELECT statement provides the *query* in the Structured Query Language.

The SELECT statement is included in a *query-expression*. A query-expression can be a simple table-expression that is terminated with a semicolon, as shown in many of the examples in this chapter. A query-expression can also contain multiple table-expressions that are linked with one or more set operators. Think of each table-expression as producing a set of data, which you can combine with the optional SQL set operators UNION, INTERSECT, EXCEPT, and OUTER UNION.

A *table-expression* is composed of the SELECT and FROM clauses, as well as other optional clauses. The SELECT statement derives its name from this first clause.

```
SELECT <DISTINCT> object-item-list     /* SELECT clause */
   <INTO macro-variable-list>          /* INTO clause * /
   FROM from-list                      /* FROM clause */
   <WHERE sql-expression>              /* WHERE clause */
   <GROUP BY group-by-item-list>       /* GROUP BY clause */
   <HAVING sql-expression>             /* HAVING clause */
```

See **Components of the SQL Procedure Statements** later in this chapter for more information on the query-expression and on the components named in this table-expression.

A summary function, such as SUM or AVG, is one of the operands included in an *sql-expression*. However, a WHERE clause cannot contain a summary function unless it is part of a subquery (that is, a nested query-expression). Thus, a WHERE clause can contain a subquery, and a summary function can appear in the SELECT or FROM clause of that subquery.

The SELECT statement can also be used to retrieve data from an external database management system (DBMS) using SAS/ACCESS software. You can use this software to create SAS/ACCESS views, which describe data from a DB2 table, for example, to the SAS System. This software also enables you to create and load DBMS tables for processing without leaving your SAS session. You can use SAS/ACCESS views as you would PROC SQL tables, with some restrictions, as noted in the INSERT, DELETE, and UPDATE statement descriptions elsewhere in this chapter. See the SAS/ACCESS interface guide for your database management system for more information on using SAS/ACCESS views.

Example

This example retrieves data from the SQL.SALARIES table and sorts it in ascending order according to the LASTNAME column. The following statements produce **Output 34.5**:

```
libname sql 'SAS-data-library';

proc sql;
title 'Employees with Midrange Salaries';
select lastname, fname, ssnumber
   from sql.salaries
   where salary>2000 and salary<3999.99
   order by lastname;
```

Output 34.5 SQL.SALARIES Table in Sorted Order

```
                     Employees with Midrange Salaries                          1

             LASTNAME        FNAME        SSNUMBER
             ----------------------------------------------
             Johnston        Lois         276-11-6745
             Rodriguez       Jose         123-99-4563
             Stein           Joel         323-09-3467
```

UPDATE Statement

UPDATE *table-name* | *<libref.>sas-access-view* **<AS** *alias>*
    SET *column-name=sql-expression* *<,column-name=sql-expression>*...
    *<***SET** *column-name=sql-expression* *<,column-name=sql-expression>*...*>*
    *<***WHERE** *sql-expression>*;

The UPDATE statement modifies the values in a column in existing rows of a table or DBMS table described by a SAS/ACCESS view,* according to the values specified in the SET clause. Any column that is not modified retains its original values, except in certain queries using the case-expression. See **case-expression** in Chapter 5, "SQL Procedure," of the SAS *Guide to the SQL Procedure* for more information.

To add, drop, or modify a column's definition or attributes, you must use the ALTER statement, described earlier in this chapter.

Notice in the syntax that multiple SET clauses are not separated by commas.

In the SET clause, a column reference on the left side of the equal sign can also appear as part of the expression on the right side of the sign. That is, it is possible to modify a column in terms of itself. For example, you could use this expression to give employees a $1000 holiday bonus:

```
set salary=salary + 1000
```

All the rows specified in the WHERE clause are updated. If the WHERE clause is omitted, all the rows in the table are updated.

When you update a column and an index has been defined for that column, the values in the updated column continue to have the index defined for them.

Using SAS/ACCESS Views in the UPDATE Statement

You can reference a SAS/ACCESS view (or view descriptor) in the UPDATE statement in the following cases:

- You have been granted the appropriate authorization by the external database management system (for example, DB2) to update data in a table.
- The SAS/ACCESS view accesses data from an external database table (such as a DB2 table). The UPDATE statement modifies the data in the external database table.
- The SAS/ACCESS view accesses data from an external database view (such as a DB2 view) that is based on a single database table. The UPDATE statement modifies the data in the single database table.
  You cannot use the UPDATE statement when referencing a SAS/ACCESS view that accesses data from an external database view that is based on multiple database tables or database views.

See the SAS/ACCESS interface guide for your database system for more information.

---

* For simplicity, *table* is used in the rest of this description to mean *table* or *SAS/ACCESS view*. The UPDATE statement cannot update a PROC SQL view.

Examples

This example updates the data in the UPDATED table, which is a temporary table based on the SQL.SALARIES table. A temporary table is used here so that the chapter's sample table is not modified.

This example updates the data to reflect a 10% raise for employees earning less than $2,000 per month. The SELECT statement retrieves and displays the table, sorting its rows in ascending order by the SALARY column. The following statements produce **Output 34.6**:

```
libname sql 'SAS-data-library';

proc sql;
create table updated as
select * from sql.salaries;

update updated
   set salary = salary * 1.1
   where salary < 2000;

update updated
   set annsal = salary * 12
   where salary < 2000;

title 'Updated Table with Raises';
select * from updated
   order by salary;
```

Output 34.6   WORK.UPDATED Table

```
                      Updated Table with Raises                        1

                                          Monthly    Annual
      LASTNAME   FNAME      SSNUMBER       Salary     Salary
      ------------------------------------------------------------
      Schneyer   Samantha   321-53-8796   $1,402.50  $16,830.00
      Wong       William    321-68-4532   $1,977.80  $23,733.60
      Johnston   Lois       276-11-6745   $2,444.00  $29,328.00
      Stein      Joel       323-09-3467   $3,211.00  $38,532.00
      Rodriguez  Jose       123-99-4563   $3,356.00  $40,272.00
      Conway     Kathryn    224-22-3312   $4,325.00  $51,900.00
```

The next example adds values to the GENDER column, as defined in **Example** in **ALTER Statement** earlier in this chapter. The following statements produce **Output 34.7**:

```
libname sql 'SAS-data-library';

update sql.altertab
   set gender='F' where lastname in ('Conway','Schneyer','Johnston');

update sql.altertab
   set gender='M' where gender is missing;

title 'Altertab Table';
select lastname, fname, gender, ssnumber, salary, annsal
   from sql.altertab;
```

Output 34.7   SQL.ALTERTAB Table with Added Values

```
                             Altertab Table                          1

                                            Monthly    Annual
   LASTNAME    FNAME      GENDER   SSNUMBER   Salary     Salary
   --------------------------------------------------------------
   Conway      Kathryn    F       224-22-3312  $4,325.00  $51,900.00
   Schneyer    Samantha   F       321-53-8796  $1,275.00  $15,300.00
   Stein       Joel       M       323-09-3467  $3,211.00  $38,532.00
   Rodriguez   Jose       M       123-99-4563  $3,356.00  $40,272.00
   Johnston    Lois       F       276-11-6745  $2,444.00  $29,328.00
   Wong        William    M       321-68-4532  $1,798.00  $21,576.00
```

VALIDATE Statement

VALIDATE *query-expression*;

The VALIDATE statement checks the correctness of a query-expression's syntax without executing the expression. If the syntax of the query is valid, a message to that effect is written to the SAS log; if invalid, a syntax error message is written to the log. The VALIDATE statement is useful in interactive applications for determining whether an SQL procedure query is likely to succeed if submitted.

The VALIDATE statement can also be included in applications that use the macro facility. When used in such an application, VALIDATE returns a value indicating the query-expression's validity. The value is returned through the macro variable SQLRC (short for SQL return code). For example, if a SELECT statement is valid, the macro variable SQLRC returns a value less than or equal to 4.

Example

This example validates the syntax of the following query. A note is written to the SAS log indicating that the syntax of the query is valid.

```
libname sql 'SAS-data-library';

proc sql;
validate
select ssnumber, salary, annsal
   from sql.salaries
   where salary<2000;
```

NOTE: PROC SQL statement has valid syntax.

COMPONENTS OF THE SQL PROCEDURE STATEMENTS

This section describes the components used in SQL procedure statements. Most components are contained in clauses within the statements. For example, the basic SELECT statement is composed of the SELECT and FROM clauses, where each contains one or more components. Components can also contain other components. Therefore, the components are presented in alphabetic order, and some terms are referred to before they are defined.

The clauses and components used in the SQL procedure are fully described in the *SAS Guide to the SQL Procedure: Usage and Reference*.

column-definition

The *column-definition* component defines the SQL procedure's data types and dates. It can take any one of the following forms:

> column **CHARACTER | VARCHAR** < (*width*)> <column-modifier>
> <,column-modifier>...>
> column **INTEGER | SMALLINT** <column-modifier <,column-modifier>...>
> column **DECIMAL | NUMERIC | FLOAT** < (*width* <,*ndec*>)>
> <column-modifier <,column-modifier>...>
> column **REAL | DOUBLE PRECISION** <column-modifier <,column-modifier>...>
> column **DATE** <column-modifier>

column-modifier

The *column-modifier* component sets column attributes. You can use any of the following options:

> <INFORMAT=*informatw.d*>
> <FORMAT=*formatw.d*>
> <LABEL='*label*'>

column-name

The *column-name* component defines the valid forms of a column name. It can take any one of the following forms:

> *column*
> *table.column*
> *tablealias.column*
> *view.column*
> *viewalias.column*
> *sas-access-view.column*
> *sas-access-viewalias.column*

from-list

The *from-list* component specifies source tables or views. It can take any one of the following forms:

> *table-name* <<AS> *alias*>
> <*libref.*>*view* <<AS> *alias*>
> <*libref.*>*sas-access-view* <<AS> *alias*>
> *joined-table*
> (*query-expression*) <<AS> *alias*> <(*column-name* <,*column-name*>...)>

group-by-item

The *group-by-item* component specifies the groups of column values that the summary function processes. It can take any one of the following forms:

> *integer*
> *column*
> *sql-expression*

in-condition

The *in-condition* component tests set membership and is used in WHERE clauses for subqueries. It can take either of the following forms:

sql-expression <NOT> IN (*constant* <,*constant*>...)
sql-expression <NOT> IN (*query-expression*)

join-expression

The *join-expression* component lists operands that can be used in the ON clause when joining tables. It can take any one of the following forms:

constant
column-name
SAS-function
USER
<ALL | ANY> (*query-expression*)

joined-table

The *joined-table* component joins a table with itself or with other tables. It can take any one of the following forms:

table <<**AS**> *alias*>, *table* <<**AS**> *alias*> <,*table* <<**AS**> *alias*>...>
table <**INNER**> **JOIN** *table* **ON** *join-expression*
table **LEFT JOIN** *table* **ON** *join-expression*
table **RIGHT JOIN** *table* **ON** *join-expression*
table **FULL JOIN** *table* **ON** *join-expression*

where *table* can be any one of the following:

table-name
<*libref.*>*view*
<*libref.*>*sas-access-view*
query-expression

object-item

The *object-item* component lists items allowed in the SELECT clause. It can take any one of the following forms:

*
*table.**
*tablealias.**
*view.**
*viewalias.**
*sas-access-view.**
*sas-access-viewalias.**
column-name <**AS** *alias*> <*column-modifier* <*column-modifier*>...>
sql-expression <**AS** *alias*> <*column-modifier* <*column-modifier*>...>

order-by-item

The *order-by-item* component specifies the order in which rows are displayed in a result table. It can take any one of the following forms:

integer <ASC> | <DESC>
column-name <ASC> | <DESC>
sql-expression <ASC> | <DESC>

query-expression

The *query-expression* component retrieves data and may perform set operations on table-expressions.

> *table-expression* <*set-operator table-expression*>...

where *set-operator* and optional keywords are any one of the following:

    <INTERSECT <CORRESPONDING> <ALL>>
    <OUTER UNION <CORRESPONDING>>
    <UNION <CORRESPONDING> <ALL>>
    <EXCEPT <CORRESPONDING> <ALL>>

sql-expression

The *sql-expression* component lists operands that can be used in functions and expressions. It can take any one of the following forms:

> *constant*
> *column-name*
> *summary-function*
> *SAS-function*
> USER
> <ALL | ANY> (*query-expression*)

where *SAS-function* can be any SAS function except LAG, DIF, or SOUND.

Operators used in the SQL procedure are comparable to those used in expressions in the SAS DATA step. See the *SAS Guide to the SQL Procedure* for a detailed description of the available operators.

summary-function

The *summary-function* component performs statistical calculations.

> *summary-function* (<DISTINCT> *sql-expression*)

where *summary-function* can be any one of the following summarizing or aggregate functions: AVG, MEAN, COUNT, FREQ, N, CSS, CV, MAX, MIN, NMISS, PRT, RANGE, STD, STDERR, SUM, SUMWGT, T, USS, or VAR.

Notice that the SQL function name, as well as the SAS name, is listed with some of the functions. For example, COUNT and FREQ are the SQL function names for the SAS function N.

table-expression

The *table-expression* component defines a query's result table.

    SELECT <DISTINCT> object-item <,object-item>...   /* SELECT clause */
      <INTO :macroname <,:macroname>...>   /* INTO clause */
    FROM from-list   /* FROM clause */
    <WHERE sql-expression>   /* WHERE clause */
    <GROUP BY group-by-item <,group-by-item>...>   /* GROUP BY clause */
    <HAVING sql-expression>   /* HAVING clause */

table-name

The *table-name* component defines the valid forms of a table name.

> <*libref.*>*table* <(*dataset-option-list*)>

The STANDARD
Procedure

ABSTRACT

The STANDARD procedure standardizes some or all of the variables in a SAS data set to a given mean and standard deviation and produces a new SAS data set containing the standardized values.

INTRODUCTION

Standardizing is a technique for removing location and scale attributes from a set of data. Sometimes you need to center the values on a variable to a mean of 0 and a standard deviation of 1. Some statistical techniques begin the analysis by standardizing the data in this way. If your data are normally distributed, standardizing is also studentizing, since the result has a Student's t distribution.

SPECIFICATIONS

The STANDARD procedure is controlled by the following statements:

PROC STANDARD *standardization-option-list* <*option-list* >;
BY *variable-list*;
FREQ *variable*;
VAR *variable-list*;
WEIGHT *variable*;

PROC STANDARD Statement

PROC STANDARD *standardization-option-list* <*option-list*>;

The options shown in **Table 35.1** can appear in the PROC STANDARD statement. You must use the MEAN=, STD=, or REPLACE option in order to prevent your output SAS data set from becoming an exact copy of your input data set. The options below are described in alphabetic order following the table.

Table 35.1   PROC STANDARD Statement Options

Task	Options
Specify data set details	DATA= OUT=
Choose standardization method	MEAN= STD= REPLACE
Specify variance divisor	VARDEF=
Control printed output	PRINT

DATA=*SAS-data-set*
> gives the name of the data set to be used by PROC STANDARD. If the DATA= option is omitted, PROC STANDARD uses the most recently created SAS data set.

MEAN=*mean-value*
M=*mean-value*
> requests that all variables specified in the VAR statement (or all the numeric variables if the VAR statement is omitted) be standardized to a mean of *mean-value*. If you don't use the MEAN= option, the mean of the output values will be the same as the mean of the input values.
>
>   Note: You must use at least one standardization option (MEAN=, STD=, or REPLACE) or your output SAS data set will be an exact copy of your input data set.

OUT=*SAS-data-set*
> gives the name of the new SAS data set to contain the standardized variables. If the OUT= option is omitted, the SAS System names the new data set using the DATA*n* naming convention. The OUT= data set contains all the variables from the input data set, including those not standardized. If you want to create a permanent SAS data set, you must supply a two-level name in the OUT= option.

PRINT
> prints the input frequency, mean, and standard deviation for each variable standardized. Unless you specify the PRINT option, these statistics do not appear on your output.

REPLACE
> requests that all missing values be replaced with the variable mean. If MEAN=*mean-value* is also specified, missing values are set instead to *mean-value*.

STD=*std-value*
S=*std-value*

standardizes all variables specified in the VAR statement (or all numeric variables if the VAR statement is omitted) to a standard deviation of *std-value*. If you do not use the STD= option, the standard deviation of the output values is the same as the standard deviation of the input values. The REPLACE option does not affect the actions of the STD= option.

VARDEF=DF
      |N
      |WDF
      |WEIGHT|WGT

specifies the divisor to be used in the calculation of variances. The default value is VARDEF=DF. The values and associated divisors are shown below:

Value	Divisor	Formula
DF	degrees of freedom	$n - 1$
N	number of observations	n
WDF	sum of weights minus one	$(\Sigma_i \, w_i) - 1$
WEIGHT | WGT	sum of weights	$\Sigma_i \, w_i$

BY Statement

BY *variable-list*;

A BY statement can be used with PROC STANDARD to obtain separate analyses on observations in groups defined by the BY variables. When a BY statement appears, the procedure expects the input data set to be sorted in order of the BY variables or to have an appropriate index. If your input data set is not sorted in ascending order, you can do one of the following:

- Use the SORT procedure with a similar BY statement to sort the data.
- If appropriate, use the BY statement option NOTSORTED or DESCENDING.
- Create an index on the BY variables you want to use. For more information on using the BY statement with indexed data sets, see Chapter 17, "The DATASETS Procedure."

FREQ Statement

FREQ *variable*;

The FREQ statement specifies a numeric variable in the input SAS data set. If a FREQ statement is used, each observation in the input data set is assumed to represent *n* observations, where *n* is the value of the FREQ variable. If the value is not an integer, it is truncated to the integer portion. An observation is not used in the calculation of the mean and standard deviation if the FREQ value is less than one or is missing. However, the variables to be standardized for the observation are still adjusted.

VAR Statement

VAR *variable-list*;

The VAR statement specifies the variables to be standardized. If the VAR statement is omitted, all the numeric variables in the data set are standardized.

WEIGHT Statement

WEIGHT *variable*;

The WEIGHT statement specifies a numeric variable in the input SAS data set, the values of which are used to weight each observation. Only one variable can be specified. The WEIGHT variable values can be nonintegers and are used to calculate a weighted mean and a weighted variance. If the value of the WEIGHT variable is less than zero or is missing, a value of zero is assumed. The FREQ and WEIGHT statements can both be used in a single PROC STANDARD step.

DETAILS

Missing Values

Missing values are excluded from the standardization process. Unless the REPLACE option is specified, missing values are left as missing in the output data set. When the REPLACE option is specified, missing values are replaced with the variable mean, or if you use the MEAN= option, with the *mean-value* you specify.

Output Data Set

The STANDARD procedure produces an output SAS data set containing the standardized variables for a given variable. The standardized values are created as follows:

$$x_i' = \frac{S * (x_i - \bar{x})}{s_x} + M$$

where

x_i' is the new standardized value.

S is the STD= value.

M is the MEAN= value.

x_i is the observation's value.

$\bar{x}$ is the variable's mean.

s_x is the variable's standard deviation.

PROC STANDARD calculates $\bar{x}$ and s_x, the variable's mean and standard deviation. The resulting standardized variable has a mean equal to the MEAN= value and a standard deviation equal to the STD= value. See **EXAMPLE** for an illustration of the MEAN= and STD= options.

Printed Output

If you specify the PRINT option, the STANDARD procedure prints the following:

1. the variable name
2. the mean
3. the standard deviation
4. the input frequency for each variable standardized in the procedure output.

If you do not use the PRINT option, no printed ouput is produced. The standardized variable values are output to the OUT= data set, which you can print using the PRINT procedure.

EXAMPLE

Standardizing Test Scores

The data in this example consist of three test scores for students in two sections of a course. For each section, you want to standardize all three test scores to a mean of 80 and a standard deviation of 5. To keep the original test scores with the standardized scores in the same SAS data set, create the three variables NEWTEST1 through NEWTEST3 to contain the new, standardized test scores.

The PROC STANDARD statement includes the MEAN= and STD= options and gives the name NEWSCORE to the new SAS data set containing the standardized values. Since only NEWTEST1 through NEWTEST3 appear in the VAR statement, they are the only variables standardized; the original variables, TEST1 through TEST3, are not standardized. The BY statement asks that the standardization be done separately for each section of the course. The PROC PRINT statement prints the new data set, and the PROC MEANS output shows in both sections that NEWTEST1 through NEWTEST3 have means of 80 and standard deviations of 5. The following statements produce **Output 35.1**:

```
data score;
   input student section test1-test3;
   newtest1=test1;
   newtest2=test2;
   newtest3=test3;
   cards;
238900545 1 94 91 87
254701167 1 95 96 97
238806445 2 91 86 94
999002527 2 80 76 78
263924860 1 92 40 85
459700886 2 75 76 80
416724915 2 66 69 72
999001230 1 82 84 80
242760674 1 75 76 70
990001252 2 51 66 91
;
run;

proc sort data=score;
   by section;
run;
```

```
proc standard data=score mean=80 std=5 print out=newscore;
   by section;
   var newtest1-newtest3;
   title 'Output Generated with PROC STANDARD and the PRINT Option';
run;

proc print data=newscore;
   by section;
   title 'Standardized Test Scores';
run;

proc means data=newscore(drop=student) maxdec=2 n mean std;
   by section;
   title 'Output from PROC MEANS';
run;
```

Output 35.1   Standardizing Test Scores: PROC STANDARD

```
                   Output Generated with PROC STANDARD and the PRINT Option                          1
----------------------------------------------- SECTION=1 --------------------------------------------
              ❶                    ❷                    ❸            ❹

              NAME                MEAN                 STD            N

              NEWTEST1         87.600000            8.734987          5
              NEWTEST2         77.400000           22.221611          5
              NEWTEST3         83.800000            9.884331          5

----------------------------------------------- SECTION=2 --------------------------------------------

              NAME                MEAN                 STD            N

              NEWTEST1         72.600000           15.076472          5
              NEWTEST2         74.600000            7.733046          5
              NEWTEST3         83.000000            9.219544          5
```

```
                                    Standardized Test Scores                                         2
----------------------------------------------- SECTION=1 --------------------------------------------

       OBS     STUDENT     TEST1    TEST2    TEST3    NEWTEST1    NEWTEST2    NEWTEST3

        1     238900545      94       91       87      83.6634     83.0601     81.6187
        2     254701167      95       96       97      84.2358     84.1851     86.6772
        3     263924860      92       40       85      82.5186     71.5848     80.6070
        4     999001230      82       84       80      76.7945     81.4850     78.0778
        5     242760674      75       76       70      72.7876     79.6850     73.0193

----------------------------------------------- SECTION=2 --------------------------------------------

       OBS     STUDENT     TEST1    TEST2    TEST3    NEWTEST1    NEWTEST2    NEWTEST3

        6     238806445      91       86       94      86.1022     87.3710     85.9656
        7     999002527      80       76       78      82.4542     80.9052     77.2884
        8     459700886      75       76       80      80.7959     80.9052     78.3730
        9     416724915      66       69       72      77.8112     76.3792     74.0344
       10     990001252      51       66       91      72.8365     74.4394     84.3386
```

```
                          Output from PROC MEANS                                      3
--------------------------------------------- SECTION=1 -------------------------------------------------

                 Variable   N      Mean      Std Dev
                 -------------------------------------------
                 TEST1      5      87.60        8.73
                 TEST2      5      77.40       22.22
                 TEST3      5      83.80        9.88
                 NEWTEST1   5      80.00        5.00
                 NEWTEST2   5      80.00        5.00
                 NEWTEST3   5      80.00        5.00
                 -------------------------------------------

--------------------------------------------- SECTION=2 -------------------------------------------------

                 Variable   N      Mean      Std Dev
                 -------------------------------------------
                 TEST1      5      72.60       15.08
                 TEST2      5      74.60        7.73
                 TEST3      5      83.00        9.22
                 NEWTEST1   5      80.00        5.00
                 NEWTEST2   5      80.00        5.00
                 NEWTEST3   5      80.00        5.00
                 -------------------------------------------
```

The SUMMARY
Procedure

ABSTRACT

The SUMMARY procedure computes descriptive statistics on numeric variables in a SAS data set and outputs the results to a new SAS data set. PROC SUMMARY does not produce printed output except when you specify the PRINT option. The SUMMARY procedure performs tasks similar to the MEANS procedure. Refer to Chapter 21, "The MEANS Procedure," for specific information on statement and option syntax for PROC SUMMARY, and for examples.

INTRODUCTION

The SUMMARY procedure creates a SAS data set containing summary statistics. You can optionally display the computed statistics. Each observation in the new data set contains the statistics for a different subgroup of the observations in the input data set. These subgroups represent all possible combinations of the levels of the variables specified in the CLASS statement.

The MEANS procedure also computes descriptive statistics and creates a SAS data set. A major difference between PROC MEANS and PROC SUMMARY is in the default setting of the PRINT option. By default, the SUMMARY procedure does not produce printed output. The MEANS procedure always prints the computed statistics except when the NOPRINT option is specified in the PROC MEANS statement.

SPECIFICATIONS

The SUMMARY procedure is controlled by the following statements:

PROC SUMMARY <*option-list*> <*statistic-keyword-list*>;
    VAR *variable-list*;
    CLASS *variable-list*;
    FREQ *variable*;
    WEIGHT *variable*;
    ID *variable-list*;
    BY *variable-list*;
    OUTPUT <OUT=*SAS-data-set*> <*output-statistic-list*>
                <MAXID <(*var-1*<(*id-list-1*)> <...*var-n*<(*id-list-n*)>>)>=*name-list*>;
                <MINID <(*var-1*<(*id-list-1*)> <...*var-n*<(*id-list-n*)>>)>=*name-list*>;

If you omit the VAR statement with PROC SUMMARY, a simple count of observations is produced. This differs from the MEANS procedure. If you omit the VAR statement with PROC MEANS, all numeric variables in the input data set are analyzed except for those variables used in the BY, ID, FREQ, WEIGHT, or CLASS statements. For more information on the SUMMARY procedure syntax, refer to Chapter 21, "The MEANS Procedure."

Chapter 37

The TABULATE Procedure

ABSTRACT

The TABULATE procedure displays descriptive statistics in tabular format. The value in each table cell is calculated from the variables and statistics that define the pages, rows, and columns of the table. The statistic associated with each cell is calculated on values from all observations in that category. PROC TABULATE computes many of the same statistics that are computed by other descriptive statistical procedures such as MEANS, FREQ, and SUMMARY. PROC TABULATE provides

- simple but powerful methods to create tabular reports
- flexibility in classifying the values of variables and establishing hierarchical relationships between the variables
- mechanisms for labeling and formatting variables and procedure-generated statistics.

This chapter briefly describes the TABULATE procedure. Detailed information and examples of how to use the TABULATE procedure are given in the *SAS Guide to TABULATE Processing, 1987 Edition*.

SPECIFICATIONS

The TABULATE procedure is controlled by the following statements:

> **PROC TABULATE** <*option-list*>;
>> **CLASS** *class-variable-list*;
>> **VAR** *analysis-variable-list*;
>> **TABLE**<<*page-expression,*> *row-expression,*> *column-expression*
>>> </ *table-option-list*>;
>> **BY** <NOTSORTED> <DESCENDING> *variable-1*
>>> <...<DESCENDING> *variable-n*>;
>> **FORMAT** *variable-list-1 format-1* <...*variable-list-n format-n*>;
>> **FREQ** *variable*;
>> **KEYLABEL** *keyword-1='description-1'* <...*keyword-n='description-n'*>;
>> **LABEL** *variable-1='label-1'* <...*variable-n='label-n'*>;
>> **WEIGHT** *variable*;

Table 37.1 summarizes which statements and options to use to perform specific functions with the TABULATE procedure. Use the options listed in the last column of the table with the statements listed in the middle column.

Table 37.1   Summary of PROC TABULATE Functions

Function	Statements	Options
Print frequencies for combinations of variable values	CLASS, TABLE	
Calculate statistics other than frequency on values of a numeric variable	VAR, TABLE	
Calculate statistics other than frequency on values of a numeric variable within classes of other variable values	CLASS, VAR, TABLE	
Format values in table cells	PROC TABULATE, TABLE (F=)	FORMAT=
Format values of class variables in row and column headings	FORMAT	
Change appearance of table	PROC TABULATE, TABLE	FORMCHAR=, NOSEPS, ORDER= BOX, CONDENSE, ROW=, RTSPACE=
Change treatment of missing values	PROC TABULATE, TABLE	MISSING MISSTEXT=, PRINTMISS
Change row and column headings	KEYLABEL, LABEL	
Change default computations	PROC TABULATE, TABLE, FREQ, WEIGHT	VARDEF= FUZZ=

The PROC TABULATE statement is always accompanied by one or more TABLE statements specifying the tables to be produced. In addition, you must use either a VAR statement or a CLASS statement or both. All variables used in the TABLE statement must be specified in either the VAR statement or the CLASS statement, but not both. The WEIGHT, FREQ, and BY statements are optional; each can be specified once for the entire TABULATE procedure step. The FORMAT, LABEL, and KEYLABEL statements are also optional; if you repeat one of these statements, the value in the last statement applies to the entire step.

PROC TABULATE Statement

PROC TABULATE <*option-list*>;

You can specify the following options in the PROC TABULATE statement:

DATA=*SAS-data-set*
specifies the SAS data set used by PROC TABULATE. If you omit the DATA= option, PROC TABULATE uses the SAS data set created most recently in the current job or session.

DEPTH=*number*
specifies the maximum depth of any dimension's crossing. (Refer to **TABLE Statement** later in this chapter for an explanation of crossings.) The default depth is 10. You may need to increase the value for the DEPTH= option, but there is no benefit to decreasing the value. The depth of a crossing refers to the number of elements, including the default statistic, that are crossed with each other within any single dimension of the TABLE statement. For example, the depth of the following TABLE statement is 3 because the default statistic must be included in the crossing:

```
table a*b;
```

Note: Format modifiers are also counted in the crossings. Therefore, the maximum depth of the following TABLE statement is 5:

```
table a*b,x*y*z*sum*f=10.0;
```

FORMAT=*format-name*
specifies a default format for formatting the value in each table cell. You can use any valid SAS or user-defined format. If you omit the FORMAT= option, PROC TABULATE uses BEST12.2 as the default format. The default format is overridden by any formats specified in a TABLE statement. This option is especially useful for decreasing the number of print positions used to print a table. Refer to Chapter 5, "Controlling the Table's Appearance," in the *SAS Guide to TABULATE Processing* for more information on formatting output.

FORMCHAR<(*index-list*)>='*string*'
FC<(*index-list*)>='*string*'
defines the characters used for constructing the table outlines and dividers. The value is a string 11 characters long defining the two bar characters, vertical and horizontal, and the 9 corner characters: upper left, upper middle, upper right, middle left, middle middle (cross), middle right, lower left, lower middle, and lower right. The default value is FORMCHAR= '│----│+│---'. You can substitute any character or hexadecimal string to customize the table's appearance. You can replace the entire default string by specifying a full 11-character replacement string, or you can replace selected characters by including an index list that indicates which characters are to be replaced. For example, change the four corners to asterisks by using

```
FORMCHAR(3 5 9 11)= '****'
```

Specifying 11 blanks produces tables with blank outlines and dividers:

```
FORMCHAR='
```

Refer to Chapter 5 in the *SAS Guide to TABULATE Processing* for more information on formatting output.

MISSING

considers missing values as valid levels for the class variables. Special missing values are considered as different level values.* A heading for each missing value is shown in the table. Unless the MISSING option is specified, PROC TABULATE does not include observations with a missing value for one or more class variables in the analysis.

NOSEPS

eliminates horizontal separator lines from the row titles and body of the printed table. Horizontal separator lines remain in the column title section of the table. Note that the NOSEPS option completely removes the separator lines instead of substituting blank characters, as illustrated in the FORMCHAR= option discussed earlier in this chapter.

ORDER=*order*

specifies the order in which headings for class variable values are displayed in each table. The possible values for *order* are as follows:

DATA   keeps values of class variables in the order they were encountered when the input was read. Note that the order remains the same for the entire data set or BY group if a BY statement is specified.

FORMATTED

orders the class values by the formatted (external) representation of the value.

FREQ   orders the headings for class variables by descending frequency count so that class values occurring in the greatest number of observations come first.

INTERNAL   orders the headings in the same sequence as they would be ordered by the SORT procedure.

If you omit the ORDER= option, PROC TABULATE defaults to ORDER=INTERNAL.

VARDEF=DF
    |N
    |WDF
    |WEIGHT|WGT

specifies the divisor to be used in the calculation of the variances. The possible values for *divisor* are as follows:

DF   requests that the degrees of freedom ($N-1$) be used as the divisor.

N   requests that the number of observations (N) be used.

WDF   requests that the sum of the weights minus one be used.

WEIGHT | WGT   requests that the sum of the weights be used.

The default is VARDEF=DF.

---

* Special missing values are the uppercase letters A through Z and the underscore (_), which are used to represent missing *numeric* values. Refer to **Missing Values with Special Meanings** in Chapter 2, "The DATA Step," in *SAS Language: Reference, Version 6, First Edition* for more information.

BY Statement

> **BY** <NOTSORTED> <DESCENDING> *variable-1*
>   <...<DESCENDING> *variable-n*>;

Use a BY statement with PROC TABULATE to obtain separate analyses on observations in groups defined by the BY variables.

Note that the page-dimension expression of a TABLE statement can have an effect similar to using a BY statement. Your input data set need not be sorted or indexed when the page-dimension expression is used. The page dimension should be used in most cases where a new page is desired for a given level of a class variable or combination of variables. Refer to **TABLE Statement** later in this chapter for more information on the page dimension and **Comparison of BY-Group Processing to Using the Page Dimension** in Chapter 3, "Details of TABULATE Processing," in the *SAS Guide to TABULATE Processing*.

When a BY statement appears, the TABULATE procedure expects the input data set to be sorted in order of the BY variables or to have an appropriate index. If your input data set is not sorted in ascending order, you can do one of the following:

- Remove the BY statement and use the page dimension to produce the same effect as the BY statement.
- Use the SORT procedure with a similar BY statement to sort the data.
- If appropriate, use the BY statement options NOTSORTED or DESCENDING.
- Create an index on the BY variables you want to use. For more information on creating indexes and using the BY statement with indexed data sets, see Chapter 17, "The DATASETS Procedure."

The following options can be specified in the BY statement:

DESCENDING
   specifies that the data set is sorted in descending order by the variable that immediately follows the word DESCENDING in the BY statement.

NOTSORTED
   specifies that observations are not necessarily sorted in alphabetic or numeric order. This option can appear anywhere in the BY statement.

CLASS Statement

> **CLASS** *class-variable-list*;
> **CLASSES** *class-variable-list*;

Use the CLASS statement to identify variables in the input data set as class variables. Class variables may have either numeric or character values. Normally each class variable has a small number of discrete values or unique levels. Continuous values for a numeric variable can be grouped into discrete levels by using the FORMAT procedure and then including a FORMAT statement in the PROC TABULATE step. Refer to Chapter 3 in the *SAS Guide to TABULATE Processing* for more information on creating classes.

If an observation contains missing values for any variable listed in the CLASS statement, the observation is not included in the table unless you specify the MISSING option in the PROC TABULATE statement. Note that the variables listed in the CLASS statement affect observations regardless of whether the class variable appears in a TABLE statement because the CLASS statement is in effect for the entire PROC TABULATE step.

FORMAT Statement

> **FORMAT** *variable-list-1 format-1 <...variable-list-n format-n>;*

where

> *variable-list*   names one or more variables to format.
>
> *format*   specifies the format for the preceding variables.

In the TABULATE procedure, the FORMAT statement formats the values of class variables used as headings in the page, row, and column dimensions. The FORMAT statement has no effect on either analysis variables (variables specified in the VAR statement) or the content of table cells.

You can use the FORMAT statement in combination with the FORMAT procedure to group values of class variables. Keep in mind that when you use PROC FORMAT to define temporary user-written formats, you must also use the FORMAT statement in the PROC TABULATE step to associate the format with the variable.* Refer to **Setting Up Useful Classes** in Chapter 3 in the *SAS Guide to TABULATE Processing* for more information on how to use the FORMAT statement and PROC FORMAT.

FREQ Statement

> **FREQ** *variable;*

The FREQ statement specifies a numeric variable in the input SAS data set whose value represents the frequency of the observation.

If you use the FREQ statement, each observation in the input data set is assumed to represent *n* observations, where *n* is the value of the FREQ variable. If the value is not an integer, the value is truncated to the integer portion. If the FREQ variable has a value less than 1, PROC TABULATE skips the observation. You can use only one variable in a FREQ statement. The FREQ statement can be used in combination with the WEIGHT statement.

KEYLABEL Statement

> **KEYLABEL** *keyword-1='label-1' <...keyword-n='label-n'>;*

where

> *keyword*   is one of the valid keywords for statistics discussed in
> **STATISTICS AVAILABLE WITH PROC TABULATE** later in
> this chapter, or the universal class variable ALL
> (discussed in **TABLE Statement** later in this chapter).
>
> *label*   is up to 40 characters of labeling information. The *label*
> must be enclosed in single or double quotes.

PROC TABULATE uses the replacement text in the label anywhere the specified keyword is used, unless another label is assigned in the TABLE statement. The KEYLABEL statement is useful for relabeling a keyword once in a PROC TABULATE step rather than each time it occurs in a TABLE statement. Each keyword can have only one label in a particular PROC TABULATE step; if you request multiple labels for the same keyword, PROC TABULATE uses the last one specified in the step. An example of a KEYLABEL statement is

```
keylabel all='Total $'
         mean='Average'
         pctsum='Percent of Sum';
```

---

* You can also create permanent formats by assigning the format in a DATA step. In this case, you do not need the FORMAT statement in the PROC TABULATE step.

LABEL Statement

LABEL *variable-1='label-1' <...variable-n='label-n'>;*

where

    variable   names a class or analysis variable used in a TABLE statement.

    label   specifies a label of up to 40 characters, including blanks, for the variable. The *label* must be enclosed in single or double quotes.

The label specified for the variable replaces the name of the variable in the page, row, or column heading where the variable appears. Any number of pairs of variable names and labels can be specified in a LABEL statement.

TABLE Statement

TABLE *<<page-expression,> row-expression,> column-expression </ table-option-list>;*

The TABLE statement describes the table to be printed. Every PROC TABULATE step requires at least one TABLE statement. All variables used in the TABLE statement must be specified in either the VAR statement or the CLASS statement but not both.

A TABLE statement consists of one to three dimension expressions separated by commas that can be followed by an option list. If all three dimensions are specified, the leftmost dimension defines pages, the middle dimension defines rows, and the rightmost dimension defines columns. If two dimensions are specified, the left defines rows, and the right defines columns. If a single dimension is specified, it defines columns.

The *page-expression*, *row-expression*, and *column-expression* are constructed in the same way and are referred to collectively as *dimension expressions*. A dimension expression is composed of elements and operators.

The elements you can use in a dimension expression are

- analysis variables. Refer to **VAR Statement** later in this chapter for more information.
- class variables. Refer to **CLASS Statement** earlier in this chapter for more information.
- the universal class variable ALL, which summarizes all of the categories for class variables in the same parenthetical group or dimension (if the variable ALL is not contained in a parenthetical group). If the data set contains a variable named ALL, enclose the name of the universal class variable in single quotes.
- keywords for statistics. Refer to **STATISTICS AVAILABLE WITH PROC TABULATE** later in this chapter for more information.
- format modifiers, which define how to format values in cells. These have the form *f=format* and must be crossed with the elements that produce the cells you want to format. See Chapter 5 in the *SAS Guide to TABULATE Processing* for more information.
- labels, which temporarily replace the names of variables and statistics with a label. These have the form *='label'* and affect only the variable or statistic that immediately precedes the label.
- expressions formed by combining any of these elements.

A dimension expression can have any of the following forms:

element*element	(crossing)
element element	(concatenation)
(element element)	(grouping)

When you cross class variables in an expression, PROC TABULATE creates categories from the combination of values of the variables. If one of the elements in the crossing is an analysis variable, the statistics for the analysis variable are calculated for the categories created by the class variables.

Concatenating elements joins information for the elements by placing the output for the second element immediately after the output for the first element.

Grouping elements causes the operator adjacent to the parenthesis to be applied to each concatenated element inside the parentheses.

Table 37.2 lists the operators and the effects they produce.

Table 37.2   Operators Used in the TABLE Statement

Operator	Action
, (comma)	separates dimensions of a table and crosses elements across dimensions
* (asterisk)	crosses elements within a dimension
(blank space)	concatenates elements in a dimension
() (parentheses)	group elements and associate an operator with an entire group
<> (brackets)	specify denominator definitions
= (equal sign)	assigns a label to a variable or statistic, or completes a format modifier

A TABLE statement can define only one table. Multiple TABLE statements can appear in one PROC TABULATE step, each defining a separate table. Refer to Chapter 4, "Learning to Use PROC TABULATE," in the *SAS Guide to TABULATE Processing* for more information on dimension expressions and how to construct TABLE statements.

You can use the following options in the TABLE statement:

BOX=*value*
specifies the text to be placed in the empty box above the row titles. The possible values are as follows:

PAGE   causes the page-dimension text to appear in the box. If the page-dimension text does not fit, it is placed in its default position, and the box is left empty.

'*string*'   causes the quoted string to appear in the box. Any name, label, or quoted string that does not fit is truncated.

variable   causes the name or label of a variable to appear in the box.

CONDENSE
prints multiple logical pages on a single physical page. PROC TABULATE prints as many complete logical pages as fit on a single printed page. This option can be used to condense multiple pages generated by the page dimension of the TABLE statement, or multiple pages caused by

tables that are too wide to fit on a single page. The CONDENSE option has no effect on the pages generated by the BY statement.

FUZZ=*number*
supplies a numeric value against which analysis variable values and table cell values other than frequency counts are compared to eliminate trivial values (absolute values less than the FUZZ= value) from computation and printing. A number whose absolute value is less than the FUZZ= value is treated as zero in computations and printing. The default value is the smallest representable floating-point number on the computer you are using.

MISSTEXT=*'text'*
supplies up to 20 characters of text to print in table cells containing missing values.

PRINTMISS
specifies that row and column headings are the same for all logical pages of the table. The PRINTMISS option indicates that you want to print all values that occur for a class variable each time headings for that variable are printed. For example, consider a data set with the three observations below:

A	B
1	1
3	1
3	3

The following TABLE statement does not produce a column for A=1 and B=3 because this combination of values does not exist in the data set:

```
table a*b;
```

If you specify the PRINTMISS option, the table includes a column for A=1 and B=3 with missing values for all table cells in the column.

If an entire logical page contains only missing values, that page does not print regardless of the PRINTMISS option. Note: By default PROC TABULATE does not suppress a row or column with all missing values when the missing values are the result of computations on analysis variables. The PRINTMISS option affects only missing rows and columns that result from combinations of class variable values that do not exist.

ROW=*spacing*
specifies whether all title elements in a row crossing are allotted space even when they are blank. The possible values for *spacing* are as follows:

> CONSTANT | CONST   causes all row title elements to have space allotted to them, even if the title has been blanked out (for example, N=' ' in the row dimension). CONSTANT is the default.
>
> FLOAT   causes the row title space to be divided equally among the nonblank title elements in the crossing.

RTSPACE=*number*
RTS=*number*
supplies an integer value that specifies the number of print positions allotted to the headings in the row dimension. Note that this space is divided equally among all levels of row headings and includes spaces used to print outlining characters for the row headings. The default value is one-fourth of the LINESIZE= value. Refer to Chapter 5 in the

SAS Guide to TABULATE Processing for more information on controlling the row title space.

VAR Statement

> **VAR** *analysis-variable-list*;
> **VARIABLES** *analysis-variable-list*;

Use the VAR statement to identify analysis variables in the input data set. Analysis variables must be numeric and can contain continuous values.

If an observation contains missing values for a variable listed in the VAR statement, the value is omitted from calculations of all statistics except N (the number of observations with nonmissing variable values) and NMISS (the number of observations with missing variable values). For example, the missing value does not increase the SUM, and it is not counted when calculating statistics such as the MEAN.

WEIGHT Statement

> **WEIGHT** *variable*;
> **WGT** *variable*;

The WEIGHT statement specifies a numeric variable in the input data set whose value is used to weight each analysis variable. Note that the WEIGHT variable value need not be an integer and does not affect the degrees of freedom.

If you specify a WEIGHT statement, PROC TABULATE uses the value of the WEIGHT variable to calculate weighted statistics. Refer to w_i in the formulas in **STATISTICS AVAILABLE WITH PROC TABULATE** for information on how the WEIGHT value affects statistic calculations.

STATISTICS AVAILABLE WITH PROC TABULATE

A standardized set of keywords is used to refer to the descriptive statistics for PROC TABULATE. Use these keywords to request statistics in the TABLE statement. If a variable name (class or analysis) and a statistic name are the same, enclose the statistic name in single quotes.

Keywords and Formulas

The following notations are used where summation is over all nonmissing values:

x_i the *i*th nonmissing observation of the variable

w_i the weight associated with x_i if a WEIGHT statement is specified, otherwise 1

n the number of nonmissing observations

$$\bar{x} = \Sigma w_i x_i / \Sigma w_i$$

$$d = n \qquad \text{(if the option VARDEF=N is specified)}$$
$$= n - 1 \quad \text{(if VARDEF=DF)}$$
$$= \Sigma w_i \quad \text{(if VARDEF=WEIGHT or WGT)}$$
$$= \Sigma w_i - 1 \quad \text{(if VARDEF=WDF)}$$

$$s^2 = \Sigma w_i (x_i - \bar{x})^2 / d$$

$$s = \sqrt{s^2}$$

$$z_i = (x_i - \bar{x})/s, \text{ standardized variables.}$$

The formulas and standard keywords for each statistic are given below. In some formulas a keyword is used to designate the corresponding statistic. Refer to the previous notation for an explanation of the symbols used in these formulas.

CSS	$\Sigma w_i(x_i-\overline{x})^2$, the sum of squares corrected for the mean
CV	$100s/\overline{x}$, the percent coefficient of variation
MAX	the maximum value
MEAN	$\overline{x}$, the arithmetic mean
MIN	the minimum value
N	the number of observations with nonmissing variable values
NMISS	the number of observations with missing variable values
PCTN	the percentage that one frequency represents of another frequency
PCTSUM	the percentage that one sum represents of another sum
PRT	the two-tailed p-value for Student's t with $n-1$ degrees of freedom, the probability under the null hypothesis of obtaining an absolute value of t greater than the t value observed in this sample
RANGE	$MAX-MIN$, the range
STD	s, the standard deviation
STDERR	$s/\sqrt{(n)}$, the standard error of the mean
SUM	$\Sigma w_i x_i$, the weighted sum
SUMWGT	Σw_i, the sum of weights
USS	$\Sigma w_i x_i^2$, the uncorrected sum of squares
T	$t=\overline{x}\sqrt{(n)}/s$, Student's t for H_0: population mean$=0$
VAR	s^2, the variance.

Computational Requirements for Statistics

The following requirements are computational requirements and do not describe recommended sample sizes.

Statistics are reported as missing if they cannot be computed. The specific requirements for statistics follow:

- N and NMISS do not require any nonmissing observations.
- SUM, MEAN, MAX, MIN, RANGE, USS, and CSS require at least one nonmissing observation.
- VAR, STD, STDERR, CV, T, and PRT require at least two observations.
- T and PRT require that STD is greater than zero.
- CV requires that MEAN is not equal to zero.

EXAMPLE

This example illustrates how to use the CLASS, VAR, and TABLE statements to obtain totals and percentages of project hours. Note that the default column headings have been overridden by the labels embedded in the TABLE statement and the labels defined on the KEYLABEL statement. This example also uses the FORMAT= option on the PROC TABULATE statement to modify the format of the values in the cells.

The universal class variable ALL provides summaries of all project hours in addition to the individual summaries by employee. The statements below produce **Output 37.1**.

```
data timerec;
   input employee $ week $ phase $ hours;
   cards;
Chen      11SEP89 Analysis 8
Chen      11SEP89 Analysis 7
Chen      11SEP89 Coding   2.5
Chen      11SEP89 Testing  8
Chen      11SEP89 Coding   8.5
Chen      11SEP89 Testing  6
Chen      11SEP89 Coding   4
Stewart   11SEP89 Coding   8
Stewart   11SEP89 Testing  4.5
Stewart   11SEP89 Coding   4.5
Stewart   11SEP89 Coding   10.5
Stewart   11SEP89 Testing  10
;
run;

proc tabulate data=timerec format=8.1;
   class employee week phase;
   var hours;
   table week, employee all, sum*hours=' '*(phase all);
   table week, employee all, pctsum*hours=' '*(phase all);
   keylabel sum='Total Hours'
            pctsum='Percentage of Hours';
   title 'Summary of Project Hours';
run;
```

Output 37.1 Summary of Employee Hours by Project

```
                         Summary of Project Hours                          1
     WEEK 11SEP89
     -------------------------------------------------------------
     |                         |         Total Hours              |
     |                         |---------------------------------|
     |                         |           PHASE          |      |
     |                         |--------------------------|      |
     |                         |Analysis| Coding |Testing | ALL  |
     |-------------------------|        |        |        |      |
     |EMPLOYEE                 |        |        |        |      |
     |-------------------------|        |        |        |      |
     |Chen                     |   15.0 |  15.0  |  14.0  | 44.0 |
     |-------------------------|--------|--------|--------|------|
     |Stewart                  |     .  |  23.0  |  14.5  | 37.5 |
     |-------------------------|--------|--------|--------|------|
     |ALL                      |   15.0 |  38.0  |  28.5  | 81.5 |
     -------------------------------------------------------------
```

```
                         Summary of Project Hours                          2
     WEEK 11SEP89
     -------------------------------------------------------------
     |                         |       Percentage of Hours        |
     |                         |---------------------------------|
     |                         |           PHASE          |      |
     |                         |--------------------------|      |
     |                         |Analysis| Coding |Testing | ALL  |
     |-------------------------|        |        |        |      |
     |EMPLOYEE                 |        |        |        |      |
     |-------------------------|        |        |        |      |
     |Chen                     |   18.4 |  18.4  |  17.2  | 54.0 |
     |-------------------------|--------|--------|--------|------|
     |Stewart                  |     .  |  28.2  |  17.8  | 46.0 |
     |-------------------------|--------|--------|--------|------|
     |ALL                      |   18.4 |  46.6  |  35.0  |100.0 |
     -------------------------------------------------------------
```

The TAPECOPY Procedure

ABSTRACT

The TAPECOPY procedure copies an entire tape volume or files from one or more tape volumes to one output tape volume. This procedure is described in system-dependent documentation.

The TAPELABEL
Procedure

ABSTRACT

The TAPELABEL procedure lists the label information of an IBM standard-labeled tape volume under the MVS operating system. This procedure is described in system-dependent documentation.

The TIMEPLOT
Procedure

ABSTRACT

The TIMEPLOT procedure plots one or more variables over time intervals.

INTRODUCTION

For each plot requested, the TIMEPLOT procedure produces a plot and a listing of observations in the data set similar to those produced by the PLOT and PRINT procedures. However, PROC TIMEPLOT has several distinctive features:

- The vertical axis always represents the sequence of observations in the data set; thus, if the observations are arranged in date or time order, the vertical axis represents time.
- The horizontal axis represents the values of the variable you are examining. Like PROC PLOT, PROC TIMEPLOT can overlay multiple plots on one set of axes, so that each line of the plot can contain values for more than one variable.
- A plot produced by PROC TIMEPLOT may occupy more than one page.
- Each observation appears sequentially on a separate line of the plot; no observations are hidden, as may occur with PROC PLOT.
- Each observation in the plot is accompanied by a printing of the values plotted.

Output 40.1 illustrates one type of plot produced by PROC TIMEPLOT. In this example, the plot contains the high, low, and closing values of the Dow Jones Index of prices on the New York Stock Exchange. The symbols for the variables are joined by a line. The minimum and maximum values label the horizontal axis; a vertical reference line appears at the mean of the low values. The listing on the left side of the output contains, for each observation, the date, the volume of stocks traded, and the low, closing, and high prices. The statements that produce this output follow:

```
data dow;
   input date date7. volume high low close;
   label volume='Volume in Thousands of Shares';
   format date date7.;
   cards;
03AUG81 3219.3 955.48 940.45 946.25
04AUG81 2938.5 951.39 937.40 945.97
05AUG81 4177.8 958.81 942.16 953.58
06AUG81 3975.7 961.47 947.30 952.91
07AUG81 3884.3 954.15 938.45 942.54
10AUG81 2937.7 948.82 935.88 943.68
11AUG81 5262.9 955.48 939.50 949.30
12AUG81 4005.2 955.86 942.26 945.21
13AUG81 3680.8 952.91 938.55 944.35
14AUG81 3714.1 947.77 933.79 936.93
17AUG81 3432.7 939.40 924.37 926.75
18AUG81 4396.7 932.74 916.38 924.37
19AUG81 3517.3 932.08 918.38 926.46
20AUG81 3811.9 935.31 923.52 928.37
21AUG81 2625.9 930.65 917.14 920.57
24AUG81 4736.1 917.43 896.97 900.11
25AUG81 4714.4 904.30 887.46 901.83
26AUG81 3279.6 908.39 893.65 899.26
27AUG81 3676.1 900.49 883.66 889.08
28AUG81 3024.2 898.78 884.80 892.22
;
run;

proc timeplot data=dow;
   plot low close high / overlay hiloc ref=mean(low)
                         axis=880 to 966 by 2;
   id date volume;
   format volume 6.1 high low close 6.2;
   title 'HIGH-LOW-CLOSE Stock Market Data';
run;
```

Output 40.1   High-Low-Close Stock Market Report

```
                                    HIGH-LOW-CLOSE Stock Market Data                              1
         DATE    Volume in        LOW     CLOSE     HIGH     min                           max
                 Thousands                                   880.00                        966.00
                 of Shares                                   *-----------------------------------*
        03AUG81    3219.3        940.45   946.25   955.48    |                  |     L--C---H    |
        04AUG81    2938.5        937.40   945.97   951.39    |                  |   L---C-H       |
        05AUG81    4177.8        942.16   953.58   958.81    |                  |       L----C--H |
        06AUG81    3975.7        947.30   952.91   961.47    |                  |      L--C---H   |
        07AUG81    3884.3        938.45   942.54   954.15    |                  |   L-C-----H     |
        10AUG81    2937.7        935.88   943.68   948.82    |                  |  L---C--H       |
        11AUG81    5262.9        939.50   949.30   955.48    |                  |   L----C--H     |
        12AUG81    4005.2        942.26   945.21   955.86    |                  |    LC----H      |
        13AUG81    3680.8        938.55   944.35   952.91    |                  |   L--C---H      |
        14AUG81    3714.1        933.79   936.93   947.77    |                  | L-C----H        |
        17AUG81    3432.7        924.37   926.75   939.40    |                  |LC-----H         |
        18AUG81    4396.7        916.38   924.37   932.74    |              L-- |C---H            |
        19AUG81    3517.3        918.38   926.46   932.08    |              L-|-C--H             |
        20AUG81    3811.9        923.52   928.37   935.31    |               L--C--H            |
        21AUG81    2625.9        917.14   920.57   930.65    |             L-C |---H             |
        24AUG81    4736.1        896.92   900.11   917.43    |      L-C-------H |                 |
        25AUG81    4714.4        887.46   901.83   904.30    |   L------C-H     |                 |
        26AUG81    3279.6        893.65   899.26   908.39    |     L--C----H    |                 |
        27AUG81    3676.1        883.66   889.08   900.49    | L--C-----H       |                 |
        28AUG81    3024.2        884.80   892.22   898.78    | L---C--H         |                 |
                                                             *-----------------------------------*
```

SPECIFICATIONS

The following statements control the TIMEPLOT procedure:

PROC TIMEPLOT <*option-list*>;
    PLOT *request-list* </ *option-list*>;
    CLASS *variable-list*;
    BY *variable-list*;
    ID *variable-list*;

A PLOT statement must be present to tell the procedure which variables to plot. You can specify any number of PLOT statements each time you invoke the procedure, and you can request any number of plots on one PLOT statement. No more than one ID and BY statement should appear.

PROC TIMEPLOT Statement

PROC TIMEPLOT <*option-list*>;

The PROC TIMEPLOT statement supports the following options:

DATA=*SAS-data-set*
    specifies the SAS data set to use. If you do not use the DATA= option, PROC TIMEPLOT uses the most recently created SAS data set.

MAXDEC=*number*
    specifies the maximum number of decimal positions to print for a number. A decimal specification in a format overrides a MAXDEC= specification. The default is MAXDEC=2.

UNIFORM

> uniformly scales the horizontal axis across all BY groups. If you do not use the UNIFORM option and you do use a BY statement, PROC TIMEPLOT determines the scale of the axis for each BY group separately. The UNIFORM option also indicates that the REF= option in the form MEAN(*variable-list*) represents the mean over all observations for all BY groups. (See **PLOT Statement** later in this chapter.)

BY Statement

> **BY** *variable-list*;

You can use a BY statement with PROC TIMEPLOT to obtain separate plots for observations in different BY groups. When a BY statement appears, the procedure expects the input data set to be sorted in order of the BY variables or to have an appropriate index. If your input data set is not sorted in ascending order, you can do one of the following:

- Use the SORT procedure with a similar BY statement to sort the data.
- If appropriate, use the BY statement option NOTSORTED or DESCENDING.
- Create an index on the BY variables you want to use. For more information on creating indexes and using the BY statement with indexed data sets, see Chapter 17, "The DATASETS Procedure."

The BY statement should appear only once.

CLASS Statement

> **CLASS** *variable-list*;

You can use the CLASS statement to group your data according to the values of the class variables. You do not need to sort the data by the class variables, but the output may be more meaningful if you group the data according to values of the class variables. (The grouping of data is similar to applications of other procedures that use the NOTSORTED option in a BY statement.)

Class variables can be numeric or character. PROC TIMEPLOT prints values of the class variables in the listing but does not plot them.

When you use a CLASS statement, PROC TIMEPLOT prints and plots one line each time the combination of values of the class variables changes. Therefore, if the data are sorted by the class variables, PROC TIMEPLOT prints and plots one line for each combination of class variable values. However, the contents of the listing and the plot vary depending on whether or not you specify a symbol variable:

- If you do not specify a symbol variable, PROC TIMEPLOT prints and plots only the first observation for a combination of class variable values.
- If you do specify a symbol variable, PROC TIMEPLOT makes a separate column for each value of the symbol variable and prints the value of the variable being plotted in the column with the appropriate value of the symbol variable. Each row of the plot contains a point for each value of the symbol variable. PROC TIMEPLOT uses the first character of the formatted value of the symbol variable as the plotting symbol. If more than one observation within a class has the same value of a symbol variable, the TIMEPLOT procedure plots and prints only the first occurrence of that value and writes a warning message to the SAS log.

The CLASS statement is normally used in conjunction with a symbol variable. **Example 2** later in this chapter illustrates the use of the CLASS statement with a symbol variable.

You can use any number of CLASS statements. If you use more than one CLASS statement, the TIMEPLOT procedure simply concatenates all variables from all of the CLASS statements. The following CLASS statement includes three variables:

```
class variable-1 variable-2 variable-3;
```

It produces the same results as the following CLASS statements:

```
class variable-1;
class variable-2;
class variable-3;
```

ID Statement

ID *variable-list*;

The ID statement prints the values of the ID variables in the listing but does not plot them. The ID statement should appear only once.

PLOT Statement

PLOT *request-list* </ *option-list*>;

The PLOT statement specifies the plots to produce. Remember that you can include many PLOT statements and specify many plot requests in one PLOT statement.

Each element in *request-list* specifies the variable or variables to plot and, optionally, the symbol to use to mark the points on the plot. Each PLOT statement produces a separate plot. Unless you use the OVERLAY option in the PLOT statement, each variable in a *request-list* also appears in a separate plot. All plotting variables must be numeric.

An element in *request-list* can have the following forms:

variable-list
   names the variables to plot. PROC TIMEPLOT uses the first character of the variable name as the plotting symbol. For example, the following statement plots the values of HIGH with an H, the value of LOW with an L, and the value of CLOSE with a C:

```
plot high low close;
```

(variable-list)='*plotting-symbol*'
   names the variables to plot and specifies the plotting symbol to use for the variables in the list. You can omit the parentheses if the list contains only one variable. For example, the following statement plots the values of LOW and HIGH with an exclamation point (!) and the values of CLOSE with an asterisk (*):

```
plot (low high)='!' close='*';
```

(variable-list)=*symbol-variable*
   names the variables to plot and specifies a symbol variable. PROC TIMEPLOT uses the first nonblank character of the formatted value of the symbol variable as the plotting symbol for the variables in the list. The symbol variable may be either character or numeric. You can omit the parentheses if the list contains only one variable. For example, the following statement plots the values of CLOSE with the first nonblank character of the formatted value of VOLUME for that observation:

```
plot close=volume;
```

You can mix different styles of requests in one PLOT statement. For example, the following statement plots values of LOW with an L (the default), values of HIGH with an asterisk (*), and values of CLOSE with the first nonblank character of the formatted value of VOLUME:

```
plot low high='*' close=volume;
```

The PLOT statement supports a variety of options. **Table 40.1** summarizes these options. More detailed descriptions follow.

Table 40.1 Summary of PLOT Statement Options

Class	Option	Function
Axis options	AXIS=	specifies the range of values to plot and, by default, the interval represented by each tick mark on the horizontal axis
	REVERSE	reverses the order of the values on the horizontal axis
Sizing option	POS=	specifies the number of print positions to use in the plot
Reference line options	REF=	draws lines on the plot perpendicular to the specified values on the horizontal axis
	REFCHAR=	specifies the character for drawing reference lines
Appearance options	HILOC	connects the leftmost plotting symbol to the rightmost plotting symbol with a line of hyphens
	JOINREF	connects the leftmost symbol to the rightmost symbol with a line of hyphens
	NOSYMNAME	suppresses the name of the symbol variable in column headings when you use a CLASS statement
	NPP	suppresses printing of the values of the variables specified in the PLOT statement
Overlaying options	OVERLAY	plots all variables specified in the PLOT statement on one plot
	OVPCHAR=	specifies the character to print if two plotting symbols coincide (the default is @)

AXIS=*interval-list*

specifies the range of values to plot and, by default, the interval represented by each tick mark on the horizontal axis. PROC TIMEPLOT labels the first and last tick mark on the axis with the appropriate values if space permits. If you specify the POS= option, the value of that option determines the total number of tick marks on the axis and, therefore, the interval each tick mark represents, while the AXIS= option determines only the range of values to plot. (See the description of the POS= option for more information.)

Examples of axis specifications are given in the table below.

Form of the AXIS= Option	Tick Marks
axis=10 to 100 by 10	10, 20, 30, . . . , 100
axis=10,30,40	10, 30, 40
axis=10,20,30 to 40 by 2	10, 20, 30, 32, . . . , 40
axis='01JAN85'd to '01JAN86'd by month	01JAN85, 01FEB85, . . . , 01JAN86
axis='01JAN85'd to '01JAN86'd by qtr	01JAN85, 01APR85, . . . , 01JAN86

In the last two examples, the values in the range can be any of the valid SAS date, time, or datetime values described for the SAS functions INTCK and INTNX. The BY value can be any of the valid values listed for the *interval* argument in the SAS functions INTCK and INTNX. You must use a FORMAT statement to label the first and last tick marks in an understandable form.

If an AXIS= list is given, the scale of the plot is not modified to encompass all values of plotting variables or reference lines. Any plotting value outside the range specified by the AXIS= option is indicated by a < or > on the left or right border of the plot, respectively. A REF= value outside the AXIS= range is ignored.

The following example illustrates the interaction between the AXIS= and POS= options. These statements produce **Output 40.2**.

```
data axispos;
   do i=1 to 20;
      output;
   end;
run;

proc timeplot data=axispos;
   plot i / axis=0 to 20 by 2;
   title 'Range and Interval between Tick Marks';
   title2 'Specified by the AXIS= Option';
run;
```

```
proc timeplot data=axispos;
   plot i / axis=0 to 20 by 2 pos=21;
   title 'Range Determined by AXIS=';
   title2 'Interval between Tick Marks Determined by POS=';
run;
```

Output 40.2   Interaction between the VAXIS= and the POS= Options

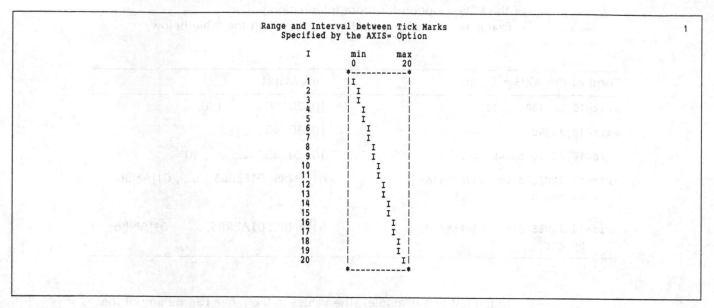

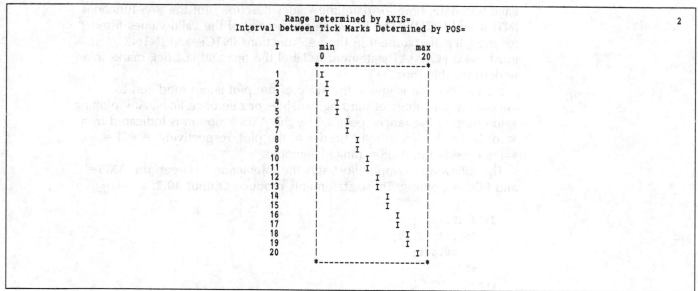

The first PROC step produces a plot with a range of 0 to 20. The interval between tick marks is 2. Thus, the horizontal axis contains 11 tick marks (for 0, 2, 4 and so on up to 20). The second PROC step also produces a plot with a range of 0 to 20. However, in this case, the POS= option specifies 21 print positions on the horizontal axis. Thus, the horizontal axis contains 21 tick marks, one for each integer from 0 to 20.

HILOC

connects the leftmost plotting symbol to the rightmost plotting symbol with a line of hyphens (-). If you specify the JOINREF option, PROC TIMEPLOT ignores the HILOC option.

JOINREF

connects the leftmost symbol to the rightmost symbol with a line of hyphens, regardless of whether the symbols are reference symbols or plotting symbols. However, if a line contains only reference symbols, PROC TIMEPLOT does not connect the symbols.

NOSYMNAME

suppresses the printing of the name of the symbol variable in column headings when you use a CLASS statement. If you use the NOSYMNAME option, only the value of the symbol variable appears in the column heading:

VALUE
PLOTTING VARIABLE

If you omit the NOSYMNAME option, headings have the following form:

SYMBOLNAME: VALUE
PLOTTING VARIABLE

(See **Output 40.4** where the symbol variable is SELLER.) The TIMEPLOT procedure ignores the NOSYMNAME option if you do not use a CLASS statement.

NPP

suppresses the printing of the values of the variables specified in the PLOT statement.

OVERLAY

overlays all variables specified in the PLOT statement on one plot. Otherwise, PROC TIMEPLOT produces a separate plot for each variable.

OVPCHAR='character'

specifies the character to print if two plotting symbols coincide. If you do not use the OVPCHAR= option, the *at sign* (@) is used. If a plotting symbol and a character in a reference line coincide, PROC TIMEPLOT prints the plotting symbol. The TIMEPLOT procedure never actually overprints two symbols.

POS=print-positions-for-plot

specifies the number of print positions to use in the plot. If you specify POS=0 and also specify the AXIS= option, the plot is expanded to fill the page, with each axis value possibly comprising several plot positions instead of just one. If you omit both the POS= and the AXIS= options, an initial POS= value of 20 is assumed. However, if space permits, PROC TIMEPLOT increases this value so that the plot fills the available space. See **DETAILS** later in this chapter for more information.

REF=reference-list

draws lines on the plot perpendicular to the specified values on the horizontal axis. The values for *reference-list* may be constants, or you may use the form

MEAN(variable-list)

If you use this form of the REF= option, the TIMEPLOT procedure evaluates the mean for each variable in *variable-list* and draws a reference line for each mean.

If you use the UNIFORM option in the PROC TIMEPLOT statement, the procedure calculates the mean values for the variables over all observations for all BY groups. If you do not use the UNIFORM option, the procedure calculates the mean for each variable for each BY group.

If any REF= value is less than the minimum value of any plotting variable, or if any REF= value is greater than the maximum of any plotting variable, the scale of the plot is adjusted to allow the reference line to be printed (unless the AXIS= option is used). If a plotting symbol and a reference character coincide, PROC TIMEPLOT prints the plotting symbol.

REFCHAR=*'character'*

specifies the character for drawing reference lines. If you do not use the REFCHAR= option, PROC TIMEPLOT uses the vertical bar (|). If you are using the JOINREF or HILOC option, do not specify a value for the REFCHAR= option that is the same as a plotting symbol because PROC TIMEPLOT will interpret the plotting symbols as reference characters and will not connect the symbols as you expect.

REVERSE

reverses the order of the values on the horizontal axis so that the largest value is in the leftmost position. PROC TIMEPLOT also uses this order on the axis if the AXIS= values are in descending order. Therefore, if the AXIS= option is specified with descending values, the procedure ignores the REVERSE option.

DETAILS

Missing Values

A missing value of a plotting variable appears in the listing as a missing value (.) or as one of the special missing values (A through Z or an underscore). It is not plotted.

If a CLASS statement and a symbol value are used, the observations in a given class may not contain all values of the symbol variable. For example, if the symbol variables are PREDICTED and ACTUAL, classes representing future dates may not have a value for ACTUAL. In this case, the value of ACTUAL is represented in the listing by a blank and is not plotted.

A missing value of a class variable is treated as a valid level of the variable and defines a class of observations. The missing value appears as a missing value in the listing. A missing value of an ID variable is printed as a missing value. A missing value of a symbol variable is treated like any other value of that variable. A column for that value appears in the listing and the value is plotted. However, even if the missing value is a blank (as occurs when the symbol variable is a character variable), the column heading and the plot represent the value as a period (.) .

Input Data Set

The input data set usually contains a date variable to use as either a class or an ID variable. Although the data set does not have to be sorted by date, the output is usually more meaningful if the data are in chronological order. In addition, if you use a CLASS statement, the output is more meaningful if observations are grouped according to combinations of class variable values.

Printed Output

The TIMEPLOT procedure prints one or more pages of printed values and plots for each plot request. The page is divided into two sections: the listing and the plot.

PROC TIMEPLOT determines the arrangement of the page as follows:

1. If you use the POS= option, the procedure
   - determines the size of the plot from the POS= value
   - determines the space for the listing from the width of the columns of printed values, equally spaced and with a maximum of five positions between columns
   - centers the output on the page.

2. If you do not use the POS= option, the procedure
   - determines the width of the listing by default or from the AXIS= option
   - expands the plot to fill the rest of the page.

If there is not sufficient room to print all values along with a plot, PROC TIMEPLOT writes an error message to the SAS log. That plot is not printed; however, other plots are not affected.

The listing on the left side of the output contains different information depending on whether or not you use a CLASS statement. If you do not use a CLASS statement (see **Output 40.1**), PROC TIMEPLOT prints (and plots) each observation on a separate line. If you do use a CLASS statement, the form of the output varies depending on whether or not you specify a symbol variable (see **CLASS Statement**).

The listing contains the following items:

1. column headings for class and ID variables. These headings consist of either variable labels (if they are present and if space permits) or variable names. To suppress variable labels in column headings, use the NOLABEL system option. (See the OPTIONS statement in Chapter 9, "SAS Language Statements," in *SAS Language: Reference* for a description of the NOLABEL system option.)
2. column headings for plotting variables, unless the NPP option has been specified. These headings consist of two parts: the variable label or name, and the name (unless NOSYMNAME is used) and value of the symbol variable (if a class statement and a symbol variable are both used). If a format is associated with a variable, the value is printed using that format.
3. values for class variables.
4. values for ID variables. If you use a CLASS statement, the value printed for each ID variable is the first value in that class.
5. values for plotting variables, unless the NPP option has been specified.

The plot contains

6. plotted values of variables.
7. tick marks.
8. labels on the first and last tick marks if space permits.
9. reference lines.

EXAMPLES

Example 1:   How Well a Model Fits the Data

This example uses PROC TIMEPLOT to demonstrate how well a model fits actual data. First, the REG procedure analyzes the data, fits the model, and calculates residual and predicted values. Then, PROC TIMEPLOT overlays the plot of a predicted and an actual value. The mean of the actual values is given as a reference line. Next, the procedure shows how residuals digress from the origin by using the REF=0 option to produce a reference line at the origin and the JOINREF option to connect the residuals with the origin. The following statements produce **Output 40.3**:

```
data grunfeld;
   input year i f c @@;
   label i='Gross Investment GE'
         c='Capital Stock Lagged GE'
         f='Value of Shares GE Lagged';
   cards;
1935  33.1  1170.6  97.8   1936  45.0  2015.8 104.4
1937  77.2  2803.3 118.0   1938  44.6  2039.7 156.2
1939  48.1  2256.2 172.6   1940  74.4  2132.2 186.6
1941 113.0  1834.1 220.9   1942  91.9  1588.0 287.8
1943  61.3  1749.4 319.9   1944  56.8  1687.2 321.3
1945  93.6  2007.7 319.6   1946 159.9  2208.3 346.0
1947 147.2  1656.7 456.4   1948 146.3  1604.4 543.4
1949  98.3  1431.8 618.3   1950  93.5  1610.5 647.4
1951 135.2  1819.4 671.3   1952 157.3  2079.7 726.1
1953 179.5  2371.6 800.3   1954 189.6  2759.9 888.9
;
run;

proc reg data=grunfeld noprint;
  model i=f c ;
  output out=c r=resid p=pred;
  title 'Grunfeld''s Investment Model';
run;

proc timeplot data=c;
  id year;
  plot pred='P' i='A' / overlay ref=mean(i) axis=32 to 200 by 3;
  plot resid        / joinref ref=0 axis=-60 to 60 by 2;
run;
```

Output 40.3   Fitting a Model to Actual Data

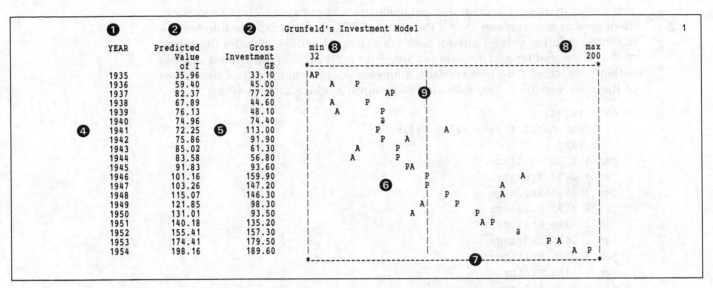

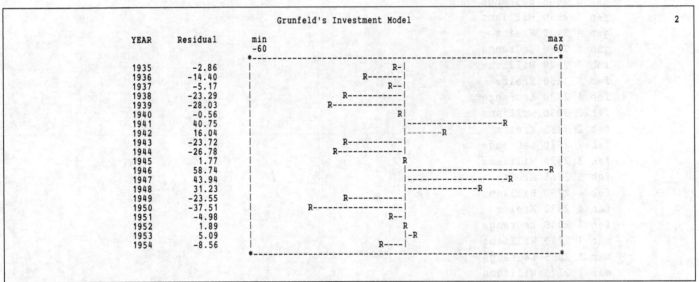

Example 2:   Using the CLASS Statement

This example uses a CLASS statement to illustrate sales figures. The CLASS statement groups observations by MONTH and WEEK. The symbol variable SELLER has three different values, one for each sales clerk. The listing includes the values of the class variables and the value of SALES for each value of the symbol variable within each class. The plot contains a line for each combination of the values of the class variables. The following statements produce **Output 40.4**:

```
data sales;
   input month $ week sales seller $;
   cards;
jan 1 2780 Williams
jan 1 3450 Kreitz
jan 1 2520 LeGrange
jan 2 2895 Williams
jan 2 3240 Kreitz
jan 2 2675 LeGrange
jan 3 2925 Williams
jan 3 3160 Kreitz
jan 3 2805 LeGrange
jan 4 2890 Williams
jan 4 3400 Kreitz
jan 4 2870 LeGrange
feb 1 2920 Williams
feb 1 3550 Kreitz
feb 1 2730 LeGrange
feb 2 3030 Williams
feb 2 3385 Kreitz
feb 2 2670 LeGrange
feb 3 2620 Williams
feb 3 3055 Kreitz
feb 4 2790 Williams
feb 4 2830 Kreitz
feb 4 2935 LeGrange
mar 1 2740 Williams
mar 1 2895 LeGrange
mar 2 2775 Williams
mar 2 2750 Kreitz
mar 2 2800 LeGrange
mar 3 3050 Williams
mar 3 3175 Kreitz
mar 3 2850 LeGrange
mar 4 2740 Williams
mar 4 2900 Kreitz
mar 4 2875 LeGrange
;
run;
```

```
proc timeplot data=sales;
   plot sales=seller;
   class month week;
   format sales dollar16.;
   title 'Using the CLASS Statement with a Symbol Variable';
run;
```

Output 40.4 Using the CLASS Statement with a Symbol Variable

```
                                      Using the CLASS Statement with a Symbol Variable                                 1
           ❶             SELLER :Williams     SELLER :Kreitz      SELLER :LeGrange       min    ❽                    ❽    max
 MONTH         WEEK     ❷     SALES               SALES               SALES            $2,520                        $3,550
                                                                                       *-----------------------------------*
 jan            1          $2,780              $3,450              $2,520             |L         W                     K  |
 jan            2          $2,895              $3,240              $2,675             |      L        W          K         |
 jan            3          $2,925              $3,160              $2,805             |          L     W       K          K|
 jan            4          $2,890              $3,400              $2,870             |             LW        K             |
 feb            1          $2,920              $3,550              $2,730             |          L     W             K    K|
 feb   ❸        2          $3,030         ❺    $3,385              $2,670             |      L           W     ❻    K     |
 feb            3          $2,620              $3,055                                 |   W           K                    |
 feb            4          $2,790              $2,830              $2,935             |         W K L                      |
 mar            1          $2,740                                  $2,895             |       W   L                        |
 mar            2          $2,775              $2,750              $2,800             |       KWL                          |
 mar            3          $3,050              $3,175              $2,850             |         L      W    K              |
 mar            4          $2,740              $2,900              $2,875             |       W   LK                       |
                                                                                     *------------------------❼----------*
```

The TRANSPOSE
Procedure

ABSTRACT

The TRANSPOSE procedure transposes a SAS data set, changing observations into variables and vice versa.

INTRODUCTION

The TRANSPOSE procedure reads a SAS data set and creates an output data set as its only output. The rows of the original data matrix become columns, and columns become rows. Observations in the output data set correspond to variables in the input data set. The output data set contains three kinds of variables:

- variables copied from the input data set. These variables have the same names and values as they do in the input data set.
- variables created by transposing observations in the input data set. This chapter refers to these variables as *transposed variables*.
- variables created by PROC TRANSPOSE to identify the source of the values in each observation in the output data set.

For example, these statements produce **Output 41.1**:

```
data a;
   input a b c;
   cards;
1 2 3
4 5 6
;
run;

proc transpose data=a out=atransp;
run;

proc print data=atransp;
   title 'Simple Example of PROC TRANSPOSE';
run;
```

Output 41.1   A Transposed Data Set

```
                    Simple Example of PROC TRANSPOSE                         1

            OBS    _NAME_    COL1    COL2

             1       A        1       4
             2       B        2       5
             3       C        3       6
```

In this simple example, PROC TRANSPOSE creates three variables in the output data set:

NAME   contains the name of the variable being transposed. In the first observation, the value of _NAME_ is **A**, the name of the first variable in the input data set; in the second observation, the value of _NAME_ is **B**, the name of the second variable in the input data set; and so on.

COL1   contains the value of the variable identified by _NAME_ in the first observation in the input data set.

COL2   contains the value of the variable identified by _NAME_ in the second observation in the input data set.

You can use PROC TRANSPOSE with a BY statement to rearrange complex data sets in a variety of ways. The following example uses measurements of length and weight for samples of two species of fish, *Mugil curema* (white mullet) and *Brevoortia tyrannus* (Atlantic menhaden). During data collection it was convenient to enter the date and species once and to string the measurements along the same line. Each line, therefore, represents a particular sample group and date.

What you need, however, are two data sets: one containing a separate observation for each length value, and one containing a separate observation for each weight value. Each data set must also indicate the group, species, and date corresponding to each length or weight measurement. These statements produce the output shown in **Output 41.2**:

```
libname fish 'SAS-data-library';

data fish.rawdata;
   input group date date7. species $
         length1 width1 length2 width2 length3 width3 length4 width4;
   format date date7.;
   cards;
1  2JUN84 CUR 31 .25 32 .3  32 .25 33 .3
2  2JUN84 CUR 30 .20 36 .45 33 .25 36 .35
3  2JUN84 CUR 32 .35 32 .25 33 .30  .  .
1 11JUL84 MEN 72 4.0 82 5.5 70 4.0 79 4.3
1 14JUL84 MEN 79 4.1 78 3.8 80 3.8 74 3.6
1 13AUG84 MEN 86 5.0 83 4.8 89 5.7 80 4.2
;
run;

proc sort data=fish.rawdata out=fish.rawsort;
   by species date group;
run;

proc print data=fish.rawsort;
   title 'The Data Set FISH.RAWSORT';
run;

proc transpose data=fish.rawsort out=fish.length;
     /* Do not transpose variables listed in the BY statement. */
   by species date group;
     /* Transpose all variables listed in the VAR statement.   */
   var length1-length4;
run;

proc print data=fish.length;
   title 'Output Data Set with Length Measurements';
run;

proc transpose data=fish.rawsort out=fish.weight;
     /* Do not transpose variables listed in the BY statement. */
   by species date group;
     /* Transpose all variables listed in the VAR statement.   */
   var width1-width4;
run;

proc print data=fish.weight;
   title 'Output Data Set with Weight Measurements';
run;
```

Output 41.2   PROC TRANSPOSE Converts the Data into a More Usable
Form

The Data Set FISH.RAWSORT   1

OBS	GROUP	DATE	SPECIES	LENGTH1	WIDTH1	LENGTH2	WIDTH2	LENGTH3	WIDTH3	LENGTH4	WIDTH4
1	1	02JUN84	CUR	31	0.25	32	0.30	32	0.25	33	0.30
2	2	02JUN84	CUR	30	0.20	36	0.45	33	0.25	36	0.35
3	3	02JUN84	CUR	32	0.35	32	0.25	33	0.30	.	.
4	1	11JUL84	MEN	72	4.00	82	5.50	70	4.00	79	4.30
5	1	14JUL84	MEN	79	4.10	78	3.80	80	3.80	74	3.60
6	1	13AUG84	MEN	86	5.00	83	4.80	89	5.70	80	4.20

Output Data Set with Length Measurements   2

OBS	SPECIES	DATE	GROUP	_NAME_	COL1
1	CUR	02JUN84	1	LENGTH1	31
2	CUR	02JUN84	1	LENGTH2	32
3	CUR	02JUN84	1	LENGTH3	32
4	CUR	02JUN84	1	LENGTH4	33
5	CUR	02JUN84	2	LENGTH1	30
6	CUR	02JUN84	2	LENGTH2	36
7	CUR	02JUN84	2	LENGTH3	33
8	CUR	02JUN84	2	LENGTH4	36
9	CUR	02JUN84	3	LENGTH1	32
10	CUR	02JUN84	3	LENGTH2	32
11	CUR	02JUN84	3	LENGTH3	33
12	CUR	02JUN84	3	LENGTH4	.
13	MEN	11JUL84	1	LENGTH1	72
14	MEN	11JUL84	1	LENGTH2	82
15	MEN	11JUL84	1	LENGTH3	70
16	MEN	11JUL84	1	LENGTH4	79
17	MEN	14JUL84	1	LENGTH1	79
18	MEN	14JUL84	1	LENGTH2	78
19	MEN	14JUL84	1	LENGTH3	80
20	MEN	14JUL84	1	LENGTH4	74
21	MEN	13AUG84	1	LENGTH1	86
22	MEN	13AUG84	1	LENGTH2	83
23	MEN	13AUG84	1	LENGTH3	89
24	MEN	13AUG84	1	LENGTH4	80

Output Data Set with Weight Measurements   3

OBS	SPECIES	DATE	GROUP	_NAME_	COL1
1	CUR	02JUN84	1	WIDTH1	0.25
2	CUR	02JUN84	1	WIDTH2	0.30
3	CUR	02JUN84	1	WIDTH3	0.25
4	CUR	02JUN84	1	WIDTH4	0.30
5	CUR	02JUN84	2	WIDTH1	0.20
6	CUR	02JUN84	2	WIDTH2	0.45
7	CUR	02JUN84	2	WIDTH3	0.25
8	CUR	02JUN84	2	WIDTH4	0.35
9	CUR	02JUN84	3	WIDTH1	0.35
10	CUR	02JUN84	3	WIDTH2	0.25
11	CUR	02JUN84	3	WIDTH3	0.30
12	CUR	02JUN84	3	WIDTH4	.
13	MEN	11JUL84	1	WIDTH1	4.00
14	MEN	11JUL84	1	WIDTH2	5.50
15	MEN	11JUL84	1	WIDTH3	4.00
16	MEN	11JUL84	1	WIDTH4	4.30
17	MEN	14JUL84	1	WIDTH1	4.10
18	MEN	14JUL84	1	WIDTH2	3.80
19	MEN	14JUL84	1	WIDTH3	3.80
20	MEN	14JUL84	1	WIDTH4	3.60
21	MEN	13AUG84	1	WIDTH1	5.00
22	MEN	13AUG84	1	WIDTH2	4.80
23	MEN	13AUG84	1	WIDTH3	5.70
24	MEN	13AUG84	1	WIDTH4	4.20

For each BY group in the input data set, PROC TRANSPOSE creates four observations in each output data set, one for each variable being transposed. (In this example, each observation in the input data set is a BY group because each one has a unique combination of values for the three BY variables.) Each observation in the output data set consists of the following:

- values for the three variables listed in the BY statement. The procedure does not transpose these variables.
- a value for the variable _NAME_. This value is the name of the variable in the input data set that is being transposed into the current observation.
- the value of the variable being transposed.

For more information on transposing with a BY statement, see **Using a BY Statement** later in this chapter.

SPECIFICATIONS

The following statements control the TRANSPOSE procedure:

> **PROC TRANSPOSE** <*option-list*>;
> **VAR** *variable-list*;
> **ID** *variable*;
> **IDLABEL** *variable*;
> **COPY** *variable-list*;
> **BY** *variable-list*;

PROC TRANSPOSE Statement

> **PROC TRANSPOSE** <*option-list*>;

Table 41.1 summarizes the options available with the PROC TRANSPOSE statement. Detailed descriptions follow the table in alphabetic order.

Table 41.1   Summary of PROC TRANSPOSE Statement Options

Class	Option	Function
Specifying data set names	DATA=	names the SAS data set to transpose
	OUT=	names the output data set
Naming options	PREFIX=	specifies the prefix to use in constructing names of transposed variables in the output data set
	NAME=	specifies the name of the variable in the output data set that contains the name of the variable being transposed to create the current observation

(continued)

Table 41.1   (continued)

Class	Option	Function
	LABEL=	specifies the name of the variable in the output data set that contains the label of the variable being transposed to create the current observation
Using ID- and BY-statement processing	LET	allows duplicate values of an ID variable in the input data set or within a BY group

DATA=*SAS-data-set*
   names the SAS data set to transpose. If you do not use the DATA= option, PROC TRANSPOSE uses the most recently created SAS data set.

LABEL=*name*
   specifies the name of the variable in the output data set that contains the label of the variable being transposed to create the current observation. If you do not specify the LABEL= option and at least one variable you are transposing has a label, the name of this variable is _LABEL_.

LET
   allows duplicate values of an ID variable within the DATA= data set or, if you use a BY statement, within a BY group. The TRANSPOSE procedure transposes the observation containing the last occurrence of a particular ID value within the data set or BY group.

NAME=*name*
   specifies the name of the variable in the output data set that contains the name of the variable being transposed to create the current observation. If you do not specify the NAME= option, the name of this variable is _NAME_.

OUT=*SAS-data-set*
   names the output data set. If you want to create a permanent SAS data set, you must specify a two-level name. (See Chapter 6, "SAS Files," in *SAS Language: Reference, Version 6, First Edition* for more information on permanent SAS data sets.) If you omit the OUT= option, the SAS System still creates an output data set and automatically names it according to the DATA*n* naming convention, just as if you omitted a data set name in a DATA statement.

PREFIX=*name*
   specifies a prefix to use in constructing names for transposed variables in the output data set. For example, if PREFIX=VAR, the names of the transposed variables are VAR1, VAR2, . . . ,VAR*n*, where the value of *n* is the number of observations in the data set or, if you use a BY statement, the number of observations in the largest BY group.

BY Statement

BY *variable-list*;

When you use a BY statement, PROC TRANSPOSE generates an observation for each variable being transposed for each BY group. The BY variables are included in the output data set but are not transposed. The statements below produce **Output 41.3**:

```
data b;
  input b x $ y $;
  cards;
1 X1a Y1a
1 X1b Y1b
2 X2a Y2a
3 X3a Y3a
3 X3b Y3b
3 X3c Y3c
;
run;

proc transpose data=b out=btransp;
  var x y;
  by b;
run;

proc print data=btransp;
  title 'Transposing with a BY Statement';
run;
```

Output 41.3   Using the BY Statement

```
                      Transposing with a BY Statement                           1

        OBS    B    _NAME_    COL1    COL2    COL3

         1     1      X       X1a     X1b
         2     1      Y       Y1a     Y1b
         3     2      X       X2a
         4     2      Y       Y2a
         5     3      X       X3a     X3b     X3c
         6     3      Y       Y3a     Y3b     Y3c
```

In this example, the TRANSPOSE procedure generates two observations for each BY group in the input data set, one for each variable you transpose. The first two observations include values for COL1 and COL2 because the first BY group contains two observations and therefore has two values for each variable being transposed. The third and fourth observations include values only for COL1 because the second BY group contains only one observation. The fifth and sixth observations include values for COL1, COL2, and COL3 because the third BY group contains three observations and therefore has three values for each variable being transposed.

When a BY statement appears, the TRANSPOSE procedure expects the input data set to be sorted in order of the BY variables or to have an appropriate index. If your input data set is not sorted in ascending order, you can do one of the following:

- Use the SORT procedure with a similar BY statement to sort the data.
- If appropriate, use the BY statement option NOTSORTED or DESCENDING.
- Create an index on the BY variables you want to use. For more information on creating indexes and using the BY statement with indexed data sets, see Chapter 17, "The DATASETS Procedure."

For more information on the BY statement, see Chapter 6 in *SAS Language: Reference* and **Using a BY Statement** later in this chapter.

COPY Statement

COPY *variable-list*;

PROC TRANSPOSE copies all variables in the COPY statement directly from the input data set to the output data set without transposing them. The procedure pads the output data set with missing values if necessary. For example, these statements produce **Output 41.4**:

```
data c;
   input a b c;
   cards;
1  2  3
4  5  6
7  8  9
11 22 33
;
run;

proc transpose data=c out=ctransp;
   copy c;
run;

proc print data=ctransp;
   title 'Transposing with a COPY Statement';
run;
```

Output 41.4 Using the COPY Statement

```
                       Transposing with a COPY Statement                              1
           OBS    C    _NAME_    COL1    COL2    COL3    COL4

            1     3      A        1       4       7       11
            2     6      B        2       5       8       22
            3     9                .       .       .        .
            4    33                .       .       .        .
```

The TRANSPOSE procedure creates one observation for each value of the variable listed in the COPY statement. Thus, the output data set contains four observations. However, because you are transposing only two variables, only the first two observations have values for the transposed variables. The third and fourth observations have missing values for both transposed variables.

ID Statement

ID *variable*;

An ID statement specifies a variable in the input data set. PROC TRANSPOSE uses the formatted values of the ID variable as the names of the transposed variables in the output data set. Each formatted ID value should occur only once in the input data set or, if you use a BY statement, only once within a BY group. Duplicate values cause PROC TRANSPOSE to issue a warning message and stop unless you use the LET option.

PROC TRANSPOSE changes a formatted ID value into a valid SAS name whenever necessary. If the formatted value looks like a numeric constant, the TRANSPOSE procedure changes the characters "+", "−", and "." to "P","N", and "D", respectively. If the first character is numeric, an underscore is prefixed to the value, truncating the last character of an eight-character value. Any remaining invalid characters are replaced by underscores.

If you use an ID statement, PROC TRANSPOSE writes an error message to the SAS log when it encounters an observation with a missing value for the ID variable. The TRANSPOSE procedure omits these observations from the output data set. For example, the statements below produce the log shown in **Output 41.5** and the output shown in **Output 41.6**:

```
data d;
   input a 1 b 3 c $ 5;
   cards;
1 2 x
3 4 y
5 6 z
7 8
;
run;

proc transpose data=d out=dtransp;
   id c;
run;

proc print data=dtransp;
   title 'Transposing with an ID Statement';
run;
```

Output 41.5 Log Produced with Missing Value for the ID Variable

```
5              data d;
6                  input a 1 b 3 c $ 5;
7                  cards;
NOTE: The data set WORK.D has 4 observations and 3 variables.

12             ;
13             run;
14
15             proc transpose data=d out=dtransp;
16                 id c;
17             run;
WARNING: 1 observations omitted due to missing ID values.
NOTE: The data set WORK.DTRANSP has 2 observations and 4 variables.

18
19             proc print data=dtransp;
20                 title 'Transposing with an ID Statement';
21             run;

NOTE: The PROCEDURE PRINT printed page 1.
```

Output 41.6 Output Produced Using the ID Statement

```
                     Transposing with an ID Statement                           1
                     OBS    _NAME_    X    Y    Z

                      1       A       1    3    5
                      2       B       2    4    6
```

The values of the variable C in the input data set (**x** in the first observation, **y** in the second, and **z** in the third) determine the names of the transposed variables in the output data set.

IDLABEL Statement

> **IDLABEL** *variable*;
> **IDL** *variable*;

If you use an ID statement, you can use the IDLABEL statement to specify a character or numeric variable to provide labels for the transposed variables in the output data set.

VAR Statement

> **VAR** *variable-list*;

The VAR statement lists the variables to transpose.

If you omit the VAR statement, the TRANSPOSE procedure transposes all numeric variables in the input data set that are not listed in another statement. The TRANSPOSE procedure omits variables that are not transposed from the output data set unless listed in the COPY or BY statement.

You must list character variables in a VAR statement if you want to transpose them. If you use the VAR statement, PROC TRANSPOSE transposes only those variables listed in the statement. The list can include both numeric and character variables.

For example, these statements produce **Output 41.7**:

```
data e;
   input a 1 b 3 x $ 5;
   cards;
1 2 X
3 4 Y
5 6 Z
;
run;

   /* No VAR statement--transpose all numeric variables not */
   /* in another statement.                                 */
proc transpose data=e out=trannum;
run;

proc print data=trannum;
   title 'Numeric Variables Transposed by Default';
run;

   /* Transpose only the variable X. */
proc transpose data=e out=tranchar;
   var x;
run;

proc print data=tranchar;
   title 'Character Variable Transposed Using the VAR Statement';
run;
```

Output 41.7 Using the VAR Statement

```
                    Numeric Variables Transposed by Default                    1

            OBS    _NAME_    COL1    COL2    COL3

             1       A        1       3       5
             2       B        2       4       6
```

```
            Character Variable Transposed Using the VAR Statement             2

            OBS    _NAME_    COL1    COL2    COL3

             1       X        X       Y       Z
```

The first PROC TRANSPOSE step transposes all numeric variables from the input data set because the VAR statement is absent and no variables appear in a subordinate statement. The second PROC TRANSPOSE step transposes only the variable X because it is the only variable listed in the VAR statement.

DETAILS

Output Data Set

Contents

The output data set contains a character variable whose values are the names of the variables transposed from the input data set. The name of the variable is specified by the NAME= option. If you omit the NAME= option, the name of the variable is _NAME_.

If the variables being transposed from the input data set have labels, the output data set contains a character variable whose values are the variable labels. The name of the variable is specified by the LABEL= option. If you omit the LABEL= option, the name of the variable is _LABEL_.

Note: If the variables referenced by the NAME= or LABEL= option (or, if you omit these options, the variables whose values are used for _NAME_ or _LABEL_) are listed in the COPY or BY statement, PROC TRANSPOSE does not create variables with duplicate names containing the names or labels of the transposed input variables.

All transposed variables are the same type and length. If all input variables are numeric, the transposed variables are numeric. **If any input variable is character, all transposed variables are character**. The character values of transposed numeric variables in the output data set are the formatted values of the input numeric variables. The length of the transposed variables is equal to the length of the longest variable being transposed.

PROC TRANSPOSE copies all variables listed in the COPY statement to the output data set.

Naming Transposed Variables

PROC TRANSPOSE names transposed variables in one of four ways:

1. An ID statement specifies a variable in the input data set. The TRANSPOSE procedure uses the formatted values of this variable as names for the transposed variables.
2. The PREFIX= option in the PROC TRANSPOSE statement specifies a prefix to use in constructing the names of transposed variables. For example, if you request PREFIX=VAR, PROC TRANSPOSE assigns the names VAR1, VAR2, . . . , VARn to the transposed variables.
3. If you do not use an ID statement or the PREFIX= option, PROC TRANSPOSE looks for an input variable called _NAME_ from which to get the names of the transposed variables. If variable _NAME_ results from a previous execution of PROC TRANSPOSE, the variable names are identical to the variable names in the original (untransposed) data set.
4. If you do not use an ID statement or the PREFIX= option, and the input data set does not contain a variable named _NAME_, PROC TRANSPOSE assigns the names COL1, COL2, . . . , COLn to the transposed variables.

Using a BY Statement

When you use a BY statement with PROC TRANSPOSE, the output data set contains one observation for each variable in each BY group in the input data set.

If the transposed variables are named by the PREFIX= option or by the default prefix COL, the number of transposed output variables is the maximum number of observations in any BY group of the input data set. If a BY group in the input data set has fewer than the maximum number of observations, the BY group in the output data set has missing values for the variables with no corresponding input observations. The following example shows the use of a BY statement and the PREFIX= option with the data set FISH.RAWDATA. These statements produce the output shown in **Output 41.8**:

```
libname fish 'SAS-data-library';

proc sort data=fish.rawdata out=fish.sortgrp;
   by group;
run;

proc print data=fish.sortgrp;
   title 'Fish Data Sorted by Group';
run;

proc transpose data=fish.sortgrp out=fish.transgrp prefix=var;
   var length1-length4 width1-width4;
   by group;
run;

proc print data=fish.transgrp;
   title 'Fish Data Transposed with BY Groups';
   title2 'Using the PREFIX= Option';
run;
```

Output 41.8   FISH.SORTGRP Is Transposed and the Output Data Set Is Called FISH.TRANSGRP

```
                                        Fish Data Sorted by Group                                            1
   OBS   GROUP    DATE     SPECIES   LENGTH1   WIDTH1   LENGTH2   WIDTH2   LENGTH3   WIDTH3   LENGTH4   WIDTH4

    1      1     02JUN84    CUR        31      0.25       32      0.30       32      0.25       33      0.30
    2      1     11JUL84    MEN        72      4.00       82      5.50       70      4.00       79      4.30
    3      1     14JUL84    MEN        79      4.10       78      3.80       80      3.80       74      3.60
    4      1     13AUG84    MEN        86      5.00       83      4.80       89      5.70       80      4.20
    5      2     02JUN84    CUR        30      0.20       36      0.45       33      0.25       36      0.35
    6      3     02JUN84    CUR        32      0.35       32      0.25       33      0.30       .        .
```

```
                        Fish Data Transposed with BY Groups                    2
                             Using the PREFIX= Option

        OBS     GROUP     _NAME_      VAR1      VAR2      VAR3      VAR4

         1        1       LENGTH1     31.00     72.0      79.0      86.0
         2        1       LENGTH2     32.00     82.0      78.0      83.0
         3        1       LENGTH3     32.00     70.0      80.0      89.0
         4        1       LENGTH4     33.00     79.0      74.0      80.0
         5        1       WIDTH1       0.25      4.0       4.1       5.0
         6        1       WIDTH2       0.30      5.5       3.8       4.8
         7        1       WIDTH3       0.25      4.0       3.8       5.7
         8        1       WIDTH4       0.30      4.3       3.6       4.2
         9        2       LENGTH1     30.00       .         .         .
        10        2       LENGTH2     36.00       .         .         .
        11        2       LENGTH3     33.00       .         .         .
        12        2       LENGTH4     36.00       .         .         .
        13        2       WIDTH1       0.20       .         .         .
        14        2       WIDTH2       0.45       .         .         .
        15        2       WIDTH3       0.25       .         .         .
        16        2       WIDTH4       0.35       .         .         .
        17        3       LENGTH1     32.00       .         .         .
        18        3       LENGTH2     32.00       .         .         .
        19        3       LENGTH3     33.00       .         .         .
        20        3       LENGTH4       .         .         .         .
        21        3       WIDTH1       0.35       .         .         .
        22        3       WIDTH2       0.25       .         .         .
        23        3       WIDTH3       0.30       .         .         .
        24        3       WIDTH4        .         .         .         .
```

Each of the three BY groups in the input data set generates eight observations, one for each variable being transposed. Because the largest BY group (where GROUP=1) contains four observations, the output data set contains four transposed variables. The PREFIX= option names these variables VAR1, VAR2, VAR3, and VAR4. BY groups with fewer than four observations have missing values for some of the transposed variables.

If you use an ID statement to name the transposed variables, the output data set contains one variable for each distinct value of the ID variable. The TRANSPOSE procedure orders the transposed variables according to the first appearance of their names in the input data set. If a BY group does not contain a value for the ID variable, the corresponding transposed variable has missing values in that BY group. For example, the following program transposes the data set FISH.SORTGRP with an ID statement:

```
libname fish 'SAS-data-library';

proc transpose data=fish.sortgrp out=fish.transid;
   id date;
   var length1-length4 width1-width4;
   by group;
run;

proc print data=fish.transid;
   title 'FISH.SORTGRP Transposed with BY Groups and ID Statement';
run;
```

The output data set appears in **Output 41.9**.

Output 41.9   FISH.SORTGRP Is Transposed and the Output Data Set Is
Called FISH.TRANSID

```
                 FISH.SORTGRP Transposed with BY Groups and ID Statement                        1
     OBS     GROUP     _NAME_      _02JUN84     _11JUL84     _14JUL84     _13AUG84

       1       1       LENGTH1      31.00        72.0         79.0         86.0
       2       1       LENGTH2      32.00        82.0         78.0         83.0
       3       1       LENGTH3      32.00        70.0         80.0         89.0
       4       1       LENGTH4      33.00        79.0         74.0         80.0
       5       1       WIDTH1        0.25         4.0          4.1          5.0
       6       1       WIDTH2        0.30         5.5          3.8          4.8
       7       1       WIDTH3        0.25         4.0          3.8          5.7
       8       1       WIDTH4        0.30         4.3          3.6          4.2
       9       2       LENGTH1      30.00          .            .            .
      10       2       LENGTH2      36.00          .            .            .
      11       2       LENGTH3      33.00          .            .            .
      12       2       LENGTH4      36.00          .            .            .
      13       2       WIDTH1        0.20          .            .            .
      14       2       WIDTH2        0.45          .            .            .
      15       2       WIDTH3        0.25          .            .            .
      16       2       WIDTH4        0.35          .            .            .
      17       3       LENGTH1      32.00          .            .            .
      18       3       LENGTH2      32.00          .            .            .
      19       3       LENGTH3      33.00          .            .            .
      20       3       LENGTH4        .            .            .            .
      21       3       WIDTH1        0.35          .            .            .
      22       3       WIDTH2        0.25          .            .            .
      23       3       WIDTH3        0.30          .            .            .
      24       3       WIDTH4        .             .            .            .
```

   Output 41.9 is identical to the second page of **Output 41.8** except for the
names of the transposed variables. In **Output 41.8**, the PREFIX= option names
the transposed variables. In **Output 41.9**, the ID statement names the transposed
variable.

EXAMPLES

Example 1:   Transposing a Data Set Twice

This example shows that transposing a data set twice can produce a data set similar
to the original data set, except for the new variable _NAME_. The following statements produce the output shown in **Output 41.10**:

```
data f;
   input a b c;
   cards;
1  2  3
4  5  6
7  8  9
10  11  12
;
run;

proc print data=f;
   title 'Before Transposing';
run;
```

```
proc transpose data=f out=ftransp;
run;

proc print data=ftransp;
   title 'After Transposing Once';
run;

proc transpose data=ftransp out=dbltrans;
run;

proc print data=dbltrans;
   title 'After Transposing Twice';
run;
```

Output 41.10   Transposing a Data Set Twice

```
                                Before Transposing                                    1

                         OBS      A      B      C

                          1       1      2      3
                          2       4      5      6
                          3       7      8      9
                          4      10     11     12
```

```
                                After Transposing Once                                2

                 OBS    _NAME_    COL1    COL2    COL3    COL4

                  1       A        1       4       7      10
                  2       B        2       5       8      11
                  3       C        3       6       9      12
```

```
                                After Transposing Twice                               3

                     OBS    _NAME_    A      B      C

                      1      COL1     1      2      3
                      2      COL2     4      5      6
                      3      COL3     7      8      9
                      4      COL4    10     11     12
```

Example 2:   Converting a List to a Table

The data below are a list of cities with temperatures in January, July, or August. The desired output is a table with cities as rows and two columns showing minimum winter and maximum summer temperatures. The cities should be ordered from coldest to hottest mean temperature. The following statements produce the output shown in **Output 41.11**:

```
    /* Create the data set. */
data list;
   input city $15. month $15. temp;
   cards;
Raleigh        July             77.5
Raleigh        January          40.5
Miami          August           82.9
Miami          January          67.2
Los_Angeles    August           69.5
Los_Angeles    January          54.5
Juneau         July             55.7
Juneau         January          23.5
Phoenix        July             91.2
Phoenix        January          51.2
Bismarck       January           8.2
Bismarck       July             70.8
Chicago        August           71.1
Chicago        January          22.9
Wichita        July             80.7
Wichita        January          31.3
Honolulu       August           80.7
Honolulu       January          72.3
Boston         July             73.3
Boston         January          29.2
Duluth         July             65.6
Duluth         January           8.5
;
run;
```

```
     /* Sort the data by CITY. */
proc sort;
   by city;
run;


   /* Print the data set. */
proc print data=list;
   title 'Original Data in List Form';
run;


   /* Transpose the data set by CITY. Name the transposed  */
   /* variables from the values of the ID variable, MONTH. */
proc transpose data=list out=listtran;
   by city;
   id month;
run;


   /* Print the transposed data set. */
proc print data=listtran;
   title 'The Transposed Data Set LISTTRAN';
run;


   /* Create a new data set from LISTTRAN. Create a variable  */
   /* named WINTER that contains the value of the variable    */
   /* JANUARY. Create a variable named SUMMER that contains   */
   /* the value of the variable JULY or AUGUST, whichever is  */
   /* greater. Create a variable named MEAN that contains the */
   /* the mean temperature for the months for which data are  */
   /* available.                                              */
data table;
   set listtran;
   winter=january;
   summer=max(july,august);
   mean=mean(january,july,august);
run;


   /* Sort the new data set by MEAN to put the cities in order */
   /* of increasing mean temperature.                          */
proc sort data=table;
   by mean;
run;


   /* Print the new data set. */
proc print data=table;
   title 'Tabular Data';
   id city;
   var winter summer;
run;
```

Output 41.11   Converting Data in List Form to Tabular Form

```
                        Original Data in List Form                              1

                   OBS    CITY          MONTH      TEMP

                    1     Bismarck      January      8.2
                    2     Bismarck      July        70.8
                    3     Boston        July        73.3
                    4     Boston        January     29.2
                    5     Chicago       August      71.1
                    6     Chicago       January     22.9
                    7     Duluth        July        65.6
                    8     Duluth        January      8.5
                    9     Honolulu      August      80.7
                   10     Honolulu      January     72.3
                   11     Juneau        July        55.7
                   12     Juneau        January     23.5
                   13     Los_Angeles   August      69.5
                   14     Los_Angeles   January     54.5
                   15     Miami         August      82.9
                   16     Miami         January     67.2
                   17     Phoenix       July        91.2
                   18     Phoenix       January     51.2
                   19     Raleigh       July        77.5
                   20     Raleigh       January     40.5
                   21     Wichita       July        80.7
                   22     Wichita       January     31.3
```

```
                     The Transposed Data Set LISTTRAN                           2

              OBS   CITY          _NAME_   JANUARY    JULY   AUGUST

               1    Bismarck      TEMP        8.2    70.8      .
               2    Boston        TEMP       29.2    73.3      .
               3    Chicago       TEMP       22.9      .     71.1
               4    Duluth        TEMP        8.5    65.6      .
               5    Honolulu      TEMP       72.3      .     80.7
               6    Juneau        TEMP       23.5    55.7      .
               7    Los_Angeles   TEMP       54.5      .     69.5
               8    Miami         TEMP       67.2      .     82.9
               9    Phoenix       TEMP       51.2    91.2      .
              10    Raleigh       TEMP       40.5    77.5      .
              11    Wichita       TEMP       31.3    80.7      .
```

```
                              Tabular Data                                      3

                  CITY          WINTER    SUMMER

                  Duluth          8.5      65.6
                  Bismarck        8.2      70.8
                  Juneau         23.5      55.7
                  Chicago        22.9      71.1
                  Boston         29.2      73.3
                  Wichita        31.3      80.7
                  Raleigh        40.5      77.5
                  Los_Angeles    54.5      69.5
                  Phoenix        51.2      91.2
                  Miami          67.2      82.9
                  Honolulu       72.3      80.7
```

Example 3:   Rearranging Data from a Factorial Design

The data below are from a subject-by-drug-by-exercise factorial design. This example shows how PROC TRANSPOSE can rearrange a more complicated data set using BY groups and ID variables. The following statements produce the output shown in **Output 41.12**:

```
data a1;
   input subject $ drug $ exercise $ response;
   cards;
Smith      Aspirin     Light     5
Smith      Aspirin     Medium    8
Smith      Aspirin     Heavy     9
Smith      Placebo     Light     4
Smith      Placebo     Heavy     7
Jones      Aspirin     Light     6
Jones      Aspirin     Medium    7
Jones      Aspirin     Heavy     9
Jones      Placebo     Light     3
Jones      Placebo     Medium    4
Jones      Placebo     Heavy     6
;
run;

proc sort;
   by subject drug;
run;

proc print data=a1;
   by subject;
   title 'Data Set A1';
run;

proc transpose data=a1 out=a2 name=respname;
   by subject drug;
   id exercise;
   var response;
run;

proc print data=a2;
   by subject;
   title 'Data Set A2';
run;

proc transpose data=a2 out=a3 name=exercise;
   by subject respname;
   id drug;
   var light medium heavy;
run;

proc print data=a3;
   by subject;
   title 'Data Set A3';
run;
```

```
proc transpose data=a3 out=a4 name=drug;
   by subject exercise notsorted;
   id respname;
run;

proc print data=a4;
   by subject;
   title 'Data Set A4';
run;
```

Output 41.12   Data from a Subject-by-Drug-by-Exercise Factorial Design

```
                                    Data Set A1                                          1
-------------------------------- SUBJECT=Jones --------------------------------

                  OBS    DRUG      EXERCISE    RESPONSE

                   1    Aspirin    Light          6
                   2    Aspirin    Medium         7
                   3    Aspirin    Heavy          9
                   4    Placebo    Light          3
                   5    Placebo    Medium         4
                   6    Placebo    Heavy          6


-------------------------------- SUBJECT=Smith --------------------------------

                  OBS    DRUG      EXERCISE    RESPONSE

                   7    Aspirin    Light          5
                   8    Aspirin    Medium         8
                   9    Aspirin    Heavy          9
                  10    Placebo    Light          4
                  11    Placebo    Heavy          7
```

```
                                    Data Set A2                                          2
-------------------------------- SUBJECT=Jones --------------------------------

            OBS    DRUG      RESPNAME    LIGHT    MEDIUM    HEAVY

             1    Aspirin    RESPONSE      6        7         9
             2    Placebo    RESPONSE      3        4         6


-------------------------------- SUBJECT=Smith --------------------------------

            OBS    DRUG      RESPNAME    LIGHT    MEDIUM    HEAVY

             3    Aspirin    RESPONSE      5        8         9
             4    Placebo    RESPONSE      4        .         7
```

```
                                    Data Set A3                                          3
-------------------------------- SUBJECT=Jones --------------------------------

            OBS    RESPNAME    EXERCISE    ASPIRIN    PLACEBO

             1    RESPONSE     LIGHT          6          3
             2    RESPONSE     MEDIUM         7          4
             3    RESPONSE     HEAVY          9          6


-------------------------------- SUBJECT=Smith --------------------------------

            OBS    RESPNAME    EXERCISE    ASPIRIN    PLACEBO

             4    RESPONSE     LIGHT          5          4
             5    RESPONSE     MEDIUM         8          .
             6    RESPONSE     HEAVY          9          7
```

```
                                Data Set A4                                          4
---------------------------------- SUBJECT=Jones ----------------------------------
                OBS   EXERCISE   DRUG      RESPONSE

                 1    LIGHT      ASPIRIN       6
                 2    LIGHT      PLACEBO       3
                 3    MEDIUM     ASPIRIN       7
                 4    MEDIUM     PLACEBO       4
                 5    HEAVY      ASPIRIN       9
                 6    HEAVY      PLACEBO       6


---------------------------------- SUBJECT=Smith ----------------------------------
                OBS   EXERCISE   DRUG      RESPONSE

                 7    LIGHT      ASPIRIN       5
                 8    LIGHT      PLACEBO       4
                 9    MEDIUM     ASPIRIN       8
                10    MEDIUM     PLACEBO       .
                11    HEAVY      ASPIRIN       9
                12    HEAVY      PLACEBO       7
```

Chapter 42

The UNIVARIATE Procedure

ABSTRACT

The UNIVARIATE procedure produces simple descriptive statistics (including quantiles) for numeric variables.

INTRODUCTION

The UNIVARIATE procedure differs from other SAS procedures that produce descriptive statistics because it provides greater detail on the distribution of a variable. PROC UNIVARIATE can provide the following:

- details on the extreme values of a variable
- quantiles, such as the median
- frequency tables

- several plots to illustrate the distribution
- paired comparison tests
- tests of central location
- a test to determine whether the data are normally distributed.

If a BY statement is used with PROC UNIVARIATE, descriptive statistics are calculated separately for groups of observations. PROC UNIVARIATE can also create one or more data sets containing the statistics it calculates.

SPECIFICATIONS

The UNIVARIATE procedure is controlled by the following statements:

PROC UNIVARIATE <*option-list*>;
   VAR *variable-list*;
   BY *variable-list*;
   FREQ *variable*;
   WEIGHT *variable*;
   ID *variable-list*;
   OUTPUT <OUT=*SAS-data-set*> <*output-statistic-list*>
           <PCTLPTS=*percentiles* PCTLPRE=*prefix-name-list*>
           <PCTLNAMES=*suffix-name-list*>;

Several OUTPUT statements are permitted, but the other statements can only be used once each in a PROC UNIVARIATE step. The VAR statement is required when you use the OUTPUT statement. The statements after the PROC UNIVARIATE statement can be listed in any order. In the sections that follow, the PROC UNIVARIATE statement is described first; descriptions of the other statements follow in alphabetic order.

PROC UNIVARIATE Statement

   PROC UNIVARIATE <*option-list*>;

The PROC UNIVARIATE statement starts the procedure and is the only required statement. The options that can appear in the PROC UNIVARIATE statement are described below.

DATA=*SAS-data-set*
   names the SAS data set to be used by PROC UNIVARIATE. If the DATA= option is omitted, the most recently created SAS data set is used.

FREQ
   requests a frequency table consisting of the variable values, frequencies, percentages, and cumulative percentages.

NOPRINT
   suppresses all printed output. The NOPRINT option is useful when the only purpose for executing the UNIVARIATE procedure is to create new data sets.

NORMAL
   computes a test statistic for the hypothesis that the input data come from a normal distribution. The NORMAL option also computes and prints the probability of a more extreme value of the test statistic.

PCTLDEF=*value*
> specifies which of the five definitions presented in **Computational Methods** later in this chapter is used to calculate percentiles. The PCTLDEF= value can be 1, 2, 3, 4, or 5. By default, PCTLDEF=5.

PLOT
> produces a stem-and-leaf plot (or a horizontal bar chart), a box plot, and a normal probability plot. If a BY statement is used, side-by-side box plots labeled **Schematic Plots** appear for groups defined by the BY variables.

ROUND=*round-off-unit-1<...round-off-unit-n>*
> specifies units for rounding variable values. The ROUND= option reduces the number of unique values for each variable and hence reduces the memory required for temporary storage.
>
> If only one round-off unit is specified, that unit is used for all variables. If more than one round-off unit is specified, you must use a VAR statement, and the units are used for the corresponding variables in the VAR statement. For example, in the following statements, a round-off unit of 1 is used for RESP1, a round-off unit of 0.5 is used for RESP2, and a round-off unit of 2 is used for RESP3:

```
proc univariate round=1 .5 2;
   var resp1 resp2 resp3;
run;
```

> The value of the round-off unit must be greater than or equal to 0. If the round-off unit is equal to 0, the ROUND= option has no effect on the corresponding variables.
>
> When a variable value is located at a point midway between the two nearest rounded points, the value is rounded to the nearest even multiple of the round-off unit. For example, with a round-off unit of 1, the values of -2.5, -2.2, and -1.5 are rounded to -2; the values of -0.5, 0.2, and 0.5 are rounded to 0; and the values of 0.6, 1.2, and 1.4 are rounded to 1.
>
> If you do not use the ROUND= option, the original values are used.

VARDEF=DF
> | N
> | WDF
> | WEIGHT | WGT
>
> specifies the divisor to be used in the calculation of variances and covariances. By default, VARDEF=DF. The values and associated divisors are shown below:

Value	Divisor	Formula
DF	degrees of freedom	$n - 1$
N	number of observations	n
WDF	sum of weights minus one	$(\Sigma_i w_i) - 1$
WEIGHT	WGT	sum of weights	$\Sigma_i w_i$

BY Statement

BY *variable-list*;

A BY statement can be used with PROC UNIVARIATE to obtain separate analyses on observations in groups defined by the BY variables.

When a BY statement appears, the UNIVARIATE procedure expects the input data set to be sorted in order of the BY variables or to have an appropriate index. If your input data set is not sorted in ascending order, you can do one of the following:

- Use the SORT procedure with a similar BY statement to sort the data.
- If appropriate, use the BY statement options NOTSORTED or DESCENDING.
- Use the DATASETS procedure to create an index on the BY variables you want to use. For more information on using the BY statement with indexed data sets, see Chapter 17, "The DATASETS Procedure."

FREQ Statement

FREQ *variable*;

When a FREQ statement appears, each observation in the data set being analyzed is assumed to represent *n* observations, where *n* is the value of the FREQ variable. If the FREQ variable has a value that is less than 1 or is missing, the observation is not used in the analysis. If the value is not an integer, only the integer portion is used.

The statistics calculated using a FREQ statement are identical to an analysis produced using a data set that contains *n* observations in place of each observation in the input data set.

ID Statement

ID *variable-list*;

The ID statement names a variable that identifies the five largest and five smallest observations in the printed output. However, the values of these ID variables are written in their entirety to any OUTPUT data set specified.

If you use one or more OUTPUT statements, the values of the ID variables are placed in each OUT= data set. The values of the ID variables used in the output data set are taken either from the first observation in the data set analyzed by PROC UNIVARIATE or, if a BY statement is used, from the first observation in the current BY group.

See **Census Data Analysis Using PROC UNIVARIATE** later in this chapter for an illustration.

OUTPUT Statement

OUTPUT <OUT=*SAS-data-set*> <*output-statistic-list*>
       <PCTLPTS=*percentiles* PCTLPRE=*prefix-name-list*>
       <PCTLNAMES=*suffix-name-list*>;

The OUTPUT statement saves summary statistics in a new SAS data set. Any number of OUTPUT statements can be used with each execution of PROC UNIVARIATE. Each OUTPUT statement creates a new data set. When you use the OUTPUT statement, you must also use the VAR statement. The options name the new data set and specify the variables to be included.

The number of observations in the new data set corresponds to the number of BY groups for which statistics are calculated. If a BY statement is not used, the new data set contains only one observation. The variables in the BY statement and the ID statement, as well as the computed statistics, are included in the new data set.

You can use the following options in the OUTPUT statement:

output-statistic-list

specifies the statistics you want in the new data set and names the new variables that contain the statistics. Write the keyword for the desired statistic, an equal sign, and the variable or variables to contain the statistic. In the output data set, the first variable listed after a keyword in the OUTPUT statement contains the statistic for the first variable listed in the VAR statement, the second variable contains the statistic for the second variable in the VAR statement, and so on. The formulas are given in Chapter 1, "SAS Elementary Statistics Procedures."

The valid keywords and the statistics they represent are as follows:

N	the number of observations on which the calculations are based.
NMISS	the number of missing values.
NOBS	the number of observations.
MEAN	the mean.
STDMEAN	the standard deviation of the mean.
SUM	the sum.
STD	the standard deviation.
VAR	the variance.
CV	the coefficient of variation.
USS	the uncorrected sum of squares.
CSS	the corrected sum of squares.
SKEWNESS	skewness.
KURTOSIS	kurtosis.
SUMWGT	the sum of the weights.
MAX	the largest value.
MIN	the smallest value.
RANGE	the range.
Q3	the upper quartile or the 75th percentile.
MEDIAN	the median or the 50th percentile.
Q1	the lower quartile or the 25th percentile.
QRANGE	the difference between the upper and lower quartiles, that is, $Q3 - Q1$.
P1	the 1st percentile.
P5	the 5th percentile.
P10	the 10th percentile.
P90	the 90th percentile.
P95	the 95th percentile.
P99	the 99th percentile.
MODE	the most frequent value. If there is more than one mode, the smallest mode is used. If your data are continuous and there are no replicated values, PROC UNIVARIATE reports the smallest value as the mode. In this case, the mode is of little use.
T	Student's *t* value for testing the hypothesis that the population mean is 0.
PROBT	probability of a greater absolute value for the Student's *t* value.

MSIGN   the sign statistic.

PROBM   probability of a greater absolute value for the sign statistic.

SIGNRANK

     the signed rank statistic.

PROBS   probability of a greater absolute value for the centered signed rank statistic.

NORMAL   the test statistic for normality. If the sample size is less than or equal to 2000, this is the Shapiro-Wilk statistic. Otherwise, it is the Kolmogorov statistic.

PROBN   probability for testing the hypothesis that the data come from a normal distribution.

OUT=*SAS-data-set*

    names an output data set. If you want to create a permanent SAS data set, you must specify a two-level name (see Chapter 6, "SAS Files," in *SAS Language: Reference, Version 6, First Edition* for more information on permanent data sets). If the OUT= option is omitted, the new data set is created and named using the DATA*n* naming convention.

You can use the following percentile options in the OUTPUT statement to produce percentiles other than the default percentiles. PROC UNIVARIATE automatically computes the 1st, 5th, 10th, 90th, 95th, and 99th percentiles. All percentiles can be saved in an output data set using the OUT= option.

PCTLNAME=*suffix-name-list*

    provides suffix names for the new variables created by the PCTLPTS= option. These suffixes are added to the prefixes specified in the PCTLPRE= option. The PCTLPRE= option is required if you use the PCTLPTS= option. List the suffixes in the same order in which you specify the percentiles. For example, the following statements create the variables ACLASS1 and A40 in the output data set:

```
proc univariate;
   var grade;
   output out=newa pctlpts=20 40  pctlpre=a b
   pctlname=class1;
run;
```

The first value of the PCTLNAME= option, CLASS1, is used for the first percentile, 20, in the PCTLPTS= list. This suffix is added to the values specified in the PCTLPRE= option to generate new variable names. The variable ACLASS1 contains the 20th percentiles for GRADE. The variable A40 contains the 40th percentile for GRADE. The default percentile name, 40, is used in this case since only one name appears in the PCTLNAME= option. Notice that the second prefix, B, is ignored since only one variable appears in the VAR statement.

Examples of various OUTPUT statements are shown here:

```
proc univariate data=students;
   var height weight;
   output mean=hmean std=hstddev out=means;
   output mean=hmean wmean out=stats;
   output mean=hmean wmean out=stat2 pctlpts=20 pctlpre=H W;
run;
```

The first OUTPUT statement saves the variables HMEAN and HSTDDEV (the mean and standard deviation of HEIGHT) in a data set named using the DATA*n* convention. PROC UNIVARIATE calculates statistics for the variable WEIGHT but does not save these values in the output data set since new variable names are not given. The second OUTPUT statement saves the variables HMEAN and WMEAN (the means of HEIGHT and WEIGHT) in the data set STATS. The third OUTPUT statement saves the means once again and uses the PCTLPTS= option to compute a percentile that is not automatically computed by PROC UNIVARIATE. The PCTLPRE= option gives prefixes for the new variables that contain percentiles. The PCTLPRE= option is required if you use the PCTLPTS= option.

PCTLPRE=*prefix-name-list*

specifies prefixes used to create variable names for percentiles requested with the PCTLPTS= option. The designated prefix is combined with the percentile name (either a default or the name specified with the PCTLNAME= option) to create the output variable name. The default percentile names are the values listed in the PCTLPTS= option (converting the decimal points to underscores if necessary). If you request percentiles for more than one variable in the input data set, then specify prefixes in the same order that the variables appear in the VAR statement. The PCTLPRE= option is required if you use the PCTLPTS= option. For example, in the following statement, the new variables for the 33rd and 66th percentiles of the variables HEIGHT and WEIGHT are NEWH33 and NEWW33 and NEWH66 and NEWW66, respectively:

```
var height weight;
output pctlpts=33 66  pctlpre=newh neww;
run;
```

If combining the prefix (specified in the PCTLPRE= option) and percentile name (specified in the PCTLNAME= option) results in a name longer than eight characters, the prefix is truncated to the necessary length. For example, in the following statement, the new variable created is named NCCOUN75:

```
output pctlpts=75 pctlpre=nccounty;
run;
```

If you use a BY statement, the BY variables, as well as the computed statistics, are included in the new data set. For example, consider these statements:

```
proc univariate;
    var grade1 grade2;
    by sex;
    output out=new mean=ave1 ave2 var=var1
           pctlpre=one two pctlpts=33.3 66.7;
run;
```

If the BY variable SEX has two values, **F** and **M**, the data set NEW contains two observations. Each of these observations contains the variables SEX, AVE1, AVE2, VAR1, ONE33_3, ONE66_7, TWO33_3, and TWO66_7. Since default names are used and the names contain decimals (such as 33.3), the decimals are converted to underscores.

PCTLPTS=*percentiles*

specifies percentiles not automatically computed by the UNIVARIATE procedure. The PCTLPTS= option generates additional percentiles and outputs them to a data set specified in the OUT= option; percentiles are not automatically printed. Values allowed are any decimal number between 0 and 100, inclusive.

If you use the PCTLPTS= option, you must also use the PCTLPRE= option to provide a prefix for the new variable names. For example, to create variables that contain the 20th, 40th, 60th, and 80th percentiles for the variable GRADE, use the following statements:

```
var grade;
output out=newdata pctlpts=20 40 60 80 pctlpre=new;
run;
```

This creates the output data set NEWDATA with variables NEW20, NEW40, NEW60, and NEW80, whose values are the corresponding percentiles of GRADE. NEW, specified by the PCTLPRE= option, is the prefix for the new variable names. You can also specify a range of percentiles, as in this example:

```
var pop;
output out=census pctlpts=50, 95 to 100  by 2.5 pctlpre=pop_;
run;
```

This creates the output data set CENSUS that contains the following percentiles: 50, 95, 97.5, and 100. See **Census Data Analysis Using PROC UNIVARIATE** later in this chapter for an illustration.

In addition to using the PCTLPRE= option, which is required, you can also use the PCTLNAME= option to create names for the new variables created by the PCTLPTS= option.

VAR Statement

VAR *variable-list*;

Univariate descriptive measures and tests are calculated for all numeric variables listed in the VAR statement. If no VAR statement appears, all numeric variables in the data set are analyzed. A VAR statement must be included when an OUTPUT statement is used.

WEIGHT Statement

WEIGHT *variable*;

The WEIGHT statement specifies a numeric variable in the input SAS data set whose values are used to weight each observation. Only one variable can be specified. Both the FREQ and WEIGHT statements can be used. When a WEIGHT statement is specified, PROC UNIVARIATE uses the value of the WEIGHT variable, w_i, to calculate a weighted mean $\bar{x}_w$, a weighted variance s^2_w, and a weighted sum $\Sigma w_i x_i$. The sample mean and sample variance are then represented as

$$\bar{x}_w = \Sigma_i w_i x_i / \Sigma_i w_i$$

and

$$s^2_w = \Sigma_i w_i (x_i - \bar{x}_w)^2 / d$$

where the x_i values are the variable values and the divisor d is controlled by the VARDEF= option. The divisor can be $n-1$ (VARDEF=DF), Σw_i

(VARDEF=WEIGHT | WGT), n (VARDEF=N), or $\Sigma w_i - 1$ (VARDEF=WDF), where n is the number of values. VARDEF=DF is the default.

The WEIGHT variable values can be nonintegers. If the value of the WEIGHT variable is less than 0 or is missing, a value of 0 is assumed for the weight.

The value of the WEIGHT variable is used only to calculate the first two sample moments and related statistics. Hence, if a WEIGHT statement is used, measures of skewness and kurtosis are not calculated and are reported as missing values. The WEIGHT variable has no effect on the calculation of quantiles or extremes.

DETAILS

Missing Values

If a variable for which statistics are to be calculated has a missing value, that value is ignored in the calculation of statistics, and the missing values are tabulated separately. See **Output 42.1** later in this chapter for an illustration. A missing value for one such variable does not affect the treatment of other variables in the same observation.

If the WEIGHT variable has a missing value, the weight is taken to be zero. However, the observation is still used to calculate quantiles and extremes. If the FREQ variable has a missing value, the observation is not used at all.

If a variable in a BY or ID statement has a missing value, the UNIVARIATE procedure treats it as it would treat any other value of a BY or ID variable.

Output Data Sets

If an OUTPUT statement is used, the corresponding output data set contains an observation for each unique set of values of the variables in the BY statement or a single observation if there is no BY statement. The variables in each observation consist of the variables in the BY statement, the variables in the ID statement, the statistics selected in the OUTPUT statement, and the requested percentiles as described in **OUTPUT Statement** earlier in this chapter.

The values of the variables listed in the BY statement are taken as those of the corresponding BY group. The values of the ID variables are taken from the first observation of each BY group. The values of the statistics are computed from the values of the variables within each BY group or across all the data if there is no BY statement.

Computational Methods

Standard algorithms (Fisher 1973) are used to compute the moment statistics (such as the mean, variance, skewness, and kurtosis).

Using the PCTLDEF= option, you can specify one of five methods for computing quantile statistics. Let n be the number of nonmissing values for a variable, and let $x_1, x_2, \ldots, x_n$ represent the ordered values of the variable. For the tth percentile, let $p=t/100$. For definitions 1, 2, 3, and 5 below, let

$$np = j + g$$

where j is the integer part and g is the fractional part of np. For definition 4, let

$$(n + 1)p = j + g$$

For example, the *t*th percentile, *y*, is defined as follows:

PCTLDEF=1   weighted average at x_{np}

$$y = (1 - g) x_j + gx_{j+1}$$

where x_o is taken to be x_1

PCTLDEF=2   observation numbered closest to *np*

$$y = x_i$$

where *i* is the integer part of $np+1/2$ if $g \neq 1/2$. If $g=1/2$, then $y=x_j$ if *j* is even, or $y=x_{j+1}$ if *j* is odd.

PCTLDEF=3   empirical distribution function

$$y = x_j \quad \text{if } g = 0$$
$$y = x_{j+1} \quad \text{if } g > 0$$

PCTLDEF=4   weighted average aimed at $x_{p(n+1)}$

$$y = (1 - g) x_j + gx_{j+1}$$

where x_{n+1} is taken to be x_n

PCTLDEF=5   empirical distribution function with averaging

$$y = (x_j + x_{j+1}) / 2 \quad \text{if } g = 0$$
$$y = x_{j+1} \quad \text{if } g > 0$$

The Wilcoxon signed rank statistic S is computed as

$$S = \Sigma r_i^+ - n(n + 1) / 4$$

where r_i^+ is the rank of $|x_i|$ after discarding values of $x_i=0$, *n* is the number of nonzero x_i values, and the sum (Σ) is over the values of x_i greater than 0. Average ranks are used for tied values.

If *n* is less than or equal to 20, the significance level of S is computed from the exact distribution of S, where the distribution of S is a convolution of scaled binomial distributions. When *n* is greater than 20, the significance of level S is computed by treating

$$S \sqrt{n - 1} / \sqrt{nV - S^2}$$

as a Student's *t* variate with $n-1$ degrees of freedom. V is computed as

$$V = (n(n + 1)(2n + 1) - 0.5 \Sigma t_i (t_i + 1)(t_i - 1)) / 24$$

where the sum is calculated over groups tied in absolute value and t_i is the number of tied values in the *i*th group (Iman 1974; Conover 1980).

If you are testing the hypothesis that the distribution mean or median is equal to 0, the Wilcoxon signed rank test assumes that the distribution is symmetric. If the assumption is not valid, the sign test may be used.

The UNIVARIATE procedure calculates the sign test as follows:

$$M(\text{Sign}) = p - n / 2$$

where

> p is the number of values greater than 0.

> n is the number of nonzero values.

Under the null hypothesis that the population median is zero, the probability of a sign statistic as, or more, extreme in absolute value than the observed value is:

$$2 \sum_{j=0}^{\min(p, n-p)} \binom{n}{j} 0.5^n$$

Test of Normality

When the NORMAL option is specified in the PROC UNIVARIATE statement, the procedure produces a test statistic for the null hypothesis that the input data values are a random sample from a normal distribution. One of two tests may be used depending on the sample size, as described below. However, to determine whether to reject the null hypothesis of normality, it is only necessary to examine the probability associated with the test statistic. This probability is labeled PROB<W for the Shapiro-Wilk test or PROB>D for the Kolmogorov test. If this value is less than the level you have chosen (such as 0.10), then the null hypothesis is rejected, and you can conclude that the data do not come from a normal distribution.

If the sample size is less than or equal to 2000, the Shapiro-Wilk statistic, W, is computed. The W statistic is the ratio of the best estimator of the variance (based on the square of a linear combination of the order statistics) to the usual corrected sum of squares estimator of the variance. W must be greater than zero and less than or equal to one, with small values of W leading to rejection of the null hypothesis of normality. Note that the distribution of W is highly skewed. Seemingly large values of W (such as 0.90) may be considered small and lead to the rejection of the null hypothesis. When the sample size is greater than six, the coefficients for calculating the linear combination of the order statistics are approximated by the method of Shapiro and Wilk (1965).

With a sample size of three, the probability distribution of W is known and is used to determine the significance level. When the sample size is greater than three, simulation results are used to determine the significance levels. For sample size n (between four and six), the W statistic, W_n, is transformed into an equivalent W statistic of sample size three, W_3, where the significance levels can be evaluated (Royston 1982). For sample size, n, greater than six, the significance level of W is obtained by Royston's approximate normalizing transformation

$$Z_n = ((1 - W_n)^\gamma - \mu) / \sigma$$

where

> Z_n is a standard normal variate. Large values of Z_n indicate departure from normality.

> γ, μ, and σ are functions of n, obtained from simulation results.

If the sample size is greater than 2000, the data are tested against a normal distribution with mean and variance equal to the sample mean and variance. The usual Kolmogorov D statistic is computed and printed. The probability of a larger test statistic is obtained by forming the value

$$\left[\sqrt{n} - 0.01 + (0.85/\sqrt{n}) \right] D$$

where n is the number of nonmissing values. This value is used to interpolate linearly within the range of simulated critical values given in Stephens (1974).

Note: When interpreting your output, if the modified Kolmogorov statistic is sufficiently large or small, the probability appears as less than .01 or greater than .15. This occurs when the value of the statistic is not within the range of critical values given by Stephens (1974).

Plots

When the PLOT option is specified in the PROC UNIVARIATE statement, the procedure generates three data plots.

The first plot is a stem-and-leaf plot (Tukey 1977) if no more than 48 observations fall into a single interval. Otherwise, the UNIVARIATE procedure plots a horizontal bar chart.

The second plot is a box plot or schematic plot. The bottom and top edges of the box are located at the sample 25th and 75th percentiles. The center horizontal line is drawn at the sample median and the central plus sign (+) is at the sample mean. It is possible for all of these statistics to fall on the same printer line. The central vertical lines, called *whiskers*, extend from the box as far as the data extend, to a distance of at most 1.5 interquartile ranges. (An *interquartile range* is the distance between the 25th and the 75th sample percentiles.) Any value more extreme than this is marked with a zero if it is within three interquartile ranges of the box, or with an asterisk (*) if it is still more extreme. For more explanation about this plot, see Tukey (1977). When a BY statement also appears, PROC UNIVARIATE produces side-by-side box plots in order of the BY variables after the separate analyses of each BY group.

The third plot, a normal probability plot, is a quantile-quantile plot of the data. The empirical quantiles are plotted against the quantiles of a standard normal distribution. Asterisks (*) mark the data values. The plus signs (+) provide a reference straight line that is drawn using the sample mean and standard deviation. If the data are from a normal distribution, the asterisks tend to fall along the reference line. The vertical coordinate is the data value, and the horizontal coordinate is

$$\Phi^{-1}((r_i - 3/8) / (n + 1/4))$$

where

r_i is the rank of the data value.

Φ^{-1} is the inverse of the standard normal distribution function.

n is the number of nonmissing data values.

An excellent description and interpretation of these plots is provided in *SAS System for Elementary Statistical Analysis.*

Rounding Algorithm in Stem-and-Leaf Plots

For a stem-and-leaf plot, the variable value is rounded to the nearest leaf. If the variable value is exactly halfway between two leaves, the value is rounded to the nearest leaf with an even integer value. For example, a variable value of 3.15 has a stem of 3 and a leaf of 2.

Computer Resources

In the following discussion, let

> N   be the number of observations in the data set
>
> V   be the number of variables in the VAR list (or the number of numeric variables in the DATA= data set if the VAR list is omitted)
>
> U_i be the number of unique values for the ith variable.

The following factors determine the time requirements:

- The observations for each variable are stored internally in a tree structure. The time needed to organize the observations into V tree structures is proportional to NV log(N).
- The time needed to compute the moments and quantiles for the jth variable is proportional to U_j.
- The time needed to compute the Shapiro-Wilk statistic is proportional to N.
- Additional time may be required to compute the exact significance level of the sign rank statistic if the number of nonzero values is less than or equal to 20.

Each of the above factors has a different constant of proportionality.

Printed Output

For each variable, PROC UNIVARIATE prints the following:

1. the name of the variable.
2. the variable label.
3. the number of observations on which the calculations are based.
4. the sum of the weights of these observations.
5. the mean.
6. the sum.
7. the standard deviation.
8. the variance.
9. the measure of skewness.
10. the measure of kurtosis.
11. the uncorrected sum of squares.
12. the corrected sum of squares.
13. the coefficient of variation.
14. the standard error of the mean.
15. the Student's t value for testing the hypothesis that the population mean is 0.
16. the probability of a greater absolute value for this t-value.
17. the number of nonzero observations.
18. the number of positive observations.
19. the centered (the expected value is subtracted) sign statistic for testing the hypothesis that the population median is 0.
20. the probability of a greater absolute value for the sign statistic under the hypothesis that the population median is 0.
21. the centered (the expected value is subtracted) Wilcoxon signed rank statistic for testing the hypothesis that the population mean and median are 0.
22. the probability of a greater absolute value for this statistic under the hypothesis that the population mean and median are 0.
23. the largest value.
24. Q3, Q1, and Med, the upper and lower quartiles, and the median.
25. the smallest value.

26. the range.
27. the difference between the upper and lower quartiles.
28. the mode.
29. the 1st, 5th, 10th, 90th, 95th, and 99th percentiles.
30. the five largest and five smallest values. The five largest and five smallest values of variables in the VAR statement are printed by PROC UNIVARIATE. If an ID statement is used, the values of the ID variable are used to identify these ten values for each VAR variable. If an ID statement is not used, the observation number identifies the values.

If missing values occur for a variable, the following are printed:

31. the missing value
32. count, the number of occurrences
33. %Count/Nobs, the count as a percentage of the total number of observations
34. %Count/Nmiss, the count as a percentage of the total number of missing values (not shown).

If the NORMAL option is used, PROC UNIVARIATE prints the following:

35. W:NORMAL or D:NORMAL, test statistics
36. associated probabilities, PROB<W or PROB>D, for testing the hypothesis that the data come from a normal distribution.

If the PLOT option is used, PROC UNIVARIATE prints the following:

37. a stem-and-leaf plot (if any value's count is greater than 48, a horizontal bar chart is printed instead)
38. a box plot
39. a normal probability plot
40. side-by-side box plots for groups defined by the BY variables.

If the FREQ option is used, PROC UNIVARIATE prints the following:

41. a list of variable values
42. frequencies of variable values
43. percentages of variable values
44. cumulative percentages of variable values.

EXAMPLE

Census Data Analysis Using PROC UNIVARIATE

In the following example, descriptive statistics are produced for the 1970 and 1980 census populations by sex for the 50 states (plus 2 fictional states to illustrate missing values). Several OUTPUT statements are used in the DATA step to create the necessary BY groups for schematic plots. **Output 42.1** contains the descriptive statistics for one of the BY groups, DECADE=70 SEX=FEMALE (others are omitted for brevity). **Output 42.2** contains schematic plots for all groups defined by the BY variables. **Output 42.3** illustrates an output data set from PROC UNIVARIATE containing percentile values.

```
data pf70 pm70 pf80 pm80;
    input state $ pop_f70 pop_m70 pop_f80 pop_m80 @@;
    drop pop_m70 pop_f70 pop_m80 pop_f80;
    decade= 70;
    sex= 'Female';
    pop= pop_f70;  output pf70;
```

```
         sex= 'Male';
         pop= pop_m70;  output pm70;
         decade= 80;
         pop= pop_m80;  output pm80;
         sex= 'Female';
         pop= pop_f80;  output pf80;
         cards;
     ALA    1.78   1.66   2.02   1.87  ALASKA 0.14   0.16   0.19   0.21
     ARIZ   0.90   0.87   1.38   1.34  ARK    0.99   0.93   1.18   1.10
     CALIF 10.14   9.82  12.00  11.67  COLO   1.12   1.09   1.46   1.43
     CONN   1.56   1.47   1.61   1.50  DEL    0.28   0.27   0.31   0.29
     FLA    3.51   3.28   5.07   4.68  GA     2.36   2.23   2.82   2.64
     HAW    0.37   0.40   0.47   0.49  IDAHO  0.36   0.36   0.47   0.47
     ILL    5.72   5.39   5.89   5.54  IND    2.66   2.53   2.82   2.67
     IOWA   1.45   1.37   1.50   1.41  KAN    1.15   1.02   1.21   1.16
     KY     1.64   1.58   1.87   1.79  LA     1.87   1.77   2.17   2.04
     ME     0.51   0.48   0.58   0.55  MD     2.01   1.92   2.17   2.04
     MASS   2.97   2.72   3.01   2.73  MICH   4.53   4.39   4.75   4.52
     MINN   1.94   1.86   2.08   2.00  MISS   1.14   1.07   1.31   1.21
     MO     2.42   2.26   2.55   2.37  MONT   0.35   0.35   0.39   0.39
     NEB    0.76   0.72   0.80   0.77  NEV    0.24   0.25   0.40   0.41
     NH     0.38   0.36   0.47   0.45  NJ     3.70   3.47   3.83   3.53
     NM     0.52   0.50   0.66   0.64  NY     9.52   8.72   9.22   8.34
     NC     2.59   2.49   3.03   2.86  ND     0.31   0.31   0.32   0.33
     OHIO   5.49   5.16   5.58   5.22  OKLA   1.31   1.25   1.55   1.48
     ORE    1.07   1.02   1.34   1.30  PA     6.13   5.67   6.18   5.68
     RI     0.48   0.46   0.50   0.45  SC     1.32   1.27   1.60   1.52
     SD     0.34   0.33   0.35   0.34  TENN   2.03   1.90   2.37   2.22
     TEXAS  5.72   5.48   7.23   7.00  UTAH   0.54   0.52   0.74   0.72
     VT     0.23   0.22   0.26   0.25  VA     2.35   2.30   2.73   2.62
     WASH   1.72   1.69   2.08   2.05  W.VA   0.90   0.84   1.00   0.95
     WIS    2.25   2.17   2.40   2.31  WYO    0.16   0.17   0.23   0.24
     XX       .      .      .      .   YY       .      .      .      .
     ;
     run;


     data popstate;
       set pf70 pm70 pf80 pm80;
       label pop= 'Census Population In Millions';
     run;

     proc univariate data=popstate freq plot normal;
        by decade sex;
        var pop;
        id state;
        output out= univout mean= popnmean median= popn50
                 pctlpre= pop_  pctlpts= 50, 95 to 100 by 2.5;
     run;

     proc print data= univout;
        title 'Output Dataset From PROC UNIVARIATE';
        format popn50 pop_50 pop_95 pop_97_5 pop_100 best8.;
     run;
```

Output 42.1   Descriptive Statistics for State Census Population Date

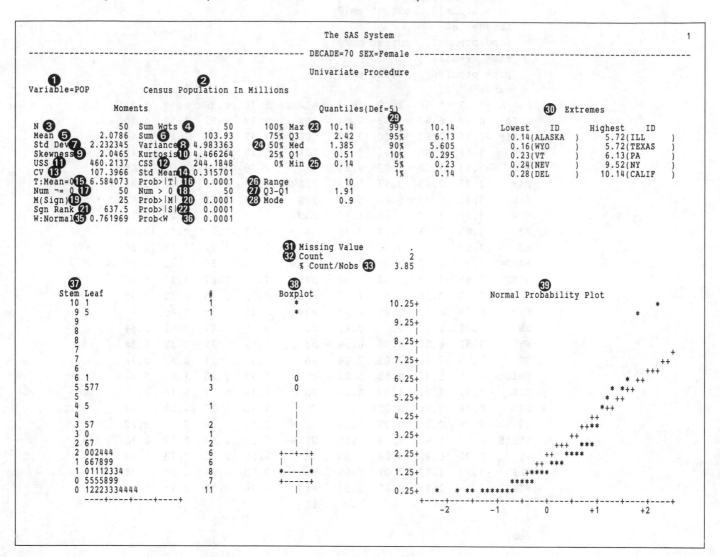

Output 42.2   Producing Schematic Plots

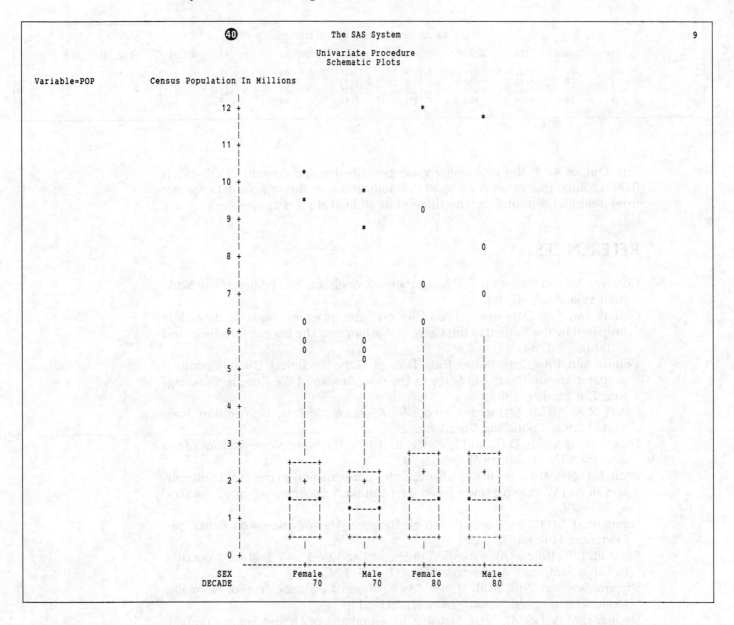

Output 42.3   Producing an Output Data Set

				Output Dataset From PROC UNIVARIATE						10
OBS	DECADE	SEX	STATE	POPNMEAN	POPN50	POP_50	POP_95	POP_97_5	POP_100	
1	70	Female	ALA	2.0786	1.385	1.385	6.13	9.52	10.14	
2	70	Male	ALA	1.9704	1.32	1.32	5.67	8.72	9.82	
3	80	Female	ALA	2.3230	1.575	1.575	7.23	9.22	12	
4	80	Male	ALA	2.1958	1.49	1.49	7	8.34	11.67	

In **Output 42.1**, the probability value contained in the column PROB<W is 0.0001. Since this value is close to 0, it indicates that the sample data are not from a normal distribution. The three plots all indicate this as well.

REFERENCES

Conover, W.J. (1980), *Practical Nonparametric Statistics*, 2nd Edition, New York: John Wiley & Sons, Inc.

County and City Data Book, 1983 Files on Tape (machine-readable data file)/ prepared by the Bureau of the Census. Washington: The Bureau (producer and distributor), 1984.

County and City Data Book, 1983 Files on Tape Technical Documentation/ prepared by the Data User Services Division, Bureau of the Census. Washington: The Bureau, 1984.

Fisher, R.A. (1973), *Statistical Methods for Research Workers*, 14th Edition, New York: Hafner Publishing Company.

Frigge, M., Hoaglin, D.C., and Iglewicz, B. (1989), "Some Implementations of the Boxplot," *The American Statistician*, 43.

Iman, R.L. (1974), "Use of a t-statistic as an Approximation to the Exact Distribution of the Wilcoxon Signed Ranks Test Statistic," *Communications in Statistics*, 3, 795–806.

Lehmann, E.L. (1975), *Nonparametrics: Statistical Methods Based on Ranks*, San Francisco: Holden-Day, Inc.

Royston, J.P. (1982), "An Extension of Shapiro and Wilk's W Test for Normality to Large Samples," *Applied Statistics*, 31, 115–124.

Shapiro, S.S. and Wilk, M.B. (1965), "An Analysis of Variance Test for Normality (complete samples)," *Biometrika*, 52, 591–611.

Stephens, M.A. (1974), "EDF Statistics for Goodness of Fit and Some Comparisons," *Journal of the American Statistical Association*, 69, 730–737.

Tukey, J.W. (1977), *Exploratory Data Analysis*, Reading, Massachusetts: Addison-Wesley.

U.S. Bureau of the Census (1977), *County and City Data Book, 1977* (machine-readable data file), Washington, D.C.: U.S. Government Printing Office.

The V5TOV6 Procedure

ABSTRACT

The V5TOV6 procedure converts members of a SAS data library or a file of formats from Version 5 format to Version 6 format on the same operating system. Operating systems that do not support Version 5 of the SAS System do not support this procedure. The V5TOV6 procedure is supported on the following operating systems: AOS/VS, CMS, MVS, PRIMOS, VMS, and VSE.

INTRODUCTION

Because Version 6 of the SAS System supports a variety of new features, the structure (or format) of many SAS files has changed since Version 5. With the exceptions of data sets on all operating systems and of formats and informats on the CMS operating system, you cannot directly access a Version 5 SAS file when you are running Version 6 of the SAS System. The V5TOV6 procedure copies SAS files from a Version 5 SAS data library to a Version 6 SAS data library, changing the formats of the files as necessary so that you can use them in Version 6. The original Version 5 library remains intact.

The V5TOV6 procedure can convert the following types of SAS files to their Version 6 equivalents:

- data sets
- formats and informats
- SAS/IML matrices and modules
- SAS/ETS models
- SAS/GRAPH graphics catalogs
- SAS/AF and SAS/FSP catalogs, excluding FSCALC catalog entries.

Note: The V5TOV6 procedure converts files, but you cannot use it to move files from one operating system or host to another. For information on moving files across operating systems and hosts, see Chapter 16, "The CPORT Procedure;" Chapter 10, "The CIMPORT Procedure;" and the discussion of the Version 5 transport engine in *SAS Language: Reference, Version 6, First Edition*.

Version 5 SAS Files and Their Version 6 Counterparts

This section explains the relationship between files in a Version 5 SAS data library and their counterparts in a Version 6 SAS data library. For information on file types in Version 5, refer to Chapter 17, "SAS Files," in *SAS User's Guide: Basics, Version 5 Edition*. For information on file types in Version 6, refer to Chapter 6, "SAS Files," in *SAS Language: Reference*.

SAS Data Sets

In both Versions 5 and 6, the SAS System stores data sets in SAS files of type DATA. When you convert a data set from its Version 5 to its Version 6 format, the file retains its name and type.

Note: You can access a Version 5 data set from Version 6 with the Version 5 compatibility engine without actually converting the file. See Chapter 6 in *SAS Language: Reference*.

SAS/AF and SAS/FSP Catalogs

In both Versions 5 and 6, files created by SAS/AF and SAS/FSP software are catalogs, but the internal formats of Version 5 and Version 6 catalogs differ.

With the few exceptions shown in **Table 43.1**, each entry retains its type when converted to its Version 6 format.

Table 43.1 Entry Types that Change When You Convert a Version 5 Catalog to a Version 6 Catalog

Version 5 Entry Type	Version 6 Entry Type
CBTGO	AFGO
CBTSAVE	AFCBT
TRANSAVE	AFGO

In addition, when you convert an entry of type PROGRAM from Version 5 to Version 6, each ### macro in the entry is converted to a separate catalog entry of type AFMACRO. Each entry's name is the name of the original ### macro.

A converted catalog retains its name and, in most cases individual entries retain their names. However, if an entry name contains special characters that were allowed in Version 5 entry names but are not allowed in Version 6 entry names, the Version 6 name contains an underscore instead of the special character. Therefore, catalog entries that have different names in Version 5 can have the same name and type when you convert them to Version 6. *In such a case, a newly converted catalog entry replaces an existing catalog entry of the same name.*

Note: If your user profile catalog (SASUSER.PROFILE) contains forms used by entries of type LETTER in other catalogs, you must convert the user profile catalog before you convert any other catalogs. Otherwise, entries of type LETTER cannot find the correct FORM entry and may be reformatted.

Refer to Technical Report P-195: *Transporting SAS Files between Host Systems* for information on the changes made when you convert a PROGRAM entry from Version 5 to Version 6 format.

Formats and Informats

In Version 5 of the SAS System, different operating systems store formats and informats differently. The V5TOV6 procedure converts each format or informat to an entry in a catalog named FORMATS. Each type of format and informat is assigned a particular entry type (see **Table 43.2**).

Table 43.2 Conversion of Formats and Informats

Format or Informat	Corresponding Version 6 Entry Type
numeric format	FORMAT
character format	FORMATC
numeric informat	INFMT
character informat	INFMTC

For example, the V5TOV6 procedure converts a Version 5 file named PRODFMTS that contains a numeric format to an entry in a Version 6 catalog named FORMATS. The entry's name is PRODFMTS; its entry type is FORMAT.

If the name of a format or informat contains special characters that were allowed in Version 5 names but are not allowed in Version 6 names, the V5TOV6 procedure drops the special character from the Version 6 name.

Note: You can access a Version 5 format or informat from Version 6 on the CMS operating system. Refer to the SAS documentation for the CMS operating system for details.

Other File Types

In Version 5, SAS/ETS models, SAS/GRAPH graphics catalogs, and SAS/IML matrices and modules are separate types of files. In Version 6, they are all stored in catalogs, but each has a different entry type. Thus, when you convert one of these Version 5 files to its Version 6 counterpart, the entire file becomes one or more entries in a catalog. If the corresponding catalog does not exist in the Version 6 SAS data library, the SAS System creates it. If the catalog already exists, PROC V5TOV6 adds the selected entries to the catalog.

Table 43.3 shows how PROC V5TOV6 names these new catalog entries and what entry types it assigns to them.

Note: Version 5 *objects* are called *entries* in Version 6.

Table 43.3   Relationship between Version 5 Files and Version 6 Catalogs

Version 5 File			Version 6 Catalog		
Filename	File Type	Object Name	Catalog Name	Entry Name	Entry Type
OLDNAME	MODEL		MODELS	OLDNAME	MODEL
OLDNAME	GCAT	OBJNAME	OLDNAME	OBJNAME	GRSEG
OLDNAME	GCAT	OBJNAME	OLDNAME	OBJNAME1	GRSEG
OLDNAME	GCAT	OTHRNAME	OLDNAME	OTHRNAME	GRSEG
OLDNAME	IMLWK		OLDNAME	*matrix name* or *module name*	MATRIX

For example, the V5TOV6 procedure converts a Version 5 file of type MODEL named SALESMOD to an entry in a Version 6 catalog named MODELS. The entry's name is SALESMOD; its entry type is MODEL.

A Version 5 graphics catalog named BOOKS converts to a Version 6 catalog named BOOKS. Each entry in the catalog retains its name unless the Version 6 catalog already contains an entry with that name. In such a case, PROC V5TOV6 appends a number to the name to create a unique entry name. If appending the number makes the name too long, the V5TOV6 procedure drops characters from the end of the original name. The type of all entries in the catalog is GRSEG.

Conversion of files of type IMLWK is discussed in **Converting SAS/IML Matrices and Modules** later in this chapter.

SPECIFICATIONS

You can use the following statements in the V5TOV6 procedure:

PROC V5TOV6 *source=identifier* OUT=*V6-libref* <*option-list*>;
    SELECT *member-list* </ <MEMTYPE=(*mtype-list*)> <READ=*password*>>;
    EXCLUDE *member-list* </ <MEMTYPE=(*mtype-list*)>>;
    CAT SELECT *select-list* </ ENTRYTYPE=(*etype-list*)>;
    CAT EXCLUDE *exclude-list* </ ENTRYTYPE=(*etype-list*)>;
    GCAT SELECT *select-list*;
    GCAT EXCLUDE *exclude-list*;

Table 43.4 summarizes the basic functions of these statements. You can combine statements and options to perform more complicated conversions. You can also perform the same task a variety of ways. Descriptions of these statements follow.

Table 43.4 Basic Functions of PROC V5TOV6 Statement

Function	Statements	Options
Convert an entire SAS data library (see **Example 1**) or file of formats (see **Example 11**)	PROC V5TOV6	
Select files by type (see **Example 2**)	PROC V5TOV6	MEMTYPE=
Select files by name (see **Example 3**)	PROC V5TOV6, SELECT, EXCLUDE	
Select files by type and by name (see **Example 4**)	PROC V5TOV6, SELECT, EXCLUDE	MEMTYPE=
Convert all entries in a catalog (see **Example 5**)	PROC V5TOV6, CAT SELECT	
Select catalog entries by type (see **Example 6**)	PROC V5TOV6	MEMTYPE=CAT ENTRYTYPE=
Select catalog entries by name (see **Example 7**)	PROC V5TOV6, CAT SELECT, CAT EXCLUDE	
Select catalog entries by type and by name (see **Example 8**)	PROC V5TOV6, CAT SELECT, CAT EXCLUDE	ENTRYTYPE=
Convert all entries in a graphics catalog (see **Example 9**) or select graphics catalogs by name (see **Example 10**)	PROC V5TOV6, GCAT SELECT, GCAT EXCLUDE	

PROC V5TOV6 Statement

PROC V5TOV6 *source=identifier* OUT=*V6-libref* <*option-list*>;

Requirements

The V5TOV6 procedure requires the following arguments, which specify the library or file of formats to read from and the destination for the converted files:

source=identifier
  specifies the Version 5 source to convert. This argument takes two different forms: one for converting formats and informats under the CMS, MVS, and VSE operating systems; one for converting everything else.

  FORMAT=SASLIB
    You must use the argument FORMAT=SASLIB to convert formats and informats under the CMS, MVS, and VSE operating systems because Version 5 formats and informats on those systems are not stored in SAS data libraries. This argument is not valid on other operating systems.

    Before starting your SAS session, use the FILEDEF command (under CMS), the ALLOCATE command or DD statement (under MVS), or the LIBDEF command (under VSE) to associate the fileref of SASLIB with the file of formats. Under MVS, the file of formats is a load module library; under CMS, it is a TXTLIB; under VSE, it is a VSE library.

    Note: Under CMS, you must global the TXTLIB before you start your SAS session. Refer to the *SAS Companion for the CMS Environment, Version 6, First Edition* for more information on converting formats and informats under CMS.

    You must use either the FORMAT= or the IN= argument, but you cannot use both.

  IN=*libref*
    specifies the Version 5 SAS data library to read from. Use the LIBNAME statement to associate a *libref* with the SAS data library. For details on the LIBNAME statement, see *SAS Language: Reference*.

    You must use either the IN= or the FORMAT= argument, but you cannot use both.

OUT=*V6-libref*
  specifies the Version 6 SAS data library to write to. Use the LIBNAME statement to associate a *libref* with the SAS data library. For details on the LIBNAME statement, see *SAS Language: Reference*.

Options

The PROC V5TOV6 statement supports four options. **Table 43.5** summarizes the functions of these options. Descriptions of these options follow in alphabetic order.

Table 43.5   Functions of PROC V5TOV6 Statement Options

Function	Option
Specify member types to convert	MEMTYPE=
Specify catalog entry types to convert	ENTRYTYPE=
Specify READ password for data sets to convert	READ=
List selected files and catalog entries, but do not convert them	LIST

ENTRYTYPE=(etype-list)
ETYPE=(etype-list)
ET=(etype-list)
   specifies one or more Version 5 catalog entry types. Note that etype-list
   can be a single entry type or a list of entry types. If you specify a single
   entry type, you do not need to enclose it in parentheses. Valid values
   for etype-list include one or more of the following:

ALL	all valid entry-types.
CBT	an entry containing the text, which may include questions and possible responses, of an application created with the SAS/AF software BUILD procedure.
CBTGO	a specialized entry type produced by the DISPLAY procedure for use in displaying the entry. This entry type does not exist in Version 6. The V5TOV6 procedure converts all CBTGO entries to the corresponding type in Version 6: AFGO.
CBTSAVE	a specialized entry type produced by PROC DISPLAY for use in displaying the entry. This entry type does not exist in Version 6. The V5TOV6 procedure converts all CBTSAVE entries to the corresponding type in Version 6: AFCBT.
FORM	an entry containing printer information for SAS/AF, SAS/FSP, or base SAS software.
GCMAP	an entry containing a color map created by the GREPLAY procedure in SAS/GRAPH software. This entry type does not exist in Version 6. The V5TOV6 procedure converts all GCMAP entries to the corresponding type in Version 6: CMAP.
HELP	an entry containing help information for applications developed with the BUILD procedure in SAS/AF software.
KEYS	an entry containing function-key settings for any of a variety of full-screen procedures or applications, including the SAS Display Manager System.
LETTER	an entry containing text created, edited, and output with the FSLETTER procedure in SAS/FSP software.
LIST	an entry that lists valid values for fields in an application created by the BUILD procedure in SAS/AF software.

MENU   an entry containing a menu created by the BUILD
        procedure in SAS/AF software.

PROGRAM

        an entry containing a program, a display, or both
        created by the BUILD procedure in SAS/AF software.

SCREEN   an entry containing a screen created by the FSEDIT or
        FSBROWSE procedure in SAS/FSP software.

TEMPLATE   an entry containing a template or layout created with
        the GREPLAY procedure for graphs displayed with
        SAS/GRAPH software.

TRANSAVE

        a specialized entry type produced by PROC DISPLAY
        used in displaying the entry. This entry type does not
        exist in Version 6. The V5TOV6 procedure converts all
        TRANSAVE entries to the corresponding type in
        Version 6: AFGO.

For example, the following statements use the ENTRYTYPE= option
to convert all entries of types HELP and MENU in all catalogs (specified
by the MEMTYPE= option, described later in this chapter) in the
Version 5 SAS data library SOURCE to their equivalents in the Version 6
SAS data library DEST:

```
libname source 'V5-SAS-data-library';
libname dest 'V6-SAS-data-library';

proc v5tov6 in=source out=dest memtype=cat
                           entrytype=(help menu);
run;
```

You can also specify the ENTRYTYPE= option in the CAT SELECT and
CAT EXCLUDE statements. For more information on how the options
interact when you use them in more than one statement, refer to **Using
Options in Subordinate Statements** later in this chapter.

If you do not specify an entry type for a catalog, the default is ALL.

LIST

lists in the SAS log the names of the files and entries you specify but
does not convert any files. Use the LIST option if you want to verify that
you are selecting the items you intend to convert.

For example, the following statements list all entries of types HELP
and MENU in all catalogs in the Version 5 SAS data library SOURCE but
do not convert them:

```
libname source 'V5-SAS-data-library';

proc v5tov6 in=source out=work list memtype=cat
                              entrytype=(help menu);
run;
```

Note: You must always use the required argument OUT=. When
you are using the LIST option, it is convenient to specify OUT=WORK.

MEMTYPE=(*mtype-list*)
MTYPE=(*mtype-list*)
MT=(*mtype-list*)

specifies one or more Version 5 member types. Note that *mtype-list* can
be a single member type or a list of member types. If you specify a
single member type, you do not need to enclose it in parentheses. Valid

values for *mtype-list* include one or more of the following:

ALL	all supported member types
CAT	SAS/AF, SAS/FSP, and base SAS catalogs
DATA	SAS data sets
FORMAT	all formats and informats
FORMATC	all character formats
FORMATN	
	all numeric formats
NFORMATC	
	all character informats
NFORMATN	
	all numeric informats
GCAT	SAS/GRAPH graphics catalogs
IMLWK	SAS/IML workspaces
MODEL	SAS/ETS models

For example, the following statements convert all the SAS data sets in the Version 5 SAS data library SOURCE to their equivalents in the Version 6 SAS data library DEST:

```
libname source 'V5-SAS-data-library';
libname dest 'V6-SAS-data-library';

proc v5tov6 in=source out=dest memtype=data;
run;
```

You can also specify the MEMTYPE= option in the SELECT or EXCLUDE statement. For more information on how the options interact when you use them in more than one statement, refer to **Using Options in Subordinate Statements** later in this chapter.

If you do not specify a member type, the default is ALL.

READ=*password*

specifies the default value of the READ= password for all SAS data sets selected for conversion.

For example, the following statements convert all SAS files in the Version 5 SAS data library SOURCE to their equivalents in the Version 6 SAS data library DEST. The READ= option in the PROC V5TOV6 statement specifies that the password for all SAS data sets in SOURCE is SECRET.

```
libname source 'V5-SAS-data-library';
libname dest 'V6-SAS-data-library';

proc v5tov6 in=source out=dest read=secret;
run;
```

If you do not specify a password for a file that has password protection or if data sets within the library have different passwords, the SAS System prompts you when it needs a password if you are running interactively. If you are not running interactively, the V5TOV6 procedure cannot convert that data set and sends an error message to the SAS log.

You can also use the READ= option in the SELECT statement. For more information on how the options interact when you use them in more than one statement, refer to **Using Options in Subordinate Statements** later in this chapter.

Note: As of Release 6.06, Version 6 of the SAS System does not support password protection. Therefore, although you must specify the read password to convert a password-protected Version 5 SAS data set, the resulting Version 6 data set has no password.

CAT EXCLUDE Statement

CAT EXCLUDE *exclude-list* </ ENTRYTYPE=(*etype-list*)>;

The CAT EXCLUDE statement excludes catalog entries from conversion. Each element of *exclude-list* has the form *member.entry*, where

member   is the name of a catalog to process. You can use wild-card characters to specify the member. For more information, see **Using Wild-Card Characters** later in this chapter.

entry   is the name of an entry in *member* to exclude from conversion. You can use wild-card characters to specify the entry. For more information, see **Using Wild-Card Characters** later in this chapter.

For example, the following PROC V5TOV6 step converts all entries in the catalogs SOFTWARE and BOOKS in the Version 5 SAS data library SOURCE except for entries of any type named WRITE:

```
libname source 'V5-SAS-data-library';
libname dest 'V6-SAS-data-library';

proc v5tov6 in=source out=dest;
   cat exclude software.write books.write;
run;
```

You can use the ENTRYTYPE= option in the CAT EXCLUDE statement or the PROC V5TOV6 statement to specify one or more entry types to exclude from conversion. For more information on using this option, see **Options** earlier in this chapter and **Using Options in Subordinate Statements** later in this chapter.

You can use both the CAT EXCLUDE statement and the CAT SELECT statement in the same PROC V5TOV6 step as long as they specify different catalogs (see **Example 7** and **Example 8**).

CAT SELECT Statement

CAT SELECT *select-list* </ ENTRYTYPE=(*etype-list*)>;

The CAT SELECT statement selects catalog entries for conversion. Each element of *select-list* has the form *member.entry*, where

member   is the name of a catalog to process. You can use wild-card characters to specify the member. For more information, see **Using Wild-Card Characters** later in this chapter.

entry   is the name of an entry in *member* to select for conversion. You can use wild-card characters to specify the entry. For more information, see **Using Wild-Card Characters** later in this chapter.

For example, the following PROC V5TOV6 step converts all catalog entries named SOFTWARE.WRITE and BOOKS.WRITE from the Version 5 SAS data library SOURCE to their equivalents in the Version 6 SAS data library DEST:

```
libname source 'V5-SAS-data-library';
libname dest 'V6-SAS-data-library';

proc v5tov6 in=source out=dest;
   cat select software.write books.write;
run;
```

You can use the ENTRYTYPE= option in the CAT SELECT statement or the PROC V5TOV6 statement to specify one or more entry types to convert. For more information on using this option, see **Options** earlier in this chapter and **Using Options in Subordinate Statements** later in this chapter.

You can use both the CAT SELECT statement and the CAT EXCLUDE statement in the same PROC V5TOV6 step as long as they specify different catalogs (see **Example 7** and **Example 8**).

EXCLUDE Statement

EXCLUDE *member-list* </ <MEMTYPE=*(mtype-list)*>>;

The EXCLUDE statement excludes members of a SAS data library or of a file of formats from conversion, where

> *member-list*   specifies the members to exclude from conversion. You can use wild-card characters to specify the members. For more information, see **Using Wild-Card Characters** later in this chapter.

For example, the following SAS statements convert all SAS files in the Version 5 SAS data library SOURCE except those named SOFTWARE to their equivalents in the Version 6 SAS data library DEST:

```
libname source 'V5-SAS-data-library';
libname dest 'V6-SAS-data-library';

proc v5tov6 in=source out=dest;
   exclude software;
run;
```

You can use the MEMTYPE= option in the EXCLUDE statement or the PROC V5TOV6 statement to specify one or more member types to exclude from conversion. For more information on using this option, see **Options** earlier in this chapter and **Using Options in Subordinate Statements** later in this chapter.

You do not need to specify the password of a data set that you want to exclude from conversion. Therefore, the EXCLUDE statement does not support the READ= option. However, you do need to specify the password of a data set that you want to convert if a password exists. When you use the EXCLUDE statement, you can use the READ= option in the PROC V5TOV6 statement to specify the passwords of the data sets you want to convert. For more information on using this option, see **Options** earlier in this chapter.

Note: When used in the PROC V5TOV6 statement in conjunction with the EXCLUDE statement, the READ= option applies to all data sets being converted. If different data sets have different read passwords, you must select them for conversion with the SELECT statement, which allows you to specify different passwords for different data sets.

You cannot use both the EXCLUDE and SELECT statements in the same PROC V5TOV6 step.

GCAT EXCLUDE Statement

GCAT EXCLUDE *exclude-list*;

The GCAT EXCLUDE statement excludes entries in graphics catalogs from conversion. Each element of *exclude-list* has the form *member.entry*, where

member is the name of a graphics catalog to process. You can use wild-card characters to specify the member. For more information, see **Using Wild-Card Characters** later in this chapter.

entry is the name of an entry in *member* to exclude from conversion. You can use wild-card characters to specify the entry. For more information, see **Using Wild-Card Characters** later in this chapter.

For example, the following statements convert all the entries in the graphics catalogs SOFTWARE and BOOKS in the Version 5 SAS data library SOURCE except the ones named OLDGRAPH to their equivalents in the Version 6 SAS data library DEST:

```
libname source 'V5-SAS-data-library';
libname dest 'V6-SAS-data-library';

proc v5tov6 in=source out=dest;
   gcat exclude software.oldgraph books.oldgraph;
run;
```

You can use both the GCAT EXCLUDE statement and the GCAT SELECT statement in the same PROC V5TOV6 step as long as they specify different graphics catalogs.

GCAT SELECT Statement

GCAT SELECT *select-list*;

The GCAT SELECT statement selects entries from graphics catalogs for conversion. Each element of *select-list* has the form *member.entry*, where

member is the name of a graphics catalog to process. You can use wild-card characters to specify the member. For more information, see **Using Wild-Card Characters** later in this chapter.

entry is the name of an entry in *member* to select for conversion. You can use wild-card characters to specify the entry. For more information, see **Using Wild-Card Characters** later in this chapter.

For example, the following statements convert the graphics catalog entries SOFTWARE.GRAPH1, SOFTWARE.GRAPH2, and SOFTWARE.GRAPH3 from their formats in the Version 5 SAS data library SOURCE to their equivalents in the Version 6 SAS data library DEST:

```
libname source 'V5-SAS-data-library';
libname dest 'V6-SAS-data-library';

proc v5tov6 in=source out=dest;
   gcat select software.graph1 software.graph2 software.graph3;
run;
```

SELECT Statement

SELECT *member-list* </ <MEMTYPE=*(mtype-list)*> <READ=*password*>>;

The SELECT statement selects members of a SAS data library or a file of formats to convert, where

member-list   specifies the members to convert. You can use wild-card characters to specify the members. For more information, see **Using Wild-Card Characters** later in this chapter.

For example, the following SAS statements convert all SAS files named SOFTWARE in the Version 5 SAS data library SOURCE to their equivalents in the Version 6 SAS data library DEST:

```
libname source 'V5-SAS-data-library';
libname dest 'V6-SAS-data-library';

proc v5tov6 in=source out=dest;
   select software;
run;
```

You can use the MEMTYPE= option in the SELECT statement and the PROC V5TOV6 statement to specify one or more member types to convert. For more information on using this option, see **Options** earlier in this chapter and **Using Options in Subordinate Statements** later in this chapter.

You can use the READ= option in the SELECT statement and the PROC V5TOV6 statement to specify the password or passwords of the data sets you want to convert. For more information on using this option, see **Options** earlier in this chapter and **Using Options in Subordinate Statements** later in this chapter.

You cannot use the SELECT and EXCLUDE statements in the same PROC V5TOV6 step.

DETAILS

Using Options in Subordinate Statements

The ENTRYTYPE=, MEMTYPE=, and READ= options are supported not only by the PROC V5TOV6 statement but also by some subordinate statements. When used with a subordinate statement, the options all follow similar rules, which are described here.

Using the MEMTYPE= and READ= Options

You can use the MEMTYPE= and the READ= options in the SELECT statement. You can also use the MEMTYPE= option in the EXCLUDE statement. Each of these options can appear

- in parentheses immediately after a member name
- after a slash (/) at the end of the statement.

When used in parentheses, these options can have only one value and refer only to the member name immediately preceding the option. For example, the following statements convert the data sets SOFTWARE and BOOKS as well as all entries in the catalog BOOKS from their formats in the Version 5 SAS data library SOURCE to their equivalents in the Version 6 SAS data library DEST:

```
libname source 'V5-SAS-data-library';
libname dest 'V6-SAS-data-library';

proc v5tov6 in=source out=dest;
   select software(memtype=data)
          books(memtype=data)
          books(memtype=cat);
run;
```

When used following a slash, the MEMTYPE= and READ= options refer to all members named in the statement unless the same option appears in parentheses after a member name. In this position the MEMTYPE= option can have multiple values, in which case you must enclose the values for the option in parentheses (see below). For example, the following statements convert the data sets SOFTWARE and BOOKS as well as all entries in the catalogs SOFTWARE and BOOKS from the Version 5 SAS data library SOURCE to their equivalents in the Version 6 SAS data library DEST:

```
libname source 'V5-SAS-data-library';
libname dest 'V6-SAS-data-library';

proc v5tov6 in=source out=dest;
   select software books / memtype=(data cat);
run;
```

The READ= option functions the same way as the MEMTYPE= option although it can never have multiple values. Remember, too, that passwords apply only to data sets.

You can use the MEMTYPE= and READ= options in multiple places. When you do so, the V5TOV6 procedure determines the type of each member and password of each data set as described below:

1. By the value of the option in parentheses immediately following the member name, if present
2. Otherwise, by the value of the option after the slash in the SELECT or EXCLUDE statement, if present
3. Otherwise, by the value of the option in the PROC V5TOV6 statement, if present
4. If you do not specify a member type, the V5TOV6 procedure uses the default member type, ALL. No default for the READ= option exists. You must specify the password to convert a file that has read protection. If you do not specify a password for a file that has password protection, the SAS System prompts you for the password if you are running interactively. If you are not running interactively, the V5TOV6 procedure cannot convert that data set and sends an error message to the SAS log.

Note: Remember that the EXCLUDE statement does not support the READ= option. If you inadvertently specify the READ= option in the EXCLUDE statement, the V5TOV6 procedure ignores it.

The following SAS statements illustrate the use of the MEMTYPE= and READ= options in multiple places:

```
libname source 'V5-SAS-data-library';
libname dest 'V6-SAS-data-library';

proc v5tov6 in=source out=dest memtype=data;
   select software books(memtype=cat)
          maillist(read=top) / read=secret;
run;
```

Table 43.6 shows which files these statements convert and the password associated with each data set.

Table 43.6   Using the MEMTYPE= and READ= Options in Multiple Places

Member Name	Member Type	Source of Type	Password	Source of Password
SOFTWARE	DATA	MEMTYPE= option in PROC V5TOV6 statement	SECRET	READ= option after slash in SELECT statement
BOOKS	CAT	MEMTYPE= option in parentheses after member name		
MAILLIST	DATA	MEMTYPE= option in PROC V5TOV6 statement	TOP	READ= option in parentheses after the name of the file

Using the ENTRYTYPE= Option

You can use the ENTRYTYPE= option in the CAT SELECT and CAT EXCLUDE statements. This option can appear

- in parentheses immediately after an entry name
- after a slash (/) at the end of the statement.

When used in parentheses, this option can have only one value and refers only to the entry name immediately preceding the option. For example, the following statements convert the entry SOFTWARE.MAIN of type MENU and the entry SOFTWARE.REPORTS of type HELP in the Version 5 SAS data library SOURCE to their equivalents in the Version 6 SAS data library DEST:

```
libname source 'V5-SAS-data-library';
libname dest 'V6-SAS-data-library';

proc v5tov6 in=source out=dest;
   cat select software.main(entrytype=menu)
              software.reports(entrytype=help);
run;
```

When used following a slash, this option refers to all members named in the statement unless the same option appears in parentheses after a member name. In this position the option can have multiple values, in which case you must enclose the option and its values in parentheses (see below). For example, the following statements convert the entries SOFTWARE.MAIN of types HELP and MENU as well as the entries SOFTWARE.REPORTS of types HELP and MENU from the Version 5 SAS data library SOURCE to their equivalents in the Version 6 SAS data library DEST:

```
libname source 'V5-SAS-data-library';
libname dest 'V6-SAS-data-library';

proc v5tov6 in=source out=dest;
   cat select software.main software.reports
                / entrytype=(help menu);
run;
```

You can use these options in multiple places. When you do so, the V5TOV6 procedure determines each entry type as follows:

1. By the value of the option in parentheses immediately following the entry name, if present
2. Otherwise, by the value of the option after the slash in the CAT SELECT or CAT EXCLUDE statement, if present
3. Otherwise, by the value of the option in the PROC V5TOV6 statement, if present
4. If you do not specify an entry type, the V5TOV6 procedure uses the default entry type, ALL.

For instance, consider the following statements, which use the ENTRYTYPE= option in three different places:

```
libname source 'V5-SAS-data-library';
libname dest 'V6-SAS-data-library';

proc v5tov6 in=source out=dest entrytype=(program);
   cat select software.text software.reports(entrytype=menu)
               software.write / entrytype=(help program);
   cat exclude books.add;
run;
```

Table 43.7 shows the entries these statements convert and their types. It also shows which use of the ENTRYTYPE= option determines each entry's type.

Table 43.7 Using the ENTRYTYPE= Option in Multiple Places

Entry Name	Entry Types	Source of Entry Types
SOFTWARE.TEXT	HELP, PROGRAM	ENTRYTYPE= option after the slash in the CAT SELECT statement
SOFTWARE.REPORTS	MENU	ENTRYTYPE= option in parentheses after the entry name
SOFTWARE.WRITE	HELP, PROGRAM	ENTRYTYPE= option after the slash in the CAT SELECT statement
BOOKS.ADD	PROGRAM (exclude)	ENTRYTYPE= option in the PROC V5TOV6 statement

Using Wild-Card Characters

You can use wild-card characters to specify multiple characters in the following situations:

- when you specify a member name
- when you specify an entry name
- when you specify a value for the MEMTYPE= or the ENTRYTYPE= option.

In a Member or Entry Name

Table 43.8 shows the meanings of the wild-card characters you can use to specify multiple member or entry names.

Table 43.8 Wild-Card Characters in Member and Entry Names

Character	Meaning
* (asterisk)	All member or entry names
: (colon)	All member or entry names beginning with the string of characters immediately preceding the colon
- (hyphen)	All member or entry names falling lexigraphically between the names on either side of the hyphen (you can use this wild-card character only between two names that begin with the same string of characters and end in a number)

For example, to select all member names beginning with a *b*, use the following statement:

```
select b:;
```

To select all entry names beginning with a *b* in the catalog BOOKS, use this statement:

```
cat select books.b:;
```

The following statement selects all entry names beginning with a *b* in all catalogs in the source library:

```
cat select *.b:;
```

And, the following statement selects the entries GRAPH1, GRAPH2, and GRAPH3 from the graphics catalog BOOKS:

```
gcat select books.graph1-graph3;
```

In the MEMTYPE= or ENTRYTYPE= Option

You can use the asterisk (*) as a wild-card character when you specify a value for the MEMTYPE= or the ENTRYTYPE= option. The asterisk stands for the type ALL.

For example, the following statements convert all the entries of type PROGRAM in the catalog BOOKS and all entries in the catalog SOFTWARE from the Version 5 SAS data library SOURCE to their equivalents in the Version 6 SAS data library DEST:

```
libname source 'V5-SAS-data-library';
libname dest 'V6-SAS-data-library';

proc v5tov6 in=source out=dest memtype=cat entrytype=program;
   cat select books.* software.*(entrytype=*);
run;
```

Selecting a File Whose Name Contains Special Characters

The Version 5 SAS System creates some files and entries whose names contain characters that are not allowed in Version 6 names. Entry names in catalogs created by SAS/AF and SAS/FSP software can contain a variety of special characters. However, when you use any of the subordinate statements to select or exclude entries, the names you specify must be valid SAS names. Therefore, you cannot directly select or exclude entries whose names contain special characters. To select these entries for conversion, you must use only the PROC V5TOV6 statement to make the conversion or use wild-card characters in subordinate statements.

When the V5TOV6 procedure converts an entry whose name contains a special character, it must change the name as described earlier in **Version 5 SAS Files and Their Version 6 Counterparts**.

Note: On some operating systems, the filename of a character format begins with a dollar sign ($) and the filename of an informat with an at sign (@). The V5TOV6 procedure ignores the special characters in these cases. Therefore, when you select these files for conversion, you should ignore these characters as well.

Honoring System Options

When converting SAS data sets, the V5TOV6 procedure honors the following system options:

- COMPRESS=
- FIRSTOBS=
- OBS=
- REPLACE and NOREPLACE
- REUSE=

Note: The V5TOV6 procedure honors these options for data sets only. Thus, newly converted files of any other type replace existing files of the same name and type. Newly created catalog entries, except those of type GRSEG, replace existing entries of the same name and entry type.

Converting SAS/IML Matrices and Modules

Version 5 of the SAS System stores SAS/IML matrices and modules in a member of type IMLWK. The member can contain multiple matrices and modules; however, the only way to determine the number and names of the matrices and modules within the member is to use the SHOW STORAGE command in the IML procedure. In addition, in Version 5 you cannot store a module directly. Before you can store it, you must convert it to a character matrix. Thus, a character matrix in a member of type IMLWK may be either a genuine character matrix or the stored version of a module.

Version 6 of the SAS System stores each matrix and module as an individual entry within a catalog. Thus, you can use either the CATALOG procedure or the IML procedure to manage them. Matrices have an entry type of MATRIX, and modules have an entry type of IMOD.

When you convert a member of type IMLWK from Version 5 to Version 6, you get a separate catalog entry for each matrix and module in the original member. However, initially all entries are of type MATRIX. Use the CALL PUSH command in PROC IML to compile the matrix into a module and the STORE command to store it permanently as an entry of type IMOD. For example, consider the following SAS program:

```
libname source 'V5-SAS-data-library';
libname dest 'V6-SAS-data-library';

proc v5tov6 in=source out=dest memtype=imlwk;
   select books;
run;

proc iml;
   reset storage="dest.books";
   load mod1;              /* Load Version 6 character matrix */
   call push(mod1);        /* Compile matrix into a module    */
   store module=mod1;      /* Store module as MOD1.IMOD;      */
quit;
```

In these SAS statements, the V5TOV6 procedure converts the Version 5 member BOOKS.IMLWK in the SAS data library SOURCE to its equivalent in the Version 6 SAS data library DEST. The equivalent of the original member is a Version 6 catalog (BOOKS) containing one entry of type MATRIX for each module and matrix in the original member.

PROC IML then loads one catalog entry (BOOKS.MOD1) resulting from that conversion and compiles it into a module (a catalog entry of type IMOD). The

STORE command stores it as an entry in the catalog BOOKS. This catalog now contains two entries named MOD1—one of type MATRIX and one of type IMOD. The entry of type MATRIX is no longer useful and should be deleted.

Note: To successfully convert Version 5 modules, which are stored as character matrices, to Version 6 modules, you must follow the steps outlined in this section. Therefore, someone must know which items in the original Version 5 member are genuine character matrices and which are compiled modules. Neither PROC IML nor the SAS System can distinguish them.

Compiling PROGRAM Entries

If you convert a catalog that contains entries of type PROGRAM, you must compile the entries before execution. To compile all the PROGRAM entries in a catalog, submit the following statements to the SAS System:

```
proc build cat=libref.member-name batch;
    compile;
run;
```

where *libref* identifies the SAS data library containing the catalog and *member-name* identifies the catalog.

EXAMPLES

The statements and options that the V5TOV6 procedure supports combine to make the procedure extremely versatile. As you become familiar with the V5TOV6 procedure, you will see that you can combine statements and options in a variety of ways to perform the same task. The examples in this section show one way of accomplishing each task, although other valid ways exist.

The V5TOV6 procedure sends messages to the SAS log as it converts files. Because the messages in the log are always similar, the log is not always shown in the following examples.

Note: By adding the LIST option to the PROC V5TOV6 statement in any of these examples, you can obtain a list of the files you have selected for conversion without actually converting them.

Example 1: Converting an Entire SAS Data Library

The following SAS statements convert all SAS files in the Version 5 SAS data library SOURCE to their equivalents in the Version 6 SAS data library DEST:

```
libname source 'V5-SAS-data-library';
libname dest 'V6-SAS-data-library';

proc v5tov6 in=source out=dest;
run;
```

The messages in the SAS log document the conversion (see **Output 43.1**).

Output 43.1 Log Produced by Converting an Entire SAS Data Library

```
10        libname source V5-SAS-data-library;
NOTE: Libref SOURCE was successfully assigned as follows:
      Engine:        V5
      Physical Name: V5-SAS-data-library
11        libname dest V6-SAS-data-library;
NOTE: Libref DEST was successfully assigned as follows:
      Engine:        V606
      Physical Name: V6-SAS-data-library

12        proc v5tov6 in=source out=dest;
13        run;

WARNING: A new catalog DEST.BOOKS has been created.
NOTE: SOURCE.BOOKS.CAT.MAIN.CBT has been converted to DEST.BOOKS.MAIN.CBT.
NOTE: SOURCE.BOOKS.CAT.TEXT.FORM has been converted to DEST.BOOKS.TEXT.FORM.
NOTE: SOURCE.BOOKS.CAT.WRITE.FORM has been converted to DEST.BOOKS.WRITE.FORM.
NOTE: SOURCE.BOOKS.CAT.PICTURES.GCMAP has been converted to DEST.BOOKS.PICTURES.CMAP.
NOTE: SOURCE.BOOKS.CAT.ADD.HELP has been converted to DEST.BOOKS.ADD.HELP.
NOTE: SOURCE.BOOKS.CAT.MAIN.HELP has been converted to DEST.BOOKS.MAIN.HELP.
NOTE: SOURCE.BOOKS.CAT.PICTURES.HELP has been converted to DEST.BOOKS.PICTURES.HELP.
NOTE: SOURCE.BOOKS.CAT.REPORTS.HELP has been converted to DEST.BOOKS.REPORTS.HELP.
NOTE: SOURCE.BOOKS.CAT.TEXT.HELP has been converted to DEST.BOOKS.TEXT.HELP.
NOTE: SOURCE.BOOKS.CAT.WRITE.HELP has been converted to DEST.BOOKS.WRITE.HELP.
NOTE: SOURCE.BOOKS.CAT.MAIN.KEYS has been converted to DEST.BOOKS.MAIN.KEYS.
NOTE: SOURCE.BOOKS.CAT.WRITE.LETTER has been converted to DEST.BOOKS.WRITE.LETTER.
NOTE: SOURCE.BOOKS.CAT.MAIN.MENU has been converted to DEST.BOOKS.MAIN.MENU.
NOTE: SOURCE.BOOKS.CAT.REPORTS.MENU has been converted to DEST.BOOKS.REPORTS.MENU.
NOTE: SOURCE.BOOKS.CAT.ADD.PROGRAM has been converted to DEST.BOOKS.ADD.PROGRAM.
NOTE: SOURCE.BOOKS.CAT.PICTURES.PROGRAM has been converted to DEST.BOOKS.PICTURES.PROGRAM.
NOTE: SOURCE.BOOKS.CAT.TEXT.PROGRAM has been converted to DEST.BOOKS.TEXT.PROGRAM.
NOTE: SOURCE.BOOKS.CAT.WRITE.PROGRAM has been converted to DEST.BOOKS.WRITE.PROGRAM.
NOTE: SOURCE.BOOKS.CAT.ADD.SCREEN has been converted to DEST.BOOKS.ADD.SCREEN.
NOTE: SOURCE.BOOKS.CAT.WRITE.SCREEN has been converted to DEST.BOOKS.WRITE.SCREEN.
NOTE: SOURCE.BOOKS.CAT.PICTURES.TEMPLATE has been converted to DEST.BOOKS.PICTURES.TEMPLATE.
NOTE: Use the BUILD procedure available in SAS/AF software to compile converted program screens before attempting execution.
      To invoke proc BUILD, type

          PROC BUILD CATALOG=DEST.BOOKS BATCH; COMPILE; RUN;

NOTE: The data set DEST.BOOKS has 2 observations and 1 variables.
```

```
2                                      The SAS System

NOTE:  Segment originally created for IBM3279.
NOTE:  DEVICE DEFAULT CBACK = BLACK
NOTE: SOURCE.BOOKS.GCAT.GRAPH1 has been converted to DEST.BOOKS.GRAPH1.GRSEG.
NOTE:  Segment originally created for IBM3279.
NOTE: SOURCE.BOOKS.GCAT.GRAPH2 has been converted to DEST.BOOKS.GRAPH2.GRSEG.
NOTE:  Segment originally created for IBM3279.
NOTE:  DEVICE DEFAULT CBACK = BLACK
NOTE: SOURCE.BOOKS.GCAT.GRAPH3 has been converted to DEST.BOOKS.GRAPH3.GRSEG.
NOTE:  Segment originally created for IBM3279.
NOTE:  DEVICE DEFAULT CBACK = BLACK
NOTE: SOURCE.BOOKS.GCAT.OLDGRAPH has been converted to DEST.BOOKS.OLDGRAPH.GRSEG.
NOTE: SOURCE.BOOKS.IMLWK has been converted to DEST.BOOKS.MOD1.MATRIX.
      and DEST.BOOKS.MOD2.MATRIX.
      and DEST.BOOKS.MOD3.MATRIX.
NOTE: The data set DEST.MAILLIST has 2 observations and 2 variables.
WARNING: A new catalog DEST.SOFTWARE has been created.
NOTE: SOURCE.SOFTWARE.CAT.MAIN.CBT has been converted to DEST.SOFTWARE.MAIN.CBT.
NOTE: SOURCE.SOFTWARE.CAT.TEXT.FORM has been converted to DEST.SOFTWARE.TEXT.FORM.
NOTE: SOURCE.SOFTWARE.CAT.WRITE.FORM has been converted to DEST.SOFTWARE.WRITE.FORM.
NOTE: SOURCE.SOFTWARE.CAT.PICTURES.GCMAP has been converted to DEST.SOFTWARE.PICTURES.CMAP.
NOTE: SOURCE.SOFTWARE.CAT.ADD.HELP has been converted to DEST.SOFTWARE.ADD.HELP.
NOTE: SOURCE.SOFTWARE.CAT.MAIN.HELP has been converted to DEST.SOFTWARE.MAIN.HELP.
NOTE: SOURCE.SOFTWARE.CAT.PICTURES.HELP has been converted to DEST.SOFTWARE.PICTURES.HELP.
NOTE: SOURCE.SOFTWARE.CAT.REPORTS.HELP has been converted to DEST.SOFTWARE.REPORTS.HELP.
NOTE: SOURCE.SOFTWARE.CAT.TEXT.HELP has been converted to DEST.SOFTWARE.TEXT.HELP.
NOTE: SOURCE.SOFTWARE.CAT.WRITE.HELP has been converted to DEST.SOFTWARE.WRITE.HELP.
NOTE: SOURCE.SOFTWARE.CAT.MAIN.KEYS has been converted to DEST.SOFTWARE.MAIN.KEYS.
NOTE: SOURCE.SOFTWARE.CAT.WRITE.LETTER has been converted to DEST.SOFTWARE.WRITE.LETTER.
NOTE: SOURCE.SOFTWARE.CAT.MAIN.MENU has been converted to DEST.SOFTWARE.MAIN.MENU.
NOTE: SOURCE.SOFTWARE.CAT.REPORTS.MENU has been converted to DEST.SOFTWARE.REPORTS.MENU.
NOTE: SOURCE.SOFTWARE.CAT.ADD.PROGRAM has been converted to DEST.SOFTWARE.ADD.PROGRAM.
NOTE: SOURCE.SOFTWARE.CAT.PICTURES.PROGRAM has been converted to DEST.SOFTWARE.PICTURES.PROGRAM.
NOTE: SOURCE.SOFTWARE.CAT.TEXT.PROGRAM has been converted to DEST.SOFTWARE.TEXT.PROGRAM.
NOTE: SOURCE.SOFTWARE.CAT.WRITE.PROGRAM has been converted to DEST.SOFTWARE.WRITE.PROGRAM.
NOTE: SOURCE.SOFTWARE.CAT.ADD.SCREEN has been converted to DEST.SOFTWARE.ADD.SCREEN.
NOTE: SOURCE.SOFTWARE.CAT.WRITE.SCREEN has been converted to DEST.SOFTWARE.WRITE.SCREEN.
NOTE: SOURCE.SOFTWARE.CAT.PICTURES.TEMPLATE has been converted to DEST.SOFTWARE.PICTURES.TEMPLATE.
```

```
3                                          The SAS System
NOTE: Use the BUILD procedure available in SAS/AF software to compile converted program screens before attempting execution.
      To invoke proc BUILD, type

                PROC BUILD CATALOG=DEST.SOFTWARE BATCH; COMPILE; RUN;
NOTE: The data set DEST.SOFTWARE has 2 observations and 1 variables.
NOTE:  Segment originally created for IBM3279.
NOTE:  DEVICE DEFAULT CBACK = BLACK
NOTE: SOURCE.SOFTWARE.GCAT.OLDGRAPH has been converted to DEST.SOFTWARE.OLDGRAPH.GRSEG.
```

Example 2:   Selecting Files by Type

The following example uses the MEMTYPE= option to convert all data sets in the Version 5 SAS data library SOURCE to their equivalents in the Version 6 SAS data library DEST:

```
libname source 'V5-SAS-data-library';
libname dest 'V6-SAS-data-library';

proc v5tov6 in=source out=dest memtype=data;
run;
```

Example 3:   Selecting Files by Name

The following example converts all files named BOOKS and SOFTWARE in the Version 5 SAS data library SOURCE to their equivalents in the Version 6 SAS data library DEST. Because neither the MEMTYPE= nor the ENTRYTYPE= option is present, member type and entry type both default to ALL. Therefore, the V5TOV6 procedure converts all files regardless of type and all entries within catalogs, regardless of entry type.

```
libname source 'V5-SAS-data-library';
libname dest 'V6-SAS-data-library';

proc v5tov6 in=source out=dest;
   select books software;
run;
```

Example 4:   Selecting Files by Type and by Name

The following example combines the MEMTYPE= option and the SELECT statement to convert the data sets named BOOKS and SOFTWARE in the Version 5 SAS data library SOURCE to their equivalents in the Version 6 SAS data library DEST:

```
libname source 'V5-SAS-data-library';
libname dest 'V6-SAS-data-library';

proc v5tov6 in=source out=dest memtype=data;
   select books software;
run;
```

The SAS log documenting this conversion appears in **Output 43.2**.

Output 43.2 Log Produced by Selecting Files by Type and by Name

```
7          libname source V5-SAS-data-library;
NOTE: Libref SOURCE was successfully assigned as follows:
      Engine:        V5
      Physical Name: V5-SAS-data-library
8          libname dest V6-SAS-data-library;
NOTE: Libref DEST was successfully assigned as follows:
      Engine:        V606
      Physical Name: V6-SAS-data-library

9          proc v5tov6 in=source out=dest memtype=data;
10            select books software;
11         run;

NOTE: The data set DEST.BOOKS has 2 observations and 1 variables.
NOTE: The data set DEST.SOFTWARE has 2 observations and 1 variables.
```

Example 5:   Converting All Entries in a Catalog

The following statements convert all entries in the catalog SOFTWARE from their formats in the Version 5 SAS data library SOURCE to their equivalents in the Version 6 SAS data library DEST:

```
libname source 'V5-SAS-data-library';
libname dest 'V6-SAS-data-library';

proc v5tov6 in=source out=dest;
   cat select software.*;
run;
```

The SAS log produced by these statements appears in **Output 43.3**.

Output 43.3 Log Produced by Converting All Entries in a Catalog

```
7          libname source V5-SAS-data-library;
NOTE: Libref SOURCE was successfully assigned as follows:
      Engine:        V5
      Physical Name: V5-SAS-data-library
8          libname dest V6-SAS-data-library;
NOTE: Libref DEST was successfully assigned as follows:
      Engine:        V606
      Physical Name: V6-SAS-data-library

9          proc v5tov6 in=source out=dest;
10            cat select software.*;
11         run;

WARNING: A new catalog DEST.SOFTWARE has been created.
NOTE: SOURCE.SOFTWARE.CAT.MAIN.CBT has been converted to DEST.SOFTWARE.MAIN.CBT.
NOTE: SOURCE.SOFTWARE.CAT.TEXT.FORM has been converted to DEST.SOFTWARE.TEXT.FORM.
NOTE: SOURCE.SOFTWARE.CAT.WRITE.FORM has been converted to DEST.SOFTWARE.WRITE.FORM.
NOTE: SOURCE.SOFTWARE.CAT.PICTURES.GCMAP has been converted to DEST.SOFTWARE.PICTURES.CMAP.
NOTE: SOURCE.SOFTWARE.CAT.ADD.HELP has been converted to DEST.SOFTWARE.ADD.HELP.
NOTE: SOURCE.SOFTWARE.CAT.MAIN.HELP has been converted to DEST.SOFTWARE.MAIN.HELP.
NOTE: SOURCE.SOFTWARE.CAT.PICTURES.HELP has been converted to DEST.SOFTWARE.PICTURES.HELP.
NOTE: SOURCE.SOFTWARE.CAT.REPORTS.HELP has been converted to DEST.SOFTWARE.REPORTS.HELP.
NOTE: SOURCE.SOFTWARE.CAT.TEXT.HELP has been converted to DEST.SOFTWARE.TEXT.HELP.
NOTE: SOURCE.SOFTWARE.CAT.WRITE.HELP has been converted to DEST.SOFTWARE.WRITE.HELP.
NOTE: SOURCE.SOFTWARE.CAT.MAIN.KEYS has been converted to DEST.SOFTWARE.MAIN.KEYS.
NOTE: SOURCE.SOFTWARE.CAT.WRITE.LETTER has been converted to DEST.SOFTWARE.WRITE.LETTER.
NOTE: SOURCE.SOFTWARE.CAT.MAIN.MENU has been converted to DEST.SOFTWARE.MAIN.MENU.
NOTE: SOURCE.SOFTWARE.CAT.REPORTS.MENU has been converted to DEST.SOFTWARE.REPORTS.MENU.
NOTE: SOURCE.SOFTWARE.CAT.ADD.PROGRAM has been converted to DEST.SOFTWARE.ADD.PROGRAM.
NOTE: SOURCE.SOFTWARE.CAT.PICTURES.PROGRAM has been converted to DEST.SOFTWARE.PICTURES.PROGRAM.
```

(continued on next page)

(continued from previous page)

```
NOTE: SOURCE.SOFTWARE.CAT.TEXT.PROGRAM has been converted to DEST.SOFTWARE.TEXT.PROGRAM.
NOTE: SOURCE.SOFTWARE.CAT.WRITE.PROGRAM has been converted to DEST.SOFTWARE.WRITE.PROGRAM.
NOTE: SOURCE.SOFTWARE.CAT.ADD.SCREEN has been converted to DEST.SOFTWARE.ADD.SCREEN.
NOTE: SOURCE.SOFTWARE.CAT.WRITE.SCREEN has been converted to DEST.SOFTWARE.WRITE.SCREEN.
NOTE: SOURCE.SOFTWARE.CAT.PICTURES.TEMPLATE has been converted to DEST.SOFTWARE.PICTURES.TEMPLATE.
NOTE: Use the BUILD procedure available in SAS/AF software to compile converted program screens before attempting execution.
      To invoke proc BUILD, type

          PROC BUILD CATALOG=DEST.SOFTWARE BATCH; COMPILE; RUN;
```

Example 6:   Selecting Catalog Entries by Type

The following statements convert all entries of type HELP and MENU in all catalogs from their formats in the Version 5 SAS data library SOURCE to their equivalents in the Version 6 SAS data library DEST:

```
libname source 'V5-SAS-data-library';
libname dest 'V6-SAS-data-library';

proc v5tov6 in=source out=dest memtype=cat entrytype=(help menu);
run;
```

Example 7:   Selecting Catalog Entries by Name

The following statements convert all entries named WRITE in the catalog
SOFTWARE and all entries except those named WRITE in the catalog BOOKS
from their formats in the Version 5 SAS data library SOURCE to their equivalents
in the Version 6 SAS data library DEST:

```
libname source 'V5-SAS-data-library';
libname dest 'V6-SAS-data-library';

proc v5tov6 in=source out=dest;
   cat select software.write;
   cat exclude books.write;
run;
```

Example 8:   Selecting Catalog Entries by Type and by Name

The following statements combine the CAT SELECT and CAT EXCLUDE state-
ments with the ENTRYTYPE= option to convert all entries named WRITE of type
HELP and LETTER in the catalog SOFTWARE and all entries except those named
WRITE of type HELP and PROGRAM in the catalog BOOKS from their formats
in the Version 5 SAS data library SOURCE to their equivalents in the Version 6
SAS data library DEST:

```
libname source 'V5-SAS-data-library';
libname dest 'V6-SAS-data-library';

proc v5tov6 in=source out=dest;
   cat select software.write / entrytype=(help letter);
   cat exclude books.write / entrytype=(help program);
run;
```

The SAS log produced by these statements appears in **Output 43.4**.

Output 43.4   Log Produced by Selecting Catalog Entries by Type and by
Name

```
7           libname source V5-SAS-data-library;
NOTE: Libref SOURCE was successfully assigned as follows:
      Engine:       V5
      Physical Name: V5-SAS-data-library
8           libname dest V6-SAS-data-library;
NOTE: Libref DEST was successfully assigned as follows:
      Engine:       V606
      Physical Name: V6-SAS-data-library

9           proc v5tov6 in=source out=dest;
10              cat select software.write / entrytype=(help letter);
11              cat exclude books.write / entrytype=(help program);
12          run;

WARNING: A new catalog DEST.BOOKS has been created.
NOTE: SOURCE.BOOKS.CAT.MAIN.CBT has been converted to DEST.BOOKS.MAIN.CBT.
NOTE: SOURCE.BOOKS.CAT.TEXT.FORM has been converted to DEST.BOOKS.TEXT.FORM.
NOTE: SOURCE.BOOKS.CAT.WRITE.FORM has been converted to DEST.BOOKS.WRITE.FORM.
NOTE: SOURCE.BOOKS.CAT.PICTURES.GCMAP has been converted to DEST.BOOKS.PICTURES.CMAP.
NOTE: SOURCE.BOOKS.CAT.ADD.HELP has been converted to DEST.BOOKS.ADD.HELP.
NOTE: SOURCE.BOOKS.CAT.MAIN.HELP has been converted to DEST.BOOKS.MAIN.HELP.
NOTE: SOURCE.BOOKS.CAT.PICTURES.HELP has been converted to DEST.BOOKS.PICTURES.HELP.
NOTE: SOURCE.BOOKS.CAT.REPORTS.HELP has been converted to DEST.BOOKS.REPORTS.HELP.
NOTE: SOURCE.BOOKS.CAT.TEXT.HELP has been converted to DEST.BOOKS.TEXT.HELP.
NOTE: SOURCE.BOOKS.CAT.MAIN.KEYS has been converted to DEST.BOOKS.MAIN.KEYS.
NOTE: SOURCE.BOOKS.CAT.WRITE.LETTER has been converted to DEST.BOOKS.WRITE.LETTER.
NOTE: SOURCE.BOOKS.CAT.MAIN.MENU has been converted to DEST.BOOKS.MAIN.MENU.
NOTE: SOURCE.BOOKS.CAT.REPORTS.MENU has been converted to DEST.BOOKS.REPORTS.MENU.
NOTE: SOURCE.BOOKS.CAT.ADD.PROGRAM has been converted to DEST.BOOKS.ADD.PROGRAM.
NOTE: SOURCE.BOOKS.CAT.PICTURES.PROGRAM has been converted to DEST.BOOKS.PICTURES.PROGRAM.
NOTE: SOURCE.BOOKS.CAT.TEXT.PROGRAM has been converted to DEST.BOOKS.TEXT.PROGRAM.
NOTE: SOURCE.BOOKS.CAT.ADD.SCREEN has been converted to DEST.BOOKS.ADD.SCREEN.
NOTE: SOURCE.BOOKS.CAT.WRITE.SCREEN has been converted to DEST.BOOKS.WRITE.SCREEN.
NOTE: SOURCE.BOOKS.CAT.PICTURES.TEMPLATE has been converted to DEST.BOOKS.PICTURES.TEMPLATE.
NOTE: Use the BUILD procedure available in SAS/AF software to compile converted program screens before attempting execution.
      To invoke proc BUILD, type

          PROC BUILD CATALOG=DEST.BOOKS BATCH; COMPILE; RUN;

WARNING: A new catalog DEST.SOFTWARE has been created.
NOTE: SOURCE.SOFTWARE.CAT.WRITE.HELP has been converted to DEST.SOFTWARE.WRITE.HELP.
NOTE: SOURCE.SOFTWARE.CAT.WRITE.LETTER has been converted to DEST.SOFTWARE.WRITE.LETTER.
```

Example 9:   Converting All Entries in a Graphics Catalog

The following statements convert all entries in the graphics catalog SOFTWARE
in the Version 5 SAS data library SOURCE to their equivalents in the Version 6
SAS data library DEST:

```
libname source 'V5-SAS-data-library';
libname dest 'V6-SAS-data-library';

proc v5tov6 in=source out=dest;
  gcat select software.*;
run;
```

Example 10:   Selecting Graphics Catalog Entries by Name

The following example converts all entries named OLDGRAPH in all graphics
catalogs in the Version 5 SAS data library SOURCE to their equivalents in the Version 6 SAS data library DEST. Each entry in a Version 5 graphics catalog becomes
an entry in a Version 6 file of type CATALOG. The catalog retains its original
name. Each entry in the catalog retains its name unless the Version 6 catalog
already contains an entry with that name. In such a case, PROC V5TOV6

appends a number to the name to create a unique entry name. The type of all entries in the catalog is GRSEG.

```
libname source 'V5-SAS-data-library';
libname dest 'V6-SAS-data-library';

proc v5tov6 in=source out=dest;
   gcat select *.oldgraph;
run;
```

Example 11:   Converting Formats and Informats

Because of the difference in the way different operating systems store formats and informats in Version 5, the way you convert them depends on your operating system (see **Requirements** earlier in this chapter).

Under the CMS, MVS, and VSE Operating Systems

The following example converts all the formats and informats in the file of formats referenced by the fileref SASLIB to the catalog FORMATS in the Version 6 SAS data library DEST. The file contains a character format named $PRODUCT; three numeric formats named CURRNCYA, CURRNCYB, and CURRNCYC; a numeric informat named @IDGROUP; and a character informat named @$STATES. Each format and informat retains its name (although special characters are dropped) and is assigned the appropriate entry type: FORMAT, FORMATC, INFMT, or INFMTC.

   Note: You must reference SASLIB with the FILEDEF command (CMS), the ALLOCATE command or the DD statement (MVS), or the LIBDEF command (VSE) before starting your SAS session and, under CMS, you must global the TXTLIB before you start your SAS session.

```
libname dest 'V6-SAS-data-library';

proc v5tov6 format=saslib out=dest;
run;
```

On Other Operating Systems

On other operating systems, formats are stored in a SAS data library. You perform the same task with these statements, replacing the allocation of the file of formats with a LIBNAME statement and the FORMAT= argument in the PROC V5TOV6 statement with the IN= argument. The MEMTYPE= option restricts the conversion to formats and informats.

```
libname source 'V5-SAS-data-library';
libname dest 'V6-SAS-data-library';

proc v5tov6 in=source out=dest memtype=format;
run;
```

SAS® Statements Used with Procedures

INTRODUCTION

In addition to the statements in this book described with each procedure, you can also use the SAS statements listed below in any PROC step:

ATTRIB	FOOTNOTE	OPTIONS
comment	FORMAT	RUN
DM	%INCLUDE	TITLE
ENDSAS	LABEL	WHERE
FILENAME	LIBNAME	X

Most of these statements work in the PROC step just as they do in the DATA step. Exceptions are noted below. Refer to *SAS Language: Reference, Version 6, First Edition* for detailed information on using these statements.

ASSIGNING ATTRIBUTES IN THE PROC STEP

When you use one of the following statements in a PROC step, the attribute is associated with the variable only for the duration of that PROC step and in any output data sets created by the procedure. The attributes for the variable in the input data set are not changed.

ATTRIB
FORMAT
LABEL

USING THE WHERE STATEMENT IN THE PROC STEP

The WHERE statement works on the input data set in the PROC step as it does in the DATA step. Note that the following procedures have multiple input data sets:

- the APPEND procedure
- the CALENDAR procedure
- the COMPARE procedure
- the DATASETS procedure with an APPEND statement.

Refer to the description of these procedures for information on how the WHERE statement works with them.

Engines and Processing Capabilities

INTRODUCTION

This appendix assumes that you are familiar with the SAS data model and with the concept of engines. For information on these topics, refer to Chapter 6, "SAS Files," in *SAS Language: Reference, Version 6, First Edition.*

The V606 engine supports every processing capability of the SAS data model for noncompressed data sets. However, not all engines support all these capabilities. Therefore, procedures that require certain processing capabilities may not work with all engines. If you are writing an application, be sure that the procedures and engines you choose are compatible.

Each section in this appendix addresses one commonly used processing capability that is not supported by all engines. Sections include a list of the base SAS procedures that use the processing capability and, if a procedure uses the capability only under certain circumstances, descriptions of those circumstances. **If you use a procedure that uses one of these processing capabilities, you must use an engine that supports that capability.** If you are using a SAS/ACCESS product, refer to the chapter on using external data in SAS programs in the documentation for your SAS/ACCESS product. This chapter includes information on restrictions on using individual procedures with that SAS/ACCESS engine.

Note: The output from the CONTENTS procedure tells you the name of the engine used to access the data set and whether or not the data are compressed.

UPDATING A SAS DATA SET IN PLACE

You update a SAS data set in place when you change the data values in one or more observations without re-creating the entire data set. The following base SAS procedures update in place:

- the APPEND procedure
- the DATASETS procedure with a REPAIR statement or with the MODIFY statement and a FORMAT, INFORMAT, LABEL, or RENAME statement
- the SQL procedure with the UPDATE statement.

For example, if you are using a data set created by a sequential engine such as the SAS tape engine, you cannot update in place.

DELETING, RENAMING, OR MOVING A SAS DATA SET

The following procedures delete, rename, or move a SAS data set:

- the COPY procedure with the MOVE option
- the DATASETS procedure with the KILL option or with an AGE, DELETE, CHANGE, EXCHANGE, or SAVE statement
- the SQL procedure with the DROP statement.

For example, if you are using a data set created by a sequential engine such as the SAS tape engine, you cannot delete, rename, or move a SAS data set.

CHANGING A VARIABLE'S ATTRIBUTES

The following procedures change a variable's attributes:

- the DATASETS procedure with the MODIFY statement and a FORMAT, INFORMAT, LABEL, or RENAME statement
- the SQL procedure with the ALTER statement.

For example, if you are using a data set created by a sequential engine such as the SAS tape engine, you cannot change a variable's attributes.

EQUATING OBSERVATION NUMBERS WITH INTERNAL RECORD IDS

The following procedures equate an observation number with an internal record ID:

- the COMPARE procedure
- the PRINT procedure.

If you use these procedures with a compressed data set, the output may differ slightly from the output generated by a noncompressed data set, depending on whether or not the engine supports this capability. (The integrity of the data is not compromised; the procedures simply number the observations differently.)

CREATING AND DELETING INDEXES

The following procedures create or delete indexes:

- the COPY procedure when copying a file with an index
- the DATASETS procedure with the MODIFY statement and an INDEX CREATE or INDEX DELETE statement
- the SQL procedure with the CREATE statement.

For example, if you are using the Version 5 compatibility engine or a sequential engine such as the SAS tape engine, you cannot create or delete an index. Therefore, if you use the COPY procedure to copy an indexed Version 6 data set to a Version 5 data library, the procedure copies the data set but cannot copy the index.

NONSEQUENTIAL ACCESS

The following procedures use nonsequential access to the data:

- the CHART procedure with a BY statement
- the PLOT procedure with a BY statement
- the RANK procedure with a BY statement
- the SQL procedure whenever it uses an index
- the STANDARD procedure with a BY statement.

For example, when you are using a data set created by a sequential engine such as the SAS tape engine, you generally cannot use nonsequential access.

CONCURRENT ACCESS

By default, the following procedures disallow concurrent access to a SAS data set:

- the CHART procedure
- the COMPARE procedure when you compare the whole comparison data set to each BY group in the base data set
- the PLOT procedure
- the PRINT procedure with the UNIFORM option, and then only if not all variables have formats that explicitly specify a width
- the RANK procedure
- the STANDARD procedure.

You may not use these procedures with an engine that supports concurrent access if another user is updating the same data set at the same time.

Index

P

Q

X

Z

Special Characters

Your Turn

If you have comments or suggestions about the *SAS Procedures Guide, Version 6, Third Edition* or SAS software, please send them to us on a photocopy of this page.

Please return the photocopy to the Publications Division (for comments about this book) or the Technical Support Division (for suggestions about the software) at SAS Institute Inc., SAS Campus Drive, Cary, NC 27513.